A Statistical portrait of
the United States

A Statistical Portrait of the United States

Contributors

MARK S. LITTMAN is a senior data analyst and editor with Bernan Associates. Mr. Littman retired from the federal government in 1995 after 27 years of service. Most of his government career was spent in the Population Division at the U.S. Bureau of the Census, where he served as a demographic statistician in several arenas. He has been the recipient of a Blue Pencil Award from the National Association of Government Communicators, and of a Klein Award from the Bureau of Labor Statistics. Mr. Littman holds a B.A. and an M.A. degree in sociology from American University and has completed coursework for a Ph.D. in sociology at the University of Maryland.

DAVID E. BLOCKSTEIN is a senior scientist with the Committee for the National Institute for the Environment (CNIE) and was the organization's first Executive Director. Mr. Blockstein holds a Ph.D. in ecology from the University of Minnesota, is a frequent contributor to both technical and popular literature about science and environmental policy, and is chair of the Ornithological Council.

RICHARD E. DODGE is a data analyst and editor with Bernan Associates. He is a co-editor of the forthcoming 2nd edition of *Places, Towns and Townships* (Bernan Press) and has assisted in producing *County and City Extra* (Bernan Press) since its first edition. Before coming to Bernan, Mr. Dodge was involved with a variety of statistical programs at the Bureau of the Census and the Bureau of Justice Statistics during his 31 years of government service. While at the Census Bureau, Mr. Dodge helped plan the content and analyzed data for a number of voting surveys, beginning with the first such survey covering the November 1964 election. He holds a Ph.D. in political science from the University of Michigan.

BILL DOWNS has 35 years of experience producing and analyzing housing statistics, principally with the Housing Division in the U.S. Bureau of the Census. His last position was as Chief of the Decennial Planning and Data Services Branch in the Housing and Household Economic Statistics Division. Mr. Downs holds a B.A. degree in economics from the University of Maryland.

PAUL O. FLAIM worked for the Bureau of Labor Statistics (BLS) of the U.S. Department of Labor from 1966 until his retirement in 1994. For many years before his retirement, Mr. Flaim served as the Chief of the Division of Labor Force Statistics at BLS, where he was responsible for analyzing U.S. employment and unemployment figures. States. He is the author of many articles that focus on the labor force and that have appeared in the *Monthly Labor Review* and elsewhere. Mr. Flaim holds an M.A. degree in economics from Johns Hopkins University.

GEORGE E. HALL is a managing editor with Bernan Associates. During his 25 years of government service (with various agencies), Mr. Hall was, among other things, responsible for the United States social indicators program, and was the first Director of what is now called the Bureau of Justice Statistics. Mr. Hall holds a B.A. degree in economics from Howard University.

JENNIFER L. PRICE is a graduate student in environmental policy at Georgetown University, and worked as a staff member for the Committee for the National Institute for the Environment during 1997. Ms. Price holds a B.S. degree in Forestry and Wildlife Resources from Virginia Polytechnic Institute.

HENRY WULF is Chief of the Census Management Staff in the Governments Division at the U.S. Bureau of the Census. He has 27 years of experience with that agency. Mr. Wulf has contributed chapters to several other books, including *The Book of the States* (Council of State Governments), as well as *Proceedings of the American Statistical Association*. Mr. Wulf holds a B.A. degree from Tufts University and an M.A. degree from the University of Massachusetts in political science, where he also completed the coursework toward a Ph.D.

A Statistical Portrait of the United States

Social Conditions and Trends

Edited by Mark S. Littman

Bernan Press
Lanham, MD

ISBN: 0-89059-076-1

Library of Congress Catalog Card Number: 98-72991

Book design and composition by Bremmer & Goris Communications, Inc., Alexandria, VA.

Printed in the United States of America on acid-free paper that meets the American National Standards Institute Z39-48 standard.

99 98   4 3 2 1

Bernan Press
An Imprint of Bernan Associates
4611-F Assembly Drive
Lanham, MD 20706-4391
(800) 274-4447
e-mail: info@bernan.com

Contents

Chapter 1: Population Characteristics

Population

Distribution and Density

Age and Race Distribution, Vital Rates, and International Migration

Chapter 2: Living Arrangements

Marital Status

Household Composition

Chapter 3: Education

School Enrollment

Chapter 4: Health

Chapter 5: Labor Force and Job Characteristics

Chapter 6: Income, Wealth, and Poverty

Chapter 7: Housing

Chapter 8: Crime and Criminal Justice

Chapter 9: Voting

Voting

Chapter 10: Leisure, Volunteerism, and Religiosity

Leisure

Volunteerism

Religiosity

Chapter 11: Environment

Environment

Chapter 12: Government

Government

Government (Continued)

Appendix: Detailed Tables

Figures and Tables

Chapter 3: Education

Chapter 4: Health

Chapter 5: Labor Force and Job Characteristics

Chapter 6: Income, Wealth, and Poverty

Chapter 6: Income, Wealth, and Poverty (Continued)

Chapter 7: Housing

Chapter 8: Crime and Criminal Justice

Chapter 9: Voting

Chapter 10: Leisure, Volunteerism, and Religiosity

Chapter 11: Environment

Chapter 11: Environment (Continued)

Chapter 12: Government

Chapter 12: Government (Continued)

Introduction

The first edition of *A Statistical Portrait of the United States: Social Conditions and Trends* is an approach to depicting societal change over the past several decades. Through a combination of written exposition, graphics, and detailed tabulations, this volume presents statistical indicators from a multitude of government and private sources on a wide variety of subjects that affect the lives of residents of the United States. Included are chapters not only on demographic topics such as population growth, fertility, and immigration, but also on economic subjects such as labor force measures and income. This volume also covers such arenas as education, crime, recreation and leisure, voting, environmental trends, and changes in government programs, taxes, and spending.

Each chapter in *A Statistical Portrait of the United States* summarizes major changes over the past quarter century, with emphasis on the 1990s. In addition, international comparisons are presented when comparable data are available so that trends in the United States can be viewed from a global perspective. Chapters include current summary statistics, graphics depicting trends over time, and bibliographic references to use for further information. More detailed data underlying each chapter are included in appendix tables.

In the late 1960s a movement among social scientists to gauge societal progress and change in quality of life with "social indicators," akin to various economic indicators championed by economists, began to take shape. This movement was not confined to the United States. Various nations from Australia to Sweden produced reports on social indicators of conditions in their respective countries by the mid-1970s. Additionally, international organizations such as the United Nations (UN) and Organization of Economic Cooperation and Development (OECD) produced volumes on gauging social indicators.[1] The U.S. government produced three volumes on social indicators in the United States beginning in 1973 and ending with *Social Indicators III* published in 1980.[2] While some other nations and international organizations have continued to produce a social indicators report, the United States government has not.[3] Nor has any single government agency attempted to include in one volume the breadth of subjects covered in the original Social Indicators reports. It is this task that we have undertaken in *A Statistical Portrait of the United States: Social Conditions and Trends*.

Various U.S. government agencies have, however, produced profiles for their particular domain. Prominent among these are various reports of the Census Bureau, the National Center for Education Statistics, the National Center for Health Statistics, and the Bureau of Labor Statistics. The authors of this report have drawn heavily from and synthesized these data sources.

---

[1] See, for example UN. *Social Indicators-Preliminary Guidelines and Illustrative Series*. ST/ESA/STAT/SER.M/63. New York. 1978; and OECD. *Measuring Social Well-Being: A Progress Report on the Development of Social Indicators*. Paris. 1976.

[2] Office of Management and Budget and Bureau of the Census. *Social Indicators* (triennial, published in 1974,1977 and 1980, United States Government Printing Office).

[3] See for example the European communities' report by Eurostat, *Social Portrait of Europe*. Office for Official Publications of the European Communities. Luxembourg. 1996.

Acknowledgments

Particular thanks go out to George E. Hall, whose past and present work, and whose encouragement inspired this volume.

In addition to the authors, several people contributed to the production of this volume. Many of the graphics and tables were prepared by Candace Feit and Hongwei Zhang. Sean Long coordinated the editing and production of this volume, with editorial support from Gary Kessler, Kathy Kelly, Gayle Young, and Paige Hull, and production support from Elaine Clem, Renee Bocko-Dexter, and Joyce Goodwine.

We are indebted to several organizations and individuals that reviewed parts of the manuscript. They include Gary Liles of the National Marine Fisheries Service, Scott Burns of the World Wildlife Fund, and Jeff Dunckel. We also appreciate several private organizations granting us permission to use their materials. These organizations include: Independent Sector, National Sporting Goods Association, the Gallup Organization, and The Nature Conservancy.

Mark S. Littman

CHAPTER 1

Population Characteristics

MARK S. LITTMAN

POPULATION

RANK OF THE UNITED STATES AMONG THE WORLD'S MOST POPULOUS COUNTRIES:	3RD
TOTAL U.S. POPULATION AS OF JULY 1996:	265,253,000 PERSONS
PERCENTAGE OF TOTAL WORLD POPULATION:	4.6 PERCENT
AVERAGE ANNUAL RATE OF GROWTH IN THE 1990S—	
UNITED STATES:	1.0 PERCENT
DEVELOPED COUNTRIES AS A GROUP:	0.4 PERCENT
LESS-DEVELOPED COUNTRIES AS A GROUP:	1.7 PERCENT
PROJECTED U.S. POPULATION IN 2020:	322,742,000 PERSONS
THREE MOST POPULOUS U.S. STATES IN—	
1996:	CALIFORNIA, TEXAS, NEW YORK
2020:	CALIFORNIA, TEXAS, FLORIDA

INTRODUCTION

The importance of population size to the social and economic health of nations has been debated for centuries, some claiming population growth has a positive influence and others condemning continued increases in these numbers. The debate continues today, with many, particularly economists, proclaiming that "market forces and human ingenuity will always take care of shortages," and others emphasizing that a single species (Homo sapiens) has now become a "vast destructive ecological force" with human population growth "a driving force behind many environmental and social problems."[1] This section presents basic population information in current and historical perspective both for the United States alone, and for the United States in the context of the rest of the world. The population indicators include not only the total population, but also the basic determinants of population growth (births, deaths, and migration), as well as distribution of the population both by age and by a variety of geographic categories of interest (that is, in cities, farms, and states).

TOTAL POPULATION

The U.S. population reached 265 million in 1996, approximately twice as many people as were U.S. residents at the time of the 1940 census. The U.S. population now represents about 4.6 percent of the world's estimated total population of about 5.8 billion people. Even with such a relatively small proportion of the world's inhabitants, the United States is the third most populous country in the world (prior to its dissolution, the former Soviet Union claimed the number three population rank), China and India being the first and second most populous. Most of the world's population (about 80 percent) lives in what are characterized as "developing" or "less developed" countries according to the United Nation's scheme of development status, with "more developed" countries (including the United States, most of Europe, and such countries as Japan and Australia) composing the remaining 20 percent. Since the U.S. annual growth rate is below the world's growth rate (1.4 percent per year), the share of the world's population that lives in the United States is projected to decrease slightly to about 4.3 percent by the year 2020 when the U.S. population will approach 323 million. Similarly, the share of the world's population living in developed countries is projected to decline to about 16.4 percent by 2020, but this assumes that the characterization of the development status of countries will not change in the next 25 years. In reality, some countries that are now characterized as "developing" will become "developed" by that time.

---

[1] For the former view, see Robert Whelan in Victor Anderson, *Alternative Economic Indicators* (London: Routledge, 1991); for the latter, see Lester R. Brown, et al., *State of the World 1997* (New York: W. W. Norton, 1997).

TABLE 1.1

U.S. AND WORLD POPULATION: 1996–2020

(NUMBERS IN THOUSANDS)

YEAR	WORLD POPULATION	UNITED STATES POPULATION (MIDDLE SERIES)	PERCENT OF WORLD POPULATION	POPULATION OF DEVELOPED COUNTRIES EXCLUDING THE UNITED STATES	PERCENT OF WORLD POPULATION	POPULATION OF LESS-DEVELOPED COUNTRIES	PERCENT OF WORLD POPULATION	POPULATION OF MORE-DEVELOPED COUNTRIES	PERCENT OF WORLD POPULATION
1996	5,772,351	265,253	4.6	905,728	15.7	4,601,370	79.7	1,170,981	20.29
2000	6,091,000	274,634	4.5	914,366	15.0	4,903,000	80.5	1,189,000	19.52
2005	6,480,500	285,981	4.4	924,760	14.3	5,269,760	81.3	1,210,741	18.68
2010	6,862,000	297,716	4.3	930,284	13.6	5,634,000	82.1	1,228,000	17.90
2015	7,239,238	310,134	4.3	931,733	12.9	5,997,372	82.8	1,241,867	17.15
2020	7,600,000	322,742	4.2	926,258	12.2	6,351,000	83.6	1,249,000	16.43

Source: U.S. Bureau of the Census, *World Population Profile: 1996*, Series WP/96, and unpublished data from the U.S. Bureau of the Census.

The U.S. growth rate in the 1990s of about 1 percent per year is only slightly higher than the annual growth rate in the 1980s of about .9 of 1 percent. This annual growth rate approached 1.7 percent during the 1950s baby boom era, the highest rate for the United States since early this century. The baby boom era birthrate in the United States was comparable to that of the world's developing countries today (about 1.7 percent per year in 1996).

Growth rates in all regions of the world, for both developed and less-developed countries, appear to have peaked. Average annual growth rates peaked in the 1950s for developed countries and in the 1960s for less-developed countries, and have been declining for both groups ever since.

FIGURE 1.1

PROPORTION OF THE WORLD POPULATION IN MORE-DEVELOPED COUNTRIES, LESS-DEVELOPED COUNTRIES, AND THE UNITED STATES: 1996–2020

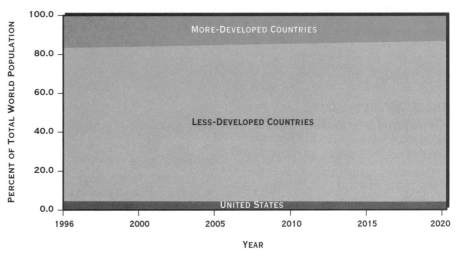

Source: U.S. Bureau of the Census, World Population Profile: 1996, Series WP/96 , and unpublished data from the U.S. Bureau of the Census.

TABLE 1.2

AVERAGE ANNUAL RATES OF GROWTH FOR THE UNITED STATES AND FOR THE WORLD: 1950–2000

PERIOD	WORLD	LESS-DEVELOPED COUNTRIES	MORE-DEVELOPED COUNTRIES	UNITED STATES
1950–1959	1.7	2.0	1.2	1.7
1960–1969	2.0	2.4	1.0	1.2
1970–1979	1.8	2.2	0.7	1.1
1980–1989	1.7	2.0	0.6	0.9
1990–1999	1.4	1.7	0.4	1.0

Source: U.S. Data from P-25 #1130 Table D. World data from *World Population Profile:1996*, U.S. Bureau of the Census, Series WP/960.

FIGURE 1.2

AVERAGE ANNUAL RATES OF GROWTH FOR THE WORLD AND FOR THE UNITED STATES: 1950–2000

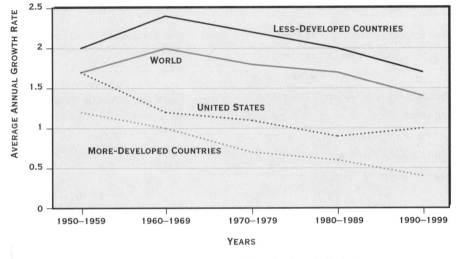

Source: U.S. Data from P-25 #1130 Table D. World data from World Population Profile: 1996, U.S. Bureau of the Census, Series, WP/960.

POPULATION BY STATE

The South and West regions combined will account for 80 percent of U.S. growth between 1996 and 2025. The South will remain the most populous region in the United States, and Western states will replace the Midwest as the second most populous region in the United States by the year 2000. California, currently the nation's most populous state, accounted for about 13 percent of the nation's population in 1996. Texas became the nation's second most populous state during the 1990s, while New York dropped to third. (As recently as the mid-1960s, New York had the largest state population.) According to current projections, Florida will replace New York as the third largest state in the next 20 years. At the other end of the size spectrum, Vermont, Delaware, the Dakotas, Wyoming, Alaska, and the District of Columbia are projected to still have total populations of under 1 million in 2020.

TABLE 1.3

POPULATION ESTIMATES AND PROJECTIONS OF THE LARGEST AND SMALLEST 10 STATES IN THE U.S.: 1995 AND 2025.

(NUMBERS IN THOUSANDS)

	1995 LARGEST 10 STATES NAME	POPULATION		2025 LARGEST 10 STATES NAME	POPULATION
1	CALIFORNIA	31,589	1	CALIFORNIA	49,285
2	TEXAS	18,724	2	TEXAS	27,183
3	NEW YORK	18,136	3	FLORIDA	20,710
4	FLORIDA	14,166	4	NEW YORK	19,830
5	PENNSYLVANIA	12,072	5	ILLINOIS	13,440
6	ILLINOIS	11,830	6	PENNSYLVANIA	12,683
7	OHIO	11,151	7	OHIO	11,744
8	MICHIGAN	9,549	8	MICHIGAN	10,078
9	NEW JERSEY	7,945	9	GEORGIA	9,869
10	GEORGIA	7,201	10	NEW JERSEY	9,558

	1995 SMALLEST 10 STATES NAME	POPULATION		2025 SMALLEST 10 STATES NAME	POPULATION
1	WYOMING	480	1	DISTRICT OF COLUMBIA	655
2	DISTRICT OF COLUMBIA	554	2	VERMONT	678
3	VERMONT	585	3	WYOMING	694
4	ALASKA	604	4	NORTH DAKOTA	729
5	NORTH DAKOTA	641	5	DELAWARE	861
6	DELAWARE	717	6	SOUTH DAKOTA	866
7	SOUTH DAKOTA	729	7	ALASKA	885
8	MONTANA	870	8	MONTANA	1,121
9	RHODE ISLAND	990	9	RHODE ISLAND	1,141
10	NEW HAMPSHIRE	1,148	10	MAINE	1,423

Source: U.S. Bureau of the Census.

DISTRIBUTION AND DENSITY

RANK OF U.S. LAND AREA AMONG THE WORLD'S LARGEST COUNTRIES:	4TH
U.S. POPULATION PER SQUARE MILE, 1991:	71
PERCENT OF THE WORLD'S POPULATION CLASSIFIED AS URBAN IN 1995:	46 PERCENT
PERCENT OF THE U.S. POPULATION CLASSIFIED AS URBAN IN 1995:	76 PERCENT
PERCENT OF THE U.S. POPULATION LIVING IN CITIES* OF 2 MILLION OR MORE:	22 PERCENT
PERCENT OF THE U.S. POPULATION LIVING IN METROPOLITAN AREAS:	80 PERCENT
PERCENT OF METROPOLITAN POPULATION LIVING IN SUBURBAN AREAS IN 1996:	63 PERCENT
PERCENT OF U.S. POPULATION LIVING ON FARMS IN THE 1990S:	2 PERCENT
PERCENT OF THE U.S. POPULATION THAT CHANGED RESIDENCES 1993–1994:	17 PERCENT
STATE WITH HIGHEST PROPORTION OF ITS 1990 RESIDENTS BORN IN THAT STATE:	PENNSYLVANIA
STATE WITH LOWEST PROPORTION OF ITS 1990 RESIDENTS BORN IN THAT STATE:	FLORIDA

* See note to Figure 1.4

DENSITY

Based on the relationship between their respective land areas and populations, not only cities, but also countries can be considered large or small, crowded or not crowded. Russia, for example, has by far the largest land area of any country, but it has "only" the sixth largest population of any country. The United States is the fourth largest country in land area, behind Russia, China, and Canada. Persons per square kilometer is one measure of population density at the national level. Of the world's 10 most populous countries, Bangladesh is the most crowded. The United States is among the least crowded of the world's 25 largest countries, with only Brazil and Russia having lower population density.

FIGURE 1.3

POPULATION PER SQUARE MILE (25 LARGEST COUNTRIES): 1991

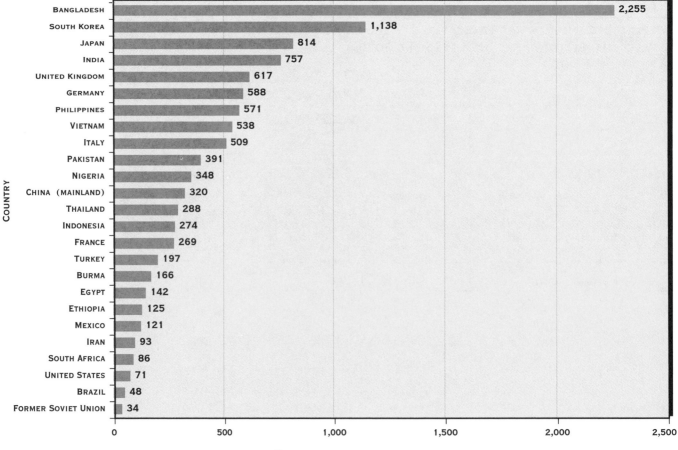

Source: World Population Profile: 1991, U.S. Bureau of the Census. WP/91.

FIGURE 1.4

PERCENTAGE OF NATIONS' POPULATION LIVING IN CITIES OF 2 MILLION OR MORE POPULATION: 2000 (PROJECTED)

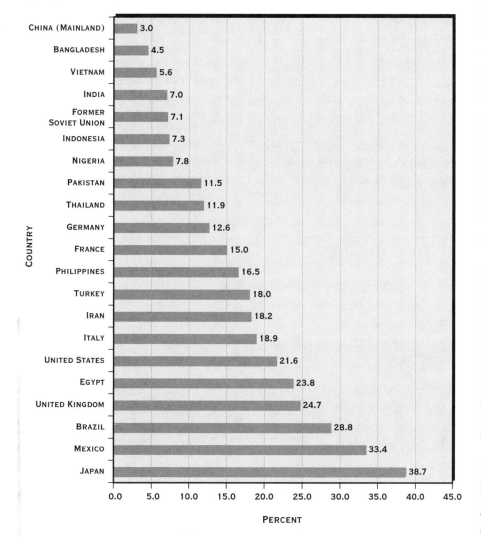

Note: For the purpose of these projections, the Census Bureau defined "cities" as population clusters of continuous built-up area with a population density of at least 5,000 persons per square mile, ignoring political and administrative boundaries. For further details see table 10 in the report. Countries shown are those with 50 million or more population and one or more "city" of 2 million or more population, U.S. Bureau of the Census. WP/91.

Source: World Population Profile: 1991, U.S. Bureau of the Census. WP/91.

URBAN, METROPOLITAN POPULATION

About 80 percent of the U.S. population is now classified as living within metropolitan areas. As defined by the U.S. Office of Management and Budget, these areas typically contain a city with a population of 50,000 or more, and contain one or more whole central counties.[2] In 1970 only about two-thirds of the U.S. population was classified as metropolitan. Part of this proportionate increase in metropolitan population is attributable to changes in the definition of metropolitan area. These changes increased the total percentage of U.S. land area categorized as metropolitan, from 11 percent in 1970 to nearly 20 percent in 1995, by adding 28 new metropolitan areas (243 metropolitan areas in 1973, 271 in 1995).[3] Within U.S. metropolitan areas, suburban growth continues unabated, with the suburban population inching up from 54 percent to 63 percent of the total metropolitan population between 1970 and 1996 (using the metropolitan area definition at each of those times). Much of this suburban growth is attributable to the significant movement of the population from central cities to suburban areas, with, for instance, 2.9 million persons moving from cities to suburbs between 1993 and 1994.

Historically, the growth of metropolitan areas has been fueled by rural to urban migration.[4] But recent metropolitan growth has not occurred in this way—there was essentially no net migration from rural areas into metropolitan areas between 1993 and 1994, the latest available figures. Rather, nearly all migrants moving into metropolitan areas came from abroad: in fact, throughout the 1990s international migration has accounted for nearly 90 percent of the metropolitan growth attributable to migration.

Using a simple urban/rural dichotomy, the population of the world as a whole, 46

---

2 For a more detailed definition and history, see Donald C. Dahmann and James D. Fitzsimmons, ed., "Metropolitan and Nonmetropolitan Areas: New Approaches to Geographic Definition," Working paper no. 12 (Washington, DC: U.S. Bureau of the Census, Population Division, September, 1995). Components of individual areas are shown in Appendix C of George E. Hall and Deirdre A. Gaquin, ed., 1997 County and City Extra (Lanham, MD: Bernan Press, 1997).

3 Since metropolitan areas are defined in terms of whole counties (except in New England), the boundaries of some metropolitan areas include territory beyond what might ordinarily be considered metropolitan (e.g., much of the Mojave Desert, including Death Valley National Monument, is part of the Los Angeles-Anaheim-Riverside CMSA).

4 Douglas S. Massey, "The Age of Extremes: Concentrated Affluence and Poverty in the Twenty-First Century," Demography, no. 4 (November 1996), 395-412.

percent of which is classified as urban, is considerably less urban than the United States as a whole, 76 percent of which is classified as urban (1995 estimates).[5] But the world figure is expected to pass the 50 percent mark sometime within the next 20 years. As is the case in the United States, European nations also are experiencing an exodus from large cities. The proportion of their respective populations living in urban areas with a population of 2 million or more is projected to decline between 1991 and 2000 in such countries as the United Kingdom, France, and Germany.[6]

FARM, RURAL, AND NONMETROPOLITAN POPULATION

At the turn of the century, nearly two of every five Americans (40 percent) lived on a farm. Today, persons living on farms represent fewer than 2 percent of the U.S. population. Although part of this shift reflects industrial changes (fewer than half of the persons living on farms are employed in farm occupations today, and only about a third of the persons doing farm work live on farms), most of this shift in residence is attributable to Americans moving from rural to urban settings.[7]

While about one out of four Americans still live in rural settings (defined negatively as living outside places that have a population of 2,500 or more), most of these people now have no involvement with agriculture per se, and only about 7 percent of rural residents live on farms. As in the United States, the shift away from agriculture and the tendency toward urbanization of the population is occurring worldwide, but there are still vast differences by country: in China, for example, about 70 percent of the population now live in rural areas, the vast majority of whom are involved with agriculture.

FIGURE 1.5

DISTRIBUTION OF POPULATION IN THE UNITED STATES: 1990

Source: U.S. Department of Commerce, Economics and Statistics Administration, U.S. Bureau of the Census.

---

[5] In the United States, the urban population is defined essentially as that living in places of 2,500 or more population; the rural population is that which is not living in such places. There is no internationally agreed-upon definition of urban and rural, but it is generally based on size of locality. For a detailed U.S. definition, see Appendix A, Area Classifications, in the *1990 Census Volumes*. For a discussion of international definitions, see United Nations, *Demographic Yearbook: 1992*.

[6] Ellen Jamison, *World Population Profile: 1991*, Series WP/91 (Washington, DC: U.S. Bureau of the Census).

[7] Laarni T. Dacquel and Donald C. Dahmann, *Residents of Farms and Rural Areas: 1991*, Current Population Reports, Series P-20 no. 472 (Economic Research Service, U.S. Department of Agriculture, and U.S. Bureau of the Census/ERS joint publication).

NONMETROPOLITAN GROWTH

During the 1970s, nonmetropolitan counties (that is, the land area in the United States that is not in metropolitan counties, some of which is rural, but much of which is urban) grew faster than metropolitan areas, prompting discussion of a rural renaissance in the United States. It was short-lived, although some researchers feel that we are now in the middle of another turnaround. Using the 1993 metropolitan area designation, nonmetropolitan population increased by 13.6 percent during the 1970s compared with 10.8 percent for metropolitan areas, but during the 1980s the population in nonmetropolitan areas grew only 2.7 percent compared with 11.8 percent for metropolitan areas. So far in the 1990s (between 1990 and 1994), the population in metropolitan areas has grown about 5.8 percent compared with 5.1 percent for nonmetropolitan areas. Nonmetropolitan counties in the West and Northeast are growing faster than metropolitan areas in those regions, and, based on recent data, net migration rates for nonmetropolitan areas are, once again, higher than rates for metropolitan areas. More than half of nonmetropolitan growth between 1990 and 1994 is the result of net in-migration from metropolitan areas. Because of these trends, some researchers feel that we are in the midst of a new nonmetropolitan turnaround.[8]

U.S. REGIONAL GROWTH AND MIGRATION

During the mid-1990s, the only region that appears to have had more people moving in than moving out (from other regions of the United States) is the South. Including international migration, no region of the United States is losing population because of migration largely because of the propensity of immigrants from abroad to move to a handful of states. (See the next subsection

FIGURE 1.6

PERCENTAGE OF THE U.S. POPULATION LIVING IN RURAL AREAS AND ON FARMS: 1900–1992

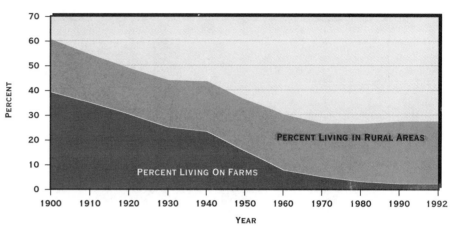

Source: *Residents of Farms and Rural Areas: 1991*, U.S. Bureau of the Census. Series P-20, no. 472, and unpublished data.

on international migration.) According to the most recent survey, taken between 1993 and 1994, 17 percent of the U.S. population did move, but the majority of those moves were of short distance—over 60 percent within the same county, with only 16 percent to a different state. One gauge of the propensity to move over a lifetime is the proportion of persons in a state who were born in that state. Americans have a cosmopolitan view of the United States, but there are several states in which over three-fourths of their populations were born in the state in which they live. Pennsylvania heads the list, with 80 percent of its 1990 population having been born in that state. Most states with low proportions of their populations born there were concentrated in the West, but one Southern state, Florida (with only 30.5 percent of its population born in that state), ranked lowest because of both its large retirement-age population from other states and its large numbers of immigrants (principally from Cuba).

---

[8] See Calvin Beale and Kenneth Johnson, Nonmetropolitan Population Continues Post-1990 Rebound, *Rural Conditions and Trends* (spring 1995); Glenn L. Fuguitt and Calvin L. Beale, "Recent Trends in Nonmetropolitan Migration: Toward New Turnaround?" *Growth and Change* 27 (spring 1996).

FIGURE 1.7

IN-MIGRANTS AND OUT-MIGRANTS IN THE UNITED STATES, BY REGION: 1993–1994

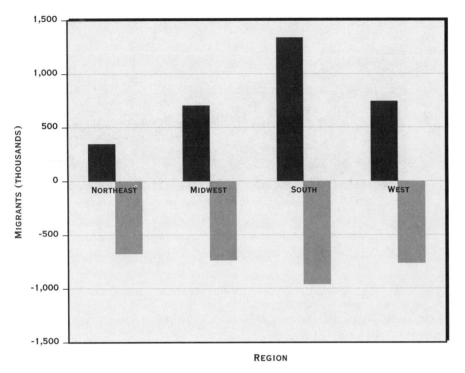

REGION

■ IN-MIGRANTS   ■ OUT-MIGRANTS

Note: Excludes movers from abroad.

Source: 1994 Current Population Survey data available on the U.S. Bureau of the Census Website at <http://www.census.gov>.

AGE AND RACE DISTRIBUTION, VITAL RATES, AND INTERNATIONAL MIGRATION

MEDIAN AGE IN THE UNITED STATES IN 1995:	34.3 YEARS
PERCENTAGE OF THE U.S. POPULATION AGED 65 AND OVER IN—	
1996:	13.0 PERCENT
2030:	20.0 PERCENT (PROJECTED)
PERCENTAGE OF THE U.S. POPULATION UNDER AGE 18 IN—	
1996:	26.0 PERCENT
2030:	24.0 PERCENT (PROJECTED)
TOTAL FERTILITY RATE IN 1995 FOR THE—	
U.S.:	2.0
WORLD:	2.9
PERCENTAGE OF BIRTHS IN U.S. TO	
UNMARRIED WOMEN—	
1970:	11.0 PERCENT
1995:	32.9 PERCENT
TEENAGE MOTHERS—	
1970:	18.0 PERCENT
1995:	13.0 PERCENT
LIFE EXPECTANCY AT BIRTH IN THE U.S. IN 1996:	76 YEARS
PERCENTAGE OF THE U.S POPULATION THAT WAS	
FOREIGN-BORN IN—	
1910:	14.8 PERCENT
1994:	9.0 PERCENT
PERCENTAGE OF U.S. POPULATION GROWTH ATTRIBUTABLE	
TO IMMIGRATION IN—	
1995–1996:	33.0 PERCENT
1996–2020:	60.0 PERCENT (PROJECTED)

AGE AND DEPENDENCY

As is the case worldwide, the population of the United States is slowly aging. At the turn of the century, only about 4 percent of the U.S. population was over age 65. This percentage has increased to about 13 percent today, and will likely reach 20 percent by the year 2030. The median age (that is, the age that divides the population in half, one half being younger than that age, the other half being older) in the United States has increased from about 22.9 years at the turn of the century to 34.3 years in 1995, and is expected to be about 38.5 by 2030.

European countries in general have slightly older populations than the United States. The United Kingdom, for example, had a median age of 34.5 in 1988, while Germany and Denmark had even older populations. About 7 percent of the world's total population is estimated to be 65 years and over in 1996, and an estimated 9 percent will be 65 and over by the year 2020. Developed countries tend to have higher proportions of older persons in their populations than developing countries (about 14 percent versus 5 percent in 1996).

During this century, the U.S. dependency ratio (that is, the number of children and elderly persons per 100 persons 18 to 64 years of age) was at its highest point during the early 1960s as a result of the baby boom.[9] There were about 82 dependents per 100 persons aged 18 to 64 years during the early 1960s. Since that time the dependency ratio has been declining (63 per 100 in 1996), and is forecast to continue declining until about the year 2010: its rise at that point will be fueled by the increasing aging of the population as well as the (projected) increasing number of births. In 2030 the dependency ratio is projected to be about where it was in 1970, but the mix of dependents will be considerably different. In 1970 about three-fourths of dependents were children, and the remainder were elderly, but by the year 2030 only about 53 percent of dependents will be children, with the remaining 47 percent being elderly. The overall dependency ratio in the United States is similar to that for developed countries as a group, and is considerably less than that of developing countries, which, as a group, had a dependency ratio of about 94 in 1996.

---

[9] The notion of a dependency ratio is that persons in the "nondependent" age groups are performing the economic support of the "dependent" age groups. It should be remembered that many persons over and under the nondependent age groups provide some or all of the economic support for their families or particular members of their families, and that persons are retiring earlier, so that persons in the nondependent ages may actually be retired. See, for example, *Who's Helping Out? Support Networks Among American Families*, Series P-70, no. 13 (Washington, DC: U.S. Bureau of the Census).

FIGURE 1.8

U.S. DEPENDENCY RATIO: 1990–2030

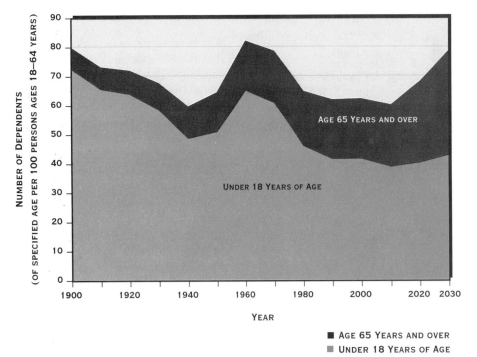

Source: U.S. Bureau of the Census, Middle Series Projections.

TABLE 1.4

RATIO OF DEPENDENTS TO PERSONS AGES 18 TO 64 YEARS IN THE UNITED STATES: 1900–2030

YEAR	TOTAL DEPENDENTS	UNDER 18 YEARS OF AGE	AGE 65 YEARS AND OVER
1900	79.9	72.6	7.3
1910	73.2	65.7	7.5
1920	72.0	64.0	8.0
1930	67.7	58.6	9.1
1940	59.7	48.8	10.9
1950	64.5	51.1	13.4
1960	82.2	65.3	16.9
1970	78.7	61.1	17.6
1980	64.9	46.2	18.7
1990	62.0	41.7	20.3
2000	62.4	41.8	20.5
2010	60.2	39.0	21.2
2020	68.2	40.4	27.7
2030	78.7	43.0	35.7

Source: U.S. Bureau of the Census, Middle Series Projections.

TABLE 1.5

STATES WITH THE LARGEST AND SMALLEST PROPORTIONS OF THEIR POPULATIONS AGE UNDER 18 YEARS AND 65 YEARS AND OVER: 1995

STATES WITH LARGEST PROPORTION		STATES WITH SMALLEST PROPORTIONS	
UNDER 18 YEARS		**UNDER 18 YEARS**	
	PERCENT		PERCENT
UTAH	34.5	DIST. OF COLUMBIA	20.6
ALASKA	31.5	WEST VIRGINIA	23.1
IDAHO	29.9	MASSACHUSETTS	23.6
NEW MEXICO	29.7	FLORIDA	23.8
TEXAS	28.8	RHODE ISLAND	24.0
65 YEARS AND OVER		**65 YEARS AND OVER**	
	PERCENT		PERCENT
FLORIDA	18.6	ALASKA	4.9
PENNSYLVANIA	15.9	UTAH	8.8
RHODE ISLAND	15.8	COLORADO	10.0
WEST VIRGINIA	15.3	GEORGIA	10.0
IOWA	15.2	TEXAS	10.2

Source: U.S. Bureau of the Census Website at <http://www.census.gov>.

DIFFERENCES IN AGE DISTRIBUTION BY STATE

There is considerable variation by state in age distribution, as is evident by the percentage of the population who are children or the percentage who are 65 years of age or older. For example, in 1995 the percentage of the population 65 years and over varied from a high of 18.6 percent in Florida to a low of 4.9 percent in Alaska. Other states with relatively high proportions of elderly persons include Pennsylvania, Rhode Island, Iowa, and West Virginia (all between 15 and 16 percent). The only state other than Alaska with fewer than 10 percent of its populace over age 65 is Utah, with 8.8 percent in that age range. Utah and Alaska are the only states with over 30 percent of their populations under age 18. The District of Columbia, West Virginia, and Florida have the smallest proportions of their populations who are children. (As is the case in the District of Columbia, large American cities typically have relatively small proportions of their populations who are children.)

TABLE 1.6

SELECTED FERTILITY INDICATORS FOR THE UNITED STATES: 1940–1994

YEAR	NUMBER OF BIRTHS (THOUSANDS)	CRUDE BIRTH RATE (PER 1,000 POPULATION)	FERTILITY RATE (PER 1,000 WOMEN AGED 15 TO 44)	TOTAL FERTILITY RATE (IMPLIED LIFETIME BIRTHS PER 1,000 WOMEN)
1994	3,953	15.2	66.7	2,046
1990	4,158	16.7	70.9	2,081
1985	3,761	15.8	66.3	1,844
1980	3,612	15.9	68.4	1,840
1975	3,144	14.6	66.0	1,774
1970	3,731	18.4	86.1	2,480
1965	3,760	19.4	96.3	2,622
1960	4,258	23.7	118.0	3,449
1955	4,097	25.0	118.3	3,580
1950	3,632	24.1	106.2	3,091
1945	2,858	20.4	85.9	2,491
1940	2,559	19.4	79.9	2,301

Source: National Center for Health Statistics.

BIRTHS AND FERTILITY

The number of births in the United States has declined in each of the past 5 years, after peaking at about 4.2 million in 1990. The rise in the number of births during the 1980s (1989 was the first year since the height of the baby boom era that the number of births had exceeded 4 million) was the result of an increase in the number of women of childbearing age rather than an increase in the birth rate. The crude birth rate in the United States, 14.8 births per 1,000 people in 1995, was close to 25 births per 1,000 people in the late 1950s, at the peak of the baby boom.

FIGURE 1.9

NUMBER OF BIRTHS AND TOTAL FERTILITY RATE IN THE UNITED STATES: 1940–1994

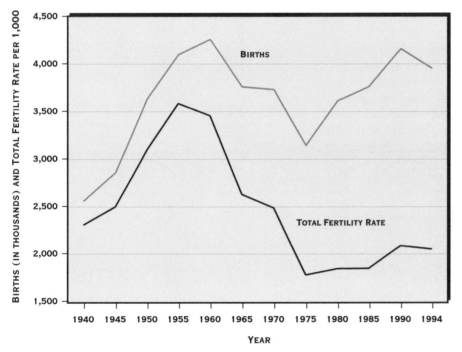

Source: National Center for Health Statistics.

FIGURE 1.10

TOTAL FERTILITY RATES FOR SELECTED COUNTRIES: 1996

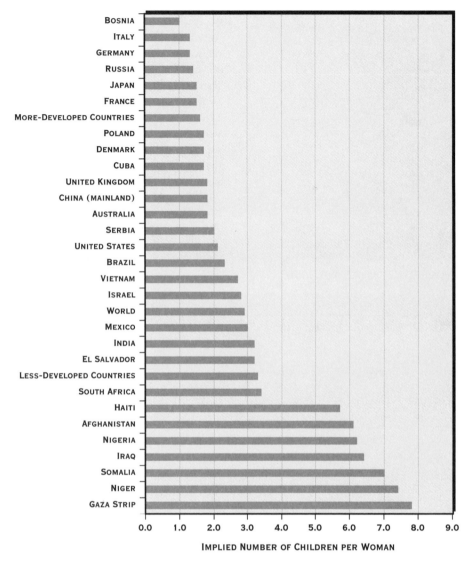

IMPLIED NUMBER OF CHILDREN PER WOMAN

Source: World Population Profile: 1996, U.S. Bureau of the Census. Series WP/96.

Another gauge of fertility is the total fertility rate (TFR), a hypothetical measure, which is the expected number of lifetime births that 1,000 women would have based on age-specific fertility rates in a given year. In 1995, the TFR in the United States was a little over 2.0, which implies about two births per woman. The average TFR for the world was 2.9 births, but there is considerable variation by country, with several Asian and African nations having TFRs of 6 or higher, and Western European countries as a group having TFRs averaging 1.5 births, well below replacement level. Both developing and more-developed nations have seen decreases in their total fertility rates over the past decade, and decreases for developing nations are forecast to continue. In 1996, out of 227 countries, the United States ranked 150th in TFR, the highest being in the Gaza Strip (7.0 TFR) and the lowest in Bosnia (with a total fertility rate of 1.0).[10] Several factors affect the number and rate of births, including the number of women of child-bearing age and the average age of women giving birth for the first time.

---

10 Thomas M. McDevitt, *World Population Profile: 1996*. Series WP/96 (Washington, DC: U.S. Agency for International Development and U.S. Bureau of the Census joint publication).

FIGURE 1.11

PERCENTAGE OF ALL BIRTHS THAT WERE TO UNMARRIED WOMEN, BY SELECTED COUNTRY: 1970–1993

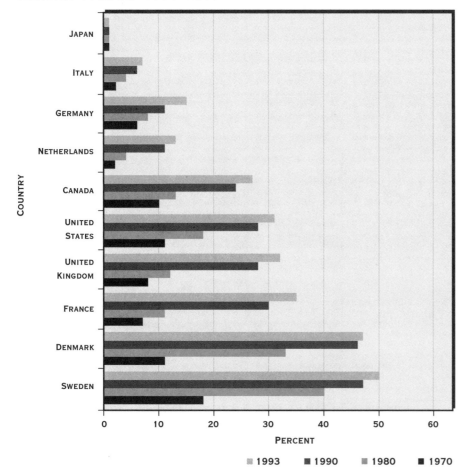

Source: National Center for Health Statistics and U.S. Bureau of the Census, *Statistical Abstract 1996* .

FIGURE 1.12

TEEN BIRTHS AS A PERCENT OF ALL BIRTHS IN THE U.S.: 1970–1993

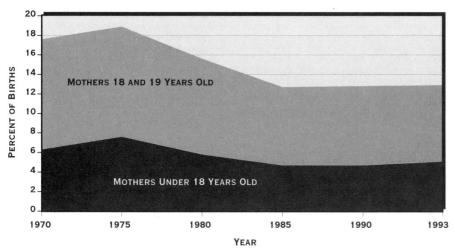

Source: National Center for Health Statistics and U.S. Bureau of the Census. Statistical Abstract 1996.

NONMARITAL BIRTHS, TEEN BIRTHS

The proportion of all births in the United States that were to unmarried women has increased considerably in the past several decades, but appears to have leveled off in the 1990s. This increase has not been confined to America, but has occurred worldwide. In 1970, about 11 percent of births in the United States were to unwed mothers. This fraction increased fairly steadily, reaching 32.6 percent in 1994, but declined slightly, to 32.0 percent, in 1995. The decrease in 1995 was the first ever recorded. The proportion of births that are to unmarried women varies enormously among developed countries, ranging from nearly 50 percent in the Scandinavian nations to only 1 percent in Japan, both relatively developed countries. Thus, cultural factors, rather than simply economic development per se, also influence the incidence of unwed births.

The proportion of all births that are to teenage mothers has not increased as much as one might think from the amount of press coverage such births get: teen births represented only 13 percent of all births in 1995 in the United States, down from about 18 percent in 1970. However, since marriage rates have decreased and the average age at marriage has increased over the past several decades (from 20.3 years in 1950 to 24.5 years in 1993), a considerably higher proportion of births to teen mothers are to unmarried teenagers. This has prompted society's concern not only for these young mothers, but also for their offspring. The United States is grappling with questions such as who will provide financial support to these unwed, teenage mothers, and who will provide health insurance coverage for their children? The birth rate for teenagers was about 60 births per 1,000 teenage women in 1993, down from about 68 in 1970 and 89 per 1,000 teenage women in 1960.

MORTALITY AND LIFE EXPECTANCY

The crude death rate in the United States has not changed much in the past 20 years, hovering between 8 and 9 deaths per 1,000 population on an annual basis since 1975. However, when changes in age distribution are controlled by using an age-adjusted death rate, the *1995 death rate was at a record low level*.[11] Worldwide, the crude death rate is about 9 deaths per 100 population. Age distribution can affect the crude death rate so that a country with relatively low mortality can appear to have high mortality levels (and vice versa). For example, the overall crude death rate may be high in a society with a proportionately large number of elderly, but the death rates for each age group taken separately may be relatively low (relative to other countries). Age-adjusted death rates and death rates by cause are discussed in the chapter on health.

Life expectancy (which is the average number of years that a group of infants born in a given year would live if they were to experience the age-specific death rates prevailing during the year of their birth) is now 76 in the United States. For women, life expectancy is about 79 years, for men about 73 years.[12] For both sexes combined, life expectancy has increased by nearly 10 years since the end of World War II. Among the world's 25 largest countries, the United States has the sixth highest life expectancy, although the spread among the top six countries is only about 3 years. The average life expectancy for all countries combined is only 62 years, and that for all developed countries combined, 74 years, is below the U.S. average. Japan has one of the highest life expectancies in the world (80 years). Two small nations have life expectancy even higher than that of Japan: Hong Kong (82 years) and San Marino (81 years). There are still many countries, principally in Africa, that have life expectancy at birth of below 50 years. Among this latter group, Haiti is the only country in the Western Hemisphere with a life expectancy of 49 years (in 1996).

FIGURE 1.13

LIFE EXPECTANCY AT BIRTH IN SELECTED COUNTRIES: 1996

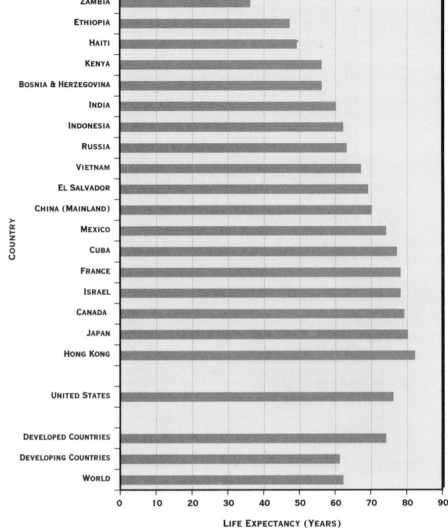

Source: World Population Profile 1996 U.S. Bureau of the Census. Series WP/96.

---

[11] National Center for Health Statistics, "Monthly Vital Statistics Report,"*1995 Annual Summary*, 3.

[12] Stephanie J. Ventura et al., "Births and Deaths: United States, 1996," *Monthly Vital Statistics Reports* 46, no. 1 (September 1997).

FIGURE 1.14

FOREIGN-BORN POPULATION AS A PERCENTAGE OF THE TOTAL POPULATION IN THE UNITED STATES: 1900–1990

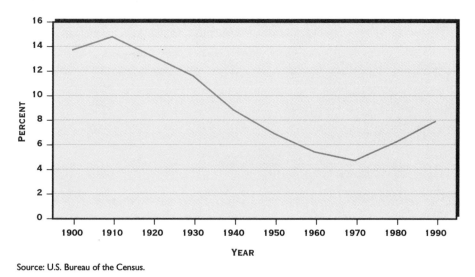

Source: U.S. Bureau of the Census.

FIGURE 1.15

PROPORTION OF IMMIGRATION TO THE UNITED STATES, BY WORLD REGION: 1955–1995

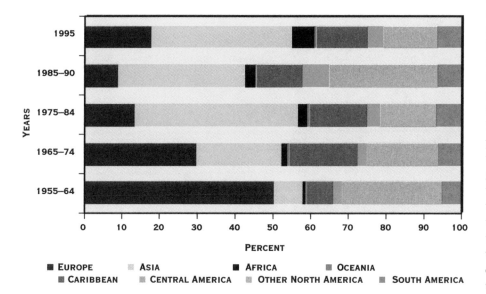

■ EUROPE   ▨ ASIA   ■ AFRICA   ▨ OCEANIA
■ CARIBBEAN   ▨ CENTRAL AMERICA   ▨ OTHER NORTH AMERICA   ▨ SOUTH AMERICA

Source: Statistical Yearbook: 1995, Immigration and Naturalization Service.

LEGAL IMMIGRATION

The number of births minus the number of deaths (dubbed "natural increase" by demographers) and net migration are the determinants of growth for a country. One or both of these components can be the driving force of population change depending on the country and the point-in-time of interest. In the United States, net immigration is projected to be a predominant factor in our future population growth. At levels presumed by the Census Bureau's middle projection series (which assume net immigration at current levels), immigrants and the offspring of immigrants who come to the United States between 1994 and the middle of the next century will be responsible for 60 percent of our total population growth during that period.

Despite arguments or opinions that suggest U.S. immigration policy is either too restrictive or too permissive, the United States, according to one estimate, was receiving nearly twice as many immigrants (at the beginning of the decade) as the rest of the world's countries combined.[13] Recent concern about immigration has been fueled not only by the number of immigrants, but by their perceived and actual influence on the lives of nonimmigrants. Historically, immigrants have borne the brunt of public scorn when economic conditions worsen. However, economic conditions in general have been good for the past several years, yet immigration remains a hotly contested issue in the media and at various levels of government. Part of the reason for this topicality is the differential effect of recent immigration on the resident population; much of the negative impact is on minorities, according to some research, because the jobs recent immigrants are taking are concentrated at the bottom of the occupational ladder, where minorities are disproportionately represented.[14]

While the level of immigration is high by recent standards, the proportion of foreign-born persons in the population is not at record levels for the United States. In 1994, about 9 percent of the population

---

13 Joseph A. McFalls Jr., "Population: A Lively Introduction," *Population Bulletin* 46, no. 2 (Washington, DC: Population Reference Bureau, October 1991).

14 See George J. Borjas, "The New Economics of Immigration," *Atlantic Monthly* (November 1996).

was foreign born, nearly double the percentage of foreign born in 1970 (about 5 percent) but considerably less than the figure at the turn of the century (about 15 percent).

The number of immigrants admitted to the United States has varied considerably throughout the past decade, increasing from about 600,000 in the mid-1980s to nearly 900,000 in 1993 (excluding IRCA legalizations[15]). In the next 2 years the number began decreasing, approaching 720,000 by 1995. The Immigration Act of 1990 placed a "flexible" cap on immigration of 700,000 in 1992–94, and 675,000 thereafter. Roughly two-thirds of immigrants are admitted based on their family relationship to a U.S. citizen, while most of the remaining immigrants are admitted based on job skills. Beginning in the early 1990s, Congress mandated a new "diversity" program that guaranteed about 55,000 visas to countries that had been "adversely affected" by the 1965 Immigration Act.[16]

During this century, there has been a fairly dramatic shift in the countries of origin of immigrants, away from Europe and toward Central America and Asia. As has been the case throughout the 1990s, Mexico remains the source country for the largest group of immigrants (even excluding IRCA legalizations, which were predominantly from Mexico as well), representing about 13 percent of all immigrants in 1995. The other countries in the top five in 1995 include the Philippines (7 percent of immigrants), Vietnam (6 percent), and the Dominican Republic, China, and India (all with about 5 percent). Immigrants tend to cluster in a relatively small number of states, with three-fourths of those admitted in 1995 concentrated in 10 states. The most popular are California, home to 23 percent of immigrants in 1995, New York (18 percent), Florida (9 percent), Texas (7 percent), New Jersey (6 percent), and Illinois (5 percent).

It is important to note that many persons legally enter the United States each year who are not immediately enumerated as "immigrants" in official statistics, despite the fact that many end up staying in the United States permanently. Some "classes" of persons can "adjust" to permanent status (and are thus counted as immigrants) after being in the United States for 1 year (e.g., people granted asylum or refugee status). Such persons are counted as "immigrants" only after they take this adjustment step even though they may have been in the United States for several years.

FIGURE 1.16

RANGE OF ESTIMATED UNDOCUMENTED ALIEN POPULATION IN THE UNITED STATES: 1980–1990

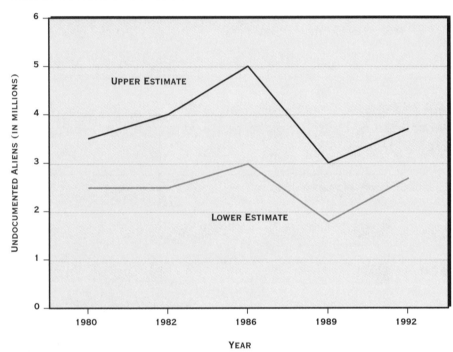

Source: Michael Fix and Jeffrey S. Passel. *Immigration and Immigrants.* Urban Institute. 1994.

---

15 IRCA is an acronym for Immigration Reform and Control Act of 1986. This legislation legalized the immigration of approximately 3 million persons (roughly 1 percent of the U.S. population) who had entered the United States illegally or as temporary visitors after January 1, 1982. The size of the illegal immigrant population likely peaked in the mid-1980s, prior to the IRCA legalization program, declined for a few years, and now appears to be increasing again. One indication is the number of apprehensions of aliens. The number of apprehensions (arrests of aliens who are in violation of immigration law), which had peaked in the 1980s prior to IRCA and which then declined sharply after IRCA, has begun to increase again in the 1990s. Apprehensions totaled about 1.3 million in 1993, the country of origin of 96 percent of whom was Mexico. The law also created sanctions against employers for hiring aliens not authorized to work in the United States. For further discussion, see Michael Fix and Jeffrey S. Passel, *Immigration and Immigrants* (Washington, DC: The Urban Institute, 1994) and Immigration and Naturalization Service, *1994 Statistical Yearbook,* as well as the yearbook for various other years.

16 Forty percent of the visas allocated under the diversity program must be allocated to natives of Ireland. Prior to 1965 there had been quotas by country that dictated how many immigrants were to be admitted from each.

ILLEGAL IMMIGRATION

The term "illegals" conjures up notions of undocumented (i.e., without visa or other permit to enter the United States) persons sneaking across the Rio Grande at night, carrying their belongings in a sack over their heads. In fact *the majority of illegal immigrants enter the United States legally* and simply overstay their visit when their visas expire. Immigrants most often enter the United States as students, visitors, or temporary workers: in 1994, over 20 million persons were admitted to the U.S. on a temporary basis, 17 million as visitors and, about 3 million on business. Such persons represent about 60 percent of undocumented immigrants.[17] Nevertheless, the size of the illegal immigrant population, estimated to be somewhere in the 3.5 to 4 million range in 1994 by the Census Bureau, is a significant figure (between 1 and 2 percent of the resident population) not only because of its size and the geographic concentration of undocumented persons in a few states, with something on the order of half concentrated in California, but also because of the concentration of source countries, the majority coming from Mexico and Central America (over 60 percent).

EMIGRATION

Not all immigrants stay in the United States. In fact, at some times in our history (e.g., during the 1930s depression era), more persons left the United States to live in another country than entered the United States. Since World War II, however, the ratio of emigrants (persons leaving the country) to immigrants (persons entering the country to live) has been about one to four; that is, one person left for every four who entered the United States. During the 1980s, for example, about 7.3 million persons immigrated to the United States, while 1.6 million left for another country, leaving a net immigration figure of 5.7 million persons. The countries receiving the largest numbers of emigrants from the United States were Mexico, the country to which nearly one of four émigrés returned during the 1980s, followed by the United Kingdom and Germany.

FIGURE 1.17

IMMIGRATION AND EMIGRATION IN THE UNITED STATES: 1901–1990

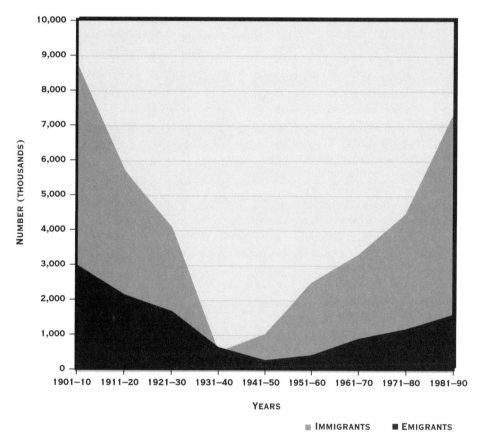

■ IMMIGRANTS   ■ EMIGRANTS

Source: 1992 Statistical Yearbook, Immigration and Naturalization Service.

---

17 Fix and Passel, *Immigration and Immigrants.*

RACIAL AND ETHNIC COMPOSITION

By the time of the birth of the United States as a nation, the predominant race among its approximately 4 million residents had already been transformed from Native American Indian to White. European settlers and their descendants composed about 80 percent of the U.S. population enumerated in the first U.S. Census in 1790, with Black slaves from Africa making up the bulk of the remainder. Indians were not included in the census figures until the 1890 census (the Constitution of the United States specifically excluded "Indians not taxed" from the apportionment of representatives in Congress and, thus, Congress made no earlier attempt to enumerate Indians on reservations or in Indian Territory). In 1890, there were only about 248,000 American Indians enumerated, less than 1 percent of the population in the continental United States. They compose under 1 percent of the country's inhabitants in the mid-1990s as well. Although Blacks have remained the largest racial minority group in the United States, the proportion of the U.S. population that was of African American origin actually declined from 1790 until the turn of the 20th century. Blacks represented less than 10 percent of the U.S. population in 1950 before their proportion of the U.S. population began to increase once again. In 1996, Blacks represented about 13 percent of the U.S. population.[18]

Recent trends in immigration and accompanying fertility differentials portend major changes in the racial and ethnic composition of the U.S. population in the next 50 years, with the proportion of the population that is White and not of Hispanic origin (the "Anglo" population) expected to decline significantly. The Latino population is projected to account for about one out of four U.S. residents by the year 2050 using the Census Bureau's middle projection series.

Hispanics now represent about 9 percent of the U.S. population. Also increasing proportionately will be the Asian American population, which will increase from about 3 percent to 8 percent of the U.S. population by 2050. The representation of African Americans is forecast to increase only slightly in the next 50 years, from 13 to 13.5 percent of the U.S. population by 2050. Because of these increases, the Anglo population is likely to decline from about 74 percent to 53 percent of the U.S. population by 2050. Latinos will become the largest minority group in the U.S. within the next decade.

FIGURE 1.18

PERCENTAGE DISTRIBUTION OF THE U.S. POPULATION, BY RACE AND HISPANIC ORIGIN: 1990–2050 (PROJECTED)

(RACE SHOWN FOR PERSONS NOT OF HISPANIC ORIGIN)

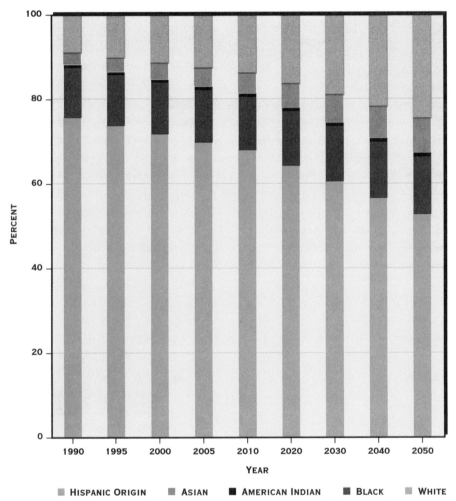

Source: Population Projections of the United States by Age, Sex, Race and Hispanic Origin: 1995 to 2050, U.S. Bureau of the Census, Series P-25.

---

18 The concept of race used here is based on self-identification of persons into one of five racial groups (White; Black; American Indian, including Eskimo and Aleut; Asian, including Pacific Islanders; and a residual category identified as other "races") based on response to survey or decennial census questions. Persons are also asked to self-identify as being of Hispanic origin or not of Hispanic origin. Persons of Hispanic, or Latino, origin (the terms are used interchangeably here) can be of any race and can include persons of Mexican, Puerto Rican, Cuban, Central or South American, and other Spanish culture or origin. Since most of the data on race and ethnicity used in this report derive from U.S. government sources, the racial classification used generally adheres to the guidelines in Federal Statistical Directive No. 15, issued by the Office of Management and Budget. The subject of race has been the topic of several studies and conferences in the 1990s, including whether to revise the race categories required by the Office of Management and Budget in Directive 15 to include the option of indicating a multiracial category or allowing respondents to mark all racial categories that apply. See, for example, *Challenges of Measuring an Ethnic World: Proceedings of the Joint Canada-United States Conference on the Measurement of Ethnicity*, April 1-3, 1992; "Recommendations from the Interagency Committee for the Review of Racial and Ethnic Standards to the Office of Management and Budget Concerning Changes to the Standards for the Classification of Federal Data on Race and Ethnicity," available at Website <www.whitehouse.gov>; and Stephen Barr and Michael A. Fletcher, "U.S. Proposes Multiple Racial Identification for 2000 Census," *Washington Post* (9 July 1997).

FOR FURTHER INFORMATION SEE:

1993 STATISTICAL YEARBOOK OF THE IMMIGRATION AND NATURALIZATION SERVICE. WASHINGTON, DC: IMMIGRATION AND NATURALIZATION SERVICE (SEPTEMBER, 1994).

BORJAS, GEORGE J. "THE NEW ECONOMICS OF IMMIGRATION." *ATLANTIC MONTHLY* (NOVEMBER 1996).

DACQUEL, LAARNI T., AND DONALD C.DAHMANN. *RESIDENTS OF FARMS AND RURAL AREAS: 1991.* CURRENT POPULATION REPORTS, SERIES P-20, NO. 472. WASHINGTON, DC: U.S. DEPARTMENT OF AGRICULTURE, ECONOMIC RESEARCH SERVICE, AND U.S. BUREAU OF THE CENSUS BUREAU JOINT REPORT.

FIX, MICHAEL, AND JEFFREY S. PASSEL. *IMMIGRATION AND IMMIGRANTS.* WASHINGTON, DC: THE URBAN INSTITUTE, 1994.

FORSTALL, RICHARD, AND JAMES FITZSIMMONS. *METROPOLITAN GROWTH AND EXPANSION IN THE 1980S.* TECHNICAL WORKING PAPER NO. 6. WASHINGTON, DC: U.S. BUREAU OF THE CENSUS, POPULATION DIVISION, APRIL 1993.

McFALLS, JOSEPH A. JR. "POPULATION: A LIVELY INTRODUCTION." *POPULATION BULLETIN* 46, NO. 2. POPULATION REFERENCE BUREAU (OCTOBER 1991).

MONTHLY VITAL STATISTICS REPORTS (VARIOUS). DEPARTMENT OF HEALTH AND HUMAN SERVICES, CENTERS FOR DISEASE CONTROL AND PREVENTION, NATIONAL CENTER FOR HEALTH STATISTICS.

"POPULATION PROJECTIONS OF THE UNITED STATES BY AGE, SEX, RACE, AND HISPANIC ORIGIN: 1995 TO 2050." SERIES P-25, NO. 1130. WASHINGTON, DC: U.S. BUREAU OF THE CENSUS.

SWANSON, LINDA L., ED. *RACIAL AND CULTURAL MINORITIES IN RURAL AREAS, PROGRESS AND STAGNATION: 1980-1990.* WASHINGTON, DC: U.S. DEPARTMENT OF AGRICULTURE, ECONOMIC RESEARCH SERVICE, 1997.

"STATE POPULATION PROJECTIONS BY AGE, SEX, RACE, AND HISPANIC ORIGIN: 1995 TO 2025." PPL-47. WASHINGTON, DC: U.S. BUREAU OF THE CENSUS.

THOMAS M. McDEVITT. *WORLD POPULATION PROFILE: 1996.* SERIES WP/96. WASHINGTON, DC: U.S. AGENCY FOR INTERNATIONAL DEVELOPMENT AND U.S. BUREAU OF THE CENSUS.

WEBSITES:

IMMIGRATION AND NATURALIZATION SERVICE WEBSITE AT<WWW.USDOJ.GOV/INS/PUBLIC/STATS>.

INTERNATIONAL DATABASE, U.S. BUREAU OF THE CENSUS, AVAILABLE ON THE INTERNET AT <HTTP://WWW.CENSUS.GOV>.

NATIONAL CENTER FOR HEALTH STATISTICS WEBSITE AT <HTTP://WWW.CDC.GOV/NCHSWWW>.

U.S. BUREAU OF THE CENSUS WEBSITE AT <HTTP://WWW.CENSUS.GOV>.

U.S. DEPARTMENT OF AGRICULTURE, ECONOMIC RESEARCH SERVICE WEBSITE AT <WWW.ECON.AG.GOV>.

CHAPTER 2
Living Arrangements

MARK S. LITTMAN

MARITAL STATUS

MEDIAN AGE AT FIRST MARRIAGE FOR MEN—	
1970:	23.2
1995:	26.9
MEDIAN AGE AT FIRST MARRIAGE FOR WOMEN—	
1970:	20.8
1995:	24.5
DIVORCE RATE PER 1,000 POPULATION—	
1970:	3.5
1979:	5.3 (RATE AT RECENT PEAK)
1994:	4.6
PERCENTAGE OF MALES 15 YEARS AND OVER WHO WERE NEVER MARRIED IN 1995—	
WHITE:	28.7
BLACK:	46.5
MEDIAN LENGTH OF MARRIAGE FOR COUPLES DIVORCING IN 1990:	7.2 YEARS

AGE AT MARRIAGE

Age at marriage has effects beyond ceremony: it influences the number and timing of births, household formation, and consumer purchases, and it can influence such life events as educational attainment, career goals, and the likelihood of divorce, as well as the eventual total population of a nation. Age at first marriage has been increasing in the United States since the mid-1960s and is now at the highest level recorded during this century. For men, the median age at first marriage approached 27 years in 1995, for women it was 24.5 years. During the baby boom era, median age at first marriage was between 4 and 5 years younger than the current figure for men and between 3 and 4 years younger for women. Some demographers feel that the baby boom era, rather than the current era, is the exception, since at the turn of the 20th century, the median age at first marriage was relatively as high (about 26 years for men and 22 years for women) as it is today.[1] The delay in age of marriage can also be seen in the percentage of young adults who have never married: 39 percent of men and 27 percent of women aged 25 to 34 in 1995 were never married. Both figures are considerably higher than they had been in the past several decades. Although there is a general tendency toward later marriage throughout the world, the majority of women in many African nations, as well as the majority of women in some Asian and Central American countries, marry as teenagers.[2]

---

1 See, for example, Andrew Cherlin, *Marriage, Divorce, and Remarriage* (Cambridge: Harvard University Press, 1992).

2 United Nations, *The World's Women 1995: Trends and Statistics.* Social Statistics and Indicators, Series K, no. 12 (New York: United Nations Publications, 1995).

FIGURE 2.1

PERCENTAGE OF 15 TO 19 YEAR OLDS WHO ARE MARRIED, BY WORLD REGION: 1990

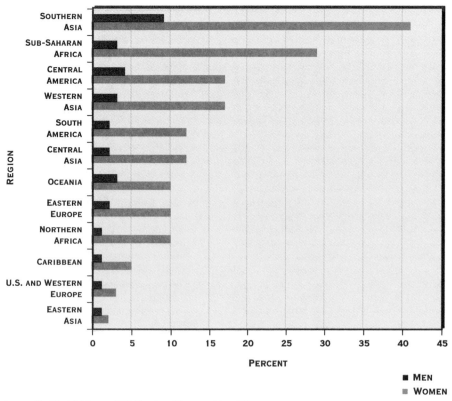

Source: The World's Women 1995: Trends and Statistics, United Nations.

Note: See Annex II in the publication above for lists of countries included in each area of the world.

PROPENSITY TO MARRY

Despite this tendency to delay marriage, the vast majority of today's young adults can be expected to marry, although at slightly lower rates than previous generations. In 1995, for example, in the United States only about 7 percent of men and 5 percent of women aged 45 to 64 years had never married. It is estimated that the percent of adults who will eventually marry has declined in recent years from about 95 percent to about 90 percent.[3] Because of this propensity to marry, increased divorce rates in the United

States have resulted in a relatively higher proportion of the populace in a remarriage. In 1970, 69 percent of marriages performed were first marriages for both the bride and groom. Only 54 percent of marriages begun in 1988 were first marriages, with nearly one of four marriages involving remarriage for both the bride and groom.

However, a major exception to this eventual tendency to marry has occurred among Blacks. In 1950, similar proportions of Black and White males 15 years and over were unmarried (28 percent for Blacks, 26

percent for Whites). By 1995, the comparable proportion for Black men had increased to 46 percent, while for Whites it was only 3 percentage points above their 1950 figure (29 percent). Several theories have been advanced for this change among Blacks, often focusing on the diminished capacity of Black men to support families because of increased mechanization decreasing the number of relatively high-paying jobs not requiring college education, and the movement of relatively high-paying industrial sector jobs overseas.[4]

---

[3] *Marriage, Divorce and Remarriage in the 1990s*, Current Population Reports, Series P-23, no. 180 (Washington, DC: U.S. Bureau of the Census, 1992).

[4] See William Julius Wilson, *The Truly Disadvantaged* (Chicago: University of Chicago Press, 1987); W. J. Wilson, *When Work Disappears* (Chicago: University of Chicago Press, 1997); and Cherlin, *Marriage*.

FIGURE 2.2

PERCENTAGE OF MALES AGES 15 YEARS AND OVER WHO WERE NEVER MARRIED, BY RACE: 1950–1995

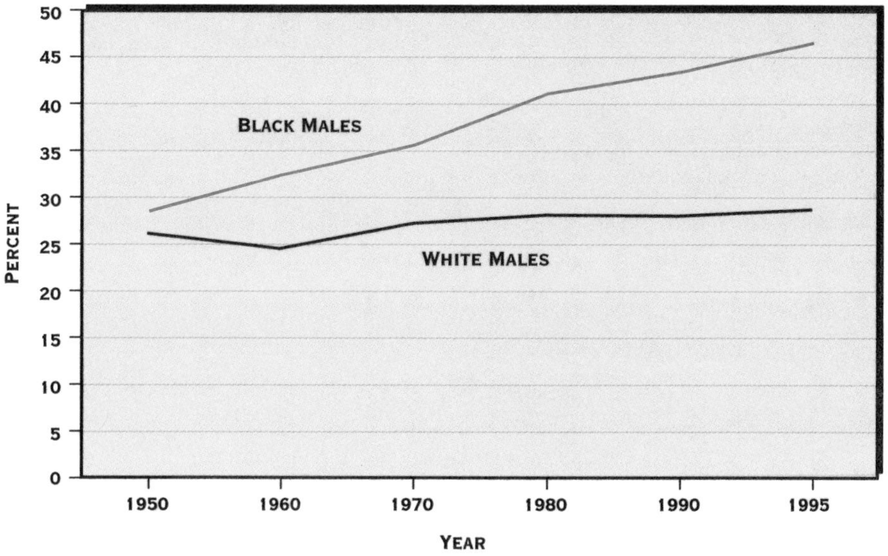

Source: U.S. Bureau of the Census.

DIVORCE RATE

The overall divorce rate seems to have leveled off in the 1990s after reaching a level nearly twice that of the 1950s and 1960s. In 1994 the overall divorce rate was 4.6 divorces per 1,000 population. It is estimated that about half of marriages begun in 1995 will eventually end in divorce. Marriages ending in divorce in 1990 had lasted an average (median) of 7.2 years, a figure that has increased only slightly in the past 25 years. Because of this high incidence of divorce, more than a few in American society have come to question the relevance of marriage in the modern world, while others continue to see it as the mainstay of civilization, with rather awkward arrangements of bedfellows at times. The latter includes a variety of religious groups, including the often antihomosexual religious right, as well as some in the gay rights community itself who are fighting for the recognition of their unions as legal marriage.

HOUSEHOLD COMPOSITION

MARRIED-COUPLE HOUSEHOLDS AS A PERCENTAGE OF ALL HOUSEHOLDS—	
1960:	**74.3 PERCENT**
1995:	**54.4 PERCENT**
NONFAMILY HOUSEHOLDS AS A PERCENTAGE OF ALL HOUSEHOLDS—	
1960:	**15.0 PERCENT**
1995:	**30.0 PERCENT**
FEMALE-HEADED FAMILIES AS A PERCENTAGE OF ALL FAMILIES—	
1960:	**9.8 PERCENT**
1995:	**17.6 PERCENT**
PERCENTAGE OF CHILDREN UNDER 18 LIVING WITH ONLY	
ONE PARENT OR WITH NEITHER PARENT IN 1995—	
ALL RACES:	**31.3 PERCENT**
BLACK CHILDREN:	**66.9 PERCENT**
WHITE CHILDREN:	**24.2 PERCENT**
AVERAGE HOUSEHOLD SIZE IN 1995:	**2.65 PERSONS**
AVERAGE FAMILY SIZE IN 1995:	**3.19 PERSONS**

NONFAMILY HOUSEHOLDS, UNMARRIED COUPLES

As a result of the tendency to delay marriage (or avoid it entirely) indicated in the previous section, as well as the increased divorce rates, there has been a proliferation of single-person households as well as nonfamily households. In 1960, at the height of an era that has come to epitomize the positive attributes of marriage and the two-parent family in America, married-couple families were 75 percent of all households, and represented 87 percent of all families. Nonfamily households were 15 percent of households. By 1995, married-couple families represented only 54 percent of all households, while nonfamily households had doubled their representation among all households.[5] Households maintained by women only (without benefit of spouse) have increased from about 10 percent to 18 percent of all families during this same period, and those sustained by a man with no spouse present have also increased and now represent 5 percent of all families.

FIGURE 2.3

PERCENTAGE DISTRIBUTION OF FAMILIES IN THE UNITED STATES, BY TYPE: 1960 AND 1995

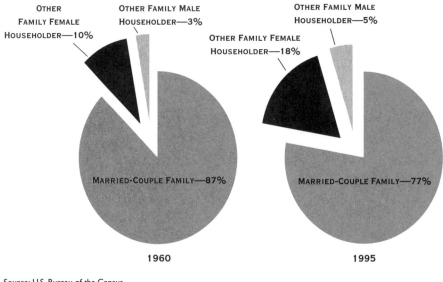

OTHER FAMILY FEMALE HOUSEHOLDER—10%
OTHER FAMILY MALE HOUSEHOLDER—3%
MARRIED-COUPLE FAMILY—87%
1960

OTHER FAMILY MALE HOUSEHOLDER—5%
OTHER FAMILY FEMALE HOUSEHOLDER—18%
MARRIED-COUPLE FAMILY—77%
1995

Source: U.S. Bureau of the Census.

---

[5] The definitions of "household," "family," and "nonfamily household" used here are those used in U.S. Census Bureau publications. Much of the data cited in this section are from the *Current Population Survey* conducted by the Census Bureau in March of each year and available in various publications or on the Census Bureau Website at <http://www.census.gov>. A household consists of all persons who occupy a housing unit. A housing unit may be a house, an apartment, or other group of rooms in which the occupants eat and live separately from other persons in the structure. The "householder" is generally the person or one of the persons in whose name the housing unit is owned or rented. Household members can be related to the householder, but they can also include unrelated persons, such as boarders or foster children. A family refers to a group of two or more persons who are related and live together in the same household. Conversely, a nonfamily household is one in which the householder lives alone or with nonrelatives only.

FIGURE 2.4

PERCENTAGE DISTRIBUTION OF HOUSEHOLDS IN THE UNITED STATES, BY TYPE: 1995

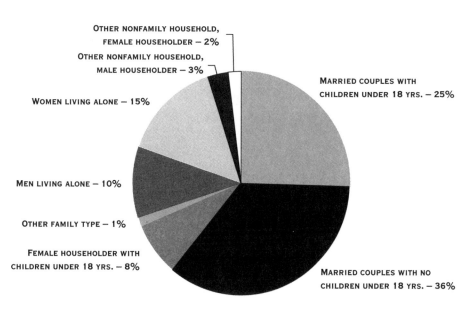

OTHER NONFAMILY HOUSEHOLD, FEMALE HOUSEHOLDER — 2%

OTHER NONFAMILY HOUSEHOLD, MALE HOUSEHOLDER — 3%

WOMEN LIVING ALONE — 15%

MEN LIVING ALONE — 10%

OTHER FAMILY TYPE — 1%

FEMALE HOUSEHOLDER WITH CHILDREN UNDER 18 YRS. — 8%

MARRIED COUPLES WITH CHILDREN UNDER 18 YRS. — 25%

MARRIED COUPLES WITH NO CHILDREN UNDER 18 YRS. — 36%

Source: U.S. Bureau of the Census.

A subset of nonfamily households is composed of those who are unmarried couples, defined as persons of the opposite sex sharing living quarters. Since there are no questions directly relating to intimacy between such persons in most surveys, it is generally assumed that such persons are in fact "a couple" even though they may consist of an elderly widow renting a room to a college student, for example. The number of unmarried couples has increased from about half a million in 1970 to about 3.7 million in 1995. Unmarried couples now represent about 6 percent of all couples (married and unmarried) in the United States, up from only about 1 percent 25 years ago. Children under age 15 are living in a little over a third of these households.

Most nonfamily households, which accounted for 43 percent of the growth in the number of households during the 1990s, consist of persons living alone (about 83 percent). Men living alone tend to be younger than women (in 1995 the median age was about 44 years for men, and about 66 for women). The largest group of women living alone were widowed, with 30 percent over age 75 years.

Both household and family size have tended to shrink over the past three decades, influenced by the increase in nonfamily households, divorce, the incidence of female householders without a spouse, and the fertility declines indicated in the previous chapter. The average household size has declined from about 3.33 to 2.65 between 1960 and 1995, while family size on average has declined from 3.67 to 3.19 persons. The average number of children under 18 years (for families with children in the household) has declined from about 2.33 to 1.84.

Thus, the likelihood that children will experience life in a single-parent family at some time in their childhood has increased considerably in the past several decades. In 1995, 27 percent of children under 18 years were living with only one parent (and an additional 4 percent were living with a relative other than their parents, or with a nonrelative), whereas in 1970 about 12 percent of children lived with only one parent. Life in a single-parent family is even more probable for Black children: in 1995 nearly 67 percent lived with only one parent or with neither parent.

FIGURE 2.5

AVERAGE NUMBER OF CHILDREN PER FAMILY IN THE UNITED STATES, BY STATE: 1990

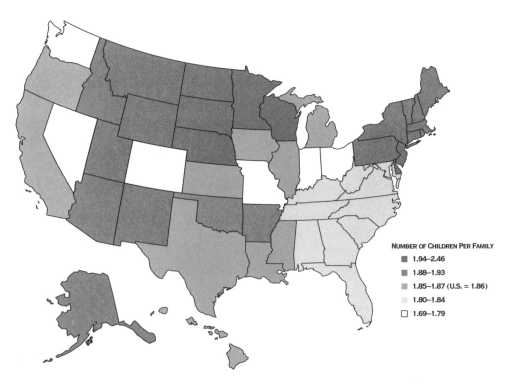

NUMBER OF CHILDREN PER FAMILY
- ■ 1.94–2.46
- ■ 1.88–1.93
- ■ 1.85–1.87 (U.S. = 1.86)
- ■ 1.80–1.84
- □ 1.69–1.79

Source: "General Population Characteristics," U.S. Bureau of the Census, 1990 Census of Population, 1990, CP-1-1, Table 263.

YOUNG ADULTS STILL IN THEIR PARENTAL HOUSEHOLD

The proportion of young *adult* children continuing to live in their parental household appears to have leveled off after increasing between 1960 and the early 1980s. In 1995, about 58 percent of young men 18 to 24 and 47 percent of young women of similar age were still living in their parental household. This figure is about 6 percentage points higher for men and 12 percentage points higher for women than it was in 1960. Several factors tend to influence the likelihood of young adult's continued living in the parental home, including delay in the age at first marriage, a reluctance to incur the expense of setting up one's own household due to economic conditions (or perhaps psychological ones), and a tendency for young adults to return to their parental home after divorce. For 25- to 34-year-old women, there has been virtually no change in the percent living in their parental home since 1960 (about 8 percent in 1995), while for men of comparable age, the percentage living with their parents (or parent) has increased from 11 percent in 1960 to 15 percent in 1995.

CHILDCARE ARRANGEMENTS

There are no widespread government-run child care centers in the United States. Yet, the increased incidence of mothers of young children who are in the labor force over the past several decades has meant an increased need for childcare arrangements, particularly for families with preschoolers. In 1993, there were 8 million families with preschoolers who required care during the time their mothers were at work (according to one survey).[6] Of these families, about 56 percent paid for childcare, which averaged to about $74, or 8 percent of their monthly family income in 1993. For families with more than one preschooler, the cost averaged about $110, or 11 percent of their income, compared with $66 (7 percent of family income) for those with one preschooler. For single-parent families, paid childcare was relatively more burdensome, averaging about 12 percent of their income. And poor families, the most burdened, paid more than twice as much proportionately for childcare (about 18 percent of their income) as did nonpoor families (7 percent), even though the amount paid was less.

Who in the United States provided the care for children under age 5 when their mothers were at work? In 1993, about 16 percent were cared for by their fathers, 17 percent by a grandparent, 9 percent by another relative, 21 percent were cared for by a nonrelative, and 30 percent were in a nursery school or daycare center. The remaining 6 percent of children under age 5 were cared for by their mothers while they worked, most of whom worked at home. There are few clear trends in these proportions. The proportion cared for by fathers, for example, was no higher in 1993 than it had been in 1985, after appearing to increase to 20 percent by the early 1990s. One discernible trend, however, is the apparent increase in the proportion of preschoolers attending daycare centers, and a decline in those cared for in the homes of nonrelatives since the mid-1980s.[7]

FIGURE 2.6

PERCENTAGE DISTRIBUTION OF CHILDCARE ARRANGEMENTS FOR PRESCHOOL CHILDREN USED BY FAMILIES WITH EMPLOYED MOTHERS IN THE UNITED STATES: 1993

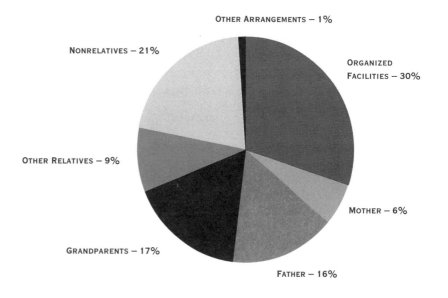

Source: *Who's Minding Our Preschoolers?*, U.S. Bureau of the Census. Series P-70, no. 53.

Note: An **organized childcare facility** is a daycare center, a nursery school, or a preschool. **Nonrelatives** include those who provide care in the child's home and family daycare providers who care for one or more children in the care provider's home. The **other** category includes preschoolers who are in kindergarten and school-based activities. **Mother** includes mothers working both at home and away from home.

---

6 See, Lynne M. Casper, *What Does It Cost to Mind Our Preschoolers?* Current Population Reports, Series P-70, no. 52 (Washington, DC: U.S. Bureau of the Census).

7 See historical table available on the Census Bureau Website at <http://www.census.gov/population/socdemo/child/cctab1/txt>.

FOR FURTHER INFORMATION SEE:

BIANCHI, SUZANNE, AND DAPHNE SPAIN. *AMERICAN WOMEN IN TRANSITION.* NEW YORK: RUSSELL SAGE FOUNDATION, 1986.

BIANCHI, SUZANNE. *AMERICA'S CHILDREN: MIXED PROSPECTS.* POPULATION REFERENCE BUREAU, 1990.

CASPER, LYNNE M. *WHAT DOES IT COST TO MIND OUR PRESCHOOLERS?* CURRENT POPULATION REPORTS, SERIES P-70, NO. 52. WASHINGTON, DC: U.S. BUREAU OF THE CENSUS.

CASPER, LYNNE M. *WHO'S MINDING OUR PRESCHOOLERS?* CURRENT POPULATION REPORTS, SERIES P-70, NO. 53. WASHINGTON, DC: U.S. BUREAU OF THE CENSUS.

CHERLIN, ANDREW. *MARRIAGE, DIVORCE, AND REMARRIAGE.* (CAMBRIDGE: HARVARD UNIVERSITY PRESS, 1992).

HOUSEHOLD AND FAMILY CHARACTERISTICS. CURRENT POPULATION REPORTS, SERIES P-20 (VARIOUS YEARS). WASHINGTON, DC: U.S. BUREAU OF THE CENSUS.

MARITAL STATUS AND LIVING ARRANGEMENTS. CURRENT POPULATION REPORTS, SERIES P-20 (VARIOUS YEARS). WASHINGTON, DC: U.S. BUREAU OF THE CENSUS.

WEBSITES:

NATIONAL CENTER FOR HEALTH STATISTICS WEBSITE AT <HTTP://WWW.CDC.GOV/NCHSWWW>.

U.S. BUREAU OF THE CENSUS WEBSITE AT <HTTP://WWW.CENSUS.GOV>.

CHAPTER 3

Education

MARK S. LITTMAN

SCHOOL ENROLLMENT

TOTAL SCHOOL ENROLLMENT (NURSERY THROUGH COLLEGE) IN 1994:	**69.3 MILLION**
PERCENTAGE OF ALL PERSONS AGE 3 AND OVER ENROLLED IN 1994:	**28.0 PERCENT**
PERCENTAGE OF ELEMENTARY AND HIGH SCHOOL STUDENTS ENROLLED IN PUBLIC SCHOOL IN 1994:	**90.0 PERCENT**
HIGH SCHOOL DROPOUT RATE IN 1993–1994:	**5.0 PERCENT**
PERCENTAGE OF HIGH SCHOOL GRADUATES AGE 18–24 WHO ENROLLED IN COLLEGE IN 1994:	**42.0 PERCENT**
WOMEN AS A PERCENTAGE OF ALL COLLEGE STUDENTS IN 1993–1994:	**55.0 PERCENT**
PROPORTION OF ELEMENTARY STUDENTS RECEIVING REMEDIAL HELP IN READING IN 1993–1994:	**13.0 PERCENT**
PROPORTION OF ELEMENTARY STUDENTS ENROLLED IN GIFTED AND TALENTED PROGRAMS IN 1993–1994:	**6.0 PERCENT**

AGE OF STUDENTS

In the Fall of 1994, more than one out of four persons in the United States was currently enrolled in school. While the vast majority of these students were in what historically are considered customary school attendance ages (between age 5 and 34 years), there were 3.9 million children under age 5 enrolled in preprimary school and 2.8 million persons over the age of 34 enrolled (for the most part) in college in 1994. These groups at the enrollment age extremes have seen the largest proportional increases in school attendance in the past several decades.

About 53 percent of the population 3 to 34 years of age was enrolled in 1994, down slightly from 56 percent in 1970. However, this "decline" is actually due to the changing age distribution within this age universe. In actuality, enrollment rates are higher in most age groups, more than doubling in some, and lower in none. Rates have increased from about 21 percent to 47 percent for 3 and 4 year olds, for example, and from 48 to 60 percent for 18 and 19 year olds. Over 95 percent of children in the United States between the ages of 5 and 17 were in school in 1994. These high enrollment rates are the rule for both boys and girls in the United States, which is not the case in many countries of the world, particularly in Asia and Africa, and particularly at the high school (or equivalent) level.[1]

FIGURE 3.1

SCHOOL ENROLLMENT RATES IN THE UNITED STATES, BY AGE: 1970 AND 1994

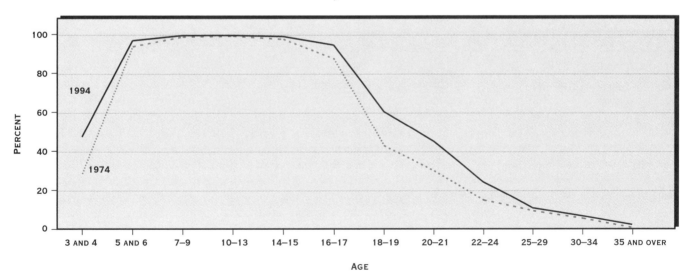

Source: U.S. Bureau of the Census.

---

[1] See *1996 UNESCO Statistical Yearbook* (Lanham, MD: Bernan Press, 1997), Table 3.2.

FIGURE 3.2

PERCENTAGE OF 3 AND 4 YEAR OLDS ENROLLED IN NURSERY SCHOOL IN THE UNITED STATES, BY MOTHERS' LEVEL OF EDUCATION: OCTOBER 1995

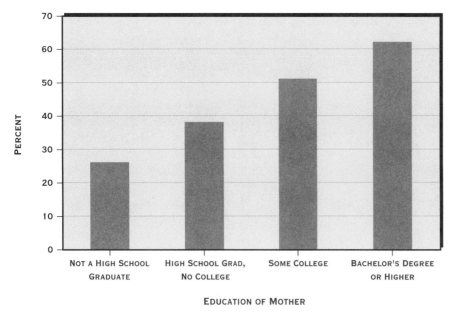

EDUCATION OF MOTHER

Source: Current Population Survey Press Release CB97-FS. 08, 8/18/97, U.S. Bureau of the Census.

TYPE OF SCHOOL

In addition to the enrollment in regular schools indicated above, an additional 4 million persons 15 and over in the United States were enrolled in vocational training. Such training, which was typically received by persons who had already earned a high school diploma but who were not in college, includes enrollment in business, trade, technical, and secretarial courses.

The vast majority of students at all levels, except for preprimary, are enrolled in the public school system in the United States. At the primary and secondary levels, 9 of 10 students were in public schools, a figure that has increased only a little since 1970. At the college level, about 78 percent of students were in public institutions in 1994. At the prekindergarten level, about 47 percent were enrolled in public programs.

Preprimary enrollment is still linked to income despite government efforts such as Head Start and other state and locally administered preprimary programs to make preprimary education available to any student who desires it. Such government programs are typically restricted to families with low incomes. About 59 percent of 3- and 4-year olds in families with an income over $40,000 were enrolled in 1995, compared with about 34 percent of comparable children in families with incomes under $20,000, for example. Similarly, children with more educated mothers tended to be enrolled at higher rates: about 62 percent of 3- and 4-year-old offspring of college-educated mothers were enrolled compared with 26 percent of those whose mother did not finish high school. Given these enrollment rate disparities, it is likely that these income and educational attainment differences will be perpetuated in the next generation.

HIGH SCHOOL DROPOUTS

At the other end of the enrollment spectrum, high school dropout rates have tended to decline in the past 20 years, to an annual figure of about 5 percent of 9th through 11th graders between 1993 and 1994. Using this gauge of the high school dropout rate, the annual dropout rate is somewhat lower overall than it was around 1970. For Whites, the rate has not changed much (after increasing during the 1970s it has come back down); for Blacks, the dropout rate is now nearly half their 1970 rate, but remains higher than that for Whites (6.1 percent for Blacks, 4.7 percent for Whites between 1993 and 1994). The annual dropout rate for Hispanics (9.2 percent in 1994) is higher than that for either Blacks or Whites.[2]

Annual dropout rates do not show the cumulative effect dropping out of school has on the population: in 1994, 13 percent of 18 to 24 year olds were not enrolled and were not attending school. However, the trend is the same as the annual rate: this figure has decreased since the 1970s.

COLLEGE ENROLLMENT AND COMPOSITION OF STUDENT BODY

The proportion of high school graduates who go on to enroll in college (although not necessarily to receive a degree of any sort) has risen to about 42 percent of high school graduates in the 18- to 24-year-old age group in 1994 (up from 31 percent in 1974). The number of 18- and 19-year olds enrolled in college in 1994 was very similar to the comparable figure in 1975—about 3 million. Yet, total college enrollment has increased from 10.9 to 15 million during that period, fueled largely by older students. The number of college students who are 35 and over has increased from 1.2 to 2.7 million, and these now represent 18 percent of all college students. While the college enrollment rate for 18- to 24-year-old high school graduates was higher for Whites (about 44

---

2 The dropout rate for Hispanics between 1993 and 1994 was unusually high relative to other years during this decade and may be an aberration. The rate for Hispanics in other years during the 1990s average about 7.4, still higher than that for Whites or Blacks, but lower than the dropout rate for Hispanics in the early 1970s (between 10 and 11 percent), when data for Hispanics were first collected.

FIGURE 3.3

ANNUAL HIGH SCHOOL DROPOUT RATES IN THE UNITED STATES, BY RACE AND HISPANIC ORIGIN: 1970–1994

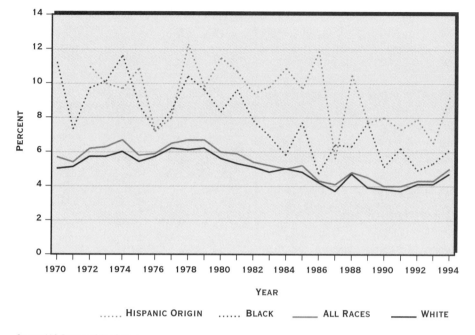

...... HISPANIC ORIGIN   ...... BLACK   —— ALL RACES   —— WHITE

Source: U.S. Bureau of the Census.

FIGURE 3.4

SELECTED CHARACTERISTICS OF U.S. COLLEGE STUDENTS: 1974 AND 1994

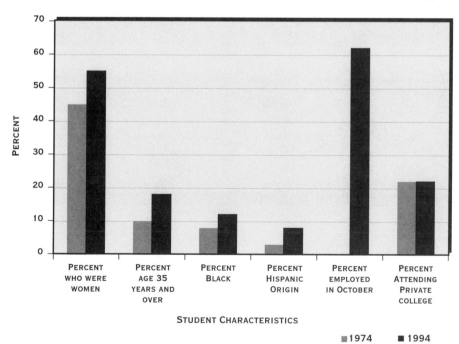

■ 1974   ■ 1994

Source: U.S. Bureau of the Census.

Note: Employment data for college students in 1974 are not available.

percent in 1994) than for Blacks (36 percent) or Hispanics (33 percent), at older ages the enrollment rates for these minority groups were equal to or actually higher than those of Whites. At ages of 35 and higher, 3.5 percent of Blacks and 4.3 percent of Hispanics were enrolled in college compared with 2.5 percent for Whites. This is not a new phenomenon, however, as minorities generally have had enrollment rates equal to or greater than those of Whites at older ages since the early 1970s.

Both Blacks and Hispanics represented larger proportions of the total college population in 1994 than they did in the early 1970s: Blacks had increased from about 8 percent to about 12 percent of all college students and Hispanics had increased from about 3 percent to about 8 percent of all persons enrolled in college. Both groups were still somewhat underrepresented in college compared with their proportions among the total population (about 13 percent Black, 10 percent Hispanic).

Women, who represented about one-third of all college students in 1950, became the majority of all college students in the United States during the late 1970s, and, by 1994, represented about 55 percent of total college enrollment. Women typically outnumber men in higher education in Latin America, but not yet in many Western European nations, Japan, or much of the developing world. In 1990, there were 63 women enrolled for every 100 men enrolled in higher education in Japan, 80 per 100 in Switzerland, and 68 per 100 in Germany. Less-developed regions tend to have considerably lower ratios: sub-Saharan Africa and southern Asia (including India, Pakistan, and Iran), for example, typically have fewer than 40 women per 100 men enrolled in higher education.[3]

3 See United Nations, *The World's Women 1995: Trends and Statistics*, Social Statistics and Indicators, Series K, no. 12 (New York: United Nations Publications, 1995).

GAUGING PROGRESS IN SCHOOL

One gauge of how well students are doing in school is the proportion enrolled below their modal grade. Modal grade is the year of school in which the largest proportion of students of a given age is enrolled.[4] By the time they were 15 to 17 years old, 31 percent of students were enrolled below their modal grade in 1994. When they were 6 to 8 year olds in 1985, only 18 percent of this same cohort were enrolled below their modal grade. Since 1971, the proportion of students enrolled below their modal grade has been increasing for each age group.

Another gauge of progress in school is the proportion of students who need remedial assistance for their particular grade, as well as the proportion in programs for the gifted and talented: about 13 percent of students in public elementary schools were receiving remedial reading assistance in 1993–94 while about 6 percent were enrolled in gifted and talented programs. Remedial instruction was offered by 78 percent of colleges and universities in 1996, a figure which has increased by 5 percentage points since the 1987–88 school year.[5]

Comparisons over time on standardized test scores are an additional gauge of progress in school and of how well our educational system is preparing students for an increasingly technical world of work. Average mathematics and science proficiency scores given to 17 year olds between 1977 and 1992 indicate an increase in proficiency in these areas, while reading proficiency scores have remained stable. The Scholastic Assessment Test (SAT) is used as an admission criterion for college and has been taken by students who are contemplating college attendance. It is usually taken in the senior year of high school. The proportion of high school graduates who take the SAT has increased, from 34 percent to 42 percent between 1972 and 1995, as

the availability of college education has increased. The proportion of minorities who take the SAT has increased as well, from 15 percent to 31 percent of test-takers during this period. Even though the average scores of minorities (with the exception of Asian-American math scores) were lower than those of Whites, the average scores in 1995 for all test-takers, regardless of race, are as high, in both mathematics and verbal areas, as they have been since the early 1970s (although not as high as they were in 1972). Average SAT scores have increased considerably for minority test-takers, while average scores for Whites have fallen a few percentage points in the past 20 years.[6]

COMPUTER USAGE

Computer literacy is likely to influence the employment opportunities available to

today's students and is likely to restrict the opportunities of those without computer skills. The proportion of households with a computer has increased from about 8 percent in 1984 to 23 percent in 1993. The proportion of working adults indicating use of computers on the job has nearly doubled during this same period, from about 25 percent to 46 percent in 1993. About 61 percent of students aged 3 to 17 used computers at school, with three out of four students at some ages (within the 3 to 17 year old group) using computers in school in 1993. Eight- to 11-year-olds reported higher usage rates at school than those in high school or younger children in 1993. Students from higher-income families were considerably more likely to have computer access at home and to use computers for homework.

FIGURE 3.5

PERCENTAGE OF 3 TO 17 YEAR OLDS IN THE U.S. WITH COMPUTER ACCESS AT SCHOOL OR AT HOME: 1984, 1989, AND 1993

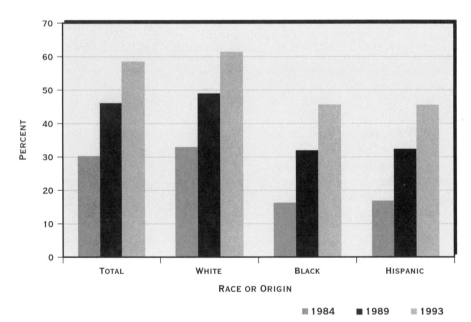

Source: U.S. Bureau of the Census, Survey of Income and Program Participation Data available at <http://www.census.gov.>.

4 Progress in school is only one reason a student may be enrolled below the modal grade for his or her age. Some parents choose to start their children's schooling later, enrollment-age cutoffs may delay the enrollment of a particular student, etc. See *School Enrollment-Social and Economic Characteristics of Students: October, 1994*, Current Population Reports, Series P-20, no.487 (Washington, DC: U.S. Bureau of the Census).

5 See *Digest of Education Statistics 1996*. National Center for Education Statistics publication no. 96-133 (Washington, DC: U.S. Department of Education , National Center for Education Statistics), Tables 57 and 304.

6 See *Condition of Education 1996* and *Youth Indicators: 1996* (Washington, DC: U.S. Department of Education, National Center for Education Statistics).

EDUCATIONAL ATTAINMENT AND OUTCOMES

PERCENTAGE OF YOUNG ADULTS COMPLETING HIGH SCHOOL—	
1970:	75 PERCENT
1995:	87 PERCENT
PERCENTAGE OF YOUNG ADULTS COMPLETING COLLEGE—	
1970:	16 PERCENT
1995:	25 PERCENT
AVERAGE EARNINGS IN 1994—	
HIGH SCHOOL GRADUATE, NO COLLEGE:	$20,248
PERSONS WITH A BACHELOR'S DEGREE:	$37,224
PERSONS WITH A DOCTORATE DEGREE:	$67,685

CHANGE AND CONTINUED VARIATION

It was not until the mid-1960s that over half of the adult population of the United States had completed 4 or more years of high school. The increase in average educational attainment of the U.S. population has continued over the past two decades, with the proportion of young adults (25 to 29 years) who have completed high school increasing from 75 to 87 percent between 1970 and 1995, and the proportion completing 4 or more years of college increasing from about 16 to 25 percent. The proportion of young Black adults who have completed at least high school is essentially the same as that of young Whites, although the proportion completing college is still considerably lower than that of Whites (15 percent for Blacks, 26 percent for Whites). Young adults of Hispanic origin trail both their White and Black peers, with only 57 percent having graduated from high school and 9 percent having graduated from college in 1995.

Overall, 82 percent of the population 25 years of age and over were high school graduates in 1995. This fraction is lower than that for the younger ages indicated above, since only about half of the persons at older ages, particularly over the age of 75, were high school graduates. For minorities, the fraction of the population age 25 and over who were high school graduates was considerably smaller in 1995: for example, only slightly more than a fourth of both Hispanics and Blacks over the age of 65 had

graduated from high school. There is still considerable variation among states in part because of these racial and ethnic differences, and in part because of the varied racial composition among states. One of four persons in many southern states—such as Alabama, Georgia, the Carolinas, and

Mississippi—was not a high school graduate, while in several states with relatively small minority populations—Utah and Washington—over 90 percent of the adult population were high school graduates.

Nearly one-half of the U.S. population age 25 and over had attended college for at least one course, and about one out of four had a bachelor's or higher degree in 1995. A bachelor's degree typically takes 4 years of full-time study beyond the high school level, although there is some variation (in both directions) in this time. Here again, there is considerable variation by state, with more than 30 percent of the population of some states (Colorado, Connecticut, Massachusetts, and Vermont) holding a bachelor's or higher degree, while fewer than 18 percent in other states (Arkansas, Indiana, Mississippi, Nevada, Tennessee, and West Virginia) had such a degree.

FIGURE 3.6

PERCENTAGE OF ADULT POPULATION IN THE U.S. WITH A BACHELOR'S DEGREE OR HIGHER: 1995

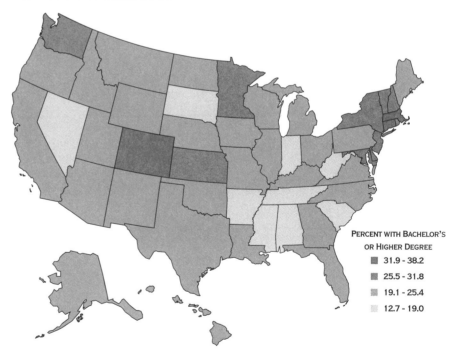

PERCENT WITH BACHELOR'S OR HIGHER DEGREE
- 31.9 - 38.2
- 25.5 - 31.8
- 19.1 - 25.4
- 12.7 - 19.0

Source: U.S. Bureau of the Census, Current Population Reports, Series P-20, no. 489. Educational Attainment in the United States: March 1995.

The economic returns to additional schooling appear to be considerable. As of March 1995, persons (18 years old and over) who had completed high school but no college had average earnings in 1994 of about $20,248,while those with a bachelor's degree could expect earnings of about $37,224, and those individuals with a doctorate had average earnings in 1994 of $67,685. In addition, the average number of months with work activity tends to increase with educational attainment, indicating a greater likelihood of periodic unemployment with lower education.

INTERNATIONAL COMPARISONS

In terms of education (as well as other subjects), how well the United States compares to other nations depends a great deal upon which countries are compared. Often, comparisons are made among what are referred to as the "G-7" countries, ostensibly because these countries are "similar to the United States in terms of size and are viewed as major economic competitors."[7] The G-7 countries include Canada, France, Germany, Italy, Japan, the United Kingdom, and the United States. Note, however, that there are many large countries that are not on this list (India or Russia, for example), and that there are many countries in which at least some segment of our economy is in competition that are not on this list (e.g., Mexico or China). The United States had the highest proportion of its 25- to 64-year-old population that had completed "upper secondary" or higher education (equivalent to a high school education or above in the United States), the highest proportion among the G-7 countries in 1992. Furthermore, the United States was second only to Canada in the proportion of the

FIGURE 3.7

PERCENTAGE OF THE POPULATION 25 TO 64 YEARS OLD AMONG G-7 COUNTRIES THAT HAS COMPLETED SPECIFIED LEVEL OF EDUCATION: 1992

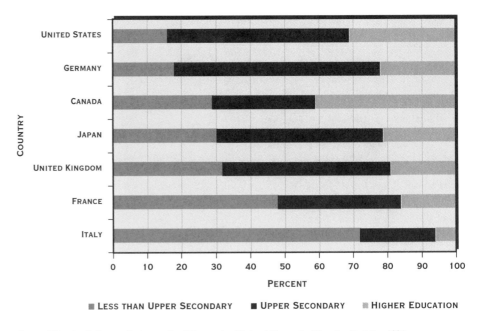

Source: Education Indicators: An International Perspective, National Center for Education Statistics, 1996.

Note: Upper Secondary is equivalent to grades 10–12 in the U.S. Higher Education includes study beyond secondary school at an institution that offers programs terminating in an associate, baccalaureate or higher degree.

population that had completed "higher education" in 1992, which is equivalent to having completed a college or vocational program beyond the high school level (including 2-year, 4-year, graduate, and professional programs).

In reading literacy, students in the United States outscored students in all of the G-7 countries, as well as a group of 25 additional countries for which comparable scores were available in 1991–92 (with the exception of Finland, whose students

scored highest in reading literacy among all comparable countries). U.S. students' scores in mathematics and science were not as high as in reading relative to other countries (although data for only two other G-7 countries were available). Scores in mathematics were below those for both Canada and France for ages 9 and 13, as well as age 13 in science. At age 9, science scores were higher in the United States than in Canada in 1991. These differences were not particularly large, however.

---

7 *Education Indicators: An International Perspective*. National Center for Education Statistics publication no. 96-003 (Washington, DC: U.S. Department of Education, National Center for Education Statistics, 1996), 3. See definitions section on page 19 for educational concepts such as "upper secondary" and "higher education."

EXPENDITURES ON EDUCATION AND TEACHERS

AVERAGE TEACHER SALARY (PUBLIC ELEM. AND SECONDARY)—	
1972:	$36,000 (1995 DOLLARS)
1995:	$37,400
RANK OF AVERAGE TEACHER SALARY IN UNITED STATES AMONG G-7 COUNTRIES:	2ND
PER-PUPIL EXPENDITURES—	
1970:	$3,200 (1995 DOLLARS)
1993:	$5,500 (1995 DOLLARS)

TEACHERS: QUANTITY AND QUALITY

Recently, there has been concern that, in general, the skills of U.S. students have deteriorated. Some people feel that it is important for the United States to rank first internationally in all educational subjects, and they blame deterioration in the quality of public school education for what they feel is the poor showing of American students. The previous section dealt with the scores of U.S. students relative to some other countries on a few measures. But what about public schools in the United States and the feeling that the quality of teachers in those schools has deteriorated in recent decades?

An estimated 3.1 million teachers were engaged in elementary and secondary classroom instruction in 1996, 2.7 million of whom were teaching in public schools. The number of teachers has increased by 18 percent over the past decade, an increase that is slightly higher than the increase in the number of students. Consequently, the student/teacher ratio has declined slightly, from 17.7 to 17.4 students per teacher in public schools.[8]

There is at worst mixed evidence that teacher quality has deteriorated in recent years. Some past research indicates that persons entering the teaching field had lower SAT scores than their nonteaching, college-graduating peers and that those leaving the profession had higher scores than those remaining as teachers.[9] However, recent data from the 1992 National Adult Literacy Survey (NALS) indicates that teachers have similar literacy scores to many other professionals, including executives, physicians, writers, social workers, and nurses. Another gauge of teacher qualification for the specific field in which they are teaching is their major in college. At the high school level in 1993–94, generally about three-fourths or more of teachers had majored in the specific field in which they were teaching: the lowest proportions of these teachers were in mathematics and biology, in which about two-thirds of the teachers held degrees in those fields. In terms of qualifications for teaching specific subject matter, there was no clear relationship between teaching at private schools versus public schools. Math teachers at public schools were more likely

to have majored in that field than were teachers at private schools, for example. Students from schools in relatively poorer areas (as gauged by the proportion of students who were receiving free or reduced-price school lunches, which is tied to family income) were less likely to be taught by teachers who majored in the specific class subject they taught.

TEACHER SALARIES

Teacher salaries are one gauge of the public's willingness (or ability) to invest in education. As did the salaries of other professions, teacher salaries actually declined (in real terms) during the 1970s, and have only reached their 1972 levels in the past few years. In 1995, the average salary for all public school teachers was $37,400. The average salary for beginning teachers in 1995 was still below its 1972 level in real terms (as is the case in other fields). And compared with other persons with a bachelor's degree, teacher salaries were among the lowest, averaging about two-thirds of the amount received by all full-time workers in 1991 with a bachelor's degree.[10]

Viewed internationally, teacher salaries in the United States are among the highest in absolute terms. The starting salary at the elementary level in the United States was about $21,200 in 1992, higher than all but two countries (Germany and Spain) out of 16 for which comparable data were available.[11] Relative to the size of per capita Gross Domestic Product (GDP), however, teacher salaries in the United States rank relatively low (last among the G-7 countries).

---

8 *Digest of Education Statistics 1996* (Washington, DC: U.S. Department of Education, National Center for Education Statistics), 1.

9 *Condition of Education 1996*, (Washington, DC: U.S. Department of Education, National Center for Education Statistics), ix.

10 Ibid., 174.

11 Teacher salaries were converted to U.S. dollars using purchasing power parities. See *Education Indicators: An International Perspective.* National Center for Education Statistics publication no. 96-003 (Washington, DC: U.S. Department of Education, National Center for Education Statistics, 1996), Table 40a.

FIGURE 3.8

AVERAGE ELEMENTARY SCHOOL TEACHER SALARIES, BY SELECTED COUNTRY

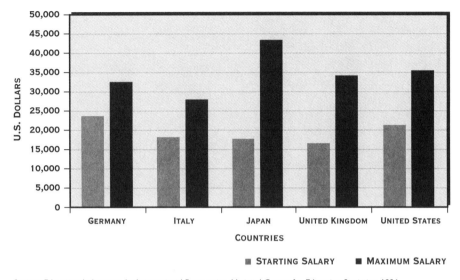

■ STARTING SALARY ■ MAXIMUM SALARY

Source: Education Indicators: An International Perspective, National Center for Education Statistics, 1996.
Teacher salaries were converted to U.S. dollars using purchasing power parities. See the report above for description.

FIGURE 3.9

PERCENTAGE CHANGE IN EXPENDITURES PER PUPIL IN THE UNITED STATES BETWEEN 1989–1990 AND 1993–1994

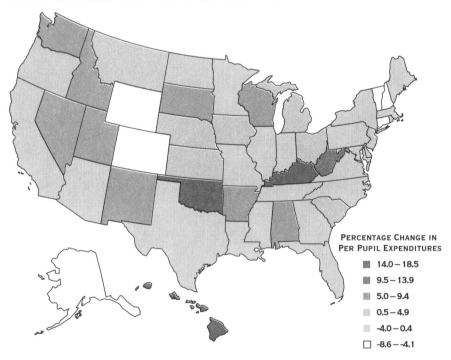

PERCENTAGE CHANGE IN
PER PUPIL EXPENDITURES

■ 14.0 – 18.5
■ 9.5 – 13.9
▦ 5.0 – 9.4
▨ 0.5 – 4.9
□ -4.0 – 0.4
□ -8.6 – -4.1

Source: National Center for Education Statistics.

Note: Figures represent current expenditures per pupil in average daily attendance for elementary and secondardy students in public education.

EXPENDITURES ON EDUCATION

Expenditures per pupil are another gauge of the public investment that is devoted annually (on average) to each student's education. Actual expenditures per pupil (in constant 1995 dollars) have increased from about $3,200 to $5,500 between 1970 and 1993 for elementary and secondary education.[12] However, during the 1990s, there has been little change, with per pupil expenditures increasing less than 1 percent in real terms between the 1989–90 and 1993–94 school years. Nearly half the states have experienced real decreases in per pupil expenditures at the elementary and secondary level during that period. Furthermore, as a percent of the GDP in the United States, there has been little change in public investment in education, with education expenditures representing about 4.2 percent of GDP in 1970 and 4.1 percent in 1993. A further gauge of change in expenditures on education is the ratio of public revenues per student to per capita personal income (called the "national index"). This index shows some improvement at the elementary and secondary level, increasing from 20.7 to 25.9 between 1970 and 1993 (indicating a relative increase in spending on education). For higher education, all three of these measures show declines in expenditures at the college level.

---

12 *Condition of Education 1996*, National Center for Education Statistics.

FOR FURTHER INFORMATION SEE:

SCHOOL ENROLLMENT-SOCIAL AND ECONOMIC CHARACTERISTICS OF STUDENTS: OCTOBER 1994. CURRENT POPULATION REPORTS, SERIES P-20, NO. 487. WASHINGTON, DC: U.S. BUREAU OF THE CENSUS.

EDUCATIONAL ATTAINMENT IN THE U.S.: 1995. CURRENT POPULATION REPORTS, SERIES P-20, NO. 489. WASHINGTON, DC: U.S. BUREAU OF THE CENSUS.

THE CONDITION OF EDUCATION 1996. NATIONAL CENTER FOR EDUCATION STATISTICS PUBLICATION NO. 96-304. WASHINGTON, DC: U.S. DEPARTMENT OF EDUCATION, NATIONAL CENTER FOR EDUCATION STATISTICS.

DIGEST OF EDUCATION STATISTICS: 1996. NATIONAL CENTER FOR EDUCATION STATISTICS PUBLICATION NO. 96-133. WASHINGTON, DC: U.S. DEPARTMENT OF EDUCATION, NATIONAL CENTER FOR EDUCATION STATISTICS.

DROPOUT RATES IN THE UNITED STATES: 1994. NATIONAL CENTER FOR EDUCATION STATISTICS PUBLICATION NO. 96-863. WASHINGTON, DC: U.S. DEPARTMENT OF EDUCATION, NATIONAL CENTER FOR EDUCATION STATISTICS.

EDUCATION INDICATORS: AN INTERNATIONAL PERSPECTIVE. NATIONAL CENTER FOR EDUCATION STATISTICS PUBLICATION NO. 96-003. WASHINGTON, DC: U.S. DEPARTMENT OF EDUCATION, NATIONAL CENTER FOR EDUCATION STATISTICS.

EDUCATION STATISTICS ON DISK: 1996. NATIONAL CENTER FOR EDUCATION STATISTICS PUBLICATION NO. 97-076. WASHINGTON, DC: U.S. DEPARTMENT OF EDUCATION, NATIONAL CENTER FOR EDUCATION STATISTICS.

YOUTH INDICATORS: 1996. NATIONAL CENTER FOR EDUCATION STATISTICS PUBLICATION NO. 96-027. WASHINGTON, DC: U.S. DEPARTMENT OF EDUCATION, NATIONAL CENTER FOR EDUCATION STATISTICS.

UNITED NATIONS. *THE WORLD'S WOMEN 1995: TRENDS AND STATISTICS.* SOCIAL STATISTICS AND INDICATORS, SERIES K, NO. 12. NEW YORK: UNITED NATIONS PUBLICATIONS, 1995.

WEBSITES:

U.S. BUREAU OF THE CENSUS WEBSITE AT <HTTP://WWW.CENSUS.GOV>.

NATIONAL CENTER FOR EDUCATION STATISTICS WEBSITE AT <HTTP://WWW.ED.GOV/NCES>.

CHAPTER 4

Health

MARK S. LITTMAN

MORTALITY, ILLNESS, AND BEHAVIORS CONDUCIVE TO BOTH

EXPECTED YEARS OF "HEALTHY LIFE" AT BIRTH—	
1990:	**64.0 YEARS**
1993:	**63.5 YEARS**
LEADING CAUSE OF DEATH FOR—	
ALL AGES:	**DISEASES OF THE HEART**
CHILDREN UNDER AGE 15:	**ACCIDENTS**
ADULTS 25–44 YEARS:	**HIV INFECTION**
PROPORTION OF U.S. RESIDENTS WHO ARE	
OVERWEIGHT, BETWEEN 1988 AND 1991:	**ONE-THIRD**
PERCENTAGE OF POPULATION 18 YEARS OF AGE AND OVER	
THAT SMOKES CIGARETTES—	
1974:	**37 PERCENT**
1994:	**25 PERCENT**
PERCENTAGE OF PERSONS 12 YEARS OF AGE AND OVER WHO	
ENGAGED IN BINGE-DRINKING IN THE LAST MONTH, 1995:	**16 PERCENT**
PERCENTAGE OF HIGH SCHOOL SENIORS USING	
MARIJUANA IN THE LAST MONTH, 1995:	**21 PERCENT**

HEALTHY LIFE

Is the American population more or less healthy today than it was a few decades ago? Clearly in terms of life expectancy (see chapter 1) the U.S. population lives longer on average, life expectancy having increased by 5 years since 1970 to nearly 76 years in 1995. Yet there are new health concerns today that were virtually nonexistent 25 years ago (e.g., HIV and AIDS), and there is now emphasis on risk factors to a healthy life that were only peripheral concerns a few decades ago (e.g., lowering fat intake, obesity). The U.S. Department of Health and Human Services (DHHS) has developed the concept of "healthy life" as that portion of life expectancy spent in a state free from disabilities, disease or injury,

estimated to be about 85 percent of life expectancy for children born in 1990, or about 64.0 years at that time. This figure has declined, however, in the 1990s, to 63.5 years in 1993. The goal set by DHHS was 65.0 years by the year 2000. DHHS has developed an initiative entitled *Healthy People 2000* with the goals of "increasing the span of healthy life for all Americans, decreasing health disparities among Americans, and achieving access to preventive services for all Americans."[1]

MORTALITY

Death rates for the United States have continued to decline in the past 25 years for the population as a whole when changes in age composition are taken into account (age-adjusted death rate). The crude death rate in 1995 of 880 deaths per 100,000 population was slightly higher than the rate in 1994 of 875 but considerably below the rate for 1970 of 945. When changes in the age composition of the population are taken into account by using the age-adjusted death rate, the rate for 1995 of 504 deaths was the lowest ever recorded. The figure in 1994 was 507 deaths per 100,000 and in 1970 it was 714.[2]

The infant mortality rate in the United States, 7.5 per 1,000 live births in 1995, was one of the lowest in the world, although several European and Asian nations had infant mortality rates of around 5. The average infant mortality rate for developed countries was about 11 in 1996, while less-developed countries averaged 66 infant deaths per 1,000 live births.

---

1 National Center for Health Statistics, *Healthy People 2000 Review 1992*, Department of Health and Human Services publication no. (PHS) 93-1232-1.

2 Age-adjusted death rates are per 100,000 U.S. standard million population, which relates to the age distribution as of the 1940 census. See the technical notes of, "Births and Deaths: United States, 1995," *Monthly Vital Statistics Report* 45, no. 3, Supplement 2 (National Center for Health Statistics, 4 October 1996), 36.

FIGURE 4.1

LEADING CAUSE OF DEATH IN THE UNITED STATES, BY AGE: 1995

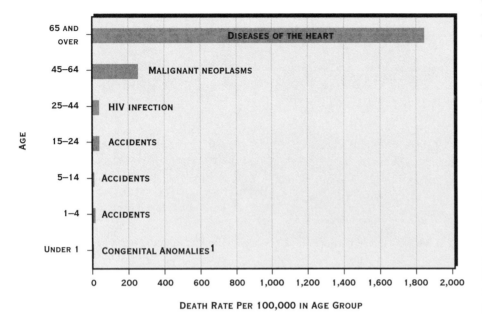

[1] Deaths of infants under 1 year per 1,000 live births.

Source: Rosenburg, H.M., Ventura, S.J., Mauer, J.D., et. al, "Births and Deaths: United States, 1995, "Monthy Vital Statistics report vol. 45 no. 3, supp 2. (1996): Hyattsville, MD: National Center for Health Statistics. 1996.

Cause of death varies considerably by age. Since nearly three out of four deaths in a year are to persons over age 65 (about 1.7 million of the 2.3 million deaths in 1995), their causes of death predominate when causes of death are not disaggregated by age. Thus, the major causes of death are: diseases of the heart, at 32 percent of deaths; malignant neoplasms (various forms of cancer), at 23 percent of deaths; cerebrovascular diseases (stroke), at 7 percent of deaths; chronic obstructive pulmonary diseases (such as emphysema), at 5 percent of deaths; and accidents, which cause 4 percent of deaths. Human Immunodeficiency Virus (HIV) infection, which ranked eighth overall, caused 2 percent of deaths for all age groups combined. As a point of reference, the number of deaths caused by HIV and the number caused by car accidents are comparable.

Some causes of death are among the top 10 causes for each age group, including accidents, cancers, diseases of the heart, and pneumonia. Others, such as diabetes, HIV infection, or congenital anomalies, are primarily causes of death for particular age groups. For any given age group, the top five causes of death account for the vast majority of deaths, with the 10th most common cause of death typically contributing only about 1 percent of deaths in a group in a given year. For children under 15, accidents remain the leading cause of death, accounting for about two of every five deaths: motor vehicle accidents predominate for 5 to 14 year-olds, while other types of accidents are more common for younger children. Homicide and suicide are the third and fifth most common causes of death for children 5 to 14, with HIV infection ranked seventh. For young adults aged 15 to 24, motor vehicle accidents are still the number one cause of death (and account by themselves for nearly a third of deaths in this group), followed by homicide and suicide. HIV infection is the sixth most common killer in this age group. HIV infection is the number one cause of death in the 25 to 44 year-old-age group, accounting for about one out of five deaths in 1995; accidents are second, followed by cancers and heart disease. For 45 to 64 year olds, cancers and heart disease are the first and second most frequent killers, with HIV infection dropping to eighth place. The top four most common causes of death are the same for the elderly as those for all age groups, with pneumonia in fifth place for the elderly.

FIGURE 4.2

ESTIMATED DEATHS AMONG PERSONS WITH AIDS IN THE UNITED STATES: 1984–JUNE 1996

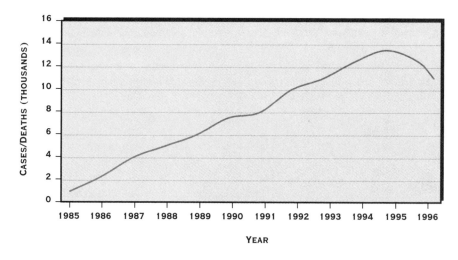

YEAR

Source: CDC, Morbidity and Mortality Weekly Report, vol 46, no. 8 (February 28, 1997).

Note: Estimates include persons age <13 years.

FIGURE 4.3

NUMBER OF PERINATALLY ACQUIRED AIDS CASES AMONG CHILDREN UNDER AGE 13 IN THE UNITED STATES: 1986–1996

(SMOOTHED PLOT BY QUARTER OF DIAGNOSIS WITHIN YEAR)

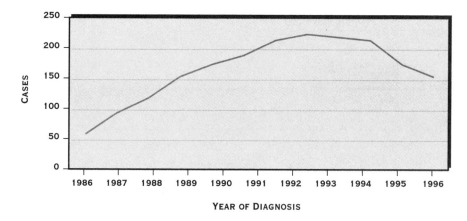

YEAR OF DIAGNOSIS

Source: CDC, Morbidity and Mortality Weekly Report. vol. 45, no. 46.

Note: Estimates are based on cases reported through September 1996, adjusted for reporting delays and unreported risk but not for incomplete reporting of diagnosed AIDS cases.

Deaths (for all ages combined) from Acquired Immunodeficiency Syndrome (AIDS) declined in 1995 for the first time since such deaths were separately recorded. The number of deaths from AIDS increased steadily from 1984, when such data were first gathered, through 1994. However the number of such deaths tapered off in 1995 and declined over the first part of 1996 compared to the same time period a year earlier. There were about 30,000 such deaths in 1990, increasing to 44,000 in 1994. The comparable figure for 1995 was about 31,000. While prevalence of AIDS in the United States has increased, this is related to declines in AIDS deaths rather than an increase in the incidence of AIDS. The incidence of AIDS has been stable, while the number of deaths from AIDS declined for the first time in 1995.[3] In the first half of 1996, about 46 percent of new AIDS cases were attributed to homosexual contact, 29 percent were to heterosexual injecting-drug users, and 17 percent were infected through heterosexual contact. For the remainder, the risk category was unknown (but includes combinations of the categories above as well as transfusion recipients). In 1995, about 84 percent of persons who died from AIDS were men, most typically in their 30s. Women were about 10 percent of AIDS victims in 1990, but nearly 16 percent by 1995. Slightly more than half of the persons who died of AIDS in 1995 were Black or Hispanic, a change from the beginning of this decade, when a small majority were White.

Most children under age 13 with AIDS were infected from their mothers around the time of their birth. During the 1988–93 period, an estimated 1,000 to 2,000 children each year were born infected with HIV, which leads to AIDS. In 1994 treatment with the drug zidovudine (ZDV) was found to reduce perinatal HIV transmission, and since that time the number of AIDS cases among children has declined.

3 Centers for Disease Control and Prevention, *Morbidity and Mortality Weekly Report* 46, no. 8 (February 28, 1997).

Changes in the quality of the environment and effects of pollution on health and death rates have been of particular concern over the past 25 years. Concern for illness born of the environment takes an extraordinarily broad sweep—from sick building syndrome (in which building occupants experience acute health problems that appear to be linked to time spent in a particular structure) exposure to lead (left in the pilings of long-closed mines in Idaho, which sift onto school yards) to public water systems that carry unsafe bacteria levels (recently reported in Washington, D.C.). Some environmental disease occurs naturally (e.g., mosquito-borne malaria), some is man-made. The fraction of all deaths attributable to environmental causes has decreased dramatically in the United States throughout this century, with 40 percent of deaths due to environmental causes at the turn of the century but only 5 percent of deaths due to such causes in 1970. There is little evidence that the proportion has changed much since 1970.[4]

The U.S. Public Health Service Year 2000 goals (which were set in 1990) in the environmental health area include reducing asthma hospitalizations, reducing the incidence of mental retardation in children, reducing the number of outbreaks of waterborne diseases, broadening the proportion of the population that is not exposed to various air pollutants, and lessening the exposure of the population to a variety of health risks such as radon, lead-based paint, and hazardous waste sites. To date the only goal reached has been the reduction in the number of outbreaks of waterborne disease, which decreased from 16 to 11.[5] However, some progress has been made toward reaching these goals: the pro-

portion of persons residing in counties that met national ambient air quality standards for all pollutants has improved from about half the population in 1988 to nearly 77 percent of the population in 1993.[6]

Since 1980, suicide rates have tended to increase for men (both Black and White) and decrease or remain constant for women. Suicide rates are considerably higher for men than for women (by a factor of between four and six times, depending on race). The death rates by suicide for Whites are considerably higher than those

for Black men over age 45, while for women death rates by suicide are higher than those for Blacks in all age groups. Death rates for drug-induced causes (excluding alcohol) have increased since 1980 and are higher for minorities than for Whites. On the other hand, death rates for alcohol-related causes have declined since 1980, considerably for Blacks and only marginally for Whites.[7]

FIGURE 4.4

MOST FREQUENTLY REPORTED CHRONIC CONDITION PER 1,000 PERSONS IN THE UNITED STATES, BY SEX AND AGE: 1994

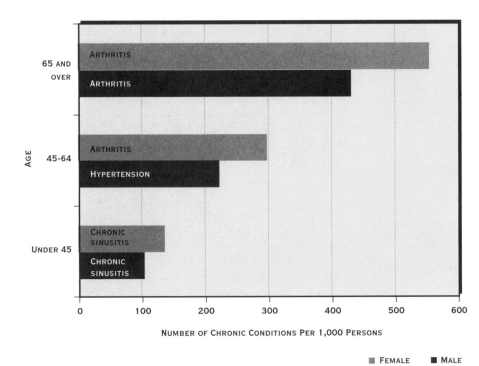

NUMBER OF CHRONIC CONDITIONS PER 1,000 PERSONS

■ FEMALE   ■ MALE

Source: Adams P. F., Marano M.A., current estimates from the "National Health Interview Survey, 1994." National Center for Health Statistics, Vital Health Stat 10 #193 (1995): pp. 83–4.

4 See Jesse H. Ausubel, Perrin S. Meyer, and Iddo K. Wernick, "Death and the Human Environment: The United States in the 20th Century" (unpublished paper, The Rockefeller University, Program for Human Environment, June 1997).

5 National Center for Health Statistics, *Healthy People 2000: 1995-96*, Department of Health and Human Services publication no. (PHS) 96-1256, Table 11.

6 National Center for Health Statistics, *Health 1995*, data tables on diskette, Table 72.

7 See U.S. Bureau of the Census, *Statistical Abstract of the United States: 1996*, (116th) edition (Washington, DC: U.S. Bureau of the Census), 103.

ILLNESS, EXERCISE, AND OVERWEIGHT

Chronic illnesses, those health conditions that have long duration or frequent recurrence, are associated with age, as are causes of death, and tend to occur more frequently with advancing age. Arthritis, which in 1994 affected about 43 out of 100 men over age 65 and 55 out of 100 women; hearing impairments; and heart disease were the most prevalent chronic conditions for the elderly. Furthermore, the incidence of these illnesses often doubled for persons age 65 and over when compared with persons age 45 to 64. For example, hearing impairment affected about 43 out of 1,000 men under age 45, 192 out of 1,000 age 45 to 64, but 354 out of 1,000 who were 65 years and over in 1994. About the only ailment that decreases in incidence with age is acne, which affected about 32 out of 1,000 women under age 45 but only 7 out of 1,000 women in the 45- to 64-year-old age group.

Health experts feel that regular exercise, coupled with healthful diet, can help to prevent some and ameliorate other health conditions: "Regular physical activity can help to prevent and manage coronary heart disease, hypertension, non-insulin-dependent diabetes mellitus, osteoporosis, obesity, and mental health problems such as depression and anxiety."[8] It does not appear that all Americans are listening to this advice. Physical inactivity and poor diet together account for at least 300,000 deaths in the United States each year.[9] Despite what would appear to be an American fetish with fitness—the U.S. consumer spends considerable amounts of money on fitness equipment, health clubs, and weight reduction programs—the average American was less fit in the 1990s than his or her counterpart 20 or 30 years ago. This appears to be the case regardless of age, sex, or race. About 24 percent of Americans were overweight in the 1960–62 period. According to the most recent data,

compiled in the 1988–91 period, this fraction has crept up to the point where about one out of three U.S. residents was overweight.[10] The percentage is slightly higher for women than men and tends to become progressively more common with advancing age, peaking at about 42 percent for men in the 65 to 74 year-old age group and

at 49 percent of women overweight in the 55 to 64 year age group. While about the same proportion of Black men, White men and White women are overweight (about a third), Black women and Mexican-American women are considerably more likely to be overweight.

FIGURE 4.5

PERCENTAGE OF THE ADULT POPULATION IN THE UNITED STATES THAT IS OVERWEIGHT, BY SEX AND RACE: 1960–62 AND 1988–91

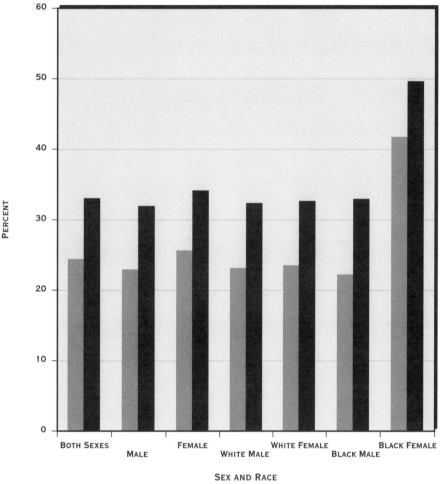

Source: CDC, National Center for Health Statistics, unpublished data and Health, United States, 1995.

Note: Overweight is defined for men as body mass index greater than or equal to 27.8 kilograms/meters, and for women as body mass index greater than or equal to 27.3 kilograms/meters. For additional information see the source indicated.

---

8 National Center for Health Statistics, *Healthy People 2000 Review 1992*, U.S. Department of Health and Human Services publication no. (PHS) 93-1232-1.

9 "Physical Activity and the Health of Young People," National Center for Health Statistics Fact sheet, NCHS Website <http://www.cdc.gov/nchswww/> (March 1997).

10 Based on physical examination data. See National Center for Health Statistics, *Health, United States, 1995.*

If being overweight had no side effect other than to make clothing purchases more difficult, it would be of little more than aesthetic concern. But being overweight is associated with a host of other ailments, including high cholesterol readings, which in turn can lead to high blood pressure, heart disease, and other chronic conditions. Despite the increased proportion of the population that is overweight, the percentage of the population that has high serum cholesterol readings has actually declined in the past 30 years, from about 32 percent to 20 percent in the 1988–91 period. For men, the proportion with high cholesterol readings has declined from about 29 to 19 percent; for women, from 35 percent to 20 percent. Similarly, the percentage of the population that suffers from hypertension has declined as well, from about 37 percent of adults (20 to 74 years of age) in the early 1960s to 23 percent in the early 1990s. Hypertension rates remain higher for men, but the proportion suffering from this disorder has declined for both men and women. All of this decline, for both men and women, has occurred since 1980. The fraction suffering from this malady actually increased between 1960 and 1980. What is behind this paradoxical increase in overweight but decrease in cholesterol levels and hypertension? One partial explanation that has been offered is that a large fraction of adults have stopped smoking over this same period. Former smokers have long complained that they gained weight when they stopped smoking, and a recent study appears to confirm this injustice.[11] Former smokers who had quit in the past 10 years were found to be considerably more likely to have become overweight than their peers who had never smoked. For men, about a fourth and for women about a sixth of the increase in the number of persons who are overweight could be attributed to their stopping smoking.

FIGURE 4.6

SERUM CHOLESTEROL LEVELS AMONG PERSONS AGES 20 YEARS AND OVER IN THE UNITED STATES, BY SEX AND RACE: 1960–1991
(SELECTED YEARS)

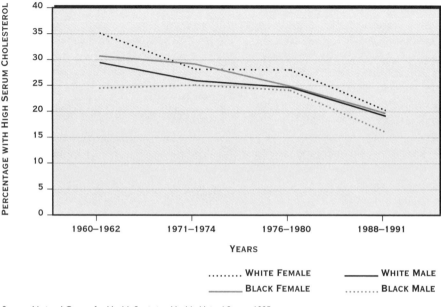

Source: National Center for Health Statistics. Health, United States, 1995.
Hyattsville, MD: Public Health Service, 1996, p 182.

FIGURE 4.7

HYPERTENSION AMONG PERSONS AGES 20 YEARS AND OVER IN THE UNITED STATES, BY SEX AND RACE: 1960–1991
(SELECTED YEARS)

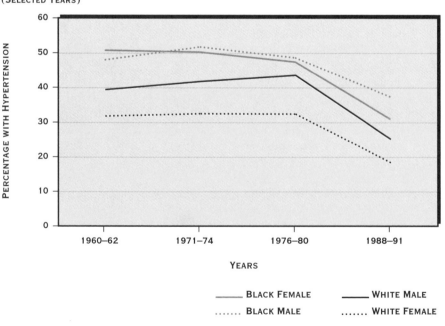

Source: National Center for Health Statistics. Health, United States, 1995.
Hyattsville, MD: Public Health Service, 1996.

---

11 See Katherine M. Flegal et al., "The Influence of Smoking Cessation on the Prevalence of Overweight in the United States," *New England Journal of Medicine* 333 (1995), 1165-70.

This theory (smoking cessation) does not, however, explain the large increase in the occurrence of overweight children and adolescents. In the past 30 years, the percentage of 6 to 17 year olds who are overweight has doubled, with much of this increase occurring (as in adults) since the late 1970s. About 11 percent of these children are classified as "seriously overweight." Obese children are likely to become obese adults and suffer the health consequences of being overweight, and they are likely to attempt dangerous weight-reducing activities: about 5 percent of youth in a 1995 survey had taken laxatives or vomited to lose or maintain weight during the previous month.[12]

Decreased participation in physical activity with increasing age is part of the problem for children as well as adults. Regular participation in vigorous physical activity was reported by about 7 out of 10 youngsters between 12 and 13 years old, but only about 4 of 10 persons aged 18 to 21.[13] Similarly about 80 percent of 9th graders but only 42 percent of 12th graders were enrolled in a physical education class in 1996. In American adults the problem intensifies, with more than 60 percent not achieving recommended levels of regular physical activity, and one out of four achieving the ultimate "couch-potato" status of essentially no physical activity during an average week during 1992.[14]

DRUG AND ALCOHOL USE

Being overweight and lack of exercise are not the only factors contributing to serious health problems in the United States. *Use of drugs*—including cigarettes and alcohol as well as illegal substances—persists. *Alcohol* is the most pervasive, with a fairly constant proportion of the population reporting its use in the past month. In 1994, 54 percent of the population reported using alcohol in the past month, about the same proportion as 20 years ago. During that 20-year period, alcohol use appears to have peaked around 1980, at about 60 percent. Alcohol usage has declined considerably among young teenagers: nearly one out of four 12 and 13 year olds reported alcohol consumption in 1974. In 1994 only 4 percent reported such usage. Similarly, older teens' usage (16–17 year olds) has dropped to about one of four in 1994, while half reported alcohol use in the past month in 1974. Alcohol use was and remains highest in the 18 to 34 year old age group, in which about two-thirds reported use in the past month in 1974 as well as today. Certain historical patterns persist: for example, for persons 18 to 25 years of age, alcohol usage remains more prevalent in men than women (70 percent versus 58 percent), and more prevalent in Whites than in Blacks (71 percent versus 40 percent) or Hispanics (53 percent).

FIGURE 4.8

ALCOHOL USE IN THE PAST MONTH AMONG PERSONS AGES 12 YEARS AND OVER IN THE UNITED STATES, BY AGE: 1974–1994

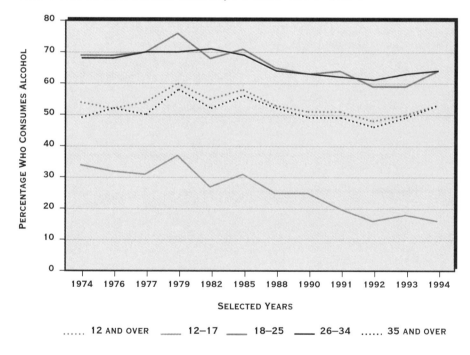

...... 12 AND OVER   ____ 12–17   ____ 18–25   ____ 26–34   ...... 35 AND OVER

Source: National Household Survey on Drug Abuse: Main Findings, 1979, Fishburne, P.M., Abelson, H.I., and I Cisin. DHHS Pub. No. (ADM) 80-976. Alcohol, Drug Abuse Abuse, and Mental Health Administration, Washington, D.C. U.S. Government Printing Office, 1980; and National Household Survey on Drug Abuse: Main Findings, 1982–1994.

---

12 *1995 Youth Risk Behavior Surveillance Survey*. Data from National Center for Health Statistics Website at <http://www.cdc.gov/nchswww/>.

13 See "Physical Activity and the Health of Young People," National Center for Health Statistics Fact Sheet, NCHS Website <http://www.cdc.gov/nchswww/> (March 1997).

14 "Physical Activity and Health: A Report of the Surgeon General," data from the *1992 Behavioral Risk Factor Survey* of the Centers for Disease Control. "Regular vigorous activity" is defined here as sustained activity for 20 minutes a day, three times a week, and could include such activities as gardening for 30 minutes or more, walking a mile in 20 minutes, raking leaves for 30 minutes, as well as such sports activities as swimming laps for 20 minutes, biking four miles in 15 minutes, or playing basketball for 30 minutes.

FIGURE 4.9

ALCOHOL USE IN THE PAST MONTH AMONG PERSONS AGES 12 YEARS AND OVER IN THE UNITED STATES, BY TYPE OF DRINKER: 1995

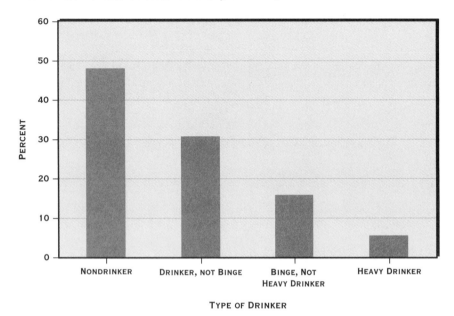

TYPE OF DRINKER

Heavy drinker = Five or more drinks on the same occasion on at least five different days in the past month

Binge, not heavy drinker = Five or more drinks on the same occasion at least once in the past month but on fewer than five different days.

Drinker, not binge = At least one drink in the past month but fewer than five on any single occasion.

Nondrinker = No drinks in the past month

Source: NCADI: 1995 National Household Survey, Data Sheet on Alcohol Use available at <www.health.org/pubs/95hhs/alcohol.htm>.

The vast majority of users of alcohol are neither "binge" drinkers nor can their drinking be characterized as "heavy use." "Binge drinkers" are those who indicated they have had five or more drinks on the same occasion at least once in the last month. "Heavy use" drinkers are those who indicate they have had five or more drinks on the same occasion on five or more different days in the past month.[15] However, about 32 million persons, or 16 percent of the U.S. population 12 years and over, engaged in binge drinking in 1995. An additional 11 million persons, or 5.5 percent of the population, were heavy drinkers based on the definition above.

While possible consequences of alcohol abuse—both health and societal—are widely known, only recently have groups such as Mothers Against Drunk Driving (MADD) brought to public awareness issues that had not formerly been discussed about drinking, such as the consequences of driving while intoxicated. In 1995, about 17,000 persons died in alcohol-related traffic crashes, over 40 percent of all traffic fatalities were attributable to alcohol use, and slightly over 1 million persons were injured in alcohol-related automobile crashes. As stark as these figures are, they represent considerable improvement since the mid-1980s. Automobile crash-related deaths have declined by 24 percent since 1985.

After alcohol, the most pervasive drug use is *cigarette smoking*. Cigarette smoking has declined in the past 20 years among all age groups, among both men and women, and for both Whites and Blacks. Still, about one out of four Americans smoked cigarettes in 1994, down from about 37 percent in 1974. When data on smoking were first collected in 1965, half of adult men and about a third of adult women smoked. The proportion for both sexes was considerably smaller by 1994, with less of a sex differential (about 28 percent of men and 23 percent of women smoked in that year).

15 *1995 National Household Survey on Drug Abuse*, National Clearinghouse for Alcohol and Drug Information Website at <http://www.health.org/pubs/nhsda/index.htm> (May 1998).

FIGURE 4.10

AGE-ADJUSTED PREVALENCE OF CURRENT CIGARETTE SMOKING AMONG PERSONS AGES 25 YEARS AND OVER IN THE UNITED STATES, BY SEX AND LEVEL OF EDUCATION: 1974–1993

(SELECTED YEARS)

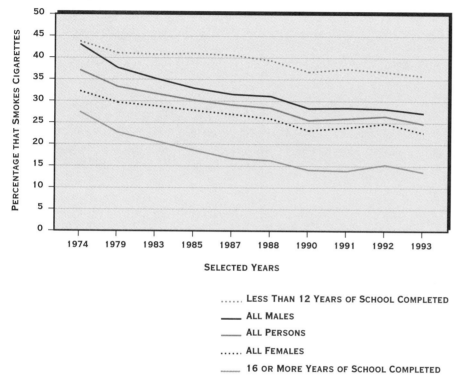

SELECTED YEARS

...... LESS THAN 12 YEARS OF SCHOOL COMPLETED
——— ALL MALES
——— ALL PERSONS
...... ALL FEMALES
------- 16 OR MORE YEARS OF SCHOOL COMPLETED

Source: Data computed by the Centers for Disease Control and Prevention, National Center for Health Statistics, Division of Health and Utilization Analysis, from data compiled by the Division of Health Interview Statistics.

Cigarette use (persons were asked about use in the past month) has declined for youths 12 to 17 years old, from 25 percent in 1974 to 10 percent in 1994, and does not appear to have increased subsequently in the 1990s, despite the increase in use of other drugs in recent years. Years of school completed is strongly associated with cigarette smoking, with persons who have not completed high school having the highest rates and college graduates having the lowest usage. For example, about 41 percent of men (25 years old and over) who were not high school graduates smoked in 1994, compared with only 15 percent of those with 4 or more years of college. This relationship was true in 1974 as well. But even high school dropouts are smoking less now than in the 1970s.

Perhaps one of the biggest societal attitude changes that has occurred since 1980 is that toward smoking. The U.S. Surgeon General's report of 1964 was the first significant government blast against smoking, linking smoking causally to lung cancer as well as other ailments. Yet prior to 1980 smoking cigarettes, pipes or cigars was still common in most workplaces and in such public accommodations as restaurants and airplanes. After 1980, amid mounting evi-

dence of the health effects of smoking, effects of secondhand smoke in the workplace, and the legal right and obligation of employers to protect their workers, smoking in the workplace began to be severely limited, first restricted by employers to particular locations, then banned entirely from the interior of buildings. By the end of 1994, 48 states and the District of Columbia had laws restricting smoking in public places. In addition, most states restrict smoking in government workplaces, and 23 have extended those limitations to private sector workplaces.[16]

Among *illicit drugs*, marijuana is the most widely used in the United States in the 1990s, as it has been for the past several decades. Heroin, which was the largest single source of drug treatment admissions in government-funded programs since 1980 (accounting for about 40 percent), has been supplanted by cocaine in its various forms in the 1990s. In 1995, about 35 percent of the admissions were for cocaine use, 28 percent for heroin, 22 percent for marijuana, about 10 percent for stimulants such as amphetamines, and the remainder for abuse of such drugs as PCP, tranquilizers, and sedatives. The largest single admissions category is alcohol, either alone or in combination with a secondary drug. Such admissions were about 52 percent of admissions to drug and alcohol treatment facilities that were state monitored in 1992.[17]

Most drug and alcohol treatment clients attend outpatient clinics (about 87 percent).[18] In September 1992, there were an estimated 945,000 persons receiving substance abuse treatment, which amounts to 432 clients per 100,000 persons in the population. This is a point-in-time estimate. A much larger proportion of the population would have received treatment during that year (or during their lifetime, for example). Among persons receiving treatment, about 38 percent reported abuse of both alcohol and drugs, an additional 37 percent had only an alcohol abuse problem,

16 American Lung Association Fact Sheet at <htttp://www.lungusa.org>.

17 *The Treatment Episode Data Set*, U.S. Department of Health and Human Services, Substance Abuse and Mental Health Services Administration, Office of Applied Studies Website at <http://www.samhsa.gov/oas/teds>

18 *National Drug and Alcoholism Treatment Unit Survey 1992*, U.S. Department of Health and Human Services, Substance Abuse and Mental Health Services Administration, Office of Applied Studies.

FIGURE 4.11

USE OF SELECTED SUBSTANCES IN THE PAST MONTH BY U.S. HIGH SCHOOL SENIORS: 1980–1995

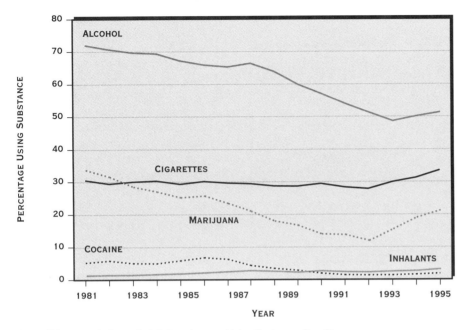

Source: "Monitoring the Future Study," Annual surveys, National Institute on Drug Abuse.

Note: The use of substances from the "National Household Survey on Drug Abuse" and the "Monitoring the Future Study" differ because of different methodologies, sampling frames, and tabulation categories.

and about 25 percent abused only drugs other than alcohol.

Drug use among youths had shown signs of decline between the mid-1970s and 1990, but such use appears to have increased during the 1990s. For example, among high school seniors, self-reported marijuana use in the past month declined from about one out of three students in 1980 to 12 percent in 1992. However, in 1995, about 21 percent reported using marijuana in the past month, and 1 in 20 high school seniors reported daily marijuana use.[19] Some researchers fear the increased use of cigarettes and marijuana, because these drugs are considered "gateways" to the use of more dangerous substances.[20]

But drug abuse is not confined to the young. The National Household Survey on Drug Abuse shows the proportion of drug users who are 35 years and over continues to increase as a proportion of all drug users because of the aging of the baby boom cohort. This group, whose members were teenagers and young adults in the 1960s and 1970s, has a continuing presence in the drug arena. In 1979, 12 percent of emergency room visits for cocaine episodes were to persons 35 years and over. In 1985 this fraction was 19 percent, and, by 1995, 43 percent of emergency room treatment of persons for cocaine episodes were to persons 35 years and over.

---

19 *Monitoring the Future: National High School Drug Use Study*, University of Michigan, Institute for Social Research (various years). *Monitoring the Future* results can be found on National Clearinghouse for Alcohol and Drug Information Website at <http://www.health.org>.

20 *Monitoring the Future*; and "Trends in Adolescent Use of Gateway Drugs" (Columbia University, National Center on Addiction and Substance Abuse, 1994).

CONTRACEPTIVE USE, ABORTION, AND SEXUALLY TRANSMITTED DISEASES

PERCENTAGE OF UNPLANNED BIRTHS IN THE UNITED STATES, 1990:	**40 PERCENT**
PERCENTAGE OF WOMEN RELYING ON OWN STERILIZATION:	**30 PERCENT**
PERCENTAGE OF WOMEN RELYING ON PARTNER'S STERILIZATION:	**13 PERCENT**
NUMBER OF ABORTIONS IN THE UNITED STATES—	
1979:	**1.5 MILLION**
1993:	**1.3 MILLION**
NUMBER OF ABORTIONS PER 1,000 LIVE BIRTHS, 1992:	**379**
FIVE MOST FREQUENTLY TREATED SEXUALLY TRANSMITTED DISEASES IN THE 1990S:	**CHLAMYDIA, GONORRHEA, AIDS, SYPHILIS, HEPATITIS B**

CONTRACEPTIVE USE

The U.S. Government's involvement in family planning services in the 1960s was intended as an aid in its war on poverty that was declared by President Johnson in 1964. It first began as funds to provide family planning services to women receiving public assistance. In 1970, Title X of the Public Health Service Act created a comprehensive federal program to provide family planning services (but prohibited abortion as a family planning method). Despite cutbacks, congressional appropriations have continued for this program. The single largest source of funding for family planning by 1992, however, was the Medicaid program, which is a health insurance program for low-income Americans that reimburses physicians and health-care providers for health care, including family planning. Medicaid provided about half the public funds for family planning in 1992, Title X provided about 17 percent, state funds about 24 percent, and a variety of smaller programs contributed the remainder. It is estimated that publicly funded contraceptive services help to prevent 1.3 million unintended pregnancies a year, which would otherwise result in 534,000 births, 632,000 abortions and 165,000 miscarriages.[21]

As indicated in a previous chapter (Chapter 2, Living Arrangements), average family size in the United States has decreased considerably over the past several decades. A major contributor to the decrease in the number of children born to American women has been the increased use of and improvements in contraceptives. Yet, it is estimated that the majority of *pregnancies* are unplanned, and that 40 percent of *eventual births* as recently as 1990 were unplanned.[22] Despite the family planning efforts indicated above, economic status and education of women are still factors in the use of contraception, as well as in the incidence of unplanned pregnancies, with poorer and less educated women having more unplanned births and using contraception less frequently.

FIGURE 4.12

METHOD OF BIRTH CONTROL USED BY WOMEN: 1990

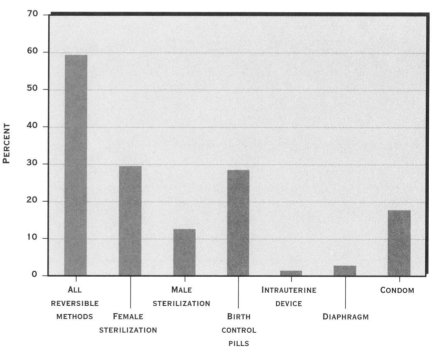

Source: "National Survey of Family Growth," Center for Disease Control and Prevention, National Center for Health Statistics, Division of Vital Statistics.

21 "Issues in Brief: the Impact of Publicly Funded Family Planning," Alan Guttmacher Institute Website at <http://agi-usa.org> (October 1996).

22 "Contraceptive Use," Briefing paper, Guttmacher Website at <http://www.agi-usa.org>.

Nine of 10 sexually active women in the 15- to 44-year-old age group (who are not pregnant and do not wish to become so) report using some contraceptive method. Forty-two percent of the women who used contraception relied on sterilization—either their own (29.5 percent) or their partner's vasectomy (12.6 percent). The remaining 58 percent used a reversible method, with 29 percent using oral contraceptives, 18 percent using condoms, about 3 percent using abstinence or the diaphragm, and the remainder using other techniques. The use of sterilization for women increased from 23 to 30 percent during the 1980s.[23] While no contraceptive technique is 100 percent effective (although sterilization comes closest with a failure rate under 1 percent, and the "pill" 6 percent), the 10 percent of women who use no birth control method account for over half of all unintended pregnancies.[24]

ABORTION TRENDS

Since the passage of the landmark abortion decision *Roe v. Wade* in 1972, the actual number of induced abortions has tended to decline, as has the ratio of abortions to live births, after initial increases in the late 1970s. Between 1975 (when such data were first collected) and 1979 the number of abortions increased from about 1 million to 1.5 million and the ratio of abortions to live births increased from 331 to 420 per 1,000 live births. Since 1979, the actual number of abortions has been relatively stable—varying by only about 100,000 between 1979 and 1992—despite a large increase in the number of women of childbearing age, from 52 to 59 million during this period. The number of abortions has continued to decline in the 1990s and is estimated to have been 1.3 million in 1994. Since the number of abortions has remained relatively flat and the number of women of childbearing age has increased, the abortion rate per 1,000 women has declined, from about 29 around 1980 to about 26 in 1992. The ratio of abortions to live births, which jumped from 331 to 420 abortions per 1,000 live births during the latter half of the 1970s, peaked in the early 1980s and has since declined. In 1992 there were 379 abortions per 1,000 live births.[25]

FIGURE 4.13

NUMBER OF ABORTIONS PER 1,000 LIVE BIRTHS IN THE UNITED STATES, BY STATE: 1992

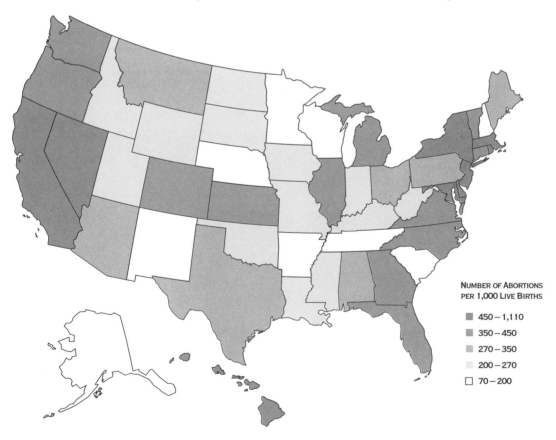

NUMBER OF ABORTIONS PER 1,000 LIVE BIRTHS

- 450 – 1,110
- 350 – 450
- 270 – 350
- 200 – 270
- 70 – 200

Source: Allan Guttmacher Institute.

[23] National Center for Health Statistics, *National Survey of Family Growth in Health* (1995).

[24] "Issues in Brief: Contraception Counts and Contraceptive Use," Alan Guttmacher Institute Website at <http://agi-usa.org>.

[25] U.S. Bureau of the Census. *Statistical Abstract* 1996, Table 115.

SEXUALLY TRANSMITTED DISEASES

Sexually transmitted diseases (STDs) have become more of a public health problem in the United States in the past two decades. Despite the fact that the number of cases per 100,000 for syphilis and gonorrhea have declined throughout the 1990s, five such diseases are among the 10 most frequently treated infections and include chlamydia, gonorrhea, AIDS, syphilis and hepatitis B.[26] Women are more likely than men to become infected with an STD. Serious, and at times fatal, health complications, such as pelvic inflammatory disease, occur more often in women infected with STDs and often do not have any initial symptoms. For example, in 1995 there were six times more cases of chlamydia reported in women than in men. Some STDs are curable; others, such as genital herpes, are not. Once infected, individuals are at risk of infecting their partners for the rest of their lives. The number of initial visits to physicians' offices for treatment of genital herpes, which increased by a factor of 10 between 1970 and 1990 from less than 25,000 to nearly 250,000, appears to have peaked in the early 1990s and fallen off since that time.[27]

Typically, STD rates are higher among minorities than the non-Hispanic White population. Gonorrhea rates were 27 times higher among young Black males than Whites in 1995, for example, and 79 percent of all reported gonorrhea cases were among Blacks. These persistent race differences in part explain why gonorrhea and syphilis are more prevalent in the South than in other regions of the country, since Blacks represent a higher proportion of the total population in that region. According to the U.S. Public Health Service "there are no known biologic reasons to explain why racial or ethnic factors alone should alter risk for STDs. Rather, race and ethnicity in the United States are risk markers that correlate with other more fundamental determinants of health status such as poverty, access to quality health care, health care–seeking behavior, illicit drug use, and living in communities with high prevalence of STDs."[28]

Compared with older adults, teenagers and young adults are at higher risk of acquiring STDs, because they are more likely to have multiple partners and more likely to engage in sex without appropriate protection. And they are less likely to seek treatment because of loss of confidentiality, transportation, and ability to pay. Between 1970 and 1990, there was a steady rise in the proportion of teenage women who indicated they had ever had sexual intercourse, from 29 percent in 1970 to 55 percent in 1990. This rise contributes to the increase in the spread of STDs. In 1995, however, that proportion dropped for the first time, to 50 percent. A comparable drop has been reported for men in another survey.[29] In addition, the proportion of teens reporting use of contraception in general and condoms in particular has increased dramatically, from about 18 percent using condoms in 1970 to 54 percent in 1995. Aside from abstinence, the use of condoms is the most effective means of minimizing the risk of sexually transmitted diseases. The increased use of birth control at first intercourse is often cited as the reason that the teenage birth rate has begun to decline.

---

26 National Center for Health Statistics, *Health 1995,* data tables on diskette, Table 55; and Patricia Donovan, "Confronting a Hidden Epidemic: the Institute of Medicine's Report on Sexually Transmitted Diseases," *Family Planning Perspectives* 29, no. 2 (March/April 1997).

27 "Sexually Transmitted Disease Surveillance, 1995," U.S. Department of Health and Human Services, Centers for Disease Control and Prevention, Division of STD Prevention Website at <http://www.cdc.gov.> (September 1996).

28 "Sexually Transmitted Disease Surveillance, 1995: STDs in Minorities," U.S. Department of Health and Human Services, Centers for Disease Control and Prevention, Division of STD Prevention Website at <http://www.cdc.gov.>.

29 See *1995 National Survey of Family Growth,* National Institute of Child Health and Human Development; and National Institute of Child Health and Human Development Research reported in HHS press release, "Teen Sex Down, New Study Shows" (May 1, 1997).

DISABILITY

PERCENTAGE OF THE U.S. POPULATION WITH A DISABILITY IN 1992*:	**19 PERCENT**
PERCENTAGE OF CHILDREN UNDER 3 WITH A DISABILITY:	**2 PERCENT**
PERCENTAGE OF 45–64 YEAR OLDS WITH A DISABILITY:	**29 PERCENT**
NUMBER OF PERSONS WHO CANNOT HEAR NORMAL SPEECH LEVELS:	**900,000**
NUMBER OF PERSONS USING A WHEELCHAIR:	**1.5 MILLION**
NUMBER OF PERSONS NEEDING DAILY ASSISTANCE WITH GETTING DRESSED, TAKING A BATH, GETTING IN AND OUT OF BED:	**3.8 MILLION**
NUMBER OF PERSONS WITH A MENTAL OR EMOTIONAL DISABILITY:	**6.9 MILLION**

* All figures relate to noninstitutional population.

DEFINING AND GAUGING DISABILITY

The term "disability" has many connotations and can be defined very broadly or narrowly. The proportion of the population that has a disability varies considerably, depending on the definition. A relatively narrow definition, that employed or formerly employed persons are considered to be disabled if they are "unable to engage in substantial gainful activity," is used by the U.S. government in the Social Security Disability program. A considerably broader definition is used in the far-reaching Americans with Disabilities Act of 1990 (ADA), which defines disability as a "physical or mental impairment that substantially limits one or more of the major life activities." Early surveys relating to disability concentrated on the presence of a physical, mental, or other health condition that limited the kind or amount of work a person could do. In recent surveys to determine the extent of disability, the ADA definition is typically operationalized by asking questions relating to: (a) "limitations in functional activities" (for example seeing, hearing, using stairs, lifting, and carrying); (b) "activities of daily living" (ADLs), such as washing, eating, and dressing; and (c) "instrumental activities of daily living

(IADLs), such as difficulty going outside the home or in keeping track of money or bills. ADA assessment also includes questions relating to ability to work and, for children,

limitations in their ability to do school work and other usual activities.[30]

In 1992, about 19 percent of the U.S. population, or 49 million persons (excluding persons living in nursing homes and other institutions), could be characterized as having a disability, using an ADA-like definition. About half of these persons had a disability that was characterized as severe. Severe disabilities include those that limit an individual to a wheelchair for 6 months or longer, that render an individual unable to perform one or more functional activities, or that prevent an individual from working at a job or doing housework.

FIGURE 4.14

PERCENTAGE OF PERSONS IN THE UNITED STATES WITH DISABILITIES, BY AGE GROUP: 1991–1992

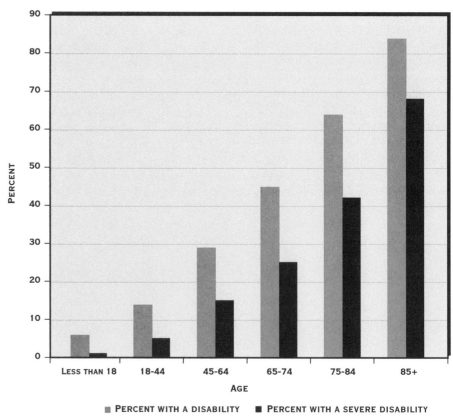

Source: U.S. Department of Commerce.

30 For a more detailed discussion, see John M. McNeil, *Americans with Disabilities: 1991-92*, Series P-70, no. 33 (Washington, DC: U.S. Bureau of the Census).

The likelihood of having some type of disability increases with age: in 1992, about 2 percent of children under 3 years of age had a disability, compared with 29 percent of adults 45 to 64 years and 84 percent of persons 85 years old and over. Because of this increased likelihood with advancing age, persons 65 years and over composed 34 percent of all persons reporting a disability and 43 percent of persons reporting a severe disability. For children, boys tended to have slightly higher disability rates than girls, and for adults, the rates by sex were similar, although women tended to have slightly higher proportions with a severe disability. For older adults, women tended to have slightly higher disability rates.

TYPES OF DISABILITY AND EFFECTS ON LIVELIHOOD

Among the limitations reported by persons 15 years and over in 1992 were about 1.6 million persons who indicated an inability to see words or letters, nearly 1 million who reported an inability to hear normal conversational speech; and 3.8 million who reported needing personal assistance with such activities of daily living as getting dressed, taking a bath, or getting in and out of bed. Also, 1.5 million persons reported using a wheelchair and nearly 4 million used a cane, crutches, or walker for 6 months or longer. About 3.5 percent of the adult population (6.9 million persons) reported a mental or emotional disability, including 1.2 million reported as mentally retarded.

Data for 1994 for persons 21 to 64 years of age indicate that 82 percent of persons in this age group with no reported disability were employed in the last quarter of that year. For persons who reported having a disability, the proportion employed was considerably less at 52 percent. However, for the disabled who reported their problem was not severe, the employment rate was similar to those reporting no disability (about 77 percent). For those reporting a severe disability, employment was relatively rare, with only 26 percent employed.

The earnings level of those with a work disability was adversely affected, even when weeks worked and educational attainment were taken into account. Persons 25 to 64 years of age who worked year-round full-time and reported no work disability had mean earnings in 1995 of $36,400, compared with earnings of about $30,800 for those reporting a work disability, and $25,900 for those reporting a severe disability. On average, persons who reported a disability but who worked year-round full-time made about 85 percent as much as persons without a disability. Those with a college education fared better, earning on average 95 percent as much as their nondisabled counterparts, and they represented about 9 percent of all persons working with a reported disability. Since 1980, the relative economic status of disabled workers has worsened, as indicated by the drop in the ratio of earnings of disabled to nondisabled (such data were first collected in 1980).[31]

---

[31] See U.S. Bureau of the Census, *Labor Force Status and Other Characteristics of Persons with a Work Disability: 1981 to 1988*, Series P-23, no. 160 (Washington, DC: U.S. Bureau of the Census).

HEALTH INSURANCE COVERAGE

NUMBER OF PERSONS WITHOUT HEALTH INSURANCE COVERAGE AT ANY TIME DURING 1995:	**40 MILLION**
PERCENTAGE OF THE U.S. POPULATION WITHOUT HEALTH INSURANCE COVERAGE IN 1995:	**15 PERCENT**
OF THE INSURED, PERCENTAGE WITH PRIVATE HEALTH INSURANCE:	**83 PERCENT**
MOST LIKELY AGE GROUP TO LACK HEALTH INSURANCE:	**YOUNG ADULTS**

WHO IS NOT COVERED

Unlike some countries, there is no national health insurance program in the United States that covers all persons regardless of age or income. Thus, for many persons in the United States, the greatest impediment to a healthy life is lack of adequate health insurance. Lack of health insurance coverage can delay or prevent treatment for a specific ailment as well as impede access to information or preventive services. While not having health insurance is associated with having low income, as well as underemployment and unemployment, some people choose not to have health insurance. For example, presumably persons in households with income of $75,000 or more (which is approximately twice the U.S. average household income) should be able to afford insurance, yet 7 percent of such persons lacked health coverage in 1995. And some young adults, for example, weigh the probability of illness against their relatively tight budgets and opt not to get health insurance.

In 1995, about 15 percent of the U.S. population (40 million people) had no health insurance (at any time during that year). This fraction has increased from about 13 percent in 1987, when comparable information was first collected.[32] In addition, some people were covered by health insurance only part of the year. They may not be covered by health insurance because of unemployment, change in employment, or failure to pay their insurance premium, for example. Other survey data indicated that about 21 percent of the population in 1993 had no insurance or experienced a lapse in coverage of one or more months in that year.[33]

FIGURE 4.15

PERCENTAGE OF PERSONS IN THE UNITED STATES NEVER COVERED BY HEALTH INSURANCE: 1995

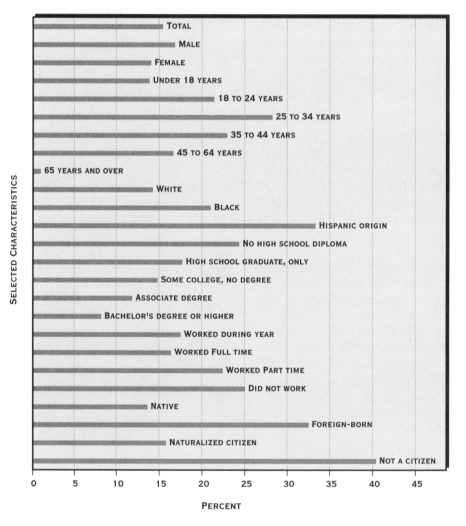

Source: "Current Population Survey", U.S. Bureau of the Census, March 1996.

---

[32] "Health Insurance Historical Table HI-1," Current Population Survey estimates on U.S. Bureau of the Census Website at <http://www.census.gov>.

[33] *Survey of Income and Program Participation*, data available on U.S. Bureau of the Census Website at <http://www.census.gov>.

Men were somewhat more likely than women to be uninsured in 1995. Young adults (18 to 34) were more likely to lack insurance than other age groups. Hispanics were more likely than Blacks or non-Hispanic Whites to lack insurance, with one out of three Hispanics lacking health insurance in 1995. Hispanic males were particularly vulnerable. Immigrants in general were more than twice as likely as natives to lack insurance, with over half of foreign-born persons with poverty-level income lacking health insurance in 1995.

SOURCES OF COVERAGE

There are three main government health insurance programs: one to provide coverage for the elderly (that is, persons 65 years old and older) regardless of income level (Medicare), one to provide coverage for low-income Americans (Medicaid), and a third group of programs that provide care for the military and veterans. These programs provide health insurance coverage to about one-fourth of the U.S. population, with Medicare covering 13 percent, Medicaid about 12 percent, and military health insurance covering about 4 percent.

The vast majority of the insured (83 percent), representing 70 percent of the total population, have private health insurance of one sort or another. Since there are gaps in the insurance coverage of government-sponsored programs, some persons who have Medicare coverage, for example, also have private health insurance.

Generally, private health insurance was obtained through employment. Persons with unstable employment or with part-time work were considerably more likely than full-time workers to be uninsured or to have periods when they were uninsured. Such persons may not be eligible immediately for a government program like Medicaid, because their income was too high (or has recently been too high), but they may not feel that they can afford to continue private insurance coverage. Working for small companies also tends to be associated with a greater likelihood of being uninsured. Many small employers do not offer an employee health insurance plan. For example, about 28 percent of persons working for a company with fewer than 25 employees had private health-insurance policies in their name compared with 65 percent of persons working for a company with 100 or more employees in 1995.

In the United States coverage varies considerably between health plans. Some plans only cover catastrophic illnesses and may have large copayment amounts that must be paid by the insured individual, while other plans cover virtually everything from prescriptions to long-term hospital care. In addition, while a plan may "cover" virtually all health conditions, health insurance plans have caps that limit the amount the health-care provider will be paid for a particular service, which may be considerably less than the actual charge. In some cases, the insured individual is responsible for any amount above the charge allowed by the insurance company; in some instances the health-care provider will accept the insurance company's allowed charges as full payment.[34]

---

[34] For a discussion of the varieties of and access to health insurance in the United States, see U.S. Department of Health and Human Services, *Access to Health Care* (3 parts), U.S. Department of Health and Human Services publication no. (PHS) 97-1526, 1997.

FOR FURTHER INFORMATION:

DONOVAN, PATRICIA. "CONFRONTING A HIDDEN EPIDEMIC: THE INSTITUTE OF MEDICINE'S REPORT ON SEXUALLY TRANSMITTED DISEASES." *FAMILY PLANNING PERSPECTIVES* 29, NO. 2 (MARCH/APRIL 1997).

MCNEIL, JOHN. *AMERICANS WITH DISABILITIES: 1991-92.* SERIES P-70, NO. 33. WASHINGTON, DC: U.S. BUREAU OF THE CENSUS.

NAGI, SAAD. "DISABILITY CONCEPTS REVISITED: IMPLICATIONS FOR PREVENTION." IN *DISABILITY IN AMERICA: TOWARD A NATIONAL AGENDA FOR PREVENTION.* NATIONAL ACADEMY PRESS, 1991.

NATIONAL CENTER FOR HEALTH STATISTICS. *HEALTHY PEOPLE 2000 REVIEW 1995-96.* DEPARTMENT OF HEALTH AND HUMAN SERVICES PUBLICATION NO. (PHS) 96-1256.

NATIONAL CENTER FOR HEALTH STATISTICS. *HEALTH 1995* (TABLES ON DISKETTE).

U.S. BUREAU OF THE CENSUS. *STATISTICAL ABSTRACT OF THE UNITED STATES: 1996.* (116TH) EDITION. WASHINGTON, DC: U.S. BUREAU OF THE CENSUS.

U.S. BUREAU OF THE CENSUS. *HEALTH INSURANCE, 1991 TO 1993.* SERIES P-70, NO. 43.

U.S. BUREAU OF THE CENSUS. *HEALTH INSURANCE COVERAGE: 1995.* SERIES P-60, NO. 195.

U.S. BUREAU OF THE CENSUS. *LABOR FORCE STATUS AND OTHER CHARACTERISTICS OF PERSONS WITH A WORK DISABILITY: 1981 TO 1988.* SERIES P-23, NO. 160.

WEBSITES:

ALAN GUTTMACHER INSTITUTE WEBSITE AT <HTTP://WWW.AGI-USA.ORG>.

CENTERS FOR DISEASE CONTROL WEBSITE FOR DATA ON STDS AT <HTTP://WWW.CDC.GOV>.

NATIONAL CENTER FOR HEALTH STATISTICS WEBSITE AT <HTTP://WWW.CDC.GOV/NCHSWWW/>.

NATIONAL CLEARINGHOUSE FOR ALCOHOL AND DRUG INFORMATION WEBSITE AT <HTTP://WWW.HEALTH.ORG>.

SUBSTANCE ABUSE AND MENTAL HEALTH SERVICES ADMINISTRATION WEBSITE AT <HTTP://WWW.SAMHSA.GOV>.

U.S. BUREAU OF THE CENSUS WEBSITE FOR HEALTH INSURANCE DATA AT <HTTP://WWW.CENSUS.GOV>.

CHAPTER 5

Labor Force and Job Characteristics

PAUL O. FLAIM

LABOR FORCE

U.S. LABOR FORCE—	
1970:	82.9 MILLION
1996:	133.9 MILLION
PROPORTION OF LABOR FORCE THAT WERE WOMEN—	
1970:	38.1 PERCENT
1996:	46.2 PERCENT
PROPORTION OF WOMEN THAT WERE IN THE LABOR FORCE—	
1970:	43.3 PERCENT
1996:	59.3 PERCENT
UNEMPLOYMENT RATE IN 1996 (ANNUAL AVERAGE)—	
ALL WORKERS:	5.4 PERCENT
MEN:	4.6 PERCENT
WOMEN:	4.8 PERCENT
TEENAGERS (16–19):	16.7 PERCENT
PERCENTAGE OF WORKERS IN 1995 WHO WORKED YEAR-ROUND FULL-TIME:	63 PERCENT
MEDIAN YEARS WITH CURRENT EMPLOYER FOR MEN AGED 55–64—	
1983:	15.3 YEARS
1996:	10.5 YEARS
PERCENTAGE OF WAGE AND SALARY WORKERS WHO WERE UNION MEMBERS—	
1983:	20.1 PERCENT
1996:	14.5 PERCENT
RATIO OF SERVICE-PROVIDING TO GOODS-PRODUCING JOBS—	
1970:	2.0 TO 1
1996:	3.9 TO 1
AVERAGE COMMUTING TIME TO WORK IN 1990:	22.4 MINUTES

INTRODUCTION

The extent to which a nation's inhabitants are actively engaged in the production of goods and the provision of services for others—that is, are gainfully employed—is a critical gauge of the nation's economic standing and of the socioeconomic conditions of its people. This is so because it is through employment that most persons obtain the means with which to satisfy their and their families' material requirements as well as, at least in many cases, their own psychic needs.

The degree of difficulty that people encounter in entering or reentering these work activities, that is, in finding a job, is also a very important indicator of the economic health of a nation and of the general well-being of its people. And when the number of persons who are trying to find a job—that is, are unemployed—is added to the number of those who are already in jobs, we have yet another important national statistic. It relates to what is generally referred to as "the economically active population" or (more commonly in the United States) "the labor force." In terms of the course of these indicators, the United States has fared relatively well in recent decades when compared with other industrialized nations, and particularly so in the 1990s.

LABOR FORCE GROWTH

The labor force of the United States has expanded at a remarkable pace in recent decades. In 1996, an average of 133.9 million Americans were in the labor force, 51 million more than in 1970. This impressive expansion is attributable in large part to two factors: the growth of the population of working age, and women's sustained increase in labor force participation.

While men have slightly reduced their participation in the labor force in recent decades, by retiring earlier in their lives than in the past as well as by living longer after retirement, women have continued to increase their job market roles. (See Figure 5.1 and Table 5.1.)

FIGURE 5.1

LABOR FORCE PARTICIPATION RATE IN THE UNITED STATES, BY SEX: 1970–1996

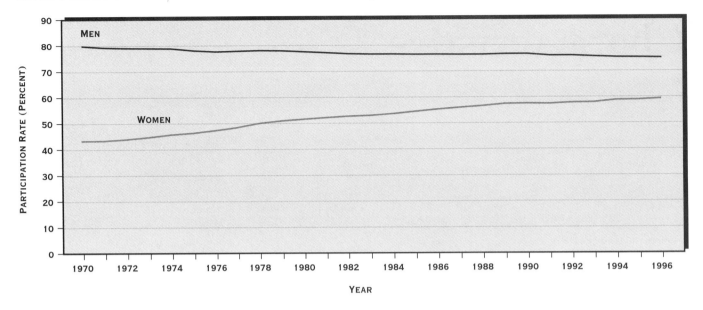

Source: U.S. Bureau of Labor Statistics.

The proportion of the female population 16 years and over that was either working or actively looking for work increased from 43.3 percent in 1970 to 59.3 percent in 1996. This sharp rise in work activity, combined with the increase in the female population, has practically doubled the number of American women in the labor force in the last quarter of the century, taking it from 31.5 million in 1970 to 61.9 million in 1996.

Of course, owing to the rapid growth of their population, the number of men in the labor force increased as well over this period, from 51.2 million in 1970 to 72.1 million in 1996. This increase occurred despite the slow downdrift in the rate of labor force participation among men.

The sustained and very strong increase in the rate of labor force participation among women over the past quarter of a century has more than offset the slight decline among men, resulting in a rise in the rate of labor force participation among all persons from 60.4 percent in 1970 to 66.8 percent in 1996.

TABLE 5.1

GROWTH OF THE U.S. POPULATION AND LABOR FORCE, BY SEX: 1970–1996

(SELECTED YEARS; IN THOUSANDS OF PERSONS)

GROUP	CIVILIAN NON-INSTITUTIONAL POPULATION 16 YEARS AND OVER	CIVILIAN LABOR FORCE	LABOR FORCE PARTICIPATION (PERCENT)
BOTH SEXES			
1970	137,085	82,771	60.4
1975	153,153	93,775	61.2
1980	167,745	106,940	63.8
1985	178,206	115,461	64.8
1990	189,164	125,840	66.5
1995	198,584	132,304	66.6
1996	200,591	133,943	66.8
MEN			
1970	64,304	51,228	79.7
1975	72,291	56,299	77.9
1980	79,398	61,453	77.4
1985	84,469	64,411	76.3
1990	90,377	69,011	76.4
1995	95,178	71,360	75.0
1996	96,206	72,087	74.9
WOMEN			
1970	72,782	31,543	43.3
1975	80,860	37,475	46.3
1980	88,348	45,487	51.5
1985	93,736	51,050	54.5
1990	98,787	56,829	57.5
1995	103,406	60,944	58.9
1996	104,385	61,857	59.3

Source: U.S. Bureau of Labor Statistics

TABLE 5.2

FAMILIES IN THE UNITED STATES WITH CHILDREN UNDER 6 YEARS OF AGE, BY EMPLOYMENT STATUS OF PARENTS: 1996

(ANNUAL AVERAGES)

CHARACTERISTIC	NUMBER (IN THOUSANDS)	PERCENT DISTRIBUTION
ALL FAMILIES WITH CHILDREN UNDER 6	15,286	100.0
PARENT(S) EMPLOYED	13,405	87.7
NO PARENT EMPLOYED	1,881	12.3
MARRIED-COUPLE FAMILIES	11,562	100.0
PARENT(S) EMPLOYED	11,174	96.6
MOTHER EMPLOYED	7,053	61.0
BOTH PARENTS EMPLOYED	6,641	57.4
MOTHER EMPLOYED, NOT FATHER	412	3.6
FATHER EMPLOYED, NOT MOTHER	4,121	35.6
NEITHER PARENT EMPLOYED	388	3.4
FAMILIES MAINTAINED BY WOMEN	3,076	100.0
MOTHER EMPLOYED	1,699	55.2
MOTHER NOT EMPLOYED	1,378	44.8
FAMILIES MAINTAINED BY MEN	648	100.0
FATHER EMPLOYED	532	82.2
FATHER NOT EMPLOYED	115	17.8

Source: U.S. Bureau of Labor Statistics.

MOTHERS IN THE LABOR FORCE

The rapid expansion of the female labor force has been fueled in large part by an increasingly stronger attachment to jobs on the part of women of child-bearing and child-rearing ages. Relative to the past, women are marrying at later ages, and, on average, they are postponing having children to later ages. In addition, whereas in the past mothers of young children tended to stay away from the job market for many years, this is no longer typical.

As shown in Table 5.2, the majority of women with children under 6 years of age were actually employed in 1996. This was the case whether they were part of a married-couple family—in which case often both parents were working—or whether they had no spouse and maintained their own family. Indeed, there were over 400,000 married-couple families with children under 6 years of age in 1996 where the mother was the only working parent.

The fact that women have developed ever stronger attachment to their jobs, with many having also attained relatively high-paying positions, may be one of the driving forces leading to the slight but persistent decline in the labor force participation among men of prime working age. For men 35 to 44, for example, the participation rate has declined from 96.9 percent in 1970 to 92.4 in 1996. While the slow downdrift in the labor force participation among these men may be largely attributable to other factors (such as an easing of the rules allowing those with some disability to cease working), some men have, no doubt, assumed the role of homemakers, while their wives have assumed the role of the primary family earner.

GROWTH IN EMPLOYMENT

Just as impressive as the growth of the labor force (which includes unemployed persons) has been the actual rise in the number of persons with jobs over the past quarter of a century. In 1996, an average of 126.7 million persons were employed in the United States, up from 78.7 million in 1970. Over the same period, the proportion of the population 16 years and over that was employed expanded gradually from 57.4 to 63.2 percent (again driven largely by gains in the employment of women).

TABLE 5.3

EMPLOYED PERSONS AGES 16 YEARS AND OVER IN THE UNITED STATES, BY SEX: 1970–1996

(ANNUAL AVERAGES)

CHARACTERISTIC	EMPLOYED (IN THOUSANDS)	EMPLOYED AS PERCENT OF POPULATION
BOTH SEXES		
1970	78,678	57.4
1975	85,846	56.1
1980	99,303	59.2
1985	107,150	60.1
1990	118,793	62.8
1995	124,900	62.9
1996	126,708	63.2
MEN		
1970	48,990	76.2
1975	51,857	71.7
1980	57,186	72.0
1985	59,891	70.9
1990	65,104	72.0
1995	67,377	70.8
1996	68,207	70.9
WOMEN		
1970	29,688	40.8
1975	32,989	42.0
1980	42,117	47.7
1985	47,259	50.4
1990	53,689	54.3
1995	57,523	55.6
1996	58,501	56.0

Source: U.S. Bureau of Labor Statistics.

There have been sharply contrasting trends in the employment trends for men and women. Primarily because men have tended to leave their jobs at a gradually lower age, the employed proportion of the male population 16 years of age and over shrank from 76.2 percent in 1970 to 70.9 percent in 1996. On the other hand, the proportion of the female population with jobs increased at an astounding pace, rising from 40.8 percent in 1970 to 56.0 percent in 1996.

TRENDS IN UNEMPLOYMENT

In 1996, with the American economy continuing to expand vigorously, the ranks of the unemployed—persons without a job who were actively looking for work—continued to shrink. The proportion of the labor force that was unemployed averaged only 5.4 percent for the year. By contrast, the unemployment rate had generally been much higher during most of the preceding quarter of a century, having approached 10 percent in the early 1980s. (During 1997 the unemployment rate dropped even further, dipping slightly below 5.0 percent by midyear.)

Of course, unemployment is a highly cyclical phenomenon, rising sharply when economic growth slackens and dropping quickly as the economy recovers its productive rhythm. This largely explains the fluctuations in the unemployment rate as shown in Figure 5.2.

Some population groups are, likewise, much more likely to encounter unemployment than are other groups. Teenagers, who may be trying to insert themselves in the world of work or who may merely look for temporary jobs while studying and preparing for a career, have by far the highest rate of unemployment among the major population groups. In 1996, the teenage unemployment rate averaged 16.7 percent. For adult workers, unemployment is a much more infrequent phenomenon. As shown in Table 5.4, in 1996 the jobless rate averaged 4.6 percent for men 20 years of age and over 4.8 percent for women in this age bracket.

TABLE 5.4

UNEMPLOYMENT RATES IN THE UNITED STATES, BY SEX AND MAJOR AGE GROUP: 1996

(ANNUAL AVERAGE)

AGE-SEX GROUP	UNEMPLOYMENT RATE
TOTAL, ALL WORKERS	5.4
MEN, 20 YEARS AND OVER	4.6
WOMEN, 20 YEARS AND OVER	4.8
TEENAGERS (BOTH SEXES)	
AGE 16 TO 19	16.7

Source: U.S. Bureau of Labor Statistics.

FIGURE 5.2

UNEMPLOYMENT RATE IN THE UNITED STATES: 1970–1996

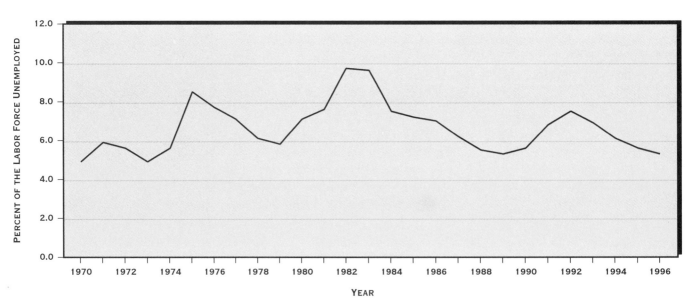

Source: U.S. Bureau of Labor Statistics.

Note: Annual averages for civilian workers 16 years and over.

The fact that jobless rates for adult men and women have recently been nearly equal is another reflection of the progress made by women in becoming a very large and relatively permanent portion of the nation's labor force. Only a few decades ago, by contrast, women were more likely to be considered as a "secondary" source of workers. Indeed, women were then much more likely than men to leave and reenter the labor force many times in response to changes in demand or in their family situations. Because of their relatively frequent transitions into and out of the labor force, adult women had a generally higher unemployment rate than men. In 1970, for example, when unemployment averaged only 3.5 percent for men 20 years and over, the rate for women in the same age group was 4.8 percent.

INTERNATIONAL COMPARISONS

A few decades ago, unemployment in the United States was generally much higher than in other major industrialized countries. In 1970, for example, when the rate of unemployment for the United States averaged 4.9 percent, Japan and the major European countries exhibited much lower jobless rates. By the mid-1990s, the situation had practically reversed itself. While the unemployment rate for Japan is still much lower than that for the United States, as shown in Table 5.5, the jobless rates for the major European countries have, in recent years, risen to much higher levels than the rate for the United States.

Even in terms of the actual employment trends, that is, in the proportion of persons with jobs among the principal population groups, the United States has performed comparatively well. By 1996, for example, the overall proportion of the population 16 years and over that was actually employed reached 63.2 percent in the United States. As shown in Table 5.6, this was somewhat higher than the employment/population ratio for Japan and considerably higher than the comparable ratios for the major European countries.

On average, 70.9 percent of American men age 16 and over held jobs in 1996. While the comparable ratio for Japan was even higher (74.9 percent), the employment ratios for men in the major industrialized countries of Europe were generally lower. Women in the United States were employed at particularly high rates compared with other countries. In 1996, after decades of impressive increases in their participation in the labor market, the proportion of American women with jobs—most often in addition to their traditional household duties—averaged 56.0 percent. Of the selected countries for which 1995 data are shown in Table 5.6, only Sweden, a country with a historically high proportion of women in the labor force, approached the United States in terms of this important socioeconomic indicator.

TABLE 5.5

UNEMPLOYMENT RATES FOR THE UNITED STATES AND OTHER INDUSTRIALIZED COUNTRIES: 1970–1995

(SELECTED YEARS)

YEAR	UNITED STATES	JAPAN	FRANCE	GERMANY	ITALY	SWEDEN	UNITED KINGDOM
1970	4.9	1.2	2.5	0.5	3.2	1.5	3.1
1975	8.5	1.9	4.2	3.4	3.4	1.6	4.6
1980	7.1	2.0	6.5	2.8	4.4	2.0	7.0
1985	7.2	2.6	10.5	7.2	6.0	2.8	11.2
1990	5.6	2.1	9.1	5.0	7.0	1.8	7.0
1995	5.6	3.2	11.5	6.5	12.0	9.1	8.8

Source: U.S. Bureau of Labor Statistics.

Note: The data for foreign nations has been adjusted by B.L.S. to render them conceptually comparable to those for the United States.

TABLE 5.6

EMPLOYMENT TO POPULATION RATIOS FOR THE UNITED STATES AND SELECTED COUNTRIES, BY SEX: 1995

(ANNUAL AVERAGES)

POPULATION GROUP	UNITED STATES	JAPAN	FRANCE	GERMANY	ITALY	SWEDEN	UNITED KINGDOM
BOTH SEXES	62.9	60.9	49.0	49.7	41.8	58.5	56.7
MEN	70.8	75.0	58.2	N/A	N/A	62.3	N/A
WOMEN	55.6	48.0	40.7	N/A	N/A	54.9	N/A

Source: U.S. Bureau of Labor Statistics.

TABLE 5.7

UNEMPLOYMENT RATES IN THE UNITED STATES, BY RACE AND HISPANIC ORIGIN: 1970–1996

(SELECTED YEARS)

YEAR	TOTAL, ALL GROUPS	WHITE	BLACK	HISPANIC ORIGIN
1970	4.9	4.5	8.2	N/A
1975	8.5	7.8	13.8	12.2
1980	7.1	6.3	13.1	10.1
1985	7.2	6.2	13.7	10.5
1990	5.6	4.8	10.1	8.2
1995	5.6	4.9	9.6	9.3
1996	5.4	4.7	10.5	8.9

Source: U.S. Bureau of Labor Statistics.

EMPLOYMENT STATUS OF BLACKS AND HISPANICS

Although the general labor market indicators for the United States have performed particularly well in recent years, there are some groups of workers that continue to lag far behind the national averages. This is particularly the case for Black workers and, to a lesser extent, for those of Hispanic origin. The unemployment rates for these two groups, as well as for Whites, are shown in Table 5.7.

The substantial differential between the unemployment rates of White workers and those of Blacks and Hispanics has changed little over the past several decades. The percentage of Black workers trying to find a job has consistently run two to two-and-one-half times the comparable statistic for White workers. Persons of Hispanic origin, a group that has been growing rapidly in the United States, have generally experienced unemployment rates that are lower than those for Blacks but still much higher than those for Whites.

EXTENT OF WORK DURING THE YEAR

The statistics examined thus far relate to the average number of persons employed or unemployed during a given year. These numbers, while very important, do not fully reflect the dynamics of labor force activity. Since many persons work or look for work for only a part of the year, the total number with some labor force activity during a given year is generally much greater than is reflected in the averages for that year.

In 1995, for example, while the "average" number of persons with jobs was 124.9 million, the total number with at least some employment during the year was 139.0 million. And while the "average" number of persons looking for work during the year was 7.4 million and the "average" unemployment rate was 5.6 percent, the "total" number of persons encountering some unemployment during the course of the year was 18.1 million, equaling 12.8 percent of all those with some labor force activity during the year.

Of all the persons with a job during 1995, about 63 percent worked full time the entire year (see Table 5.8). Approximately 16 percent also worked predominantly on a full-time basis, but not the entire year. The remainder, about 21 percent, worked predominantly on a part-time basis for periods that varied from a few weeks to the entire year. As shown in Table 5.8, the numbers for 1994 were very similar to those for 1995, indicating that this is a fairly typical pattern of the labor force dynamics for the U.S. population.

PERSONS WITH MORE THAN ONE JOB

Many American workers hold more than one job. In fact, nearly 8 million managed to hold two or more jobs simultaneously during 1995. These "multiple jobholders" accounted for 6.3 percent of the average number of employed persons for the year.

The reasons that workers cite for holding more than one job vary considerably. Financial necessity is usually cited by about two-fifths of such workers—specifically 37 percent in a special 1979 survey and 44 percent in a similar survey conducted in 1989. The other multiple jobholders cited a variety of nonfinancial motivators, such as getting experience in a new field or building up a "side business."

As shown in Table 5.9, the tendency to hold more than one job increases with education. Whereas only 3 percent of the workers with less than a high school education held more than one job in 1995, the multiple jobholding rate rose to nearly 10 percent for persons with a Ph.D.

TABLE 5.8

EXTENT OF LABOR FORCE ACTIVITY IN THE UNITED STATES DURING COURSE OF YEAR: 1994–1995

(THOUSANDS OF PERSONS AND PERCENT DISTRIBUTION)

EXTENT OF LABOR FORCE ACTIVITY	1994	1995
CIVILIAN NONINSTITUTIONAL POPULATION 16 YEARS AND OVER	198,022	199,925
WORKED AND/OR LOOKED FOR WORK DURING YEAR	140,441	141,659
PERCENT OF POPULATION	70.9	70.9
WORKED ALL OR PART OF YEAR	137,584	138,971
PERCENT OF POPULATION	69.5	69.5
ENCOUNTERED SOME UNEMPLOYMENT	18,944	18,063
PERCENT OF TOTAL WITH LABOR FORCE ACTIVITY	13.5	12.8
PERCENT DISTRIBUTION BY EXTENT OF EMPLOYMENT		
TOTAL WHO WORKED	100.0	100.0
WORKED FULL TIME	78.0	78.7
ALL YEAR	61.7	62.9
PART OF YEAR	16.2	15.8
WORKED PART TIME	22.0	21.3
ALL YEAR	9.4	9.1
PART OF YEAR	12.6	12.2

Source: U.S. Bureau of Labor Statistics.

YEARS WITH CURRENT EMPLOYER

The average number of years that the typical worker has been with the same employer has changed little over the past two decades. For all workers 25 years of age and over—men and women combined—the median years with the current employer was 5.0, as reported in a 1996 survey, about the same as reported in previous "job tenure" surveys in 1983, 1987, and 1991. However, the stability of these "average" numbers masks important changes in tenure for some groups of workers, namely a general increase for women and a rather sharp and disturbing decline for men in the middle age groups and preretirement years.

When the job tenure numbers are broken down by sex, they show clearly that women are staying in their jobs longer and longer, whereas men have seen a rather sharp decline in the average number of years spent with the same employer. While for men in the advanced age groups this may be largely a reflection of the voluntary trend toward earlier retirement, this cannot be said for the men in the middle age groups, who have also exhibited large declines in job tenure. For these men, there has been an obvious decline in job security, probably as the inevitable result of the "downsizing" of many American firms, which has forced many of them to restart their careers with new employers.

As the result of these developments, the traditional gap in average job tenure between men and women has shrunk significantly. Whereas in 1983 the median years of tenure in one's job were 5.9 for men 25 and over, but only 4.2 for women of the same age, the numbers for the two groups are now nearly equal. The February 1996 survey yielded a median job tenure of 5.3 years for men 25 and over and 4.7 years for women in the same age bracket.

Naturally, the job tenure numbers tend to increase with age. But they dip again for persons 65 and over, many of whom are evidently found in postretirement jobs of relatively short duration. It is interesting to note in this context that for workers 55 and over, the tenure numbers are now virtually the same for women as for men.

TABLE 5.9

MULTIPLE JOBHOLDERS IN THE UNITED STATES, BY EDUCATIONAL ATTAINMENT: 1995

(ANNUAL AVERAGES)

EDUCATIONAL ATTAINMENT	TOTAL EMPLOYED	MULTIPLE JOBHOLDERS	PERCENT OF EMPLOYED WHO ARE MULTIPLE JOBHOLDERS
TOTAL EMPLOYED	125,004	7,924	6.3
LESS THAN HIGH SCHOOL	15,968	519	3.3
HIGH SCHOOL GRADUATES	40,821	2,077	5.1
SOME COLLEGE, NO DEGREE	26,101	1,940	7.4
ASSOCIATE DEGREE	10,096	793	7.9
BACHELOR'S DEGREE	21,470	1,683	7.8
MASTER'S DEGREE	7,109	648	9.1
PROFESSIONAL DEGREE	2,036	132	6.5
PH.D.	1,402	132	9.4

Source: U.S. Bureau of Labor Statistics.

TABLE 5.10

MEDIAN YEARS WITH CURRENT EMPLOYER FOR U.S. WAGE AND SALARY WORKERS AGES 25 YEARS AND OVER: 1983–1996

(SELECTED YEARS)

SEX AND AGE	JANUARY 1983	JANUARY 1987	JANUARY 1991	FEBRUARY 1996
BOTH SEXES				
TOTAL, 25 YEARS AND OVER	5.0	5.0	4.8	5.0
25–34 YEARS	3.0	2.9	2.9	2.8
35–44 YEARS	5.2	5.5	5.4	5.3
45–54 YEARS	9.5	8.8	8.9	8.3
55–64 YEARS	12.2	11.6	11.1	10.2
65 YEARS AND OVER	9.6	9.5	8.1	8.4
MEN				
TOTAL, 25 YEARS AND OVER	5.9	5.7	5.4	5.3
25–34 YEARS	3.2	3.1	3.1	3.0
35–44 YEARS	7.3	7.0	6.5	6.1
45–54 YEARS	12.8	11.8	11.2	10.1
55–64 YEARS	15.3	14.5	13.4	10.5
65 YEARS AND OVER	8.3	8.3	7.0	8.3
WOMEN				
TOTAL, 25 YEARS AND OVER	4.2	4.3	4.3	4.7
25–34 YEARS	2.8	2.6	2.7	2.7
35–44 YEARS	4.1	4.4	4.5	4.8
45–54 YEARS	6.3	6.8	6.7	7.0
55–64 YEARS	9.8	9.7	9.9	10.0
65 YEARS AND OVER	10.1	9.9	9.5	8.4

Source: U.S. Bureau of Labor Statistics.

TABLE 5.11

MEANS OF TRANSPORTATION TO WORK IN THE UNITED STATES FOR PERSONS WHO WORKED IN THE PAST WEEK: 1980 AND 1990

MEANS OF TRAVEL TO WORK	1980	1990
TOTAL	100.0	100.0
CAR, TRUCK, OR VAN	84.1	86.5
DROVE ALONE	64.4	73.2
CARPOOLED	19.7	13.4
PUBLIC TRANSPORTATION	6.4	5.3
WALKED	5.6	3.9
USED OTHER MEANS	1.6	1.3
WORKED AT HOME	2.3	3.0

Source: 1980 and 1990 Censuses, U.S. Bureau of the Census.

HOW AMERICANS TRAVEL TO THEIR JOBS

Most American workers drive alone to and from their jobs, and their tendency to do so has been increasing. Nearly three-fourths used this mode of transportation in 1990, up considerably from 1980. (See Table 5.11.)

In contrast, the proportion riding with others or using public transportation has continued to shrink despite public and private efforts to reverse this trend (through the subsidization of fares, the institution of special traffic lanes, and prioritized parking for car pools). Only 13 percent of the American workers carpooled in 1990, down from 20 percent in 1980, and there was also a further decline—to only 5 percent—in the proportion of workers using public transportation. The small proportion of workers who walked to their jobs or used other means (such as bicycles, motorcycles, etc.) also shrank further between 1980 and 1990.

Average commuting time did not change much between 1980 and 1990. Data from the 1990 census show that the average (mean) travel time was about 22.5 minutes compared with 21.7 minutes in 1980. However, as Table 5.12 and Figure 5.3 shows, there was a wide variation in reported travel time: about 4 percent of the workers (excluding those working at home)

reported it took them less than 5 minutes to reach their jobs. At the other extreme, about 6 percent of the workers surveyed had to travel in excess of 1 hour to reach their jobs.

TABLE 5.12

TRAVEL TIME TO WORK IN THE UNITED STATES: 1990

TRAVEL TIME TO WORK (MINUTES)	PERCENT
TOTAL, WORKING AWAY FROM HOME	100
LESS THAN 5 MINUTES	3.9
5 TO 9	12.5
10 TO 14	16.1
15 TO 19	17.0
20 TO 24	14.5
25 TO 29	5.5
30 TO 34	12.8
35 TO 39	2.4
40 TO 44	2.8
45 TO 59	6.4
60 TO 89	4.5
90 OR MORE	1.6
MEAN TRAVEL TIME (MINUTES)	22.4

Source: 1990 Census, U.S. Bureau of the Census.

FIGURE 5.3

TRAVEL TIME TO WORK IN THE UNITED STATES: 1990

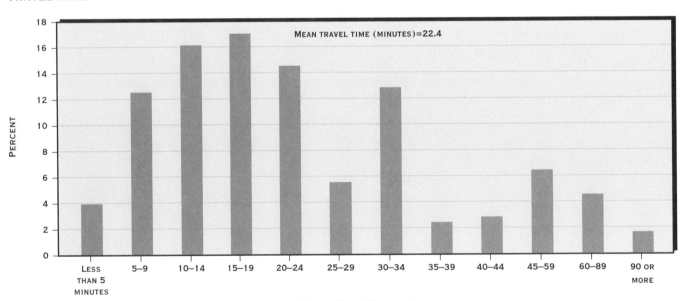

Source: 1990 Census, U.S. Bureau of the Census.

UNION REPRESENTATION

American workers are less likely to belong to a union than they were in the past. While the extent of union membership differs significantly across the industrial spectrum, the proportion of all wage and salary workers belonging to unions or employee associations similar to labor unions has declined from nearly a fourth in the late 1970s to only 14.5 percent in 1996 (see Table 5.13 and Figure 5.4). The proportional decline is related both to the rapid increase in employment in services-providing industries, where participation in the union movement has traditionally been very low, and to the decline or relative stagnation in employment in those goods-producing industries where union membership had tended to be more prevalent.

TABLE 5.13

UNION OR ASSOCIATION MEMBERS IN THE UNITED STATES AS A PERCENTAGE OF WAGE AND SALARY EMPLOYMENT: 1977–1996

YEAR	WAGE AND SALARY EMPLOYEES WHO WERE UNION OR EMPLOYEE ASSOCIATION MEMBERS (IN THOUSANDS)	TOTAL WAGE AND SALARY EMPLOYMENT (IN THOUSANDS)	UNION OR ASSOCIATION MEMBERS AS A PERCENT OF WAGE AND SALARY EMPLOYMENT
1977	19,335	81,334	23.8
1978	19,548	84,968	23.0
1979	20,986	87,117	24.1
1980	20,095	87,480	23.0
1981	N/A	N/A	N/A
1982	N/A	N/A	N/A
1983	17,717	88,290	20.1
1984	17,340	92,194	18.8
1985	16,996	94,521	18.0
1986	16,975	96,903	17.5
1987	16,913	99,303	17.0
1988	17,002	101,407	16.8
1989	16,960	103,480	16.4
1990	16,740	103,905	16.1
1991	16,568	102,786	16.1
1992	16,390	103,688	15.8
1993	16,598	105,067	15.8
1994	16,748	107,989	15.5
1995	16,360	110,038	14.9
1996	16,269	111,960	14.5

Source: Data from the Current Population Survey: May, 1977-80, U.S. Bureau of Labor Statistics, Annual Averages, 1983-96.

Note: Data on union membership are not available for 1981 and 1982, and, because of some survey changes, the data for 1983 may not be directly comparable with the data for 1980 and prior years. Furthermore, the data beginning with 1994 may also not be strictly comparable with those for prior years.

FIGURE 5.4

UNION OR ASSOCIATION MEMBERS IN THE UNITED STATES AS A PERCENTAGE OF WAGE AND SALARY EMPLOYMENT: 1977–1996

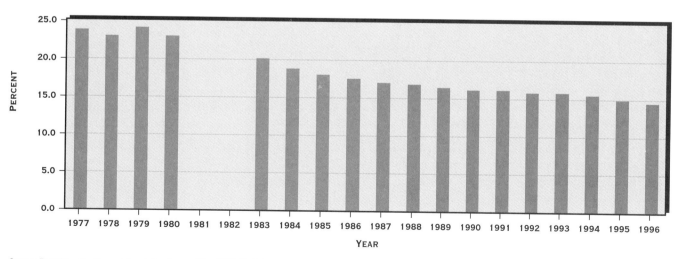

Source: Data from the Current Population Survey: May, 1977–80, U.S. Bureau of Labor Statistics, Annual Averages, 1983–96.

Note: Data on union membership are not available for 1981 and 1982, and, because of some survey changes, the data for 1983 may not be directly comparable with the data for 1980 and prior years. Furthermore, the data beginning with 1994 may also not be strictly comparable with those for prior years.

The actual number of workers belonging to unions has remained fairly stable, in absolute terms, during the 1990s, after declining rapidly in the 1980s. However, because total wage and salary employment has continued to increase rapidly, the proportion of workers belonging to unions has continued to shrink as a percentage of the total.

PRODUCTION OF GOODS VERSUS PROVISION OF SERVICES

As a nation's prosperity increases, the consumption of various services—in the fields of education, health, utilities, transportation, lodging, amusement, etc.—tends to increase much more rapidly than the consumption of goods. In line with this trend, the proportion of the labor force engaged in the provision of services will also tend to increase, while the percentage engaged in the production of goods will shrink. Of course, these trends, which are highly visible in the historical statistics for the United States, may also be affected by changes in productivity and in international trade. For example, the United States has become a large importer of manufactured goods in recent decades, and this has had a further negative impact on employment in its goods-producing sector.

As shown in Figure 5.5, which relates to nonagricultural payroll employment, while the number of jobs in goods-producing industries has remained relatively flat (in absolute terms) over the past quarter of a century, the number of jobs in industries engaged in the provision of various services has expanded at a very rapid pace. And, as shown by the data for the most recent period, this trend is continuing.

TRENDS IN EMPLOYMENT BY OCCUPATION

Reflecting the rapid increase in the proportion of the economy dedicated to the provision of services, there has been a gradual transformation of the occupational landscape, with a rapid increase in white-collar and services occupations and a relative decline in the traditional blue-collar occupations.

FIGURE 5.5

EMPLOYMENT IN GOODS-PRODUCING AND SERVICE-PROVIDING INDUSTRIES IN THE UNITED STATES: 1970–1996

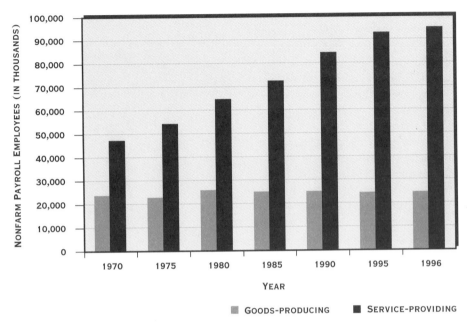

Source: U.S. Bureau of Labor Statistics.

TABLE 5.14

DISTRIBUTION OF EMPLOYMENT FOR MEN AND WOMEN IN THE UNITED STATES, BY OCCUPATIONAL GROUP: 1972, 1983, AND 1996

(ANNUAL AVERAGES)

OCCUPATIONAL GROUP	1972	1983	1996
MEN			
TOTAL EMPLOYED:			
NUMBER (IN THOUSANDS)	50,896	56,787	68,207
PERCENT	100.0	100.0	100.0
MANAGERS AND PROFESSIONALS	21.2	24.5	27.5
TECHNICAL, SALES, AND ADMINISTRATIVE SUPPORT	18.8	19.5	19.8
SERVICE OCCUPATIONS	8.3	9.7	10.2
PRECISION PRODUCTION, CRAFT, AND REPAIR	19.4	19.9	18.1
OPERATORS, FABRICATORS, AND LABORERS	25.9	20.8	20.2
FARMING, FORESTRY, AND FISHING	6.4	5.5	4.2
WOMEN			
TOTAL EMPLOYED:			
NUMBER (IN THOUSANDS)	31,257	44,047	58,501
PERCENT	100.0	100.0	100.0
MANAGERS AND PROFESSIONALS	17.0	21.9	30.3
TECHNICAL, SALES, AND ADMINISTRATIVE SUPPORT	45.0	45.8	41.4
SERVICE OCCUPATIONS	21.2	18.9	17.5
PRECISION PRODUCTION, CRAFT, AND REPAIR	1.6	2.3	2.1
OPERATORS, FABRICATORS, AND LABORERS	13.4	9.7	7.6
FARMING, FORESTRY, AND FISHING	1.9	1.3	1.2

Source: U.S. Bureau of Labor Statistics.

Most notable over the past quarter of a century has been the increase in white-collar employment, particularly in managerial and professional occupations. At the same time, there has been a steady erosion in the proportion of workers in lower-skill jobs, particularly in the blue-collar sector.

As women have increased their general job attachment over the past quarter of a century, they have also made considerable upward progress on the occupational ladder. For example, whereas only 17 percent of the women were in managerial or professional jobs in 1970, the proportion in such occupations exceeded 30 percent in 1996. Nevertheless, there are some occupations, such as the highly skilled blue-collar crafts, into which women have not yet made wide inroads, and other occupations, such as the generally lower-skilled administrative support positions, where women still predominate. Clearly, although much progress toward equality has been made, there are still wide differences in the distribution of employment by occupation for men and women.

ADVANCES IN EDUCATION

The gradual movement of workers into the higher skill occupations has been accompanied by substantial advances in educational levels: about 29 percent of persons 25 years of age and over who were in the labor force in 1996 boasted a college degree (see figure 5.15). The proportion of such highly educated workers has been rising gradually for many years and the trend appears to be continuing.

Labor force participation tends to rise as the level of education increases, and the probability of becoming unemployed is reduced. In 1996, for example, the unemployment rate for workers age 25 and over varied from 8.7 percent for those with less than a high school diploma to only 2.2 percent for those who had graduated from college, and it was even lower for those with a professional or doctoral degree. Furthermore, the latter were, understandably, likely to have much higher earnings than the less educated.

TABLE 5.15

EDUCATIONAL ATTAINMENT OF PERSONS 25 YEARS OF AGE AND OVER IN THE U.S. LABOR FORCE: 1996

(ANNUAL AVERAGES)

EDUCATIONAL ATTAINMENT	NUMBER (IN THOUSANDS)	PERCENT DISTRIBUTION
TOTAL, 25 YEARS AND OVER	112,760	100.0
LESS THAN HIGH SCHOOL	12,394	11.0
HIGH SCHOOL GRADUATES, NO COLLEGE	37,026	32.8
SOME COLLEGE, NO DEGREE	21,437	19.0
ASSOCIATE DEGREE	9,722	8.6
COLLEGE GRADUATES, TOTAL	32,181	28.5
BACHELOR'S DEGREE	21,251	18.8
MASTER'S DEGREE	7,409	6.6
PROFESSIONAL DEGREE	2,049	1.8
PH.D.	1,472	1.3

Source: U.S. Bureau of Labor Statistics.

OCCUPATION-RELATED INJURIES, ILLNESSES, AND FATALITIES

Although, with the advances in education noted above, an increasing share of the American work force has moved to the white-collar field, where the risk of injuries and work-related illnesses has traditionally been very low, millions of Americans are still in jobs where such risk is relatively high. And, although relatively rare, fatalities stemming from work-related injuries are still a problem in certain fields of work.

Concern about the safety and health of American workers has increased significantly in recent decades, and it is now incumbent upon employers in the United States to report any injury or job-related illnesses among their employees. According to such reports, there were 6.6 million nonfatal injuries and work-related illnesses among American workers in 1995. Of these, nearly 3 million required either recuperation away from work or restriction of duties.

TABLE 5.16

NONFATAL OCCUPATIONAL INJURIES AND ILLNESSES IN PRIVATE INDUSTRY IN THE UNITED STATES: 1995

INDUSTRY DIVISION	TOTAL CASES (IN THOUSANDS)	WITH LOST WORKDAYS[1] (IN THOUSANDS)
TOTAL, PRIVATE INDUSTRY	6,575.4	2,972.1
AGRICULTURE, FORESTRY, AND FISHING	120.8	53.5
MINING	37.8	23.4
CONSTRUCTION	484.9	221.9
MANUFACTURING	2,122.6	970.7
DURABLE GOODS	1,370.1	595.2
NONDURABLE GOODS	752.4	375.5
TRANSPORTATION AND PUBLIC UTILITIES	523.6	299.2
WHOLESALE AND RETAIL TRADE	1,632.1	693.8
WHOLESALE TRADE	458.9	221.6
RETAIL TRADE	1,173.2	472.2
FINANCE, INSURANCE, AND REAL ESTATE	155.5	59.3
SERVICES	1,498.1	650.2

[1] INCLUDES CASES OF RESTRICTED WORK ACTIVITY.

Source: U.S. Bureau of Labor Statistics.

The major occupational group with the highest relative risk of injury is that which includes operators, fabricators, and laborers. These blue-collar workers are more than twice as likely as the average worker to sustain an injury or illness resulting in lost work days. The relative risk of work-related injuries or illnesses is higher for men than for women, particularly in the younger age groups (16 to 34). In the upper age groups, the risk is only slightly higher for men than for women (See Figure 5.6).

There were 6,210 fatal work injuries during 1995, averaging about 17 for each day of the year. Transportation incidents were the major cause of deaths, accounting for 42 percent of the total. About half of those deaths occurred among truck drivers.

Homicides were the second leading cause of fatalities at work. Among the other leading causes of fatal injuries were the falls of workers, the falls of various objects upon workers, and accidental electrocutions.

THE RETIREMENT YEARS

Americans are spending more and more years in retirement. This is because their life span has increased considerably over the past century, while, at the same time, there has been a tendency to retire from their jobs at an ever earlier age (despite some legislative changes aimed to counteract this trend). The result of these two crosscurrents has been a large increase in the number of years that the average worker is expected to spend in retirement. For this reason, the eventual availability of retirement benefits—and their amount—has become of paramount importance and concern to American workers.

Social Security benefits, under a government-sponsored program, have been available to most retired workers since about 1940, and the coverage of this program has been expanded significantly over the years, becoming gradually almost universal. For many retirees, however, the benefits available under this program have not been sufficient to maintain the desired living standards. To relieve this problem, additional retirement benefits provided through employer-specific or union-sponsored pension plans have become increasingly popular and their coverage has expanded significantly in recent decades.

For government workers—be it at the federal, state, or local level—employer-sponsored pension plans have long been prevalent. In the private sector, however, the proportion of workers covered by employer-specific or union-sponsored pension plans has been much lower. Since the early 1970s, that proportion has averaged about 50 percent among full-time workers, rising steadily for women but declining slightly for men. (See Table 5.18.)

FIGURE 5.6

FATAL OCCUPATIONAL INJURIES IN THE UNITED STATES, BY MAJOR EVENT OR EXPOSURE: 1996

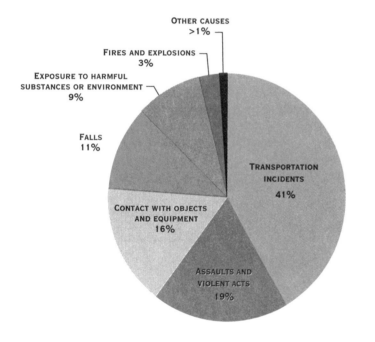

Source: U.S. Bureau of Labor Statistics.

TABLE 5.17

FATAL OCCUPATIONAL INJURIES IN THE UNITED STATES, BY MAJOR EVENT OR EXPOSURE: 1996

EVENT OR EXPOSURE	NUMBER OF FATALITIES
TOTAL	6,112
TRANSPORTATION INCIDENTS	2,556
ASSAULTS AND VIOLENT ACTS	1,144
CONTACT WITH OBJECTS AND EQUIPMENT	1,005
FALLS	684
EXPOSURE TO HARMFUL SUBSTANCES OR ENVIRONMENT	523
FIRES AND EXPLOSIONS	184
OTHER CAUSES	16

Source: U.S. Bureau of Labor Statistics.

TABLE 5.18

RETIREMENT PLAN COVERAGE RATES IN THE UNITED STATES FOR FULL-TIME, PRIVATE-SECTOR WAGE AND SALARY WORKERS: 1972–1993

(PERCENT WITH COVERAGE, SELECTED YEARS)

GROUP	1972	1979	1983	1988	1993
ALL FULL-TIME WORKERS	48	50	48	48	50
MEN	54	55	52	51	51
WOMEN	38	40	42	44	48

Source: U.S. Bureau of Labor Statistics.

There are essentially two broad categories of private-sector retirement plans: defined-benefit and defined-contribution. A defined-benefit plan obligates the employer (or union) to pay retirees an annuity at retirement age, with the amount based on a formula specified in the plan. Defined-contribution plans generally specify the amount of the employer contributions as well as what the employees may contribute, but not the actual benefits to be paid upon retirement, which will depend on the amount of funds available at the time. The amount of funds available will hinge largely on the success with which these funds are invested.

Of paramount importance for individual workers is the extent to which retirement benefits will replace their preretirement earnings. This depends on various factors: the amount of time of participation in one's retirement plan, one's age upon retirement, and one's earnings in the year preceding retirement. For workers age 65 and over, the average "replacement ratios" are shown in Table 5.19, and indicate that, after 40 years of participation, retirement benefits range from about 46 percent of the earnings of persons whose final preretirement earnings were $15,000 per year to about 35 percent for those with annual earnings of $65,000. Coupled with Social Security, the retirement benefits after 40 years in the plan rise to 97 percent of the annual preretirement earnings of low-income workers to about 57 percent for those with the highest earnings in their last year of work.

The well-being of retirees will become an issue of even greater importance very early in the next century, when the great wave of baby boomers—persons born in the two decades immediately following World War II—will join the ranks of the retired. Unless the retirement age is raised, or unless the ranks of the younger workers are increased substantially—perhaps through immigration—the ratio of workers to retirees will narrow considerably, and some estimates indicate that, unless there are some substantial changes in retirement patterns or in the amounts of contributions set aside for the eventual payment of pensions, the Social Security retirement trust fund might become exhausted some time between the year 2015 and 2029. Thus, in the years to come our nation will face the growing challenge of how to maintain the standard of living of the retired population in view of the demographic trends, which will likely multiply the number of retirees.

TABLE 5.19

AVERAGE REPLACEMENT RATIOS OF DEFINED-BENEFIT PLANS FOR FULL-TIME WORKERS AT AGE 65, BY ANNUAL EARNINGS AND YEARS OF PARTICIPATION: 1995

FINAL ANNUAL EARNINGS AND RECEIPT OF SOCIAL SECURITY	YEARS OF PARTICIPATION						
	10	15	20	25	30	35	40
PENSION ONLY							
$ 15,000	12.2	18.5	24.5	30.9	36.8	41.6	45.6
$ 25,000	10.7	16.2	21.4	26.9	32.0	35.9	39.1
$ 35,000	10.1	15.3	20.1	25.3	30.0	33.7	36.7
$ 45,000	9.8	14.8	19.4	24.5	29.2	32.8	35.6
$ 55,000	9.6	14.4	19.0	24.0	28.8	32.3	34.9
$ 65,000	9.6	14.5	19.2	24.2	28.9	32.3	34.9
PENSION PLUS SOCIAL SECURITY							
$ 15,000	39.3	52.1	62.8	73.7	84.2	92.8	96.8
$ 25,000	31.1	42.1	51.9	62.0	71.7	79.3	82.6
$ 35,000	28.1	37.9	47.3	56.3	64.6	70.4	73.4
$ 45,000	25.9	35.4	43.8	51.9	58.1	62.8	65.7
$ 55,000	24.5	33.2	40.9	47.6	53.3	57.7	60.4
$ 65,000	22.2	30.4	37.7	44.1	49.7	53.9	56.6

Source: U.S. Bureau of Labor Statistics.

FOR FURTHER INFORMATION SEE:

JACOBS, EVA E., ED. *HANDBOOK OF U.S. LABOR STATISTICS.* LANHAM, MD: BERNAN PRESS, 1997.

REICH, ROBERT B. *THE WORK OF NATIONS: PREPARING OURSELVES FOR 21ST CENTURY CAPITALISM.* NEW YORK: VINTAGE BOOKS, 1992.

SPAIN, DAPHNE, AND SUZANNE M. BIANCHI. *BALANCING ACT: MOTHERHOOD, MARRIAGE, AND EMPLOYMENT AMONG AMERICAN WOMEN.* NEW YORK: RUSSELL SAGE, 1996.

U.S. DEPARTMENT OF LABOR. *REPORT ON THE AMERICAN WORKFORCE.* WASHINGTON, DC: GPO, 1995.

U.S. DEPARTMENT OF LABOR, BUREAU OF LABOR STATISTICS. *EMPLOYEE BENEFITS SURVEY: A BLS READER.* BULLETIN 2459 (1995).

WEBSITES:

INTERNATIONAL LABOUR ORGANIZATION WEBSITE AT <HTTP://WWW.ILO.ORG>.

U.S. BUREAU OF THE CENSUS WEBSITE AT <HTTP://WWW.CENSUS.GOV>.

U.S. BUREAU OF LABOR STATISTICS WEBSITE AT <HTTP://STAT.BLS.GOV>.

U.S. BUREAU OF TRANSPORTATION STATISTICS WEBSITE AT <HTTP://WWW.BTS.GOV>.

CHAPTER 6

Income, Wealth, and Poverty

MARK S. LITTMAN

INCOME

MEDIAN INCOME OF MEN WITH A HIGH SCHOOL DIPLOMA, NO COLLEGE—	
1973:	$34,975 (IN 1995 DOLLARS)
1995:	$23,365
MEDIAN INCOME OF MEN WITH 4 OR MORE YEARS OF COLLEGE—	
1973:	$47,476 (IN 1995 DOLLARS)
1995:	$43,322
RATIO OF MEDIAN INCOME OF WOMEN WHO WORKED YEAR-ROUND FULL-TIME TO INCOME OF COMPARABLE MEN—	
1973:	.57
1995:	.74
MEDIAN INCOME IN 1995 OF—	
MARRIED-COUPLE FAMILIES:	$47,062
WITH WIFE IN PAID LABOR FORCE:	$55,823
WITH WIFE NOT IN PAID LABOR FORCE:	$32,375
FEMALE HOUSEHOLDER, NO HUSBAND PRESENT:	$19,691
EMPLOYER COSTS FOR EMPLOYEE BENEFITS AS A PERCENTAGE OF TOTAL COMPENSATION IN—	
1950:	15 PERCENT
1991:	30 PERCENT

TRENDS IN INCOME

The standard of living of the average worker in the United States increased steadily between the end of World War II and the early 1970s. After the mid-1970s, the direction changed. Not only were wages not increasing, they were decreasing for some groups (after adjusting for inflation). In addition, what is termed "income inequality" was increasing, whereas in the 1960s income inequality had been decreasing. While the well-educated typically have earned more than those without a high school education in the United States, trends in income and earnings in the past 20 years have expanded the earnings differential between those with a college education and those persons with no education beyond high school.

Many theories have evolved to explain these trends. They range from the intransigence of U.S. business to respond to the growth of a global economy by innovation rather than downsizing, to swings in the business and productivity cycles, and to the size of the baby boom cohort, marriage patterns, and the entrance of women into the labor force in large numbers. No single theory is broadly accepted as explaining "the great u-turn" in earnings.[1] Despite these trends, there is evidence from longitudinal data that Americans are not necessarily confined to a particular income "class" during their entire lifetimes. There is considerable movement along the income spectrum, both up and down.

---

[1] See such works as Bennett Harrison and Barry Bluestone, *The Great U-Turn* (New York: Basic Books, 1990); and Robert Reich, *The Work of Nations: Preparing Ourselves for 21st Century Capitalism* (New York: Vintage Books, 1992).

FIGURE 6.1

MEDIAN INCOME OF MEN AND WOMEN IN THE UNITED STATES: 1967–1995

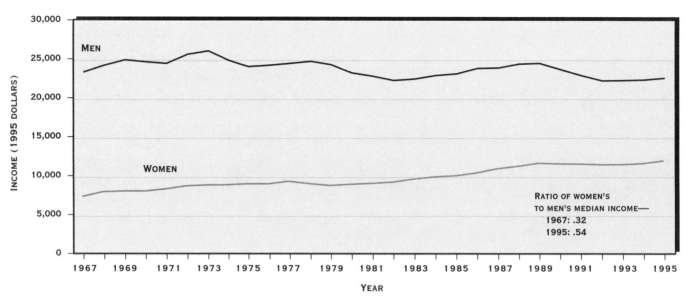

Source: U.S. Bureau of the Census.

FIGURE 6.2

MEDIAN INCOME FOR MEN IN THE UNITED STATES, BY RACE AND HISPANIC ORIGIN: 1972–1995

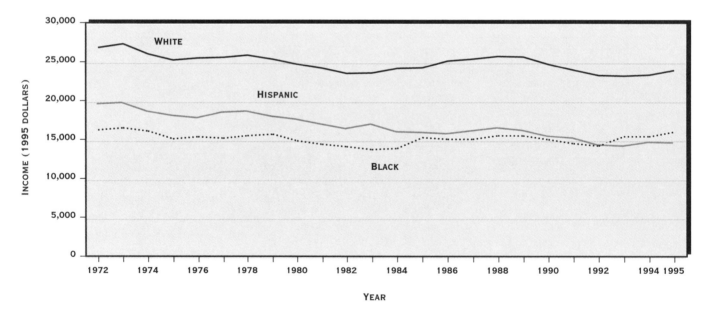

Source: U.S. Bureau of the Census.

Because of changing household composition, family size, and the increasing proportion of women who work and who work more hours, different income trends are evident for households, families, and persons during the past couple of decades. For men, median income peaked in 1973 at about $26,000 (adjusted for inflation in 1995 dollars using the CPI-U-X1). Since that time it has declined to approximately $22,600 in 1995, fluctuating to some extent with the business cycle (see Figure 6.1). For example, after bottoming out in 1982 at $22,200, the median income for men rose to $24,400 by 1989, but has not yet approached that

figure in the 1990s. The pattern for Hispanic men is similar to that for Whites, dipping from a median of $20,000 in 1973 to $14,800 in 1995 (see Figure 6.2). Black men experienced similar trends in income during this period, but their median income in 1995 ($16,000) is closer to their median income in 1973 ($16,500) than is the case for Hispanics or Whites. As a consequence, the ratio of Black to White median income for men has increased from .60 to .67 during this period.

As mentioned in the previous chapter (Labor Force), educational attainment appears to be playing an increasingly

important role in determining income (see Figure 6.3). Men 25 years and over who had a high school diploma but no college had a median income of nearly $34,000 in 1972. That figure declined to $23,400 by 1995, a decline of 31 percent.[2] Comparable men with a college degree (4 years or more) also had an income decrease during this period, but from $48,500 to $43,300, an 11 percent decline. As a consequence, the income of men with only a high school diploma, whose income was 70 percent of that of college-educated men in 1972, was on average only 54 percent of college-educated men by 1995.

FIGURE 6.3

MEDIAN INCOME OF MEN IN THE UNITED STATES, BY EDUCATIONAL ATTAINMENT: 1972–1995

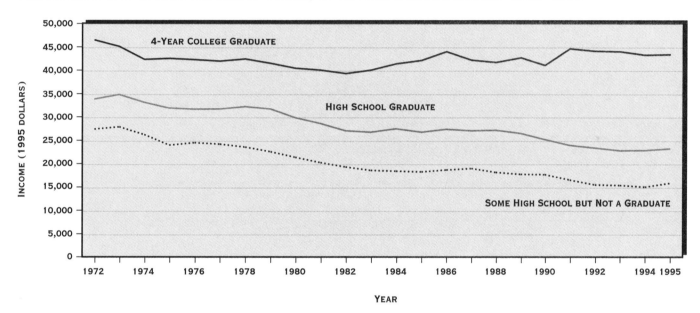

Source: U.S. Bureau of the Census.

2 U.S. Census Bureau Website at <http://www.census.gov/hhes/income/histinc/p07a.html>.

FIGURE 6.4

MEDIAN INCOME OF WOMEN IN THE UNITED STATES: 1972 AND 1995

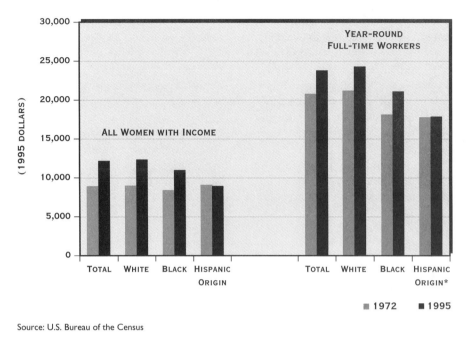

Source: U.S. Bureau of the Census

* Data indicated as 1972 are for 1974 for Hispanic year-round full-time workers.

INCOME OF WOMEN

For women, on the other hand, median income has continued to grow during the past several decades, from about $9,000 in 1973 to $12,000 in 1995 (see Figure 6.1). This is true for Black as well as White women, but not for Hispanic women (whose median income is similar to what it was 20 years ago), likely because of the relatively low earnings of recent immigrants in this group (see Figure 6.4). The increase in the earnings of women is not simply a function of women working more hours (although on average they are doing so). The median income of women who worked year-round full-time increased from $20,900 in 1973 to $23,800 by 1995 in real terms, while the income for comparable men declined from $37,000 to $32,200. As a consequence of the decline in men's income and the increase in women's income, the median income in 1995 of women who worked year-round full-time has increased to about 74 percent of that for comparable men, a 17 percent increase since 1973. Throughout the 1960s and 1970s there was little change in this

FIGURE 6.5

RATION OF FEMALE TO MALE MEDIAN EARNINGS FOR YEAR-ROUND FULL-TIME WORKERS IN THE UNITED STATES: 1972–1995

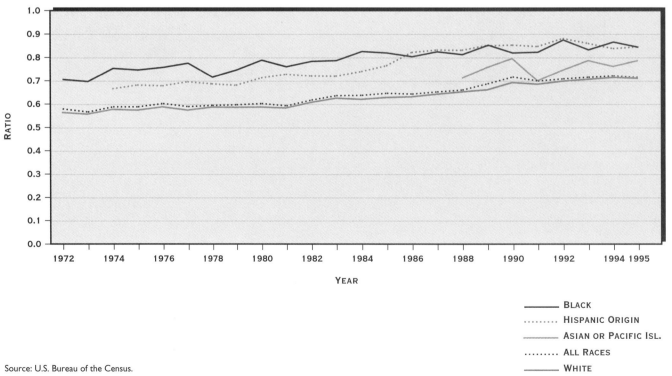

Source: U.S. Bureau of the Census.

ratio of female to male income. The 1990s was the first decade in which this ratio reached the .7 mark. (See Figure 6.5.) In general the earnings of minority women have been closer to the earnings of minority men than has been true for those who are White, non-Hispanic (also referred to as Anglo). Both Black and Hispanic women who worked year-round full-time in 1995 earned about 85 percent of what Black and Hispanic men earned, respectively, while Anglo women earned about 69 percent of the earnings of Anglo men in that year.

INCOME INEQUALITY

Another trend was evident during the 1970–95 period: that of increasing "income inequality." This tendency was not restricted to the United States: income inequality increased in the Organization for Economic Cooperation and Development (OECD) countries as well during this period.[3] What does this often-used term mean and why is it important to persons in the United States? American society is firmly rooted in the belief in equality of opportunity. But that does not mean that Americans believe in general that income should be equal regardless of skill, effort, and education (nor that certain segments of society— Blacks or women, for example—were not excluded from that belief). And at the same time, residents of the United States seem to hold the belief that differences in lifestyle between the poorest Americans and the richest Americans should be diminishing over time, not increasing. Similarly, Americans tend to believe that extremes of poverty, if not wealth, are somehow foreign to U.S. culture, despite the persistent appearance of both. Thus, for example, few would argue against the Chief Executive Officer (CEO) of a large company earning more than an assembly-line worker in one of the company plants. But, what is the appropriate ratio of their incomes? Should the CEO make 10 times that of the assembly-line worker, 50 or 100 times as much? And should that gap be increasing or

FIGURE 6.6

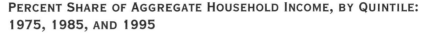

PERCENT SHARE OF AGGREGATE HOUSEHOLD INCOME, BY QUINTILE: 1975, 1985, AND 1995

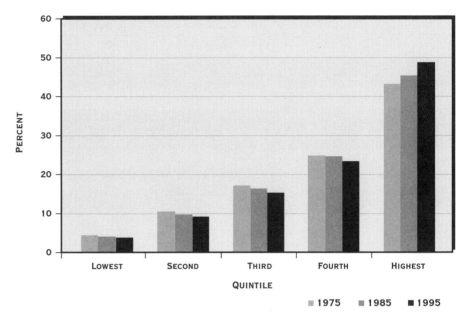

Source: U.S. Bureau of the Census.

diminishing, and under what conditions? A recent article indicated that the CEOs of many large corporations, including Lockheed Martin, Black and Decker, Fannie Mae, CSX, Gannett, and Mobil earn annual salary, bonus, and stock options ranging from $4 to $24 million. Executive salaries of that magnitude range between 80 and 800 times the average income of U.S. workers in 1995.[4] While some feel such income differences are obscene, there is no sign of revolution.

In the aggregate, income inequality has come to be measured (and defined) in several ways. One means is to arrange households (or families or persons) in order of income (or earnings) and then divide the distribution into pieces of equal size (deciles, quintiles, and quartiles are often used). Then the aggregate income of each group (e.g., each quintile) can be compared to see if any given quintile receives more or less than its "share," that is, more or less

than 20 percent of the pie if quintiles are used (see Figure 6.6). Using this measure, the poorest quintile received 3.7 percent of aggregate income in 1995, while the richest quintile received nearly 49 percent of income. This disparity has increased in the past 20 years. In 1975 the poorest quintile received 4.4 percent of the pie, the richest quintile 43 percent. A derivative of this approach is to compare the ratio of total income received by the top 20 percent of the population to the ratio of total income received by the bottom 20 percent. With this approach one can say that the aggregate income of the richest 20 percent of households is about 13 times that of the poorest 20 percent in 1995. Another indicator of change in income inequality is the ratio of the upper limit of the bottom fifth income level to the lower limit of the top fifth, over time. For example, in 1973 the income level separating the bottom fifth from the next fifth was $14,265 (in 1995

---

3 See A.B. Atkinson, L. Rainwater, and T.M. Smeeding, "Income Distribution in OECD Countries: Evidence from the Luxembourg Income Study," OECD publication (1995).

4 Peter Behr, "It Pays to Be a Top Executive," *Washington Post, Washington Business Section* (16 June 1997). For comparison, the median income of male precision-production employees who worked year-round full-time in 1995 was about $30,000. For all male year-round full-time workers with a college degree, regardless of occupation, the median income was $50,500 in 1995.

dollars) and the income level separating the fourth from the highest income fifth for households was $58,070. Every household in the bottom fifth had income below $14,265, every household in the top fifth had income over $58,070. The ratio of these two figures was about .25. By 1995, the comparable limits were $14,400 for the bottom fifth but $65,124 for the top fifth and the ratio of these two figures had dropped to .22.

Another technique used to gauge income inequality is the Gini index, also called the index of income concentration. The Gini index ranges from 0 to 1, with 0 indicating perfect equality (i.e., everyone receives the same income) and with 1 indicating perfect inequality (all income is received by one recipient, family, etc.).[5] This index has shown continued increase (meaning more income inequality) since 1973, from a Gini ratio of .397 to .450 in 1995. During the years immediately after World War II, income inequality either

declined or remained stable and economists wondered about the consequences of too much equality.[6] The increases in inequality in the past 25 years were unanticipated. Predictions of future trends at this point range from the pessimistic predictions of increased crime, riots, and terrorism due to continuing and increasing inequality, to those who feel that inequality will stabilize and have no ill effects on society.

Running somewhat counter to these gauges of income inequality are trends in per capita income. Per capita income was higher in 1995 than in 1973 ($9,300 versus $7,924 in 1995 dollars), and rose steadily through the 1970s before vacillating in the 1980s. Much of the per capita increase can be attributed to the increasing labor force participation of women—a larger proportion of the population working leads to an increase in per capita income.[7] However, per capita income peaked in 1989 at $10,312 and shows no predisposition to return to that figure in the 1990s.

INCOME OF FAMILIES

Trends in the income of families are not only affected by macroeconomic conditions but also by such factors as the increasing employment of women, the decreasing number of births, and the increasing incidence of divorce. The income trend for married-couple families is not the same as that for families sustained by women without a spouse (see Figure 6.7). Married-couple families in 1995 had a median income higher than that of comparable families in 1973 ($47,100 versus $42,100), although not as high as in 1989 ($47,400). The relative well-being of these families was, however, typically balanced on the backs of more than one worker: married-couple families in which the wife was in the paid labor force had higher income in 1995 ($55,800) than any prior year, and 13 percent higher than comparable families in 1973. On the other hand, married-couple families, in which the wife was not in the labor force, had a median income in 1995

FIGURE 6.7

MEDIAN INCOME IN THE UNITED STATES, BY TYPE OF FAMILY: 1972–1995

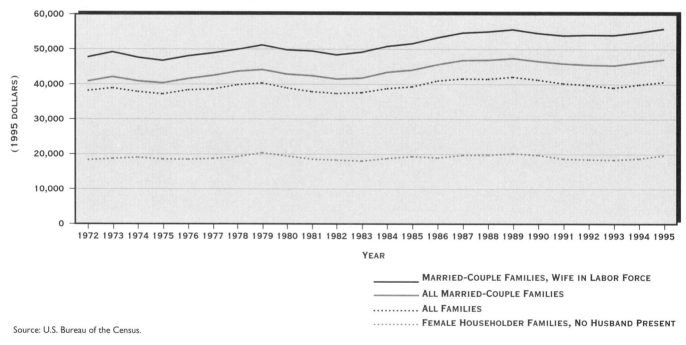

Source: U.S. Bureau of the Census.

- ————— MARRIED-COUPLE FAMILIES, WIFE IN LABOR FORCE
- ————— ALL MARRIED-COUPLE FAMILIES
- ·········· ALL FAMILIES
- ·········· FEMALE HOUSEHOLDER FAMILIES, NO HUSBAND PRESENT

---

[5] For a detailed definition of the Gini index, see Current Population Reports, Series P-60, no. 123 (Washington, DC: U.S. Bureau of the Census).

[6] See studies cited in Sheldon Danziger and Peter Gottschalk, "Increasing Inequality in the United States: What We Know and What We Don't," *Journal of Post Keynesian Economics* 11, no. 2 (winter 1988-89), 174-95.

[7] See Reynolds Farley, *The New American Reality* (New York: Russell Sage, 1997).

of $32,400, 12 percent lower than comparable families in 1973, and only 58 percent of the median in 1995 for married couples in which the wife worked.

Fueled by increased divorce and a decrease in the social stigma associated with unmarried motherhood, the number of families headed by women with no spouse has nearly doubled and has increased from 12 to 18 percent of all families during the 1973–1995 period. About a third of all families with never-married children under age 21 are now single-parent families, with the vast majority (over 85 percent) of these families sustained by a custodial mother. The income of such families was only about 42 percent of the median for married-couple families in 1973 as well as in 1995. Their median income has, however, increased in 1995 to about $19,700, about $1,000 more than their 1973 figure in real terms. The median income of families headed by women had dropped to the 1973 level during the first half of the 1990s, after fluctuating with the business cycle during the 1970s and 1980s. This change does not appear to be related to any increase in child support payments, as only about half of such families have a child support agreement and were supposed to receive payments, and, of those, only about half actually received the full amount due. Nearly one-fourth of those who were supposed to receive child support payments actually received nothing.[8]

CHANGES IN INCOME OVER LIFETIME

Income level in the United States is not static. Thus, discussions about the poor or the rich in the 1970s versus the 1990s does not mean that those groups are composed of the same individuals at both time periods. There is considerable evidence of large annual as well as lifetime shifts in income level. Such life cycle events as leaving the parental home, graduating from college, getting one's first "real" job, marriage, divorce, disability, and retirement (not nec-

essarily in that order) can have profound impact on income. Typically, income peaks in the ages between 45 to 54 and then begins to taper off (on average) as people begin to retire. But patterns vary by sex, for example, with women more likely to maintain a family due to divorce or death of a spouse and thus have reduced income. One longitudinal study indicates that in the course of a decade one-third of Americans will have at least 1 year in which their income doubles, and nearly a third will experience a year in which their income drops by 50 percent.[9] In order to compare changes in income over time, an "equivalence-adjusted income concept" is often used. Such concepts make it possible to compare changes by taking into account the living arrangements of persons over

time (since the resources available to people with similar incomes but different family sizes typically are not the same). The equivalence-adjusted income concept in the data used here takes account of family size and composition by using the economy of scale built into the federal government's poverty definition and is expressed as a ratio of their income to their appropriate poverty threshold (that is, their income is two times, one and one-half times, or three times their poverty threshold, for example).[10] Using this gauge, three-fourths of Americans have had a change of 5 percent or more in their incomes between 1992 and 1993, with half of these experiencing an increase and the other half a decrease (see Figure 6.8). During the mid-1980s, the proportion experiencing an

FIGURE 6.8

PERCENTAGE DISTRIBUTION OF PERSONS IN THE U.S., BY THE YEAR-TO-YEAR PERCENTAGE CHANGE IN THEIR FAMILY INCOME-TO-POVERTY RATIO: 1984–1993

(SELECTED YEARS)

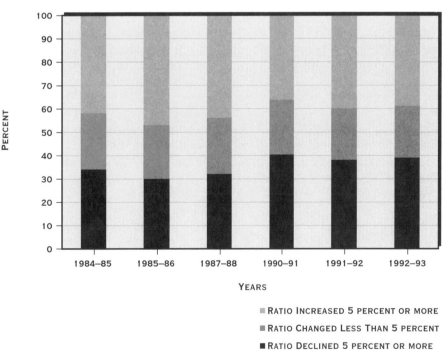

YEARS

■ RATIO INCREASED 5 PERCENT OR MORE
■ RATIO CHANGED LESS THAN 5 PERCENT
■ RATIO DECLINED 5 PERCENT OR MORE

Source: U.S. Bureau of the Census.

8   See *Child Support for Custodial Mothers and Fathers: 1991*, Current Population Reports, Series P-60, no. 187 (Washington, DC: U.S. Bureau of the Census).

9   Greg J. Duncan, "On the Slippery Slope," *American Demographics* 9, no. 5 (May 1987).

10 For further discussion, see *Transitions in Income and Poverty Status: 1984-85*, Current Population Reports, Series P-70, no. 15-RD-1 (Washington, DC: U.S. Bureau of the Census).

FIGURE 6.9

EMPLOYEE BENEFITS AS A PERCENT OF TOTAL COMPENSATION IN THE UNITED STATES: 1929–1991

(SELECTED YEARS)

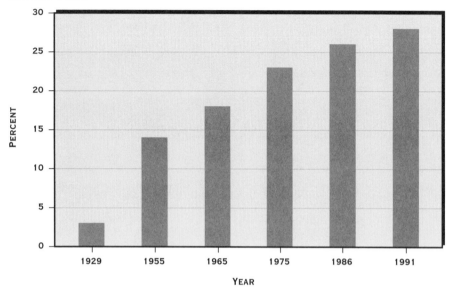

Source: U.S. Bureau of Labor Statistics.

increase in income was higher than that experiencing a decrease in income (e.g., between 1987 and 1988 about 44 percent had an increase, 32 percent a decrease), while in the 1990s similar proportions tended to have increases and decreases.[11] Other studies have looked at changes in income quintiles over time and have found that the proportion changing quintiles— whether an annual, 5- or 9-year mobility period was used—was similar in the 1970s and 1980s, and conclude that mobility rates in the United States have not changed in the past 25 years.[12]

NONCASH BENEFITS

One trend complicating the comparison of income over time is the increased tendency of employers to offer noncash benefits as partial compensation for work. Employer costs for employee benefits as a percentage of total compensation have increased from less than 15 percent in the 1950s to about 30 percent in 1991 (see Figure 6.9).[13] Such compensation can take the form of paid holidays, sick leave, childcare, medical insurance, pension plans, and life insurance. The United States' public pension plan (Social Security) has existed for about 60 years and is financed by both employer and employee mandatory contributions. About 133 countries have a public pension program akin to the U.S. system, which combines old age/disability and survivors' programs. However, such programs cover only about 30 percent of the world's older population, and coverage outside industrialized countries is often limited to selected workers (for example government employees) principally in urban areas.[14] In the United States the vast majority of employed persons are covered by Social Security.

In addition, many persons in the United States contribute to a private pension plan. Such plans take two principal forms: "defined-benefit" and "defined-contribution." *Defined-benefit plans* offer a predetermined formula to calculate retirement benefits (e.g., 50 percent of the highest salary paid to the employee after 25 years of service). About two of every five workers in the United States were covered by a defined-benefit plan in 1992. Thirty-one percent of U.S. workers in that year were covered by a *defined-contribution plan.* Such plans specify the employer's and employee's contributions to the plan but not the benefits at retirement, since the level of benefits may depend on the return on the investments of such plans or in the company itself in the case of deferred profit sharing plans.[15] For a variety of reasons, not all employees of a company that offers a pension plan are covered by that plan. According to one survey, about a fourth of persons not participating in a pension plan offered by their employer chose not to participate, while a third had not worked long enough for that company to participate, and another fourth worked less than full-time and were not eligible to participate.[16]

Paid leave for holidays and vacations was available to about three-fourths of U.S. workers (although the number of days of leave varies by employer, number of years on the job, and other factors). In addition, about 58 percent of workers received a set number of days of sick leave (see Figure 6.10). A considerably smaller fraction received paid maternity or paternity leave (1 percent), although 29 percent were granted unpaid maternity leave. This fraction will increase in the future with the enactment of a new federal law (Family and Medical Leave Act of 1993) that will mandate large employers to grant up to 12 weeks of unpaid leave for birth, adoption,

11 *Dynamics of Economic Well-Being: Income 1992-1993*, Current Population Reports, Series P-70, no. 56 (Washington, DC: U.S. Bureau of the Census).

12 See Isabel V. Sawhill and Danniel P. McMurrer, "How Much Do Americans Move Up and Down the Economic Ladder?" Urban Institute Website at <http://www.urban.org/oppor/opp_031.htm>; and "Economic Mobility in the United States," Urban Institute Paper no. 6722 (Washington, DC: The Urban Institute, 1996).

13 Bureau of Labor Statistics, *Employee Benefits in a Changing Economy: A BLS Chartbook*, Bulletin no. 2394 (September 1992).

14 See Kevin Kinsella and Yvonne J. Gist. "Older Workers, Retirement and Pensions: A Comparative International Chartbook," IPC/95-2 (Washington, DC: U.S. Bureau of the Census); and U.S. Social Security Administration, "Social Security Programs Throughout the World 1995," SSA Publication, no. 13-11805 (July 1995).

15 Ann C. Foster, "Employee Benefits in the United States, 1991-92," Bureau of Labor Statistics Website at <http://stats.bls.gov/special.requests/ocwc/ebs>.

16 U.S. Bureau of the Census, "Preparing for Retirement: Who Had Pension Coverage in 1991," SB/93-6 (Washington, DC: U.S. Bureau of the Census, April 1993).

FIGURE 6.10

PERCENTAGE OF U.S. EMPLOYEES PARTICIPATING IN SELECTED BENEFIT: 1993

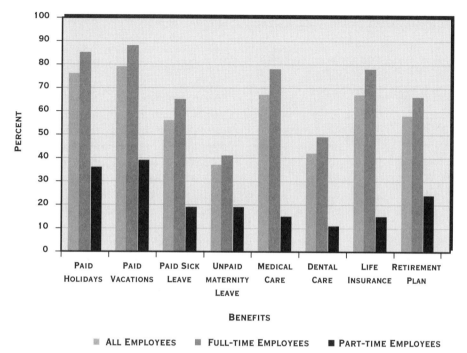

Source: U.S. Bureau of Labor Statistics.

or care of a sick family member. Still another type of benefit often provided by employers was further education: about one-half of workers were offered job-related educational assistance by their employers. A relatively small number of employers also offer some form of childcare benefit for employees with children, and a few (7 percent) medium-to-large employers offered on-site childcare arrangements.

The majority of U.S. workers are offered some form of medical, dental, and life insurance benefits by their employers as well as the leave benefits indicated above. While such plans vary considerably, 68 percent of all employees were covered by a medical care plan, with 52 percent of those

covered in plans paid entirely by their employer, and 29 percent in family plans paid entirely by their employer. Furthermore, about 7 out of 10 employees have a life insurance plan offered by their employer, with employers who offer such insurance paying the entire amount for 84 percent of insured employees.

WEALTH

MEDIAN NET WORTH, ALL FAMILIES—	
1989:	**$56,500 (IN 1995 DOLLARS)**
1995:	**$56,400**
MEDIAN NET WORTH, ALL FAMILIES, 1995—	
WITH A COLLEGE-EDUCATED HEAD OF HOUSEHOLD:	**$104,100**
WITH AN ANGLO HEAD OF HOUSEHOLD:	**$73,900**
WITH A MINORITY HEAD OF HOUSEHOLD:	**$16,500**
WITH A HOUSEHOLD HEAD UNDER AGE 35 YEARS:	**$11,400**
WITH A HOUSEHOLD HEAD AGED 55–64 YEARS:	**$110,800**
PERCENT OF FAMILIES HAVING CREDIT CARD DEBT AFTER PAYING THEIR MOST RECENT BILL:	
1989:	**40 PERCENT**
1995:	**48 PERCENT**
MEDIAN CREDIT CARD BALANCE—	
1989:	**$1,100**
1995:	**$1,500**

NET WORTH

Income is not the only influence on the economic well-being of an individual. Wealth is another factor, and one gauge of wealth that is often used is "net worth," which is the value of assets (for example, equity in one's home, automobiles, stocks, savings, and checking account balances, etc.) minus liabilities (for example, debt on credit cards). The median net worth for all U.S. families in both 1989 and 1995, after a period of decline earlier this decade, was about $56,400.[17] Families with income under $10,000 had a median net worth of about $4,800, while those with income over $100,000 had a median net worth of nearly $486,000.

For White, non-Hispanic (also referred to as Anglo) households, median net worth in 1995 ($74,000) was about four and a half times the median net worth of minority households in 1995 ($17,000). However, this disparity has declined in the 1990s: the net worth of minority households has increased from a median of about $7,000 in 1989, at which time it was less than half its current figure and only 1/12th of the White, non-Hispanic median (see Figure 6.11). White, non-Hispanic households, on the other hand, have experienced a decline in net worth during the 1990s, from a median of $85,000 in 1989 to the current $74,000. Thus, the return to the 1989 median net worth figure for all races combined, after a decline in the early 1990s, appears to be driven by increases in net worth for minorities only.

Since the passage of time offers increased opportunity to accumulate wealth, it is not surprising that net worth

FIGURE 6.11

MEDIAN NET WORTH OF FAMILIES IN THE UNITED STATES, BY RACE AND HISPANIC ORIGIN: 1989, 1992, AND 1995

(CONSTANT 1995 DOLLARS)

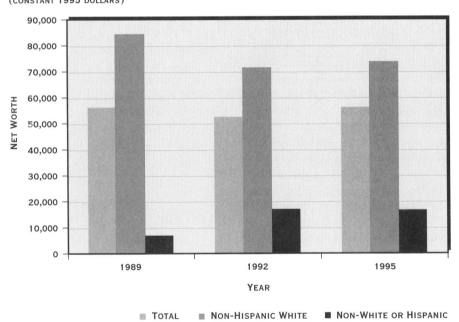

Source: Survey of Consumer Finances, Board of Governors of the Federal Reserve System.

---

17 Data from the *1995 Survey of Consumer Finances*. See Arthur B. Kennickell et al., "Family Finances in the U.S.: Recent Evidence from the Survey of Consumer Finances," *Federal Reserve Bulletin* (January 1997).

increases with age of the householder until retirement age. The median net worth in 1995 of households in which the head was under 35 was only about $11,000 in 1995 but increased to $111,000 for householders in the 55 to 64 age group before beginning to taper off for older households (see Figure 6.12). As is the case with income, the net worth of married-couple households typically was more than either households maintained by a man or woman without benefit of a spouse in the household. Regardless of age of householder, those maintained by a married couple typically had four to five times the net worth of other household types. Households headed by a woman under age 35 had the lowest median net worth.[18] Education is also strongly associated with wealth: the median net worth of households in which the householder was a college graduate ($104,000) was twice that for households in which the head had completed only high school ($50,000).

TYPES OF ASSETS

The nation's homeowners, who represent about 65 percent of households in the United States, had a median net worth of $102,000 in 1995, which was over 20 times the net worth of households that rent (about $5,000). The median net worth of homeowners, however, has declined in the 1990s, while the net worth of renters has nearly doubled. The apparent stagnation of net worth for homeowners is probably not driven by a decline in housing value, but it may actually be driven by increased opportunities to buy homes for lower income households. The percentage of U.S. households that own their own home has increased in the 1990s, from 63.8 percent in 1989 to 64.7 percent in 1995. In the 1990s, families have come to hold less of their assets in regular savings or checking accounts, while holding more in tax-deferred retirement accounts, publicly traded stocks, and mutual funds. The proportion of families holding one of the latter assets has increased from 38 percent in 1989 to 56 percent in 1995. (See Figure 6.13.)

FIGURE 6.12

MEDIAN NET WORTH OF FAMILIES IN THE UNITED STATES, BY AGE OF HOUSEHOLDER: 1995

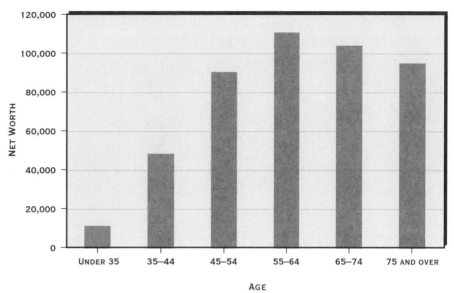

Source: Survey of Consumer Finances, Board of Governors of the Federal Reserve System.

FIGURE 6.13

PERCENTAGE DISTRIBUTION OF HOUSEHOLD NET WORTH IN THE UNITED STATES, BY ASSET TYPE: 1993

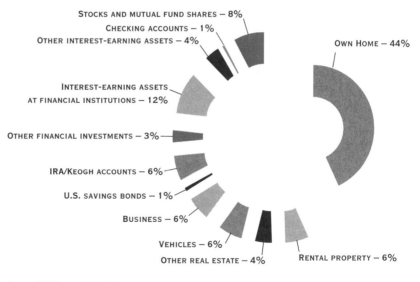

Source: U.S. Bureau of the Census.

---

[18] *Asset Ownership of Households: 1993*, Current Population Reports, Series P-70, no. 47 (Washington, DC: U.S. Bureau of the Census).

TABLE 6.1

PERCENTAGE OF FAMILIES HOLDING DEBT IN THE UNITED STATES, BY TYPE OF DEBT AND MEDIAN AMOUNT OF DEBT: 1995

TYPE OF DEBT	PERCENT WITH SPECIFIED DEBT	MEDIAN AMOUNT
MORTGAGE AND HOME EQUITY LOANS	39.1	$47,400
INSTALLMENT LOANS	46.1	$5,000
OTHER LINES OF CREDIT	2.4	$2,200
CREDIT CARD BALANCES	43.8	$1,100
INVESTMENT REAL ESTATE MORTGAGES	7.8	$26,000
OTHER DEBT	8.8	$2,700
ANY DEBT	73.6	$19,500

Source: Survey of Consumer Finances, Board of Governors of the Federal Reserve System.

FIGURE 6.14

PERCENTAGE DISTRIBUTION OF DEBT FOR FAMILIES IN THE UNITED STATES, BY TYPE OF DEBT: 1995

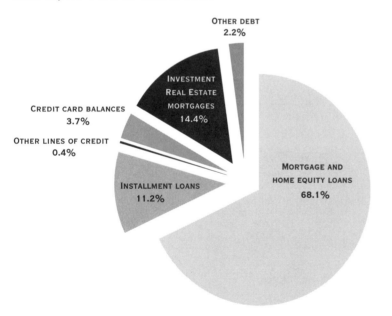

Source: Survey of Consumer Finances, Board of Governors of the Federal Reserve System

Ownership of vehicles (including cars, trucks, and motorcycles as well as mobile homes, boats, and airplanes) is one of the most pervasive assets—with 84 percent of households having one or more with a median value of $10,000. There has been a slight decrease in the tendency of families to own such assets, with an increased tendency for households to lease rather than buy their automobiles, particularly among higher-income households. In 1995, about 5 percent of households leased an automobile. For households with income over $100,000, about 17 percent leased a vehicle.

DEBT

While the assets of households in 1995 have returned to their 1989 level, so too has the amount of debt. The debt of the average household in 1995 represented about 16 percent of its assets. This fraction (known as the "leverage ratio") has not changed much in the 1990s. Another gauge of debt, known as the "debt burden," is the ratio of total debt to total household income. The median debt burden increased slightly between 1989 and 1995, from 16.0 to 16.7 percent. The median debt for all households, including such debt as mortgage and home equity loans, credit card debt and installment purchases was about $22,500 in 1995 (see Table 6.1 and Figure 6.14). The median credit card debt (that is, the outstanding balance after paying the most recent bill) was about $1,500 in 1995, up from $1,100 in 1992. The proportion of households that have credit card debt has increased from about 40 percent to 48 percent between 1989 and 1995. Intensive marketing of credit cards, coupled with a decline in interest rates, has been as successful in seducing households with middle-aged householders as it has in inducing the young to hold credit card debt: in 1992, households with a head under age 35 had the highest proportion of those with any credit card debt. By 1995, households with a 45- to 54-year-old head were just as likely as the young to have credit card debt.

POVERTY

POVERTY THRESHOLD FOR A FAMILY OF FOUR IN 1995:	$15,569
NUMBER OF FAMILIES BELOW THE POVERTY LEVEL IN 1995:	7.5 MILLION
POVERTY RATE IN 1995 FOR—	
ALL FAMILIES:	10.8 PERCENT
FAMILIES WITH A FEMALE HOUSEHOLDER, NO HUSBAND PRESENT:	32.4 PERCENT
CHILDREN UNDER 18 YEARS:	20.2 PERCENT
PERSONS 65 YEARS AND OVER:	10.5 PERCENT
BLACKS:	26.4 PERCENT
PERSONS OF HISPANIC ORIGIN:	27.0 PERCENT
PERSONS RECEIVING—	
AID TO FAMILIES WITH DEPENDENT CHILDREN (APRIL 1997):	11 MILLION
FOOD STAMPS (1995):	27 MILLION
MEDICAID BENEFITS (1995):	36 MILLION

DEFINING POVERTY

Official poverty in America began in the mid-60s during the presidency of Lyndon Johnson: it was the advent of his administration's "War on Poverty" that introduced a variety of antipoverty programs. Prior to the mid-60s, no official government gauge of the extent and distribution of poverty in the United States existed, despite Franklin D. Roosevelt's pronouncement: "I see one-third of a nation ill-housed, ill-clad, ill-nourished."[19] An often-used gauge of poverty during the early 1960s had been the number of families with annual incomes below $3,000 combined with the number of unrelated persons with annual income below $1,500. Such a fixed gauge did not take into account differences in family size (and thus the varying living expenses) or changes over time in the amount of income required to sustain a family.

During the 1960s, Mollie Orshansky, an economist at the Social Security Administration (SSA), devised a gauge that did factor in differences in size and composition of families. She also devised a mechanism for adjusting the poverty "thresholds" for inflation. Within a few years, the Orshansky, or SSA, poverty definition was

being used as a budget and planning tool by federal agencies and as the basis for eligibility for certain programs. And in 1969 the SSA definition of poverty was adopted by the Budget Bureau for use in the official statistical series for the U.S. Government to be published by the U.S. Census Bureau.[20] The poverty definition provides a sliding scale of income thresholds by family size and number of related children under 18 years of age. (See Table 6.2.) The original basis for these income thresholds was in an Agriculture Department devised minimally adequate food budget and in the ratio of food to total spending for a typical family around 1969 (which was about a third). Thus, minimum food requirements for various family compositions were multiplied by a factor of three to come up with the original poverty thresholds. Families or individuals with income below their appropriate threshold are classified as poor; those with income above their poverty threshold are classified as not poor. In 1995, for example, the average poverty threshold for a family of four was $15,569; and other average thresholds varied from a low of $7,763 for a person living alone to $31,280 for a family of nine or more members. Poverty thresholds are updated every year to reflect

TABLE 6.2

WEIGHTED AVERAGE POVERTY THRESHOLD FOR FAMILIES IN THE UNITED STATES, BY SIZE OF FAMILY: 1995

SIZE OF FAMILY UNIT	WEIGHTED AVERAGE POVERTY THRESHOLD
ONE PERSON (UNRELATED INDIVIDUAL)	$7,763
UNDER 65 YEARS	$7,929
65 YEARS AND OVER	$7,309
TWO PERSONS	$9,933
HOUSEHOLDER UNDER 65 YEARS	$10,259
HOUSEHOLDER 65 YEARS AND OVER	$9,219
THREE PERSONS	$12,158
FOUR PERSONS	$15,569
FIVE PERSONS	$18,408
SIX PERSONS	$20,804
SEVEN PERSONS	$23,552
EIGHT PERSONS	$26,237
NINE PERSONS OR MORE	$31,280

Source: U.S. Bureau of the Census.

---

19 *Inaugural Addresses of the Presidents of the United States from George Washington 1789 to George Bush 1989*, Bicentennial Edition (Washington, DCC: GPO, 1989), 277.

20 Budget Bureau Circular no. A-46, transmittal memorandum no. 9, 29 August 1969. The Budget Bureau was the predecessor of the present-day Office of Management and Budget.

FIGURE 6.15

AVERAGE U.S. POVERTY THRESHOLD FOR A FOUR-PERSON FAMILY, AND CONSUMER PRICE INDEX (CPI-U): 1959–1995

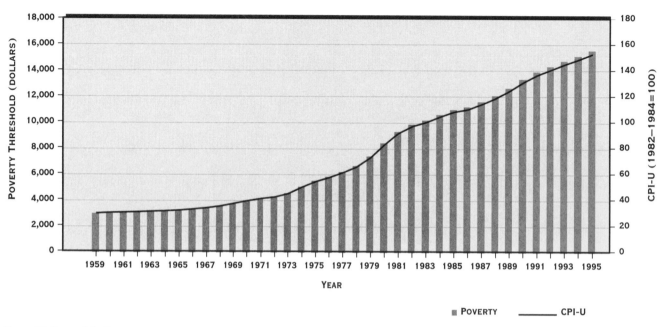

Source: U.S. Bureau of the Census.

changes in cost of living using the Consumer Price Index (CPI–U). Thus, for example, the poverty threshold for a family of four was $2,973 in 1959, $10,989 in 1985, $12,675 in 1989, and $15,569 in 1995. (See Figure 6.15.) Over the years, the SSA definition of poverty has been attacked by those who think it is too stringent as well as those who think it is too lenient. The definition has been the subject of several major studies examining what some perceive to be technical deficiencies, although most criticisms have been around since the definition was first proposed.[21] Some of these criticism were anticipated by Ms. Orshansky in her original research.[22] To date, there has not been a convergence of both the technical/programmatic need for a change in the definition of poverty

and the political climate necessary for such a change to occur. (No president wants an increase in poverty—a likely product of a change in definition—on their "watch," whether or not it was statistically induced.) For example, the poverty threshold for a family of four cited above was essentially the same as that already used for all families, $3,000, at the time of its adoption as the official measure.

TRENDS IN THE NUMBER OF POOR

Using the official definition of poverty, the number of poor decreased dramatically in the 1960s and the early 1970s, down from a high of nearly 40 million persons in 1960 to a low of 23 million by 1973 (see Figure 6.16). The proportion of the U.S. popula-

---

[21] The latest such study was that of the National Research Council's Panel on Poverty and Family Assistance, Constance F. Citro and Robert T. Michael, ed., *Measuring Poverty: A New Approach* (Washington, DC: National Academy Press, 1995). Earlier effort in the 1970s was the U.S. Department of Health, Education and Welfare, *The Measure of Poverty* (Washington, DC: GPO, 1976); and also U.S. Bureau of the Census, *Proceedings of the Conference on the Measurement of Noncash Benefits* (Washington, DC, 12 to 14 December 1985).

[22] See Mollie Orshansky, "Counting the Poor: Another Look at the Poverty Profile," *Social Security Bulletin* 28, no. 1 (January 1965); and "Who's Who Among the Poor: A Demographic View of Poverty," *Social Security Bulletin* 28, no. 7 (July 1965).

tion living in households with poverty-level income fell as well, from a high of 22 percent in 1960 to half that figure by 1973. As discussed in the income section, the early 1970s marked a turning point in income growth in the United States—a point at which income, adjusted for inflation, began to stagnate. While there has been some fluctuation (with business cycles) in the number and proportion of poor since the early 1970s, neither the number of poor nor the poverty rate has returned to the lowest levels of that period. Although there have been declines in the number of poor in 1994 and 1995, the number remains well above its level at the beginning of the decade (31.5 million poor in 1989, 36.4 million in 1995). The number of poor in the United States has not been as high as it was in 1995 since the mid-1960s. The poverty rate has averaged over 14 percent in the 1990s (and stands at 13.8 percent in 1995), 3 percentage points above the early 1970s low point.

Why poverty in America has not been eradicated despite government efforts is the subject of considerable debate. Conservatives tend to assert that government intervention has perpetuated poverty and created a dependent class. Liberal arguments tend to put the blame on insufficient government assistance, along with environmental influences and economic conditions that perpetuate poverty. Data can be brought forth to support either position.[23] An often lost detail in these arguments is that there is considerable movement up and down the income ladder and that the poor in 1995 are not the same persons who were poor in 1965. About one out of four persons who were poor the previous year were not poor the next, according to some longitudinal data for the mid-1980s and early 1990s. Conversely, a considerably larger proportion of the total U.S. population than the current 14 percent have ever experienced poverty in their lifetimes.[24]

WHO IS POOR?

One of the groups that has experienced considerable reduction in poverty since 1959 is the elderly. Persons 65 years and over had a poverty rate over 35 percent in 1959, higher than any other age group. However, by 1995 the poverty rate for the elderly had declined to less than a third of its 1959 level (10.5 percent) and has been lower than that for all ages combined since the early 1980s. Much of this reduction has been attributed to the automatic inflation adjustment of Social Security benefits that began in the early 1970s, as well as an increasing proportion of the aged eligible for such benefits.[25] A larger than average proportion of the elderly have incomes just above the poverty level, however, and thus are at risk of falling below that subsistence level if faced with unavoidable and unusually large expenses.

Children, on the other hand, have experienced little reduction in poverty since government figures have been available,

FIGURE 6.16

NUMBER OF POOR PERSONS AND POVERTY RATE IN THE UNITED STATES: 1959–1995

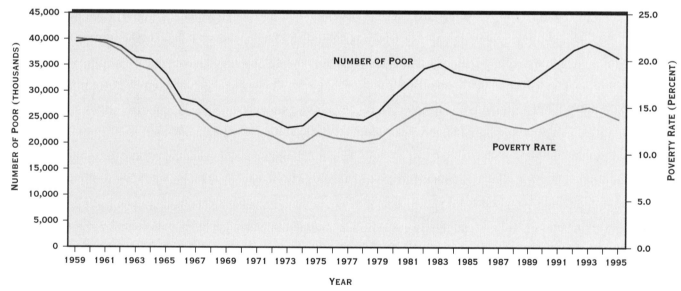

Source: U.S. Bureau of the Census.

[23] See Charles Murray, *Losing Ground: American Social Policy 1950-80.* (BasicBooks, 1984); and Isabelle Sawhill, "Poverty in the United States: Why Is It So Persistent?" *Journal of Economic Literature* 26, no. 3 (September 1988).

[24] See K. Short and M. Littman, *Transitions in Income and Poverty Status: 1984-85*, Current Population Reports, Series P-70, no. 15-RD-1 (Washington, DC: U.S. Bureau of the Census); and M. Shea, *Dynamics of Economic Well-Being: Poverty, 1991-1993*, Current Population Reports, Series P-70, no. 45 (Washington, DC: U.S. Bureau of the Census). Data from the University of Michigan's *Panel Survey of Income Dynamics* can be used to take even longer looks at lifetime income and poverty. See Greg Duncan, *Years of Poverty, Years of Plenty* (Ann Arbor: University of Michigan, 1984).

[25] See Reynolds Farley, *The New American Reality: Who We Are, How We Got There, Where We Are Going* (New York: Russell Sage, 1996).

FIGURE 6.17

POVERTY RATE FOR PERSON AGES UNDER 18 YEARS AND PERSONS AGES 65 YEARS AND OVER IN THE UNITED STATES: 1959–1995

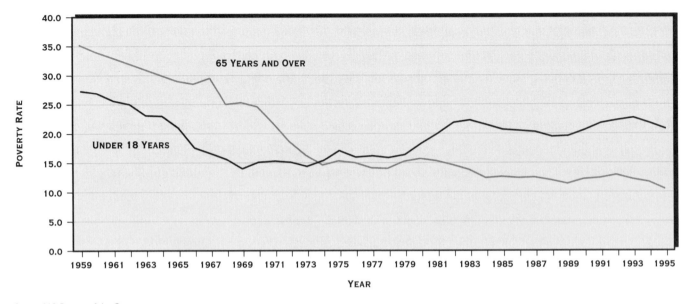

Source: U.S. Bureau of the Census.

with a poverty rate in 1995 (about 21 percent) the same as it was in 1965. (See Figure 6.17.) The poverty rate for children under 18 years was lower than that of the elderly until the early 1970s, but it is now roughly twice that of older age groups. One of four American children under age 6 lived in a poor household in 1995. Because of their relatively high poverty rate, children under 18 years of age represented 40 percent of all poor persons in 1995.

Blacks are another group for whom official poverty has declined considerably in the past 30 years. Over half (55 percent) of Blacks were poor in 1959, when poverty statistics were first tabulated. The poverty rate for this group declined to 29 percent in 1995, the first time it has been lower than 30 percent (the poverty rate for Blacks has hovered between 30 and 35 percent since the late 1960s). This progress has been made despite the presence of several countervailing trends that tend to increase poverty in this group, particularly the incidence of single-parent families. Much of the original concern with measuring poverty at the Social Security Administration had been with women left alone to sustain their children without benefit of a spouse, since historically such families have had poverty rates higher than married-couple families. Originally, this concern was fostered by widowhood, but the number of children growing up in single-parent families is now driven by divorce and childbearing outside of marriage rather than death of a spouse. The incidence of single-parent families is particularly high among Blacks, where 47 percent of all families, and 80 percent of poor families were single parent in 1995.

(See Figure 6.18.) The poverty rate is as high for Hispanic families headed by women (49 percent) as for Black families (45 percent), whereas for Whites the poverty rate for families with a woman householder and no spouse present was considerably lower, at 26 percent, but still high compared with the poverty rate for married couples. For all races combined, only about 6 percent of married-couple families were poor in 1995. Hispanic married-couple families had a poverty rate more than three times that of Anglo families (19 versus 5 percent) and twice that of Black families. Even though the poverty rate for Hispanic families was higher than that for Blacks within each family type, the overall poverty rate for families with an Hispanic householder was about the same as that for Black families (27 percent) because of the vastly different family composition of these two groups: only one-fourth of Hispanic families are maintained by women without hus-

bands, and fewer than half of poor Hispanic families (about 47 percent) are headed by women alone.

Unrelated individuals (that is, persons living alone or with persons who are not related to them—such as a roommate, boarder, etc.) have increased both in absolute terms and as a proportion of all poor persons. About one of five of these unrelated persons was poor in 1995, less than half of their poverty rate in the early 1960s (when a larger proportion of them were elderly persons living alone). The number of poor unrelated individuals have increased from about 5 million to 8 million and were about 23 percent of the poor in 1995, about twice their representation in 1959. This fraction likely would be even larger if homeless persons, who are largely missed in survey counts of the poor (which are typically household surveys), were included in official counts. Estimates of

how many homeless persons there are vary considerably, from approximately 500,000 as a point-in-time estimate in 1988 to a figure of 12 million who have experienced homelessness (or had to double up with relatives or friends) at some point in their lifetime.[26] The causes associated with increasing homelessness are as varied as the estimates of the number of homeless and include stagnating or falling wages and diminished work opportunities for the low-skilled, the lack of affordable low-rent housing, the demolition of millions of single room occupancy (SRO) housing units in flop houses and cubicle hotels, the increased tendency to deinstitutionalize the mentally ill, and drug and alcohol abuse.[27]

Other characteristics (other than membership in a minority group or living in a single-parent family) are also associated with higher than average poverty rates. (See Figure 6.19.) Recent immigrants have poverty rates twice those of persons born in

FIGURE 6.18

POVERTY RATE FOR FAMILIES IN THE UNITED STATES, BY TYPE AND RACE/HISPANIC ORIGIN OF HOUSEHOLDER: 1995

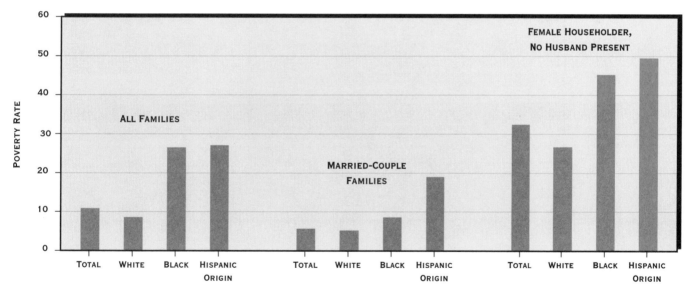

Source: U.S. Bureau of the Census.

---

[26] See Martha Burt and Barbara Cohen, *America's Homeless: Numbers, Characteristics and Programs That Serve Them* (Washington, DC: Urban Institute Press, 1989); and Bruce Link et al., "Lifetime and Five-Year Prevalence of Homelessness in the United States," *American Journal of Public Health* (December 1994).

[27] See Christopher Jencks, *The Homeless* (Cambridge: Harvard University Press, 1995); and "Why Are People Homeless," Fact sheet no. 1, National Coalition for the Homeless Website at <http://nch.ari.net/causes.html>.

FIGURE 6.19

POVERTY RATE FOR SELECTED GROUPS OF PERSONS IN THE UNITED STATES: 1995

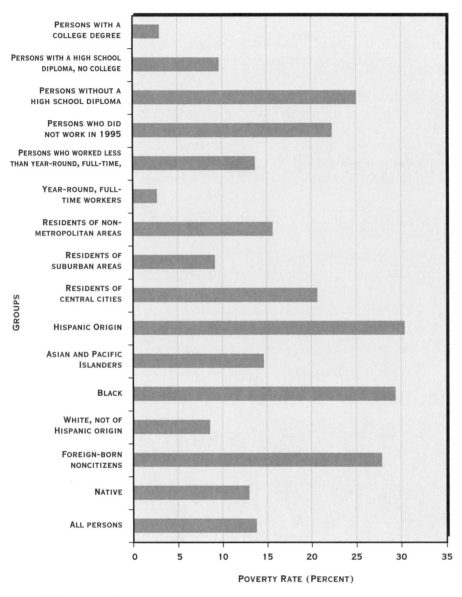

Source: U.S. Bureau of the Census.

the United States (28 percent versus 13 percent);[28] persons living in large cities have poverty rates twice those of persons living in suburban areas, while those living in rural areas have an intermediate rate that falls between the city and suburban rates; persons living in the South historically have had higher poverty rates than other regions (in part because of its rurality and because of its relatively higher concentration of minority population, but the states in the West region now have an overall poverty rate indistinguishable from the South); work effort is highly correlated with poverty status, as only 3 percent of persons who worked year-round full time were poor in 1995 compared with 14 percent who worked, but not year-round, and 22 percent who did not work at all; and educational attainment is strongly associated with poverty status, with the poverty rate for persons 25 years and over without a high school diploma more than twice that of those with a high school diploma and no college, and college graduates having a poverty rate a third of that of high school graduates.

Many of these same characteristics are found among the poor in other countries as well: that is, minorities, the rural population, and the less well educated are more likely to be poor. Single-mother families, a large fraction of the poor in the United States, are, however, better off (relative to two-parent families) in many European countries (relative to the United States), although U.S. single-parent families are about as well off as their counterparts in Australia and Canada.[29] Using some measures of living conditions (such as housing and availability of consumer durables), however, the U.S. poor appear to be at least as well off as their European counterparts.[30] For programs that aid the poor, European countries tend to rely more on nonmeans-tested (defined below) programs, such as child allowances, universal childcare, and national health insurance than do U.S. programs.

---

28 Foreign-born persons who are not citizens are used here as proxies for recent immigrants. Some foreign-born persons have been in the United States long enough to become citizens but have not done so.

29 See Ying-Ling Irene Wong, Irwin Garfinkel, and Sara McLanahan, "Single-Mother Families in Eight Countries: Economic Status and Social Policy," *Social Service Review* (June 1993).

30 See Susan E. Mayer, "A Comparison of Poverty and Living Conditions in Five Countries," Discussion paper no. 987-92 (University of Wisconsin Madison, Institute for Research on Poverty, 1992).

FIGURE 6.20

NUMBER OF PERSON IN THE UNITED STATES BELOW POVERTY LEVEL WHO RECEIVED AID TO FAMILIES WITH DEPENDENT CHILDREN (AFDC) OR FOOD STAMPS: 1960–1995

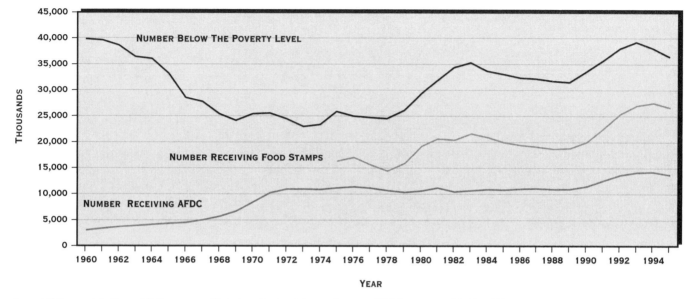

Source: U.S. Bureau of the Census, U.S. Department of Agriculture, Food and Nutrition Service, and U.S. Department of Health and Human Services, Administration for Children and Families.

AID TO THE POOR

Much of U.S. aid to the poor takes the form of "means-tested" assistance, rather than universal programs that have no eligibility criteria. "Means-testing" means that the income and/or assets of the prospective recipients of assistance from a program are compared with a standard for the program. Eligibility criteria vary considerably between programs. Means-tested programs transfer income in the form of cash, goods, or services to persons who typically make no recompense for this aid. Nonmeans-tested programs are those such as Social Security, in which the eligibility criteria are not related to current income but rather to work history and age in the case of Social Security or age alone in the case of Medicare.

There are about 80 means-tested programs in the United States.[31] Major programs designed to assist the poor in the United States include Aid to Families with Dependent Children (AFDC), a program that provides cash as well as other assistance to poor families; Medicaid, a health insurance program for persons with limited income; the Food Stamp program, which provides coupons that can be traded for food at grocery stores; Supplemental Security Income (SSI), which provides cash to eligible persons who are aged (65 and over), blind, or disabled; the Earned Income Tax Credit program (EITC), a program for low-income workers with children that reduces the taxes of those with gross income below a specified amount and provides a "refund" for those whose credit is

larger than their tax liability; and low-income housing assistance, which provides housing subsidies for low-income households and housing accommodations in public housing for other poor families.

Although there is considerable overlap in program eligibility, participation in one program does not typically make one eligible for participation in another. (Although recipients of AFDC are automatically eligible for Medicaid and Food Stamps, the reverse is not the case, for example.) Furthermore, a family may be eligible for housing assistance, for example, but there may not be any housing units available. The official poverty definition is used for statistical purposes only, and though it is the basis of eligibility for some programs, eligibility may be more or less restrictive based on other factors.

31 For a description see Vee Burke, "Cash and Noncash Benefits for Persons with Limited Income: Eligibility Rules, Recipient and Expenditure Data, FY 1992-94," Series 96-159 EPW, Congressional Research Service.

Trends in the number of means-tested program participants have not paralleled changes in the number of poor, largely due to program changes, particularly the eligibility criteria (see Figure 6.20). The number of AFDC recipients increased rather dramatically in the 1960s and early 1970s, from 3 million to over 11 million by 1975, before leveling off.[32] During the early 1990s the number of AFDC recipients increased dramatically again, from about 10.9 million in 1989 to 14.2 million by 1994, but declined to about 11 million once again by April 1997. These changes preceded recent welfare reform and, despite political rhetoric, presumably have little to do with those reforms. As has been the case historically, benefit levels in 1996 for the AFDC program were lower than the poverty level. Since the benefit levels are set by the individual state, they vary considerably. In Alabama, for example, the maximum AFDC cash assistance for a family of three was $164 a month in 1996, only about 15 percent of the federal poverty guideline for a family of that size; in Alaska the same family would receive $923 a month, about 68 percent of the federal poverty guideline. The median state would give such a family about $389 a month in 1996. As states have struggled with increasing AFDC caseloads and decreasing revenues, a common reaction has been to cut AFDC benefit levels. For a three-person family, the median state has cut its benefits by about $51 in real terms since 1970.[33]

A second program that offers cash assistance, but to the aged, blind, and disabled rather than to families with children (as does AFDC), is the Supplemental Security Income Program (SSI), which began in 1974. The number of SSI recipients has risen from about 4 million in 1974 to about 6.5 million in 1995. At its inception, the majority of SSI recipients qualified because of age, but the mix of recipients

FIGURE 6.21

COMPOSITION OF MEANS-TESTED BENEFITS IN THE UNITED STATES: FY 1968 AND 1994

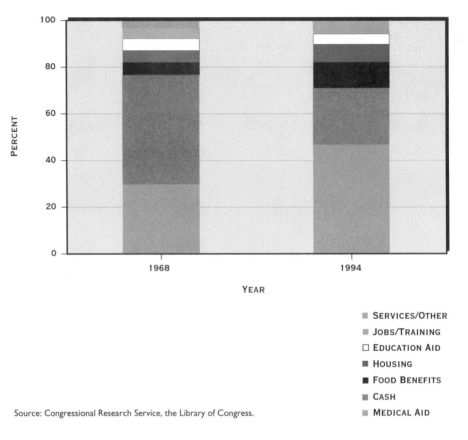

Source: Congressional Research Service, the Library of Congress.

■ SERVICES/OTHER
■ JOBS/TRAINING
□ EDUCATION AID
■ HOUSING
■ FOOD BENEFITS
■ CASH
■ MEDICAL AID

has changed considerably since then: in 1995 three-fourths of recipients qualified for SSI because of a disability.[34]

The Food Stamp program, which became a nationwide program in 1975, is another major assistance program in the United States in which the recipients are given coupons that can be redeemed for food at grocery stores. While the vast majority of AFDC recipients receive food stamps (approximately 9 out of 10), about half of food stamp recipients do not receive AFDC, because the universe of persons eligible for food stamps is broader than that of those who receive AFDC. For example, single

adults and childless couples are eligible for food stamps but not AFDC. In addition, the income/asset eligibility for the food stamp program is less stringent than that for the AFDC program, so that some families with children may receive food stamps but not AFDC. Because of differences in the population that these programs were designed to serve, about twice as many people receive food stamps as receive AFDC (27 million versus 14 million in 1995). As with the AFDC program, the number of participants in the food stamp program increased considerably in the early 1990s to historic highs but appears to have tapered off after 1994

---

32 As a result of welfare reform in 1996 (the Personal Responsibility and Work Opportunity Reconciliation Act of 1996), the name of the AFDC program was officially changed to Temporary Assistance for Needy Families (TANF) as of July 1997.

33 U.S. Congress, House, Committee on Ways and Means, 1996 Greenbook, background Material and Data on Programs within the Jurisdiction of the Committee on Ways and Means (November 1996), Table 8-12, and Table 8-15. Data on number of recipients from the Administration for Children and Families Website at <http://www.acf.dhhs.gov/news/afdc6097.htm>.

34 U.S. Congress, House, Committee on Ways and Means, 1996 Greenbook, background Material and Data on Programs within the Jurisdiction of the Committee on Ways and Means (November 1996), Table 4-1.

(again in advance of welfare reform measures put in place in 1996). One out of 10 persons in the United States received food stamps during 1995. Average monthly food stamp benefits per person were about $71 in 1995 (using the face value of the stamps).

By far the most expensive federal programs in aid to the poor do not provide food, cash, or housing assistance, but medical assistance. Medical assistance accounted for about 48 percent of means-tested benefits in 1994 (federal, state, and local expenditures combined), up from about 30 percent in 1968 (see Figure 6.21), the largest program of which is called Medicaid.[35] Medicaid was initially designed to provide medical care for poor children and their mothers, but a variety of low-income groups have become eligible for this assistance since the program's inception. AFDC and SSI recipients are generally eligible for Medicaid benefits as are pregnant women, children, and the "medically needy," who do not receive AFDC or SSI benefits but who meet certain other (low-income) requirements. Medicaid plays an important role in financing nursing home care for the elderly, which is not generally available under Medicare. In 1995, about 36 million people (about 14 percent of the U.S. population) received some type of medical assistance from Medicaid.

As indicated earlier, the official government definition of poverty is based on money income only. When that definition of poverty was devised, noncash programs in aid of the poor were relatively small, but because aid to the poor has increasingly taken the form of noncash benefits, as indicated by the medical benefits and food stamps discussed above, researchers have attempted to value in-kind benefits in order to evaluate their effectiveness.[36] In 1995, using the official definition of poverty, there were 36.4 million poor, representing 13.8 percent of the population. This figure already includes the value of government cash transfer programs (both means-tested, such as AFDC, and nonmeans-tested, such as Social Security), but not noncash programs (such as food stamps), or the EITC. Factoring in the value of medical benefits as well as food stamps, the EITC, and several other programs reduces the number of poor to about 21.4 million in 1995, or 8.1 percent of the population; but it is Social Security that has more effect than any other program in reducing poverty.[37] Although a poverty standard that includes the value of noncash benefits would produce lower counts of the poor and a lower poverty rate, similar trends in the number of poor and poverty rate over the past decade are evident whether noncash benefits are valued or not.[38]

---

[35] See Vee Burke, "Cash and Noncash Benefits," 17-18. Also see chapter on medical benefits starting on page 33.

[36] Much of the early work in this area was conducted at the Census Bureau. See Timothy Smeeding, "Alternative Methods for Valuing Selected In-Kind Transfer Benefits and Measuring Their Effect on Poverty," Technical paper no. 50 (Washington, DC: U.S. Bureau of the Census, 1982); and also U.S. Bureau of the Census, *Proceedings of the Conference on the Measurement of Noncash Benefits* (Washington, DC, 12 to 14 December 1985); and Harold W. Watts, "Have Our Measures of Poverty Become Poorer?" *Focus* 9, no. 2 (Madison: University of Wisconsin, Institute for Research on Poverty, summer 1986).

[37] See *Poverty in the United States: 1995*, Series P-60, no. 194 (Washington, DC: U.S. Bureau of the Census), Table 6.

[38] See Mark S. Littman, "Poverty in the 1980s: Are the Poor Getting Poorer," *Monthly Labor Review* (June 1989). Some definitional issues surrounding the government's definition of poverty, which are not taken into account here, would tend to increase the number of poor. For example, the homeless are typically excluded from poverty figures because the CPS is a household survey, the food-to-total income ratio inherent in the current definition is not correct according to some analysts, and whether or not lower poverty income thresholds should be used for the elderly in one and two person households is in question.

FOR FURTHER INFORMATION SEE:

Chafel, Judith A., ed. *Child Poverty and Public Policy*. Washington, DC: Urban Institute Press, 1993.

Jencks, Christopher. *The Homeless*. Cambridge: Harvard University Press, 1995.

Kennickell, Arthur B., Martha Starr-McCluer, and Annika E. Sunden. "Family Finances in the U.S.: Recent Evidence from the Survey of Consumer Finances." *Federal Reserve Bulletin* 83, no. 10 (January 1997).

Orshansky, Mollie. "Counting the Poor: Another Look at the Poverty Profile." *Social Security Bulletin* 28, no. 1 (January 1965). Reprinted in *Social Security Bulletin* (October 1988).

———."Who's Who Among the Poor: A Demographic view of Poverty." *Social Security Bulletin* 28, no. 7 (July 1965).

Ruggles, Patricia. *Drawing the Line: Alternative Poverty Measures and Their Implications for Public Policy*. Washington, DC: Urban Institute Press, 1990.

U.S. Bureau of the Census. *Asset Ownership of Households: 1993*. Current Population Reports, Series P-70 , no. 47.

U.S. Bureau of the Census. *Money Income in the United States: 1995*. Series P-60, no. 193.

U.S. Bureau of the Census. *Poverty in the United States: 1995*. Series P-60, no. 194.

U.S. Department of Labor, U.S. Bureau of Labor Statistics. *Employee Benefits Survey: A BLS Reader*. Bulletin 2459 (1995).

U.S. Congress, House Committee on Ways and Means. *1996 Greenbook*. Background Material and Data on Programs within the Jurisdiction of the Committee on Ways and Means (November 1996).

WEBSITES:

Administration on Children and Families, Department of Health and Human Services Website at <HTTP://WWW.ACF.DHHS.GOV>.

Bureau of Labor Statistics Website at <HTTP://STAT.BLS.GOV>.

Federal Reserve Board Website at <HTTP://WWW.BOG.FRB.FED.US>.

Health Care Financing Administration Website at <HTTP://WWW.HCFA.GOV/MEDICAID>.

National Coalition for the Homeless Website at <HTTP://NCH.ARI.NET>.

U.S. Bureau of the Census Website at <HTTP://WWW.CENSUS.GOV>.

The Urban Institute Website at <HTTP://WWW.URBAN.ORG>.

CHAPTER 7

Housing

BILL DOWNS

HOUSING

NUMBER OF HOUSING UNITS IN THE UNITED STATES IN 1995:	109.5 MILLION
MEDIAN AGE OF HOUSING UNITS IN THE UNITED STATES IN 1995:	28 YEARS
PERCENT OF UNITS THAT ARE OWNER-OCCUPIED—	
1970:	62.9 PERCENT
1995:	65.0 PERCENT
HOMEOWNERSHIP RATE IN 1995 FOR HOUSEHOLDS—	
WITH A WHITE HOUSEHOLDER:	69.2 PERCENT
WITH A BLACK HOUSEHOLDER:	43.6 PERCENT
WITH AN HISPANIC HOUSEHOLDER:	41.8 PERCENT
FOR NATIVE-BORN CITIZENS:	67.4 PERCENT
FOR FOREIGN-BORN CITIZENS:	66.9 PERCENT
FOR NONCITIZENS:	33.1 PERCENT
PERCENT OF RENTERS WHOSE GROSS RENT WAS 30 PERCENT OR MORE OF HOUSEHOLD INCOME—	
1985:	43.0 PERCENT
1995:	49.0 PERCENT
HOUSING COSTS IN 1995 AS A PERCENT OF CURRENT INCOME (MEDIAN)—	
RENTERS:	28.0 PERCENT
OWNERS:	18.0 PERCENT
MEDIAN GROSS RENT IN 1995 FOR RENTER-OCCUPIED UNITS:	$537
MEDIAN VALUE IN 1995 OF OWNER-OCCUPIED UNITS:	$92,500

INTRODUCTION

Perhaps the earliest example of housing as a social indicator was the work of social reformer Jacob Riis, whose graphic descriptions (in 1890) of slum conditions in the United States led to passage of legislation to cure tenement ills.[1] Since that time, there has been a considerable amount of study and legislation on all aspects of housing. For the majority of householders, slum conditions are unknown today. Their home is likely to be the largest expenditure they will make in a lifetime. Housing is the largest component of family budgets; for most owners it is the best vehicle for accumulating wealth.

At the end of 1995 the nation's housing inventory included more than 109 million homes, apartments, and mobile homes, more than double the number just 40 years earlier. Like population, the greatest increase in housing units is in the Sunbelt regions of the South and West. (See Table 7.1.) These two regions continue to increase their share of the housing stock at the expense of the Northeast and Midwest. These latter areas are growing as well, but at a slower rate.

TABLE 7.1

REGIONAL DISTRIBUTION OF HOUSING UNITS IN THE UNITED STATES: 1985 AND 1995

(THOUSANDS OF UNITS)

	1985		1995	
REGIONS	HOUSING UNITS	PERCENT	HOUSING UNITS	PERCENT
NORTHEAST	20,684	20.9	21,461	19.6
MIDWEST	24,565	24.6	26,056	23.6
SOUTH	34,815	34.8	39,148	35.8
WEST	19,687	19.7	22,791	20.8

Source: U.S. Bureau of the Census, Series H-150, *American Housing Survey for the United States.*

---

1 See Fried Lewis, *Makers of the City* (Amherst: University of Massachusetts Press, 1990).

TABLE 7.2

METRO/NONMETRO DISTRIBUTION OF HOUSING UNITS IN THE UNITED STATES: 1985 AND 1995

(THOUSANDS OF UNITS)

	1985		1995	
REGIONS	HOUSING UNITS	PERCENT	HOUSING UNITS	PERCENT
IN METROPOLITAN AREAS:				
CENTRAL CITIES	32,665	32.7	33,153	30.6
SUBURBS	43,188	43.2	49,386	45.5
OUTSIDE METROPOLITAN AREAS:	24,078	24.1	26,108	23.9

Source: U.S. Bureau of the Census, Series H-150, *American Housing Survey for the United States.*

In 1995, more than 45 percent of all housing was in suburban locations, while 31 percent was in central cities. The remaining 24 percent was outside metropolitan areas. (See Table 7.2.)

The nation's 109 million housing units include 97.8 million occupied units and nearly 12 million vacant units, of which slightly more than 4 million were part of the active housing market. The remaining units were held off the market for various reasons, mostly as second or vacation homes.

The American householder's preference for a single-family home continues undiminished. In 1995, about 95 percent of owners lived in single-family or mobile homes, while just 37 percent of renters were in one-family units. There are substantial size differences in single-family owner and renter units. The typical single detached owner home is about 1,814 square feet, and the smaller renter unit is about 1,270 square feet. However, there is virtually no difference in lot size. The typical owner lot is slightly smaller at 18,700 square feet than the 19,200 square-foot renter lot.

HOMEOWNERSHIP

Since early in the 20th century, public policy at various levels of government has encouraged both construction and ownership of the single-family home. Homeownership has often been cited as a major part of the American Dream. However, that dream has been realized for the majority of Americans only in the past three decades, and significant gaps exist among household groups.

Measurement of homeownership in the United States began in the last decade of the 19th century, when 47.8 percent of households were occupied by their owners. As vast numbers of immigrants moved into mostly rented quarters in American cities, the homeownership rates slipped downward to 45.6 percent in 1920. The boom times of the 1920s reversed that trend, but the disastrous effects of the Great Depression in the 1930s fell particularly hard on housing, where the 1940 Census found 43.6 percent of households owner-occupied.

The decades after World War II were ones of unprecedented growth in homeownership. Between 1940 and 1950 the United States went from a nation of renters to one of homeowners. The 1950 Census found 55.0 percent and the 1960 Census found 61.9 percent of households owner occupied. Homeownership rate increases in the two following decades showed slight gains: up 1 percent to 62.9 in 1970 and up 1.5 percent to 64.4 percent in 1980. (See Figure 7.1.) This apparently modest increase in the rate represented a net addition of 19 million new homeowners.

FIGURE 7.1

PERCENTAGE OF HOMEOWNERSHIP IN THE UNITED STATES: 1890–1995

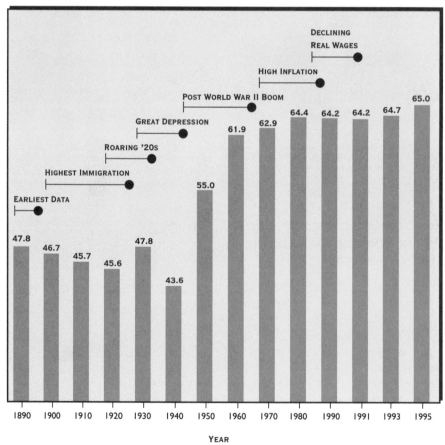

Source: U. S. Bureau of the Census, "Housing Characteristics for States and Small Areas," *Census of Housing, 1960,* Vol. I; U.S. Bureau of the Census, "General Housing Characteristics," *1970, 1980, 1990 Census of Housing*; and U.S. Bureau of the Census, *American Housing Survey for the United States,* Series H–150A.

TABLE 7.3

PERCENTAGE OF OWNER-OCCUPIED HOUSING IN THE UNITED STATES, BY AGE OF HOUSEHOLDER: 1981, 1991, AND 1995

AGE	1981	1991	1995
UNDER 25 YEARS	20.9	13.9	14.2
25 TO 29	41.9	35.6	34.5
30 TO 34	59.4	50.2	53.4
35 TO 44	71.0	65.7	65.5
45 TO 54	76.9	74.3	75.5
55 TO 64	79.8	80.6	79.4
65 TO 74	76.7	80.8	81.3
75 YEARS AND OLDER	70.1	72.7	74.5

Source: U.S. Bureau of the Census, *American Housing Survey for the United States*, Series H-150.

TABLE 7.4

PERCENTAGE OF OWNER-OCCUPIED HOUSING IN THE UNITED STATES, BY RACE AND HISPANIC ORIGIN OF HOUSEHOLDER: 1980, 1990, AND 1995

RACE/ETHNICITY	1980	1990	1995
WHITE	67.8	68.2	69.2
BLACK	44.4	43.4	43.6
NATIVE AMERICAN	52.4	53.8	47.8
ASIAN AND PACIFIC ISLANDER	51.4	52.1	53.3
HISPANIC	43.3	42.4	41.8

Source: U.S. Bureau of the Census, *American Housing Survey for the United States*, Series H-150.

TABLE 7.5

HOMEOWNERSHIP RATES IN THE UNITED STATES, BY CITIZENSHIP AND YEAR OF ENTRY: 1996

YEAR OF ENTRY	FOREIGN BORN	
	CITIZEN	NON CITIZEN
TOTAL	66.9	33.1
1990 OR LATER	36.1	14.7
1985 TO 1989	46.3	27.0
1980 TO 1984	53.1	36.7
1970 TO 1979	63.8	47.2
1969 OR EARLIER	77.1	61.1

Source: U.S. Bureau of the Census, *Current Housing Reports*, Series H121/97-2.

However, a decline in the homeownership rate was recorded in the 1990 Census, which, survey data reveals, actually began in the early 1980s. Younger householders in the United States were particularly hard hit and have not yet returned to earlier levels of homeownership. Older age groups of householders were not affected by the downturn and continue to show increasing ownership rates. (See Table 7.3.)

To what extent do the foreign born, described in this discussion as helping to drive down the homeownership rate earlier in this century, participate in the American Dream today? Currently foreign-born persons who became U.S. citizens are as successful in achieving homeownership status as the native born. In 1996, the homeownership rate was 67.4 percent for native born citizens and 66.9 percent for foreign-born citizens. The rate for noncitizens in 1996 was about 33 percent. (See Table 7.5.) In general, the longer the immigrants have lived in this country, the more likely they are to be owners. The ownership rate in 1996 for those who have been in the United States for 30 years or more was 77 percent. For immigrants who came to the United States since 1990 (and became citizens), about 36 percent were homeowners by 1996.

Foreign-born Hispanic and Black citizens were more likely to own than native-born Hispanic and Black citizens, while the opposite was true for White citizens. (See Figure 7.2.)

FIGURE 7.2

HOMEOWNERSHIP RATES IN THE UNITED STATES, BY CITIZENSHIP, RACE, AND HISPANIC ORIGIN

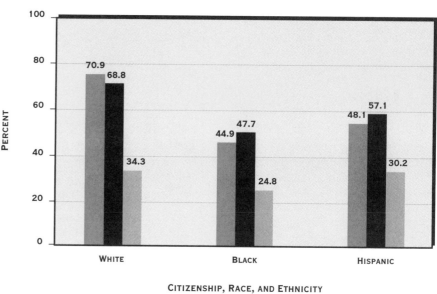

Source: U.S. Bureau of the Census, *Current Housing Reports*, Series H121/97-2, Moving to America—Moving to Homeownership," (September 1997).

TABLE 7.6

PERCENTAGE OF SUBSTANDARD HOUSING UNITS IN THE UNITED STATES: 1940–1990

	1940	1950	1960	1970	1980	1990
SUBSTANDARD:	48.6	35.4	16.0	8.8	N/A	N/A
NEED REPAIR; DILAPIDATED	18.1	9.1	4.6	3.7	N/A	N/A
LACKING COMPLETE PLUMBING	44.6	34.0	14.7	5.5	2.7	1.1

Source: U.S. Bureau of the Census, *Census of Housing, 1940 to 1990*, variously titled.

TABLE 7.7

YEAR U.S. HOUSING BUILT, BY SELECTED CHARACTERISTIC OF HOUSEHOLDER: 1995

	BEFORE 1930	1930 TO 1959	1960 TO 1989	1990 OR LATER	MEDIAN YEAR BUILT
ALL	14%	26%	52%	8%	1967
BLACK	15%	33%	48%	4%	1961
HISPANIC	11%	34%	50%	5%	1963
ELDERLY	16%	34%	46%	4%	1960
BELOW POVERTY	17%	31%	48%	4%	1961

Source: U.S. Bureau of the Census, *American Housing Survey for the United States*, Series H-150.

INDICATORS OF HOUSING QUALITY

When Franklin Roosevelt stated in his second inaugural address in 1936 "I see one-third of a nation ill-housed, ill-clad, ill-nourished,"[2] little was known about the characteristics of the housing stock. Congress responded by authorizing housing questions in the 1940 Census. That first comprehensive look at housing quality focused almost exclusively on physical aspects. Standard housing required complete plumbing and was required to be not in need of major repair (later not dilapidated), and thus "substandard" became lacking complete plumbing or dilapidated. (See Table 7.6.)

While interviewer ratings of structural conditions (sound, deteriorating, dilapidated) were dropped after the 1970 census, the use of complete plumbing continues. However, its usefulness in the United States as an indicator of quality is limited because of very low incidence. There are no appreciable differences among population subgroups.

AGE OF HOUSING

In 1940, the average age of housing units in the United States was about 25 years, indicating that one-half were built before 1915. The average age dropped to 23 years in 1970 and 1980 after several decades of high residential construction rates, but in recent years has gradually moved upward to 28 years. (See Table 7.7.) Elderly householders tend to live in older housing, but low-income households are slightly more likely to live in the very oldest homes—those built before 1930.

CROWDING

The persons-per-room ratio has been used as a housing quality measure at least since 1940. There is no official definition of "overcrowding"; some users have suggested that more than 1 person per room is crowded, while more than 1.5 persons per room is more seriously crowded. The 1940 Census found that more than one-fifth of all households exceeded the 1 person-per-room criteria. Smaller household size and larger homes reduced that rate by 1995 to 2.6 percent, but there were important differences among household types. Hispanic households, regardless of income level, had the highest proportion of crowding, nearly twice that for low-income households in general. An extremely low proportion of the elderly were in crowded units, since such a large number were in one-person households. (See Figure 7.3.)

FIGURE 7.3

PERCENTAGE OF U.S. HOUSEHOLDS WITH MORE THAN ONE PERSON PER ROOM, BY HOUSEHOLD CHARACTERISTIC: 1940 AND 1995

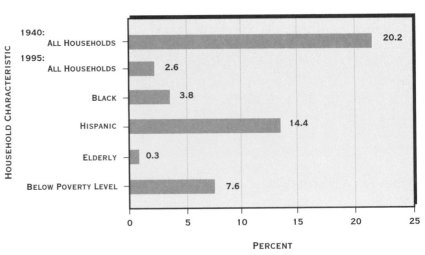

Source: U. S. Bureau of the Census, *American Housing Survey for the United States*, Series H–150.

---

2 *Inaugural Addresses of the Presidents of the United States from George Washington 1789 to George Bush 1989*, Bicentennial Edition (Washington, DC: GPO, 1989), 277.

FIGURE 7.4

PERCENTAGE OF U.S. HOUSEHOLDS LACKING CENTRAL HEAT, BY HOUSEHOLD CHARACTERISTIC: 1940, 1985, AND 1995

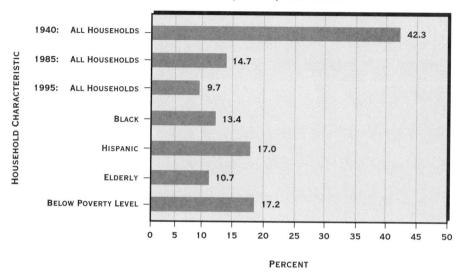

Source: U. S. Bureau of the Census, *1940 Census of Housing*, and U. S. Bureau of the Census, *American Housing Survey for the United States*, Series H-150A.

FIGURE 7.5

PERCENTAGE OF U.S. HOUSING UNITS WITH REPORTED PHYSICAL PROBLEMS, BY HOUSEHOLD CHARACTERISTIC: 1980 AND 1995

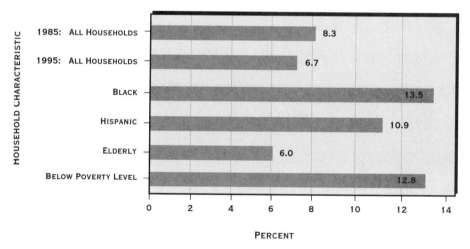

Source: U. S. Bureau of the Census, *American Housing Survey for the United States*, Series H-150A.

HEATING EQUIPMENT

The presence and type of heating equipment in the nation's homes has long been viewed as directly related to the health and safety of the occupants. In 1940, about 42 percent of occupied units did not have central heat, but in 1995, less than 10 percent of households lacked central heat. (See Figure 7.4.) There are more than 1.6 million households—mostly in the rural parts of the South—using unvented space heaters as the main heating equipment.

RECENT QUALITY TRENDS

The American Housing Survey (formerly the Annual Housing Survey) became operational in 1973. It contains a number of housing quality indicators designed, in part, to replace items no longer collected after the 1970 Census as part of the old substandard measure. These items include plumbing, heating, water and sewer systems, and service breakdowns, as well as upkeep and maintenance questions. When tabulated in different combinations, they are known variously as housing that is "inadequate," "with severe physical problems," "needing rehabilitation" or "substandard."

Data from the 1995 American Housing Survey suggest considerable progress in reducing much of the physical and structural problems of the housing stock reported in earlier decades. Less than 7 percent of households reported physical problems with their housing, just 2 percent with "severe physical problems." Yet substantial difficulties remain for certain subpopulations, especially Black and low-income households. (See Figure 7.5.)

TABLE 7.8

PERCENTAGE OF OBSERVED PROBLEM CONDITIONS IN U.S. HOUSING: 1985 AND 1995

	1985		1995	
CONDITIONS	OWNER	RENTER	OWNER	RENTER
BUILDINGS VANDALIZED	2.4	5.8	3.2	4.6
BARS ON WINDOWS	5.0	9.9	12.5	14.1
STREET REPAIRS NEEDED	32.7	38.4	16.2	23.0
TRASH OR LITTER PRESENT	22.3	38.3	14.9	27.2

Source: U.S. Bureau of the Census, *American Housing Survey for the United States*, Series H-150A.

TABLE 7.9

PERCENTAGE OF U.S HOUSEHOLDS REPORTING OPINION OF STRUCTURE: 1985 AND 1995

	1985		1995	
OPINION	OWNER	RENTER	OWNER	RENTER
PERCENT OF HOUSEHOLDS:				
WORST	0.9	6.2	0.8	3.5
BEST	79.1	56.6	81.9	59.3

Source: U.S. Bureau of the Census, *American Housing Survey for the United States*, Series H-150A.

Note: Respondents were asked how they would rate their structure as a place to live on a scale of 1 to 10, where 1 is worst and 10 is best.

TABLE 7.10

PERCENTAGE OF U.S HOUSEHOLDS WITH SELECTED DEFICIENCIES IN STRUCTURE: 1985 AND 1995

	1985		1995	
DEFICIENCIES	OWNER	RENTER	OWNER	RENTER
SIGNS OF RATS	3.5	8.0	1.9	4.4
HOLES IN FLOORS	0.8	3.1	0.8	1.7
CRACKS IN WALLS	3.6	11.0	3.1	7.6
BROKEN PLASTER	3.5	9.4	2.6	5.9

Source: U.S. Bureau of the Census, *American Housing Survey for the United States*, Series H-150A.

TABLE 7.11

PERCENTAGE OF U.S HOUSEHOLDS REPORTING OPINION OF NEIGHBORHOOD: 1985 AND 1995

	1985		1995	
OPINION	OWNER	RENTER	OWNER	RENTER
WORST	2.5	7.2	1.9	5.9
BEST	75.6	59.0	76.1	58.2

Source: U.S. Bureau of the Census, *American Housing Survey for the United States*, Series H-150A.

Note: Respondents were asked how they would rate their neighborhood as a place to live on a scale of 1 to 10, where 1 is worst and 10 is best.

TABLE 7.12

PERCENTAGE OF REPORTED NEIGHBORHOOD PROBLEM CONDITIONS IN THE UNITED STATES: 1985 AND 1995

	1985		1995	
CONDITIONS	OWNER	RENTER	OWNER	RENTER
CRIME	3.0	7.3	4.6	11.7
NOISE	5.9	10.9	5.5	11.4
TRAFFIC	6.9	8.1	7.0	8.3
PEOPLE	12.2	15.4	9.6	14.7

Source: U.S. Bureau of the Census, *American Housing Survey for the United States*, Series H-150A.

American Housing Survey interviewers observed certain conditions of neighborhoods surrounding multiunit buildings. Interviewers noted a lower incidence of problems in owner-occupied households, mostly condominium and cooperative buildings. Improvement was observed between 1985 and 1995 in street conditions and cleanliness. (See Table 7.8.)

What do American families think of their homes and neighborhoods? When asked to rate their homes and neighborhoods on a scale of 1 to 10, with 1 being the worst and 10 the best, most of the persons questioned seemed satisfied with their housing conditions. Owners rate their homes higher than renters and also report a lower incidence of deficiencies. In the tables below, "worst" is a rating of 1, 2, or 3, and "best" is a rating of 8, 9, or 10. (See Tables 7.9 and 7.10.)

Americans are not quite as satisfied with their surroundings as they are with their personal living space. A higher percentage of both owners and renters rate their neighborhood in the "worst" category. (See Table 7.11.) The number of householders who reported crime as a neighborhood problem increased from 1985 for both owners and renters, but "people" continue to be the problem identified by most households. (See Table 7.12.)

HOUSING AMENITIES

The amenities and equipment that provide for the health, safety, and comfort of families and individuals has changed dramatically over the past few decades. Questions about the availability of some household items (for example, electricity, lighting, and radios) have been dropped from the decennial census and other surveys because they are virtually universal in the United States.

For example, in 1940 about 44 percent of households reported having a mechanical refrigerator. By 1995, more than 99 percent had the appliance, and there was no discernible difference among owners, renters, or household groups.

Dishwashers, clothes washers, and clothes dryers were much more prevalent among owners than renters in 1995. (See Table 7.13 and Figure 7.6.)

HOUSEHOLD ENERGY USE

Over the past five decades, there have been vast changes in the way families in the United States heat their homes. In 1940, more than three out of four households used the solid fuels, coal, and wood. By 1995, coal had virtually disappeared and the use of wood was down to 4 percent. Utility gas ("natural" gas), the use of which increased substantially after World War II with the extension of gas pipelines to suburban areas, has leveled off at about 50 percent.

TABLE 7.13

PERCENTAGE OF OWNERS AND RENTERS IN THE UNITED STATES WITH SELECTED EQUIPMENT: 1985 AND 1995

EQUIPMENT	OWNER	RENTER
1985		
REFRIGERATOR	99.9	99.9
DISHWASHER	52.5	28.0
CLOTHES WASHER	91.8	40.5
CLOTHES DRYER	81.9	29.9
TELEPHONE	96.2	86.4
DISPOSAL	36.3	34.5
AIR CONDITIONING	66.6	55.9
1995		
REFRIGERATOR	99.9	99.5
DISHWASHER	63.3	35.9
CLOTHES WASHER	94.5	46.0
CLOTHES DRYER	89.9	39.7
TELEPHONE	97.1	87.5
DISPOSAL	45.3	39.9
AIR CONDITIONING	79.1	68.7

Source: U.S. Bureau of the Census, *American Housing Survey for the United States*, Series H-150.

FIGURE 7.6

PERCENTAGE OF U.S. HOUSEHOLDS WITH SELECTED EQUIPMENT, BY HOUSEHOLD CHARACTERISTIC: 1995

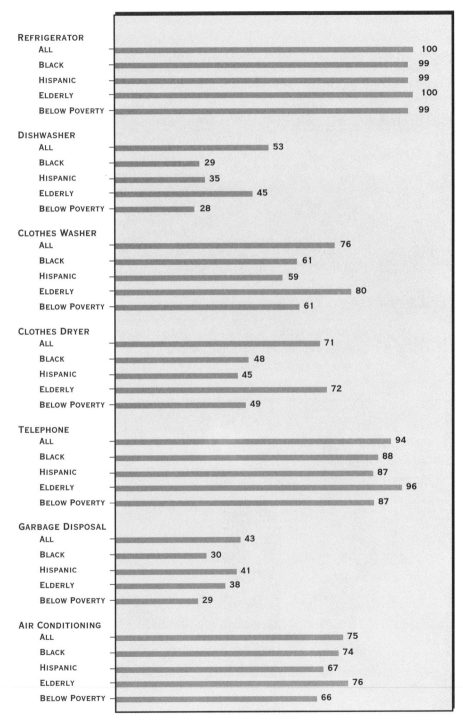

PERCENT

Source: U. S. Bureau of the Census, *American Housing Survey for the United States*, Series H-150A.

The development of more efficient reverse-cycle heating and cooling equipment, together with high population and housing growth in warmer areas of the country where the equipment is most effective, has resulted in a rapid increase in the number of households using electricity as the main house-heating fuel. In 1995, there were more than 20 million all-electric homes, nearly two-thirds of which were located in the South. (See Table 7.14.)

TABLE 7.14

TYPE OF HOUSEHOLD HEATING FUEL: 1940–1995
(PERCENT)

HEATING FUEL	1940	1960	1980	1995
ALL HOUSEHOLDS	100	100	100	100
UTILITY GAS	11	43	53	50
LP GAS	0	5	6	5
ELECTRICITY	0	2	18	27
FUEL OIL, KEROSENE	10	32	18	12
COAL	55	12	1	0
WOOD	23	4	3	4
OTHER, NONE	1	2	1	2

Source: U.S. Bureau of the Census, *1940, 1960, 1980 Census of Housing*, variously titled, and U.S. Bureau of the Census, *American Housing for the United States*, Series H-150A.

FIGURE 7.7

AVERAGE ANNUAL HOUSEHOLD ENERGY EXPENDITURES IN THE UNITED STATES, BY TYPE OF FUEL: 1984 AND 1993
(ADJUSTED BY DEGREE-DAYS AND PRICE CHANGES)

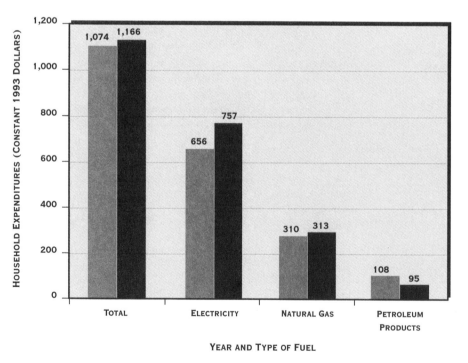

Source: U. S. Department of Energy, Energy Information Administration, *Household Energy Consumption and Expenditures*, DOE/EIA–0464(94), August 1997.

HOUSEHOLD ENERGY EXPENDITURES

How much are U.S. families paying for household energy? Are these expenditures increasing or decreasing over time? Figure 7.7, presenting data from the Residential Energy Consumption Survey, shows average expenditures by type of fuel. These data are adjusted for both price changes and degree-days. From 1984 to 1993, average expenditures were up $92, a 9 percent increase. Electricity, which accounts for more than one-half of household energy expense, was up $101, an amount greater than the total average increase. This was offset by a decline in petroleum products (excluding motor fuel) from about $108 to $95 between 1984 and 1993.

Owners averaged fuel expenditures of about $1,457 in 1993 compared with about $950 for renters. The type of fuel used, and, consequently, the fuel expenditures, varied by race and Hispanic origin. White householders had the largest expenditure for electricity, while Black householders spent more on natural gas. (See Table 7.15.)

TABLE 7.15

AVERAGE ANNUAL FUEL EXPENDITURES IN THE UNITED STATES, BY SELECTED CHARACTERISTIC: 1993

CHARACTERISTIC	MAJOR SOURCES	ELECTRICITY	NATURAL GAS
RACE OF HOUSEHOLD			
ALL	1,282	840	546
WHITE	1,307	863	547
BLACK	1,205	750	622
OTHER	988	670	391
HISPANIC	1,065	704	395
OWNERSHIP			
OWNER	1,457	951	614
RENTER	953	628	424
BELOW POVERTY			
LEVEL	1,055	669	481

Source: U.S. Department of Energy, Energy Information Administration, *Household Energy Consumption and Expenditures*, DOE/EIA-0464(94), August 1997.

HOUSEHOLD VEHICLE USE

The total number of household vehicles rose to 147 million in 1994, up 6 percent from 1988. However the average number of vehicles per household (1.8) did not change during that period. "Household vehicles" are those that are either owned or used on a regular basis by household members for personal transportation.

American householders drove more miles and consumed more fuel in 1994 than in 1988: per household, vehicle miles traveled, average fuel consumption, and expenditures for gasoline all increased between 1988 and 1994. (See Table 7.16.)

Households with children tend to have more vehicles, drive more miles, and consequently use more fuel than households without children. Not surprisingly, households with children of driving age show the highest number of vehicles, miles traveled, and fuel consumption. (See Table 7.17.)

HOUSING COSTS AND AFFORDABILITY

In recent years, the issue of affordability has begun to overshadow physical condition in discussions of housing quality. "Affordability" in the context of housing quality generally means the relationship of gross rent or homeowner cost to household income. The traditional view of household budget experts in the United States was that more than 25 percent of income spent for housing was excessive and evidence of housing or affordability problems. That somewhat arbitrary standard has edged upward to the currently used 30 percent level. Most federal and local housing assistance programs require households to contribute 30 percent of their income toward rent. (Prior to 1981, the standard was 25 percent.) Eligible-income households that spend more than 50 percent of income for rent are considered to have "worst case needs" and have top priority for federal aid.

Data in earlier sections have suggested that there has been substantial improvement in the quality of the nation's housing stock. Data in Table 7.18, however, show that in 1995 a larger proportion of householders were paying an amount for shelter above the affordability criterion indicated above than was the case in 1985. Nearly half of all renters were paying more than 30 percent of income in 1995; close to one in

TABLE 7.16

CHARACTERISTICS OF HOUSEHOLD VEHICLE USE: 1988 AND 1994

VEHICLES	1988	1994
TOTAL	147.5	156.8
AVERAGE PER HOUSEHOLD	1.8	1.8
AVERAGE MILES PER VEHICLE	10,200	11,400
AVERAGE MILES PER GALLON	18.3	19.8
ANNUAL FUEL USE PER VEHICLE, GALLONS	559	578
AVERAGE ANNUAL FUEL COST PER HOUSEHOLD:		
CURRENT DOLLARS	$998	$1234
CONSTANT 1994 DOLLARS	$1,218	$1,234

Source: U.S. Department of Energy, Energy Information Administration, *Household Vehicles Energy Consumption and Expenditures*, DOE/EIA-0464(94), August, 1994.

TABLE 7.17

AVERAGE NUMBER OF HOUSEHOLD VEHICLES, MILES TRAVELED, AND FUEL CONSUMPTION IN THE UNITED STATES: 1994

TYPE OF HOUSEHOLD	VEHICLES	MILES TRAVELED	FUEL CONSUMPTION (GALLONS)	EXPENDITURES
HOUSEHOLDS WITH CHILDREN	2.0	24,800	1,257	$1453
HOUSEHOLDS WITH CHILDREN AGE 16 OR 17	2.4	29,900	1,500	$1,727
HOUSEHOLDS WITHOUT CHILDREN	1.7	18,900	951	$1,100

Source: U.S. Department of Energy, Energy Information Administration, *Household Vehicles Energy Consumption and Expenditures*, DOE/EIA-0464(94), August 1994.

TABLE 7.18

GROSS RENT AS A PERCENTAGE OF HOUSEHOLD INCOME IN THE UNITED STATES: 1985 AND 1995

(NUMBERS IN THOUSANDS)

RENTER HOUSEHOLDS	HOUSEHOLDS PAYING 30 PERCENT OR MORE				HOUSEHOLDS PAYING 50 PERCENT OR MORE				MEDIAN PERCENT	
	1985		1995		1985		1995		1985	1995
	NUMBER	PERCENT	NUMBER	PERCENT	NUMBER	PERCENT	NUMBER	PERCENT		
ALL	12,867	43	15,086	49	6,128	21	7,064	23	27	29
BLACK	2,633	51	3,180	53	1,439	28	1,602	27	31	31
HISPANIC	1,440	51	2,419	58	766	27	1,216	29	30	34
ELDERLY	2,732	61	2,636	66	1,296	29	1,361	34	35	38
BELOW POVERTY LEVEL	5,727	83	5,889	82	4,038	59	4,235	59	65	62

Source: U.S. Bureau of the Census, *American Housing Survey for the United States*, Series H-150A.

FIGURE 7.8

MEDIAN MONTHLY HOUSING COSTS IN THE UNITED STATES FOR HOMEOWNERS WITH A MORTGAGE, BY HOUSEHOLD CHARACTERISTIC: 1985 AND 1995

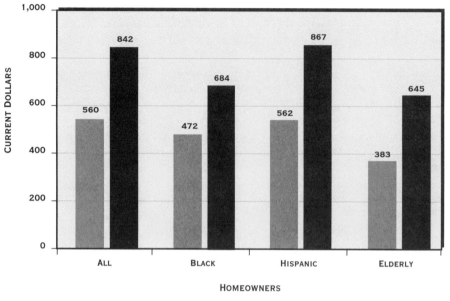

Source: U. S. Bureau of the Census, *American Housing Survey for the United States*, Series H-150A.

FIGURE 7.9

MEDIAN MONTHLY HOUSING COSTS IN THE UNITED STATES AS A PERCENTAGE OF INCOME FOR HOMEOWNERS WITH A MORTGAGE, BY HOUSEHOLD CHARACTERISTIC: 1985 AND 1995

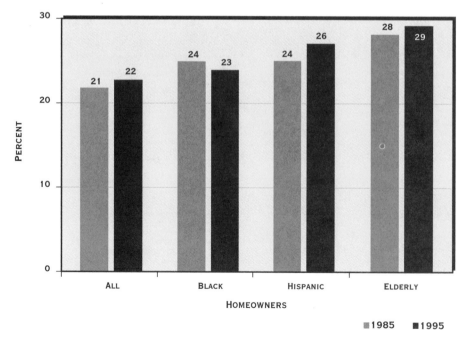

Source: U. S. Bureau of the Census, *American Housing Survey for the United States*, Series H-150A.

four were paying more than 50 percent. Some analysts argue that the data indicate declining affordability due to lack of inexpensive units or to low income or both. Another view is that some renters have made a conscious choice to live in newer rental units with more amenities and thus more costly rent.

Discussions of shelter cost and relation to income for owners are couched in slightly different terms than for renters. A distinction must be made between mortgaged and nonmortgaged homes because the cost structure is vastly different. The largest single component is principal and interest for mortgaged units. Moreover, there is the presumption of a greater range of housing choices for homeowners because of their substantially higher incomes: for example, the median household income in 1995 for renters was $20,300, for owners with a mortgage $49,600, and for owners without a mortgage $25,400.

The median monthly homeowner costs (including principal, interest, taxes, insurance, and utilities) for mortgaged homes was up 50 percent from $560 in 1985 to $842 in 1995 (current dollars in both years). This increase was slightly higher than the 45 percent increase in the Consumer Price Index over the same period. (See Figure 7.8.)

Like renters, the share of income paid for shelter increased for homeowners as well, but at a much lower rate, about 1 percent. The share of Black householders declined by 1 percent. Elderly householders, living on retirement incomes, paid the greatest share for shelter. (See Figure 7.9.)

TABLE 7.19

COMPOSITE HOUSING AFFORDABILITY INDEX FOR THE UNITED STATES

YEAR	MEDIAN PRICED HOME	INTEREST RATE	MEDIAN FAMILY INCOME	QUALIFYING INCOME	INDEX
1991	$100,300	9.30%	$35,939	$31,825	112.9
1996	$118,200	7.71%	$42,385	$32,392	130.9

Source: National Association of Realtors, news release, July 1997.

TABLE 7.20

AFFORDABILITY STATUS FOR A MODESTLY PRICED HOME IN THE UNITED STATES: 1984–1993

(SELECTED YEARS)

	PERCENTAGE WHO CAN AFFORD TO BUY	
YEAR	ALL FAMILIES	RENTER FAMILIES
1984	60.4	12.6
1988	59.7	14.0
1991	57.6	13.1
1993	57.7	11.7

Source: U.S. Bureau of the Census, "Who Can Afford to Buy a House in 1993?" Current Housing Reports, Series H121/97-1.

Affordability can also be measured by taking into account home prices, incomes, interest rates, and other factors. For example, the National Association of Realtors calculates a composite Housing Affordability Index. (See Table 7.19.) When the index measures 100, a family earning the median income has the amount needed to purchase a median-priced home. For 1996, the index was 130.9, more than enough to purchase a home.

The Bureau of the Census also issues estimates of affordability by including factors such as assets, cash on hand, and debt, in addition to price and interest rates. In 1993 about 58 percent of all families could afford a modestly priced house. Only 12 percent of renter families could afford the same house. (See Table 7.20.) A modestly priced house is priced at the 25th percentile of all owner-occupied homes in the geographic area.

The ability to purchase a modestly priced house differs significantly by race and ethnicity and by whether a family currently owns or rents. Owner families are far more likely to be able to afford to relocate than renter families, and more White renter families can afford to purchase than minority renter families. (See Figure 7.10.)

FIGURE 7.10

AFFORDABILITY STATUS FOR A MODESTLY PRICED HOME IN THE UNITED STATES, BY TENURE AND RACE/HISPANIC ORIGIN: 1993

(PERCENT OF FAMILIES WHO CAN AFFORD)

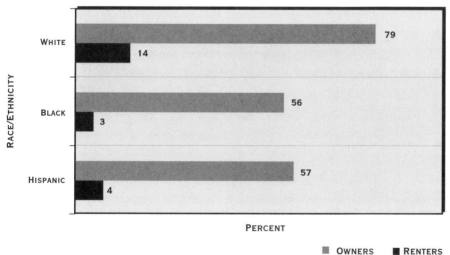

Source: U.S. Bureau of the Census, "Who Can Afford to Buy a House in 1993?," Current Housing Reports, Series H121/97-1.

TABLE 7.21

CONVENTIONAL HOME PURCHASE LOANS IN UNITED STATES, BY RACE AND ETHNIC ORIGIN: 1993–1996

BORROWER	NUMBER OF LOANS			PERCENT CHANGE	
	1993	1995	1996	1995–1996	1993–1996
AMERICAN INDIAN	8,638	10,712	11,368	61.0	31.6
ASIAN	78,671	85,571	91,547	7.0	16.4
HISPANIC	91,345	134,982	135,683	0.5	48.5
BLACK	81,322	138,034	135,944	-1.5	67.2
WHITE	1,971,153	2,205,357	2,354,024	6.7	19.4

Source: Federal Financial Institutions Examination Council, Home Mortgage Disclosure Act press release, August 1997.

TABLE 7.22

DISPOSITION OF CONVENTIONAL HOME PURCHASE LOANS IN THE UNITED STATES, BY RACE AND HISPANIC ORIGIN: 1996

RACE/ETHNICITY	DISPOSITION (PERCENTAGE)		
	APPROVED	DENIED	WITHDRAWN OR FILE CLOSED
AMERICAN INDIAN:			
ALASKA NATIVE	43.5	50.2	6.3
ASIAN, PACIFIC ISLANDER	75.0	13.8	11.2
BLACK	44.1	48.8	7.1
WHITE	68.8	24.1	7.1
HISPANIC	56.1	34.4	9.5

Source: Federal Financial Institutions Examination Council, Home Mortgage Disclosure Act press release, August 1997.

TABLE 7.23

INDEX OF RESIDENTIAL SEGREGATION (DISSIMILARITY) FOR SELECTED U.S. METROPOLITAN AREAS: 1970–1990

METROPOLITAN AREA	1970	1980	1990
CHICAGO	92	88	85
DETROIT	88	87	88
LOS ANGELES	91	81	73
NEW YORK	81	82	82
WASHINGTON, DC	81	70	66

*The percentage change of the minority group population that would have to move to each tract to reflect the composition of the entire metropolitan area.

Source: Roderick O. Harrison and Daniel Weinberg, *Racial and Ethnic Residential Segregation in 1990*, U.S. Bureau of the Census, 1992.

TABLE 7.24

MEAN RESIDENTIAL SEGREGATION (DISSIMILARITY) FOR ALL U.S. METROPOLITAN AREAS: 1980 AND 1990

GROUP	1980	1990
AMERICAN INDIAN, ESKIMO, ALEUT	36	35
ASIAN AND PACIFIC ISLANDER	40	41
BLACK	74	69
HISPANIC	50	50

Source: Douglas S. Massey and Nancy A. Denton. "Trends in the Residential Segregation of Blacks, Hispanics, and Asians: 1970-1989," *American Sociological Review 52* (1987) and Roderick O. Harrison and Daniel Weinberg, *Racial and Ethnic Residential Segregation in 1990*, U.S. Bureau of the

HOME PURCHASE LENDING TRENDS

The number of home-purchase conventional mortgage loans made to Black applicants fell in 1996. This was a reversal after a number of years of increased lending. (See Table 7.21.)

Even though lending to most minority groups has increased at a faster rate than for Whites, most minority groups were far more likely to be denied a loan than were White applicants in 1996. Less than one-half of Black and American Indian applicants were approved in 1996. Asian and Pacific Islanders were least likely to be denied a loan. (See Table 7.22.)

RESIDENTIAL SEGREGATION

"Our Nation is moving toward two societies, one black, one white, separate—and unequal" is a widely quoted sentence from the 1968 report of the National Advisory Commission on Civil Disorders. In recent years, there has been much research into, and also disagreement over, how to define and measure residential segregation. A 1988 study identified five dimensions of segregation—evenness, exposure, concentration, centralization, and clustering—with several ways of calculating each dimension. The discussion and tables that follow are restricted to perhaps the most widely used measure, the evenness dimension as determined by the index of dissimilarity. The index is calculated at the census tract level and can be defined as the percentage of the minority group population that would have to move to have each tract reflect the composition of the entire metropolitan area. Table 7.23 shows changes in the dissimilarity index over a 20-year period for five large metropolitan areas. Caution should be used in interpreting these data since the metropolitan area definition is the one existing at the time of each Census year.

Blacks continue to be the most segregated group, followed by Hispanics. There was virtually no change from 1980 to 1990, except for a modest decrease for Blacks. (See Table 7.24.)

What are the most segregated metropolitan areas for each population subgroup?

TABLE 7.25

MOST SEGREGATED METROPOLITAN AREAS IN THE UNITED STATES: 1990

GROUP	AREA	GROUP POPULATION	PERCENT OF AREA	INDEX
AMERICAN INDIAN	PHOENIX	38,017	1.8	52
ASIAN OR PACIFIC ISLANDER	STOCKTON	59,690	12.4	55
BLACK	MILWAUKEE	197,183	13.8	83
HISPANIC	NEWARK	188,234	10.3	67

Source: Douglas S. Massey and Nancy A. Denton. "Trends in the Residential Segregation of Blacks, Hispanics, and Asians: 1970-1989," *American Sociological Review* 52 (1987) and Roderick O. Harrison and Daniel Weinberg, *Racial and Ethnic Residential Segregation in 1990*, U.S. Bureau of the Census, 1992.

TABLE 7.26

DEMAND FOR HOMELESS SHELTERS IN SELECTED U.S. CITIES: 1985, 1990, AND 1996

PERCENT OF CITIES REPORTING	1985	1990	1996
INCREASE IN DEMAND FOR SHELTER OVER PREVIOUS YEAR	24	24	5
CITIES IN WHICH DEMAND INCREASED	88	80	71
CITIES WHICH EXPECT DEMAND TO INCREASE NEXT YEAR	88	97	100

Source: U.S. Conference of Mayors.

They are scattered among the West, the Midwest, and the Northeast (none in the South, the region that is often perceived to be the most segregated). (See Table 7.25.)

COUNTING THE HOMELESS

How many people are homeless in America? The answer to this frequently asked question depends on the definition used and also on the methodology employed. A 1984 Department of Housing and Urban Development (HUD) "Report to the Secretary on Homeless and Emergency Shelters" defined as homeless any person whose nighttime residence was in a shelter or on the street. The 1987 Stewart B. McKinney Homeless Assistance Act expanded that definition to include individuals in temporary or transitional living conditions. Even more expansive was a 1985 General Accounting Office (GAO) study that defined as homeless "persons who lack resources and community ties necessary to provide for their own adequate shelter." The first two definitions include persons who have been characterized as the "literal homeless." The GAO study is an example of a much broader definition that includes persons who have been described as at risk of homelessness or as precariously housed and may include persons "doubled up" with relatives or families paying a very high proportion of income for rent.

There are a number of methodological issues in measuring the homeless. Of paramount importance is the duration or reference period of the study. Evidence suggests that for many persons homelessness is a revolving door while for many others it is a one-time occurrence. Studies that are conducted at one point in time, as a snapshot, are likely to miss most of the latter people. The Street and Shelter Night enumeration, conducted as part of the 1990 census, was an example of a point-in-time count. Studies conducted over a period of time such as a month, a year, or longer, while presenting other problems such as duplication, are likely to capture more of the homeless population.

The definition and methodology issues may seem tedious to the casual reader, but they are critical to gauging the accuracy of homeless estimates. One of the most respected figures was based on a 1987 Urban Institute study that estimated 500,000 to 600,000 homeless persons in the United States at that time. Estimates range up to 12 million persons who have ever experienced homelessness (including doubling up with relatives and friends) at some point in their lifetime.[3] One indicator of whether homelessness is increasing in the United States is requests for emergency shelter. Between 1995 and 1996, requests for emergency shelter increased by an average of 5 percent in 29 large cities according to a recent report by the United States Conference of Mayors. The survey respondents were local officials or service providers. Every responding city expected an increase in requests for emergency shelter in the next year. (See Table 7.26.)

3 See Martha Burt and Barbara Cohen, *America's Homeless: Numbers, Characteristics, and Programs that Serve Them* (Washington, DC: The Urban Institute Press, 1989); Bruce Link et al. "Lifetime and Five-Year Prevalence of Homelessness in the United States," *American Journal of Public Health* (December 1994). For a discussion of causes of homelessness, see Christopher Jencks, *The Homeless* (Cambridge: Harvard University Press, 1995); and the National Coalition for the Homeless Website at <http://nch.ari.net/causes.html>.

FOR FURTHER INFORMATION SEE:

BAUMOHL, JIM, ED. *HOMELESSNESS IN AMERICA*. PHOENIX: ORYX PRESS, 1996.

CULHANE, DENNIS P., ET AL. "PUBLIC SHELTER ADMISSION RATES IN PHILADELPHIA AND NEW YORK CITY: THE IMPLICATIONS OF TURNOVER FOR SHELTERED POPULATION COUNTS." *HOUSING POLICY DEBATE* 5, NO. 2. WASHINGTON, DC: FANNIE MAE (1994).

DEVANEY, JACK. *TRACKING THE AMERICAN DREAM, 50 YEARS OF HOUSING HISTORY FROM THE CENSUS BUREAU: 1940 TO 1990*. CURRENT HOUSING REPORTS, SERIES H121/94-1. WASHINGTON, DC: U.S. BUREAU OF THE CENSUS, 1994.

FARLEY, REYNOLDS, AND WALTER ALLEN. *THE COLOR LINE AND THE QUALITY OF LIFE IN AMERICA*. NEW YORK: RUSSELL SAGE, 1987.

MASSEY, DOUGLAS S., AND NANCY A. DENTON. *AMERICAN APARTHEID: SEGREGATION AND THE MAKING OF THE UNDERCLASS*. CAMBRIDGE: HARVARD UNIVERSITY PRESS, 1993.

MYERS, DOWELL, ED. *HOUSING DEMOGRAPHY: LINKING DEMOGRAPHIC STRUCTURE AND HOUSING MARKETS*. MADISON: UNIVERSITY OF WISCONSIN PRESS, 1990.

ROSENBERRY, SARA, AND CHESTER HARTMAN, ED. *HOUSING ISSUES OF THE 1990S*. NEW YORK: PRAEGER, 1989.

SAVAGE, HOWARD A., AND PETER J. FRONCZEK. *WHO CAN AFFORD TO BUY A HOUSE IN 1991?* CURRENT HOUSING REPORTS, SERIES H121/93-3. WASHINGTON, DC: U.S. BUREAU OF THE CENSUS.

SIMMONS, PATRICK A., ED. *HOUSING STATISTICS OF THE UNITED STATES*. LANHAM, MD: BERNAN PRESS, 1997.

WALLACE, JAMES E. "FINANCING AFFORDABLE HOUSING IN THE UNITED STATES." *HOUSING POLICY DEBATE* 65, NO. 4. WASHINGTON, DC: FANNIE MAE (1995).

WEBSITES:

AMERICAN HOUSING SURVEY STATISTICS FROM THE CENSUS BUREAU WEBSITE AT <HTTP://WWW.CENSUS.GOV/HHES/WWW/AHS.HTML>.

FANNIE MAE WEBSITE AT <HTTP://WWW.FANNIEMAE.COM>.

NATIONAL ASSOCIATION OF HOMEBUILDERS WEBSITE AT <HTTP://WWW.NAHB.COM>.

NATIONAL COALITION FOR THE HOMELESS WEBSITE AT <HTTP://NCH.ARI.NET>.

U.S. DEPARTMENT OF HOUSING AND URBAN DEVELOPMENT WEBSITE AT <HTTP://WWW.HUD.GOV/> AND <HTTP:\\WWW.HUDUSER.ORG>.

CHAPTER 8

Crime and Criminal Justice

GEORGE E. HALL

CRIME

SERIOUS CRIMES KNOWN TO THE POLICE—	
1991:	**14,873,000**
1996:	**13,474,000**
VIOLENT CRIMES KNOWN TO THE POLICE—	
1991:	**1,912,000**
1996:	**1,682,000**
PERSONS ARRESTED FOR SERIOUS CRIME, 1996:	**2,041,000**
PERSONS ARRESTED FOR VIOLENT CRIME, 1996:	**548,000**
PERSONS UNDER CORRECTIONAL SUPERVISION, 1994:	**5,130,000**
PERSONS IN PRISON, 1994:	**1,017,000**
CRIMINAL JUSTICE EXPENDITURES, 1993:	**$ 97,541,826**

INTRODUCTION

Knowing about "crime" is difficult. There are serious questions of conception, definition, and measurement. In 1967, The President's Commission on Law Enforcement and Administration of Justice made the following observation: "A skid-row drunk lying in a gutter is a crime. So is the killing of an unfaithful wife. A Cosa Nostra conspiracy to bribe public officials is crime. So is a strong-arm robbery by a 15-year-old boy...These crimes can no more be linked together for purposes of analysis than can measles and schizophrenia, or lung cancer and a broken ankle...Thinking of 'crime' as a whole is futile."[1] The irony in the above statement further illustrates the difficulty in knowing about crime. Since that statement was written in 1967, many jurisdictions have decriminalized public drunkenness, making the commission's first example no longer germane. Furthermore, crime not only has a temporal dimension, but it also has a spatial dimension. For example, throughout the early decades of this century the use of marijuana, cocaine, and opium and its derivatives became ille-

gal in the United States. However, in some countries the use of these substances is not illegal, while in other countries drug use is even more severely punished than it is in the United States.

The measurement problem is equally vexing. For example, crimes such as embezzlement or drug possession cannot be identified until the perpetrator is caught. Some others cannot ever be adequately categorized. For example, if, during an inventory, a retail establishment discovers less inventory than expected, is this the result of shoplifting, employee theft, a simple error, or what? Laying these problems aside, this chapter will address what people understand crime to be, as well as the resulting criminal justice process and the outcomes of that process.

THE GREAT PARADOX

In the late 1990s the United States is confronted with a sharply declining crime rate, and, concurrently, with an exploding prison population. According to the Federal Bureau of Investigation (FBI), serious reported crime in 1996 was more than 9

percent less than in 1991 (9.4 percent). The decrease in violent crime is even greater, down 12 percent during the same period. The decrease in the crime rate per 100,000 inhabitants is even more spectacular. It is down 13.9 percent for all serious reported crimes and 16.3 percent for crimes of violence. From 1991 to 1994 the number of prisoners in Federal and state prisons rose from 0.8 million to almost 1 million, an increase of about 25 percent. Expenditures for criminal justice activities also increased significantly during this period, with an overall increase of 11 percent between 1991 and 1993.[2]

Public concern about crime has increased dramatically, notwithstanding the falling crime rate. In a series of surveys conducted by the Gallup Organization, people were asked what they considered to be the most important problems facing the country. In July 1990 only 1 percent mentioned crime. In August 1994, the number mentioning crime had risen to 52 percent. Coincidentally, this was the period when Congress and the administration were debating a major crime bill.

---

[1] President's Commission on Law Enforcement and the Administration of Justice, *The Challenge of Crime in a Free Society* (Washington, DC: GPO, 1967).

[2] Federal Bureau of Investigation, "Uniform Crime Reports," in *Crime in the United States* (Washington, DC: GPO, 1997).

CRIME AND VICTIMS

Crime may be defined as "an action or an instance of negligence…that is legally prohibited" (Webster's New Universal Unabridged Dictionary). There are many kinds of crime, including commercial crime, industrial crime, other white-collar crime, and common crime. While commercial crime, such as the savings and loan scandals of the 1980s or industrial crime involving pollution, may cost society very heavily, commercial and industrial crime are not subject to simple measurement nor do they come to mind when most people think of crime. In the United States, most people think of crime as those offenses regularly reported by the FBI in its Uniform Crime Reports (UCR).

The set of crimes reported by the UCR is called the Crime Index. "The Crime Index is composed of selected offenses used to gauge fluctuations in the overall volume and rate of crime reported to law enforcement. The offenses included are the violent crimes of murder and nonnegligent manslaughter, forcible rape, robbery, and aggravated assault and the property crimes of burglary, larceny-theft, motor vehicle theft, and arson."[3] The other principal source of national data about crime is the National Crime Victimization Survey (NCVS) from the Bureau of Justice Statistics. For the purposes of this chapter, the set of crimes making up the Crime Index will be referred to as serious crimes.

The UCR develops its data by collecting information taken from crimes reported to law enforcement agencies and provided to the FBI by virtually every police agency in the country. The NCVS is a survey of a national sample of households in which information about crime victimization is sought for each household and for each household member 12 years of age and older. Crimes, such as household burglary,

FIGURE 8.1

COMPARISON OF NATIONAL CRIME VICTIMIZATION SURVEY ESTIMATES AND UNIFORM CRIME REPORT FIGURES FOR SELECTED CRIMES IN THE UNITED STATES: 1994

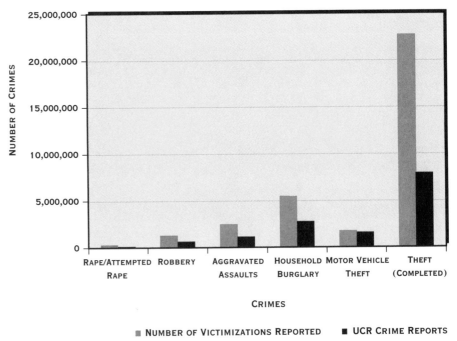

Sources: Bureau of Justice Statistics for National Crime Victimization Survey data; Federal Bureau of Investigation for Uniform Crime Reports data.

motor vehicle theft, and theft in which no victim was present are called property crimes by NCVS, and crimes where the victim is present during the commission of the crime are called personal crimes. While neither of these methods provides a perfect measure of crime, each has its own advantages. For example, because the UCR receives reports from almost all police agencies, it can provide good information on the geographic distribution of crime. Because it is based on a national sample, the NCVS does not collect data for small geographic areas but it does provide better information

on the true incidence of crime since many crimes are not reported to the police.

Every effort was made to define criminal events in the same way for both of these surveys. The major differences are that the NCVS does not include murder and nonnegligent manslaughter, since there is no living victim to interview, and that the NCVS includes simple assault in its count of violent crimes, while the UCR does not. In 1994, the NCVS showed that the violent crime rate was 51 per thousand, but if simple assault is removed, making the data roughly comparable to the UCR, the rate

---

3 Scott Butterfield, "Punitive Damages: Crime Keeps Falling, but Prisons Keep on Filling," New York Times, 28 September 1997.

TABLE 8.1

ATTITUDES TOWARD THE MOST IMPORTANT PROBLEM FACING THE UNITED STATES: 1988–1997

(SELECTED TIME PERIODS)

PROBLEM	SEPT. 9–11, 1988	MAY 4–7, 1989	NOV. 9–12, 1989	APR. 5–8, 1990	JULY 19–22, 1990	MAR. 7–10, 1991	MAR. 26–29, 1992	JAN. 8–11, 1993	JAN. 15–17, 1994	AUG. 15–16, 1994	JAN. 16–18, 1995	MAY 9–12, 1996	JAN. 10–13, 1997
HIGH COST OF LIVING; INFLATION; TAXES	2	3	2	1	1	2	6	3	4	3	7	11	6
UNEMPLOYMENT	9	6	3	3	3	8	25	22	18	6	15	13	NA
INTERNATIONAL PROBLEMS; FOREIGN AFFAIRS	4	4	3	NA	NA	1	3	8	3	4	2	4	3
CRIME; VIOLENCE	2	6	3	2	1	2	5	9	37	52	27	25	23
FEAR OF WAR/ NUCLEAR WAR; INTERNATIONAL TENSIONS	5	2	1	1	1	2	NA	NA	NA	(A)	(A)	NA	NA
MORAL DECLINE IN SOCIETY; ETHICS	1	5	3	1	2	2	5	7	8	7	6	14	9
EXCESSIVE GOVERNMENT SPENDING; FEDERAL BUDGET DEFICIT	12	7	7	6	21	8	8	13	5	3	14	15	8
DISSATISFACTION WITH GOVERNMENT	NA	2	1	1	1	NA	8	5	6	5	5	12	7
ECONOMY (GENERAL)	12	8	7	7	7	24	42	35	14	17	10	12	21
POVERTY; HUNGER; HOMELESSNESS	7	10	10	11	7	10	15	15	11	5	10	7	10
DRUGS; DRUG ABUSE	11	27	38	30	18	11	8	6	9	9	6	10	17
TRADE DEFICIT; TRADE RELATIONS	3	3	2	2	1	1	4	3	2	1	1	2	1
EDUCATION; QUALITY OF EDUCATION	2	3	2	1	2	2	8	8	7	5	5	13	10
ENVIRONMENT; POLLUTION	NA	4	3	8	5	2	3	3	1	1	1	3	1
AIDS	NA	1	NA	1	2	(A)	3	2	2	2	1	(A)	1
ABORTION	NA	(A)	3	NA	NA	NA	NA	NA	NA	1	1	0	1
RECESSION; DEPRESSION	NA	(A)	(A)	NA	NA	4	3	NA	(A)	1	0	(A)	NA
HEALTH CARE	NA	NA	NA	NA	NA	NA	12	18	20	29	12	10	7
NO OPINION; DON'T KNOW	12	7	6	9	5	6	2	2	2	2	2	7	6

(A) LESS THAN 0.5 PERCENT.

NA = NOT AVAILABLE

Note: Exact wording of response categories varies across surveys. Multiple responses are possible; the source records up to three problems per respondent. Some problems mentioned by a small percentage of respondents are not included in the tables.

Sources: George H. Gallup, *The Gallup Report*, Report No. 198, p. 27; Report No. 226, p. 17; Report No. 235, pp.20,21; Report No. 252, pp.28,29; Report No. 260, pp.6,7; Report No. 277, pp. 6,7; Report No. 285, pp.4,5; Report No. 290, p.6 (Princeton, NJ: *The Gallup Report*); George Gallup, *The Gallup Poll*, March 14, 1991, pp.2,3;April 3, 1992, pp.1,2;January 3 No. 298, p.14: No.340, p. 43; No. 352, p.7 (Princeton, NJ: *The Gallup Poll*). Bureau of Justice Statistics *Sourcebook of Criminal Justice Statistics 1996* available on the Bureau of Justice Statistics website at <www.ojp.usdoj.gov/bjs>.

drops to fewer than 20 per thousand. In the same year the UCR showed the violent crime rate as 7.2 per thousand.

Figure 8.1 shows the number of crimes reported by the FBI via the Uniform Crime Report compared to those reported by the Bureau of Justice Statistics via the NCVS. There are a number of hypotheses explaining the differences, but one thing stands out: where the victim feels that the police are powerless, or that it is not worth the effort to report the crime, the crime will not be reported to the police. That is probably why reports of theft, for example, differ so greatly between the two sources. When the victim feels that there is a chance for recovery by the police or the item is covered by insurance that would require a police report for the insurance claim (motor vehicle theft, for example), the crime is much more likely to be reported to the police.

VICTIMIZATION

A major purpose of the NCVS was not to measure crime but to identify and characterize victims of crime. For example, the most likely victim of personal crime, that is, a crime where the victim and the offender are in contact at the time of the criminal event, is male, 16 to 19 years old, black, living in an urban area, and with a household income under $7,500. (See Table 8.2.) High-income households were more likely to be victims of property crime. However, low-income households are still more likely to be victims of burglary, the most invasive of the property crimes.

TABLE 8.2

ESTIMATED RATE (PER 1,000 PERSONS AGE 12 AND OVER) OF PERSONAL VICTIMIZATION IN THE UNITED STATES, BY TYPE OF CRIME AND SELECTED CHARACTERISTICS OF VICTIM: 1994

VICTIM CHARACTERISTICS	ALL CRIME	TYPE OF CRIME							PERSONAL THEFT
		CRIMES OF VIOLENCE							
		ALL CRIMES OF VIOLENCE	RAPE/ SEXUAL ASSAULT	ROBBERY	ASSAULT				
					TOTAL	AGGRAVATED	SIMPLE		
SEX									
MALE	61.7	59.6	0.2	8.1	51.3	15.3	35.9		2.0
FEMALE	45.1	42.5	3.7	4.1	34.7	8.1	26.6		2.5
AGE									
12–15 YEARS	117.4	114.8	3.1	12.0	99.7	22.2	77.6		2.6
16–19 YEARS	125.9	121.7	5.1	11.8	104.8	33.7	71.1		4.2
20–24 YEARS	102.5	99.2	5.0	11.3	82.9	26.6	56.4		3.3
25–34 YEARS	63.2	60.9	2.9	7.5	50.6	13.7	36.9		2.3
35–49 YEARS	41.4	39.5	1.6	5.2	32.8	7.6	25.2		1.9
50–64 YEARS	16.8	15.1	0.2*	2.3	12.6	3.3	9.3		1.7
65 YEARS AND OLDER	7.2	5.1	0.1*	1.4	3.6	1.2	2.4		2.1
RACE									
WHITE	51.5	49.4	1.9	4.8	42.7	10.9	31.8		2.1
BLACK	65.4	61.8	2.7	14.0	45.0	16.6	28.4		3.6
OTHER	49.1	47.6	2.5*	9.0	36.1	11.9	24.2		1.6*
ETHNICITY									
HISPANIC	63.3	59.8	2.6	9.8	47.4	16.2	31.2		3.5
NON-HISPANIC	51.9	49.8	2.0	5.6	42.1	11.1	31.0		2.1
HOUSEHOLD INCOME									
UNDER $7,500	88.3	83.6	6.7	11.1	65.8	20.5	45.3		4.7
$7,500–$14,999	60.8	58.6	3.3	7.1	48.1	13.8	34.3		2.2
$15,000–$24,999	51.7	49.9	2.3	5.9	41.7	13.2	28.5		1.8
$25,000–$34,999	51.3	49.3	1.2	4.6	43.5	11.3	32.3		2.0
$35,000–$49,999	49.3	46.8	0.9	4.8	41.1	10.1	31.0		2.6
$50,000–$74,999	47.6	46.1	0.8	4.2	41.1	9.5	31.6		1.5
$75,000 AND OVER	42.7	40.0	0.9*	4.5	34.6	8.0	26.5		2.7
RESIDENCE									
URBAN	67.6	63.6	2.7	10.9	50.1	14.8	35.2		4.0
SUBURBAN	51.8	49.6	1.8	5.1	42.7	11.0	31.7		2.2
RURAL	39.8	39.2	1.7	2.6	34.9	9.2	25.8		0.6

* ESTIMATE IS BASED ON ABOUT 10 OR FEWER SAMPLE CASES.

Source: U. S. Department of Justice, Bureau of Justice Statistics, *Criminal Victimization 1994*, Bulletin NCJ-158022 (Washington, DC: U. S. Department of Justice, April 1996), 4.

FIGURE 8.2

VIOLENT CRIME RATES IN THE UNITED STATES, BY COUNTY: 1996

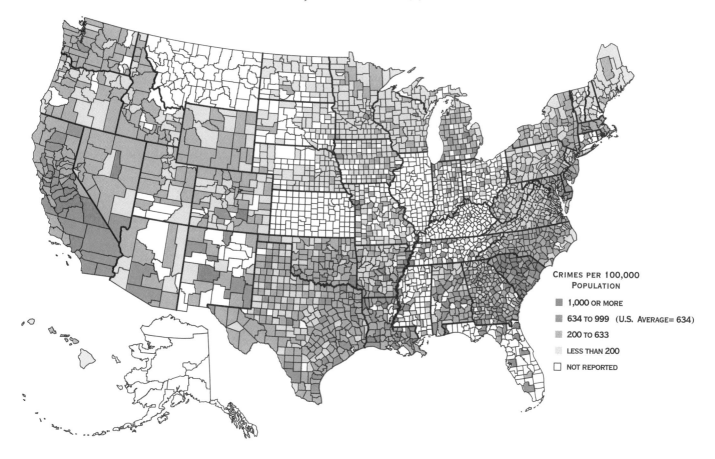

CRIMES PER 100,000 POPULATION

- 1,000 OR MORE
- 634 TO 999 (U.S. AVERAGE= 634)
- 200 TO 633
- LESS THAN 200
- NOT REPORTED

Source: Federal Bureau of Investigation.

CRIME DISTRIBUTION

Since the last year of the Eisenhower administration, the rate of serious crime in the United States, as defined by the FBI's UCR, has increased almost threefold. Violent crime has increased by almost a factor of four. However, this increase was not constant, as there was a sharp drop (18 percent) between 1980 and 1984, and between 1991 and 1996 there was a 16 percent drop in violent crime and a 14 percent decrease in serious crime. Violent crime has tended to follow the same pattern as property crime, but with much less exaggerated changes. Preliminary FBI figures indicate that crime has continued to decrease in 1997. Total index crime for the first 6 months of 1997 was 4 percent lower than the same period in the preceding year; violent crime was 5 percent lower, and property crime 4 percent lower.

Crime is not distributed evenly around the country. For example, Figure 8.2 shows that states such as California, and populous counties around the country have violent crime rates well above the average for the country as a whole. A few states such as South Carolina have an inexplicably high rate. A new, improved reporting system being introduced by the FBI has resulted in several states not being able to report for 1996.

ARRESTS

Table 8.3 shows the number of arrests in the United States in 1995 for various offenses. In addition to showing the types of offenses reflected in the Crime Index, the table shows all of the other offenses for which arrests were made, except for traffic offenses. Driving under the influence is not considered a simple traffic offense and is included on the list of offenses. The total of drug abuse violations shows up here and is second only to the index crime of larceny-theft in the number of arrests. The UCR arrest data do not differentiate between drug possession and trafficking.

TABLE 8.3

ESTIMATED NUMBER OF ARRESTS IN THE UNITED STATES, BY OFFENSE CHARGED: 1995

OFFENSE CHARGED	NUMBER OF ARRESTS
TOTAL 2	15,119,800
MURDER AND NONNEGLIGENT MANSLAUGHTER	21,230
FORCIBLE RAPE	34,650
ROBBERY	171,870
AGGRAVATED ASSAULT	568,480
BURGLARY	386,500
LARCENY-THEFT	1,530,200
MOTOR VEHICLE THEFT	191,900
ARSON	20,000
VIOLENT CRIME 3	796,250
PROPERTY CRIME 4	2,128,600
TOTAL CRIME INDEX 5	2,924,800
OTHER ASSAULTS	1,290,400
FORGERY AND COUNTERFEITING	122,300
FRAUD	436,400
EMBEZZLEMENT	15,200
STOLEN PROPERTY; BUYING, RECEIVING, POSSESSING	166,500
VANDALISM	311,100
WEAPONS; CARRYING, POSSESSING, ETC.	243,900
PROSTITUTION AND COMMERCIALIZED VICE	97,700
SEX OFFENSES (EXCEPT FORCIBLE RAPE AND PROSTITUTION)	94,500
DRUG ABUSE VIOLATIONS	1,476,100
GAMBLING	19,500
OFFENSES AGAINST FAMILY AND CHILDREN	142,900
DRIVING UNDER THE INFLUENCE	1,436,000
LIQUOR LAWS	594,900
DRUNKENNESS	708,100
DISORDERLY CONDUCT	748,600
VAGRANCY	25,900
ALL OTHER OFFENSES (EXCEPT TRAFFIC)	3,865,400
SUSPICION (NOT INCLUDED IN TOTAL)	12,100
CURFEW AND LOITERING LAW VIOLATIONS	149,800
RUNAWAYS	249,500

1 ARREST TOTALS BASED ON ALL REPORTING AGENCIES AND ESTIMATES FOR UNREPORTED AREAS.

2 BECAUSE OF ROUNDING, FIGURES MAY NOT ADD TO TOTAL.

3 VIOLENT CRIMES ARE OFFENSES OF MURDER AND NON-NEGLIGENT MANSLAUGHTER, FORCIBLE RAPE, ROBBERY, AND AGGRAVATED ASSAULT.

4 PROPERTY CRIMES ARE OFFENSES OF BURGLARY, LARCENY- THEFT, MOTOR VEHICLE THEFT, AND ARSON.

5 INCLUDES ARSON.

Source: U. S. Department of Justice, Federal Bureau of Investigation, Crime in the United States, 1995 (Washington, DC: USGPO, 1996), p. 208.

FIGURE 8.3

PERCENTAGE DISTRIBUTION OF TOTAL U.S. POPULATION AND PERSONS ARRESTED FOR ALL OFFENSES, BY AGE: 1995

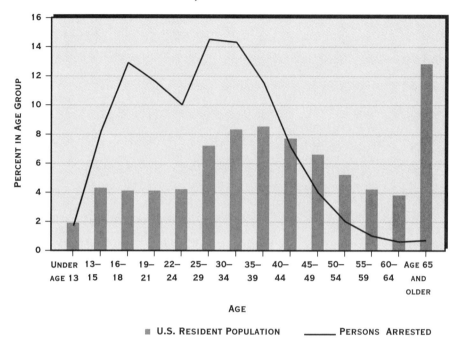

■ U.S. RESIDENT POPULATION ——— PERSONS ARRESTED

Note: This table presents data from all law enforcement agencies submitting complete reports for 12 months in 1995. Because of rounding, percentages may not add to 100.

Source: U. S. Department of Justice, Federal Bureau of Investigation, Crime in the United States, 1995 (Washington, DC: USGPO, 1996), pp. 218, 219; and "U.S. Population Estimates by Age, Sex, Race and Hispanic Origin: 1990 to 1996," Washington, DC: U.S. Bureau of the Census, 1997.

Crime is a young person's game. Figure 8.3 shows the percentage of the total population in each age group compared with the percentage of persons arrested in each age category. From age 13 to age 40 the percentage of arrestees is considerably higher than their proportion in the population.

DOES CRIME PAY?

Figure 8.4 shows that the pattern of arrests from 1971 to 1995 was much less variable than was the incidence of crime in a comparable period. (See Figure 8.5.) This was especially true for property crime. The difference between these two figures shows the large number of crimes that do not result in an arrest.

FIGURE 8.4

ARREST RATES IN THE UNITED STATES, BY TYPE OF OFFENSE: 1971–1995

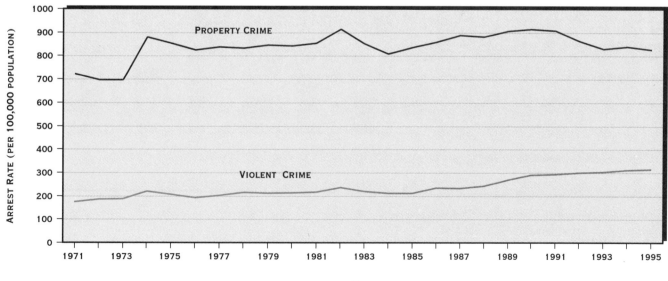

Source: Bureau of Justice Statistics. Sourcebook of Criminal Justice Statistics 1996.

FIGURE 8.5

CRIME RATE IN THE UNITED STATES, BY TYPE OF OFFENSE: 1960–1996

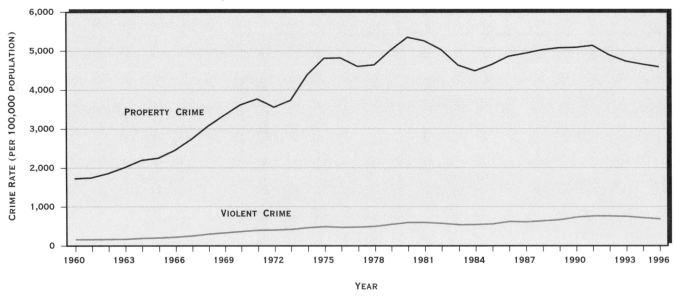

Source: Bureau of Justice Statistics. Sourcebook of Criminal Justice Statistics 1996.

The differences reflected in these figures between the number of crimes and the rate of arrests are consistent with data on crimes cleared by arrest. Figure 8.6 shows the clearance rates for index crimes in 1996. Even though the clearance rate for robbery is relatively low, the clearance rates for all of the crimes of violence are higher than for the property crimes. "To clear" is roughly equivalent to "to solve." Thus, we discover that most crimes in the United States are not solved. Although the clearance rate for murder is higher than any other, more than 30 percent of murders still go unsolved. Robbery and the property crimes—burglary, larceny, and motor vehicle theft—show extremely low clearance rates, probably because robbery is generally a stranger-to-stranger crime and property crimes are surreptitious and do not involve face-to-face contact between the offender and the victim.

CONVICTIONS AND SENTENCES

The criminal justice system in the United States divides the responsibility for judicial processing and corrections between state and local jurisdictions and the federal government. Many offenses are under federal jurisdiction, such as serious crimes that

FIGURE 8.6

OFFENSES IN THE UNITED STATES CLEARED BY ARREST, BY TYPE OF OFFENSE: 1996

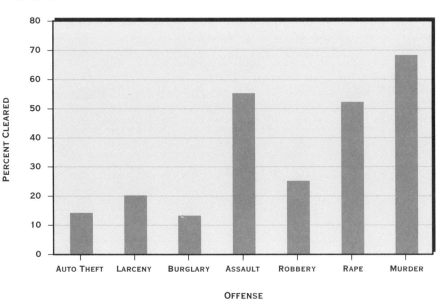

Source: Bureau of Justice Statistics. Sourcebook of Criminal Justice Statistics 1996.

FIGURE 8.7

NUMBER OF DEFENDANTS CHARGED WITH VIOLATIONS OF DRUG LAWS IN U.S. DISTRICT COURTS: 1945–1996

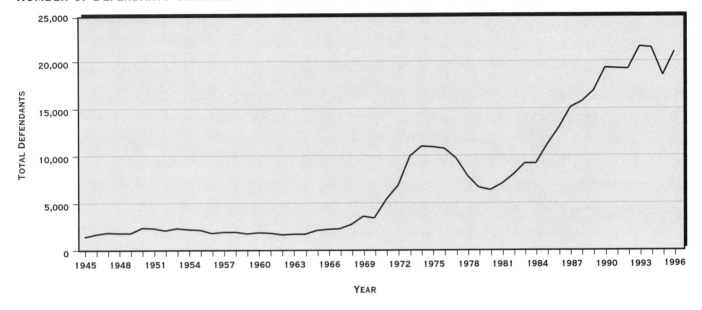

Source: Bureau of Justice Statistics. Sourcebook of Criminal Justice Statistics 1996.

FIGURE 8.8

AVERAGE SENTENCE FOR VIOLATION OF DRUG LAWS IN U.S. DISTRICT COURTS: 1945–1996

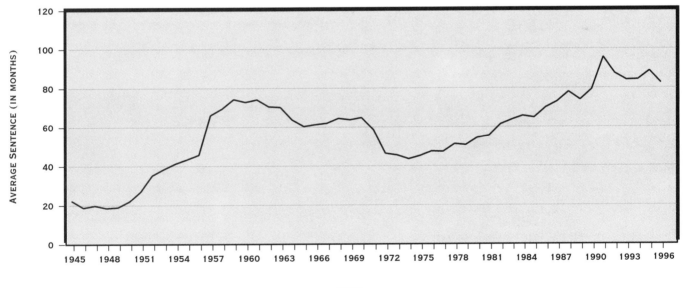

Source: Bureau of Justice Statistics. Sourcebook of Criminal Justice Statistics 1996.

TABLE 8.4

AVERAGE MAXIMUM LENGTH OF FELONY SENTENCES IMPOSED BY U.S. STATE AND FEDERAL COURTS, BY TYPE OF OFFENSE: 1994

(IN MONTHS)

| MOST SERIOUS CONVICTION OFFENSE | TOTAL | MAXIMUM SENTENCE LENGTH FOR FELONS SENTENCED TO: | | |
| | | INCARCERATION | | STRAIGHT PROBATION |
		PRISON	JAIL	
AVERAGE SENTENCE				
ALL OFFENSES	49	71	6	40
VIOLENT OFFENSES	93	118	6	45
MURDER [1]	262	269	7	59
RAPE	133	158	7	60
ROBBERY	104	116	9	51
AGGRAVATED ASSAULT	54	79	6	42
OTHER VIOLENT [2]	47	70	6	43
PROPERTY OFFENSES	39	57	6	42
BURGLARY	52	69	7	47
LARCENY [3]	29	45	6	40
FRAUD [4]	32	51	5	41
DRUG OFFENSES	40	61	6	38
POSSESSION	28	50	4	37
TRAFFICKING	48	66	7	40
WEAPONS OFFENSES	31	47	5	32
OTHER OFFENSES [5]	26	41	5	36
MEDIAN SENTENCE				
ALL OFFENSES	24	48	4	36
VIOLENT OFFENSES	60	72	6	36
MURDER [1]	300	300	6	60
RAPE	84	120	6	48
ROBBERY	72	84	9	48
AGGRAVATED ASSAULT	36	54	4	36
OTHER VIOLENT [2]	24	48	5	36
PROPERTY OFFENSES	24	42	4	36
BURGLARY	36	49	6	36
LARCENY [3]	16	36	4	36
FRAUD [4]	23	36	3	36
DRUG OFFENSES	24	48	4	30
POSSESSION	12	36	3	24
TRAFFICKING	36	48	6	36
WEAPONS OFFENSES	18	36	4	24
OTHER OFFENSES [5]	12	30	3	30

[1] INCLUDES NONNEGLIGENT MANSLAUGHTER.

[2] INCLUDES OFFENSES SUCH AS NEGLIGENT MANSLAUGHTER, SEXUAL ASSAULT, AND KIDNAPPING.

[3] INCLUDES MOTOR VEHICLE THEFT.

[4] INCLUDES FORGERY AND EMBEZZLEMENT.

[5] COMPOSED OF NONVIOLENT OFFENSES SUCH AS RECEIVING STOLEN PROPERTY AND VANDALISM.

Source: U. S. Department of Justice, Bureau of Justice Statistics, *Sourcebook of Criminal Justice Statistics 1996.*

Note: The median sentence is the sentence length that marks the point below which 50 percent of all sentence lengths fall. Average exclude sentences to death or to life in prison. Sentence length data were available for 834,124 cases sentenced to incarceration or probation.

take place on federal property, or are related to national issues only, such as violations of antitrust or customs laws. There are other crimes that have been turned into federal crimes by statute, such as the drug laws. Both states and the federal government have an interest in many of the same offenses. In general, where the state and federal interest are the same, the federal government has the jurisdictional option in individual cases.

The focus of federal interest has recently been on the prosecution of drug laws. The number of drug law defendants in 1996 totaled almost 15 times the number of such defendants at the end of World War II (1945). (See Figure 8.7.) The total number of federal cases has increased by 130 percent. Fifty-one percent of all offenders convicted in federal courts in 1982 were sent to prison. In 1992 the percentage had risen to 66. The average length of prison sentences increased from 48 months to 63 months during that same period. Sentences for drug law violations have also become more stringent. In 1982, 74 percent of persons convicted of violation of federal drug laws were sent to prison, but by 1992 that number had risen to 89 percent. (See Figure 8.8.) The actual number of persons convicted of federal drug offenses more than tripled during that period, from 5,139 to 16,757. The average sentence increased from 55 months to 80 months. From 1945 to 1995, the average prison sentence for drug offenses went from 22 months to 89 months.

Although a significant number of crimes involve the federal system, crime is still basically a state problem: more than 95 percent of all felony convictions took place in state courts in 1994. (See Table 8.4.) Sentencing patterns differ considerably between state and federal courts. Overall, an offender is more likely to be sentenced to prison in the federal system—66 percent in federal court versus 45 percent in state court. However, a prison sentence in state court is likely to be longer than in federal court. The average felony sentence in federal court is 61 months compared with 71 in state courts. For violent offenses the difference is 118 months in state court and 88 in the federal system. The situation is reversed for drug offenses, for which the average federal sentence is 80 months versus 61 months in state courts.

The huge majority of offenders convicted in state courts in 1994—85 percent—were male. For violent offenses, the percentage increases to 92 percent. The racial division is 51 percent White and 48 percent Black overall. However, the percentage is exactly reversed for all violent crimes. Over 60 percent of all offenders convicted of murder were Black, and 64 percent of rape offenders were White. Seventy-one percent of persons convicted of robbery were Black. In 1996, for every crime category, the average length of felony sentences were markedly greater for blacks than for whites.

FIGURE 8.9

AVERAGE MAXIMUM LENGTH OF FELONY SENTENCES IMPOSED BY U.S. STATE COURTS, BY RACE/HISPANIC ORIGIN FOR SELECTED OFFENSES: 1996

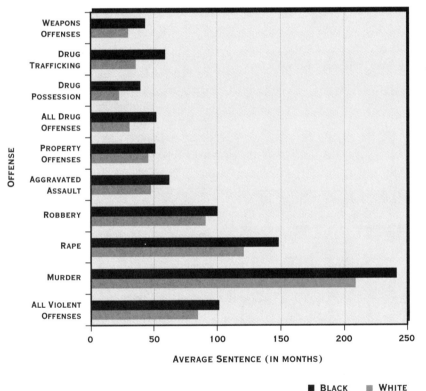

Source: United States Department of Justice, Bureau of Justice Statistics, Felony Sentences in State Courts 1996.

CORRECTIONS

The corrections system in the United States consists principally of prisons, jails, probation, and parole. Prisons are the institutions generally designed to house convicted felons and are generally managed by the federal or state governments. Jails are generally locally run and are designed to house misdemeanants with sentences of a year or less, persons being held awaiting trial, and others in temporary or short-term situations. In recent years jails have also been used to house the overflow from an overcrowded prison system. Parole is the process by which prison inmates are released before their full sentence is completed. The inmate remains under the supervision of the correctional system, usually until his original sentence is completed. Probation, either supervised or unsupervised, generally is a sentence given in lieu of either prison or jail. However, there are occasions, usually at a judge's discretion, in which the offender is given a combination of incarceration and probation.

The number of adults in custody of state or federal prisons or local jails has increased sharply. The number in federal prisons increased 260 percent between 1980 and 1994, during which period the state prison population increased by 209 percent and local jails increased by 165 percent. There was also a 165 percent increase in the number of adults on probation, and a 213 percent increase in the number on parole during the same period. According to one account, this growth in the prison population and the commensurate growth in the number of prisons constitute a new growth industry.[4] Since 1990, the number of jails and prisons has increased by about 30 percent to more than 600,000. Cities and towns are beginning to compete for new prisons with their eyes on the number of jobs prisons generate.

---

4 Scott Butterfield, "Punitive Damages: Crime Keeps Falling, but Prisons Keep on Filling," *New York Times*, 28 September 1997.

FIGURE 8.10

PERSONS UNDER CORRECTIONAL SUPERVISION IN THE UNITED STATES: 1980–1994

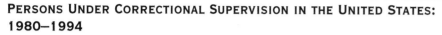
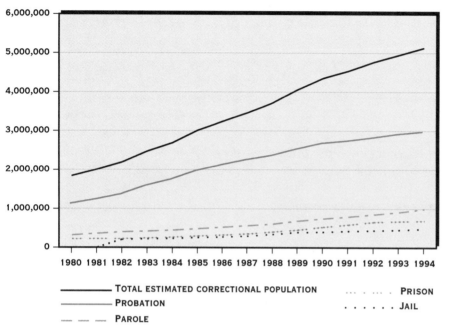

Source: Bureau of Justice Statistics. Sourcebook of Criminal Justice Statistics 1996.

FIGURE 8.11

MALES IN PRISON IN THE UNITED STATES, BY RACE: 1985–1994

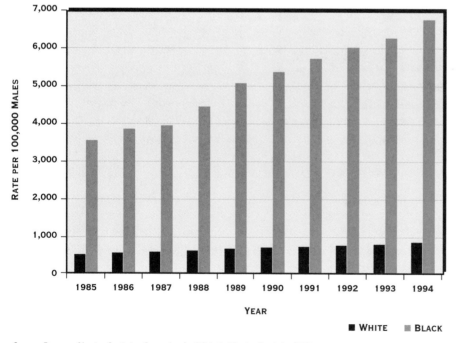

Source: Bureau of Justice Statistics. Sourcebook of Criminal Justice Statistics 1996.

This increase in the prison population is having a profound impact on many neighborhoods, especially in the inner cities. Figure 8.11 shows the incarceration rate per 100,000 for White and Black males. That figure shows that, for every 100,000 White males, 860 were incarcerated in 1994, while, for every 100,000 Black males, 6,753 were incarcerated. The White male rate increased by 63 percent between 1985 and 1994. The Black rate increased by 91 percent. The racial differences are similar for women, but they start from a much lower base. (See Figure 8.12.)

EXPENDITURES

Expenditures in all parts of the criminal justice system and at all levels of government have been rising steadily. In 1993, $97.5 billion was expended for criminal justice activities, a 172 percent increase over 1982, not corrected for inflation. During the same period, expenditures for corrections rose 253 percent, with legal and judicial expenditures rising by 178 percent and police protection by 131 percent. Federal expenditures in terms of percentage increase were rising at almost twice the rate of state and local governments, 317 percent versus 163 percent. In 1993, the United States spent $378.39 for every man, woman, and child to maintain the criminal justice system. Of this, $162.05 went to police protection, another $123.93 to corrections, and the balance to the legal and judicial functions.

FIGURE 8.12

FEMALES IN PRISON IN THE UNITED STATES, BY RACE: 1985–1994

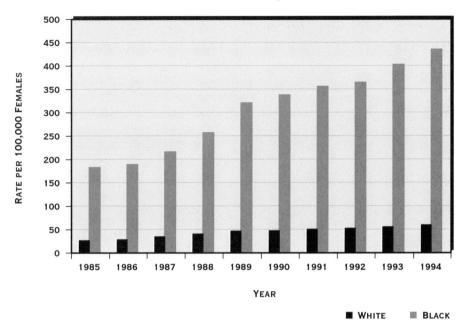

Source: Bureau of Justice Statistics. Sourcebook of Criminal Justice Statistics 1996.

FIGURE 8.13

PERCENTAGE CHANGE IN EXPENDITURES ACTIVITY, BY LEVEL OF GOVERNMENT: 1982–1993

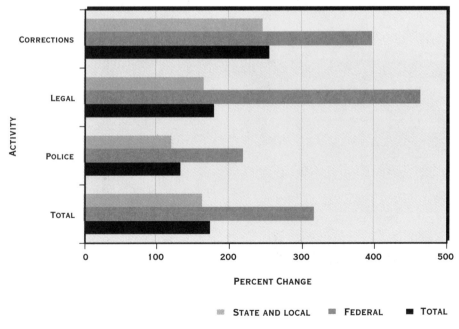

Source: Bureau of Justice Statistics. Sourcebook of Criminal Justice Statistics 1996.

TABLE 8.5

ATTITUDES TOWARD MANDATORY PRISON SENTENCES IN THE UNITED STATES, BY DEMOGRAPHIC CHARACTERISTIC: 1995

QUESTION: "IN RECENT YEARS, SOME LEGISLATURES HAVE MADE IMPRISONMENT MANDATORY FOR CONVICTIONS FOR SOME TYPES OF CRIMES. DO YOU THINK THESE MANDATORY SENTENCES ARE A GOOD IDEA, OR SHOULD JUDGES BE ABLE TO DECIDE WHO GOES TO PRISON AND WHO DOESN'T?"

CHARACTERISTIC	MANDATORY SENTENCES ARE A GOOD IDEA	JUDGES SHOULD DECIDE	BOTH	NEITHER
NATIONAL	52.9	36.4	6.0	1.3
SEX				
MALE	52.2	38.3	5.8	1.0
FEMALE	53.6	34.5	6.1	1.5
RACE				
WHITE	55.0	33.9	6.3	1.1
BLACK	45.7	48.6	3.8	1.9
HISPANIC	43.2	44.6	2.7	2.7
AGE				
18 TO 29 YEARS	47.7	44.6	5.4	0.5
30 TO 39 YEARS	53.4	35.4	9.0	0.4
40 TO 59 YEARS	55.3	35.5	2.8	1.9
60 YEARS AND OLDER	55.2	28.7	6.9	2.9
EDUCATION				
COLLEGE GRADUATE	52.7	39.8	5.4	1.1
SOME COLLEGE	56.6	31.5	6.6	0.3
HIGH SCHOOL GRADUATE	53.5	36.0	6.5	1.5
LESS THAN HIGH SCHOOL GRADUATE	39.6	44.6	5.0	4.0
INCOME				
OVER $60,000	57.0	37.1	5.9	0.0
BETWEEN $30,000 AND $60,000	53.7	35.7	6.1	1.4
BETWEEN $15,000 AND $29,999	56.1	33.1	5.9	2.1
LESS THAN $15,000	45.4	43.7	2.5	2.5
COMMUNITY				
URBAN	43.9	43.3	5.1	1.9
SUBURBAN	57.8	33.1	5.3	0.0
SMALL CITY	46.3	41.5	6.9	2.1
RURAL/ SMALL TOWN	56.4	33.1	6.6	1.3
REGION				
NORTHEAST	47.5	39.0	8.5	1.7
MIDWEST	50.0	38.7	6.7	1.3
SOUTH	59.7	28.9	5.7	1.1
WEST	49.6	43.0	3.7	1.2
POLITICS				
REPUBLICAN	59.7	31.4	6.1	0.7
DEMOCRAT	49.3	39.6	5.7	2.1
INDEPENDENT/ OTHER	51.6	37.6	5.3	1.3

Source: Bureau of Justice Statistics, Sourcebook of Criminal Justice Statistics 1995, page 181.

Note: The "don't know" category has been omitted; therefore percents may not sum to 100.

Although federal percentage increases are much larger than state and local percentage increases, the absolute numbers for states are very high. In 1993, state and local governments spent $29.5 billion on corrections alone. According to one spokesman, for example, "already California and Florida spend more to incarcerate people than to educate their college-age population. In California, where the prison population has grown from 19,000 two decades ago to 150,000 today, the state faces a new crisis, because it is caught between voters' refusal to approve more money for prison construction and an expected new influx of inmates over the next few years as more and more tough sentencing laws take effect."[5]

During the last decade, Congress and many states have begun to pass mandatory sentencing and "truth in sentencing" laws that, in effect, increase the amount of time convicted offenders will remain incarcerated, thus decreasing the number of cells available at any given time. The public seems to support the use of mandatory sentences. In a 1995 survey, about 53 percent of the survey respondents thought mandatory sentences were a good idea compared with 36 percent who felt judges should decide on sentences. (See Table 8.5.) In a survey of police chiefs on drug offenses that was conducted by the Police Foundation, only 7 percent of the nation's police chiefs thought the mandatory sentencing strategy was "very effective" and another 14 percent thought that it was "fairly effective." (See Table 8.6.) In a public survey about proposals to reduce prison overcrowding, 89 percent favored developing programs to keep more nonviolent and first offenders working in the community. In the same survey, 63 percent favored allowing prisoners to earn early release through good behavior and participation in educational and work programs, but 31 percent favored raising taxes to build more prisons. (See Table 8.7.)

Conflating the responses to the above surveys makes it appear that there is a conflict between various American value systems. On the one hand, there is the desire

5 Scott Butterfield, "Punitive Damages: Crime Keeps Falling, but Prisons Keep on Filling," New York Times, 28 September 1997.

to suppress crime and punish criminals. On the other, there is the desire to be fair to first offenders and others who appear to want to work within the system. Although various professionals do not feel that strategies such as mandatory sentences are effective, the public seems to clamor for something to be done. The political establishment appears to be listening, as more and more such laws are being enacted at the state and federal level. Only time will tell if this conflict worsens or tends to resolve itself.

TABLE 8.6

U.S. POLICE CHIEF'S ATTITUDES TOWARD THE EFFECTIVENESS OF MANDATORY MINIMUM SENTENCES FOR DRUG POSSESSION, BY SIZE OF COMMUNITY: 1996

QUESTION: "FROM YOUR PERSPECTIVE, HOW EFFECTIVE HAVE MANDATORY MINIMUM SENTENCES FOR DRUG POSSESSION BEEN IN REDUCING DRUG TRAFFICKING IN YOUR COMMUNITY—VERY EFFECTIVE, FAIRLY EFFECTIVE, ONLY SOMEWHAT EFFECTIVE, OR NOT REALLY THE ANSWER TO THE PROBLEM IN YOUR COMMUNITY?"

| | | | SIZE OF COMMUNITY | |
RESPONSES	ALL POLICE CHIEFS	LARGE CITIES	MEDIUM COMMUNITIES	SMALL TOWNS
VERY EFFECTIVE	7	10	7	6
FAIRLY EFFECTIVE	14	17	8	14
ONLY SOMEWHAT EFFECTIVE	33	31	37	33
NOT REALLY THE ANSWER	40	36	40	42
DON'T HAVE MANDATORY MINIMUM SENTENCING [1]	4	2	5	4
NOT SURE	2	4	3	1

[1] RESPONSE VOLUNTEERED.

Source: Police Foundation and Drug Strategies, Drugs and Crime Across America: Police Chiefs Speak Out (Washington, DC: Police Foundation and Drug Stategies, 1996) p.17. Reprinted in Sourcebook of Criminal Justice Statistics 1996, page 171.

TABLE 8.7

ATTITUDES TOWARD PROPOSALS TO REDUCE PRISON OVERCROWDING IN THE UNITED STATES, BY DEMOGRAPHIC CHARACTERISTIC

QUESTION: "WOULD YOU FAVOR OR OPPOSE EACH OF THE FOLLOWING MEASURES THAT HAVE BEEN SUGGESTED AS WAYS TO REDUCE PRISON OVERCROWDING?"

| | (PERCENT RESPONDING "FAVOR") | | | | |
	SHORTENING SENTENCES	ALLOWING PRISONERS TO EARN EARLY RELEASE THROUGH GOOD BEHAVIOR AND PARTICIPATION IN EDUCATIONAL AND WORK PROGRAMS	DEVELOPING LOCAL PROGRAMS TO KEEP MORE NONVIOLENT AND FIRST-TIME OFFENDERS ACTIVE WORKING IN THE COMMUNITY	GIVING THE PAROLE BOARD MORE AUTHORITY TO RELEASE OFFENDERS EARLY	INCREASING TAXES TO BUILD MORE PRISONS
NATIONAL	7.5	63.2	89.2	20.3	31.4
SEX					
MALE	10.7	70.7	88.0	26.2	34.5
FEMALE	4.4	56.3	90.4	14.8	28.6
RACE					
WHITE	6.2	63.1	88.1	17.8	33.9
BLACK	15.4	69.2	96.2	35.6	21.0
HISPANIC	5.5	60.0	91.9	23.0	24.7

Source: Bureau of Justice Statistics, Sourcebook of Criminal Justice Statistics 1995, page 179

FOR FURTHER INFORMATION SEE:

U.S. DEPARTMENT OF JUSTICE, BUREAU OF JUSTICE STATISTICS. *THE SOURCEBOOK OF CRIMINAL JUSTICE STATISTICS.* 1996.

U.S. DEPARTMENT OF JUSTICE, FEDERAL BUREAU OF INVESTIGATION. *CRIME IN THE UNITED STATES.* WASHINGTON, DC: GPO, 1996.

WEBSITES:

BUREAU OF JUSTICE STATISTICS WEBSITE AT <HTTP://OJP.USDOJ.GOV/BJS>.

FEDERAL BUREAU OF INVESTIGATION WEBSITE AT <HTTP://WWW.FBI.GOV>.

SOURCEBOOK OF CRIMINAL JUSTICE STATISTICS WEBSITE AT <HTTP://WWW.ALBANY.EDU/SOURCEBOOK.>

INTER-UNIVERSITY CONSORTIUM FOR POLITICAL AND SOCIAL RESEARCH (ICPSR) WEBSITE AT <HTTP://WWW.ICPSR.UMICH.EDU/INDEX.HTML>.

FEDERAL BUREAU OF PRISONS WEBSITE AT <HTTP://WWW.BOP.GOV>.

CHAPTER 9

Voting

RICHARD W. DODGE

VOTING

PERCENTAGE OF THE VOTING AGE POPULATION REGISTERED TO VOTE IN 1996:	73.0 PERCENT
PERCENTAGE OF PERSONS 18 YEARS AND OVER WHO VOTED FOR PRESIDENT*—	
1960:	63.1 PERCENT
1996:	49.1 PERCENT
PERCENTAGE OF PERSONS 18 YEARS AND OVER WHO VOTED IN 1996—	
WOMEN:	55.5 PERCENT
MEN:	52.8 PERCENT
PERSONS 65 YEARS AND OVER:	67.0 PERCENT
PERSONS 18–24 YEARS OLD:	32.4 PERCENT
WHITES:	56.0 PERCENT
BLACKS:	50.6 PERCENT
COLLEGE GRADUATES:	72.6 PERCENT
HIGH SCHOOL GRADUATES, NO COLLEGE:	49.1 PERCENT
STATE WITH HIGHEST PERCENT VOTING IN 1996:	MAINE (71.9 PERCENT)
STATE WITH LOWEST PERCENT VOTING IN 1996:	NEVADA (38.3 PERCENT)
PERCENTAGE OF CONTRIBUTIONS FOR CONGRESSIONAL AND SENATORIAL CANDIDATES FROM POLITICAL ACTION COMMITTEES (PACS) IN 1996:	25.5 PERCENT

* Data applies to all persons age 18 years and over.

ELIGIBILITY TO VOTE

The right to vote to elect the president, Congress, and local officials was restricted to a minority of the adult population in the United States until the 20th century: women did not gain the right to vote until 1920. Indeed, prior to this century the voting franchise was generally limited to White males. Initially, some of the states (especially in New England) required religious tests, and others required ownership of property in order to be eligible to vote. Since eligibility was determined by each state, the removal of these requirements was uneven, although they had largely disappeared by the time of the Civil War. In the aftermath of that war, Congress enacted constitutional amendments to elevate the status of former slaves to full citizenship, which included the right to vote (15th Amendment to the U.S. Constitution, enacted in 1870).

The greatest expansion of the electorate was the inclusion of females, which began in 1869 when Wyoming Territory gave women the vote. By the time the 19th Amendment was added to the Constitution in 1920, 15 states had granted women full suffrage. That amendment extended eligibility to all women, regardless of residence. After the Civil War, the attempts of Blacks to register and vote were often frustrated, especially in the South, by devices such as poll taxes and literacy tests, the latter being especially susceptible to manipulation by unsympathetic electoral officials.

Efforts to overturn discrimination against Black citizens who tried to exercise their right to vote culminated in the 24th Amendment to the U.S. Constitution in 1964. That amendment prohibited the payment of poll taxes as a requirement for voting in federal elections. The Voting Rights Act of 1965 and subsequent amendments abolished literacy tests as a prerequisite for voting and reduced the residence requirement for voting in presidential elections to 30 days.

In 1971, the 26th Amendment lowered the voting age for all persons from 21 to 18 years. At the present time, all persons who are 18 years of age or older, who are citizens of the United States, who meet local residence requirements, and who are not convicted felons or mentally incompetent, are eligible to vote in federal elections.

REGISTRATION

In most jurisdictions in the United States, becoming eligible to vote is a two-stage process.[1] First, a person must be registered to vote in order to cast a ballot on election day. Once registered, a person stays on the election rolls as long as he or she lives at the same address and meets the state requirement for frequency of voting (usually at least once every four years).

Barriers to registration have been substantially removed since World War II. Through a combination of constitutional amendments, acts of Congress, and Supreme Court decisions, registration has been greatly simplified. For example, residence requirements were as much as 2 years in some states; but the maximum residence requirement for federal elections is now 30 days. The National Voter Registration Act of 1993 is the most recent attempt to expand the core of registered voters. In the Federal Election

---

1 North Dakota does not have a registration requirement, and five other states permit election day registration in at least some jurisdictions.

Commission's (FEC) report to Congress on the impact of the act (published in June 1997), the FEC noted that there were nearly 143 million persons registered to vote in 1996, representing approximately 73 percent of the voting-age population.[2] Despite a 9.2 million increase in registered voters over 1992, the turnout in the 1996 election was 5 percentage points lower. The largest number of registration applications processed during the 1995–96 period (33 percent) were those generated by state motor vehicle departments, the so-called "motor voter" provisions of the act, whereby voter registration was simultaneously completed while applying for a driver's license. Post card registration accounted for an additional 30 percent of new registrants, registration drives about 26 percent, and 11 percent were received from public assistance agencies and other agencies designated under the law.

TURNOUT IN NATIONAL ELECTIONS

A higher proportion of eligible voters who participate in national elections is considered by some as a measure of the health of the body politic, but this is an oversimplification, since "more is better" is not necessarily indicative of a healthy democratic society. Nazi Germany routinely proclaimed voter turnouts approaching unanimity in the various referenda they conducted. Some countries attempt to guarantee high turnouts by making voting compulsory, fining nonvoters without a valid excuse. However, there is no evidence that these devices promote more beneficial results. On the other hand, an unusually low turnout in a national election would indicate a level of apathy that would be considered unhealthy in a democratic society.

Since the vote was extended to a majority of the population, the highest turnout in

an election in the United States occurred in the presidential election of 1960 when 63 percent of those eligible participated. (See Figure 9.1.) This contrasts with a 49 percent turnout in 1996, a post-World War II low. In the same election when voters choose a president, there is an approximately 5 percentage point drop-off in votes for members of the House of Representatives. Elections for president occur every 4 years (the most recent one in 1996), while elections for the House of Representatives and some local offices occur every 2 years. In elections in nonpresidential years, voting participation tends to be substantially lower, by an average of 13 to 17 percentage points since 1960. This discrepancy results from lower voter interest in these elections due to the absence of the contest for president, plus situations where incumbents are unopposed or where long-time incumbents are perceived to be invulnerable.[3]

FIGURE 9.1

VOTER TURNOUT IN U.S. NATIONAL ELECTIONS: 1960–1996

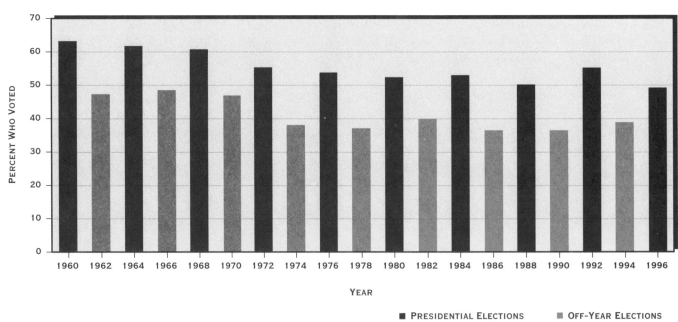

■ PRESIDENTIAL ELECTIONS   ■ OFF-YEAR ELECTIONS

Source: Federal Election Commision, "National Voter Turnout in Federal Elections: 1960-1996." internet site <www.fec.gov>

---

2 Federal Election Commission press release on a Report to Congress, *Impact of National Voter Registration Act* (19 June 1997).

3 Survey data such as that presented here from the Census Bureau's *Current Population Survey* or the University of Michigan, Center for Political Studies tend to overestimate voting participation relative to administrative data on votes cast. For a discussion, see *Voting and Registration in the Election of November 1992*, Current Population Reports, Series P-20, no. 466 (Washington, DC: U.S. Bureau of the Census).

FIGURE 9.2

VOTER TURNOUT IN THE UNITED STATES, BY STATE: 1996

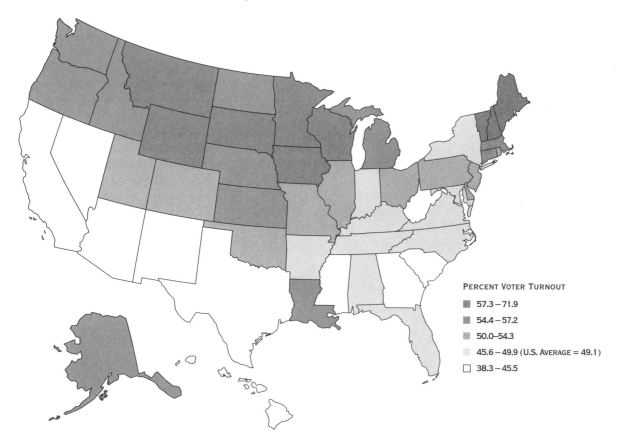

PERCENT VOTER TURNOUT

- 57.3 – 71.9
- 54.4 – 57.2
- 50.0 – 54.3
- 45.6 – 49.9 (U.S. AVERAGE = 49.1)
- 38.3 – 45.5

Source: Federal Election Commission, National Voter Turnout in Federal Elections: 1960–1996 website <http://www.fec.gov>

Voting participation differs substantially among the 50 states. For example, in 1996, Maine achieved the highest turnout at 72 percent, with Nevada bringing up the rear with 38 percent. States below the national average were disproportionately in the South. (See Figure 9.2.) The below-average turnouts for California and New York can be attributed to their sizable populations of noncitizens. Subtracting out estimates of aliens of voting age from the base, turnout for California and New York increases to 56 percent and 54 percent, respectively.

FIGURE 9.3

VOTER TURNOUT IN THE UNITED STATES, BY AGE: 1996

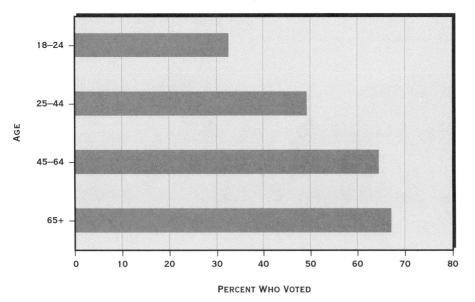

Source: U.S. Bureau of the Census, Current Population Reports, Series P-20, no. 504, "Voting and Registration in the Election of November 1996."

FIGURE 9.4

VOTER TURNOUT IN THE UNITED STATES, BY EDUCATIONAL ATTAINMENT: 1996

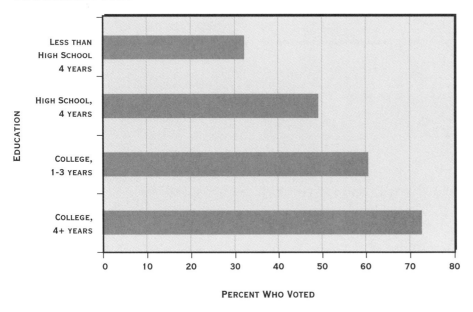

Source: U.S. Bureau of the Census, Current Population Reports, Series P-20, no. 504, "Voting and Registration in the Election of November 1996."

Numerous studies have demonstrated that participation in elections varies by population groups. Although the voting age has been lowered to 18 years, the youngest of the potentially eligible voters (those under age 25) have the lowest turnout. Persons 65 years and older voted at a rate more than twice that of those in the age 18 to 24 category in 1996. (See Figure 9.3.) Two measures that sharply differentiate voting turnout are educational level and income. Those with college degrees or more education and those with high incomes vote at levels that are up to 40 percentage points higher than persons at the opposite ends of the scale (see Figure 9.4). Members of minority groups have traditionally exhibited low electoral participation, although the gap between Blacks and Whites has narrowed since the 1960s as formal and informal barriers to registration and voting have been removed (see Figure 9.5). At first glance, Hispanic voting participation appears to be unusually low (27 percent in 1996). However, an estimated 44 percent of Hispanics 18 years old and older in the United States were noncitizens. Noncitizens are ineligible to vote in national elections in the United States. If noncitizens are excluded from the base, the voting turnout for Hispanics was only a few percentage points below that of Blacks.

Women, despite being enfranchised by the 19th Amendment in 1920, turned out in lower proportions than men until the 1970s. Since 1980, however, somewhat higher proportions of women than men have participated in the electoral process (see Figure 9.6).

Identification with the two major political parties in the United States (Democratic and Republican) has remained relatively constant for the past 25 years. Since 1972, more persons have indicated a preference for the Democratic Party than for the Republicans, although the difference has decreased in recent years. The percentage of persons who report themselves as

FIGURE 9.5

VOTER TURNOUT IN U.S. PRESIDENTIAL ELECTIONS, BY RACE: 1964–1996

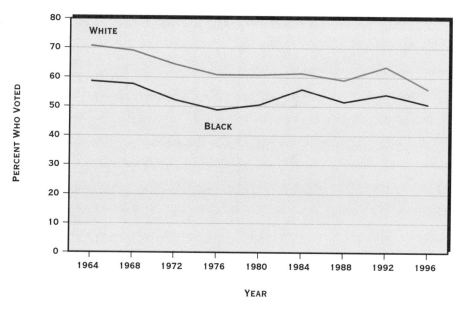

Source: U.S. Bureau of the Census, Current Population Reports, Series P-20, nos. 453, 466, and 504.

Independents has remained essentially the same during this period, even when those who lean toward one of the two major parties is taken into consideration.[4] Similarly, demographic groups have been fairly consistent in their partisan support. Preference for the Republican Party rises with increasing family income and higher educational attainment. On the other hand, Blacks have a strong and continuing attachment to the Democrats. The Democrats can usually count on the support of the youngest age group, but in 1994 there was an essentially even division in party identification among persons between 25 and 55 years of age. Older citizens expressed a strong preference for the Democrats. There has also been a tendency in recent elections for women to prefer the Democrats, whereas men have favored the Republicans.

FIGURE 9.6

VOTER TURNOUT IN U.S. PRESIDENTIAL ELECTIONS, BY SEX: 1964–1996

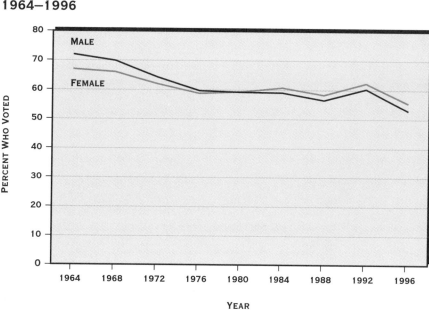

Source: U.S. Bureau of the Census, Current Population Reports, Series P-20, nos. 453, 466, and 504.

---

[4] The Center for Political Studies at the University of Michigan, which originated this concept of "leaning" toward a particular party identification, characterizes the attachment of persons who identify with either Republicans or Democrats as Strong, Weak, or Independent. There is an additional category of True Independents who do not lean toward either of the two parties.

PAYING FOR POLITICAL CAMPAIGNS

U.S. political campaigns have become increasingly expensive over the years, even when inflation is taken into consideration. (See Figure 9.7.) In the 1995–96 election cycle (January 1, 1995, through December 31, 1996), the official party committees (including national, state, and local) raised $638.1 million in federal dollars or "hard money."[5] The Republicans were more successful than the Democrats, raising $416.5 million and spending $408.5 million. The Democrats' comparable figures were $221.6 million and $214.3 million. In the aftermath of the 1996 election, each party was left with substantial debts, $15 million for the Republicans and $17.4 million for the Democrats. The Republican total of funds raised represented a 57 percent increase over the previous presidential election cycle, whereas the Democrats received 36 percent above previous levels. For both parties, the great majority of these hard money funds came from individual contributions, 87 percent for the Republicans and 77 percent for the Democrats. The remaining funds came principally from political action committees (PACs) and from the candidates themselves, in the form of either loans or gifts.

Contributions of nonfederal funds have also increased substantially in recent years. This money (popularly referred to as "soft money") is used to support the candidacy of state and local aspirants for office and to pay for the generic expenses associated with issue advocacy and party-building (e.g., get-out-the-vote drives), activities that benefit both federal and nonfederal candidates. There has been recent controversy over the fact that these funds have increasingly been diverted to advertising for the benefit of party candidates, especially presidential nominees. In so doing, these activities appear to violate the intent of campaign finance laws that banned contributions to presidential nominees who accept public funding. Individuals may,

FIGURE 9.7

FUNDS RAISED BY U.S. NATIONAL POLITICAL COMMITTEES, BY ELECTION CYCLE: 1970–80 AND 1995–96

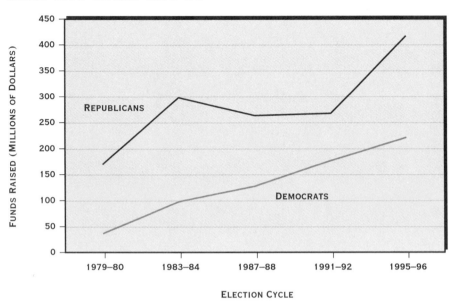

Source: Federal Election Commission, "FEC Reports Major Increase in Party Activity for 1995-96," press release March 19, 1997; website at <http://www.fec.gov>.

however, contribute up to $1,000 to a candidate's compliance fund, which helps to pay legal and accounting expenses incurred in conjunction with the campaign finance law. Independent expenditures, either for or against a specific presidential candidate, also do not count as a contribution within the meaning of the law as long as they are not made "with the cooperation or prior consent of, or in consultation with or at the request or suggestion of, any candidate or authorized committee or agent of a candidate."[6] The law also provides for the expenditure of funds by national party committees on behalf of their presidential nominees. These are called "coordinated party expenditures" and are limited by a formula that authorized the expenditure of approximately $12 million by each party in 1996. As the name implies, these funds are expended in consultation with the presidential nominee, but the funds are not transferred to the candidate or the cam-

paign committee. Coordinated party expenditures may also be made for the benefit of other candidates for federal office.

Receipts from soft money contributions to both political parties in the 1995–96 cycle increased about 200 percent over the 1992 figures, from $86 million to $262 million. The Republican Party led in both receipts and expenditures, with $138 million and $150 million, respectively, compared with the Democrats' $124 million and $122 million. These totals comprise funds handled by the national committees, the senatorial campaign committees, and the congressional campaign committees.

Because of the clamor aroused by the role of soft money in the 1996 presidential campaign, President Clinton appointed two respected public officials, former Republican Senator from Kansas Nancy Kassebaum Baker and former Democratic Vice-President Walter F. Mondale, to make

---

[5] The term "hard money" means money raised directly for candidates for federal office in accordance with the requirements of campaign finance laws.

[6] Federal Election Commission, *Campaign Guide for Political Party Committees* (August 1996), 83.

recommendations on the subject. Their first act was to call for a ban on soft money coupled with rules for enforcement.[7]

In addition to the political parties, individual candidates for the House and Senate raised a total of $790.5 million and spent $765.3 million, representing increases of 20 percent and 12 percent, respectively, over the 2-year period 1991–92. Contributions from individuals made up 56 percent of the total, contributions from PACs amounted to 25 percent, candidates gave 13 percent through gifts and loans, and the remainder came from various sources such as candidate committees, partnerships, and the political parties (see Figure 9.8).

In 1995–96, PACs raised a total of $437.4 million and spent $429.9 million. Of these amounts, PACs contributed $217.8 million to federal candidates during

this period, of which $201.4 million was for candidates currently running for the House and Senate. This compares with $188.9 million raised in 1991–92 and $60.2 million in 1979–80. Republicans received somewhat more PAC money than Democrats in 1995–96, $118.2 million compared with $98.9 million.

Paying for political campaigns out of public funds was first proposed by President Theodore Roosevelt in his 1907 State of the Union message. However, legislation to finance presidential election campaigns with tax dollars was not enacted until 1971. The law establishes a formula for determining the amounts to be granted to the presidential nominees of the two major parties. There is a basic grant of $20 million plus a cost-of-living adjustment. This resulted in a grant of $21.8 million to each major candidate in 1976, the first

presidential election to be affected by the law. For the 1996 general election campaign, each major party candidate received $61.8 million. Provision is also made for financing the campaigns of minor party candidates (those receiving between 5 percent and 25 percent of the average of the popular vote received by the two major parties in the previous election) and new party candidates. The latter qualify for partial public funding after the election if they received at least 5 percent of the average of the popular vote received by the two major parties in that election. Money is also available on a matching basis for presidential primary campaigns. Individuals may contribute up to $1,000 to a candidate in the presidential primaries and the government will match up to $250 of this amount. The national spending limit for the presidential primaries in 1996 was $30.9 million. The national nominating conventions of the two major parties are also eligible for public funding, which amounted to $12.4 million for each party in 1996.

Public funding of the presidential election process (primaries, conventions, and the general election) is financed by a voluntary $3 checkoff on individual income tax returns, raised from the original amount of $1 in 1993. Taxpayers do not earmark which candidate they want their money to support but that they wish $3 of their taxes to be allocated to the general election fund. Candidates who agree to accept public funding cannot accept private contributions but may contribute up to $50,000 of their own money. Although individuals may not contribute to a publicly funded presidential candidate, they may allot up to $1,000 to a compliance fund, as previously mentioned.

FIGURE 9.8

CONTRIBUTIONS TO CANDIDATES FOR THE U.S. SENATE AND HOUSE OF REPRESENTATIVES: 1995–1996

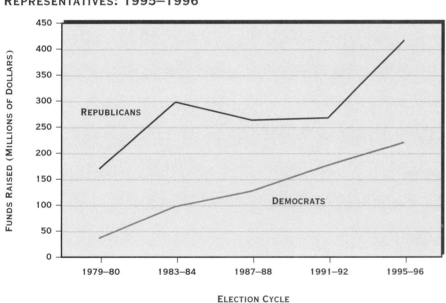

Source: Federal Election Commission, "FEC Reports Major Increase in Party Activity for 1995-96," press release March 19, 1997; website at <http://www.fec.gov>.

---

[7] Editorial, *Washington Post* (18 July 1997).

FOR FURTHER INFORMATION SEE:

BRACE, KIMBALL W., ET AL. *THE ELECTION DATA BOOK: 1992.* LANHAM, MD: BERNAN PRESS, 1993.

NATIONAL ARCHIVES AND RECORDS ADMINISTRATION, OFFICE OF THE FEDERAL REGISTER. *THE UNITED STATES GOVERNMENT MANUAL:1997/98.* LANHAM, MD: BERNAN PRESS, 1997.

VOTING AND REGISTRATION IN THE ELECTION OF NOVEMBER 1996. CURRENT POPULATION REPORTS, SERIES P-20, NO. 504. WASHINGTON, DC: U.S. BUREAU OF THE CENSUS. EARLIER ELECTION DATA ARE IN P-20 SERIES ALSO.

U.S. BUREAU OF THE CENSUS. *STATISTICAL ABSTRACT OF THE UNITED STATES: 1997.* (117TH) EDITION. WASHINGTON, DC: U.S. BUREAU OF THE CENSUS, 1997.

WEBSITES:

FEDERAL ELECTION COMMISSION WEBSITE AT <HTTP://WWW.FEC.GOV>.

U.S. BUREAU OF THE CENSUS WEBSITE AT <HTTP://WWW.CENSUS.GOV>.

NATIONAL ELECTION STUDIES AT THE UNIVERSITY OF MICHIGAN WEBSITE AT <HTTP://WWW.UMICH.EDU/~NES>.

CHAPTER 10

Leisure, Volunteerism, and Religiosity

MARK S. LITTMAN

LEISURE

AVERAGE AMOUNT OF FREE TIME PER WEEK IN 1985—	
MEN:	40 HOURS
WOMEN:	39 HOURS
CHANGE IN AVERAGE FREE TIME PER WEEK SINCE 1965—	
MEN:	+5 HOURS
WOMEN:	+5 HOURS
AVERAGE AMOUNT OF FREE TIME SPENT WATCHING TV:	40 PERCENT
PERCENT OF OLDER AMERICANS WHO WALKED FOR EXERCISE, 1994:	38 PERCENT
PERCENT OF OLDER AMERICANS WHO SWAM FOR EXERCISE, 1994:	14 PERCENT
PERCENT OF ADULTS REPORTING HOME IMPROVEMENT AS A LEISURE ACTIVITY, 1992:	48 PERCENT
PERCENT OF HIGH SCHOOL SENIORS PARTICIPATING IN EXTRACURRICULAR ACTIVITIES, 1992:	80 PERCENT
AVERAGE HOUSEHOLD EXPENDITURES ON ENTERTAINMENT AND READING, 1994:	$1,700
AVERAGE HOUSEHOLD EXPENDITURES ON ENTERTAINMENT AND READING AS A PERCENT OF TOTAL HOUSEHOLD EXPENDITURES—	
1985:	5.6 PERCENT
1994:	5.5 PERCENT

TRENDS IN LEISURE TIME

What do Americans do with their non-working, or in the case of children, non-school hours? While most nonwork time is spent in commuting and the everyday tasks of daily living, American males average about 40 hours and women average 39 hours of time per week that could be spent on leisure activities, and between 1965 and 1985, time-use studies indicated that free time is increasing.[1] Such activities can take a variety of forms, from watching television to participating in an athletic pursuit, from volunteer work to singing in the church choir. In eras before the present one, learning was the primary leisure activity.[2]

According to data from time-use studies, Americans used to spend a large fraction of their free time in civic activities such as working for a political party, in attending religious services, or in membership in such organizations as parent-teacher associations and labor unions. Membership in civic groups has declined in the past two decades, as has time spent socializing, visiting, and in church attendance, based on data from the General Social Survey and the Gallup Poll. What has increased considerably is time spent watching television. Depending on the study, Americans on average spend between 2 and 3 hours a day watching television, or approximately 40 percent of their free time. One author feels the two (declining civic association and watching television) are causally related.[3] There is a large gap between Americans' perception of how much time they have for leisure, and the actual amount of time they have, according to a recent study, with the

---

1 John P. Robinson and Geoffrey Godbey, *Time for Life: The Surprising Ways Americans Use Their Time* (University Park: Pennsylvania State University Press, 1997).

2 Thomas L. Goodale, "Leisure Apartheid," University of Waterloo, Department of Recreation and Leisure Studies, Academy of Leisure Sciences Website <http://www.geog.ualberta.ca/als/alswp2.html>.

3 See Robert D. Putnam, "The Strange Disappearance of Civic America," *The American Prospect* (winter 1996).

FIGURES 10.1 AND 10.2

CROSS-TIME DIFFERENCES IN TYPES OF TIME FOR MEN AND WOMEN IN THE UNITED STATES: 1965–1985

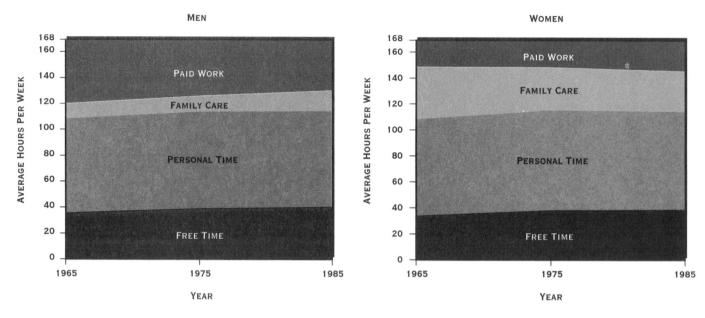

Source: John P. Robinson and Geoffrey Godbey, Time for Life, Univerity Park, PA: Pennsylvania State University Press, 1997.

Note: **Free Time** includes such activities as watching television, reading, religious and civic activities, socializing, hobbies and recreation. **Personal Time** includes such activities as eating, sleeping and bathing. Family Care includes such activities as child care, cleaning, cooking, shopping, yard work, repairs and pet care.

perception considerably short of reality.[4] Time-diary data indicate on average that both men and women were spending less time at paid work in 1985 than they did in 1965, and that free time had increased for both, whether or not they were employed. (See Figures 10.1 and 10.2.)

TYPES OF LEISURE ACTIVITY

Not only does the amount of leisure time vary throughout the life cycle, but the favorite free time activities of Americans vary by age. (See Figure 10.3.) For example, the most popular sports activities of Americans 65 years and over in 1994 were exercise walking, in which about 38 percent participated, and swimming, with

about 14 percent of this age group participating. For children between 7 and 11, bicycle riding was the most popular sports activity, with about 61 percent of this group participating, followed by swimming, with 57 percent participation. For young adults (18 to 24 years), exercising with equipment such as stationary bicycles or steppers headed the list (with about 27 percent participating), followed closely by bowling and swimming (with about 25 percent each).[5] Similar numbers of both men and women enjoyed such activities as cross-country skiing and volleyball. The participants in other sports were predominantly of one sex or the other: men predominated in football,

golf, and hunting, while more women than men participated in aerobics, for example.

Participation in athletic endeavors is only one form of leisure activity. Some other activities—which some people might think would more appropriately be classified as work—are nevertheless reported as leisure activities by large portions of the U.S. population. For example, 48 percent of adults 18 years and over indicated home improvement and repair as a leisure activity in 1992.[6] Other popular activities (engaged in at least once in the past year) include gardening (55 percent), going to movies (59 percent), and going to a sporting event of one sort or another (37 percent).[7]

---

4 Robinson and Godbey, *Time for Life*.

5 U.S. Bureau of the Census, *1996 Statistical Abstract of the United States*, Table 414. Data are from the National Sporting Goods Association.

6 U.S. Bureau of the Census, *1996 Statistical Abstract of the United States*, Tables 411, 419, and 420. Data are from "Arts Participation in America: 1982 to 1992," National Endowment for the Arts.

7 Household (as opposed to data for individuals) participation in lawn and gardening activities appears to have declined in the 1990s from about 80 to 74 percent of households. For example, vegetable gardening has declined from 37 to 31 percent, and lawn care has declined from 66 to 56 percent. Part of this decline may be attributable to the increase in condominium an cooperative apartment living.

FIGURE 10.3

PARTICIPATION IN SELECTED SPORTS IN THE UNITED STATES, BY SELECTED ACTIVITY AND AGE: 1994

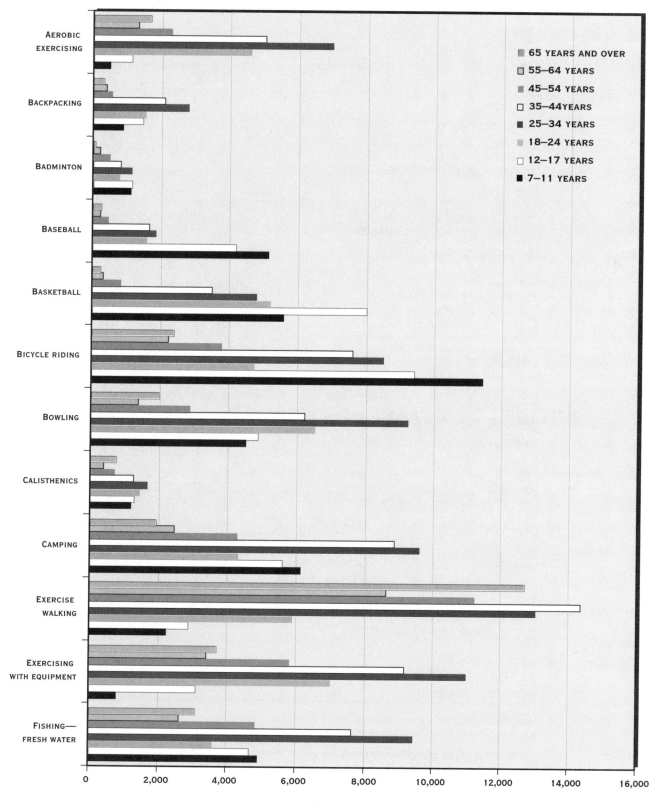

FIGURE 10.3 (CONTINUED)

PARTICIPATION IN SELECTED SPORTS IN THE UNITED STATES, BY SELECTED ACTIVITY AND AGE: 1994

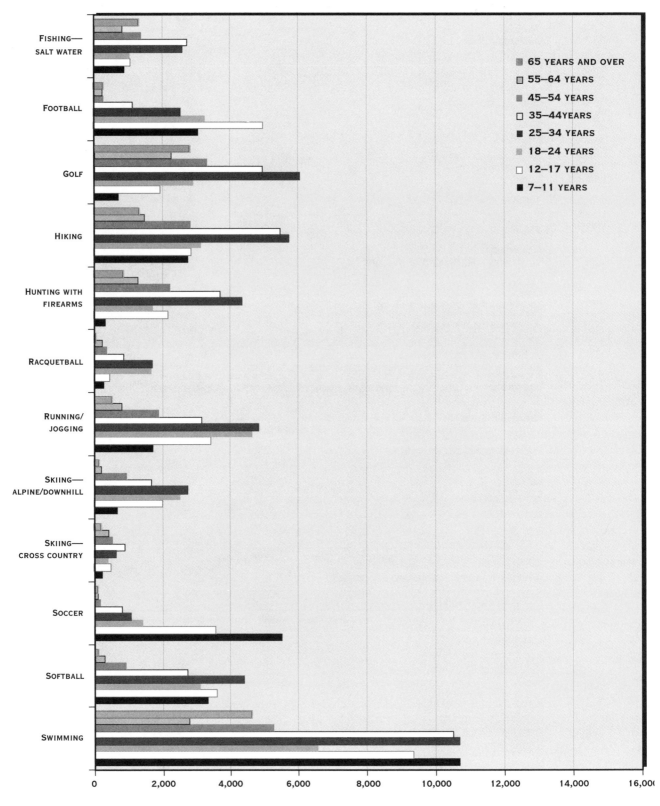

FIGURE 10.3 (CONTINUED)

PARTICIPATION IN SELECTED SPORTS IN THE UNITED STATES, BY SELECTED ACTIVITY AND AGE: 1994

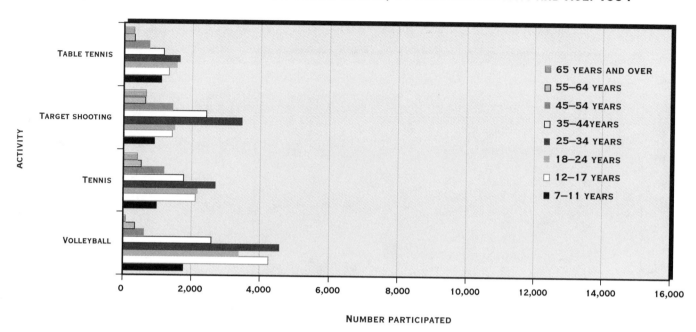

Source: National Sporting Goods Association, Mt. Prospect, IL, Sports Participation in 1994: Series I (copyright).

Participation in the arts is typically reported by a considerably smaller proportion of the population than in the activities indicated above, either in terms of attendance at an arts activity or in actual participation in the activity. While 54 percent of the adult population reported reading literature (broadly defined) in the past 12 months in 1992, only 13 percent reported attending a classical music performance, 3 percent an opera, and 5 percent a ballet. About one out of four had visited an art museum, and approximately one out of six persons had attended a play. One in four adults engaged in needlework (including weaving, quilting, crocheting, and sewing), although there was a large gap in the sex of participants, with only 5 percent of men but 43 percent of women participating in needlework in the past year. Pottery work was done recreation-

ally by 8 percent of adults, photography by 12 percent, and painting by 10 percent. Buying art was a more common activity, with 22 percent of adults engaged in this activity in the past year.[8]

Public junior and senior high schools in the United States typically have a core of extracurricular activities that students can participate in after school hours. Virtually all seniors in public high schools reported the availability of extracurricular activities at their school in the 1992 National Education Longitudinal Study conducted by the U.S. Department of Education. Included are such activities as sports; theater; band; clubs such as photography, math, or astronomy; and service clubs. Four out of five seniors reported participating in some activity, with about 42 percent participating in a sport, and about one of

[8] U.S. Bureau of the Census, *1996 Statistical Abstract of the United States*, Tables 419 and 420.

FIGURE 10.4

PERCENTAGE OF U.S. PUBLIC HIGH SCHOOL SENIORS PARTICIPATING IN SELECTED EXTRACURRICULAR ACTIVITIES: 1992

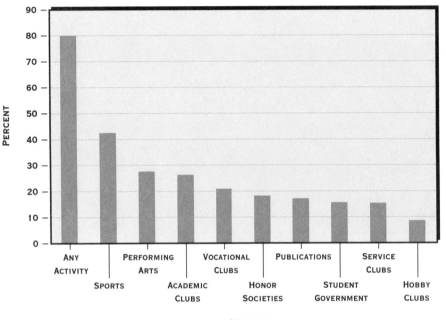

Source: National Center for Education Statistics Publication no. NCES 95-741, June 1995. "Extracurricular Participation and Student Engagement."

four participating in a performing arts club or an academic club. About 15 percent of students participated in student government, and about 15 percent in a service club. Students who participated in extracurricular activities were found to have higher school attendance than nonparticipants, to perform better on standardized math and reading tests, and to aspire to higher education at a higher rate than nonparticipants. There is some evidence to suggest that a sense of attachment to school

that is fostered by participation in extracurricular activities decreases the likelihood of school failure and dropping out.[9]

EXPENDITURES ON LEISURE

Aggregate expenditures on recreation by Americans increased from $292 billion in 1990 to $370 billion in 1994 (both figures are in 1992 dollars). American households spent an average of $1,700 on entertainment and reading in 1994, which is between 5 and 6 percent of average household total expenditures. This includes

expenditures on fees and admissions, television and sound equipment, play and sports equipment, and reading. This fraction has varied little in the past decade and has not varied much by demographic characteristics of the household (for example, one-person households spent the same proportion of their expenditures on entertainment as households with four persons), both about 5.5 percent. Households with younger heads spend proportionately more than those with older heads of households, but the difference is far from dramatic (5.9 percent of expenditures in households with a reference person under age 25, 4.1 percent in households with a reference person over age 75). Similarly, minorities tend to spend proportionately less than Anglos— both Hispanics and Blacks spend about 3.8 percent of their total expenditures on entertainment, compared with 5.7 percent for non-Hispanic Whites.[10]

These figures on consumer spending for leisure do not include spending on travel (or lodging) and thus underestimate the real expenditures on leisure. Tourism, according to some, is the world's largest industry.[11] Both "pleasure" and "vacation" travel have increased during the 1990s, with the latter increasing from 592 million to 671 million "person trips" between 1990 and 1994.[12] While the number of pleasure trips has increased in the 1990s, the average length of pleasure trips, both in terms of nights per trip and miles traveled, appears to have declined during the 1990s. The U.S. Forest Service reports that "recreation visitor days" totaled 295 million in 1993, a 6 percent increase since 1990.[13] Major activities included viewing scenery (34 percent), camping (27 percent) and hiking, and horseback riding (9 percent).

9 See National Center for Education Statistics, *Extracurricular Participation and Student Engagement*, Report no. 95-74 (Washington, DC: U.S. Department of Education, National Center for Education Statistics, June 1995).

10 U.S. Bureau of the Census, *1996 Statistical Abstract of the United States*, Table 402. Data are from the Bureau of Labor Statistics, *Consumer Expenditure Survey*.

11 See, for example, Stephen L. J. Smith, "Tourism, The Unknown Giant," University of Waterloo, Department of Recreation and Leisure Studies, Academy of Leisure Sciences Website at <http://www.geog.ualberta.ca/als/alswp9.html>; and for travel data, U.S. Bureau of the Census, *1996 Statistical Abstract of the United States*, Table 423.

12 See U.S. Bureau of the Census, *1996 Statistical Abstract of the United States*, Table 423. Data from *National Travel Survey*, U.S. Travel Data Center.

13 One recreation visitor-day is the recreation use of national forest land or water that aggregates 12 visitor-hours. See U.S. Bureau of the Census, *1996 Statistical Abstract of the United States*, Table 398.

VOLUNTEERISM

PERCENTAGE OF POPULATION VOLUNTEERING TIME IN 1995:	49 PERCENT
AVERAGE HOURS PER WEEK VOLUNTEERED FOR THOSE VOLUNTEERING:	4.2 HOURS
NUMBER OF PEACE CORPS AND VISTA VOLUNTEERS SINCE THE PROGRAMS BEGAN IN THE EARLY 1960s (APPROXIMATELY):	240,000 PERSONS
PERCENTAGE OF STUDENTS IN GRADES 6 THROUGH 12 INVOLVED IN COMMUNITY SERVICE IN THE 1995–96 SCHOOL YEAR:	49 PERCENT
PERCENTAGE OF STUDENTS REQUIRED TO PERFORM COMMUNITY SERVICE:	18 PERCENT
PERCENT OF HOUSEHOLDS CONTRIBUTING TO ONE OR MORE CHARITIES IN 1994:	73 PERCENT

HOW MANY VOLUNTEERS

Some persons feel guilty about spending time in leisure activities because of the emphasis in American society on success in the world of work. College-educated persons and other persons with relatively high income typically opt for nicer homes and cars rather than living more frugally and having more leisure time.[14] Since the image of having a strong work ethic is so highly prized in the United States, taking part in (or having time to take part in) leisure activity is equated with sloth by some people. "The ancient Athenian ideal of leisure, the absence of the necessity of being occupied, is not only rarely realized but most Americans regard contemplation as simply a waste of time—being busy has become a primary indicator of importance."[15]

Some people spend their free time not on themselves but on others through voluntary activities, some through formal organizations, others through informal assistance (for example providing childcare for a neighbor or relative). Such activities can take a wide range of forms, from volunteering to fight fires with the local fire station to assisting teachers at the local elementary school by cutting out paper circles that will

symbolize planets in the next lesson on astronomy. Volunteerism can foster a sense of doing something worthwhile with one's leisure time and of actually helping others. The extent of help that volunteers bring to their activities has recently become the subject of some debate. There is at times an inherent conflict between paid staff and volunteers, for example, because the "chain of command" is blurred. And some people feel that the amount of time offered by volunteers does more harm than good (e.g., the Big Brothers program needs long-term volunteers rather than just an hour here or there). But little is known about outcomes of volunteering since the issue of measurement has developed only recently.[16]

A frequently cited estimate of the number of adults who volunteer their assistance in one form or another is 93 million in 1995, or 49 percent of the U.S. adult population 18 years and over.[17] Volunteers averaged giving 4.2 hours per week of their time to volunteer efforts, for a total of 20.3 billion hours in that year. The estimated value of their time was $201 billion in 1995. Women tend to volunteer at higher rates than men (52 percent versus 45 percent). Persons who were employed part

time tend to volunteer at higher rates than either persons outside the labor force or those working full time. (See Figure 10.6 and 10.7.) Volunteerism is highest in the middle age groups (35 to 55 years), among college graduates (71 percent reported volunteer activity), and among households with children (74 percent of adults in such households volunteer according to a Prudential survey).

How much of this volunteering is for "human services" or "serious social problems" is the subject of some contention. Data from the Points of Light Foundation indicated that 85 percent of persons doing volunteer work in 1995 did so for "serious social problems." Other analyses imply a considerably smaller proportion of volunteering for human services, that is, 15 percent or less of volunteer activities were for such things as tutoring, counseling at homeless shelters or for substance-abuse or helping the Red Cross, and that much more volunteer effort was given to volunteering at theaters, museums and serving in administrative capacities.[18]

GOVERNMENT INVOLVEMENT IN VOLUNTEERISM

Government encouragement of volunteer efforts has expanded in the 1990s amid continued discussion about whether or not charitable organizations have sufficient resources to pick up social services when government support for such services is diminished. In the 1960s, two volunteer programs were initiated by the government—one with an international focus (the Peace Corps) and one with a domestic view (Volunteers in Service to America, or VISTA volunteers). About 140,000 Peace Corps volunteers have served since 1961, typically spending 2 years in a country requesting assistance. They have provided a wide vari-

---

14 Robinson and Godbey, *Time for Life.*

15 Geoffrey Godbey, "The Problem of Free Time—It's Not What You Think," University of Waterloo, Department of Recreation and Leisure Studies, Academy of Leisure Sciences Website at <http://www.geog.ualberta.ca/als/alswp8.html>.

16 See Michael J. Gerson, "Do Do-gooders Do Much Good?" *U.S. News and World Report* (28 April 1997); and Dale Russakoff, "Looking for Help to Even Some of Society's Odds," *Washington Post* (26 April 1997).

17 Survey data collected by the Gallup Organization for the Independent Sector and summarized at <http://vp.libertynet.org/resources/volstat.htm>. An independent survey conducted in May 1995 by the Wirthlin Group for *The Prudential* found an even higher proportion: 58 percent of adults 21 years old and over indicated they were giving some time to a community service activity. See *The Prudential Spirit of Community Adult Survey*, Prudential Website at <http://www.prudential.com/aboutpru/community>.

18 See Points of Light data, libertynet Website at <http://vp.libertynet.org/resources/volstat.htm>; and for lower estimates, see Michael J. Gerson, "Do Do-Gooders Do Much Good?" *U.S. News and World Report* (28 April 1997).

FIGURE 10.5

PERCENTAGE OF PERSONS IN THE UNITED STATES AGES 18 YEARS AND OVER WHO VOLUNTEER, BY SELECTED CHARACTERISTICS: 1996

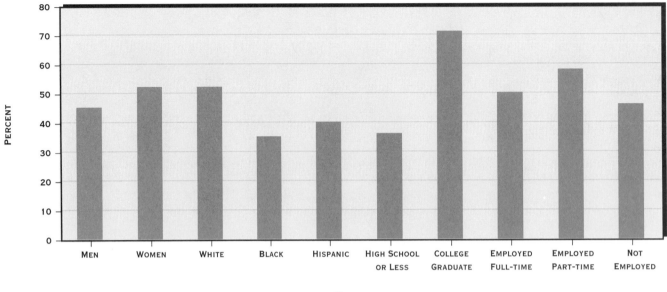

Source: The Points of Light Foundation 1995-96 Survey available at the Internet site <http://vp.libertynet.org/resources/volstat.htm>.

ety of assistance, from water, sanitation, and health programs to teaching English and helping launch small businesses. In 1997, there were about 6,500 Peace Corps volunteers serving in over 90 countries throughout the world. VISTA volunteers, who typically served for a year, have numbered about 100,000 since 1960. Both VISTA and Peace Corps volunteers were paid a small stipend on which to live during their service tour. VISTA volunteers were placed with community-based agencies involved in fighting poverty both in urban and rural settings in the United States. In 1994, VISTA became part of the AmeriCorps national service program. In addition to VISTA, the largest program of AmeriCorps is the National Civilian Community Corps (NCCC), which was modeled after the Civilian Conservation Corps (CCC). The CCC put thousands of people to work in the United States during the Great Depression in the 1930s. NCCC service is restricted to 18- to 24-year-olds, who work in teams and focus on environmental improvements, although programs are also involved in public safety, educa-

FIGURE 10.6

PERCENTAGE OF U.S. ADULTS WHO VOLUNTEER, BY AGE: 1996

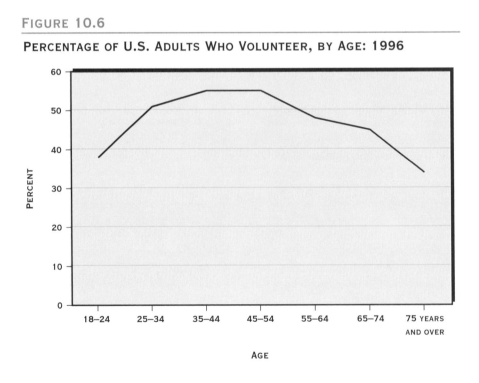

Source: The Points of Light Foundation 1995-96 Survey available at the Internet site <http://vp.libertynet.org/resources/volstat.htm>.

tion, and disaster relief. In exchange for a year of service (during which time volunteers receive a living allowance and health insurance coverage), volunteers receive an education voucher worth $4,725 for help in paying for their own education. In 1997, there were approximately 25,000 AmeriCorps members serving in over 400 programs across the Unites States.[19] At the other end of the age spectrum, the National Senior Service Corps helps persons 55 and over find volunteer activities, with three programs that receive federal funds: the Grandparents Program (which provides support to children with special needs), the Senior Companions Program (which helps frail elderly live independently), and the Retired and Senior Volunteers Program (which provides a wide range of community service).[20]

School districts in the United States are attempting to increase community service participation of students, some requiring a minimum number of hours of community service to graduate from high school, while others attempt to encourage participation without requiring students to do so. A recent survey revealed that 49 percent of students in grades 6 through 12 were involved in community service in 1995–96.[21] These students were about evenly split between those who had volunteered only once or twice during the school year and those who had volunteered more often. About 12 percent of students had volunteered more than 30 hours during the 1995–96 school year. Student participation was somewhat higher if an adult in their household also participated in community service, if their parents were college graduates, if their household income was relative-

FIGURE 10.7

PERCENTAGE OF 6TH–12TH GRADE STUDENTS IN THE UNITED STATES WHO PERFORM REGULAR COMMUNITY SERVICE DURING THE SCHOOL YEAR, BY HOURS: 1996

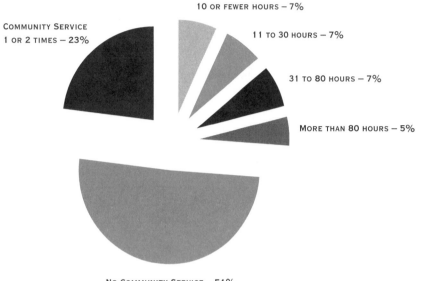

COMMUNITY SERVICE 1 OR 2 TIMES – 23%

10 OR FEWER HOURS – 7%

11 TO 30 HOURS – 7%

31 TO 80 HOURS – 7%

MORE THAN 80 HOURS – 5%

NO COMMUNITY SERVICE – 51%

Source: National Center for Education Statistics, National Household Education Survey, Spring 1996, available at the Internet site <http://www.ed.gov/nces/pubs97/97331-2.html>.

ly high, and if they were in a two-parent versus single-parent household. Differences by race of student disappeared when these other variables were controlled. Students who were asked to volunteer actually did so at considerably higher rates than those who were not asked, lending some support to the idea that schools can influence participation by simply offering the idea of service (whether or not service was mandatory, arranged, or purely voluntary). About 84 percent of students indicated that their

school arranged community service projects, with 18 percent of students indicating that their school required community service. Offering the opportunity for participation (but not requiring it) appeared to have results similar to compulsory community service: about 56 percent of students at schools that required and arranged participation had done so by the survey date, while 52 percent of students at schools that did not require but did arrange participation had participated.

19 See Websites at <http://www.peacecorps.gov> and <http://www.cns.gov>.

20 See the National Senior Service Corps description at <http://www.cns.gov/senior.html>.

21 National Center for Education Statistics, *Student Participation in Community Service Activity*, Report No. 97-331 Washington, DC: U.S. Department of Education, National Center for Education Statistics, April 1997).

RELIGIOSITY

PERCENT (1997)
INDICATING THEIR
RELIGION AS—
  CHRISTIANITY: 87 PERCENT
  CATHOLIC: 27 PERCENT
  JUDAISM: 3 PERCENT
  OTHER RELIGION: 3 PERCENT

PERCENT INDICATING
  RELIGION AS VERY
  IMPORTANT IN
  THEIR LIVES: 61 PERCENT

PERCENT ATTENDING
  SERVICES WEEKLY
  OR ALMOST WEEKLY: 43 PERCENT

PERCENT OF HOUSEHOLDS
  CONTRIBUTING MONEY
  TO A RELIGIOUS
  ORGANIZATION
  IN 1993:   49 PERCENT

AVERAGE ANNUAL
  CONTRIBUTION PER
  CONTRIBUTING
  HOUSEHOLD IN 1993: $817

TYPES OF RELIGION

Despite declines in the proportion of people who report regular attendance at religious services, religion continues to play a role in the lives of most Americans. One of four people who volunteer time (indicated in the previous section) do so through a religious activity such as teaching children's classes, gardening at their church, or singing in the choir. About 49 percent of household charitable donations (which averaged about $880, about 2 percent of household income) went to religious organizations in 1994, and this fraction has changed little in the past 15 years.[22] (See Figures 10.9 and 10.10.)

FIGURE 10.8

PERCENT OF U.S. HOUSEHOLDS GIVING TO CHARITY, BY AMOUNT: 1993

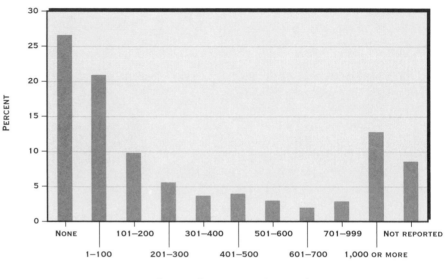

Source: Table 610, Statistical Abstract 1996. Data copyright from Independent Sector.

FIGURE 10.9

PERCENTAGE OF HOUSEHOLDS GIVING TO CHARITY, BY TYPE OF CHARITY: 1995

Source: Copyright Independent Sector. For definitions of categories see Virginia Hodkinson, et al., Giving and Volunteering in the United States: 1996 Edition. Independent Sector, Washington, D.C.

---

22 U.S. Bureau of the Census, *1996 Statistical Abstract*, Table 609; and Virginia Hodgkinson et al., *Giving and Volunteering in the United States: 1994* (Washington, DC: Independent Sector, 1994).

Christianity remains the dominant religion in the United States, with 87 percent of adults considering themselves a member of one of its denominations.[23] (See Figures 10.11 and 10.12.) About 27 percent indicated they were Catholic, with the remainder indicating adherence to Protestant denomination. (Baptist, including Southern Baptist, was the most frequently reported.) About 3 percent of the population identified themselves as Jews, and another 3 percent indicated a religion other than Christianity or Judaism, a fraction that has not changed much despite considerable immigration in recent years from countries whose predominant religion is other than Christianity.

FREQUENCY OF ATTENDANCE

One indicator of religiosity is frequency of attending religious services. While only 4 of 10 Americans say they attended church regularly in 1997, only 9 percent say they never attend a church or synagogue, and only 5 percent indicate no religious preference whatever. Two-thirds of the U.S. population maintains an affiliation with a particular church or synagogue, a fraction that has changed little in the past several decades. Another indicator of religiosity is how important individuals feel religion is in their own life. Six of 10 Americans report that religion is "very important" in their lives, a fraction that has varied between 52 and 63 percent since 1978. This proportion appears to have declined since the 1960s, when it was closer to 75 percent. At the same time, the majority of Americans (57 percent) feel that religion is losing its influence on American life in 1997.

FIGURE 10.10

PERCENTAGE DISTRIBUTION OF THE U.S. POPULATION, BY RELIGION: 1997

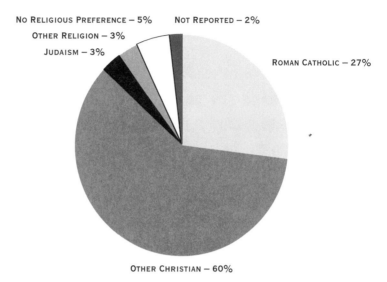

Source: The Gallup Poll of March 1997. Available at <http://www.gallup.com/poll/news/970329.html>.

FIGURE 10.11

PERCENTAGE DISTRIBUTION OF PROTESTANTS IN THE UNITED STATES, BY DENOMINATION: 1997

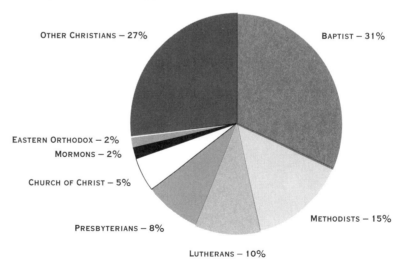

Source: The Gallup Poll of March 1997. Available at <http://www.gallup.com/poll/news/970329.html>.

---

[23] Gallup poll conducted March 1997, Gallup Website at <http://www.gallup.com/poll/news/970329.html>.

FIGURE 10.12

PERCENTAGE OF SELECTED GROUPS IN THE UNITED STATES THAT ATTEND RELIGIOUS SERVICES AT LEAST ONCE A WEEK: 1997

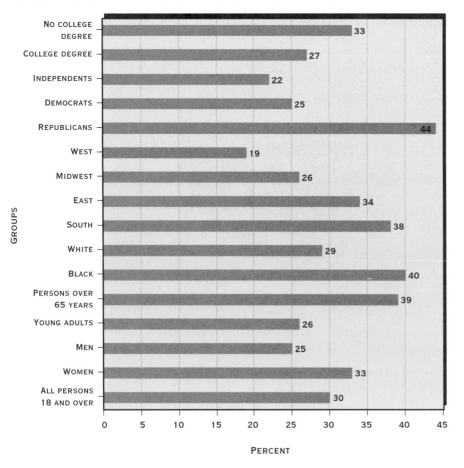

Source: Gallup Poll conducted March 24–26, 1997. Available at <http://www.gallup.com/poll/news/970329.html>.

WHO ATTENDS REGULARLY

A higher proportion of the elderly attend church regularly relative to other age groups (39 percent of those over age 65 compared with 26 percent of young adults, for example). Women tend to attend religious services more regularly than do men, with about a third of women and one-quarter of men in the United States reporting weekly attendance. (See Figure 10.13.) Blacks report weekly attendance more frequently than do Whites (40 percent versus 29 percent). Weekly attendance is considerably more likely among residents of the Southern (38 per-

cent) and the Eastern United States (34 percent) than among the Midwest (26 percent) or the Western United States, where only 19 percent report weekly church attendance. There is not much difference by educational attainment between weekly churchgoers and those who do not attend church weekly (27 percent with a college degree and 33 percent with no college degree), but there is significant difference by political affiliation. Republicans are considerably more likely to be weekly churchgoers (44 percent) than either Democrats or independents (25 percent and 22 percent, respectively).

Are Americans more or less religious than residents of other countries? A recent study comparing the United States with 14 mostly European nations indicates that both a belief in a personal god and church attendance are markedly higher in the United States.[24] Some researchers theorize that religious belief declines as a nation's populace becomes more educated, prosperous, and modern. While this appears to be the case in many European nations in recent decades, the United States appears to be an exception to this tendency. The authors of this study contend that religious beliefs endure because the religious environment of a nation shapes the religious beliefs of its citizens.

POLITICS AND RELIGION

The U.S. Constitution states that Congress cannot make any laws specifying the establishment of a state religion and that Americans are free to worship as they see fit. While politics may not shape religion in America, religious affiliation does influence political values. The general tendency is that the more devout a person is the more politically conservative he or she is, not only on matters such as abortion, homosexuality, and family, but also on national security and environmental issues.[25] While the fundamentalist classification cuts across denominations, Baptists make up the largest share of "born-again" or evangelical Christians. White evangelical Protestants have become a political force in America over the past two decades, with an increasing proportion self-identifying as Republicans. The proportion of White members of fundamentalist churches identifying themselves as Republicans has increased from about 26 in 1978 to 42 percent in 1995, with 25 percent identifying themselves as Democrats and 29 percent as Independents.

Americans report a considerable amount of direct political discussion in church regardless of race or denomination, although the issues vary by denomination and race of the parishioners. For example, 62 percent of Black Christians reported

24 See Jonathan Kelley and Nan Dirk De Graaf, "National and Parental Religiosity and Religious Belief," *American Sociological Review* 62, no. 4 (August 1997).

25 "The Dimishing Divide…American Churches , American Politics," The Pew Research Center for the People and The Press Survey Website at <www.people-press.org/relgrpt.htm> (September 1995).

hearing about health-care reform from the pulpit, compared with only 19 percent of Whites in 1995. About 75 percent of Catholics reported hearing about abortion in sermons, somewhat more than Evangelical Protestants (66 percent). About three-fourths of churchgoers (regardless of denomination) reported hearing about the issue of allowing prayer in schools.

Have a greater proportion of Americans become members of fundamentalist churches (or do a greater proportion hold fundamentalist beliefs) than in the past several decades? While such persons have become a greater proportion of registered voters (about 24 percent in 1995, up from 19 percent in 1987), evidence that they are a larger proportion of the U.S.

population is mixed. According to one study, the proportion of the U.S. population that self-identifies as Protestant (including fundamentalists as well as nonfundamentalist denominations such as Lutherans, Methodists, and Presbyterians) has been dropping over the past 40 years, with the percent reporting their religion as Catholic, "other religion," or "no religion" all gaining, despite church statistics indicating an increase in membership in fundamentalist denominations. [26] According to another poll, the fraction of Protestants who identify themselves as "born-again or evangelical" Christians has fluctuated between 39 percent and 46 percent during the 1990s, with no discernible trend.[27]

FOR FURTHER INFORMATION SEE:

DWYER, JOHN F. *CUSTOMER DIVERSITY AND THE FUTURE DEMAND FOR OUTDOOR RECREATION.* USDA TECHNICAL REPORT 252. U.S. DEPARTMENT OF AGRICULTURE, FOREST SERVICE (AUGUST 1994).

HODGKINSON, VIRGINIA, ET AL. *GIVING AND VOLUNTEERING IN THE UNITED STATES: 1994.* WASHINGTON, DC: INDEPENDENT SECTOR, 1994.

THE GALLUP POLL MONTHLY. PRINCETON: THE GALLUP POLL (VARIOUS ISSUES).

NATIONAL CENTER FOR EDUCATION STATISTICS. *COMMUNITY SERVICE PERFORMED BY HIGH SCHOOL SENIORS.* REPORT NO. 95-743. WASHINGTON, DC: U.S. DEPARTMENT OF EDUCATION, NATIONAL CENTER FOR EDUCATION STATISTICS.

NATIONAL CENTER FOR EDUCATION STATISTICS. *STUDENT PARTICIPATION IN COMMUNITY SERVICE ACTIVITIES.* REPORT NO. 97-331. WASHINGTON, DC: U.S. DEPARTMENT OF EDUCATION, NATIONAL CENTER FOR EDUCATION STATISTICS, APRIL 1997.

WEBSITES:

THE ACADEMY OF LEISURE SCIENCES WEBSITE AT <HTTP://WWW.GEOG.UALBERTA.CA/ALS/ALS1.HTML>.

THE CORPORATION FOR NATIONAL SERVICE WEBSITE AT <HTTP://WWW.CNS.GOV>.

THE GENERAL SOCIAL SURVEY WEBSITE AT <HTTP://WWW.ICPSR.UMICH.EDU/GSS>.

THE LIBERTYNET WEBSITE AT <HTTP://VP.LIBERTYNET.ORG/RESOURCES/VOLSTAT.HTM>.

THE PEACE CORPS WEBSITE AT <HTTP://WWW.PEACECORPS.GOV>.

THE PEW CHARITABLE TRUST WEBSITE AT <HTTP://WWW.PEOPLE-PRESS.ORG>.

---

[26] See Tom W. Smith, "Are Conservative Churches Growing?" *General Social Survey*, Social Change Report no. 32 (University of Chicago, National Opinion Research Center, 1991).

[27] *The Gallup Poll Monthly* (December 1995).

CHAPTER 11

Environment

DAVID E. BLOCKSTEIN AND JENNIFER L. PRICE

ENVIRONMENT

PERCENTAGE OF U.S. PLANT AND ANIMAL SPECIES IN 1995 IN SOME DANGER OF EXTINCTION:	**32 PERCENT**
PERCENTAGE OF COMMUNITY DRINKING WATER SYSTEMS IN 1994 WITH—	
NO VIOLATIONS OF HEALTH-BASED REQUIREMENTS:	**81 PERCENT**
COLIFORM VIOLATIONS:	**8 PERCENT**
OTHER VIOLATIONS:	**11 PERCENT**
CHANGE IN EMISSIONS OF SULFUR DIOXIDE, 1970–1994:	**–32 PERCENT**
CHANGE IN NUMBER OF DAYS IN WHICH AIR QUALITY STANDARDS WERE EXCEEDED, 1985–1994:	**–72 PERCENT**
CHANGE IN U.S. GREENHOUSE GAS EMISSIONS, 1990–1994:	**+4 PERCENT**
CHANGE IN TOXIC CHEMICAL RELEASES INTO THE ENVIRONMENT, 1988–1994:	**–44 PERCENT**
PER CAPITA GENERATION OF SOLID WASTE IN THE U.S. PER DAY IN—	
1960:	**2.7 POUNDS**
1994:	**4.4 POUNDS**
PERCENTAGE OF SOLID WASTE THAT WAS RECOVERED FOR RECYCLING IN—	
1960:	**7 PERCENT**
1994:	**24 PERCENT**

INTRODUCTION

In recent years, there has been increasing recognition of the importance of a diverse, healthy environment to the quality of people's lives. The connection between the environment and health and prosperity are strong. Additional research only confirms the dependence of humans on the environment.

This chapter reports on the status of the environment in the United States with respect to its natural resources: ecosystems, including forests, wetlands, and farmlands; and biological resources, such as wildlife and fish. This chapter also assesses the status of the nation's air and water. Topics addressed include waste production and management, environmental justice, and environmental economics and science. It also presents information on U.S. contribu-

tions to the global environmental problems of climate change and ozone depletion. Although population is not discussed directly in this chapter, most environmental problems are exacerbated by human population numbers (the U.S. population is growing by 2.4 million people annually during the mid-1990s, nearly equivalent to the population living in the city of Chicago) and consumption patterns. Each person that is added to the U.S. population requires, on average, about an acre of land for urbanization and highways.[1]

There are no recognized comprehensive environmental statistics or indicators akin to national economic indicators or labor statistics, although an interagency environmental monitoring initiative led by the White House Office of Science and Technology Policy is preparing a national

"environmental report card" to be presented in the year 2001. In the absence of such indicators, this chapter relies heavily on the 25th annual report of the Council on Environmental Quality (CEQ), which presents a series of summaries of particular environmental issues.[2]

In general, the quality of the environment of the United States is good. However, there are serious negative conditions and trends for many natural resources, including ecosystems, fish, and wildlife. Although there have been gains in pollution cleanup and environmental quality, continued population and economic growth and resource consumption will provide challenges to maintain this progress and to improve environmental quality in areas that have been lagging. The CEQ estimates that, "based on current trends, efficiency in the use of all resources would have to increase by more than 50 percent over the next four to five decades just to keep up with population growth."[3]

ECOSYSTEMS

Ecosystems have been described as geographically defined ecological units, consisting of plants and animals and their surrounding environment, with shared characteristics in common. Noss and Peters describe ecosystems as "a characteristic community of interdependent plants, animals, and microorganisms associated with particular kinds of soil, temperature, rainfall, and disturbance patterns."[4] Ecosystem health has become a matter of concern, because, as conversion and fragmentation of natural landscapes for agriculture, forestry, and development leaves smaller and more isolated natural areas, ecosystems

[1] See The President's Council on Sustainable Development, *Population and Consumption Task Force Report* (Washington DC: GPO, 1996). An electronic library on the linkages between population and environment is available on the Internet at <http:\\www.cnie.org>.

[2] Council on Environmental Quality, *Environmental Quality, 25th Anniversary Report* (Washington, DC, 1996), 25-26.

[3] Council on Environmental Quality, *Environmental Quality, 25th Anniversary Report* (Washington, DC, 1996), 78.

[4] Reed F. Noss and Robert L. Peters, "Endangered Ecosystems: A Status Report on America's Vanishing Habitat and Wildlife," in *Defenders of Wildlife,* (Washington, DC, 1995).

lose their ability to maintain healthy populations of plants and animals. As species disappear from these patches, biodiversity (the natural variety of plant, animal, and microbial species) is lost and the landscape becomes less resilient. Each loss of biodiversity makes it more difficult for the system to adapt to adjustments, because of human intrusion, and to continue to provide ecological goods and services (such as purification of the air and water, flood and pollutant control, soil building; and moderation of climate and weather).

In almost every corner of the United States, natural environments are being paved, plowed, drained, clear-cut, or contaminated with nonnative species. The pace of ecosystem destruction and degradation has most likely accelerated over recent decades to the point that relatively few

high-quality habitats exist outside protected areas such as wilderness areas, parks, and wildlife refuges. Even these "protected" areas are subject to a number of external threats to their long-term viability as ecological reservoirs.

Noss and Peters determined the "most-endangered" ecosystems of the United States based on four criteria: decline in original area since European settlement, present area (rarity), imminence of future threats, and number of federally listed threatened and endangered species. Of the 21 most endangered ecosystems, at least 9 of these are forests, 6 are wetlands, and 5 are grasslands. Separate sections of this chapter will provide additional information on forests and wetlands. Some endangered ecosystems have a mix of vegetation types, such as south Florida (which is ranked as

TABLE 11.1

THE 21 MOST ENDANGERED ECOSYSTEMS IN THE UNITED STATES

SOUTH FLORIDA LANDSCAPE
SOUTHERN APPALACHIAN SPRUCE-FIR FOREST
LONGLEAF PINE FOREST
EASTERN GRASSLANDS, SAVANNAS, AND BARRENS
NORTHWESTERN GRASSLANDS AND SAVANNAS
CALIFORNIA NATIVE GRASSLANDS
COASTAL COMMUNITIES IN THE LOWER 48 STATES
    AND HAWAII
SOUTHWESTERN RIPARIAN FORESTS
SOUTHERN CALIFORNIA COASTAL SAGE SHRUB
HAWAIIAN DRY FOREST
LARGE STREAMS AND RIVERS IN THE LOWER 48
    STATES AND HAWAII
CAVE AND KARST SYSTEMS
TALLGRASS PRAIRIE
CALIFORNIA RIPARIAN FORESTS AND WETLANDS
FLORIDA SCRUB
ANCIENT EASTERN DECIDUOUS FOREST
ANCIENT FOREST OF PACIFIC NORTHWEST
ANCIENT RED AND WHITE PINE FOREST, GREAT
    LAKES STATES
ANCIENT PONDEROSA PINE FOREST
MIDWESTERN WETLANDS
SOUTHERN FORESTED WETLANDS

Source: Reed F. Noss and Robert L. Peters, *Endangered Ecosystems: A Status Report on America's Vanishing Habitat and Wildlife*, (Defenders of Wildlife, Washington, DC, 1995).

FIGURE 11.1

ECOSYSTEM RISK IN THE UNITED STATES, BY STATE

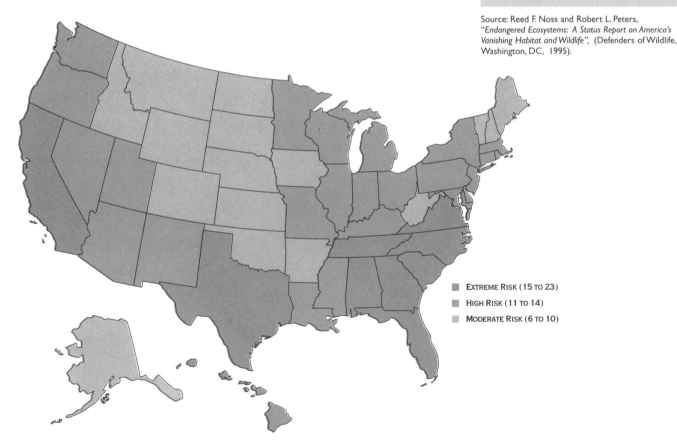

EXTREME RISK (15 TO 23)
HIGH RISK (11 TO 14)
MODERATE RISK (6 TO 10)

Source: Reed F. Noss and Robert L. Peters, *Endangered Ecosystems: A Status Report on America's Vanishing Habitat and Wildlife*, (Defenders of Wildlife, Washington, DC, 1995).

the most endangered ecosystem) and coastal communities across the lower 48 states and Hawaii.

All 50 states have serious problems with threatened or endangered ecosystems, even Alaska, where its coastal rainforest is being logged rapidly. States were ranked based on the presence of endangered ecosystems, how many rare species they contain, and the amount of development that is taking place. Florida is subject to the greatest overall ecosystem risk, followed by Hawaii and California (tied). Texas and the entire southeast region from Alabama to Virginia are also at extreme risk. Several states in the Midwest and West regions of the United States, as well as northern New England, West Virginia, and Alaska are at moderate risk, with the remainder of the states at high risk.

The former National Biological Service (NBS, now the Biological Resources Division of the U.S. Geological Survey) identified 27 types of ecosystems that have already lost 98 percent or more of their original area subsequent to European settlement.[5] A dozen of these ecosystems are primarily grasslands, which were converted to be used for agricultural purposes. Another seven are primarily forested and a half dozen are wetlands. Other ecosystems that have declined by over 85 percent include old-growth forests in all states except Alaska, limestone cedar glades in the South and Midwest, wetlands of most types in the Midwest, Gulf Coast pitcher plant bogs, coastal redwood forests and vernal pools (seasonal wetlands that dry up after the spring rains) in California, riparian forests in the Southwest and California, dry forests in Hawaii, and native beach communities and seagrass meadows in many coastal areas.

Even among relatively common ecosystems, habitat degradation is a problem. Many western grasslands and shrublands, including those in the public domain, are seriously overgrazed. This has resulted in the loss of native grasses and other plants and animals to the point that more than 340 species of the Western rangelands are listed as threatened, endangered or candidates for listing as such.[6] Nonnative pests and disease have attacked most of the dominant trees of the eastern deciduous forest, including American chestnut (virtually extinct), American elm, hemlock, and oaks, as well as understory trees, such as dogwoods.

Human activities have also adversely affected aquatic ecosystems. Between 90 and 98 percent of streams nationwide are degraded enough to be unworthy of federal designation as wild and scenic rivers, due to destruction by dams, conversion to agricultural lands, water diversion projects, urban encroachment, cattle grazing, and excessive ground water pumping. Riparian (river or streamside) habitats are particularly damaged, and much natural riparian vegetation has been either removed or replaced by nonnative species.

TABLE 11.2

ECOSYSTEMS TYPES (PLANT COMMUNITIES AND HABITATS) THAT HAVE REPORTEDLY DECLINED BY 98 PERCENT OR MORE IN THE UNITED STATES SINCE EUROPEAN SETTLEMENT

OLD GROWTH AND OTHER VIRGIN STANDS IN THE EASTERN DECIDUOUS FOREST BIOME
SPRUCE-FIR FOREST IN THE SOUTHERN APPALACHIANS
RED AND WHITE PINE FORESTS (MATURE AND OLD GROWTH) IN MICHIGAN
LONGLEAF PINE FORESTS AND SAVANNAS IN THE SOUTHEASTERN COASTAL PLAIN
PINE ROCKLAND HABITAT IN SOUTH FLORIDA
LOBLOLLY/SHORTLEAF PINE-HARDWOOD FORESTS IN THE WEST GULF COASTAL PLAIN
ARUNDINARIA GIGANTEA CANEBRAKES IN SOUTHEAST
TALLGRASS PRAIRIE EAST OF MISSOURI RIVER AND ON MESIC SITES ACROSS RANGE
BLUEGRASS SAVANNA-WOODLAND AND PRAIRIES IN KENTUCKY
BLACK BELT PRAIRIES IN ALABAMA AND MISSISSIPPI AND JACKSON PRAIRIE IN MISSISSIPPI
UNGRAZED DRY PRAIRIE IN FLORIDA
OAK SAVANNA IN MIDWEST
WET AND MESIC COASTAL PRAIRIES IN LOUISIANA
LAKEPLAIN WET PRAIRIE IN MICHIGAN
SEDGE MEADOWS IN WISCONSIN
HEMPSTEAD PLAINS GRASSLANDS ON LONG ISLAND, NEW YORK
LAKE SAND BEACHES IN VERMONT
SERPENTINE BARRENS, MARITIME HEATHLAND AND PITCH PINE-HEATH BARRENS IN NEW YORK
PRAIRIES (ALL TYPES) AND OAK SAVANNAS IN WILLAMETTE VALLEY AND FOOTHILLS OF COAST RANGE, OREGON
PALOUSE PRAIRIE (WASHINGTON, OREGON, AND IDAHO, PLUS SIMILAR COMMUNITIES IN MONTANA)
NATIVE GRASSLANDS (ALL TYPES) IN CALIFORNIA
ALKALI SINK SCRUB IN SOUTHERN CALIFORNIA
COASTAL STRAND IN SOUTHERN CALIFORNIA
UNGRAZED SAGEBRUSH STEPPE IN INTERMOUNTAIN WEST
BASIN BIG SAGEBRUSH IN SNAKE RIVER PLAIN OF IDAHO
ATLANTIC WHITE CEDAR STRANDS IN THE GREAT DISMAL SWAMP OF VIRGINIA AND NORTH CAROLINA, AND POSSIBLY ACROSS ENTIRE RANGE
STREAMS IN MISSISSIPPI ALLUVIAL PLAIN

Source: Noss, LaRoe and Scott 1995.

---

[5] Reed F. Noss, and J. M. Scott. "Endangered Ecosystems of the United States: A Preliminary Assessment of Loss and Degradation, 1995," *Biological Report* 28 (Washington, DC: U.S. Department of Interior, National Biological Service).

[6] J. Horning, *Grazing to Extinction: Endangered, Threatened, and Candidate Species Imperiled by Livestock Grazing on Western Public Lands* (Washington, DC: National Wildlife Federation, 1994).

FIGURE 11.2

U.S. WETLANDS AREA: 1780S–1980S

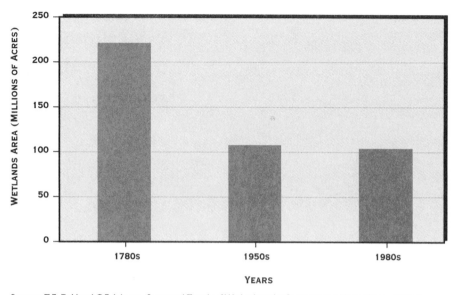

Sources: T.E. Dahl and C.E. Johnson, Status and Trends of Wetlands in the Conterminous United States, 1970s to 1980s (Washington, D.C.: U.S. Department of the Interior, Fish and Wildlife Service, Table 2, p. 8, 1991) and earlier reports, T.E. Dahl, 1780s to 1980s, Report to Congress (Washington, D.C.: U.S. Department of the Interior, Fish and Wildlife Service, 1991).

Note: Data exclude wetlands in Alaska and Hawaii.

FIGURE 11.3

PERCENTAGE OF WETLANDS LOSSES IN THE UNITED STATES, BY STATE: 1780S–1980S

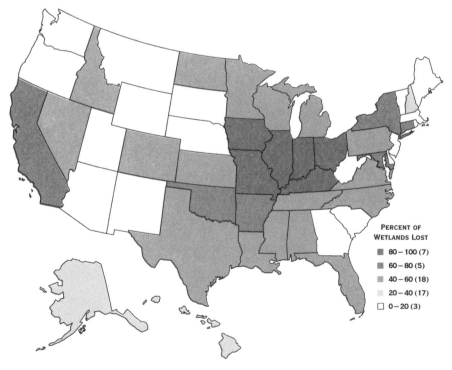

Source: T.E. Dahl, Wetlands Losses by States, 1780s to 1980s, Report to Congress (Washington, D.C.: U.S. Department of the Interior, Fish and Wildlife, 1991).

WETLANDS

Wetlands have received much attention, both because of their value as habitat and for their ecological services (such as flood protection) and because so many acres have been destroyed. More than half of the estimated 221 million acres of wetlands that existed in colonial times have been lost to agriculture, development, and other purposes. (See Figure 11.2.) Today, only 104 million acres of wetlands remain in the continental states. Virtually all of the 48 continental states have lost at least 20 percent of their original wetlands, while 30 states have lost at least 40 percent. California, Ohio, Indiana, Illinois, Iowa, Missouri, and Kentucky each have lost over 80 percent of their original wetlands.

Although wetlands occur throughout the United States, their distribution varies regionally. Alaska, with 170 million acres (nearly half the total surface area of the state), has more acres of wetlands than all other states combined. Of the remaining states, the Southeastern states (including Alabama, Arkansas, Florida, Georgia, Kentucky, Louisiana, Mississippi, North Carolina, South Carolina, and Tennessee) make up only 16 percent of the surface area of the United States, but account for 47 percent of the total wetland area and for 65 percent of the total forested wetland area.

In the 18th and 19th centuries, wetland drainage was a widespread practice. During this time, wetlands were regarded as unproductive areas that bred diseases, restricted overland travel, and restricted the production of crops. Congress supported and encouraged drainage practices to aid water transportation, farming, and grazing. The Swamp Land Acts of 1849, 1850, and 1860 granted swamps and periodically flooded lands to the states. Conversion of wetlands to agriculture has been responsible for 87 percent of national wetland losses. Most recent wetland losses can be attributed to construction of flood-control devices and reservoirs, mining and petroleum extraction, and development of urban areas, primarily housing and shopping areas. The heavy losses in the Midwest—Ohio, Indiana, Illinois, Iowa, Missouri, and Kentucky—are associated with agriculture.

We now recognize that wetlands serve

many purposes to the surrounding ecosystems and human settlements.[7] Wetlands support 5,000 plant species, 190 amphibian species, and one-third of all bird species in the United States. They provide habitat for many species on the threatened and endangered species list, including one-half of the fish, one-third of the birds, one-fourth of the plants, and one-sixth of the mammals. For many fish and shellfish, wetlands provide both spawning and rearing grounds. Wetlands help to protect habitats by safeguarding shorelines, and to improve water quality by removing excess nutrients, sediments, and pesticides from surface waters. Wetlands act as reservoirs during periods of high rainfall by slowing the overland flow of water and helping to reduce flooding and soil erosion downstream. In times of low rainfall, wetlands help to recharge the groundwater supply and to extend stream flow.

Policies toward wetlands have now turned in the direction of protection. The Clean Water Act, which prohibits most filling of wetlands and sets up a permitting process for wetland drainage, and various provisions of recent versions of the Farm Bill have helped to slow the destruction of wetlands. The latter includes "Swampbuster," which provides penalties for wetland drainage, as well as the Conservation Reserve Program (CRP) and the Wetland Reserve Program (WRP), both of which provide incentives to private landowners who restore or protect natural habitat on portions of their land. Despite this, nearly 1.2 million acres of wetlands were destroyed between 1985 and 1995; with 965,000 acres (nearly 80 percent) lost to agriculture. Although wetland destruction has slowed, more action is needed if we are to achieve the national goal of "no net loss of wetlands."

In addition, global climate change and the rise in sea level pose significant threats to wetlands by the presence of excess water and saltwater intrusion, especially coastal

wetlands along the East and Gulf Coasts, as well as bottomland hardwood and swamp forests in Florida and Louisiana. Development on the periphery of coastal wetlands has limited the ability of coastal wetlands to expand further landward as sea level rises.

FORESTS

There has been a long debate, which continues today, over forests in the United States: use or preservation? Two men, Gifford Pinchot and John Muir, personify this debate. The first career forester, Gifford Pinchot believed in conservation of forest resources, allowing use and active management of timber. This has been the guiding philosophy of the U.S. Forest Service,

which Pinchot was instrumental in founding. Development and preservation of resources for the benefit of many, and not for just a privileged few was the long-term goal of conservation. John Muir was an aesthetic conservationist, fighting for the preservation of forests. Muir believed that wilderness was a necessity, "…that mountain parks and reservations are useful not only as fountains of timber and irrigating rivers, but as fountains of life."[8] This philosophy not only embodies the Sierra Club, founded by Muir, but much of the present environmental movement as well. These differing perspectives dominate a debate about forest management that now rages across the United States, particularly in the Pacific Northwest.

FIGURE 11.4

U.S. FOREST LAND AREA: 1630–1992

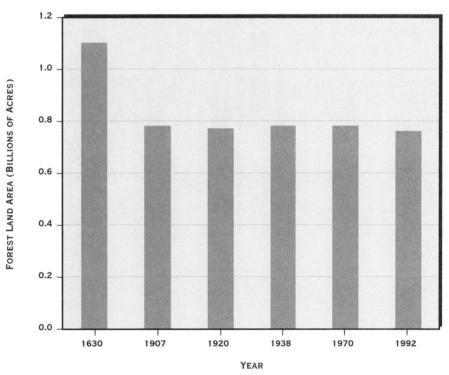

Source: D.S. Powell, J.L. Faulkner, D.R. Darr, Z. Zhu, and D.W. MacCleery, Forest Statistics of the United States, 1992 General Technical Report RM-234 (Washington, D.C.:U.S. Department of Agriculture, Forest Service, 1993).

---

[7] See National Research Council, *Wetlands: Characteristics and Boundaries* (Washington, DC: National Academy Press, 1995).

[8] John Muir, *Our National Parks* (Boston: Houghton Mifflin, 1901), 1–3.

The original forest of what is now the United States covered about 1 billion acres. During the first two centuries of colonization of America, forest area declined as land was cleared for agriculture, logging, and "settlement." Since the beginning of the 20th century, the total forested area has remained at nearly 800 million acres, but the age and distribution of forests have changed.

Increasing knowledge about timber production has led to an agriculture-like harvest of timber, with planting and restocking taking a high priority. Net growth, due to planting by industry and encouraged by various government programs, is now higher than removals, which has been decreasing due to increasing recycled pulp and paper. (See Figures 11.5 and 11.6.)

FIGURE 11.5

U.S. TREE PLANTING ACTIVITY: 1950–1995

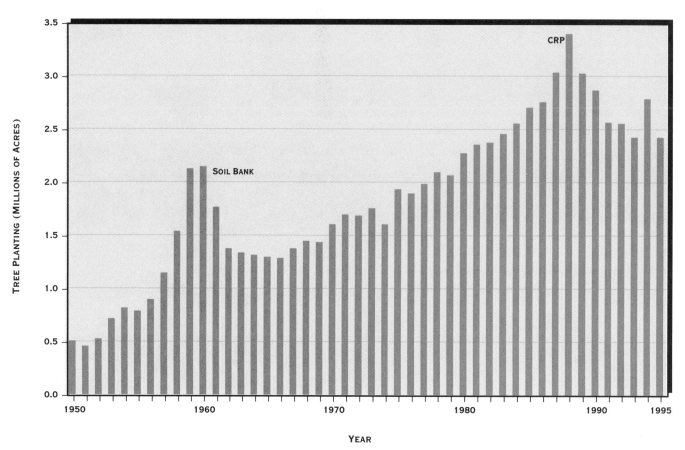

Sources: U.S. Department of Agriculture, Forest Service, "Wildfire Statistics," unpublished, (Washington, D.C.: annual), U.S. Department of Agriculture Forest Service, U.S. Forest Planting Report (Washington, D.C.: annual).

Note: CRP=Conservation Reserve Program.

FIGURE 11.6

NET GROWTH AND REMOVALS OF U.S. TIMBER: 1920–1991

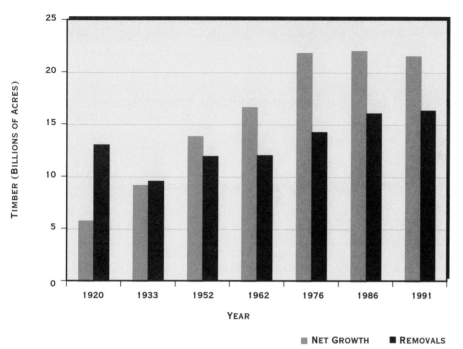

■ NET GROWTH   ■ REMOVALS

Source: D.S. Powell, J.L. Faulkner, D.R. Darr, Z. Zhu, and D.W. MacCleery, Forest Statistics of the United States, 1992, General Technical Report RM-234 (Washington, D.C.:U.S. Department of Agriculture, Forest Service, 1993).

FIGURE 11.7

U.S. TIMBERLAND, BY REGION: 1992

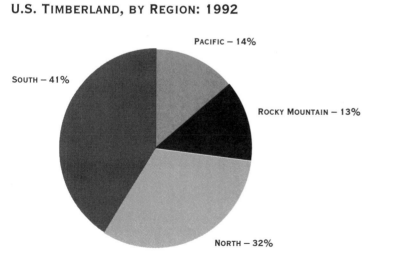

Source: D.S. Powell, J.L. Faulkner, D.R. Darr, Z. Zhu, and D.W. MacCleery, Forest Statistics of the United States, 1992, General Technical Report RM-234 (Washington, D.C.:U.S. Department of Agriculture, Forest Service, 1993).

Note: Total timberland = 489.56 million acres.

New England is much more forested than it was at the turn of the century, due to abandoned farmland that is now wooded. The South, which now has the greatest percentage of U.S. timberland, has been replanted with an industrial forest of pine plantations, which have largely replaced native forests and also covers abandoned cotton fields. (See Figure 11.7.) In many cases, short rotation of logging has left the forest much younger than the original forest. Young forests are favored by a certain type of wildlife, such as deer. Older forests have their own set of species. Many of these, such as spotted owls, have become very rare. The ancient forests (500–1,000 years old) of the West have been logged so that only 13 percent of their original area remains, almost all of it on public lands.[9] In the Pacific Northwest, old-growth forest is disappearing, and forest harvesting does not allow stands to reach the old-growth stage. Although the ancient forests west of the Cascade Mountains have gained most of the public attention, the drier forests of eastern Oregon and Washington are also in degraded condition. Presently 70 to 95 percent of the late successional/old-growth forests that remain in this region cover less than 100 acres each, which is too small to maintain most of their associated wildlife.[10] Continued logging of these forests at rates equivalent to the 1980s could reduce old-growth forests to less than 10 percent of the total forest area in the region. In most of the rest of the United States, old-growth forests are long gone.

Federal involvement in forest management began in the 1870s. Congress began by addressing the issues of preservation of forests and importance of cultivating timber. Federal involvement continued and interest increased steadily, resulting in the creation of the U.S. Forest Service in 1905. (The Forest Service currently controls 191 million acres of National Forest land, about 85 million acres of which are considered timberlands, most of the rest being high elevation wilderness.) The Multiple Use-Sustained Yield Act of 1960 (MUSYA) man-

9 Elliott A. Norse, Ancient Forests of the Pacific Northwest (Washington, DC: Island Press, 1990).

10 Mark G. Henjum et al., Interim Protection for Late-Successional Forests, Fisheries, and Watersheds: National Forests East of the Cascade Crest, Oregon, and Washington (Bethesda: The Wildlife Society, 1994).

FIGURE 11.8

U.S. LAND IN FARMS, BY FARM SIZE: 1900–1992

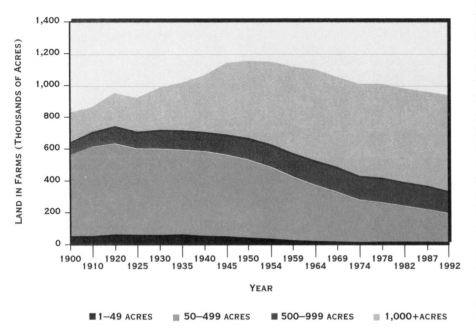

Sources: U.S. Department of Commerce, Bureau of the Census, Historical Statistics of the United States: Colonial Times to 1970 (GPO, Washington, D.C.: 1975) U.S. Department of Commerce, Bureau of the Census, Census of Agriculture for 1992 Vol. I: Geographic Area Series, Part 51 United States Summary and State Data, Table 8, p. 18, AC92-A-51 (GPO, Washington, D.C., 1994) and earlier census reports.

FIGURE 11.9

NUMBER OF U.S. FARMS, BY FARM SIZE: 1900–1992

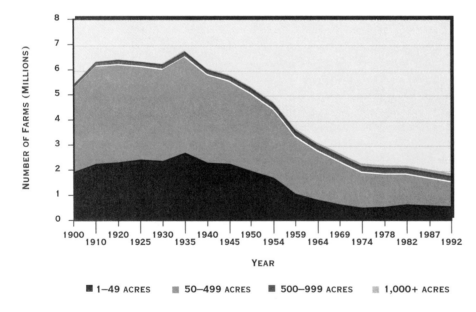

Sources: U.S. Department of Commerce, Bureau of the Census, Historical Statistics of the United States: Colonial Times to 1970 (GPO, Washington, D.C.: 1975). U.S. Department of Commerce, Bureau of the Census, Census of Agriculture for 1992, Vol. I: Geographic Area Series, Part 51 United States Summary and State Data, Table 8, p. 18, AC92-A-51 (GPO, Washington, D.C.: 1994) and earlier census reports.

dates the multiple use of National Forest land, requiring that recreation and wildlife habitat be given as much priority as timber harvest. This act was passed about the time that more people were becoming interested in forests for the aesthetics provided by outdoor activities, as well as wildlife watching. The National Forest Management Act of 1976 (NFMA) erected a procedure for planning and coordination required for successful multiple use of forests. It requires that forests maintain a natural diversity of wildlife populations. The planning process under NFMA has facilitated public involvement, which has included many legal challenges to forest plans based on different value systems and interpretations of the law.

FARMLAND

The trend of the growing population of the United States is to migrate into the urban and suburban areas, away from the rural, farm communities. The total amount of U.S. land in farms has decreased from 1.2 billion acres in the 1950s to approximately 950 million acres in 1994. (See Figure 11.8.) Although the number of farms has decreased from almost 7 million in the early 1900s to close to 2 million in 1992, the average size of those farms has increased. Farming has become increasingly specialized, mechanized, labor efficient, and capital intensive, allowing farm productivity to increase by 1.84 percent annually since World War II.

Recent efforts have been under way to protect agricultural land from development and to protect and enhance wildlife and conservation aspects of agricultural landscapes. The 1985 Farm Bill was the first of its kind with respect to provisions related directly to conservation concerns. The Conservation Reserve Program (CRP) was established in the 1985 bill to offer subsidies to farmers to protect highly erodible and other environmentally sensitive croplands by removing those fields from crop production and planting grasses or trees. The Worldwatch Institute reports that, since 1982, the registered amount of soil lost to water erosion in the United States dropped from 1.7 billion to 1.15 billion tons. Another 900 million acres are lost to wind erosion annually. Vegetative cover is the most important defense against erosion, typically limiting agriculturally induced erosion when fields are left to fallow for 7 to 15 year periods that allow vegetation to grow back.

The Wetlands Reserve Program (WRP), added in the 1990 Farm Bill, was designed to restore converted or farmed wetlands to their previous wetland conditions and to pay landowners to permanently retire the acreage. The Swampbuster provision, Section 1221 of the 1985 Farm Bill, is intended to deny all federal farm program payments to any farmer who drained wetlands to plant crops. Section 1211, also known as Sodbuster, denies the same federal payments to farmers who bring highly erodible lands, previously idle, into production without a conservation program. Land that falls under the Sodbuster provision can still be farmed, if it is farmed under an approved conservation plan.

The farm bill is one of the most important pieces of federal legislation affecting wildlife habitat on private lands in the United States.[11] A retrospective study using Breeding Bird Survey data and county agricultural statistics showed a significant population response by many grassland and upland breeding birds to the geographic distribution of CRP acreage. Some of these species include western meadowlarks, ring-necked pheasants, and bobwhite quail.[12] Mammals have also benefited from the additional grassland acreage provided by CRP lands, as greater small mammal diversity was noted compared to surrounding fields.

FIGURE 11.10

STATUS OF U.S. PLANT AND ANIMAL SPECIES: 1995

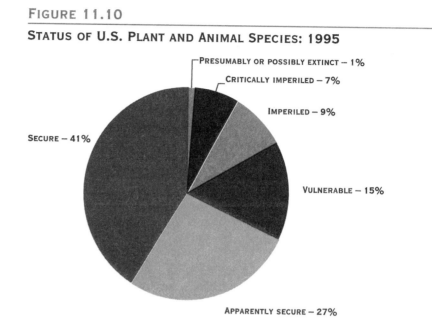

Source: The Nature Conservancy, Priorities for Conservation: 1996 Annual Report Card for U.S. Plant and Animal Species (Arlington, VA:1996).

Note: Total=20,481 species; does not include 346 species not yet ranked.

FIGURE 11.11

PORTION OF U.S. SPECIES AT RISK, BY PLANT AND ANIMAL GROUP: 1995

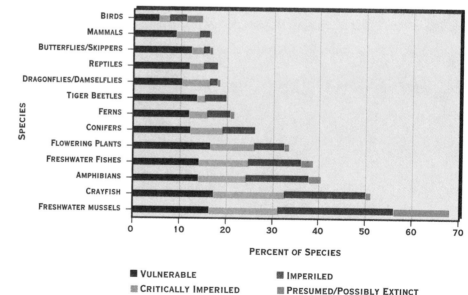

Source: The Nature Conservancy, Priorities for Conservation: 1996 Annual Report Card for U.S. Plant and Animal Species (Arlington, VA:1996).

Note: Total=20,481 species; does not include 346 species not yet ranked.

---

[11] D. L. Risley et al., "1995 Farm Bill: Wildlife Options in Agricultural Policy," *The Wildlife Society Technical Review* 95-1 (1995).

[12] T. B. Lauber, "Birds and the Conservation Reserve Program: A Retrospective Study" (Master's thesis, University of Maine, Orono, 1996).

WILDLIFE

Based on data from The Nature Conservancy, approximately one-third of U.S. plant and animal species are in some danger of extinction.[13] (See Figure 11.10.) These include 1 percent that are presumed extinct, 7 percent critically imperiled, 9 percent imperiled, and 15 percent vulnerable to extinction. The degree of species at risk varies greatly among taxonomic groups.[14] (See Figure 11.11.) The most endangered groups are associated with water.

Species in danger of extinction show up in zones or hotspots that often coincide with particularly rich and particularly imperiled ecosystems. Figure 11.12 shows the biodiversity hotspots in the United States by state.[15] California and Hawaii each have over 600 species classified as presumably extinct, critically imperiled, imperiled, or vulnerable to extinction.

Several Western states (Oregon, Nevada, Utah, and Arizona), as well as Texas, Florida, Alabama, North Carolina, Virginia, and a number of other Southern states each have from 300–600 (or more) known species in some danger. This distribution corresponds to the endangered ecosystems of the United States.

Scientists attribute species decline, endangerment, and extinction to four main causes: habitat destruction and degradation, pollution, exotic species, and direct take of the species through harvesting or hunting. Climate change is likely to be an additional force of extinction in the future. Although habitat loss is probably the greatest threat, others are also significant. For example, a conservative estimate is that 67 million birds and countless numbers of other animals are killed on agricultural lands as a result of the use of pesticides each year.[16] In many cases,

multiple factors (such as habitat loss plus climate change) put species and populations of plants and animals at risk.

One-third of flowering plants in the United States are in some danger. Half of these are regarded as vulnerable. Conifers (26 percent at risk) and ferns (21.6 percent) are only slightly better off. Many of the rarest plants naturally occur in specialized habitat in no more than a handful of locations. If these locations are disturbed, the species can be lost. As plants are the basis for animal life in ecosystems, the losses and endangerment of plants can have serious repercussions for other species.

Aquatic animals are generally more endangered than terrestrial species. Freshwater mussels are the most imperiled taxonomic group, with more than two-thirds (68 percent) at risk. Once more than 30 species of mussels and 130 snails were found only in the Mobile River basin of Alabama. Now more than half the mussels and nearly a quarter of the snails are extinct. Mussels are extremely sensitive environmental indicators, and their demise indicates the poor condition of many rivers and streams. They feed by filtering water through their bodies and concentrate large amounts of chemical contaminants. In addition, many species are subject to habitat loss due to dam construction (responsible for the loss of 30 to 60 percent of the native mussel populations in some rivers), dredging, channelization, and sedimentation. They are also subject to competition from nonnative mussels, such as zebra mussels and Asian clams, as well as direct take by humans. Crayfish, also aquatic specialists, are the second most endangered group with more than half of their species at risk.

Amphibians (frogs, toads, salamanders) are the most endangered group of vertebrates with 40 percent at risk. Amphibians are particularly vulnerable because of their lifestyle, in which they lay their eggs in water, metamorphose

FIGURE 11.12

BIODIVERSITY HOTSPOTS IN THE UNITED STATES, BY STATE: 1995

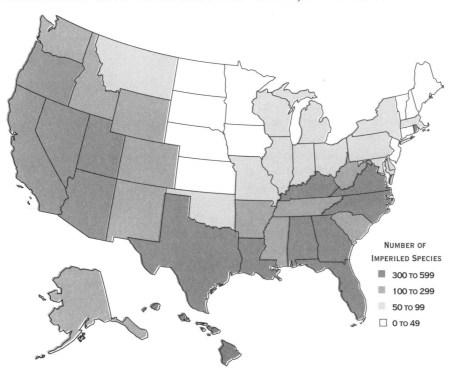

NUMBER OF
IMPERILED SPECIES

■ 300 TO 599
▨ 100 TO 299
▨ 50 TO 99
□ 0 TO 49

Source: Bruce A. Stein, "Putting Nature on the Map," The Nature Conservancy 46 (1996), 24-27.

---

[13] Bruce A. Stein and Stephanie R. Flack, *1997 Species Report Card: The State of U.S. Plants and Animals* (Arlington: The Nature Conservancy, 1997).

[14] The report includes approximately 20,500 species of plants and animals, the most comprehensive database for U.S. species, and includes information from The Nature Conservancy, state agencies in the Natural Heritage Network, and many collaborating museums, universities, and other scientific institutions.

[15] Bruce A. Stein, "Putting Porture on the Map," *The Nature Conservancy* 46 (1996), 24–27.

[16] David Pimentel, Cornell University, personal communication.

TABLE 11.3

ENDANGERED AND THREATENED SPECIES IN THE UNITED STATES

GROUP	ENDANGERED	THREATENED
MAMMALS	55	8
BIRDS	75	14
REPTILES	15	18
AMPHIBIANS	9	6
FISHES	67	40
SNAILS	15	7
CLAMS	56	6
CRUSTACEANS	15	3
INSECTS	24	9
ARACHNIDS	5	0
ANIMAL SUBTOTAL	**336**	**111**
FLOWERING PLANTS	495	110
CONIFERS	2	0
FERNS AND OTHERS	26	2
PLANT SUBTOTAL	**523**	**112**
GRAND TOTAL	**859**	**223**

TOTAL U.S. ENDANGERED:
859 (336 ANIMALS, 523 PLANTS)

TOTAL U.S. THREATENED:
223 (111 ANIMALS, 112 PLANTS)

TOTAL U.S. LISTED:
1,082 (447 ANIMALS*, 635 PLANTS)

Source: U.S. Department of the Interior, *Endangered Species Technical Bulletin*, (June 1997).

*Four animals have dual status in the United States.

from a tadpole to an adult form, and then leave water but must remain in moist habitats. They are subject to threats at all stages of their lifestyles. In addition to destruction of wetland habitats, amphibians may be particularly vulnerable to pollution, including acid rain and ozone depletion. In many cases, declines in amphibian populations are unexplained but are probably due to multiple causes acting together.

Some 39 percent of freshwater fish species are thought to be in danger, with 11 percent of those regarded as critically imperiled. Of the 30 native fish existing in Arizona, all but one are either threatened, endangered, or candidates for listing.

Causes of endangerment are similar to those for mussels but include competition from nonnative fish species or varieties that have deliberately been introduced for angling. In Arizona and other Western states, diversion of water for irrigation and other uses has also imperiled fish.

Some 18 percent of U.S. reptiles, 16 percent of mammals, and 15 percent of birds are thought to be in danger of extinction. The majority of the U.S. mammal species are classified as secure (64 percent) or apparently secure (20 percent). The U.S. bird species appear to hold a similar status; 76 percent are classified as secure and 10 percent apparently secure. However, most bird species are widespread geographically and can be subject to population declines and local extinctions in many places without endangering the species. Among birds, prairie species and aquatic species, such as ducks that nest in the far North and spend most of their lives at sea, have experienced serious population declines in recent decades. In addition to the 90 U.S. birds on the endangered species list, the U.S. Fish and Wildlife lists another 124 as "of high concern."

Invertebrates are not as well surveyed as vertebrates but appear to be in a similar situation. Some 17–20 percent of butterflies, dragonflies, and tiger beetles are at risk, with habitat destruction being the biggest cause. Many native North American species of bees have become rare or endangered because of the presence of the European honeybee. There recently appears to be a significant drop in U.S. populations of European honeybees because of an accidentally introduced virus. This, in turn, is likely to affect plants that will not be pollinated because of lack of bees. As in many ecological problems, there is a cascading of negative effects.

The Department of the Interior maintains a list of legally protected endangered and threatened species and those with recovery plans. Presently, 336 U.S. animals and 523 plants are listed as endangered, and 111 animals and 112 plants are listed as threatened. (See Table 11.3.) This only indicates the species that have gone through all of the legal steps for listing and represents just the tip of the iceberg of species at risk. An additional 600 species are biologically qualified but have not undergone all of the paperwork to be listed. (The Interior Department had listed more than 2,000 candidate endangered species before discontinuing the list in 1997.)

Alien species (nonnative plants and animals), which are introduced either intentionally or accidentally, have become leading causes of threats to U.S. species and ecosystems. Alien species degrade ecosystems by altering their physical or chemical properties and deplete native wildlife by preying on them or competing with them for food, living space, and other resources. According to the North Carolina Botanical Garden's Biota of North America Program, approximately 4,000 species of nonindigenous plants occur outside of cultivation.[17] The Congressional Office of Technology Assessment (OTA) reported that at least 2,300 alien animal species inhabit the United States.[18] People rely on some of these exotic species for cultivating crops and raising livestock. A very small percentage of these alien species actually cause environmental and economic damage, but those few species cause severe damage. Seventy-nine species have cost the United States $97 billion. Those nonnative species that cause problems were sometimes introduced to correct environmental problems, such as kudzu, which was introduced to help avoid soil erosion. Many nonnative fish species are introduced for sport and recreation, while many others land here as accidental stowaways in the mail, cargo, ballast water, or even aircraft landing gear.

---

[17] J. T. Kartesz, unpublished data reported in Bruce A. Stein and Stephanie R. Flack, ed., *America's Least Wanted: Alien Invasions of U.S. Ecosystems* (Arlington: The Nature Conservancy, 1996).

[18] U.S. Congress, Office of Technology Assessment, *Harmful Non-indigenous Species in the United States* (Washington, DC: GPO, 1993).

MARINE WILDLIFE

The marine fishing industry contributes $21 billion annually to the U.S. economy.[19] The United States maintains an exclusive economic zone (EEZ) of 200 nautical miles off the shoreline of the United States and its territories. This EEZ is the world's largest, totaling 3.5 million square miles. Beyond this zone, U.S. vessels also fish in international waters that are regulated by international and multinational agreements. From 1960 to 1995, U.S. commercial fish catches have more than doubled, from approximately 2 million metric tons to about 4.5 million metric tons. (See Figure 11.13.) The U.S. accounts for about 5 percent of the world fish catch, which exceeded 91 million tons in 1995, double the level of 1965.[20] However, there are increasing signs, nationally and globally, that this level of take is not sustainable.

Many species that once were common have declined and fishers are switching to lower-value species. The UN Food and Agriculture Organization (FAO) estimates that of 200 stocks (species fished in a particular oceanic region) that are taken worldwide, more than 25 percent are overexploited, depleted, or recovering from overfishing. An additional 35 percent are "fully exploited," meaning that maximum amounts are presently being taken. Of the 158 stock groups for which the National Marine Fisheries Service has adequate stock data, 73 groups (46 percent) have populations below what would produce long-term potential yield (the maximum long-term average catch that can be achieved from the resource). Of 157 stocks for which utilization levels are known, some 56 stocks (36 percent) are being overexploited and 70 (44 percent) are being fully utilized.

The fisheries situation is most severe in the Northeast. The fishing grounds of the North Atlantic are some of the most productive in the world. "Groundfish," such as cod, haddock, and flounder, supported a major fishing industry in New England and maritime Canada for centuries. Now most of these groundfish and others have been driven to historic low populations by overfish-

FIGURE 11.13

COMMERCIAL FISH CATCHES IN THE UNITED STATES: 1960–1995

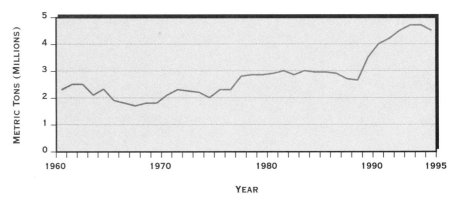

Source: National Marine Fisheries Service, *Fisheries of the United States* (Washington, D.C.: annual)

ing. One-third (18) of the overutilized stocks among U.S. fisheries are groundfish in the Northeast. Fisheries biologists refer to the "collapse" of fishery stocks, which has shifted the balance of marine ecosystems in the region and threatens the future of the fishing industry of New England and the Maritimes.

Both the United States and Canada have made significant changes in groundfishing regulations since the early 1990s in response to fishery stock declines, particularly those for cod in the North, in the Gulf of Maine, and on Georges Bank. Each country now uses a combination of adjustable measures: total allowable catches, gear restrictions, closed areas, limits on the numbers of days fished, bycatch reduction or elimination, and required reporting. Under these rules, fishing continues, but stocks have much improved chances for recovery.

A variety of other stocks are overexploited and probably declining. These include clams and other crustaceans and molluscs in the Northeast; large deep ocean fish, such as tuna (some species have declined by 90 percent in the past 20 years), marlin (down 60–80 percent in the past 20 years), and swordfish (numbers in the North Atlantic have declined 70 percent in the past 20 years and in 1995, 85 percent of the Atlantic swordfish caught were juveniles); and most reef fish. Pacific Coast

fisheries are also fully utilized for the most part. In the western Pacific, off Hawaii (where there are now over 140 fishing vessels compared with fewer than 10 in 1990) and U.S. territories such as American Samoa, most stocks of migratory open water fishes (e.g., tuna and swordfish) are near their long-term sustainable levels. California's white abalones are on the verge of extinction. Only off the Alaskan coast in the Bering Sea and Gulf of Alaska are most species in very good condition, although not without some problems (e.g., pollocks). However, with over 4,000 fishing vessels in the waters around Alaska, only careful management will prevent overfishing. Competition for fish has apparently caused Stellar's sea lion populations to dwindle in the Bering Sea.

Shark fishing, which increased in the 1970s and boomed with rising prices in the 1980s, has resulted in population declines of 50 to 75 percent in the past two decades in the dominant species of sharks (e.g., dusky and sandbar sharks) along U.S. coasts. Shark fishing is almost universally unmanaged, and there are very poor data on harvesting and population impacts. However, killing of sharks, both as targets of fishers and as unwanted "trash fish" caught unintentionally, has increased dramatically in the past two decades. Compared to most other fish species,

---

[19] National Marine Fisheries Service, *Fisheries of the United States* (1996, 1997).

[20] Food and Agricultural Organization of the United Nations, *Yearbook of Fishery Statistics* (Rome, 1996).

sharks have low reproductive potential due to biological characteristics, such as reaching reproductive stages late in life, reproducing every few years rather than annually, and having small numbers of young that are born alive. Thus, depleted shark stocks are very unlikely to recover quickly. Because sharks are top-level predators, their drastic declines are likely to affect the entire food chain. In 1997, the National Marine Fisheries Service imposed drastic reductions on the numbers of sharks that can be killed in the U.S. fishery.

Salmon present a special case because they are "anadromous," living in the oceans and returning to their natal streams to spawn. Alaskan salmon stocks have produced bumper harvests in recent years. In contrast, most continental populations have declined drastically in recent decades to the point that 18 populations have been listed and more have been proposed as endangered or threatened. Once-massive fisheries on the Columbia River and its tributaries have been reduced to numbers of fish in the hundreds or fewer. The primary causes of endangerment of these salmon are hydroelectric dams, which prevent migration of adults to their spawning streams and of hatchlings to the sea, siltation of spawning streams due to logging and other disturbances, and overfishing. Other anadromous fishes face similar obstacles. Atlantic shad were greatly depleted early in the century but are making a limited comeback in some areas. Sturgeon are almost extinct in U.S. river systems.

Fishing methods also have unintended impacts on other species. Fishermen often catch species other than their target species. For example, only 5–25 percent of a shrimper's catch is shrimp. The unwanted fish and other animals (known as bycatch) are discarded. High seas drift-netting, a practice whereby hundreds of miles of nets were left for days in the open ocean, has been banned. An international treaty in the early 1990s banned drift nets in excess of 2.5 km (1.5 miles). However, thousands of miles of nets that have broken away or were lost at sea are still "ghost fishing" and capturing fish and other marine organisms. Although some shorter drift nets are still

used, drift nets have been replaced in many cases by long-line fishing whereby lines up to 80 miles long with over 30,000 hooks are deployed beyond the fishing ship. It is estimated that 50–100 million hooks are set annually in the southern oceans.

In addition to noncommercial fish, including sharks, that are caught on these lines, tens of thousands of seabirds that are attracted by the bait fish are caught annually. This is having devastating effects on these long-lived birds such as albatrosses and petrels. Over 40,000 albatrosses are estimated to be killed annually in the southern oceans. These include the wandering albatross, a species of special concern, whose population is estimated to be declining 10 percent annually because of long-lining. More than 11,000 seabirds, including the endangered short-tailed albatross, are killed annually in the Gulf of Alaska and some 10,000 albatrosses in the waters off Hawaii. These estimates are con-

servative as in most areas there are few observers.

Sea turtles are also taken by long lines. They are among the most endangered groups of animals in the world, with six of the seven species of sea turtles listed as endangered. (Five of these occur in the United States.) Drowning in shrimp nets is a major problem for sea turtles of the world, as is development on the sandy beaches on which they spawn and the stealing of eggs on nesting beaches, although this has been reduced considerably by beach protection programs. To reduce the accidental catch of sea turtles, U.S. regulations now require shrimpers to use Turtle Excluder Devices (TEDs), which deflect turtles out of shrimp nets. There are also restrictions on the amount of time that nets can be kept in the water to prevent turtles from drowning.

Another example of unintended take is the killing of tens of thousands of dolphins that occurs with certain kinds of tuna fish-

FIGURE 11.14

SOURCES OF POLLUTION AFFECTING HARVEST-LIMITED SHELLFISH WATERS IN THE GULF OF MEXICO: 1990–1995

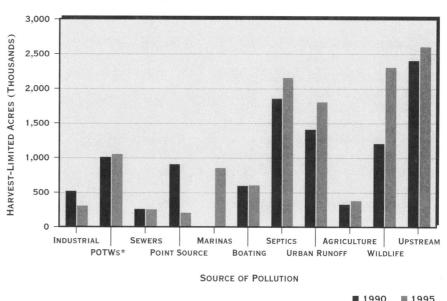

■ 1990   ■ 1995

Source: U.S. Department of Commerce, National Oceanic and Atmospheric Administration, National Ocean Survey, Ocean Assessments Division, Strategic Assessment Branch, National Shellfish Register, unpublished, (Rockville, MD, 1996).

* Publicly Owned Treatment Works.

Notes: Harvest-limited acres are shellfish growing waters that are not available for direct marketing at all times. There may be several reasons why an area is classified as harvest-limited, including water quality problems, lack of funding for complete surveying and monitoring, conservation measures, and other management or administrative actions.

ing. In the 1960s and 1970s, hundreds of thousands were killed annually. Recent U.S. legislation has restricted these kinds of fishing and authorized labeling of "dolphin-safe" tuna when appropriate methods are used. Eastern spinner dolphins and northeast spotted dolphins have suffered significant declines.

Bottom trawling, where heavy nets are dragged on the seabed for "groundfish" such as cod, haddock, and flounder, and shellfish such as mussels, is severely disruptive of marine environments. The nets dislodge marine life and change habitat by moving rocks and stirring up sand. The effect of this common practice has been compared to clear-cutting of forests.[21] It is estimated that an area equivalent to the world's continental shelf is trawled every 2 years.

There are very few monitoring methods for the hundreds of thousands of marine species that are not involved in commercial trade, but many of these are subject to habitat destruction and pollution as well as unintended take from commercial operations.

Pollution is particularly acute in certain estuaries and fisheries. Many fisheries have been shut down for oysters and other shellfish that filter contaminants as well as food from the water and accumulate them in their bodies. In 1995, 35 percent (3.3 million acres) of the 9.3 million acres of the Gulf of Mexico available for shellfish harvesting were under harvesting restrictions at least part of the year. The main problem was poor water quality, primarily from runoff of fecal bacteria from upstream farms and other sources. (See Figure 11.14.) Each summer, a huge area of the Louisiana coast becomes almost completely devoid of life as a result of the bacteria fertilizers that are washed down the Mississippi River and remove oxygen from the waters of the Gulf. Smaller "dead zones" have appeared in other bays such as the Chesapeake Bay.

An additional threat to marine and coastal ecosystems are foreign species of crabs, mussels, fish, and invertebrates that have been accidentally deposited in U.S. waters by ocean-going ships. Released from the competitive pressures in their native environment, these species often have a devastating effect on the native species in the environments in which they find themselves. The Japanese green crab is presently expanding its range up the Pacific coast of the United States at a very rapid rate, leading to losses of native crabs and other species.

WATER RESOURCES AND QUALITY

The United States has rich water resources, including 3.5 million miles of rivers and streams, 41 million acres of lakes, 34,000 square miles of estuaries (excluding Alaska), and 33,000 trillion gallons of groundwater. Most of this water is east of the Mississippi River, a region that generally receives twice as much annual rainfall as the land west of the Rocky Mountains. Of the 400 billion gallons of water used by Americans, three-quarters come from surface waters and one-quarter from groundwater. Electric utilities account for 47 percent of water use, with irrigation accounting for another 33 percent. (See Figure 11.15.) As a whole, groundwater recharge rates exceed withdrawals, but in some Western aquifers, the water table is subsiding due to overuse. Water availability shapes much of the resource use and settlement patterns of the Western states. Water quality is an issue nationwide.

America's drinking water is among the safest in the world. It is made up of more

FIGURE 11.15

WATER USE IN THE UNITED STATES, BY SECTOR: 1900–1990

(SELECTED YEARS)

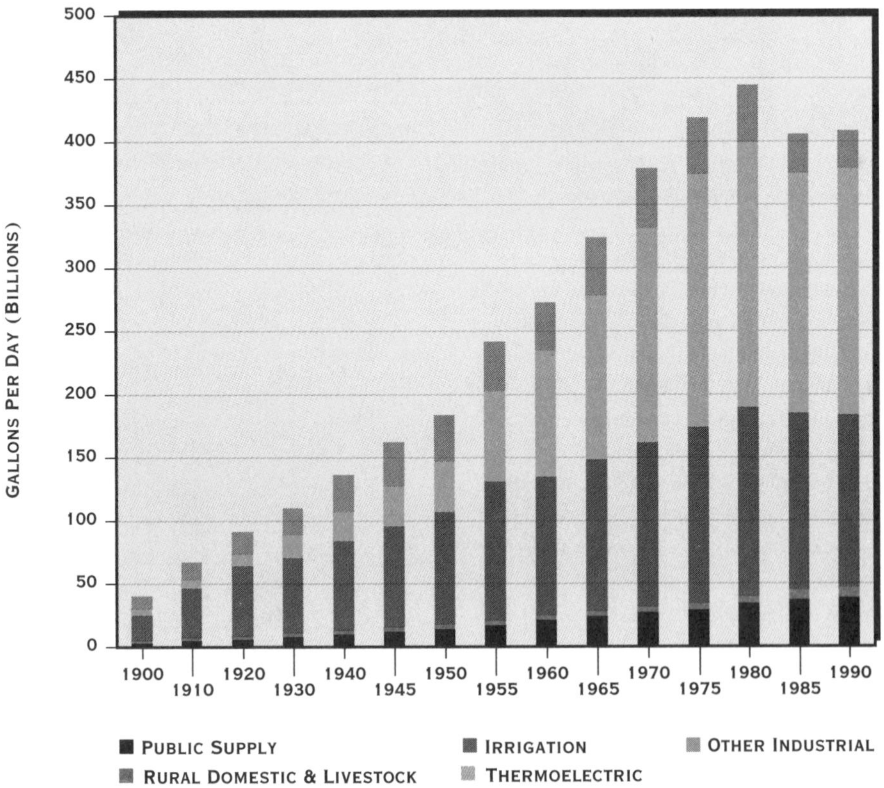

Sources: U.S. Department of Commerce, Bureau of the Census, Historical Statistics of the United States: Colonial Times to 1970, Series J 92-103 (Washington, D.C.:GPO 1975) W.B. Solley, R.R. Pierce, and H.A. Perlman, Estimated Water Use in the United States in 1990, Circular 1081 (Reston, VA: U.S. Department of the Interior, Geological Survey, 1993) and earlier reports in this series.

---

[21] Elliott A. Norse, Marine Conservation Biology Institute, Redmond, WA.

FIGURE 11.16

POPULATION IN THE UNITED STATES SERVED BY COMMUNITY DRINKING WATER SYSTEMS VIOLATING HEALTH-BASED REQUIREMENTS: 1994

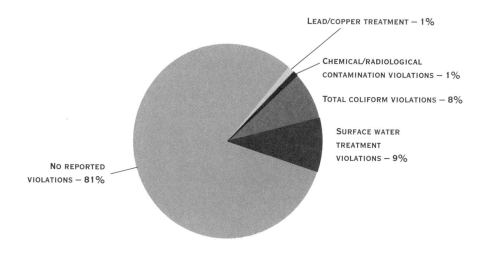

LEAD/COPPER TREATMENT — 1%

CHEMICAL/RADIOLOGICAL CONTAMINATION VIOLATIONS — 1%

TOTAL COLIFORM VIOLATIONS — 8%

SURFACE WATER TREATMENT VIOLATIONS — 9%

NO REPORTED VIOLATIONS — 81%

Source: U.S. Environmental Protection Agency, Safe Drinking Water Information System, 1994.

Notes: As many as one-fourth of the water systems did not complete required monitoring; compliance status of some of these could not be assessed. A total of 243 million people are served by community systems.

than 200,000 public water systems, including 58,000 community water systems that serve 243 million people. In 1994, more than 80 percent of the community water systems reported no violations of the health-based standards of the Safe Drinking Water Act. (See Figure 11.16.) But violations occurred in water systems that serve 40 million people. Almost all of these involved microbiological violations. In the spring of 1992, an outbreak of the parasite cryptosporidium killed 100 people and made hundreds of thousands of people ill in Milwaukee, Wisconsin. Lead in drinking water remains a problem, with about 69 million people receiving water from systems that have needed to reduce potential lead contamination to consumers.

The Federal Water Pollution and Control Act of 1972, commonly known as the Clean Water Act, sets a goal of "drinkable, swimmable, fishable" waters for the United States and provides a comprehensive framework of standards, technical assistance, and grants to meet these goals. The United States has made tremendous strides in cleaning up its waterways in the last three decades. Gross pollution from open dumping of untreated municipal wastes and industrial discharge is largely a thing of the past. In the 1960s, toxic and anoxic conditions lead to predictions of the "death" of Lake Erie and major rivers such as the Hudson. The Cuyahoga River in Cleveland, Ohio, actually caught on fire in 1969.

Today, conspicuous water pollution is essentially gone, but its legacy remains. In addition, more insidious "nonpoint sources" still fill the nation's waterways with bacteria, sediments, chemicals, fertilizers, and other contaminants. Agricultural activities are responsible for 60 percent of the identified impairment of public use or degradation of aquatic life in the nation's rivers and streams. Fertilizer use has doubled in the United States since 1950 to 40 million tons annually. There has recently been concern that runoff of nutrients and bacteria from huge commercial hog operations in North Carolina and commercial poultry operations on Maryland's eastern shore have contributed to environmental conditions where a microorganism *Pfiesteria piscicida* killed tens of thousands of fish and possibly caused human illness in the summer of 1997.

The Clean Water Act designates types of uses for the various surface waters of the United States, ranging from fishing to navigation. The Environmental Protection Agency's (EPA's) 1994 National Water Quality Inventory surveyed 17 percent of the miles of rivers and streams in the United States and assessed their ability to support the use designated for them (waters with a designated use of navigation do not need to be as clean as those with a designated use of fishing). They found 64 percent to be in good quality for their designated use, including 7 percent that may not retain their good condition unless action is taken. Another 22 percent failed at times to support their designated uses (fair condition), and 14 percent were estimated to be too polluted and frequently fail to meet the criteria for designated use (poor condition). Less than 1 percent were completely unable to support the use designated for them.

TABLE 11.4

DESIGNATED-USE SUPPORT IN SURFACE WATERS OF THE UNITED STATES: 1994

DESIGNATED-USE SUPPORT	RIVERS AND STREAMS	LAKES, PONDS AND RESERVOIRS	ESTUARIES
	MILES	ACRES	SQUARE MILES
FULLY SUPPORTING	352,828	8,598,603	15,426
THREATENED	43,454	2,184,198	1,651
PARTIALLY SUPPORTING	135,679	4,845,390	7,261
NOT ATTAINABLE	83,739	1,505,946	2,439
TOTAL SURFACE WATERS ASSESSED	615,806	17,134,153	26,847
TOTAL SURFACE WATERS NOT ASSESSED	2,932,932	23,691,911	7,541
TOTAL SURFACE WATERS	3,548,738	40,826,064	34,388

Source: U.S. Environmental Protection Agency (EPA), Office of Water (OW), *National Water Quality Inventory: 1994 Report to Congress*, Appendixes, EPA841-R-95-006 (Washington, D.C.: 1995).

TABLE 11.5

NATIONAL AMBIENT WATER QUALITY IN U.S. RIVERS AND STREAMS—VIOLATION RATE: 1980–1995

POLLUTANT	VIOLATION LEVEL	1980	1985	1989	1990	1991	1992	1993	1994	1995
FECAL COLIFORM BACTERIA	ABOVE 200 CELLS PER 100 ML	31	28	30	26	15	28	31	28	35
DISSOLVED OXYGEN	BELOW 5 MG PER LITER	5	3	3	2	2	2	(Z)	2	1
PHOSPHORUS, TOTAL, AS PHOSPHOROUS	ABOVE 1.0 MG PER LITER	4	3	2	2	2	2	2	2	4
LEAD, DISSOLVED	ABOVE 50 MG PER LITER	(Z)	(Z)	(Z)	(Z)	(Z)	(Z)	NA	NA	NA
CADMIUM, DISSOLVED	ABOVE 10 MG PER LITER	1	(Z)	(Z)	(Z)	(Z)	(Z)	NA	NA	NA

NA = NOT AVAILABLE.
Z = LESS THAN 1.

Source: U.S. Geological Survey.

Note: Violation level based on U.S. Environmental Protection Agency water quality criteria. Violation rate represents the proportion of all measurements of a specific water quality pollutant which exceeds the "violation level" for that pollutant. "Violation" does not necessarily imply a legal violation. Data based on U.S. Geological Survey's National Stream Quality Accounting Network (NASQAN) data system; for details, see source. Years refer to water years. A water year begins in October and ends in September, mg=micrograms.

There are six designated biological, chemical, physical, or economic/social conditions that prevent a river from meeting its designated use. One of the main pollutants is fecal coliform bacteria that enter water from improperly treated sewage and agricultural runoff, affecting 34 percent of all impaired river miles. In 1995, 35 percent of all measurements of U.S. rivers and streams exceeded the EPA standards of 200 cells per 100 ml. After some improvement in the mid-1980s, this level now is similar to that of the mid-1970s, with some 35 percent exceeding criteria. Excessive violations of dissolved oxygen, lead, and cadmium have largely been eliminated, while excessive

phosphorus has been reduced somewhat. Siltation from soil erosion, which reduces the river's ability to support life, also affected 34 percent of all impaired river miles.

A similar situation was found for lakes, ponds, and reservoirs, where 42 percent of the total acreage was surveyed in 1995. Of these, 63 percent were in good condition, including 13 percent threatened. Another 28 percent of the acres were fair, and 9 percent were poor. The main problems were nutrients (43 percent of all impaired lake acres), siltation (28 percent), oxygen-depleting substances (24 percent), and metals (21 percent). Some lakes were polluted by more than one factor.

Similarly for estuaries, 63 percent were in good condition and met designated use criteria, including 6 percent whose continued good condition was threatened. Another 27 percent were fair and partially met the standards; 9 percent were poor quality. Nutrients and bacteria were the most common contaminants.

The Great Lakes have recovered considerably from the dramatic problems of lack of oxygen, fish kills, and other acute problems of the 1960s and 1970s. By the mid-1990s, the near-shore waters were generally safe for swimming and as a source of drinking water (following normal treatment). However, only 3 percent of the near-

FIGURE 11.17

OVERALL DESIGNATED-USE SUPPORT IN THE GREAT LAKES: 1994

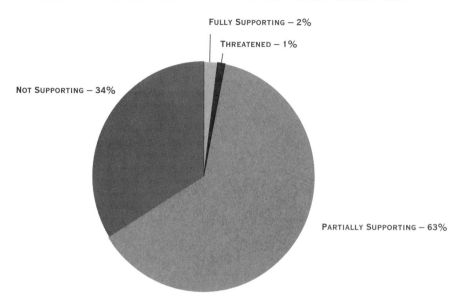

FULLY SUPPORTING – 2%

THREATENED – 1%

NOT SUPPORTING – 34%

PARTIALLY SUPPORTING – 63%

Source: U.S. Environmental Protection Agency (EPA), Office of Water (OW), National Water Quality Inventory: 1994 Report to Congress, Appendixes, EPA841-R-95-006 (Washington, D.C.: 1995).

Note: Based on an assessment of 94 of Great Lakes shoreline miles.

shore water fully supported all designated uses, including 1 percent whose future quality is threatened. Another 34 percent was in fair condition. Fully 63 percent of the Great Lakes shoreline waters did not support designated uses such as fishing. (See Figure 11.17.) Persistent toxic chemicals, especially polychlorinated biphenyls (PCBs), are ubiquitous in the Great Lakes and result in fish consumption advisories being posted along most of the shores. Many of these chemicals were deposited in the Great Lakes from atmospheric sources and runoff from rivers through the mid-1970s and persist because of their chemical stability. Although there has been a general decrease in concentration of the toxic chemicals in the past two decades, the rate of decrease has slowed recently.

Nonnative species have created havoc in Great Lakes ecosystems throughout the latter half of the 20th century. Sea lamprey, which entered the Great Lakes through the

St. Lawrence Seaway, were responsible for the elimination of the lake trout, once the dominant predatory fish of the lakes. This invasion, coupled with pollution, habitat destruction, and fishing pressure, resulted in other extinctions and a fish fauna that is very different from the native fauna. Introduced species of salmon now thrive in Lake Michigan and other lakes. The zebra mussel, accidentally introduced in the 1980s, probably from ship ballast water, has reached epidemic proportions and has inflicted major economic damage by blocking pipes on power plants, water treatment facilities, and other man-made objects, as well as drastically reducing populations of native mussels and other species.

In 1995, fish consumption advisories or bans were issued on 1,740 water bodies in 47 states. Coastal states showed more fish consumption advisories than interior states, with the Great Lakes states having the most advisories. These advisories indi-

FIGURE 11.18

NUMBER OF FISH CONSUMPTION ADVISORIES ISSUED IN THE UNITED STATES, BY STATE: 1995

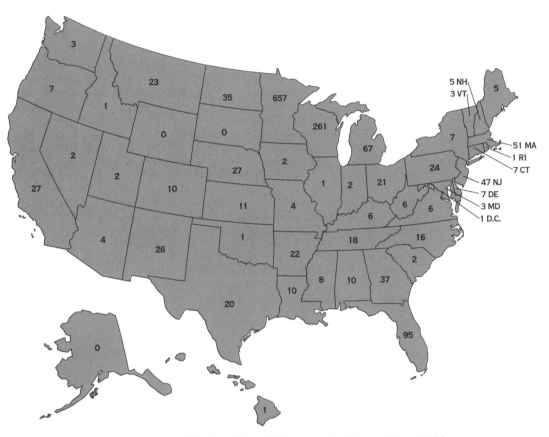

Source: U.S. Environmental Protection Agency (EPS), Office of Water (OW), Update: National Listing of Fish and Wildlife Consumption Advisories, Fact Sheet (Washington, D.C.: 1996).

Note: The numbers depicted here do not necessarily reflect the geographic extent of chemical contamination in each state not the extent of state monitorting efforts.

cated that chemical contamination of certain species of fish had reached levels that would be harmful to at least some segments of the public (such as pregnant women). Many sources of pollution contribute to the increased contamination and higher number of advisories. They range from wildlife and agriculture to urban runoff, septics and sewers, boating, and industrial areas.

Mercury accounted for 1,308 contaminated fish advisories in 35 states in 1995. Its health effects include nervous system disorders, decreased reproduction, and physiological effects. Mercury originates from coal-burning power plants, smelters,

and incineration of waste as well as inappropriate disposal of millions of batteries every year. It is transported through the atmosphere and deposited in the water, where it is chemically changed into methylmercury, which is absorbed by fish and increases in concentration up the food chain. Despite the widespread problem of this metal that does not degrade in the environment, there is no regulation of mercury emissions and few control efforts.

Regulation has been effective at reducing the deposition of acid particles of sulfur and nitrogen oxides (acid rain), which have acidified lakes and streams, particularly in

FIGURE 11.19

NUMBER OF CONTAMINATED FISH ADVISORIES IN THE UNITED STATES, BY POLLUTANT: 1993–1995

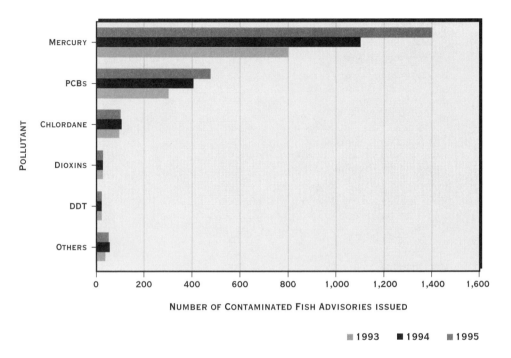

NUMBER OF CONTAMINATED FISH ADVISORIES ISSUED

■ 1993   ■ 1994   ■ 1995

Source: U.S. Environmental Protection Agency (EPA), *Update: National Listing of Fish and Wildlife Consumption Advisories* (Washington, D.C.: Office of Water, 1996).

the northern United States and eastern Canada during the past few decades. Approximately 1,000 lakes and 2,000 streams in the United States are now chronically acidic, and some 14,000 lakes in Canada are so acidic that they cannot support fish life. Acid rain is caused primarily by coal- and oil-burning power plants and by automotive exhaust. Environment Canada estimates that acid rain causes $1 billion worth of damage annually in Canada and that 50 percent of the sulfur dioxide in Canada comes from the United States. The

1990 amendments to the Clean Air Act created a national acid rain program that included reduction targets for sulfur dioxide and nitrogen oxides. Between 1970 and 1994, emissions of sulfur dioxide declined by 32 percent, with most of the reduction taking place in the last few years. The goal to reduce nonutility industrial emissions by 5.6 million tons has been met, and the goal to reduce overall emissions to 10 million tons below 1980 emissions will largely be met by 2000.

AIR QUALITY

The nation's air quality has improved considerably in the last 25 years. Many targeted air pollutants have declined, as have releases of toxic substances into the air. Nonetheless, air quality remains a significant public health concern, particularly in urban areas and among the millions of Americans who are elderly or who suffer from asthma, emphysema, and other conditions that reduce respiratory capacity.

Two types of air pollutants are regulated in the United States—common or "criteria" air pollutants and "air toxics." Under the authority of the Clean Air Act (CAA) amendments of 1970, the EPA has developed National Ambient Air Quality Standards for six criteria air pollutants: carbon monoxide (CO), lead, nitrogen dioxides (NO_2), ozone, sulfur dioxide (SO_2) and large-particulate matter (PM–10). (See Table 11.6.) In 1997, EPA announced rules to also regulate small-particulate matter (PM–2.5) as well as to tighten the standards for ozone. EPA is directed to regulate 189 toxic air pollutants. These are among the 300 chemicals whose emissions have been reported annually by manufacturing facilities with at least 10 employees, under the Toxics Release Inventory (TRI) begun in 1987.

TABLE 11.6

AIR POLLUTANTS AND THEIR IMPACT ON HEALTH IN THE UNITED STATES

CARBON MONOXIDE

SOURCES: CARBON MONOXIDE IS A COLORLESS, ODORLESS, POISONOUS GAS FORMED WHEN CARBON IN FUELS IS NOT BURNED COMPLETELY. IT IS A BYPRODUCT OF MOTOR VEHICLE EXHAUST, WHICH CONTRIBUTES MORE THAN TWO-THIRDS OF ALL CO EMISSIONS NATIONWIDE.

NAAQS: 9 PPM (MEASURED OVER 8 HOURS)

HEALTH EFFECTS: CARBON MONOXIDE ENTERS THE BLOODSTREAM AND REDUCES OXYGEN DELIVERY TO THE BODY'S ORGANS AND TISSUES. EXPOSURE TO ELEVATED CO LEVELS IS ASSOCIATED WITH VISUAL IMPAIRMENT, REDUCED WORK CAPACITY, REDUCED MANUAL DEXTERITY, POOR LEARNING ABILITY, AND DIFFICULTY IN PERFORMING COMPLEX TASKS.

LEAD

SOURCES: SMELTERS AND BATTERY PLANTS ARE THE MAJOR SOURCES OF LEAD IN AIR. INDOORS, LEAD CAN BE FOUND IN OLD BUILDINGS FROM PAINT ON WALLS.

NAAQS: 1.5 UG/M3 (MEASURED AS A QUARTERLY AVERAGE)

HEALTH EFFECTS: LEAD ACCUMULATES IN THE BODY IN BLOOD, BONE, AND SOFT TISSUE. BECAUSE IT IS NOT READILY EXCRETED, LEAD CAN ALSO AFFECT THE KIDNEYS, LIVER, NERVOUS SYSTEM, AND OTHER ORGANS. EXCESSIVE EXPOSURE TO LEAD MAY CAUSE ANEMIA, KIDNEY DISEASE, REPRODUCTIVE DISORDERS, AND NEUROLOGICAL IMPAIRMENTS SUCH AS SEIZURES, MENTAL RETARDATION, AND/OR BEHAVORIAL DISORDERS.

NITROGEN DIOXIDE

SOURCES: NITROGEN OXIDES FORM WHEN FUEL IS BURNED AT HIGH TEMPERATURES AND COME PRINCIPALLY FROM MOTOR VEHICLE EXHAUST AND STATIONARY SOURCES SUCH AS ELECTRIC UTILITIES AND INDUSTRIAL BOILERS.

NAAQS: 0.053 PPM (MEASURED AS AN ANNUAL AVERAGE)

HEALTH EFFECTS: NITROGEN DIOXIDE CAN IRRITATE THE LUNGS AND LOWER RESISTANCE TO RESPIRATORY INFECTIONS SUCH AS INFLUENZA. THE EFFECTS OF SHORT-TERM EXPOSURE ARE STILL UNCLEAR, BUT CONTINUED OR FREQUENT EXPOSURE TO CONCENTRATIONS THAT ARE TYPICALLY MUCH HIGHER THAN THOSE NORMALLY FOUND IN THE AMBIENT AIR MAY CAUSE INCREASED INCIDENCE OF ACUTE RESPIRATORY ILLNESS IN CHILDREN.

OZONE

SOURCES: UNLIKE OTHER POLLUTANTS, OZONE IS NOT EMITTED DIRECTLY INTO THE AIR BUT IS CREATED BY SUNLIGHT ACTING ON NOX AND VOC EMISSIONS IN THE AIR. THERE ARE LITERALLY THOUSANDS OF SOURCES OF THESE GASES, FROM GASOLINE VAPORS TO CHEMICAL SOLVENTS.

NAAQS: 0.12 PPM (MEASURED AT THE HIGHEST HOUR DURING THE DAY)

HEALTH EFFECTS: EXPOSURE TO OZONE SIGNIFICANTLY REDUCES LUNG FUNCTION AND INDUCES RESPIRATORY INFLAMMATION IN NORMAL, HEALTHY PEOPLE DURING PERIODS OF MODERATE EXERCISE. IT CAN BE ACCOMPANIED BY SYMPTOMS SUCH AS CHEST PAIN, COUGHING, NAUSEA, AND PULMONARY CONGESTION.

SULFUR DIOXIDE (SO2)

SOURCES: FORMED WHEN FUEL CONTAINING SULFUR (MAINLY COAL AND OIL) IS BURNED AND DURING METAL SMELTING AND OTHER INDUSTRIAL PROCESSES.

NAAQS: 0.03 PPM (ANNUAL AVERAGE) .14 PPM (OVER 24 HOURS)

HEALTH EFFECTS: SO2 CAN AFFECT BREATHING, AND CAN CAUSE RESPIRATORY ILLNESS, ALTERATIONS IN PULMONARY DEFENSES, AND AGGRAVATION OF EXISTING CARDIOVASCULAR DISEASE.

PARTICULATE MATTER (PM-10) (PM-10 REFERS TO PARTICLES WITH A DIAMETER OF 10 MICROMETERS OR LESS)

SOURCES: PARTICULATE MATTER IS THE TERM FOR SOLID OR LIQUID PARTICLES FOUND IN THE AIR. PARTICLES ORIGINATE FROM A VARIETY OF MOBILE, STATIONARY, AND NATURAL SOURCES (DIESEL TRUCKS, WOOD STOVES, POWER PLANTS, DUST, ETC.), AND THEIR CHEMICAL AND PHYSICAL COMPOSITIONS VARY WIDELY.

NAAQS: 50 UG/M3 (ANNUAL AVERAGE) 150 UG/M3 (DAILY AVERAGE)

HEALTH EFFECTS: MAJOR CONCERNS FOR HUMAN HEALTH FROM EXPOSURES TO PM-10 ARE: EFFECTS ON BREATHING AND RESPIRATORY SYSTEMS, DAMAGE TO LUNG TISSUE, CANCER, AND PREMATURE DEATH. THE ELDERLY, CHILDREN, AND PEOPLE WITH CHRONIC LUNG DISEASE, INFLUENZA, OR ASTHMA TEND TO BE ESPECIALLY SENSITIVE TO PARTICULATE MATTER.

Source: U.S. Environmental Protection Agency (EPA), Air Quality Trends (Research Triangle Park, N.C.: Office of Air Quality, Planning, and Standards, September 1995).

Note: NAAQS= National Ambient Air Quality Standards. ug/m3=Micrograms Per Cubic Meter.

Geographic areas that do not meet the primary standards designed to protect human health are referred to as nonattainment areas. In September 1996, a total of 171 areas were in nonattainment for one or more pollutant: one (Los Angeles) for NO_2, 10 for lead, 31 for CO, 43 for SO_2, 68 for ozone, and 81 for PM–10.[22] The Pollution Standard Index (PSI) indicates overall air quality for a given day among all cities with populations greater than 200,000. Between 1985 and 1994, the number of reported days per year in which at least one criteria pollutant exceeded air quality standards on a given day declined by 72 percent (excluding Los Angeles and Riverside, California).

FIGURE 11.20

URBAN AIR QUALITY IN THE UNITED STATES: 1985–1994

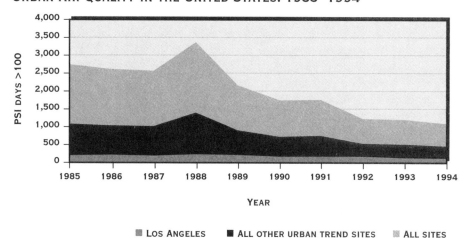

■ LOS ANGELES   ■ ALL OTHER URBAN TREND SITES   ▨ ALL SITES

Source: U.S. Environmental Protection Agency (EPA), Office of Air Quality Planning and Standards (OAQPS), National Air Quality and Emissions Trends Report, 1994, Data Appendix, Table A-13 (Research Triangle Park, N.C., 1995).

Notes: PSI=Pollutant Standards Index. The PSI index information from many pollutants across an entire monitoring network into a single number, which represents the worst daily air quality experienced in an urban area. Only carbon monoxide and ozone monitoring sites with adequate historical data are included in the PSI trend analysis above, except for Pittsburgh, where sulfur dioxide contributes a significant number of days in the PSI high range. PSI ranges and health effect descriptor words are as follows: 0 to 50 (good); 51 to 100 (moderate); 101 to 199 (unhealthful); 200 to 299 (very unhealthful); and 300 and above (hazardous). The figure above shows the number of days when the PSI was greater than 100 (= unhealthy or worse days).

TABLE 11.7

NUMBER OF PERSONS LIVING IN U.S. COUNTIES WITH AIR QUALITY LEVELS ABOVE NATIONAL AMBIENT AIR QUALITY STANDARDS: 1984–1994

POLLUTANT	1984	1985	1986	1987	1988	1989	1990	1991	1992	1993	1994
					MILLIONS OF PERSONS						
SULFUR DIOXIDE	1.7	2.2	0.9	1.6	1.7	0.1	1.4	5.2	0.0	1.4	0.0
NITROGEN OXIDE	7.5	7.5	7.5	7.5	8.3	8.5	8.5	8.9	0.0	0.0	0.0
CARBON MONOXIDE	61.3	39.6	41.4	29.4	29.5	33.6	21.7	19.9	14.3	11.6	15.3
OZONE	79.2	76.4	75.0	88.6	111.9	66.7	62.9	69.7	44.6	51.3	50.2
LEAD	4.7	4.5	4.5	1.7	1.6	1.6	5.3	14.7	4.7	5.5	4.4
PARTICULATES	32.6	47.8	41.7	21.5	25.6	27.4	18.8	21.5	25.8	9.4	13.1
ANY NAAQS	N/A	N/A	N/A	101.8	121.3	84.4	47.4	86.4	53.6	59.1	62.0

Source: U.S. Environmental Protection Agency (EPA), Office of Air Quality Planning and Standards (OAQPS), National Air Quality and Emissions Trends Report, EPA-450/F-95-003 (Research Triangle Park, N.C., 1995) and earlier reports.

Note: Particulates for 1984-86 refer to total suspended particulates. After 1986, particulates refer to PM-10 (particulate matter with a diameter 10 microns or less).

---

[22] Data for this section are from the U.S. Environmental Protection Agency, unless stated otherwise.

Air pollution is largely the result of combustion, with automobiles, power plants, and industrial processes being the primary sources. Emissions of combustion products, such as nitrogen oxides (NOX, including NO$_2$) and volatile organic compounds (VOC), which are the principal components of ozone, as well as SO$_2$, increased throughout the century. However, since 1970, concentrations of all criteria pollutants except NOX have declined. (See Figure 11.21.) Largely due to the transition to unleaded gasoline, lead emissions have declined 98 percent, from 219,500 tons in 1970 to 5,000 tons in 1994. Nonferrous smelters and other stationary sources are the primary emitters of lead at present. Carbon monoxide emissions declined 23 percent from 128 to 98 million tons per year. More than 67 percent of all CO emissions (95 percent in urban areas) result from exhaust from cars and other vehicles. Emissions of SO$_2$ declined 32 percent from 1970 to 1994, particularly after the 1990 amendments to the CAA aimed at reducing acid rain (of which SO$_2$ is a precursor) by reducing emissions from coal-burning utilities. Emissions of nitrogen oxides, including NO$_2$, increased 14 percent from 20.6 million tons in 1970 to 23.6 million tons in 1994. Since 1985, emissions of NOX from vehicles has declined by 7 percent, while emissions from power plants and other stationary sources of combustion have increased by 8 percent. Emissions of VOCs, which combine with NOX under the influence of sunlight to form ozone (smog), declined 10 percent from 1985 to 1994, and mean ozone concentrations declined from 0.124 to 0.109 parts per million. As of 1994, about 50 million people lived in counties with ozone levels that exceeded the national standard, particularly in the northeastern United States, Texas Gulf Coast and Los Angeles area. The amount of large particulates, with a diameter of 10 micrometers or less (PM–10) emitted from human-made sources, declined 78 percent from 1970 to 1994.

FIGURE 11.21

PERCENTAGE CHANGE IN U.S. EMISSIONS, BY POLLUTANT: 1970–1994

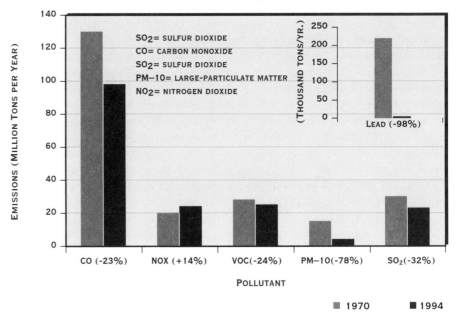

Sources: U.S. Environmental Protection Agency (EPA), Office of Air Quality Planning and Standards (OAQPS), National Air Pollutant Emission Trends, 1900-1994, Tables 3-1 through 3-6 , EPA-454/R-95-011 (Research Triangle Park, N.C., EPA, OAQPS: 1995). U.S. Environmental Protection Agency (EPA), Office of Air Quality Planning and Standards (OAQPS), National Air Quality and Emissions Trends Report, 1994, Data Appendix, Tables A-2 through A-8 (Research Triangle Park, N.C., EPA, OAQPS: 1995).

Note: PM-10 refers to particulate matter with a diameter 10 microns or less. Totals may not agree with sum of components due to independent rounding.

FIGURE 11.22

U.S. EMISSIONS OF AIR TOXICS: 1988, 1992, AND 1994

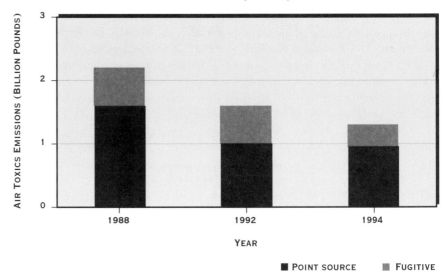

Source: U.S. Environmental Protection Agency (EPA), Office of Air Quality Planning and Standards (OAQPS), 1994 Toxics Release Inventory: Public Data Release, EPA/745-R-96-002 (EPA, Washington, D.C., 1996).

Since 1988, releases of air toxics as measured by the Toxic Release Inventory (TRI) declined by 41 percent, from 2.3 billion pounds in 1988 to 1.3 billion pounds in 1994. The TRI does not include small companies, and commercial, mobile, and residential sectors. Nine of the 10 toxic air pollutants that collectively account for more than half of the TRI emissions have declined since 1988.

Increased attention has been paid recently to indoor air pollutants. These include radon, a naturally occurring gas that EPA estimates is responsible for 7,000–30,000 deaths per year, making it the second-leading cause of lung cancer. EPA estimates that environmental tobacco smoke (ETS), or "secondhand smoke," another indoor air pollutant, is responsible for 3,000 deaths of nonsmokers annually and 150,000 to 300,000 lower respiratory tract infections in infants.

CLIMATE CHANGE

In 1995, the Intergovernmental Panel on Climate Change (IPCC), which represents the world's leading experts on climate change, concluded that "the balance of evidence suggests that human activities are having a discernible influence on global climate."[23] Emissions of "greenhouse gases" (carbon dioxide, methane, nitrous oxide, and halogenated compounds, such as chlorofluorocarbons) have added to the natural greenhouse effect of the earth's atmosphere and are warming the planet. Over the past century, the earth's surface temperature has increased by about 1 degree Fahrenheit, sea level has increased 4–10 inches, and mountain glaciers are melting worldwide.

If present trends continue, according to the IPCC, the earth's temperature is projected to increase from 2 to 6 degrees Fahrenheit (1 to 3 degrees Celsius) over the next century, the fastest rate of warming and greatest overall change in temperature since the end of the Ice Age, 10,000 years ago. The increased temperature would be accompanied by a sea level rise of 6 to 38 inches (30–91 cm) by 2100. The potential effects of rapid climate change include

stresses and disruptions on ecological and socioeconomic systems already stressed by pollution and overconsumption. These added stresses will negatively affect human health by making conditions favorable for the spread of disease borne by insects and other vectors that will thrive in a warmer, and often wetter, climate. Ecological systems that have adapted to a certain climate will be disrupted. Species extinctions will increase, as plants and animals will be unable to move fast enough over a human-dominated habitat to reach areas conducive to their requirements.

The primary cause of climate change has been an increase in emission of gases related to industrial activity. These gases are long lived in the atmosphere, and, even if atmospheric concentrations of greenhouse gases were to stabilize by the year 2100, temperatures would continue to rise for decades and sea levels would increase for centuries. Fossil fuel combustion is respon-

sible for about 88 percent of all U.S. emissions of greenhouse gases. Since the industrial era, atmospheric concentrations of carbon dioxide (CO_2) have increased by nearly 30 percent, methane has doubled and nitrous oxides have increased by 15 percent. About 65 percent of the greenhouse gas increase in the past century is due to CO_2, which is a byproduct of the burning of fossil fuels. The United States, with about 5 percent of the world's population, accounts for approximately 25 percent of global energy production and about 15 percent of world CO_2 emissions. U.S. emissions have remained fairly constant, while global emissions have tripled since 1950.

Carbon dioxide is by far the most important contributor to greenhouse gas emissions by the United States, with over 1.2 billion metric tons released into the atmosphere annually. In the United States, electric utilities (36 percent) and transportation (32 percent) are the largest

FIGURE 11.23

U.S. EMISSIONS OF CARBON DIOXIDE FROM FOSSIL FUEL COMBUSTION, BY SECTOR AND FUEL TYPE: 1994

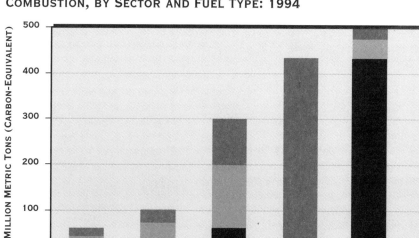

Source: U.S. Environmental Protection Agency, Inventory of U.S. Greenhouse Gas Emissions and Sinks: 1990–1994 (EPA, Washington, DC, 1995).

Note: Although not shown, U.S. territories account for slightly less than 1% of total emissions.

[23] J. T. Houghton et al., *Climate Change 1995—The Science of Climate Change: Contribution of Working Group I to the Second Assessment Report of the Intergovernmental Panel on Climate Change* (New York: Cambridge University Press, 1996). The panel is supported by a group of approximately 2,000 atmospheric scientists.

sources of CO_2 emissions, followed by other industry (21 percent), residential (7 percent), and commercial activities (4 percent). (See Figure 11.23.) Forests are an example of a "greenhouse gas sink" because they remove CO_2 from the atmosphere. The annual removal of 125 million tons of CO_2 by the 737 million acres of the United States that is forested is less than 8 percent of our gross emissions of CO_2.

Methane is 24.5 times as effective as CO_2 at trapping heat in the atmosphere over a 100-year period. The 27.1 million metric tons of methane emitted in 1990 were the greenhouse equivalent of 181 million metric tons of CO_2 emissions. U.S. methane emissions come mostly from landfills (36 percent), agriculture (33 percent), coal mining (15 percent), and production and processing of oil and gas, as well as natural sources. Nitrogen oxide has approximately 320 times the heat absorbency of CO_2. Fertilizer use is responsible for 45 percent of U.S. emissions of nitrogen oxide.

Chlorofluorocarbons (CFC) and other halogenated compounds (halons) were first manufactured in significant quantities following World War II. They are extremely long-lived in the atmosphere and stratosphere. Their greenhouse properties are more than a thousand times greater than CO_2. Conversely, ozone depletion can offset the greenhouse effect to some degree, so the overall impact of CFCs on global warming is still uncertain.[24]

In 1992, the nations of the world signed an international agreement with a "nonbinding aim" of stabilizing greenhouse gas emissions at 1990 levels by 2000. Although the United States has begun voluntary measures to reduce greenhouse gas production, emissions of CO_2 in 1994 were 4 percent greater than in 1990. In December 1997, negotiations under the International Climate Convention were expected to conclude with consideration of

FIGURE 11.24

SOURCES OF U.S. METHANE EMISSIONS: 1994

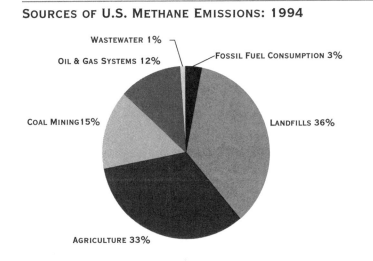

Source: U.S. Environmental Protection Agency, Inventory of U.S. Greenhouse Gas Emissions and Sinks: 1990-1994 (Washington, D.C.: 1995).

binding and verifiable targets for control of emissions.

STRATOSPHERIC OZONE

Protection of the stratospheric ozone layer is a certifiable environmental success story, where science identified a problem that was entirely caused by humans, and diplomacy, accompanied by scientific and technological advances, have led to a solution that is being implemented. In 1974, chemists Mario Molina and Sherwood Rowland (who in 1995 were awarded Nobel Prizes, along with Paul Crutzen, for this work), hypothesized that long-lived manufactured chemicals—chlorofluorocarbons (CFCs)—were destroying the layer of ozone that protects the earth from damaging ultraviolet radiation. Uses of CFCs included propellants in aerosol cans, a use that was quickly banned in the United States, Canada, and some Nordic countries. More problematic was the use of CFCs as insulating foams and cooling agents in refrigeration and air conditioners. In addition, related compounds

(halons) are used in fire extinguishers in sensitive applications (oil rigs, aircrafts, etc.) for which there are no substitutes. CFCs and halons were developed for these uses because of their chemical stability and huge heat-absorbing capacity. These properties also have led to the environmental problems. Being long-lived, CFCs float to the stratosphere, where they persist and engage in chemical reactions that destroy ozone molecules. Other compounds that destroy the ozone layer have been discovered, but much smaller quantities of these exist.

Rowland and Molina's hypothesis about the impact of CFCs on the ozone layer has been confirmed following significant additional research. After considerable political negotiation, the Montreal Protocol on Substances that Deplete the Ozone Layer (an international treaty) was signed in 1987[25] and was subsequently strengthened by several amendments that ultimately led to the effective end of production and importation of CFCs by the United States

[24] "World Meteorological Association/United Nations Environment Program/National Oceanographic and Atmospheric Administration Scientific Assessment of Ozone Depletion, Executive Summary," *World Meteorological Organization Research and Monitoring Program Publication* 37 (1994).

[25] Richard E. Benedick, *Ozone Diplomacy* (Cambridge: Harvard University Press, 1988).

TABLE 11.8

INVENTORY OF U.S. GREENHOUSE GAS EMISSIONS AND SINKS: 1990–1994

GAS / SOURCE	1990	1991	1992	1993	1994
MILLION METRIC TONS					
CARBON DIOXIDE					
FOSSIL FUEL COMBUSTION	1,336	1,320	1,340	1,369	1,390
OTHER	17	17	17	18	17
TOTAL	1,353	1,336	1,357	1,387	1,408
FORESTS (SINKS)	-125	-125	-125	NA	NA
NET TOTAL	1,228	1,211	1,232	NA	NA
METHANE					
LANDFILLS	66	67	66	67	68
AGRICULTURE	56	57	59	59	61
COAL MINING	29	28	27	24	29
OIL AND GAS SYSTEMS	22	22	22	22	22
OTHER	6	7	7	6	6
TOTAL	181	182	182	179	188
NITROUS OXIDE					
AGRICULTURE	16	17	17	17	19
FOSSIL FUEL COMBUSTION	12	12	12	12	12
INDUSTRIAL PROCESSES	8	9	8	9	9
TOTAL	37	37	37	38	41
HFCS AND PFCS	18.8	19.3	21.1	19.8	23.5
SF6	6.4	6.5	6.7	6.8	7
TOTAL U.S. EMISSIONS	1,595	1,582	1,604	1,630	1,666
NET, INCLUDING SINKS	1,470	1,457	1,479	NA	NA

Source: U.S. Environmental Protection Agency (EPA), Office of Policy, Planning and Evaluation (OPPE), *Inventory of U.S. Greenhouse Gas Emissions and Sinks: 1990-1994*, EPA-230-R-96-006 (Washington, D.C.: 1995).

Note: HFCs=hydrofluorocarbons. PFCs=perfluorocarbons. SF6=sulfur hexafluoride. NA=not available. Emissions include direct and indirect effects. Other carbon emissions come from fuel production and processing, cement and lime production, limestone consumption, soda ash production and consumption, and carbon dioxide manufacture. Total carbon dioxide does not include emissions from bunker fuels used in international transport activities. U.S. emissions from bunker fuels were approximately 23 million metric tons (carbon-equivalent) in 1994. Other methane emissions come from fuel combustion by stationary and mobile sources and from wastewater facilities.

FIGURE 11.25

CUMULATIVE PRODUCTION OF CFCS: 1958–1994

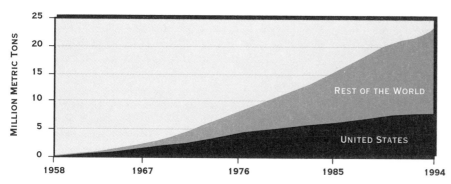

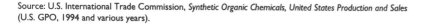

Source: U.S. International Trade Commission, *Synthetic Organic Chemicals, United States Production and Sales* (U.S. GPO, 1994 and various years).

and other industrialized countries on December 31, 1995.[26] Developing countries must complete their phase-out of CFCs by the year 2010. Most of the major producers among the developing countries are well on their way toward compliance. The phase-out has already led to a decline in the abundance of ozone-depleting chemicals in the upper atmosphere and will ultimately result in their reduction in the stratosphere. Although the abundance of ozone-depleting chemicals in the stratosphere is expected to peak in 1998, it will take another 50 or so years for stratospheric ozone concentrations to reach their previous level because of the long atmospheric lifetime of CFCs and related compounds.

The United States was the leading producer of CFCs at least through the 1980s. Production of CFCs peaked in the United States in 1987 at nearly 400,000 metric tons. Without controls, it was estimated that U.S. production would have reached nearly 3 million metric tons by 2005. However, the United States was among the first nations to ban the use of aerosol propellants and led international efforts to phase out CFC production through the Montreal protocol.

---

[26] The treaty also phases out halons and other ozone-depleting chemicals on differing timetables.

WASTE

The United States leads the world in waste generation, both in absolute and per capita terms. The average American generated 4.4 pounds of solid waste per day in 1994, a figure that has grown from 2.7 pounds in 1960 but is starting to decline. Disposing of this waste has become a serious social problem, and, to some degree, it has become an environmental problem as well. Three types of waste are generally recognized: municipal solid waste (garbage), toxic or hazardous waste (such as carcinogenic chemicals), and nuclear waste (produced by power plants and weapon production, as well as certain medical wastes).

SOLID WASTE AND RECYCLING

In 1976 the Resource Conservation and Recovery Act (RCRA) was passed to deal with the estimated more than 16,000 municipal solid waste sites, only 5,800 of which were known to be in compliance with state regulations. RCRA developed a disposal system for nonhazardous solid wastes and a cradle-to-grave management system for hazardous wastes. Better management techniques have led to a steady decline in solid waste landfills, to some 3,581 in 1995, according to EPA. (See Figure 11.28.) Landfill disposal capacity has increased as states and cities moved to larger, better designed and maintained sites. Consolidation into fewer sites has led to increased costs of transporting wastes and of maintaining landfills, with the average disposal fee increasing from $8.20 (1985) to $32.19 per ton in 1995.[27]

FIGURE 11.26

MUNICIPAL WASTE GENERATED IN THE UNITED STATES AND OTHER SELECTED OECD COUNTRIES

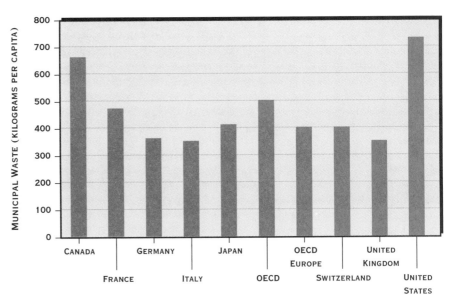

Source: OECD Environmental Data, Compendium 1995 (Paris: 1995).

Note: The definition of municipal waste and the survey methods used may vary from country to country. Data are for 1992 or latest available year.

FIGURE 11.27

U.S. SOLID WASTE PER CAPITA: 1960–2010 (PROJECTED)

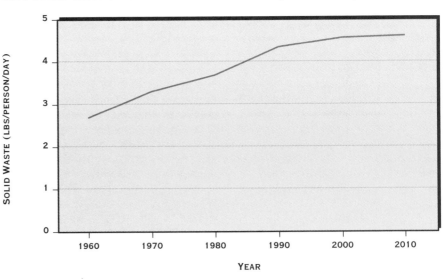

Source: U.S. Environmental Protection Agency, Office of Solid Waste and Emergency Response, Characterization of Municipal Solid Waste in the United States: 1995 Update, Table 1, p. 26, and Table 2, p. 27 (Washington, D.C.: 1996)

Note: Data are based on estimates and projections

---

27 Environmental Industries Association, data from National Solid Waste Management Association and *Solid Waste Digest* (Alexandria: Chartwell Information Publisher).

FIGURE 11.28

NUMBER OF SOLID WASTE LANDFILLS IN USE IN THE UNITED STATES: 1976–1995

(SELECTED YEARS)

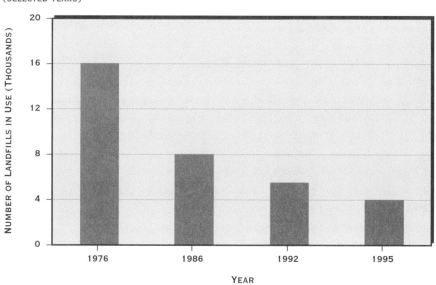

Source: U.S. Environmental Protection Agency, 1995 List of Municipal Solid Waste Landfills (1996), and unpublished data.

FIGURE 11.29

U.S. MUNICIPAL SOLID WASTE MANAGEMENT: 1960–2010 (PROJECTED)

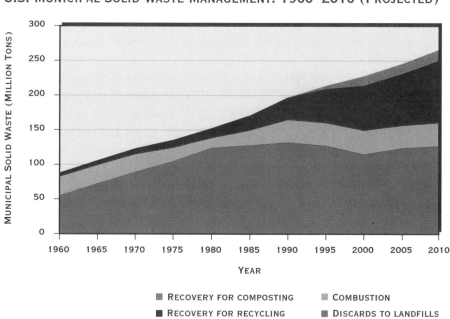

Source: U.S. Environmental Protection Agency, Office of Solid Waste and Emergency Response, Characterization of Municipal Solid Waste in the United States: 1995 Update Table 26, p. 91, and Table 38, p. 117 (Washington, D.C.: 1996).

TABLE 11.9

U.S. Municipal Solid Waste Trends: 1960–1994

Year	Gross Discards	Recovery for Recycling	Net Discards	Combustion	Discards to Landfills	Per Capita Waste Generation
	Million Tons					Lbs/Person/Day
1960	87.8	5.9	81.9	27.0	55.3	2.67
1970	121.9	8.6	113.3	25.1	89.5	3.29
1980	151.4	14.5	136.9	13.7	124.3	3.67
1990	198.0	32.9	165.1	31.9	132.3	4.33
1994	209.1	49.3	159.8	32.5	127.3	4.40

Source: U.S. Environmental Protection Agency, Office of Solid Waste and Emergency Response, *Characterization of Municipal Solid Waste in the United States: 1995 Update*, Table 26, p. 91 and Table 38, p. 117 (Washington, D.C.: 1996).

Disposal practices have shifted significantly over the past decade, with the increased use of recycling as a waste management technique. (See Figure 11.29.) In 1994, about a quarter (49.3 million tons) of all solid waste generated was recovered for recycling or composting. (See Table 11.9.) The amount of waste recovered has increased more than 350 percent since 1980. In 1995, 121 million people were served by 7,375 curbside recycling programs—a sevenfold increase in programs since 1988. Florida, Minnesota, and New Jersey are reportedly recycling more than 40 percent of their waste; nine other states indicate recycling rates of 30 percent or more. In addition, over 3,300 facilities handle grass and yard trimmings for composting. Incineration, while similar in absolute quantities to 1960 levels (presently 32 million tons), now accounts for 15 percent of the waste stream, half of the percentage in 1960. About 80 percent of these incinerators produce energy that is recovered and used. Future trends should continue in the direction of waste reduction and recovery as the pollution prevention model of "reduce, reuse, and recycle" becomes more widespread.

Hazardous Waste

The Toxic Release Inventory documents releases of more than 300 chemicals by nearly 23,000 manufacturing plants in the United States. In 1994, these facilities released 2.26 billion pounds of listed toxic chemicals into the environment. This represents a 44 percent decline since reporting began in 1988. The vast majority (69 percent) were emitted into the air, with 15 percent injected into subsurface wells, 13 percent disposed of on land, and 3 percent in water. (See Figure 11.30.) An additional 3.8 billion pounds of toxic chemicals were transferred off-site. Two-thirds of these transfers were for recycling, with only 8 percent being shipped for disposal. The leading emitters of toxics were the chemical, primary metals, and paper industries. However, the chemical industry has reduced its toxic releases by 47 percent since 1988. The greatest releases were in the manufacturing states of the Midwest and the South.

Abandoned sites contaminated with uncontrolled hazardous wastes are listed under the Superfund Law of 1980, amended in 1986 and extended in 1990, which is intended to facilitate their cleanup. Superfund created a trust fund, administered by the EPA to clean up the worst sites, which were placed on a National Priority List (NPL). Superfund also establishes liabilities for responsible parties involved in the release of hazardous substances and outlines a claims procedure for parties that have cleaned up the sites. The Superfund law does not contain any cleanup standards but applies standards from other federal or state laws.

Cleanup procedures involve treatment to significantly reduce the volume, toxicity, or mobility of hazardous substances, containment to seal the toxic material on the site from any exposure to the environment, and, in some cases, removal of contaminated dirt or other materials and destruction, usually by incineration under controlled conditions. Each of these procedures involve trained personnel working under conditions that prevent further contamination. Capital costs are high because of the extent of the contamina-

FIGURE 11.30

Percentage Distribution of Toxics Releases in the United States: 1994

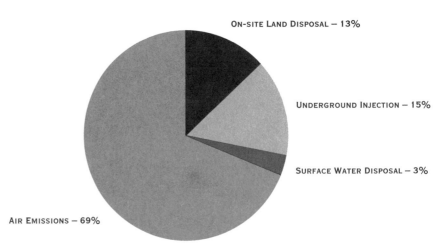

ON-SITE LAND DISPOSAL – 13%

UNDERGROUND INJECTION – 15%

SURFACE WATER DISPOSAL – 3%

AIR EMISSIONS – 69%

Source: U.S. Environmental Protection Agency, 1994 Toxics Release Inventory: Public Data Release (Washington, D.C.: 1996).

Note: Total releases=2.26 billion pounds.

tion and the technologies and personnel involved in the cleanup. However, a very small number of expensive sites account for more than half of all capital cleanup costs. In addition, Superfund has experienced considerable litigation costs to deal with lawsuits that try to determine liability for cleanup.

The EPA has identified more than 40,000 potentially hazardous waste sites across the nation. As of September 1995, a total of 1,374 of the worst sites were placed on a National Priority List for cleanup. At least 93 percent of these sites have some work under way, with permanent cleanup in progress or completed at 60 percent of these sites. Permanent cleanup had been completed at 346 (25 percent) of the NPL sites. At the end of 1995, EPA removed 24,472 low-priority sites from the Superfund list under their "brownfields" initiative, where less contaminated sites that will continue to be used for industrial purposes do not need to meet the same stringent criteria for cleanup as sites that may be used for housing and similar purposes.

NUCLEAR AND MIXED WASTE

Some of the most environmentally contaminated sites in the United States are the Department of Energy (DOE) sites of former development, testing, and production of nuclear weapons. Six major facilities, Hanford, Washington; Savannah River, South Carolina; Oak Ridge, Tennessee; Fernald, Ohio; Rocky Flats, Colorado; and the Idaho National Engineering Laboratory, account for about 80 percent of the DOE's environmental management budget, which is presently $9 billion annually and is expected to total $200–$350 billion in 1995 dollars. Cleanup costs at other agencies are expected to add another $34 to $38.5 billion. Costs at DOE facilities are so great because of the extent of the contamination and the expense of removing and storing nuclear waste and soil that has been contaminated.

Commercial nuclear power plant reactors currently generate about 2,000 metric tons of spent fuel annually, summing to 30,000 metric tons that are stored at about 70 power plants sites in lieu of a congressional decision on locating a long-term repository. Spent fuel, including plutonium,

which has a radioactive half-life of tens of thousands of years, accounts for more than 95 percent of the accumulated radioactivity in the United States. In contrast, low-level radioactive waste makes up more than 85 percent of the volume of U.S. nuclear waste but accounts for less than 0.1 percent of the radioactivity. Mixed waste includes both radioactive waste and nonradioactive hazardous waste.

States are authorized to form regional compacts for disposal of low-level waste. Presently, commercial sites are operating in Washington and South Carolina, with others pending. An interim waste-storage facility near Yucca Mountain, Nevada, is in the planning stages. Although construction is nearing completion, the necessary congressional approval has not yet been achieved.

ENVIRONMENTAL JUSTICE

Americans who are poor and members of minority groups are more at risk than other groups of suffering increased health risk and exposure to environmental hazards. In 1987, a landmark study by Charles Lee and Benjamin Chavis entitled Toxic Waste and Race in America, published by the United

Church of Christ (UCC), showed that race, not income, was the strongest correlate of residence near a commercial hazardous waste site. It found that the communities with the greatest number of commercial hazardous waste facilities had the highest composition of residents of racial and ethnic minorities. It further found that three of the five largest landfills in the United States were located in predominately Black or Hispanic communities.

The UCC study launched a movement for environmental justice and to counter environmental effects of racism. Additional research, by Mohai and Bryant, Bullard, and others has confirmed and extended the conclusions to identify disproportionate environmental risk to minorities beyond that which can be explained by income alone. (See Figure 11.31.) This includes exposure to poor air quality, lead, pesticides (particularly among migrant farm workers), as well as to hazardous waste. In addition, certain minority cultures consume larger than average quantities of fish in their diet and thus suffer greater exposure to heavy metals and other toxic chemicals that bioaccumulate in fish.

FIGURE 11.31

PERCENTAGE OF THE U.S. POPULATION EXPOSED TO POOR AIR QUALITY, BY RACE/ETHNICITY: 1993

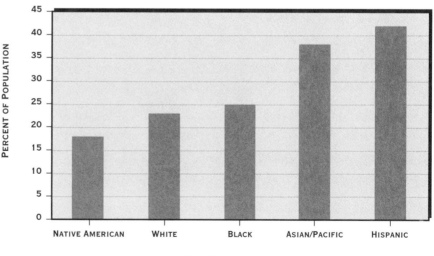

Source: Fred Seitz and Christine Plepys, Monitoring Air Quality in Healthy People 2000 , Statistical Notes No. 9 (Hyattsville, MD, National Center for Health Statistics: 1995).

Note: Data refer to proportion of population living in counties with air quality above the primary national air quality standard. Persons of Hispanic origin may be of any race.

The EPA established an Office of Environmental Justice in 1992. In 1994, President Clinton issued an executive order directing federal agencies to develop strategies for environmental justice. He also formed an interagency working group on environmental justice, chaired by the EPA.

ECONOMICS AND SCIENCE

Economic indicators of environment are difficult to establish. Costs and benefits are subject to major methodological uncertainties. Benefits are particularly hard to quantify. According to the Environmental Business Journal, approximately 59,000 U.S. private and public companies are engaged in environmental industries, including water treatment, waste management, water utilities, resource recovery, and environmental consulting and engineering. This economic sector has grown from some 463,000 employees and revenues of $52 billion in 1980 to 1,314,000 employees and $179.9 billion in 1994. There are no reliable summary statistics on economic benefits of a healthy environment in the United States. A preliminary estimate of the economic value of the world's ecosystem services (regulation of climate and atmospheric gases, water cycling, erosion control, soil formation, nutrient cycling, purification of wastes, as well as food production, raw materials, recreation, and water supply) is between $16 and $54 trillion per year.[28]

Expenditures on pollution abatement and control exceeded $117 billion in 1994, including $42.38 billion for water, $41.74 billion for solid waste, and $37.6 billion for air. This accounts for more than 2 percent of the U.S. gross domestic product. An additional $2.2 billion was spent by the government on regulation and monitoring. Government and business also spent $2 billion on research and development related to pollution. In constant dollars, expenditures on pollution abatement and control have nearly doubled since 1973, with the percentage spent on solid waste having increased dramatically over the past decade.

It has been estimated that the federal government's expenditures on environmental research and development totaled approximately $4 billion in Fiscal Year 1994.[29] Four federal departments and three independent agencies were responsible for almost all federal spending on environmental R&D. The National Aeronautics and Space Administration (NASA) was the largest spender, with just over $1 billion, most of which went to technology development of new satellite-based devices to monitor the earth at a global scale and the development of a computer-based information management system to handle the huge volume of data generated. DOE spent $662 million on environmental R&D, with most of the spending in development, particularly of technologies to clean up radioactive contamination at its own weapons development facilities. The National Science Foundation (NSF) was the leading funder of basic research on the environment, with some $595 million in grants to university-based researchers pursuing disciplinary studies. The Department of Interior spent $563 million, nearly all through its own research centers, on geological, hydrological, and biological topics of interest to the department and its state cooperators. The Department of Agriculture spent $419 million on research on environmental topics related to agriculture and forestry. A total of $344 million was spent by the National Oceanic and Atmospheric Administration (NOAA) in the Department of Commerce, mostly on climatic, weather, and oceanographic research. The EPA spent $346 million on research related to human health and environmental protection. There is concern among many scientists as well as environmentalists and business people that this collection of agencies and departments, each with a specific focus on a segment of the environment, and many with conflicting regulatory responsibilities, is insufficient to provide critical answers to the full range of environmental problems. A proposal for a National Institute for the Environment (NIE) has been slowly working through Congress. In 1997, the U.S. House of Representatives directed the National Science Foundation to study how it would establish and support an NIE.

The United States leads the world in both consumption and waste generation. Americans consumed about 4.5 billion metric tons of natural resources, or about 18 metric tons per person, and produced 730 kilograms per capita of waste in 1989. Since 1950, Americans have consumed more resources than all previous inhabitants of the earth combined. The United States, with 5 percent of the world's population in the mid-1990s, accounted for approximately 25 percent of the world's energy consumption. U.S. use of petroleum feedstocks is seven times the global per capita average. U.S. oil consumption (19.9 million barrels per day in 1994) nearly equals that of all of the remaining 24 members of the Organization for Economic Cooperation and Development in Europe and Japan (23.8 million barrels per day).

The Councils of the U.S. National Academy of Sciences and the Royal Society of London issued a joint statement in 1997 that, "For the poorer countries of the world, improved quality of life requires increased consumption of at least some essential resources. For this to be possible in the long run, the consumption patterns of the richer countries may have to change; and for global patterns of consumption to be sustainable, they must change."[30]

---

[28] Robert Costanza et al., "The Value of the World's Ecosystem Services and Natural Capital," *Nature* 387 (1997), 253–260. See also G. Daily, ed., *Nature's Services: Societal Dependence on Natural Systems* (Washington, DC: Island Press, 1997).

[29] Estimate developed by the Committee for the National Institute for the Environment, Washington DC, 1996.

[30] The Councils of the U.S. National Academy of Sciences and the Royal Society of London, *Towards Sustainable Consumption 1997*. See also National Academy of Sciences, *Environmentally Significant Consumption: Research Directions* (Washington, DC: National Academy Press, 1997).

FOR FURTHER INFORMATION, SEE:

BROWN, LESTER R., ET AL. *STATE OF THE WORLD: 1997*. NEW YORK: WORLDWATCH INSTITUTE, W.W. NORTON AND CO., 1997.

BROWN, LESTER R., ET AL. *VITAL SIGNS 1997: THE ENVIRONMENTAL TRENDS THAT ARE SHAPING OUR FUTURE*. NEW YORK: WORLDWATCH INSTITUTE. W.W. NORTON AND CO., 1997.

THE CENTERS FOR DISEASE CONTROL, NATIONAL CENTER FOR HEALTH STATISTICS. "MONITORING AIR QUALITY IN HEALTHY PEOPLE 2000." *STATISTICAL NOTES* 9 (SEPTEMBER 1995).

THE COUNCIL ON ENVIRONMENTAL QUALITY. *ENVIRONMENTAL QUALITY REPORT FOR 1994-95: THE TWENTY-FIFTH ANNIVERSARY REPORT OF THE COUNCIL ON ENVIRONMENTAL QUALITY*, 1997.

WEBSITES:

THE COMMITTEE FOR THE NATIONAL INSTITUTE FOR THE ENVIRONMENT WEBSITE AT <HTTP://WWW.CNIE.ORG>.

THE COUNCIL ON ENVIRONMENTAL QUALITY WEBSITE AT <HTTP://WWW.WHITEHOUSE.GOV/CEQ/>.

DEFENDERS OF WILDLIFE WEBSITE AT <HTTP://WWW.DEFENDERS.ORG>.

EARTHVISION WEBSITE AT <HTTP://WWW.EARTHVISION.NET>.

ENVIRONMENTAL PROTECTION AGENCY WEBSITE AT <HTTP://WWW.EPA.GOV>.

ENVIRONMENTAL RESEARCH LABORATORIES, NATIONAL OCEANIC AND ATMOSPHERIC ADMINISTRATION WEBSITE AT <HTTP://WWW.ERL.NOAA.GOV>.

ENERGY INFORMATION ADMINISTRATION, U.S. DEPARTMENT OF ENERGY WEBSITE AT <HTTP://WWW.EIA.DOE.GOV>.

FISH AND WILDLIFE SERVICE WEBSITE AT <HTTP://WWW.FWS.GOV>.

THE NATURE CONSERVANCY WEBSITE AT <HTTP://WWW.TNC.ORG>.

THE WORLD RESOURCES INSTITUTE WEBSITE AT <HTTP://WWW.WRI.ORG>.

CHAPTER 12

Government

HENRY S. WULF

GOVERNMENT

PERCENT OF U.S. LAND AREA THAT BELONGS TO THE FEDERAL GOVERNMENT:	29 PERCENT
TAX REVENUE AS A PERCENT OF GDP IN THE UNITED STATES 1994:	28 PERCENT
RANK OF UNITED STATES IN RATIO OF TAXES TO GDP AMONG 28 INDUSTRIALIZED NATIONS:	26TH LOWEST TAXES
STATE WITH THE LARGEST NUMBER OF LOCAL GOVERNMENTS:	ILLINOIS (6,723)
STATE WITH THE FEWEST NUMBER OF LOCAL GOVERNMENTS:	HAWAII (21)
PERCENTAGE OF REVENUE FROM TAXES IN 1991–92—	
FEDERAL GOVERNMENT:	52 PERCENT
STATE GOVERNMENTS:	45 PERCENT
LOCAL GOVERNMENTS:	35 PERCENT
PERSONAL INCOME TAX AS A PERCENT OF ALL FEDERAL TAXES IN—	
1960:	53 PERCENT
1990:	74 PERCENT
GOVERNMENT EMPLOYMENT (FEDERAL, STATE, AND LOCAL) AS A PERCENTAGE OF TOTAL NONFARM EMPLOYMENT IN—	
1960:	15.4 PERCENT
1995:	16.5 PERCENT

INTRODUCTION

This chapter brings some perspective, context, and background to discussions about government and government spending in the United States. Looking at American government through the prism of these statistics, this chapter will address such questions as:

- Compared to other countries, is government a large or small part of the U. S. economy?

- How many governments are there in the United States?

- Just how big is government compared to the private sector?

- What are the sources of government revenues overall? Do the sources differ much for the federal, state and local governments? Do they differ much from area to area?

- On what does government spend its money? How much does government spending vary for different areas?

- Has the emphasis of government activity changed much over the past few decades?

GOVERNMENT AND THE ECONOMY: AN INTERNATIONAL COMPARISON

The classic conservative-liberal discussions in the United States have often been framed around the issues of whether the government is too big, is too intrusive, is a drag on the economy, or needs to assist more in the care of neglected people, as well as other societal concerns such as labor/management issues or education funding. Compared with other countries, just how big is our government—federal, state, and local—relative to the economy?[1]

---

[1] It is important to be cautious in comparing government activity among different countries. First, the definition of government can vary considerably. Consider the extreme cases of a highly socialistic country where practically everything is government or a free-market country where government is minimal. In addition, it is very difficult to determine the defining line between national and subnational government activity.

FIGURE 12.1

TOTAL TAX REVENUE AS A PERCENTAGE OF GROSS DOMESTIC PRODUCT, BY SELECTED COUNTRY: 1994 (AT MARKET PRICES)

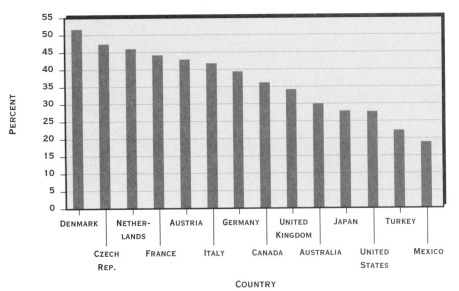

Source: OECD table <http://www.oecd.org/news_and_events/publishin/stat.pdf>.

One gauge of the size of a country's government relative to the size of its economy is a comparison of taxes relative to gross domestic product (GDP).[2] This is a fair measure because taxes are, by far, the single largest governmental revenue. Relative to other industrialized countries, the United States was ranked 26 out of 28 (OECD Countries) in 1994, a position that has varied almost not at all since 1980. To some, this low rank is positive because they see taxes as a drag on the economy—the higher the ranking, the less money for business investment. Others see this in positive terms, also, but with an entirely different slant—the United States has a much greater taxing capacity than it is using. This "extra" capacity might be available to help reduce social problems, maintain or extend infrastructure, or make important government investments in the future for activities such as education. However it is interpreted, the fact is that compared with these other industrialized countries the United States is a "low tax" nation.

GOVERNMENT AND THE ECONOMY: A STATE COMPARISON

Just as we can observe the varying economic role of government within nations, we can see the same thing within our own states. Each state can be visualized as if it were an individual entity with the economic attributes of a separate nation so that its economic growth can be gauged by the measures similar to those used for a nation's GDP. This measure is known as gross state product (GSP). Some states (California, for example) have such large economies that they would be among the world's top 10 if they were countries.

GSP is the state equivalent of the national-level GDP.[3] GSP is often expressed as the percentage of GSP that can be attributed to government. The range for 1994 is from 8.9 percent in Delaware to 39.4 percent in the District of Columbia. There are some geographic patterns among the 1994 ranking of government as a percent of each

state's GSP. For example, three of the six New England states are among the bottom five, with five of the six below the U.S. average.

Government composes a decreasing share of most states' economies in 1994 compared with 1987. The state with the greatest growth in that 7-year span was Alaska, with a 1.7 percent increase in the government share of the GSP. Vermont ranked second with a 0.4 percent rise. No other state was above a 0.1 percent increase, and five states decreased more than 3.0 percent.[4] Whether this broad trend will continue is not clear, especially in light of the discussions now taking place concerning devolution of federal responsibilities to state and local governments. At the heart of that debate is whether state and local governments will choose to continue the federal programs.

THE STRUCTURE OF GOVERNMENT

Just as government has a different economic impact in each state, the structure of government takes on a very different cast when you look in different parts of the country. Though people sometimes have a perception that government has a certain uniformity, in reality it is a series of 50 mutations. Take, for example, the case of county governments. In California the county governments definitely share responsibilities with other local governments—municipalities, school districts, special districts. Counties, on the other hand, are far and away the dominant local government in Virginia. In Connecticut and Rhode Island, county governments do not exist at all. In those two states, the primary local governments are cities and towns.

Even the federal government—ostensibly the same wherever one travels—has a different look in various parts of the country. The federal government, for example, owns a considerable portion of some states and very little of others. Of all the land area in the United States, more than one-quarter—

---

[2] Gross domestic product (GDP) is an economic measure of a country's economy. Taxes in this instance become the measure of the size of government. Though the resulting comparison requires some caution in interpretation, it is a reasonable measure of the impact of government on an economy.

[3] The Bureau of Economic Analysis produces both statistics. The most recent GSP data are available in Howard L. Friedenberg and Richard M. Beemiller, "Comprehensive Revision of Gross State Product by Industry, 1977-94," *Survey of Current Business* (Washington, DC: U.S. Department of Commerce, Bureau of Economic Analysis, June 1997).

a rather surprising 28.6 percent—belongs to the federal government. This national percentage was 33.9 percent in 1960. Between the mid-1970s and mid-1980s the percentage fell, reaching the current level in the late 1980s.

Although it might seem that the federal portion would be highest in the District of Columbia (24.1 percent), all but one of the 13 states in the Western region exceed that figure, some by a considerable amount. More than one-half the land in five of those West and Pacific area states is federally owned. (See Figure 12.2.)

Within other regions there is considerable variation in how much land belongs to the federal government. The nine Northeast states range from 0.3 percent (Connecticut) to 12.7 percent (New Hampshire). In the 12 Midwest states, the range is from 0.8 percent in Kansas to three states that top 10 percent each (Wisconsin, 10.1 percent; Minnesota, 10.5 percent; and Michigan, 12.6 percent).

The percentage of land ownership and the type of land owned (national forests, military bases, grazing lands, parks, and the like) give the federal government a very different presence among the states. These differences might influence feelings about taxes, specific laws, or media treatment that likely translate into very different social, political, and economic views by the citizens of the federal government. Whether these thoughts are extended to governments as a whole is arguable. Yet the public does have opinions about which levels of government they like and various facets of government that please or displease them.

LIKES AND DISLIKES ABOUT GOVERNMENTS AND TAXES

American attitudes toward government and taxes have been tracked for a number of decades.[5] When the three levels of government are compared to one another in terms of the public's feeling about where they get the most for their taxes, there are two

FIGURE 12.2

PERCENTAGE OF LAND IN THE UNITED STATES OWNED BY THE FEDERAL GOVERNMENT: 1996

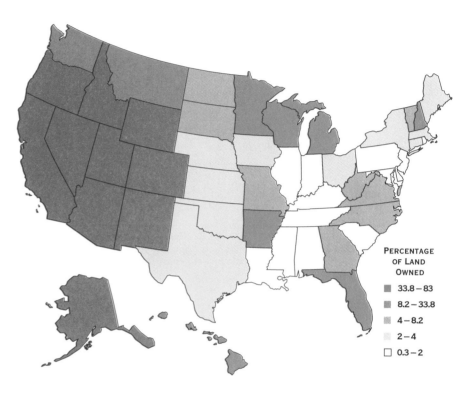

PERCENTAGE
OF LAND
OWNED

■ 33.8 – 83
■ 8.2 – 33.8
▨ 4 – 8.2
□ 2 – 4
□ 0.3 – 2

Source: U.S. General Services Administration in Statistical Abstract of the United States, 1996, table 364.

opposite trends evident in the Gallup Poll done for the U.S. Advisory Commission on Intergovernmental Relations from 1972 to 1993. They are that the percentage of Americans rating the federal government highest has declined, while the local government percentage has increased. The average for each decade of a favorable response for the federal government encapsulates the slump in support for the federal government; 35 percent for the 1970s, 31 percent for the 1980s, and 25 percent for the 1990s. Local government averages, in contrast, rose by decade from 27 percent in the 1970s, to 30 percent in the 1980s and 35 percent in the 1990s. The state government percentages showed little change over this span—20 percent in the 1970s, 23

percent in the 1980s, and 21 percent in the 1990s. The percentage of the public expressing no opinion ranged from 13 to 22 percent.

A second poll question determined which taxes the public deemed to be the least fair. These data show consistently that the federal income tax and the local property taxes are considered least fair, with state sales taxes and state income taxes trailing far behind. The averages for these taxes, from 1972 to 1993 were 32 percent for federal income tax, 29 percent for local property taxes, 17 percent for state sales taxes and 10 percent for state income taxes.

In looking at these poll results together, the public expresses increasing confidence in the ability of local governments to give them

---

[4] It will be important to determine whether some of the declining percentage of GSP attributable to government is due to the rapidly advancing economy in the private sector and a waning federal government presence.

[5] The following discussion uses Gallup Poll results as presented in U.S. Advisory Commission on Intergovernmental Relations, *Changing Public Attitudes on Governments and Taxes*, S-20 (Washington DC, 1994).

the best return for their money but shows a strong and consistent dislike for the major source of local revenue, property taxes.[6] It is also worth remarking about the position of state governments in both surveys. The two major state taxes are by far the least disliked among all major government tax sources. Comparing the three levels of government, however, the public consistently rated state governments behind both the federal and local governments in their ability to give them the most for their money. Only once, in 1984, did state governments rank as high as second in this poll.

It is difficult to draw any definitive conclusions from this information. The federal government's relative standing in both polls has declined, but it is uncertain what the implications might be. State governments appear to remain in good position with the public to continue their primary roles, financing local services. Local governments—certainly the governments closest to the public—seem to have increasing support from the public for the delivery of services. The continuing high negative ratings for local property taxes, however, might make it increasingly difficult to provide the resources to deliver those services. State and local governments have responded in some ways to the dislike of property taxes with ideas such as property tax relief programs and other funding mechanisms.

VARIATIONS IN THE STRUCTURE OF STATE AND LOCAL GOVERNMENTS

The immediacy and importance of local government today make it difficult to remember that local governments are not mentioned in our U.S. Constitution. The 10th Amendment divides all powers between just two governmental levels, a central federal government and the states. It is each of the state constitutions that sets

TABLE 12.1

RANK OF U.S. STATES, BY NUMBER OF INTERNAL GOVERNMENTS (1992) AND POPULATION (1995)

STATE	GOVERNMENTS (1992)		POPULATION (1995)		DIFFERENCE IN GOVERNMENT/ POPULATION RANK
	NUMBER	RANK	NUMBER	RANK	
ILLINOIS	6,723	1	11,830	6	5
PENNSYLVANIA	5,159	2	12,072	5	3
TEXAS	4,792	3	18,724	2	1
CALIFORNIA	4,393	4	31,589	1	3
KANSAS	3,892	5	2,565	32	27
MINNESOTA	3,580	6	4,610	20	14
OHIO	3,524	7	11,151	7	0
MISSOURI	3,310	8	5,324	16	8
NEW YORK	3,299	9	18,136	3	6
NEBRASKA	2,924	10	1,637	37	27
INDIANA	2,899	11	5,803	14	3
NORTH DAKOTA	2,765	12	641	47	35

Source: U. S. Bureau of the Census, "Government Organization," vol. I, no. I, *1992 Census of Governments*, Table 3 and press release CB 96-10.

the rules for dividing power between the state governments and their subordinate governments. Local governments are, to quote a renowned Iowa judge and local government legal commentator, John F. Dillon, "creatures of the state."[7] Using their legal authority, the states have developed a tapestry of state and local government structures that are showcases for our federal system as laboratories of government. The richness and diversity of the state and local governing institutions are the result of the different mixes of geography, history, and economic factors.

The first thing one notices about governments is just how many of them there are—about 85,000 in 1992. The largest number was in Illinois (6,723) and the fewest, excluding the District of Columbia, in Hawaii (21). The number of governments correlates roughly with population—that is, more people, more governments—with Illinois, Pennsylvania (5,159), Texas (4,792), and California (4,393) in the top

four spots and Ohio (3,524) and New York (3,299) coming in seventh and eighth. However, Kansas, Nebraska, and North Dakota—all with fairly low rankings in population—appear among the top dozen states in terms of numbers of governments. (See Table 12.1.)

The governing systems that exist today have both historical roots as well as modern origins. For example, townships in Midwestern states have a direct link to the Federal Northwest Territory Ordinance of 1787, which mandated the existence of townships.[8] The continuing growth in special district governments in California over the past two decades is attributed by some to the passage of Proposition 13 in 1978.[9]

The number of governments only begins to show the differences that exist in governing styles among the states. First, there is the division of duties—which services are provided and how to finance them—that the state governments decide. From public welfare, to public elementary

---

6 The property tax limitations movements of the late 1970s and early 1980s were some of the strongest manifestations of negative feelings about property taxes.

7 John F. Dillon, *Commentaries on the Law of Municipal Corporations* (Boston: Little, Brown and Co., 1911).

8 The Federal General Revenue Sharing Program was a direct distribution of federal funds to state and local governments during a period of about 15 years, through the 1970s to mid-1980s. One of the arguments made against the program was that the existence of this federal money would freeze in place existing but very small general purpose governments just to get this federal money. The endurance of small Midwest townships for two centuries, both before and after Federal General Revenue Sharing, seems to show the influence of historical status quo.

9 Some special districts in California were created by counties and cities to skirt the restrictions of Proposition 13. See, for example, Deborah Vrana, " 'Designer' tax districts catch on," *City and State* (26 February 1990); Lori Raineri, "Mello-Roos Bonds—California's answer to Financing Public Infrastructure in Developing Areas," *Government Finance Review* (August 1987); and Dean Misczynski, "Fiscalization of Land Use," in *California Policy Choices* 3, ed. John J. Kirland and Donald R. Winkler (Los Angeles: University of Southern California Press, 1986).

and secondary education, to highways, to sewerage treatment, there are significant differences in approaches. Some state governments take on tasks themselves based on financial, administrative, political, geographic, or historical criteria. In Hawaii, for example, all public elementary and secondary education is a state activity. Though other states fund a significant portion of elementary and secondary education, the administration in all other states is generally carried out by local governments.[10] Streets and highways in Virginia are largely a state government activity; in most other states the responsibility is more evenly divided. In Maryland, elementary and secondary school construction is a state activity, but the operation is of schools is a local government responsibility.

The states have developed two general categories of subordinate governments to provide local services, general purpose and special purpose. General purpose governments usually perform a variety of services for their citizens—public safety and health, various types of public works, social services, and the like. Usually the general purpose governments carry designations such as counties, municipalities, and townships.[11]

Special purpose governments are created to provide either a single service or a very limited number of services to a population or an area. There are two major types. The most common in terms of a type of activity is school districts. The other major group is special districts. Some special districts are very large and well known—the Port Authority of New York and New Jersey, for example. By and large, however, special districts are neither a well-known nor well-understood facet of local government and

have been described as "the dark continent of American government."[12]

While the number of some types of governments have changed considerably over the past few decades, some have changed little. Among general purpose governments, only municipalities show much change, up 14 percent from 1952 to 1992. This is due, in part, to the fact that municipalities are designed to serve populations, and, as populations grow, the number of municipalities generally do also.[13] In contrast, counties and townships, which have a geographic base, have not changed much. (See Table 12.2.)

The special purpose governments— special districts and school districts—present a considerable contrast to the general purpose governments. In 1992, there were only about one-fifth the number of school districts as there were in 1952. This largely reflects the consolidation of relatively small, multigrade schools into larger school districts to provide a more balanced and cost-effective educational system. In some states, the results of this process have been quite dramatic. Nebraska, for example, went from

6,392 school districts in 1952, to 3,264 in 1962, 1,374 in 1972, 1,069 in 1982, and 797 in 1992.

Special districts show the opposite trend from school districts, up 156 percent from 1952 to 1992. The states that used special districts the most in 1952 (Illinois and California) remain the primary users of this form of government today, each approximately doubling the number of special districts in a 40-year period. While some states have made wide use of this form of government, others have not, and the reasons are rooted in individual state politics, economies, and histories. The influence of Proposition 13 in California was cited above. New York, by way of contrast, has shown almost no change in the number of special districts in 40 years and limits the activity of this type of government to fire districts—which account for about 90 percent of the New York special district total— health districts, and a few miscellaneous activities. Nevertheless, special districts are where government structure is showing the most dynamic adaptability.

TABLE 12.2

LOCAL GOVERNMENTS IN THE UNITED STATES, BY TYPE OF GOVERNMENT: 1952–1992

(SELECTED YEARS)

YEAR	TOTAL	COUNTY	MUNICIPAL	TOWNSHIP	SPECIAL DISTRICT	SCHOOL DISTRICT
1992	84,955	3,043	19,279	16,656	31,555	14,422
1987	83,237	3,042	19,200	16,691	29,532	14,721
1982	81,831	3,041	19,076	16,734	28,078	14,851
1972	78,269	3,044	18,517	16,991	23,885	15,781
1962	91,237	3,043	17,997	17,144	18,323	34,678
1952	102,392	3,052	16,807	17,202	12,340	67,355

Source: U. S. Bureau of the Census, "Government Organization," vol. 1, no. 1, 1992 Census of Governments, vol. 1 20.1, Table 4.

---

[10] A reminder of the ultimate responsibility of the state, however, is demonstrated by the spate of state takeovers of troubled elementary and secondary school systems. The Consortium for Policy Research in Education, an education research group, has produced some useful studies on this subject. See Susan H. Fuhrman and Richard F. Elmore, "Takeover and Deregulation: Working Models of New State and Local Regulatory Relationships," no. RR-024 (April 1992); and Margaret Dolan, "State Takeover of a Local School District in New Jersey: A Case Study," no. TC-008 (April 1992).

[11] The naming convention for local governments has different manifestations. For example, county-equivalent governments in Louisiana are called parishes and in Alaska are designated boroughs. In New Jersey, boroughs are municipal corporations. There are plantation governments, not in the South but in Maine, that are almost indistinguishable from Maine towns in terms of their responsibilities.

[12] John C. Bollens, Special District Governments in the United States (Berkeley: University of California Press, 1957). This book is considered a classic among students of state and local government. A good example of a special district government that has had a very significant impact, but is not well known except among financial analysts and market observers, is the Washington Public Power Supply System. This special district government had the largest public bond default in history, about $2.25 billion in 1983, a financial move that precipitated increased power rates all over the Northwest and higher bond prices for years because of the financial uncertainty it created. It ranked as high as 6th among all state and local governments in the amount of its outstanding debt in 1980s, and still ranked 13th in 1992 despite inflation and no additional debt issues. Yet, there are very few people other than market analysts and local government scholars who know much about this public organization.

[13] The other major method that results in municipalities growing in size, if not in number, is annexation. The procedures that allow existing municipalities to annex adjacent areas where there has been population growth vary for each state. The level of difficulty in invoking annexation procedures probably has an effect on the development of new municipalities.

COMPARING PUBLIC AND PRIVATE SECTORS OF THE ECONOMY

Talk of "big" government in the United States is often directed at the size and influence of the federal government. The place of state and local governments in these discussions seems to be absent or minimized. There is another way to look at the relative size of these governments, however, that does provide a good perspective on the size of subnational governments.

The Fortune 500 is a popular and widely used listing of the biggest and most important corporations in the United States.[14] Ranking U.S. state governments against this list based on their general revenues demonstrates their size relative to the largest businesses in the United States. (See Table 12.3.) That California ranks number 4, New York number 8, and Texas number 15 might not be surprising. However, the smallest state government in terms of general revenue, South Dakota, falls in the 320th spot. And these are just the state governments. If local governments were included, in California alone five county governments (Los Angeles, Orange, San Bernardino, Santa Clara, and San Diego), two cities (Los Angeles and San Francisco), one school district (Los Angeles Unified), and one special district (Los Angeles County Transportation Commission) would each rank higher than South Dakota.

This comparison of government with the private sector holds in many different areas. In the obscure, but financially important, field of retirement or pension systems, for example, the very largest system in terms of assets is a state retirement system—the California Public Employee Retirement System—with assets about 25 percent greater than General Motors. State and local government public employee retirement systems occupy 7 of the top 10 spots in this ranking of pension/retirement systems and 28 of the top 50.[15]

A regional ranking of almost any financial activity, such as revenues, expenditures, indebtedness, assets, employment, or payroll, no matter the location, would yield similar results. State and major local governments would rank as, or among, the leaders in most categories. State and local governments are significant "businesses" and economic forces almost no matter how measured.

As one of the authors of the state governments /Fortune 500 ranking used in the previous paragraph noted: "This ranking dramatizes that the governors are the chief executive officers of some of the largest human enterprises in the country.... If you want to get a good sense of the significance of a governor's managerial responsibilities, just look at corporations that are similar in size to his or her state"[16] Though the responsibilities might be similar, there is a significant disparity in the financial compensation of public and private chief executive officers (CEOs). While the compensation of private sector executives of Fortune 500 companies extends into the hundreds of thousands or millions of dollars, the highest governor's salary is $130,000 (New York) and the lowest $59,300 (Montana). There are 36 states in which the governor's salary is less than $100,000.[17] It is also relevant, perhaps, to point out that the annual salary of the most important and powerful chief executive in the world, the president of the United States, is $200,000.

TABLE 12.3

RANK OF U.S. STATE GOVERNMENTS IN COMBINED RANKING WITH FORTUNE 500 INDUSTRIAL CORPORATIONS

(CORPORATIONS BASED ON SALES, STATE GOVERNMENTS BASED ON GENERAL REVENUE.)

STATE	COMBINED RANK OF STATES WITH FORTUNE 500 CORPORATIONS
CALIFORNIA	4
NEW YORK	8
TEXAS	15
PENNSYLVANIA	19
FLORIDA	20
ILLINOIS	21
OHIO	22
MICHIGAN	24
NEW JERSEY	25
MASSACHUSETTS	33
NORTH CAROLINA	40
WASHINGTON	42
VIRGINIA	47
GEORGIA	50
WISCONSIN	51
MINNESOTA	52
INDIANA	57
MARYLAND	60
LOUISIANA	69
CONNECTICUT	76
KENTUCKY	77
MISSOURI	80
TENNESSEE	83
ALABAMA	85
ARIZONA	88
SOUTH CAROLINA	90
OKLAHOMA	106
OREGON	108
COLORADO	111
IOWA	113
ALASKA	128
MISSISSIPPI	135
KANSAS	139
HAWAII	148
NEW MEXICO	149
ARKANSAS	151
WEST VIRGINIA	152
UTAH	165
NEBRASKA	185
MAINE	200
RHODE ISLAND	212
NEVADA	221
DELAWARE	236
IDAHO	241
MONTANA	266
NORTH DAKOTA	271
WYOMING	273
NEW HAMPSHIRE	281
VERMONT	306
SOUTH DAKOTA	320

Source: "The Fortune 500 and the Fifty States: A Combined Ranking," by Robert D. Behn and John S. Clendinen, Governors Center at Duke University, 1993.

---

[14] The following discussion is based on Robert D. Behn and John S. Clendinen, *The Fortune 500 and the Fifty States, A Combined Ranking* (Durham: The Governors Center at Duke University, 1993).

[15] "The 1,000 Largest Pension Systems," *Pensions and Investments* (20 January 1997).

[16] Press release, "Duke Study Ranks State Governments in Comparison with the Fortune 500" (January 1993).

[17] *The Book of the States*, 1996–97 ed., vol. 31 (Lexington: Council of State Governments, 1996), Table 2.3.

THE MONEY THAT FUNDS GOVERNMENT

Taxes are the largest and most visible component of governmental revenues, in addition to which there are four other identifiable types of governmental revenues: fees or charges for specific services; "contributions" for social insurance programs or retirement systems; revenues from other governments; and a miscellaneous category, some parts of which are also found in private businesses (interest earnings, rents, or sale of property) and some of which are specific to governments (fines, assessments, or lottery revenues). (See Table 12.4.)

The mix among these five components is very different depending on the level of government. The federal government gets 84 percent of its revenues from two sources, taxes and social insurance contributions. State governments have three sources that account for 84 percent of revenue—taxes, intergovernmental revenues, and social insurance contributions. Local governments rely on three sources for almost 9 of every 10 revenue dollars—taxes and intergovernmental revenues in a fairly even split, followed by charges. Since the social insurance contributions for the federal government are mostly Social Security "taxes," some analysts would include that in the tax figure for the federal government.[18]

Intergovernmental revenue—the money one level of government receives from another—takes different forms. For state governments, this is revenue they receive directly from the federal government.[19] Local governments receive federal funds both directly and indirectly (when the federal money is funneled through the state). There is also a considerable amount of money local governments receive directly from states. For local governments as a group, about $1 out of every $3 came from the federal and state governments in the early 1990s.

The matter of revenue support brings with it the hotly debated matter of control. This is a more intensely fought issue concerning federal support to state and local governments than the state support that goes to local governments. In the former case, it is an issue among parties with somewhat equal constitutional standing and a long tradition of debate concerning the meaning of the 10th Amendment, which reads, "The powers not delegated to the United States by the Constitution, nor prohibited by it to the States, are reserved to the States, respectively, or to the people."

The average of one out of every three local government revenue dollars originating in another level of government glosses over some underlying variations. These variations appear in different states and different types of local governments. If one looks at the different types of local governments, for example, one sees that school district governments obtained more than one-half (54 percent) of their revenue from other governments in 1991–92; county governments about 41 percent; and municipal, township, and special district governments somewhat over one-quarter.

Elementary and secondary education provides an illustration of the variety in intergovernmental revenue among different states.[20] Table 12.5 shows that the state support of elementary and secondary education ranges from a low in New Hampshire, where the state provides 8 per-

TABLE 12.4

REVENUE OF THE U.S. FEDERAL, STATE, AND LOCAL GOVERNMENTS, BY TYPE OF REVENUE: 1991–1992

(MILLIONS OF DOLLARS)

TYPE OF REVENUE	ALL GOVERNMENTS	FEDERAL GOVERNMENT	STATE & LOCAL GOVERNMENTS	STATE GOVERNMENTS	LOCAL GOVERNMENTS
TOTAL	2,266,765	1259,383	1189,987	743,521	655,216
TAXES	1,218,900	659,041	559,859	331,180	228,679
SOCIAL INSURANCE/ RETIREMENT SYSTEM CONTRIBUTIONS	552,172	404,562	147,610	128,150	19,460
INTERGOVERNMENTAL REVENUE	0	3,431	179,174	169,928	217,996
CHARGES	291,027	89,482	201,545	59,508	142,037
OTHER REVENUE	204,666	102,867	101,799	54,755	47,043
TOTAL	100.0%	100.0%	100.0%	100.0%	100.0%
TAXES	53.8%	52.3%	47.0%	44.5%	34.9%
SOCIAL INSURANCE/ RETIREMENT SYSTEM CONTRIBUTIONS	24.4%	32.1%	12.4%	17.2%	3.0%
INTERGOVERNMENTAL REVENUE	0.0%	0.3%	15.1%	22.9%	33.3%
CHARGES	12.8%	7.1%	16.9%	8.0%	21.7%
OTHER REVENUE	9.0%	8.2%	8.6%	7.4%	7.2%

Source: U.S. Bureau of the Census, 1992 Census of Governments.

---

[18] The discussion about the classification of Social Security contributions as "taxes" or "social insurance contributions" is technical. There are good arguments on both sides. For purposes of this discussion, it is probably not important. It does become quite important, however, in international comparisons.

[19] Primarily because of administrative adjustments, there are small amounts of funds that the federal government receives from the states. There are also many instances where state governments receive money from local governments, usually for purchase of specific services in a public works contract, for example. In general, these amounts are quite small in scale and have been discounted in this part of the discussion.

[20] The term school systems refers to governmental organizations that provide an education service. Some of these governmental organizations are independent governments and carry the designation school district. Other school systems are actually part of another government—a county, city, town or, in a few instances, the state—and are considered "dependent" parts of the "parent" government. In 1992, there were 15,834 school systems (14,422 school districts and 1,412 dependent school systems). In this part of the analysis, the matter of the varying degrees of state financial support for local government services is more clearly demonstrated using the concept of school system. Because the Hawaii elementary and secondary school system is part of the state government, it has been excluded from this part of the discussion.

cent of the funds, to Hawaii (90 percent) and New Mexico (74 percent) at the top of this ranking. What accounts for these wide differences? They likely are a mixture of factors, including the history of local education control, ability of the state to raise money that will fund this major program, and competition from other governmental programs. In New Hampshire, for example, with neither a state broad-based personal income tax nor a state general sales tax, it probably would be difficult for the state government to assume greater funding responsibility without making significant changes in its tax system. Recent changes in Michigan's funding of local education—where the state mandated a reduction in local property taxes and essentially substituted an increase in the state sales tax—demonstrate that states have the ability to change these patterns in quite dramatic ways.[21] One factor prodding some states into action on this issue is the existence of court cases and legal decisions mandating more equal funding of elementary and secondary education. In Texas, for example, there have been a whole series of court cases, funding plans, legislative actions, and proposed administrative remedies to achieve a more equal distribution of education funding.

TABLE 12.5

PERCENTAGE OF ELEMENTARY-SECONDARY EDUCATION REVENUE FUNDED BY U.S. FEDERAL, STATE, AND LOCAL GOVERNMENT SOURCES, BY STATE: 1993–1994

(RANKED BY PERCENT FROM STATE SOURCES)

AREA		ELEMENTARY-SECONDARY REVENUE			
	TOTAL (PERCENT)	PERCENT FROM FEDERAL SOURCES	PERCENT FROM LOCAL SOURCES	PERCENT FROM STATE SOURCES	RANK
HAWAII	100.0	6.9	2.7	90.5	1
NEW MEXICO	100.0	11.1	14.8	74.2	2
WASHINGTON	100.0	5.8	24.5	69.8	3
DELAWARE	100.0	7.4	27.6	65.0	4
NEVADA	100.0	4.5	30.8	64.7	5
KENTUCKY	100.0	10.4	25.1	64.5	6
WEST VIRGINIA	100.0	7.9	28.1	63.9	7
ALASKA	100.0	12.8	23.7	63.5	8
NORTH CAROLINA	100.0	8.1	29.0	62.9	9
ALABAMA	100.0	11.2	26.4	62.4	10
ARKANSAS	100.0	9.3	29.9	60.8	11
IDAHO	100.0	8.2	31.1	60.7	12
OKLAHOMA	100.0	8.0	32.0	60.0	13
KANSAS	100.0	5.0	37.5	57.5	14
CALIFORNIA	100.0	7.1	36.7	56.2	15
MISSISSIPPI	100.0	15.5	29.5	54.9	16
MINNESOTA	100.0	4.4	40.7	54.9	17
UTAH	100.0	7.0	38.1	54.9	18
LOUISIANA	100.0	12.2	34.1	53.6	19
WYOMING	100.0	5.8	42.0	52.2	20
GEORGIA	100.0	6.6	42.2	51.1	21
MONTANA	100.0	9.5	39.6	51.0	22
FLORIDA	100.0	7.2	42.8	50.0	23
IOWA	100.0	5.1	46.4	48.6	24
TENNESSEE	100.0	9.7	42.1	48.2	25
MISSOURI	100.0	6.6	46.5	46.9	26
MAINE	100.0	5.9	47.4	46.7	27
SOUTH CAROLINA	100.0	9.0	44.6	46.3	28
INDIANA	100.0	4.8	48.9	46.3	29
UNITED STATES	100.0	6.5	47.6	45.9	U.S. AVERAGE
TEXAS	100.0	7.4	49.1	43.5	30
NORTH DAKOTA	100.0	11.5	45.2	43.3	31
WISCONSIN	100.0	4.2	53.8	42.0	32
ARIZONA	100.0	9.8	48.5	41.7	33
COLORADO	100.0	4.9	54.6	40.5	34
OREGON	100.0	7.0	52.9	40.1	35
PENNSYLVANIA	100.0	5.4	54.5	40.1	36
OHIO	100.0	5.0	54.9	40.0	37
VIRGINIA	100.0	6.2	54.1	39.7	38
NEW JERSEY	100.0	3.6	56.8	39.6	39
MARYLAND	100.0	5.0	56.0	39.0	40
RHODE ISLAND	100.0	4.8	56.9	38.3	41
NEW YORK	100.0	6.1	55.6	38.3	42
CONNECTICUT	100.0	3.4	60.4	36.2	43
MASSACHUSETTS	100.0	4.9	61.9	33.2	44
ILLINOIS	100.0	5.6	61.4	33.0	45
NEBRASKA	100.0	6.1	62.0	31.8	46
VERMONT	100.0	5.0	63.7	31.3	47
MICHIGAN	100.0	5.7	64.1	30.2	48
SOUTH DAKOTA	100.0	10.3	64.2	25.5	49
NEW HAMPSHIRE	100.0	3.4	88.4	8.2	50
DISTRICT OF COLUMBIA	100.0	10.8	89.2	0.0	51

Source: U. S. Bureau of the Census, Annual Survey of Government Finance.

---

[21] In some ways, the experience in Michigan was an aberration because it was such an abrupt shift in the funding pattern. Changes of this type are usually much more gradual.

FIGURE 12.3

PERCENTAGE DISTRIBUTION OF FEDERAL TAXES IN THE UNITED STATES, BY TYPE OF TAX: 1992

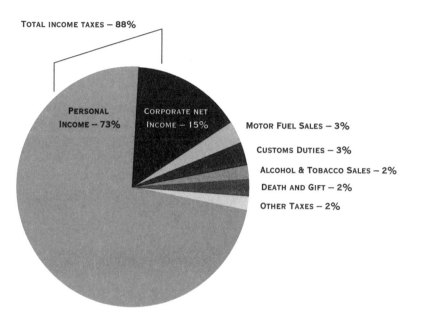

TOTAL INCOME TAXES — 88%

PERSONAL INCOME — 73%

CORPORATE NET INCOME — 15%

MOTOR FUEL SALES — 3%

CUSTOMS DUTIES — 3%

ALCOHOL & TOBACCO SALES — 2%

DEATH AND GIFT — 2%

OTHER TAXES — 2%

Source: U.S. Bureau of the Census, "Compendium of Government Finance," 1992 Census of Government, vol. 4 no. 5.

TABLE 12.6

PERCENTAGE OF FEDERAL TAXES IN THE UNITED STATES, BY TYPE OF TAX: 1960–1990

YEAR	1960	1970	1980	1990
TOTAL TAXES	100.0	100.0	100.0	100.0
INCOME TAXES	80.8	84.4	88.0	88.6
PERSONAL INCOME	52.9	61.9	69.6	73.8
CORPORATE NET INCOME	27.9	22.5	18.4	14.8
MOTOR FUEL SALES	2.6	2.6	1.4	2.1
CUSTOMS DUTIES	1.4	1.7	2.1	2.7
ALCOHOL & TOBACCO SALES	6.5	4.7	2.3	1.6
DEATH & GIFT	2.1	2.5	1.8	1.8
TOTAL TAXES	2.1	2.5	1.8	1.8

Source: U.S. Bureau of the Census, "Compendium of Government Finance," 1992 Census of Government, vol. 4 no. 5.

Note: Because of rounding a detail does not add to total.

TAXES

The contribution of taxes to overall government revenue was demonstrated earlier. But what types of taxes? Without delving into the arguments of progressivity or the effect on economic development, it is useful to look at the variations that exist in the American tax system (see Figure 12.3).

Income taxes—personal and corporate—account for seven out of every eight federal tax dollars. Individual income taxes alone provide nearly three-fourths of federal tax revenue. That is why discussions about reforming the federal government tax system start and end with individual income taxes. Even if most other specific taxes such as death and gift were eliminated entirely, the effect on total tax revenue would be relatively minor. (See Table 12.6.)

There are some interesting trends in federal taxes over the past few decades. Within the category of income taxes, the percentages derived from individual and corporate income taxes are going in opposite directions. Comparing 1990 to 1960, individual income taxes provide over 20 percent more and corporate income taxes 13 percent less of total taxes. The other noticeable trend is the decreasing percentages derived from so-called "sin taxes"—alcohol and tobacco sales taxes. The decrease for those two sales taxes as a percent of the total is almost 5 percentage points, from 6.5 percent in 1960 to less than 1.6 percent in 1990.

Economists who argue for "balanced" tax systems—that is, systems with multiple major tax sources—point out that the federal system is becoming too lopsided toward individual income taxes. There are, in addition, arguments concerning tax equity and the effect of taxes on economic growth.

State and local governments have an entirely different tax mix than the federal government. For local governments, the property tax is, without question, the dominant levy, though not as preeminent as it once was. From 1950 through 1970, property taxes composed about 85 percent of all local government taxes. From 1970 through 1980 the percentage drifted down to about 75 percent of the total, where it has remained. Though property tax restriction movements of the late 1970s, such as

TABLE 12.7

PERCENTAGE OF LOCAL TAXES IN THE UNITED STATES, BY TYPE OF TAX:1950–1990

YEAR	1950	1960	1970	1980	1990
TOTAL TAXES	100.0	100.0	100.0	100.0	100.0
PROPERTY TAX	88.2	87.4	84.9	75.9	74.5
NONPROPERTY TAXES	11.8	12.6	15.1	24.1	25.5
GENERAL SALES TAX	NA	4.8	5.0	9.4	10.7
MOTOR FUELS TAX	NA	0.2	0.1	0.1	0.3
INDIVIDUAL INCOME TAX	0.8	1.4	4.2	5.8	4.8
OTHER TAXES	11.0	6.2	5.8	8.7	9.7

Source: U.S. Bureau of the Census, Annual Survey (various years).

FIGURE 12.4

PERCENTAGE DISTRIBUTION OF STATE TAXES IN THE UNITED STATES, BY TYPE OF TAX: 1996

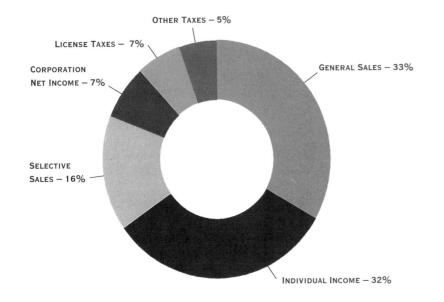

OTHER TAXES – 5%

LICENSE TAXES – 7%

CORPORATION NET INCOME – 7%

GENERAL SALES – 33%

SELECTIVE SALES – 16%

INDIVIDUAL INCOME – 32%

Source: U.S. Bureau of the Census, Annual Survey (various years).

Proposition 13 in California and Proposition Two and a Half in Massachusetts, provided additional impetus, the trend had already been firmly established earlier in that decade. (See Table 12.7.)

There were really three interrelated movements taking place in the 1970s that contributed to the reduced role of property taxes. The property tax restriction movement has already been mentioned. The second was property tax relief programs, some of which replaced property taxes with intergovernmental revenue from the states. The third was the diversification of local revenues, as state legislatures allowed local governments to impose other taxes, especially sales taxes. The states, though they allowed local governments more use of other taxes, still kept a tight rein because, in many instances, those same taxes were primary state tax producers, such as general sales taxes. (See Figure 12.4.)

State governments rely on two pillars for taxes, general sales taxes and individual income taxes, which accounted for 33 percent and 32 percent, respectively, of all state government taxes in fiscal year 1996. States supplement these with a variety of other levies, such as specific sales taxes (motor fuel, alcohol, tobacco, and utilities, for example), license taxes, death and gift taxes, severance taxes, and other imposts. These state government totals provide some good general comparisons in relationship to what is happening in federal and local government taxes. What these national totals hide, however, is some of the differences found among the state tax systems. (See Table 12.8.)

Table 12.8 provides some examples showing some of the wide variations in state tax systems. Alaska, which has built its tax system largely around its oil and gas reserves, levies neither an individual income nor a general sales tax. Delaware is the U.S. home of many large corporations, drawn there by business-friendly corporation laws. It has taken advantage of this significant corporate presence by levying corporate license taxes, and this has given it sufficient leeway so that, while Delaware does impose an individual income tax, it does not have a general sales tax. Pennsylvania has what most economists would say is a balanced tax system, with a

TABLE 12.8

RANKING OF TOP THREE TAX SOURCES IN SELECTED U.S. STATES: 1996

| | RANKING OF TAX STATE RELIES ON | | | | | |
| | FIRST | | SECOND | | THIRD | |
STATE	DESCRIPTION	PERCENT	DESCRIPTION	PERCENT	DESCRIPTION	PERCENT
ALASKA	SEVERANCE	63	CORPORATE NET INCOME	21	MOTOR FUEL SALES	2
DELAWARE	INDIVIDUAL INCOME	37	CORPORATE LICENSE	21	CORPORATE NET INCOME	10
PENNSYLVANIA	GENERAL SALES	31	INDIVIDUAL INCOME	29	CORPORATE NET INCOME	9
TEXAS	GENERAL SALES	51	MOTOR FUEL SALES	11	CORPORATE LICENSE	8
WASHINGTON	GENERAL SALES	58	PROPERTY	17	MOTOR FUEL SALES	6

Source: U.S. Bureau of the Census, Annual Survey (various years)

TABLE 12.9

RANK OF U.S. STATE AND LOCAL GOVERNMENT TAXES PER $100 PERSONAL INCOME: FY 1994

(WHOLE DOLLARS)

STATE RANK AREA	TAXES PER $100 PERSONAL INCOME (DOLLARS)	PERCENT DIFFERENCE FROM U.S. AVERAGE (PERCENT)
U.S. AVERAGE	11.67	0.00
1 NEW YORK	15.54	33.11
2 DC	14.62	25.27
3 ALASKA	14.18	21.46
4 WISCONSIN	13.73	17.68
5 HAWAII	13.71	17.49
6 NEW MEXICO	13.17	12.84
7 MINNESOTA	13.15	12.64
8 WYOMING	12.90	10.52
9 VERMONT	12.86	10.21
10 IOWA	12.60	7.96
11 MAINE	12.53	7.32
12 MICHIGAN	12.45	6.66
13 ARIZONA	12.44	6.60
14 CONNECTICUT	12.30	5.38
15 UTAH	12.21	4.58
16 WASHINGTON	12.12	3.88
17 NEW JERSEY	12.07	3.42
18 NORTH DAKOTA	11.91	2.07
19 OREGON	11.86	1.61
20 RHODE ISLAND	11.75	0.64
21 KANSAS	11.73	0.52
22 NEBRASKA	11.71	0.29
23 MASSACHUSETTS	11.64	-0.28
24 DELAWARE	11.57	-0.87
25 IDAHO	11.51	-1.36
26 KENTUCKY	11.50	-1.48
27 NORTH CAROLINA	11.49	-1.51
28 MONTANA	11.43	-2.07
29 WEST VIRGINIA	11.40	-2.30
30 MISSISSIPPI	11.35	-2.73
31 OHIO	11.24	-3.68
32 GEORGIA	11.23	-3.74
33 MARYLAND	11.20	-4.04
34 INDIANA	11.14	-4.59
35 CALIFORNIA	11.06	-5.20
36 ILLINOIS	11.03	-5.47
37 PENNSYLVANIA	11.03	-5.50
38 OKLAHOMA	10.93	-6.38
39 NEVADA	10.86	-6.98
40 TEXAS	10.80	-7.50
41 SOUTH CAROLINA	10.77	-7.69
42 FLORIDA	10.77	-7.76
43 COLORADO	10.72	-8.17
44 ARKANSAS	10.62	-9.00
45 LOUISIANA	10.42	-10.75
46 SOUTH DAKOTA	10.20	-12.62
47 VIRGINIA	10.13	-13.22
48 NEW HAMPSHIRE	9.98	-14.50
49 TENNESSEE	9.70	-16.93
50 MISSOURI	9.62	-17.61
51 ALABAMA	9.43	-19.18

Source: U. S. Bureau of the Census, Annual Survey of Government Finance.

fairly even reliance on its two major sources. Texas does not impose an individual income tax. Until recently, Texas obtained a significant percentage of its total from severance taxes, but has made a successful effort to move away from these taxes because they had become an unreliable revenue source.[22] Washington emphasizes the use of the general sales tax, with no income tax. Right next door in Oregon, just the reverse is true.

HOW ONEROUS IS THE TAX BURDEN RELATIVE TO PERSONAL INCOME?

While states obviously choose different paths for obtaining tax revenues, the question arises whether there are measures of what the states do collect compared to what they have the capacity to collect. This is especially important in arguments about equity. That is, measured against their ability to raise revenue, what efforts are states making in supplying services to citizens. Are "poor" states putting relatively less, the same, or more resources toward supplying services than "rich" states?[23]

One of the simplest and most widely used methods for measuring this is taxes as a percent of personal income. Personal income is used as a surrogate measure of wealth. Some analysts have questioned whether personal income is a proper measure of wealth in this formula, because personal income might not relate well to a state's tax sources.[24] Despite its potential shortcomings, this calculation does provide at least a rough indication of how a state's tax system measures up against the ability to pay.

Table 12.9 contains a ranking of the states for the taxes per $100 of personal income in 1994. In effect, this table is showing the state and local taxation as a percent of wealth, measured by personal income. The overall distribution of the states is not remarkable; two-thirds of them fall within plus or minus $1 of the national average ($11.70).

Two things stand out in this display, however. First, New York, at $15.50, is considerably higher than all other states and 33 percent above the national average. What makes the data for New York even

---

[22] In 1981, almost 27 percent of Texas' state taxes came from severance taxes. In 1996, it was less than 4 percent.

[23] The U. S. Advisory Commission on Intergovernmental Relations (ACIR), which no longer exists, made an effort to focus attention on this issue starting in the early 1980s. The earlier ACIR work on this subject extends back to the 1960s. Starting in 1982, the commission issued a series of reports entitled "Measuring State Fiscal Capacity," in which it developed alternatives to the tax/personal income measure. A report issued in 1986, U.S. Advisory Commission on Intergovernmental Relations, *Measuring State Fiscal Capacity: Alternative Methods and Their Uses,* Report M-150 (Washington, DC, September 1986) provides a good discussion of six potential fiscal capacity measures: per capita personal income, gross state product, total taxable resources, export-adjusted income, the representative tax system, and the representative revenue system. The last ACIR study on this subject was for 1991,"State Revenue Capacity and Effort" (Washington, DC, September 1993). A forthcoming analysis from the Federal Reserve Bank of Boston will update the ACIR study to 1994.

[24] See the discussion below about Alaska's taxes.

TABLE 12.10

EXPENDITURES FOR ALL U.S. GOVERNMENTS (FEDERAL, STATE, AND LOCAL) IN THE UNITED STATES: 1971–1992

(SELECTED YEARS; MILLIONS OF DOLLARS; RANKED BY 1991–1992 EXPENDITURES.)

ACTIVITY	1991–92		1981–82		1971–72	
	AMOUNT	PERCENT	AMOUNT	PERCENT	AMOUNT	PERCENT
TOTAL	2,488,128	100	1,233,492	100	399,098	100
INSURANCE TRUST EXPENDITURE	545,006	22	267,618	22	64,634	16
NATIONAL DEFENSE AND INTERNATIONAL RELATIONS	351,684	14	204,275	17	79,258	20
EDUCATION	348,411	14	165,766	13	70,918	18
INTEREST ON GENERAL	254,968	10	121,976	10	23,143	6
PUBLIC WELFARE	202,364	8	78,780	6	23,604	6
SUM OF TOP FIVE RANKED EXPENDITURES	1,702,433	68	2,071,907	68	660,655	66

Source: U.S. Bureau of the Census, Census of Governments (various years).

more remarkable is that the data for the District of Columbia and Alaska, second and third on the list, are statistical anomalies. The District of Columbia has unique characteristics that make it very difficult to compare with any state area. Alaska's tax data, mostly severance taxes on oil and gas holdings, probably relate the worst to personal income of any state. The best comparison for New York is with the fourth ranked state—Wisconsin—the next state without obvious anomalies. Wisconsin is 18 percent above the national average compared to New York's 33 percent. At the other end of the tax spectrum 7 of the 10 states with the lowest taxes per $100 of personal income in 1994 were in the South.

WHERE DOES THE MONEY GO?

If all government expenditures in the United States are lumped together, this brings an illuminating perspective to the major spending categories. The top five expenditure categories—insurance trust (mostly Social Security), national defense, education, interest on general debt, and public welfare—accounted for more than two out of every three dollars in 1992. All the other programs of government—police protection, sewerage, highways, community development, public hospitals, and so forth—compete for the remaining portion of public expenditures. (See Table 12.10.)

The total of the top five categories has not changed markedly in the past few decades. They amounted to slightly under 66 percent in 1972 and slightly over 68 percent in 1992. Nevertheless, the dynamic changes in this period have been within these top categories. Insurance trust expenditures now take almost 6 percent more of government expenditures, and defense an equivalent percent less. Although changes in the other three categories are of smaller magnitude, they still represent major shifts in where governments are spending funds.

What does this tell us? The interpretation is very difficult without resorting to a considerable reservoir of other information. For example, the change in interest payments—reflecting mostly increases in federal debt—represents to some an intergenerational transfer, while at the same time U.S. residents are spending a smaller proportion of government funds on education, a decrease in the investment in children. A conclusion of this sort from the data might be misleading, however. (See figure 12.5.) While it's true we are spending more of our government funds in insurance trust expenditures, mostly to older Americans, and a smaller proportion on education, demographic data allow us to see this from a very different perspective. The percentage of the population 5 to19 years of age dropped from about 29 to 21 percent from 1970 to 1990, while the percent 60 years old and above rose from about 14 to 17 percent. Thus part of this change reflects the aging of the U.S. population.

FIGURE 12.5

TOTAL FEDERAL SPENDING IN THE UNITED STATES, BY MAJOR FEDERAL SPENDING CATEGORY: 1991–1992

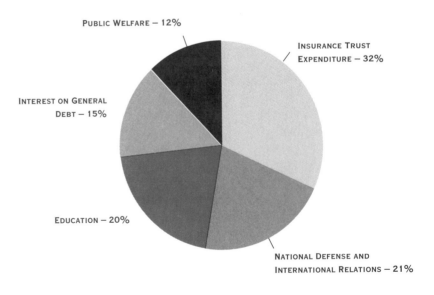

PUBLIC WELFARE – 12%
INSURANCE TRUST EXPENDITURE – 32%
INTEREST ON GENERAL DEBT – 15%
EDUCATION – 20%
NATIONAL DEFENSE AND INTERNATIONAL RELATIONS – 21%

Source: U.S. Bureau of the Census, 1992 Census of Governments.

For these five major spending categories, the federal government dominates three: insurance trust expenditures, national defense and international relations, and interest on general debt. Though the federal government funds a good portion of public welfare, most of the expenditures are actually made by the state and local governments. The federal role in education financing is fairly minimal; the state and local governments dominate here.

One way to look at federal expenditures is to limit the analysis to outlays that can be allocated to the states and outlying areas.[25] These federal expenditures can be distributed for analytical purposes in two ways, according to the type of product for which the outlay is being used, and geographically by state area.

Table 12.11 compares the allocation of these federal funds by the type of expenditure for 1996, 1986, and 1981. The distribution showed only minor changes when comparing 1981 to 1986. When comparing 1996 with 1986, however, two trends stand out. First, direct payments to individuals jumped up from 44 to 54 percent of the total. Medicare payments, which increased 162 percent in this 10-year period, were the driving force in the increased share for direct payments to individuals. Second, procurement dropped from 25 to 14 percent. Defense Department procurement showed an absolute $21 billion dollar decrease in this 10-year period, from $150 billion to $129 billion. The decline in the purchasing power of the dollar would make the $129 billion in 1996 equivalent to about $97 billion in 1986 constant dollars.

Another way to analyze federal fund-

ing is to look at the rankings of per capita distribution to each of the states. This provides a relatively simple method of comparing the effect of federal funds in the states. Virginia, Maryland, and Alaska held the top three positions, and Wisconsin, Minnesota, and Michigan the bottom ones in 1996. However, within these totals there often was considerable variation. Virginia, for example, ranked first in procurement and third in salaries and wages, but 50th in grants to state and local governments. Alaska showed similar disparities, ranking first in both grants and salaries and wages, but 50th in direct payments to individuals.

These differences in rank illustrate an important analytic point. Federal programs resulting in this geographic distribution pattern are not, for the most part, designed to be tied to geography. Thus, for example, Florida ranks first in direct payments for individuals primarily because a lot of persons who retire there receive Social Security payments. If retirees chose to live elsewhere, the federal outlays would follow.

THE FEDERAL GOVERNMENT'S BALANCE OF PAYMENTS

An extension of the federal funds per capita analysis is to consider whether a state has a surplus or deficit with regard to the money it sends to Washington and the money it receives back. One view is that states with a "deficit"—that is, that receive less than they send—are effectively subsidizing federal payments to states with a surplus.[26] In 1996, New Mexico was the top "recipient" state, receiving $1.83 from the federal government for every dollar it contributed in federal taxes.[27] New Mexico's continued position at or near the top of this scale almost every year is attributed in part to New Mexico's nuclear weapons industry. The existence of that industry contributed to the state receiving about three times the national average per capita in defense spending. Its average per capita tax payments, on the other hand, were 25 percent below the national average. At the other extreme was New Jersey, which received just $.69 in federal funds for every dollar in

TABLE 12.11

DISTRIBUTION OF FEDERAL FUNDS IN THE UNITED STATES, BY TYPE OF EXPENDITURE: 1981, 1986, AND 1996

(MILLIONS OF DOLLARS)

ACTIVITY	1996		1986		1981	
	AMOUNT	PERCENT	AMOUNT	PERCENT	AMOUNT	PERCENT
TOTAL	1,394,057	100	830,259	100	562,219	100
DIRECT PAYMENTS TO INDIVIDUALS	749,273	54	364,690	44	259,653	46
GRANTS TO STATE AND LOCAL GOVERNMENTS	227,542	16	112,596	14	94,806	17
PROCUREMENT	200,543	14	205,671	25	128,188	23
SALARIES AND WAGES	169,731	12	120,627	15	74,169	13
OTHER	46,968	3	26,675	3	5,402	1

Source: U. S. Bureau of the Census, *Federal Expenditures by State for Fiscal Year*, Various years.

---

[25] "Federal Expenditures by State for Fiscal Year 1996" (Washington DC: U.S. Bureau of the Census, April 1997). The major parts of federal expenditures that cannot be allocated to state areas are interest on federal debt, international payments and foreign aid, and expenditures for selected agencies, such as the Central Intelligence Agency and the National Security Agency.

[26] This comparison is very difficult to make and is fraught with dangers for analysts. This section is based on two studies that use basically the same information. Each presents the data in a slightly different manner that is quite useful. The more extensive analysis is provided in an annual joint report by Harvard University's Kennedy School of Government and the Office of Senator Daniel Patrick Moynihan, entitled "The Federal Budget and the States, Fiscal Year 1996." The second annual study, done by the Tax Foundation and entitled "Federal Tax Burden by State" (Washington, DC), provides some historical perspective on the changes and a slightly different view of the results. Further, the Tax Foundation provides an analysis of projected federal tax burden for two years into the future. The Kennedy School study uses the Tax Foundation tax incidence model designed to apportion the federal tax burden among the states.

[27] Because it is such an anomaly, this analysis omits the District of Columbia, which, at $5.59, is more than three times the New Mexico amount.

taxes it paid. Part of this is explained by New Jersey's high per capita tax payments and relatively limited federal spending in the state. New Jersey is also one of the states that has seen a significant decline in defense spending in the past decade.

It is important to note that in this type of "balance of payments" discussion there are some necessary caveats. First, there are measurement issues, especially where important assumptions underlie the data. Probably the most important is the great difficulty in determining the proper geographic allocation of both revenues and expenditures. Some good examples involve corporate taxes and procurement subcontracting. The proper place to allocate these geographically is problematic. The second issue, discussed briefly above, is that the imposition of taxes and allocation of revenue do not have geography as a primary driving force. Our federal system of government almost ensures that geography is a factor, but it is generally secondary to the purposes of raising revenue, supporting commerce through the transportation systems, helping the poor, paying federal employees, and the like. A defense contractor is free to relocate, a welfare recipient to move, or a local government to decide against participating in a federal program.

STATE AND LOCAL GOVERNMENT EXPENDITURES

Table 12.12 provides a good illustration of different roles played by state and local governments. One of the most prominent points that can be garnered from these data is the difference between state and local governments in providing and funding services. Almost $4 out of every $5 spent by local governments (78 percent) in 1994 was for current operations—that is, employee salaries and the direct provision of services to the public. By contrast, less than one-half of state government expenditures (48 percent) was for current operations. Local governments have the most employees (as discussed below) and spend

the highest proportion of their expenditures on salaries and wages—40 percent for local governments as compared to just 15 percent for state governments. Part of the reason for this was that a high percentage of the state expenditures (29 percent) was for intergovernmental payments to local governments. A good proportion of the revenues states raise goes for financing, but not directly providing, services.

On what types of services are state and local governments spending their money? For states, two activities predominated in 1994—education (30 percent of total) and public welfare (24 percent). There were distinct differences between what the states do in these two areas, however. In education, most of the money was split between that which states spent directly for education (mostly higher education) and that which states sent to local governments in support of elementary and secondary education. About one-third of state education money was spent directly on higher education and about 60 percent went to fund local government education services. In public welfare, the proportions were reversed—about 80 percent was spent by the state directly on welfare and 20 percent was given intergovernmentally by the state to local governments in 1994.[28] Insurance trust expenditures, mostly employee retirement and unemployment compensation, with 11 percent of the total and highways with approximately 7 percent constituted the next highest categories for state government spending.

Local governments spent about 36 percent of all outlays on education in 1994. If we exclude some of the proprietary activities of local governments, such as utilities, and insurance trust expenditures, the education total would be about 41 percent.[29] Of the other functions where local governments spend money, the distribution was remarkably even. Public welfare, hospitals, highways, police, and interest on general debt each fell in the 4 to 5 percent range of the total.

---

[28] The 20 percent of total state public welfare expenditures that is intergovernmental is a bit misleading. Two states—California and New York—account for about 70 percent of this entire amount. That emphasizes even more how heavily and broadly the states are involved in providing public welfare services.

[29] The total, excluding government-owned utility, liquor stores, and insurance trust expenditures, is called "general expenditure." Because these exclusions are erratically distributed among local governments, general expenditure is often a better construct to use for comparative purposes.

TABLE 12.12

CATEGORICAL GOVERNMENT EXPENDITURES AS A PERCENTAGE OF TOTAL EXPENDITURES, BY LEVEL OF GOVERNMENT: 1993–1994

(PERCENT)

	ALL GOVERNMENTS [1]	FEDERAL GOVERNMENT	STATE AND LOCAL GOVERNMENTS [1]	STATE GOVERNMENTS	LOCAL GOVERNMENTS
EXPENDITURE, TOTAL	100.0	100.0	100.0	100.0	100.0
INTERGOVERNMENTAL EXPENDITURE	0.0	13.4	0.3	29.0	1.2
CURRENT OPERATION	53.2	30.3	73.4	47.5	77.9
CAPITAL OUTLAY	8.1	4.9	10.9	6.8	11.8
CONSTRUCTION	4.2	0.6	8.1	5.4	8.4
EQUIPMENT, LAND, AND EXISTING STRUCTURES	4.0	4.3	2.8	1.5	3.4
ASSISTANCE AND SUBSIDIES	5.5	6.9	2.8	2.9	1.8
INTEREST ON DEBT	10.0	12.4	5.1	3.2	5.6
INSURANCE BENEFITS AND REPAYMENTS	23.1	32.1	7.6	10.7	1.8
EXHIBIT: SALARIES & WAGES	21.4	10.0	32.5	15.5	40.4
GENERAL EXPENDITURE	73.5	67.9	85.2	88.1	86.9
CURRENT EXPENDITURE	66.0	63.0	75.8	81.5	77.4
CAPITAL OUTLAY	7.5	4.9	9.4	6.5	9.5
NATIONAL DEFENSE	12.5	20.4	0.0	0.0	0.0
POSTAL SERVICE	1.7	2.8	0.0	0.0	0.0
SPACE RESEARCH	0.5	0.8	0.0	0.0	0.0
EDUCATION	14.1	3.1	27.9	29.7	36.0
LIBRARIES	0.2	0.0	0.4	0.1	0.7
PUBLIC WELFARE	8.8	10.5	14.5	23.5	5.1
HOSPITALS	2.9	0.7	5.1	3.6	5.2
HEALTH	1.7	1.1	2.8	3.7	2.3
SOCIAL INSURANCE ADMINISTRATION	0.4	0.6	0.3	0.5	0.0
VETERANS SERVICES	0.8	1.3	0.0	0.0	0.0
HIGHWAYS	2.7	1.2	5.7	6.9	3.9
AIR TRANSPORTATION	0.6	0.5	0.7	0.2	1.2
WATER TRANSPORT AND TERMINALS	0.2	0.2	0.2	0.1	0.3
OTHER TRANSPORTATION	0.0	0.0	0.1	0.0	0.1
POLICE PROTECTION	1.7	0.5	3.1	0.8	4.6
FIRE PROTECTION	0.6	0.0	1.3	0.0	2.2
CORRECTION	1.3	0.2	2.6	3.0	1.5
PROTECTIVE INSPECTION	0.2	0.0	0.5	0.6	0.3
NATURAL RESOURCES	2.4	3.3	1.1	1.5	0.4
PARKS AND RECREATION	0.7	0.1	1.3	0.4	1.9
HOUSING AND COMMUNITY DEVELOPMENT	1.3	2.3	1.6	0.4	2.5
SEWERAGE	0.8	0.0	1.7	0.3	2.8
SOLID WASTE MANAGEMENT	0.6	0.3	1.1	0.2	1.8
FINANCIAL ADMINISTRATION	1.2	0.7	1.6	1.5	1.3
JUDICIAL	0.8	0.5	1.4	1.0	1.5
PUBLIC BUILDING	0.2	0.0	0.5	0.2	0.7
OTHER GOVERNMENT ADMINISTRATION	0.5	0.1	0.9	0.3	1.1
INTEREST ON GENERAL DEBT	9.6	12.4	4.3	3.1	4.3
GENERAL EXPENDITURE, NEC	4.1	4.1	4.4	6.5	4.9
UTILITY AND LIQUOR STORES	3.4	0.0	7.2	1.3	11.3
INSURANCE TRUST EXPENDITURE	23.1	32.1	7.6	10.7	1.8
SOCIAL SECURITY AND MEDICARE	17.7	29.0	0.0	0.0	0.0
UNEMPLOYMENT COMPENSATION	1.1	0.0	2.3	3.7	0.0
EMPLOYEE RETIREMENT	3.5	2.3	4.4	5.6	1.8
OTHER INSURANCE TRUST EXPENDITURES	0.9	0.8	0.9	1.4	0.0

[1] EXCLUDES INTERGOVERNMENTAL FINANCIAL FLOWS TO AVOID DUPLICATION.

Source: U. S. Bureau of the Census, Annual Survey of Government Finance.

FIGURE 12.6

GOVERNMENT SECTOR IN THE UNITED STATES AS A PERCENTAGE OF TOTAL EMPLOYEES: 1960–1995

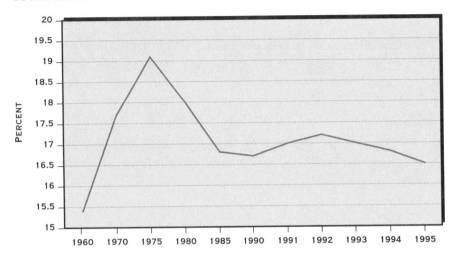

Source: U.S. Bureau of the Census, Statistical Abstract of the United States, 1996.

PUBLIC EMPLOYMENT

In the United States, approximately one out of every six nonfarm workers in 1995 was a federal, state, or local government employee. This ratio has been fairly steady for the past decade. From the mid-1970s to the mid-1980s it was slightly higher. (See Figure 12.6.)

The changes in this ratio are the result of many factors, perhaps most significantly job growth in the private sector. There are some factors we can point to, however, that affect the government sector numbers specifically. They are the requirements for particular government services, especially the largest activity, education, and the trend toward privatization of public services. Though government employment is subject to many of the same pressures as private employment—economic downturns, the downsizing/rightsizing movement, and elimination of administrative layers, for example—the resulting changes from these pressures probably occur on a different scale and with different timing than in the private sector. Among the reasons for this are the insulating effect of civil service rules; the countercyclical movement for certain public services (e.g., in bad economic times, there is a need for more government employees to help in public wel-

fare and unemployment service); the tentative relationship of economic considerations to certain services (e.g., the growth or decline of crime, and the subsequent provision of police services, is not necessarily related to economic changes); and policy changes (e.g., the "three strike" laws and their effect on correction activities).

Of the 19 million government employee total in 1995, about 3 million worked for the federal government, 5 million for state governments, and 11 million for local governments. Federal government employment has been steady since the late 1960s, staying within plus or minus 100,000 or so of 3 million. The dynamic growth in public employment has been among the state governments (up 25 percent from 1980 to 1993) and to a lesser extent local governments (up 17 percent from 1980 to 1993).

Where has this jump among state and local government employment occurred? For state governments, although education employment consistently has risen faster than noneducation, both areas have shown strong and steady growth. The average annual growth rate from 1977 to 1992 for state education was 2.1 percent (compounded, that is 37 percent) and for noneducation 1.6 percent (compounded, 28 percent).

Looking at these same categories, local governments showed a lot of variation over the 1977–92 period. Total local government employment rose almost 8 percent in this 15-year period. The noneducation sector was the real dynamic force in local government employment, increasing 21 percent in employment. The education numbers were erratic. From 1977 to 1982 they dropped (down 2 percent), had a moderate increase from 1982 to 1987 (up 9 percent), and stayed almost even from 1987 to 1992. The local noneducation employment growth rate increased steadily over the period—up 2 percent, 1977 to 1982; up 7 percent, 1982 to 1987; and up 11 percent, 1987 to 1992.

In interpreting these trends, it is useful to have recourse to other information. For example, although the education numbers probably track generally with the school-age population cohort, there are many other factors that will affect the trends. Some examples in education are changing pupil-teacher ratios, increased mainstreaming of children with special education needs and increasing numbers of adults returning for postsecondary education.

INTERGOVERNMENTAL FLOW OF FUNDS

There is considerable flow of money among governments within the U.S. governmental system. Just how large is this intergovernmental financial dimension of American government? For state governments, 23 percent of every dollar they spent in 1993 originated with another government. The comparable figure for local governments was 33 percent. Even among local governments there is a spate of funds flowing back and forth, as cities pay counties for housing prisoners in correctional facilities, counties provide financial support for school districts, and cities provide fire protection for county facilities. But there are other, less direct aspects of intergovernmental financing that need to be considered also.

Two oddities in the intergovernmental finance system provide good examples of its complexity. They are state "on-behalf-of" spending that benefits local governments and the interest exemption on municipal debt. The latter is indirect spending by the federal government that benefits state and local governments.

State "on-behalf-of" spending occurs when a state purchases goods or services that otherwise a local government would provide. One of the most common uses of this is state support of local government employee pensions. Many state-run employee retirement systems include local government employees. In many cases, the states are funding all or part of the local government share of the local government pensions. There are also other types of goods or services this state activity covers, such as certain capital expenditures. As shown in Table 12.13, which highlights "on-behalf" payments for local education agencies, these payments can be a sizeable percentage of the state intergovernmental payments. In 11 states, the "on-behalf-of" payment exceeded 10 percent of all state payments for elementary-secondary education in 1992–93.

Another aspect of the intergovernmental flow of money concerns state and local government bonds.[30] State and local government bonds are exempt from federal income taxation. Because of this, they can be issued at lower interest rates than commercial debt. The tax exemption is an inducement to investors seeking tax-free income, and the lower rate is a benefit to the state and local governments. This is also, however, a foregoing of revenue by the federal government. It is, therefore, a significant indirect intergovernmental payment by the federal government to state and local governments. In 1996, it is estimated that cost to the federal government for this was almost $25 billion.[31] There have been periodic attempts to scrap this federal tax provision, but, except for limitations in some very specific areas of debt issuance, the provision has remained intact.[32]

SOME FINAL THOUGHTS

The complicated examples of intergovernmental financial flows are in many ways good metaphors for our American governmental system. It is at the same time complex and simple, centralized and decentralized, the result of deep historical roots and current pressures, and a mix of administrative convenience and political management.

One national issue currently under debate has the potential to lead to significant changes concerning which governments will carry out tasks, which governments will pay, and whether government will be involved in certain activities at all. It goes by the term "devolution."[33] The most prominent example of this is public welfare reform. Here the change is from a federally centered open-ended grant (Aid to Families with Dependent Children, or AFDC) to a state-centered block grant (Temporary Assistance for Needy Families, or TANF).

TABLE 12.13

TOTAL REVENUE FROM STATE SOURCES AND "ON-BEHALF" STATE PAYMENTS FOR PUBLIC ELEMENTARY-SECONDARY SCHOOL SYSTEMS IN THE UNITED STATES, BY STATE: 1992–1993

(THOUSANDS OF DOLLARS)

STATE	TOTAL REVENUE FROM STATE SOURCES	STATE PAYMENTS ON BEHALF OF LOCAL EDUCATION AGENCY	"ON-BEHALF" PAYMENTS AS A PERCENT OF TOTAL REVENUE FROM STATE
MARYLAND	1,959,865	499,560	25.5
MAINE	657,885	139,786	21.2
MICHIGAN	3,326,748	696,990	21.0
MASSACHUSETTS	1,924,321	344,887	17.9
KENTUCKY	2,043,416	334,220	16.4
ALABAMA	1,729,295	282,498	16.3
NEW JERSEY	4,614,924	689,350	14.9
ARKANSAS	1,103,184	143,071	13.0
TEXAS	7,907,477	924,220	11.7
WEST VIRGINIA	1,220,263	122,931	10.1
PENNSYLVANIA	4,781,408	476,063	10.0
VERMONT	216,778	19,892	9.2
IDAHO	547,454	48,310	8.8
CONNECTICUT	1,417,328	112,617	7.9
RHODE ISLAND	351,512	25,274	7.2
ILLINOIS	3,467,071	231,340	6.7
OKLAHOMA	1,595,889	105,853	6.6
INDIANA	3,005,534	191,312	6.4
KANSAS	1,165,178	53,290	4.6
CALIFORNIA	17,090,164	768,734	4.5
SOUTH CAROLINA	1,419,961	47,780	3.4
GEORGIA	3,155,848	71,770	2.3
NEW MEXICO	1,067,410	16,685	1.6
NORTH CAROLINA	3,388,466	46,586	1.4
MISSISSIPPI	966,097	11,328	1.2
LOUISIANA	1,876,967	5,628	0.3
NEBRASKA	509,432	507	0.1
ARIZONA	1,415,429	1,002	0.1

Source: U. S. Bureau of the Census, Public Education Finances, GF93-10, table 11.

Note: Excludes states with no "on-behalf" payments.

---

[30] Often the term "municipal bonds" is used as a generic designation that encompasses all debt issued by state and local governments, not just municipalities.

[31] See "Total Revenue Loss Estimates for Tax Expenditures in the Income Tax," Budget of the United States Government, Fiscal Year 1998, Analytical Perspectives 75, Table 5-1.

[32] In the late 1970s and early 1980s, state and local governments took advantage of their ability to issue tax-exempt debt by issuing a considerable amount of industrial development bonds (IDBs). These bonds are public debt issuances intended to spur private development in communities. Governments issue the IDBs to fund the development of a private facility, and businesses pay the cost of the debt's principal and interest through the governments. The business receives a lower interest rate, and the local government receives additional economic development. The volume of IDBs grew extremely rapidly in the 1980s. The loss to the U.S. Treasury was quite significant, and led to restrictions in federal tax law on the type of development that IDBs could fund and a per capita annual cap on the amount of IDB issuance.

[33] An article by a prominent scholar of American federalism characterizes this national discussion as a "devolution revolution." See Richard P. Nathan, "The Devolution Revolution: An Overview," Rockefeller Institute Bulletin (State University of New York, Rockefeller Institute of Government, 1996), 5-13.

There are numerous other examples of similar types of changes in the past few decades.

Predicting how far this potential revolution will go should be done cautiously. The major hurdle to be overcome is the inertia inherent in such a complicated governmental system as that found in the United States. Woodrow Wilson's comment about change—"If you want to make enemies, try to change something"—sums up the major problem that devolution will encounter.

FOR FURTHER INFORMATION SEE:

NELSON A. ROCKEFELLER INSTITUTE OF GOVERNMENT, CENTER FOR THE STUDY OF THE STATES. *STATE FISCAL BRIEF, STATE REVENUE REPORT, AND STATE EMPLOYMENT.* AUGUST 1997.

BOOK OF THE STATES 1995. LEXINGTON, KY: COUNCIL OF STATE GOVERNMENTS.

DISTRICT OF COLUMBIA GOVERNMENT. *TAX RATES AND TAX BURDENS IN THE DISTRICT OF COLUMBIA: A NATIONWIDE COMPARISON.* 1995.

JOHN F. KENNEDY SCHOOL OF GOVERNMENT. *THE FEDERAL BUDGET AND THE STATES 1995.* CAMBRIDGE: HARVARD UNIVERSITY PRESS.

NATIONAL ASSOCIATION OF STATE BUDGET OFFICERS. *STATE EXPENDITURE REPORT AND FISCAL SURVEY OF THE STATES.* (VARIOUS YEARS).

NATIONAL CONFERENCE OF STATE LEGISLATURES. *STATE TAX ACTIONS AND STATE BUDGET ACTIONS.* (VARIOUS YEARS).

U.S. ADVISORY COMMISSION ON INTERGOVERNMENTAL RELATIONS. *SIGNIFICANT FEATURES OF FISCAL FEDERALISM.* (VARIOUS YEARS).

U.S. BUREAU OF THE CENSUS. *STATISTICAL ABSTRACT OF THE UNITED STATES: 1996.*

U.S. BUREAU OF THE CENSUS. *GOVERNMENT FINANCES: 1992.* SERIES GF.

U.S. BUREAU OF THE CENSUS. *FEDERAL EXPENDITURES BY STATE: 1996.* SERIES FES.

U.S. BUREAU OF THE CENSUS. *GOVERNMENT EMPLOYMENT: 1992.* SERIES GE.

U.S. EXECUTIVE OFFICE OF THE PRESIDENT. *BUDGET OF THE UNITED STATES GOVERNMENT.* (VARIOUS YEARS).

U.S. EXECUTIVE OFFICE OF THE PRESIDENT. *ECONOMIC REPORT OF THE PRESIDENT.* (VARIOUS YEARS).

WEBSITES:

COUNCIL OF STATE GOVERNMENTS WEBSITE AT <HTTP://WWW.CSG.ORG>.

GOVERNING MAGAZINE WEBSITE AT <HTTP://WWW.GOVERNING.COM>.

NATIONAL CONFERENCE OF STATE LEGISLATURES WEBSITE AT <HTTP://WWW.NCSL.ORG>.

THE BOND BUYER WEBSITE AT <HTTP://WWW.BONDBUYER.COM>.

U.S. BUREAU OF THE CENSUS WEBSITE AT <HTTP://WWW.CENSUS.GOV>.

U.S. BUREAU OF ECONOMIC ANALYSIS WEBSITE AT <HTTP://WWW.BEA.GOV>.

APPENDIX

POPULATION CHARACTERISTICS

TABLE A1.1

RESIDENT POPULATION PROJECTIONS OF THE UNITED STATES: MIDDLE, LOW AND HIGH SERIES, 1996–2050.

(NUMBERS IN THOUSANDS. CONSISTENT WITH THE 1990 CENSUS, AS ENUMERATED.)

YEAR	MIDDLE SERIES	LOW SERIES	HIGH SERIES
1996	265,253	264,869	265,646
1997	267,645	266,733	268,577
1998	270,002	268,396	271,647
1999	272,330	269,861	274,865
2000	274,634	271,237	278,129
2001	276,918	272,528	281,443
2002	279,189	273,742	284,813
2003	281,452	274,885	288,243
2004	283,713	275,965	291,742
2005	285,981	276,990	295,318
2006	288,269	277,965	298,977
2007	290,583	278,896	302,728
2008	292,928	279,790	306,575
2009	295,306	280,647	310,523
2010	297,716	281,468	314,571
2011	300,157	282,288	318,676
2012	302,624	283,104	322,834
2013	305,112	283,910	327,042
2014	307,617	284,701	331,297
2015	310,134	285,472	335,597
2016	312,658	286,216	339,939
2017	315,185	286,927	344,322
2018	317,711	287,600	348,744
2019	320,231	288,228	353,204
2020	322,742	288,807	357,702
2021	325,239	289,330	362,237
2022	327,720	289,793	366,810
2023	330,183	290,193	371,423
2024	332,626	290,525	376,079
2025	335,050	290,789	380,781
2026	337,454	290,983	385,533
2027	339,839	291,106	390,336
2028	342,208	291,161	395,195
2029	344,560	291,148	400,112
2030	346,899	291,070	405,089
2031	349,227	290,932	410,128
2032	351,544	290,737	415,231
2033	353,853	290,489	420,399
2034	356,157	290,194	425,633
2035	358,457	289,855	430,934
2036	360,756	289,478	436,301
2037	363,056	289,068	441,736
2038	365,358	288,630	447,238
2039	367,666	288,167	452,807
2040	369,980	287,685	458,444
2041	372,303	287,186	464,148
2042	374,636	286,676	469,921
2043	376,981	286,157	475,764
2044	379,339	285,633	481,679
2045	381,713	285,107	487,671
2046	384,106	284,580	493,743
2047	386,522	284,057	499,900
2048	388,962	283,538	506,142
2049	391,431	283,027	512,475
2050	393,931	282,524	518,903

Source: U.S. Bureau of the Census, Current Population Reports, Series P25-1130, *Population Projections of the United States by Age, Sex, Race, and Hispanic Origin: 1995-2050*, 1996.

TABLE A1.2

RESIDENT POPULATION OF THE UNITED STATES: ESTIMATES, BY AGE AND SEX

(NUMBERS IN THOUSANDS. CONSISTENT WITH THE 1990 CENSUS, AS ENUMERATED.)

AGE	JULY 1, 1996			JULY 1, 1990		
	TOTAL	MALE	FEMALE	TOTAL	MALE	FEMALE
TOTAL	265,185	129,540	135,645	249,403	121,593	127,810
UNDER 5 YEARS	19,423	9,941	9,482	18,849	9,646	9,203
5 TO 9 YEARS	19,563	10,017	9,546	18,062	9,246	8,816
10 TO 14 YEARS	19,093	9,777	9,316	17,189	8,804	8,385
15 TO 19 YEARS	18,570	9,523	9,047	17,750	9,104	8,646
20 TO 24 YEARS	17,369	8,827	8,542	19,135	9,746	9,388
25 TO 29 YEARS	19,030	9,530	9,499	21,233	10,658	10,575
30 TO 34 YEARS	21,363	10,648	10,716	21,906	10,901	11,005
35 TO 39 YEARS	22,501	11,203	11,297	19,975	9,900	10,075
40 TO 44 YEARS	20,756	10,260	10,495	17,790	8,777	9,013
45 TO 49 YEARS	18,416	9,037	9,379	13,820	6,777	7,044
50 TO 54 YEARS	13,909	6,754	7,155	11,368	5,520	5,848
55 TO 59 YEARS	11,352	5,448	5,904	10,473	5,004	5,469
60 TO 64 YEARS	9,993	4,709	5,284	10,619	4,948	5,671
65 TO 69 YEARS	9,897	4,508	5,389	10,077	4,512	5,564
70 TO 74 YEARS	8,788	3,821	4,968	8,022	3,423	4,599
75 TO 79 YEARS	6,870	2,819	4,051	6,145	2,411	3,734
80 TO 84 YEARS	4,559	1,664	2,895	3,934	1,365	2,569
85 TO 89 YEARS	2,382	731	1,650	2,049	611	1,439
90 TO 94 YEARS	1,011	254	758	764	188	576
95 TO 99 YEARS	285	59	226	207	44	162
100 YEARS AND OVER	57	10	47	37	8	29

Source: U.S. Bureau of the Census, Population Division, release PPL-41, *United States Population Estimates by Age, Sex, Race, and Hispanic Origin, 1990 to 1995*, 1996.

TABLE A1.3

ESTIMATES OF THE POPULATION OF STATES: ANNUAL TIME SERIES, JULY 1, 1990 TO JULY 1, 1996

(INCLUDES REVISED APRIL 1, 1990 CENSUS POPULATION COUNTS. IN THOUSANDS.)

YEAR	1996	1995	1994	1993	1992	1991	1990
UNITED STATES	265,283,783	262,889,634	260,372,174	257,795,138	255,011,287	252,106,453	249,397,990
NORTHEAST	51,580,085	51,505,491	51,426,298	51,292,552	51,097,031	50,954,026	50,857,291
NEW ENGLAND	13,351,266	13,305,111	13,265,209	13,229,548	13,197,697	13,204,213	13,219,579
MIDDLE ATLANTIC	38,228,819	38,200,380	38,161,089	38,063,004	37,899,334	37,749,813	37,637,712
MIDWEST	62,082,428	61,732,266	61,371,021	61,016,324	60,596,567	60,159,553	59,764,954
EAST NORTH CENTRAL	43,613,999	43,381,407	43,151,761	42,934,286	42,662,529	42,362,687	42,076,569
WEST NORTH CENTRAL	18,468,429	18,350,859	18,219,260	18,082,038	17,934,038	17,796,866	17,688,385
SOUTH	93,097,801	91,958,208	90,737,719	89,457,099	88,186,418	86,934,253	85,731,504
SOUTH ATLANTIC	47,615,690	47,013,137	46,396,778	45,732,755	45,096,552	44,444,010	43,757,667
EAST SOUTH CENTRAL	16,192,576	16,045,988	15,884,136	15,708,589	15,515,603	15,342,961	15,208,680
WEST SOUTH CENTRAL	29,289,535	28,899,083	28,456,805	28,015,755	27,574,263	27,147,282	26,765,157
WEST	58,523,469	57,693,669	56,837,136	56,029,163	55,131,271	54,058,621	53,044,241
MOUNTAIN	16,117,831	15,749,871	15,255,812	14,799,545	14,388,307	14,025,205	13,717,026
PACIFIC	42,405,638	41,943,798	41,581,324	41,229,618	40,742,964	40,033,416	39,327,215

TABLE A1.3 (CONTINUED)

ESTIMATES OF THE POPULATION OF STATES: ANNUAL TIME SERIES, JULY 1, 1990 TO JULY 1, 1996

(INCLUDES REVISED APRIL 1, 1990 CENSUS POPULATION COUNTS. IN THOUSANDS.)

YEAR	1996	1995	1994	1993	1992	1991	1990
ALABAMA	4,273,084	4,246,205	4,215,203	4,181,730	4,130,905	4,086,613	4,048,317
ALASKA	607,007	602,545	601,411	597,705	587,172	569,330	553,102
ARIZONA	4,428,068	4,305,016	4,091,615	3,952,954	3,841,125	3,749,569	3,679,370
ARKANSAS	2,509,793	2,484,761	2,454,811	2,426,709	2,395,956	2,371,352	2,354,301
CALIFORNIA	31,878,234	31,565,480	31,361,934	31,172,212	30,882,985	30,395,718	29,901,421
COLORADO	3,822,676	3,747,560	3,662,684	3,567,727	3,464,116	3,369,199	3,304,004
CONNECTICUT	3,274,238	3,270,740	3,273,040	3,275,568	3,276,347	3,289,115	3,288,975
DELAWARE	724,842	717,041	707,816	699,219	689,563	680,193	669,071
DISTRICT OF COLUMBIA	543,213	554,528	568,022	578,996	586,361	594,845	603,792
FLORIDA	14,399,985	14,184,155	13,964,771	13,713,523	13,513,217	13,290,697	13,018,496
GEORGIA	7,353,225	7,208,676	7,063,056	6,906,336	6,767,388	6,624,838	6,506,509
HAWAII	1,183,723	1,179,198	1,172,645	1,159,964	1,147,803	1,129,648	1,112,646
IDAHO	1,189,251	1,166,112	1,136,433	1,101,831	1,066,893	1,039,079	1,011,904
ILLINOIS	11,846,544	11,790,379	11,734,164	11,669,597	11,596,257	11,516,124	11,446,801
INDIANA	5,840,528	5,796,948	5,750,033	5,706,597	5,651,855	5,602,878	5,555,019
IOWA	2,851,792	2,843,074	2,832,360	2,822,486	2,808,185	2,791,547	2,779,652
KANSAS	2,572,150	2,563,618	2,549,972	2,531,637	2,513,609	2,491,618	2,480,630
KENTUCKY	3,883,723	3,856,877	3,825,816	3,793,968	3,752,558	3,715,011	3,692,529
LOUISIANA	4,350,579	4,338,072	4,314,630	4,290,100	4,273,734	4,241,224	4,217,362
MAINE	1,243,316	1,238,572	1,237,993	1,238,537	1,236,027	1,235,579	1,231,284
MARYLAND	5,071,604	5,038,912	4,999,632	4,952,890	4,909,389	4,859,337	4,797,676
MASSACHUSETTS	6,092,352	6,071,078	6,042,073	6,017,414	5,997,894	5,999,263	6,018,305
MICHIGAN	9,594,350	9,537,948	9,486,335	9,453,250	9,418,156	9,366,110	9,310,677
MINNESOTA	4,657,758	4,614,613	4,572,360	4,525,647	4,474,568	4,429,003	4,387,209
MISSISSIPPI	2,716,115	2,696,183	2,668,159	2,638,880	2,612,209	2,591,972	2,577,213
MISSOURI	5,358,692	5,319,335	5,275,172	5,233,149	5,188,734	5,156,936	5,126,241
MONTANA	879,372	870,351	856,519	841,188	823,287	808,230	799,826
NEBRASKA	1,652,093	1,639,213	1,625,529	1,614,829	1,604,015	1,591,528	1,580,648
NEVADA	1,603,163	1,533,478	1,464,064	1,386,258	1,333,901	1,285,597	1,218,702
NEW HAMPSHIRE	1,162,481	1,148,244	1,135,340	1,122,771	1,114,386	1,107,711	1,111,861
NEW JERSEY	7,987,933	7,949,506	7,905,880	7,859,761	7,811,316	7,767,081	7,739,502
NEW MEXICO	1,713,407	1,689,849	1,659,202	1,619,130	1,583,360	1,548,421	1,520,039
NEW YORK	18,184,774	18,190,562	18,196,829	18,170,321	18,099,081	18,036,973	18,002,719
NORTH CAROLINA	7,322,870	7,202,335	7,078,643	6,959,876	6,840,504	6,753,752	6,657,040
NORTH DAKOTA	643,539	641,506	639,695	637,066	635,326	634,101	637,369
OHIO	11,172,782	11,134,032	11,096,753	11,059,480	11,000,309	10,929,391	10,861,875
OKLAHOMA	3,300,902	3,274,870	3,253,629	3,233,549	3,207,154	3,167,748	3,147,095
OREGON	3,203,735	3,148,855	3,094,349	3,039,879	2,977,590	2,920,895	2,858,757
PENNSYLVANIA	12,056,112	12,060,312	12,058,380	12,032,922	11,988,937	11,945,759	11,895,491
RHODE ISLAND	990,225	991,701	996,112	999,861	1,001,881	1,004,545	1,004,665
SOUTH CAROLINA	3,698,746	3,667,000	3,642,968	3,628,502	3,594,586	3,555,544	3,498,970
SOUTH DAKOTA	732,405	729,500	724,172	717,224	709,601	702,133	696,636
TENNESSEE	5,319,654	5,246,723	5,174,958	5,094,011	5,019,931	4,949,365	4,890,621
TEXAS	19,128,261	18,801,380	18,433,735	18,065,397	17,697,419	17,366,958	17,046,399
UTAH	2,000,494	1,958,313	1,909,521	1,860,807	1,811,673	1,767,139	1,729,784
VERMONT	588,654	584,776	580,651	575,397	571,162	568,000	564,489
VIRGINIA	6,675,451	6,615,234	6,549,703	6,474,591	6,388,379	6,285,884	6,213,684
WASHINGTON	5,532,939	5,447,720	5,350,985	5,259,858	5,147,414	5,017,825	4,901,289
WEST VIRGINIA	1,825,754	1,825,256	1,822,167	1,818,822	1,807,165	1,798,920	1,792,429
WISCONSIN	5,159,795	5,122,100	5,084,476	5,045,362	4,995,952	4,948,184	4,902,197
WYOMING	481,400	479,192	475,774	469,650	463,952	457,971	453,397

Sources: U.S. Bureau of the Census, 1970 and 1980 data from: *Statistical Abstract of the United States 1996*, No. 27, "Resident Population - States: 1970 to 1995." Other data from: Population Estimates Program, Population Division, U.S. Bureau of the Census.

TABLE A1.4

WORLD POPULATION BY REGION: 1950–2020

(FIGURES MAY NOT ADD TO TOTALS BECAUSE OF ROUNDING. MIDYEAR POPULATION IN MILLIONS.)

REGION	1950	1960	1970	1980	1990	1996	2000	2010	2020
WORLD	2,556	3,039	3,706	4,458	5,282	5,772	6,091	6,862	7,600
LESS DEVELOPED COUNTRIES	1,749	2,129	2,703	3,377	4,139	4,601	4,903	5,634	6,351
MORE DEVELOPED COUNTRIES	807	910	1,003	1,081	1,142	1,171	1,189	1,228	1,249
AFRICA	229	283	360	470	624	732	807	1,009	1,230
SUB-SAHARAN AFRICA	185	227	289	379	504	594	659	831	1,023
NORTH AFRICA	44	56	71	91	120	137	149	178	207
NEAR EAST	43	57	74	100	134	157	175	223	276
ASIA	1,368	1,628	2,039	2,501	2,989	3,271	3,448	3,852	4,219
LATIN AMERICA AND THE CARIBBEAN	166	218	285	362	443	489	517	584	643
EUROPE AND THE NEW INDEPENDENT STATES	572	639	703	750	789	800	807	827	834
WESTERN EUROPE	304	326	352	367	377	387	391	397	394
EASTERN EUROPE	88	100	108	117	122	120	120	123	122
NEW INDEPENDENT STATES	180	214	242	266	289	293	295	307	318
NORTH AMERICA	166	199	226	252	277	295	307	333	361
UNITED STATES	152	181	205	228	250	266	277	301	326
OCEANIA	12	16	19	23	27	29	30	34	37
EXCLUDING CHINA (MAINLAND AND TAIWAN):									
WORLD	1,985	2,377	2,871	3,455	4,128	4,541	4,816	5,498	6,162
LESS DEVELOPED COUNTRIES	1,179	1,467	1,868	2,374	2,985	3,370	3,627	4,270	4,913
ASIA	797	966	1,204	1,498	1,835	2,039	2,172	2,488	2,780
LESS DEVELOPED COUNTRIES	714	872	1,099	1,382	1,711	1,914	2,046	2,361	2,657

Source: U.S. Bureau of the Census, *World Population Profile: 1996*, Appendix table A-1.

TABLE A1.5

POPULATION, VITAL EVENTS AND RATES, BY REGION AND COUNTRY: 1996

(POPULATION AND EVENTS IN THOUSANDS.   FIGURES MAY NOT ADD TO TOTALS BECAUSE OF ROUNDING.)

REGION AND COUNTRY OR AREA	MIDYEAR POPULATION	BIRTHS	DEATHS	NATURAL INCREASE	BIRTHS PER 1,000 POPULATION	DEATHS PER 1,000 POPULATION	RATE OF NATURAL INCREASE (PERCENT)
WORLD	5,772,351	133,350	53,756	79,594	23	9	1.4
LESS-DEVELOPED COUNTRIES	4,601,370	119,521	41,403	78,118	26	9	1.7
MORE-DEVELOPED COUNTRIES	1,170,981	13,829	12,354	1,475	12	11	0.1
AFRICA	731,538	28,875	10,099	18,776	39	14	2.6
SUB-SAHARAN AFRICA	594,313	24,966	9,109	15,857	42	15	2.7
NORTH AFRICA	137,225	3,908	990	2,918	28	7	2.1
NEAR EAST	157,333	4,999	929	4,070	32	6	2.6
ASIA	3,270,944	73,616	27,203	46,414	23	8	1.4
LATIN AMERICA AND THE CARIBBEAN	488,608	11,334	3,444	7,890	23	7	1.6
EUROPE AND THE NEW INDEPENDENT STATES	799,589	9,612	9,420	192	12	12	(Z)
WESTERN EUROPE	386,600	4,141	3,939	202	11	10	0.1
EASTERN EUROPE	120,190	1,356	1,352	3	11	11	(Z)
NEW INDEPENDENT STATES	292,799	4,115	4,129	-14	14	14	(Z)
NORTH AMERICA	295,424	4,381	2,448	1,933	15	8	0.7
UNITED STATES	266,476	3,995	2,241	1,754	15	8	0.7
OCEANIA	28,915	533	213	320	18	7	1.1
EXCLUDING CHINA (MAINLAND AND TAIWAN):							
WORLD	4,540,880	112,445	45,265	67,181	25	10	1.5
LESS-DEVELOPED COUNTRIES	3,369,899	98,617	32,911	65,706	29	10	1.9
ASIA	2,039,473	52,712	18,711	34,001	26	9	1.7
LESS-DEVELOPED COUNTRIES	1,914,023	51,434	17,744	33,690	27	9	1.8

(Z) BETWEEN -500 AND +500 FOR EVENTS AND BETWEEN -0.05 PERCENT AND +0.05 PERCENT FOR RATES

Source: U.S. Bureau of the Census, "World Population Profile: 1996," Appendix table A-3.

TABLE A1.6

METROPOLITAN AND NONMETROPOLITAN AREA POPULATION IN THE UNITED STATES: 1970, 1980, 1990, 1994

(AS OF APRIL 1, EXCEPT 1994, AS OF JULY 1. DATA EXCLUDE PUERTO RICO. METROPOLITAN AREAS ARE DEFINED BY U.S. OFFICE OF MANAGEMENT AND BUDGET AS OF YEAR SHOWN, EXCEPT AS NOTED.)

ITEM	1970	(SMSA's) 1980[1]	MSA's AND CMSA's[2]		
			1980	1990	1994
METROPOLITAN AREAS: NUMBER OF AREAS	243	318	271	271	271
POPULATION (1,000)	139,480	169,431	177,143	198,023	207,654
PERCENT CHANGE OVER PREVIOUS YEAR SHOWN	23.6[3]	21.5	NA	11.8	4.9
PERCENT OF TOTAL U.S. POPULATION	68.6	74.8	78.2	79.6	79.8
PERCENT OF U.S. LAND AREA	10.9	16.0	19.8	19.8	19.8
NONMETROPOLITAN AREAS, POPULATION (1,000)	63,822	57,115	49,399	50,696	52,687

NA= NOT APPLICABLE.

(1) SMSA=STANDARD METROPOLITAN STATISTICAL AREA. AREAS ARE DEFINED AS OF JUNE 30, 1981.

(2) AREAS ARE AS DEFINED JUNE 30, 1995.

(3) PERCENT CHANGE FROM 1960.

Source: Data from Statistical Abstract of the United States 1996, Table No. 40.

TABLE A1.7

U.S. INMIGRANTS, OUTMIGRANTS, AND NET MIGRATION BETWEEN 1985 AND 1990 FOR STATES AND THE DISTRICT OF COLUMBIA

UNITED STATES	INTERNAL MIGRATION AND MOVERS FROM ABROAD, FOR STATES			
	INMIGRANTS	OUTMIGRANTS	NET MIGRATION	MOVERS FROM ABROAD
UNITED STATES	21,585,297	21,585,297	0	5,108,710
ALABAMA	328,120	292,251	35,869	29,815
ALASKA	105,605	154,090	-48,485	10,899
ARIZONA	649,821	433,644	216,177	80,271
ARKANSAS	240,497	216,250	24,247	12,339
CALIFORNIA	1,974,833	1,801,247	173,586	1,498,608
COLORADO	465,714	543,712	-77,998	56,040
CONNECTICUT	291,140	342,983	-51,843	70,655
DELAWARE	94,129	68,248	25,881	7,521
DIST. OF COLUMBIA	109,107	163,518	-54,411	24,254
FLORIDA	2,130,613	1,058,931	1,071,682	389,868
GEORGIA	804,566	501,969	302,597	92,080
HAWAII	166,953	187,209	-20,256	48,417
IDAHO	137,542	157,121	-19,579	11,217
ILLINOIS	667,778	1,009,922	-342,144	202,784
INDIANA	433,678	430,550	3,128	32,464
IOWA	194,298	288,670	-94,372	17,303
KANSAS	272,213	295,663	-23,450	32,631
KENTUCKY	278,273	298,397	-20,124	26,057
LOUISIANA	225,352	476,006	-250,654	30,198
MAINE	132,006	98,688	33,318	10,773
MARYLAND	531,803	430,913	100,890	111,789
MASSACHUSETTS	444,040	540,772	-96,732	155,863
MICHIGAN	473,473	606,472	-132,999	74,307
MINNESOTA	320,725	316,363	4,362	36,175
MISSISSIPPI	193,148	220,278	-27,130	12,262
MISSOURI	448,280	420,223	28,057	34,051
MONTANA	84,523	137,127	-52,604	5,677
NEBRASKA	141,712	181,662	-39,950	12,518
NEVADA	326,919	154,067	172,852	30,245
NEW HAMPSHIRE	191,130	129,070	62,060	11,538
NEW JERSEY	569,590	763,123	-193,533	211,417
NEW MEXICO	192,761	204,218	-11,457	24,901
NEW YORK	727,621	1,548,507	-820,886	613,724
NORTH CAROLINA	748,767	467,885	280,882	65,663
NORTH DAKOTA	56,071	107,018	-50,947	6,805
OHIO	622,446	763,625	-141,179	69,106
OKLAHOMA	279,889	407,649	-127,760	32,241
OREGON	363,447	280,875	82,572	40,955
PENNSYLVANIA	694,020	771,709	-77,689	98,575
RHODE ISLAND	105,917	93,649	12,268	21,716
SOUTH CAROLINA	398,448	289,107	109,341	30,545
SOUTH DAKOTA	69,036	91,479	-22,443	5,071
TENNESSEE	500,006	368,544	131,462	30,347
TEXAS	1,164,106	1,495,475	-331,369	368,091
UTAH	177,071	213,233	-36,162	25,617
VERMONT	74,955	57,970	16,985	4,401
VIRGINIA	863,567	635,695	227,872	148,724
WASHINGTON	626,156	409,886	216,270	101,562
WEST VIRGINIA	123,978	197,633	-73,655	4,939
WISCONSIN	307,168	343,022	-35,854	32,704
WYOMING	62,286	118,979	-56,693	2,987

Source: U.S. Bureau of the Census, *Selected Place of Birth and Migration Statistics: 1990*, CPH-L-121.

TABLE A1.8

PERCENTAGE BORN IN STATE OF RESIDENCE AND RANK: 1990

UNITED STATES	PERSONS	BORN IN STATE OF RESIDENCY		
		TOTAL NUMBER	PERCENT	RANK
UNITED STATES	248,709,873	153,684,685	61.8	
ALABAMA	4,040,587	3,067,607	75.9	8
ALASKA	550,043	186,887	34.0	49
ARIZONA	3,665,228	1,252,645	34.2	48
ARKANSAS	2,350,725	1,577,038	67.1	25
CALIFORNIA	29,760,021	13,797,065	46.4	43
COLORADO	3,294,394	1,427,412	43.3	45
CONNECTICUT	3,287,116	1,874,080	57.0	33
DELAWARE	666,168	334,209	50.2	39
DIST. OF COLUMBIA	606,900	238,728	39.3	47
FLORIDA	12,937,926	3,940,240	30.5	50
GEORGIA	6,478,216	4,179,861	64.5	27
HAWAII	1,108,229	621,992	56.1	34
IDAHO	1,006,749	508,992	50.6	38
ILLINOIS	11,430,602	7,897,755	69.1	19
INDIANA	5,544,159	3,940,076	71.1	13
IOWA	2,776,755	2,154,669	77.6	3
KANSAS	2,477,574	1,519,904	61.3	30
KENTUCKY	3,685,296	2,851,449	77.4	4
LOUISIANA	4,219,973	3,332,542	79.0	2
MAINE	1,227,928	840,930	68.5	21
MARYLAND	4,781,468	2,383,427	49.8	40
MASSACHUSETTS	6,016,425	4,134,235	68.7	20
MICHIGAN	9,295,297	6,958,717	74.9	9
MINNESOTA	4,375,099	3,220,512	73.6	11
MISSISSIPPI	2,573,216	1,989,265	77.3	5
MISSOURI	5,117,073	3,563,820	69.9	17
MONTANA	799,065	470,861	58.9	31
NEBRASKA	1,578,385	1,107,280	70.2	16
NEVADA	1,201,833	261,998	21.8	51
NEW HAMPSHIRE	1,109,252	488,894	44.1	44
NEW JERSEY	7,730,188	4,232,369	54.8	35
NEW MEXICO	1,515,069	783,311	51.7	37
NEW YORK	17,990,455	12,147,209	67.5	23
NORTH CAROLINA	6,628,637	4,668,539	70.4	14
NORTH DAKOTA	638,800	467,822	73.2	12
OHIO	10,847,115	8,038,140	74.1	10
OKLAHOMA	3,145,585	1,996,579	63.5	28
OREGON	2,842,321	1,324,179	46.6	42
PENNSYLVANIA	11,881,643	9,527,402	80.2	1
RHODE ISLAND	1,003,464	636,222	63.4	29
SOUTH CAROLINA	3,486,703	2,385,744	68.4	22
SOUTH DAKOTA	696,004	488,514	70.2	15
TENNESSEE	4,877,185	3,373,365	69.2	18
TEXAS	16,986,510	10,994,794	64.7	26
UTAH	1,722,850	1,157,744	67.2	24
VERMONT	562,758	321,704	57.2	32
VIRGINIA	6,187,358	3,356,594	54.2	36
WASHINGTON	4,866,692	2,344,187	48.2	41
WEST VIRGINIA	1,793,477	1,386,139	77.3	6
WISCONSIN	4,891,769	3,737,602	76.4	7
WYOMING	453,588	193,436	42.6	46

Source: U.S. Bureau of the Census, Selected Place of Birth and Migration Statistics: 1990, CPH-L-121.

LIVING ARRANGEMENTS

TABLE A2.1

MARITAL STATUS OF THE POPULATION 15 YEARS OLD AND OVER, BY SEX AND RACE: 1950–1995

(PERCENT)

YEAR	TOTAL	MARRIED	UNMARRIED			
			TOTAL	NEVER MARRIED	WIDOWED	DIVORCED
MALES						
ALL RACES						
1995	97,704	57,750	39,953	30,286	2,284	7,383
1990	91,955	55,833	36,121	27,505	2,333	6,283
1980	81,947	51,813	30,134	24,227	1,977	3,930
1970	70,559	47,109	23,450	19,832	2,051	1,567
1960*	60,273	41,781	18,492	15,274	2,112	1,106
1950*	54,601	36,866	17,735	14,400	2,264	1,071
WHITE						
1995	82,566	50,658	31,909	23,667	1,921	6,321
1990	78,908	49,542	29,367	22,078	1,930	5,359
1980	71,887	46,721	25,167	20,174	1,642	3,351
1970	62,868	42,732	20,135	17,080	1,722	1,333
1960*	54,130	38,042	16,088	13,286	1,816	986
1950*	49,302	33,451	15,850	12,892	1,986	972
BLACK						
1995	10,825	4,632	6,193	5,031	310	852
1990	9,948	4,489	5,459	4,319	338	802
1980	8,292	4,053	4,239	3,410	308	521
1970	6,936	3,949	2,987	2,468	307	212
1960*	6,143	3,739	2,404	1,988	296	120
1950*	5,299	3,415	1,885	1,508	278	99
FEMALES						
ALL RACES						
1995	105,028	58,984	46,045	24,693	11,082	10,270
1990	99,838	56,797	43,040	22,718	11,477	8,845
1980	89,914	52,965	36,950	20,226	10,758	5,966
1970	77,766	48,148	29,618	17,167	9,734	2,717
1960*	64,607	42,583	22,024	12,252	8,064	1,708
1950*	57,102	37,577	19,525	11,418	6,734	1,373
WHITE						
1995	87,484	51,390	36,094	18,250	9,399	8,445
1990	84,508	49,986	34,522	17,438	9,800	7,284
1980	77,882	47,277	30,604	16,318	9,296	4,990
1970	68,888	43,286	25,602	14,703	8,559	2,340
1960*	57,860	38,545	19,315	10,796	7,099	1,420
1950*	51,404	34,042	17,362	10,241	5,902	1,219
BLACK						
1995	13,097	4,942	8,155	5,250	1,380	1,525
1990	11,966	4,813	7,152	4,416	1,392	1,344
1980	10,108	4,508	5,600	3,401	1,319	880
1970	8,108	4,384	3,723	2,248	1,120	355
1960*	6,747	4,038	2,709	1,456	965	288
1950*	5,698	3,534	2,164	1,178	832	154

TABLE A2.1 (CONTINUED)

MARITAL STATUS OF THE POPULATION 15 YEARS OLD AND OVER, BY SEX AND RACE: 1950–1995

(PERCENT)

| YEAR | TOTAL | MARRIED | UNMARRIED | | | |
			TOTAL	NEVER MARRIED	WIDOWED	DIVORCED
MALES						
ALL RACES						
1995	100.0	59.1	40.9	31.0	2.3	7.6
1990	100.0	60.7	39.3	29.9	2.5	6.8
1980	100.0	63.2	36.8	29.6	2.4	4.8
1970	100.0	66.8	33.2	28.1	2.9	2.2
1960	100.0	69.3	30.7	25.3	3.5	1.8
1950	100.0	67.5	32.5	26.4	4.1	2.0
WHITE						
1995	100.0	61.4	38.6	28.7	2.3	7.7
1990	100.0	62.8	37.2	28.0	2.4	6.8
1980	100.0	65.0	35.0	28.1	2.3	4.7
1970	100.0	68.0	32.0	27.2	2.7	2.1
1960	100.0	70.3	29.7	24.5	3.4	1.8
1950	100.0	67.8	32.1	26.1	4.0	2.0
BLACK						
1995	100.0	42.8	57.2	46.5	2.9	7.9
1990	100.0	45.1	54.9	43.4	3.4	8.1
1980	100.0	48.9	51.1	41.1	3.7	6.3
1970	100.0	56.9	43.1	35.6	4.4	3.1
1960	100.0	60.9	39.1	32.4	4.8	2.0
1950	100.0	64.4	35.6	28.5	5.2	1.9
FEMALES						
ALL RACES						
1995	100.0	56.2	43.8	23.5	10.6	9.8
1990	100.0	56.9	43.1	22.8	11.5	8.9
1980	100.0	58.9	41.1	22.5	12.0	6.6
1970	100.0	61.9	38.1	22.1	12.5	3.5
1960	100.0	65.9	34.1	19.0	12.5	2.6
1950	100.0	65.8	34.2	20.0	11.8	2.4
WHITE						
1995	100.0	58.7	41.3	20.9	10.7	9.7
1990	100.0	59.1	40.9	20.6	11.6	8.6
1980	100.0	60.7	39.3	21.0	11.9	6.4
1970	100.0	62.8	37.2	21.3	12.4	3.4
1960	100.0	66.6	33.4	18.7	12.3	2.5
1950	100.0	66.2	33.8	19.9	11.5	2.4
BLACK						
1995	100.0	37.7	62.3	40.1	10.5	11.6
1990	100.0	40.2	59.8	36.9	11.6	11.2
1980	100.0	44.6	55.4	33.6	13.0	8.7
1970	100.0	54.1	45.9	27.7	13.8	4.4
1960	100.0	59.8	40.2	21.6	14.3	4.3
1950	100.0	62.0	38.0	20.7	14.6	2.7

*1950 AND 1960 DATA ARE FOR THE POPULATION 14 YRS OLD AND OVER.

Source: U.S. Bureau of the Census, Current Population Reports, Series, "Marital Status and Living Arrangements: March 1995," and earlier reports.

TABLE A2.2

MARITAL STATUS AND LIVING ARRANGEMENTS OF ADULTS 18 YEARS OLD AND OVER: MARCH 1995

(NUMBERS IN THOUSANDS)

CHARACTERISTICS OF ADULTS	18 YEARS AND OVER	18 TO 24 YEARS	25 TO 34 YEARS	35 TO 44 YEARS	45 TO 64 YEARS	65 TO 74 YEARS	75 YEARS AND OVER
MARITAL STATUS							
MALES	92,008	12,545	20,589	20,972	24,900	8,097	4,908
MARRIED, SPOUSE PRESENT	54,934	1,572	10,506	13,982	19,182	6,340	3,353
MARRIED, SPOUSE ABSENT	2,796	146	718	841	763	209	121
UNMARRIED	34,277	10826	9,364	6,150	4,954	1,548	1,431
NEVER MARRIED	24,628	10,726	8,019	3,631	1,708	342	201
WIDOWED	2,282	0	17	81	428	693	1,062
DIVORCED	7,367	100	1,328	2,438	2,818	513	168
FEMALES	99,588	12,613	20,800	21,363	26,550	10,117	8,147
MARRIED, SPOUSE PRESENT	54,905	2,709	12,263	14,482	18,030	5,364	2,057
MARRIED, SPOUSE ABSENT	4,026	337	1,071	1,140	1,130	207	139
UNMARRIED	40,658	9,568	7,465	5,738	7,390	4,546	5,949
NEVER MARRIED	19,312	9,289	5,540	2,286	1,426	408	360
WIDOWED	11,080	19	86	279	2,060	3,352	5,284
DIVORCED	10,266	260	1,839	3,173	3,904	786	305
LIVING ARRANGEMENTS							
MALES	92,008	12,545	20,589	20,972	24,900	8,097	4,908
LIVING WITH RELATIVE(S)	73,720	9,927	15,265	17,036	21,009	6,767	3,718
FAMILY HOUSEHOLDER	48,534	1,400	9,009	12,339	17,052	5,705	3,022
SPOUSE OF HOUSEHOLDER	8,524	284	1,965	2,302	2,736	823	414
CHILD OF HOUSEHOLDER	12,878	7,328	3,166	1,727	618	12	28
OTHER, LIVING WITH RELATIVES	3,784	915	1,125	668	603	227	254
NOT LIVING WITH RELATIVES	18,288	2,618	5,324	3,936	3,891	1,330	1,190
NONFAMILY HOUSEHOLDER	13,178	1,246	3,345	2,928	3,270	1,224	1,164
LIVING ALONE	10,160	626	2,221	2,265	2,793	1,134	1,121
SHARING HOME WITH NONRELATIVES	3,018	620	1,124	663	477	90	43
OTHER, NOT LIVING WITH RELATIVES	5,110	1,372	1,979	1,008	621	106	26
FEMALES	99,588	12,613	20,800	21,363	26,550	10,117	8,147
LIVING WITH RELATIVE(S)	79,534	10,341	17,576	19,079	22,185	6,721	3,634
FAMILY HOUSEHOLDER	20,724	1,625	5,071	5,934	5,587	1,562	947
SPOUSE OF HOUSEHOLDER	45,309	1,943	9,845	11,876	15,308	4,594	1,743
CHILD OF HOUSEHOLDER	8,818	5,896	1,759	703	396	50	15
OTHER, LIVING WITH RELATIVES	4,683	877	901	566	894	515	929
NOT LIVING WITH RELATIVES	20,054	2,272	3,224	2,284	4,365	3,396	4,513
NONFAMILY HOUSEHOLDER	16,488	1,100	2,031	1,713	3,904	3,311	4,430
LIVING ALONE	14,640	591	1,448	1,400	3,594	3,247	4,360
SHARING HOME WITH RELATIVES	1,848	509	583	313	310	64	70
OTHER, NOT LIVING WITH RELATIVES	3,566	1,172	1,193	571	461	85	83

Source: U.S. Bureau of the Census.

TABLE A2.3

MARRIAGES AND DIVORCES IN THE U.S.: 1970 TO 1994

YEAR	MARRIAGES[1]						DIVORCES AND ANNULMENTS		
		RATE PER 1,000 POPULATION						RATE PER 1,000 POPULATION	
			MEN, 15 YRS OLD AND OVER	WOMEN, 15 YRS OLD AND OVER	UNMARRIED WOMEN				
	NUMBER (1,000)	TOTAL			15 YRS OLD AND OVER	15 TO 44 YRS OLD	NUMBER (1,000)	TOTAL	MARRIED WOMEN, 15 YRS AND OVER
1994	2,362	9.1	NA	NA	51.5	84.0	1,191	4.6	20.5
1993	2,334	9.0	NA	NA	52.3	86.8	1,187	4.6	20.5
1992	2,362	9.3	NA	NA	53.3	88.2	1,215	4.8	21.2
1991	2,371	9.4	NA	NA	54.2	86.8	1,189	4.7	20.9
1990	2,443	9.8	26.0	24.1	54.5	91.3	1,182	4.7	20.9
1989	2,403	9.7	25.8	23.9	54.2	91.2	1,157	4.7	20.4
1988	2,396	9.8	26.0	24.0	54.6	91.0	1,167	4.8	20.7
1987	2,403	9.9	26.3	24.3	55.7	92.4	1,166	4.8	20.8
1986	2,407	10.0	26.6	24.5	56.2	93.9	1,178	4.9	21.2
1985	2,413	10.1	27.0	24.9	57.0	94.9	1,190	5.0	21.7
1984	2,477	10.5	28.0	25.8	59.5	99.0	1,169	5.0	21.5
1983	2,446	10.5	28.0	25.7	59.9	99.3	1,158	5.0	21.3
1980	2,390	10.6	28.5	26.1	61.4	102.6	1,189	5.2	22.6
1975	2,153	10.0	27.9	25.6	66.9	118.5	1,036	4.8	20.3
1970	2,159	10.6	31.1	28.4	76.5	140.2	708	3.5	14.9

NA NOT AVAILABLE.

(1) BEGINNING 1980, INCLUDES NONLICENSED MARRIAGES REGISTERED IN CALIFORNIA.

Source: *Statistical Abstract of the United States 1996*, Table No. 146.

TABLE A2.4

DIVORCES AND ANNULMENTS—DURATION OF MARRIAGE, AGE AT DIVORCE, AND CHILDREN INVOLVED, (SELECTED YEARS): 1970–1990

DURATION OF MARRIAGE, AGE AT DIVORCE, AND CHILDREN INVOLVED	1990	1989	1988	1987	1986	1985	1984	1983	1980	1975	1970
MEDIAN DURATION OF MARRIAGE (YEARS)	7.2	7.2	7.1	7.0	6.9	6.8	6.9	7.0	6.8	6.5	6.7
MEDIAN AGE AT DIVORCE											
MEN (YEARS)	35.6	35.4	35.1	34.9	34.6	34.4	34.3	34.0	32.7	32.2	32.9
WOMEN (YEARS)	33.2	32.9	32.6	32.5	32.1	31.9	31.7	31.5	30.3	29.5	29.8
ESTIMATED NUMBER OF CHILDREN											
INVOLVED IN DIVORCE (1,000)	1,075	1,063	1,044	1,038	1,064	1,091	1,081	1,091	1,174	1,123	870
AVG. NUMBER OF CHILDREN PER DECREE	0.90	0.91	0.89	0.89	0.90	0.92	0.92	0.94	0.98	1.08	1.22
RATE PER 1,000 CHILDREN UNDER 18											
YEARS OF AGE	16.8	16.8	16.4	16.3	16.8	17.3	17.2	17.4	17.3	16.7	12.5

Source: U.S. Bureau of the Census, *Statistical Abstract of the United States 1996*, Table No. 150.

TABLE A2.5

PERCENTAGE DISTRIBUTION OF U.S. HOUSEHOLDS, BY TYPE: 1940–95

(NUMBERS IN THOUSANDS)

SERIES AND YEAR	TOTAL HOUSEHOLDS	FAMILY HOUSEHOLDS				NONFAMILY HOUSEHOLDS		
				OTHER FAMILY				
		TOTAL	MARRIED COUPLE	MALE HOUSEHOLDER	FEMALE HOUSEHOLDER	TOTAL	MALE HOUSEHOLDER	FEMALE HOUSEHOLDER
1995	100.0	70.0	54.4	3.3	12.3	30.0	13.3	16.7
1994	100.0	70.5	54.8	3.0	12.8	29.5	12.8	16.6
1993R	100.0	70.7	55.1	3.2	12.5	29.3	12.8	16.5
1993	100.0	70.7	55.2	3.1	12.4	29.3	12.7	16.6
1992	100.0	70.2	54.8	3.2	12.2	29.8	13.0	16.8
1991	100.0	70.3	55.3	3.1	11.9	29.7	12.9	16.8
1990	100.0	70.8	56.0	3.1	11.7	29.2	12.4	16.8
1989	100.0	70.9	56.1	3.1	11.7	29.1	12.8	16.3
1988A	100.0	71.6	56.7	3.1	11.7	28.4	12.4	16.1
1988	100.0	71.5	56.9	3.0	11.6	28.5	12.4	16.1
1987	100.0	72.1	57.6	2.8	11.7	27.9	11.9	16.0
1986	100.0	71.9	57.6	2.7	11.5	28.1	12.0	16.1
1985	100.0	72.3	58.0	2.6	11.7	27.7	11.7	16.1
1984B	100.0	72.7	58.7	2.4	11.6	27.3	11.4	15.9
1984	100.0	72.6	58.6	2.4	11.6	27.4	11.4	16.0
1983	100.0	73.2	59.5	2.4	11.3	26.8	11.3	15.5
1982	100.0	73.1	59.4	2.4	11.3	26.9	11.3	15.6
1981	100.0	73.2	59.8	2.3	11.0	26.8	11.3	15.5
1980C	100.0	73.7	60.8	2.1	10.8	26.3	10.9	15.4
1980	100.0	73.9	60.9	2.2	10.8	26.1	10.9	15.3
1979	100.0	74.4	61.6	2.1	10.6	25.6	10.4	15.2
1978	100.0	74.9	62.3	2.1	10.6	25.1	10.3	14.8
1977	100.0	76.2	64.0	2.0	10.2	23.8	9.4	14.4
1976	100.0	76.9	64.9	2.0	10.1	23.1	9.0	14.1
1975	100.0	78.1	66.0	2.1	10.0	21.9	8.3	13.6
1974	100.0	78.6	67.0	2.0	9.6	21.4	8.1	13.3
1973	100.0	79.5	67.8	2.1	9.6	20.5	7.5	13.0
1972	100.0	79.7	68.6	2.0	9.2	20.3	7.3	13.0
1971	100.0	80.4	69.4	1.9	9.1	19.6	6.8	12.8
1970	100.0	81.2	70.5	1.9	8.7	18.8	6.4	12.4
1969	100.0	81.5	70.9	2.0	8.7	18.5	6.3	12.2
1968	100.0	82.2	71.5	2.0	8.7	17.8	6.0	11.7
1967	100.0	82.9	72.2	2.0	8.7	17.1	5.8	11.4
1966	100.0	82.9	72.4	2.0	8.5	17.1	5.6	11.5
1965	100.0	83.3	72.6	2.0	8.7	16.7	5.7	11.0
1964	100.0	84.4	73.6	2.1	8.6	15.6	5.3	10.3
1963	100.0	84.8	74.0	2.3	8.5	15.2	5.1	10.1
1962	100.0	84.5	73.8	2.3	8.4	15.5	5.4	10.2
1961	100.0	84.7	74.0	2.2	8.5	15.3	5.2	10.1
1960	100.0	85.0	74.3	2.3	8.4	15.0	5.1	9.8
1959	100.0	85.5	74.7	2.5	8.3	14.5	4.8	9.8
1958	100.0	86.0	75.1	2.5	8.4	14.0	4.6	9.3
1957	100.0	87.1	75.9	2.5	8.7	12.9	4.1	8.8
1956	100.0	87.1	75.8	2.9	8.5	12.9	4.2	8.7
1955	100.0	87.2	75.7	2.8	8.7	12.8	4.3	8.5
1954	100.0	87.3	76.5	2.8	8.0	12.7	4.1	8.6
1953	100.0	87.4	76.7	2.6	8.1	12.6	4.1	8.5
1952	100.0	88.4	77.2	2.5	8.7	11.6	3.9	7.8
1951	100.0	88.4	77.0	2.6	8.9	11.6	3.9	7.7
1950	100.0	89.2	78.2	2.7	8.3	10.8	3.8	7.0
1949	100.0	90.3	78.8	2.8	8.6	9.7	3.1	6.6
1948	100.0	90.4	78.7	2.5	9.2	9.6	3.0	6.7
1947	100.0	89.4	78.3	2.9	8.2	10.6	3.5	7.0
1940D	100.0	90.1	76.0	4.3	9.8	9.9	4.6	5.3

R = REVISED USING POPULATION CONTROLS BASED ON THE 1990 CENSUS.

A = DATA BASED ON 1988 REVISED PROCESSING.

B = INCORPORATES HISPANIC-ORIGIN POPULATION CONTROLS.

C = REVISED USING POPULATION CONTROLS BASED ON THE 1980 CENSUS.

D = BASED ON 1940 CENSUS.

Source: U.S. Bureau of the Census

TABLE A2.6

UNMARRIED-COUPLE HOUSEHOLDS IN THE UNITED STATES, BY PRESENCE OF CHILDREN: 1960–95

(NUMBERS IN THOUSANDS)

YEAR	TOTAL	WITHOUT CHILDREN UNDER 15 YRS	WITH CHILDREN UNDER 15 YRS
1995	3,668	2,349	1,319
1994	3,661	2,391	1,270
1993	3,510	2,274	1,236
1992	3,308	2,187	1,121
1991	3,039	2,077	962
1990	2,856	1,966	891
1989	2,764	1,906	858
1988	2,588	1,786	802
1987	2,334	1,614	720
1986	2,220	1,558	662
1985	1,983	1,380	603
1984	1,988	1,373	614
1983	1,891	1,366	525
1982	1,863	1,387	475
1981	1,808	1,305	502
1980	1,589	1,159	431
1979	1,346	985	360
1978	1,137	865	272
1977	957	754	204
1970 CENSUS	523	327	196
1960 CENSUS	439	242	197

Source: U.S. Bureau of the Census.

TABLE A2.7

AVERAGE POPULATION PER HOUSEHOLD AND FAMILY IN THE UNITED STATES: 1940–1995

| YEAR | TOTAL (IN THOUSANDS) | HOUSEHOLDS | | | FAMILY HOUSEHOLDS | | | |
| | | POPULATION PER HOUSEHOLD | | | TOTAL (IN THOUSANDS) | POPULATION PER FAMILY | | |
		ALL AGES	UNDER 18 YEARS	18 YEARS AND OVER		ALL AGES	UNDER 18 YEARS	18 YEARS AND OVER
1995	98,990	2.65	0.71	1.93	69,305	3.19	0.99	2.20
1994	97,107	2.67	0.72	1.95	68,490	3.20	0.99	2.21
1993R	96,426	2.66	0.71	1.95	68,216	3.19	0.99	2.20
1993	96,391	2.63	0.70	1.94	68,144	3.16	0.96	2.20
1992	95,669	2.62	0.69	1.93	67,173	3.17	0.97	2.20
1991	94,312	2.63	0.69	1.94	66,322	3.18	0.96	2.22
1990	93,347	2.63	0.69	1.94	66,090	3.17	0.96	2.21
1989	92,830	2.62	0.69	1.93	65,837	3.16	0.96	2.21
1988	91,066	2.64	0.70	1.94	65,133	3.17	0.96	2.21
1987	89,479	2.66	0.71	1.96	64,491	3.19	0.96	2.22
1986	88,458	2.67	0.71	1.96	63,558	3.21	0.98	2.23
1985	86,789	2.69	0.72	1.97	62,706	3.23	0.98	2.24
1984	85,407	2.71	0.73	1.98	61,997	3.24	0.99	2.25
1983	83,918	2.73	0.74	1.99	61,393	3.26	1.00	2.26
1982	83,527	2.72	0.75	1.97	61,019	3.25	1.01	2.24
1981	82,368	2.73	0.76	1.96	60,309	3.27	1.03	2.23
1980	80,776	2.76	0.79	1.97	59,550	3.29	1.05	2.23
1979	77,330	2.78	0.81	1.97	57,804	3.31	1.08	2.23
1978	76,030	2.81	0.83	1.98	57,215	3.33	1.10	2.23
1977	74,142	2.86	0.87	1.99	56,710	3.37	1.13	2.24
1976	72,867	2.89	0.89	2.00	56,245	3.39	1.15	2.23
1975	71,120	2.94	0.93	2.01	55,712	3.42	1.18	2.23
1974	69,859	2.97	0.96	2.00	55,053	3.44	1.21	2.23
1973	68,251	3.01	1.00	2.02	54,373	3.48	1.25	2.23
1972	66,676	3.06	1.03	2.03	53,296	3.53	1.29	2.25
1971	64,778	3.11	1.07	2.04	52,227	3.57	1.32	2.25
1970	63,401	3.14	1.09	2.05	51,586	3.58	1.34	2.25
1969	62,214	3.16	1.11	2.05	50,823	3.60	1.36	2.24
1968	60,813	3.20	1.14	2.06	50,111	3.63	1.38	2.25
1967	59,236	3.26	1.17	2.08	49,214	3.67	1.41	2.27
1966	58,406	3.27	1.19	2.08	48,509	3.69	1.42	2.27
1965	57,436	3.29	1.21	2.09	47,956	3.70	1.44	2.26
1964	56,149	3.33	1.23	2.10	47,540	3.70	1.44	2.25
1963	55,270	3.33	1.22	2.10	47,059	3.68	1.43	2.25
1962	54,764	3.31	1.21	2.10	46,418	3.67	1.42	2.25
1961	53,557	3.34	1.22	2.13	45,539	3.70	1.42	2.27
1960	52,799	3.33	1.21	2.12	45,111	3.67	1.41	2.26
1959	51,435	3.34	1.20	2.14	44,232	3.65	1.39	2.26
1958	50,474	3.34	1.19	2.15	43,696	3.64	1.37	2.27
1957	49,673	3.33	1.17	2.16	43,497	3.60	1.34	2.27
1956	48,902	3.32	1.15	2.17	42,889	3.58	1.31	2.27
1955	47,874	3.33	1.14	2.19	41,951	3.59	1.30	2.29
1954	46,962	3.34	1.13	2.20	41,202	3.59	1.30	2.29
1953	46,385	3.28	1.09	2.19	40,832	3.53	1.24	2.29
1952	45,538	3.32	1.12	2.20	40,578	3.54	1.25	2.29
1951	44,673	3.34	1.10	2.23	39,929	3.54	1.23	2.31
1950	43,554	3.37	1.06	2.31	39,303	3.54	1.17	2.37
1949	42,182	3.42	1.09	2.33	38,624	3.58	1.19	2.39
1948	40,532	3.49	1.10	2.48	37,237	3.64	1.19	2.44
1947	39,107	3.56	NA	NA	35,794	3.67	NA	NA
1940	34,949	3.67	1.14	2.53	32,166	3.76	1.24	2.52

NA = NOT AVAILABLE.
R = REVISED BASED ON POPULATION FROM THE DECENNIAL CENSUS FOR THAT YEAR.

Source: U.S. Bureau of the Census.

Table A2.8

Living Arrangements in the United States of Children Under 18 Years Old: 1960–95

(Numbers in thousands. Excludes householders, subfamily reference persons, and their spouses. Also excludes inmates of institutions.)

| Year | Two Parents | Percent Living with | | | Other Relatives | Nonrelatives Only |
| | | One Parent | | | | |
		Total	Mother Only	Father Only		
1995	68.7	27.0	23.5	3.5	3.3	1.0
1994	69.2	26.7	23.5	3.2	3.1	1.0
1993	70.5	26.7	23.3	3.4	2.2	0.6
1992	70.7	26.6	23.3	3.3	2.0	0.6
1991	71.7	25.5	22.4	3.1	2.2	0.6
1990	72.5	24.7	21.6	3.1	2.2	0.5
1989	73.1	24.3	21.5	2.8	2.1	0.4
1988	72.7	24.3	21.4	2.9	2.4	0.6
1987	73.1	23.9	21.3	2.6	2.4	0.6
1986	73.9	23.5	21.0	2.5	2.1	0.4
1985	73.9	23.4	20.9	2.5	2.1	0.6
1984	74.9	22.6	20.4	2.2	2.0	0.5
1983*	74.9	22.5	20.5	2.0	2.2	0.5
1982*	75.0	22.0	20.0	1.9	2.5	0.6
1981	76.4	20.1	18.1	1.9	3.0	0.6
1980R	76.7	19.7	18.0	1.7	3.1	0.6
1980	76.6	19.7	18.0	1.7	3.1	0.6
1979	77.4	18.5	16.9	1.6	3.4	0.7
1978	77.7	18.5	17.0	1.6	3.1	0.7
1977	79.2	17.7	16.3	1.4	2.5	0.6
1976	80.0	17.1	15.8	1.2	2.3	0.6
1975	80.3	17.0	15.5	1.5	2.1	0.5
1974	81.4	15.6	14.4	1.3	2.3	0.7
1973	82.1	14.9	13.6	1.2	2.4	0.6
1972	83.1	14.0	12.8	1.2	2.3	0.6
1971	83.4	13.5	12.4	1.1	2.4	0.7
1970R	85.2	11.9	10.8	1.1	2.2	0.7
1970	85.0	12.0	10.9	1.1	2.3	0.7
1969	85.1	12.1	11.0	1.1	2.3	0.5
1968	85.4	11.8	10.7	1.1	2.4	0.4
1967	NA	NA	NA	NA	NA	NA
1966	NA	NA	NA	NA	NA	NA
1965	NA	NA	NA	NA	NA	NA
1964	NA	NA	NA	NA	NA	NA
1963	NA	NA	NA	NA	NA	NA
1962	NA	NA	NA	NA	NA	NA
1961	NA	NA	NA	NA	NA	NA
1960 Census	87.7	9.1	8.0	1.1	2.5	0.7

NA= Not available.

R=Revised based on population from the decennial census for that year.

* Introduction of improved data collection and processing procedures that helped to identify parent-child subfamilies. (See *Current Populaton Reports*, Marital Status and Living Arrangements: March 1984.)

Source: U.S. Bureau of the Census, *Current Population Reports*, Marital Status and Living Arrangements: March 1995.

TABLE A2.9

YOUNG ADULTS LIVING IN THEIR PARENTAL HOUSEHOLD: 1960–1995
(NUMBERS IN THOUSANDS)

AGE	MALE			FEMALE		
	TOTAL	TOTAL CHILD OF HOUSEHOLDER	PERCENT	TOTAL	TOTAL CHILD OF HOUSEHOLDER	PERCENT
18 TO 24 YRS						
1995	12,545	7,328	58	12,613	5,896	47
1994	12,683	7,547	60	12,792	5,924	46
1993	12,049	7,145	59	12,260	5,746	47
1992	12,083	7,296	60	12,351	5,929	48
1991	12,275	7,385	60	12,627	6,163	49
1990	12,450	7,232	58	12,860	6,135	48
1989	12,574	7,308	58	13,055	6,141	47
1988	12,835	7,792	61	13,226	6,398	48
1987	13,029	7,981	61	13,433	6,375	47
1986	13,324	7,831	59	13,787	6,433	47
1985	13,695	8,172	60	14,149	6,758	48
1984	14,196	8,764	62	14,482	6,779	47
1983	14,344	8,803	61	14,702	7,001	48
1982	14,368	NA	NA	14,815	NA	NA
1981	14,367	NA	NA	14,848	NA	NA
1980 CENSUS	14,278	7,755	54	14,844	6,336	43
1970 CENSUS	10,398	5,641	54	11,959	4,941	41
1960 CENSUS	6,842	3,583	52	7,876	2,750	35
25 TO 34 YRS						
1995	20,589	3,166	15	20,800	1,759	8
1994	20,873	3,261	16	21,073	1,859	9
1993	20,856	3,300	16	21,007	1,844	9
1992	21,125	3,225	15	21,368	1,874	9
1991	21,319	3,172	15	21,586	1,887	9
1990	21,462	3,213	15	21,779	1,774	8
1989	21,461	3,130	15	21,777	1,728	8
1988	21,320	3,207	15	21,649	1,791	8
1987	21,142	3,071	15	21,494	1,655	8
1986	20,956	2,981	14	21,097	1,686	8
1985	20,184	2,685	13	20,673	1,661	8
1984	19,876	2,626	13	20,297	1,548	8
1983	19,438	2,664	14	19,903	1,520	8
1982	19,090	NA	NA	19,614	NA	NA
1981	18,625	NA	NA	19,203	NA	NA
1980 CENSUS	18,107	1,894	10	18,689	1,300	7
1970 CENSUS	11,929	1,129	9	12,637	829	7
1960 CENSUS	10,896	1,185	11	11,587	853	7

Source: U.S. Bureau of the Census, *Current Population Reports*, Marital Status and Living Arrangements: March 1995.

EDUCATION

TABLE A3.1

SCHOOL ENROLLMENT IN THE UNITED STATES OF PERSONS 3–34 YEARS OLD, BY LEVEL AND CONTROL OF SCHOOL, RACE: OCTOBER 1955–1994

(NUMBERS IN THOUSANDS. CIVILIAN NONINSTITUTIONAL POPULATION.)

YEAR	TOTAL ENROLLED	NURSERY SCHOOL TOTAL	PUBLIC	PRIVATE	KINDERGARTEN TOTAL	PUBLIC	PRIVATE	ELEMENTARY SCHOOL TOTAL	PUBLIC	PRIVATE	HIGH SCHOOL TOTAL	PUBLIC	PRIVATE	COLLEGE TOTAL	PUBLIC	PRIVATE	COLLEGE FULL TIME
ALL RACES																	
1994	66,427	4,259	1,940	2,319	3,863	3,278	585	31,487	28,109	3,378	14,521	13,453	1,068	12,298	9,536	2,762	8,813
1993 ʀ	64,414	3,032	1,258	1,774	4,275	3,589	686	31,219	28,278	2,941	13,989	12,985	1,004	11,901	9,440	2,461	8,706
1993	62,730	3,018	1,230	1,788	4,180	3,499	681	30,604	27,688	2,914	13,522	12,542	977	11,409	9,031	2,374	8,308
1992	62,082	2,899	1,098	1,801	4,130	3,507	623	30,165	27,066	3,102	13,219	12,268	952	11,671	9,282	2,386	8,503
1991	61,276	2,933	1,094	1,839	4,152	3,531	621	29,591	26,632	2,958	13,010	12,069	945	11,589	9,078	2,511	8,461
1990	60,588	3,401	1,212	2,188	3,899	3,332	567	29,265	26,591	2,674	12,719	11,818	903	11,306	8,889	2,417	8,154
1989	59,236	2,877	971	1,906	3,868	3,293	575	28,637	25,897	2,740	12,786	11,980	806	11,066	8,576	2,490	7,905
1988	58,847	2,639	838	1,770	3,958	3,420	538	28,223	25,443	2,778	13,093	12,095	998	10,937	8,663	2,278	7,771
1987	58,691	2,587	848	1,739	4,018	3,423	595	27,524	24,760	2,765	13,647	12,577	1,070	10,915	8,556	2,361	7,560
1986	58,153	2,554	835	1,719	3,961	3,328	633	27,121	24,163	2,958	13,912	12,746	1,166	10,605	8,153	2,452	7,507
1985	58,014	2,491	854	1,637	3,815	3,221	594	26,866	23,803	3,063	13,979	12,764	1,215	10,863	8,379	2,483	7,720
1984	57,313	2,354	761	1,593	3,484	2,953	531	26,838	24,120	2,718	13,777	12,721	1,057	10,859	8,467	2,392	7,822
1983	57,745	2,350	809	1,541	3,361	2,706	656	27,198	24,203	2,994	14,010	12,792	1,218	10,825	8,185	2,640	7,711
1982	57,905	2,153	729	1,423	3,299	2,746	553	27,412	24,381	3,031	14,123	13,004	1,118	10,919	8,354	2,565	7,736
1981	58,390	2,058	663	1,396	3,161	2,616	545	27,795	24,758	3,037	14,642	13,523	1,119	10,734	8,159	2,576	7,569
1980	57,348	1,987	633	1,354	3,176	2,690	486	27,449	24,398	3,051	14,556	NA	NA	10,180	NA	NA	7,147
1979	57,854	1,869	636	1,233	3,025	2,593	432	27,865	24,756	3,109	15,116	13,994	1,122	9,978	7,699	2,280	7,010
1978	58,616	1,824	587	1,237	2,989	2,493	496	28,490	25,252	3,238	15,475	14,231	1,244	9,838	7,427	2,410	6,979
1977	60,013	1,618	562	1,056	3,191	2,665	526	29,234	25,983	3,251	15,753	14,505	1,248	10,217	7,925	2,292	7,196
1976	60,482	1,526	476	1,050	3,490	2,962	528	29,774	26,698	3,075	15,742	14,541	1,201	9,950	7,739	2,211	7,176
1975	60,969	1,748	574	1,174	3,393	2,851	542	30,446	27,166	3,279	15,683	14,503	1,180	9,697	7,704	1,994	7,105
1974	60,259	1,607	423	1,184	3,252	2,726	526	31,126	27,956	3,169	15,447	14,275	1,172	8,827	6,905	1,922	6,351
1973	59,392	1,324	400	924	3,074	2,582	493	31,469	28,201	3,268	15,347	14,162	1,184	8,179	6,224	1,955	6,089
1972	60,142	1,283	402	881	3,135	2,636	499	32,242	28,693	3,549	15,169	14,015	1,155	8,313	6,337	1,976	6,314
1971	61,106	1,066	317	749	3,263	2,689	574	33,507	29,829	3,678	15,183	14,057	1,126	8,087	6,271	1,816	6,204
1970	60,357	1,096	333	763	3,183	2,647	536	33,950	30,001	3,949	14,715	13,545	1,170	7,413	5,699	1,714	5,763
1969	59,913	860	245	615	3,276	2,682	594	33,788	29,825	3,964	14,553	13,400	1,153	7,435	5,439	1,995	5,810
1968	58,791	816	262	554	3,268	2,709	559	33,761	29,527	4,234	14,145	12,793	1,352	6,801	4,948	1,854	5,357
1967	57,656	713	230	484	3,312	2,678	635	33,440	28,877	4,562	13,790	12,498	1,292	6,401	4,540	1,861	4,976
1966	56,167	688	215	473	3,115	2,527	588	32,916	28,208	4,706	13,364	11,985	1,377	6,085	4,178	1,908	4,847
1965	54,701	520	127	393	3,057	2,439	618	32,474	27,596	4,878	12,975	11,517	1,457	5,675	3,840	1,835	4,414
1964	52,490	471	91	380	2,830	2,349	481	31,734	26,811	4,923	12,812	11,403	1,410	4,643	3,025	1,618	3,556
1963	50,356	NA	NA	NA	2,340	1,936	404	31,245	26,502	4,742	12,438	11,186	1,251	4,336	2,897	1,439	3,260
1962	48,704	NA	NA	NA	2,319	1,914	405	30,661	26,148	4,513	11,516	10,431	1,085	4,208	2,820	1,388	3,237
1961	47,708	NA	NA	NA	2,299	1,926	373	30,718	26,221	4,497	10,959	9,817	1,141	3,731	2,376	1,354	2,902
1960	46,260	NA	NA	NA	2,092	1,691	401	30,349	25,814	4,535	10,249	9,215	1,033	3,570	2,307	1,262	2,681
1959	44,370	NA	NA	NA	2,032	1,678	354	29,382	24,680	4,702	9,616	8,571	1,045	3,340	2,120	1,220	2,464
1958	42,900	NA	NA	NA	1,991	1,569	422	28,184	23,800	4,385	9,482	8,485	998	3,242	2,088	1,155	NA
1957	41,166	NA	NA	NA	1,824	1,471	353	27,248	23,076	4,172	8,956	8,059	897	3,138	2,054	1,084	NA
1956	39,353	NA	NA	NA	1,758	1,566	192	26,169	22,474	3,695	8,543	7,668	875	2,883	1,824	1,059	NA
1955	37,426	NA	NA	NA	1,628	1,365	263	25,458	22,078	3,379	7,961	7,181	780	2,379	1,515	864	NA

R = REVISED

NA = NOT AVAILABLE

Source: U.S. Bureau of the Census.

TABLE A3.2

PERCENTAGE OF PERSONS 3 TO 34 YEARS OLD ENROLLED IN SCHOOL, BY AGE: OCTOBER 1947 TO 1994

(CIVILIAN NONINSTITUTIONAL POPULATION.)

YEAR, SEX, RACE AND HISPANIC ORIGIN	TOTAL 3–34 YEARS	AGE										
		3 & 4 YEARS	5 & 6 YEARS	7-9 YEARS	10-13 YEARS	14 & 15 YEARS	16 & 17 YEARS	18 & 19 YEARS	20 & 21 YEARS	22–24 YEARS	25–29 YEARS	30–34 YEARS
ALL RACES **ALL PERSONS**												
1994	53.3	47.3	96.7	99.3	99.4	98.8	94.4	60.2	44.9	24.1	10.8	6.7
1993R	51.9	40.1	95.3	99.5	99.5	98.9	93.9	61.4	42.6	23.5	10.2	5.9
1993	51.8	40.4	95.4	99.5	99.5	98.9	94.0	61.6	42.7	23.6	10.2	5.9
1992	51.4	39.7	95.5	99.4	99.4	99.1	94.1	61.4	44.0	23.7	9.8	6.1
1991	50.7	40.5	95.4	99.6	99.7	98.8	93.3	59.6	42.0	22.2	10.2	6.2
1990	50.2	44.4	96.5	99.7	99.6	99.0	92.5	57.3	39.7	21.0	9.7	5.8
1989	49.1	39.1	95.2	99.2	99.4	98.8	92.7	56.0	38.5	19.9	9.3	5.7
1988	48.7	38.2	96.0	99.6	99.7	98.9	91.6	55.7	39.1	18.3	8.3	5.9
1987	48.6	38.3	95.1	99.6	99.5	98.6	91.7	55.6	38.7	17.5	9.0	5.9
1986	48.5	39.0	95.3	99.3	99.1	98.9	92.5	55.2	33.4	18.2	9.1	6.3
1985	48.3	38.9	96.1	99.1	99.3	98.1	91.7	51.6	35.3	16.9	9.2	6.0
1984	47.9	36.3	94.5	99.0	99.4	97.8	91.5	50.1	33.9	17.3	9.1	6.1
1983	48.4	37.5	95.4	98.9	99.4	98.3	91.7	50.4	32.5	16.6	9.6	6.3
1982	48.6	36.4	95.0	99.2	99.1	98.5	90.6	47.8	34.0	16.8	9.6	6.4
1981	48.9	36.0	94.0	99.2	99.3	98.0	90.6	49.0	31.6	16.5	9.0	6.3
1980	49.7	36.7	95.7	99.1	99.4	98.2	89.0	46.4	31.0	16.3	9.3	6.4
1979	50.3	35.1	95.8	99.2	99.1	98.1	89.2	45.0	30.2	15.8	9.6	6.4
1978	51.2	34.2	95.3	99.3	99.0	98.4	89.1	45.4	29.5	16.3	9.4	6.4
1977	52.5	32.0	95.8	99.5	99.4	98.5	88.9	46.2	31.8	16.5	10.8	6.9
1976	53.1	31.3	95.5	99.2	99.2	98.2	89.1	46.2	32.0	17.1	10.0	6.0
1975	53.7	31.5	94.7	99.3	99.3	98.2	89.0	46.9	31.2	16.2	10.1	6.6
1974	53.6	28.8	94.2	99.1	99.5	97.9	87.9	43.1	30.2	15.1	9.6	5.7
1973	53.5	24.2	92.5	99.1	99.2	97.5	88.3	42.9	30.1	14.5	8.5	4.5
1972	54.9	24.4	91.9	99.0	99.3	97.6	88.9	46.3	31.4	14.8	8.6	4.6
1971	56.2	21.2	91.6	99.1	99.2	98.6	90.2	49.2	32.2	15.4	8.0	4.9
1970	56.4	20.5	89.5	99.3	99.2	98.1	90.0	47.7	31.9	14.9	7.5	4.2
1969	57.0	16.1	88.4	99.3	99.1	98.1	89.7	50.2	34.1	15.4	7.9	4.8
1968	56.7	15.7	87.6	99.1	99.1	98.0	90.2	50.4	31.2	13.8	7.0	3.9
1967	56.6	14.2	87.4	99.4	99.1	98.2	88.8	47.6	33.3	13.6	6.6	4.0
1966	56.1	12.5	85.1	99.3	99.3	98.6	88.5	47.2	29.9	13.2	6.5	2.7
1965	55.5	10.6	84.4	99.3	99.4	98.9	87.4	46.3	27.6	13.2	6.1	3.2
1964	54.5	9.5	83.3	99.0	99.0	98.6	87.7	41.6	26.3	9.9	5.2	2.6
1963	58.5	NA	82.7	99.4	99.3	98.4	87.1	40.9	25.0	11.4	4.9	2.5
1962	57.8	NA	82.2	99.2	99.3	98.0	84.3	41.8	23.0	10.3	5.0	2.6
1961	56.8	NA	81.7	99.4	99.3	97.6	83.6	38.0	21.5	8.4	4.4	2.0
1960	56.4	NA	80.7	99.6	99.5	97.8	82.6	38.4	19.4	8.7	4.9	2.4
1959	55.5	NA	80.0	99.4	99.4	97.5	82.9	36.8	18.8	8.6	5.1	2.2
1958	54.8	NA	80.4	99.5	99.5	96.9	80.6	37.6	13.4		5.7	2.2
1957	53.6	NA	78.6	99.5	99.5	97.1	80.5	34.9	14.0		5.5	1.8
1956	52.3	NA	77.6	99.4	99.2	96.9	78.4	35.4	12.8		5.1	1.9
1955	50.8	NA	78.1	99.2	99.2	95.9	77.4	31.5	11.1		4.2	1.6
1954	50.0	NA	77.3	99.2	99.5	95.8	78.0	32.4	11.2		4.1	1.5
1953	48.8	NA	55.7	99.4	99.4	96.5	74.7	31.2	11.1		2.9	1.7
1952	46.8	NA	54.7	98.7	98.9	96.2	73.4	28.7	9.5		2.6	1.1
1951	45.4	NA	54.5	99.0	99.2	94.8	75.1	26.3	8.3		2.5	NA
1950	44.2	NA	58.2	98.9	98.6	94.7	71.3	29.4	9.0		3.0	NA
1949	43.9	NA	59.3	98.5	98.7	93.5	69.5	25.3	9.2		3.8	1.1
1948	43.1	NA	56.0	98.3	98.0	92.7	71.2	26.9	9.7		2.6	0.9
1947	42.3	NA	58.0	98.4	98.6	91.6	67.6	24.3	10.2		3.0	1.0

R = REVISED, CONTROLLED TO 1990 CENSUS-BASED POPULATION ESTIMATES; PREVIOUS 1993 DATA CONTROLLED TO 1980 CENSUS-BASED POPULATION ESTIMATES.
NA=NOT APPLICABLE

Source: U.S. Bureau of the Census.

Note: Data for 1947-53 exclude kindergarten. Nursery school was first collected in 1964. 1986 data are shown for the old and new processing system. Improvements in edits and population estimation procedure caused slight changes in the estimates.

TABLE A3.3

ANNUAL HIGH SCHOOL DROPOUT RATES IN THE UNITED STATES, BY SEX, RACE, GRADE, AND HISPANIC ORIGIN: OCTOBER 1967–1994

(NUMBERS IN THOUSANDS. CIVILIAN NONINSTITUTIONAL POPULATION.)

YEAR	TOTAL			MALE			FEMALE		
	STUDENTS		DROPOUT	STUDENTS		DROPOUT	STUDENTS		DROPOUT
	TOTAL	DROPOUTS	RATE	TOTAL	DROPOUTS	RATE	TOTAL	DROPOUTS	RATE
ALL PERSONS GRADES 10-12									
1994	9,922	497	5.0	5,048	249	4.9	4,873	247	5.1
1993[R1]	9,430	404	4.3	4,787	211	4.4	4,640	192	4.1
1993[2]	9,021	382	4.2	4,570	199	4.4	4,452	183	4.1
1992	8,939	384	4.3	4,580	175	3.8	4,357	207	4.8
1991	8,612	348	4.0	4,380	167	3.8	4,231	180	4.3
1990	8,679	347	4.0	4,356	177	4.1	4,323	170	3.9
1989	8,974	404	4.5	4,519	203	4.5	4,453	199	4.5
1988	9,590	461	4.8	4,960	256	5.2	4,628	206	4.5
1987	9,802	403	4.1	4,921	215	4.4	4,879	187	3.8
1986	9,829	421	4.3	4,910	213	4.3	4,917	208	4.2
1985	9,704	504	5.2	4,831	259	5.4	4,874	245	5.0
1984	10,041	507	5.0	4,986	268	5.4	5,054	238	4.7
1983	10,331	535	5.2	5,130	294	5.7	5,200	241	4.6
1982	10,611	577	5.4	5,310	305	5.7	5,301	271	5.1
1981	10,868	639	5.9	5,379	322	6.0	5,487	316	5.8
1981R	10,647	619	5.8	5,263	313	5.9	5,383	305	5.7
1980	10,891	658	6.0	5,445	362	6.6	5,448	296	5.4
1979	11,136	744	6.7	5,479	369	6.7	5,658	377	6.7
1978	11,116	743	6.7	5,558	415	7.5	5,558	328	5.9
1977	11,300	734	6.5	5,657	392	6.9	5,643	342	6.1
1976	10,996	644	5.9	5,534	360	6.5	5,463	285	5.2
1975	11,033	639	5.8	5,485	296	5.4	5,548	343	6.2
1974	11,026	742	6.7	5,421	402	7.4	5,605	340	6.1
1973	10,851	683	6.3	5,407	370	6.8	5,444	313	5.7
1972	10,664	659	6.2	5,305	317	6.0	5,358	341	6.4
1971	10,451	562	5.4	5,193	297	5.7	5,258	266	5.1
1970	10,281	588	5.7	5,145	288	5.6	5,138	302	5.9
1969	10,212	551	5.4	5,069	273	5.4	5,142	278	5.4
1968	9,814	506	5.2	4,831	247	5.1	4,983	259	5.2
1967	9,350	486	5.2	4,605	237	5.1	4,745	249	5.2

R = REVISED

[1] CONTROLLED TO 1990 CENSUS BASED POPULATION ESTIMANTES.

[2] CONTROLLED TO 1980 CENSUS BASED POPULATION ESTIMATES.

[3] PERSONS OF HISPANIC ORIGIN MAY BE OF ANY RACE.

Source: U. S. Bureau of the Census.

TABLE A3.4

STUDENT PROFICIENCY IN THE UNITED STATES IN READING AS GAUGED BY NATIONAL ASSESSMENT OF EDUCATIONAL PROGRESS SCORES*, BY AGE AND SELECTED CHARACTERISTICS OF STUDENTS: 1971–92

SELECTED CHARACTERISTICS OF STUDENTS	9-YEAR-OLDS				13-YEAR-OLDS				17-YEAR-OLDS			
	1971	1980	1990	1992	1971	1980	1990	1992	1971	1980	1990	1992
TOTAL	208	215	209	211	255	259	257	260	285	286	290	290
SEX												
MALE	201	210	204	206	250	254	251	254	279	282	284	284
FEMALE	214	220	215	215	261	263	263	265	291	289	297	296
RACE/ETHNICITY												
WHITE	214	221	217	218	261	264	262	266	291	293	297	297
BLACK	170	189	182	185	222	233	242	238	239	243	267	261
HISPANIC [1]	—	190	189	192	—	237	238	239	—	261	275	271
PARENTAL EDUCATION (AS REPORTED BY STUDENTS) [2]												
NOT HIGH SCHOOL GRADUATE	189	194	193	195	238	239	241	239	261	262	270	271
GRADUATED HIGH SCHOOL	208	213	209	207	256	254	251	252	283	278	283	281
POST HIGH SCHOOL	224	226	218	220	270	271	267	270	302	299	300	299
READING MATERIALS IN THE HOME [3]												
FEWER THAN 3 ITEMS	186	—	196	197	227	—	240	241	246	—	271	269
3 ITEMS	208	—	211	214	249	—	255	256	274	—	286	286
4 ITEMS	223	—	226	224	267	—	266	271	296	—	299	299
CONTROL OF SSCHOOL												
PUBLIC	—	214	208	209	—	257	255	257	—	284	289	288
PRIVATE	—	227	228	225	—	271	270	276	—	298	311	310

—— DATA NOT AVAILABLE

[1] TEST SCORES OF HISPANICS WERE NOT TABULATED SEPARATELY IN 1971.

[2] A QUARTER TO A THIRD OF THE 9-YEAR-OLDS DID NOT KNOW THEIR PARENTS' EDUCATION LEVEL.

[3] THE FOUR ITEMS IN THE SCALE WERE: NEWSPAPERS, MAGAZINES, MORE THAN 25 BOOKS, AND AN ENCYCLOPEDIA IN THE HOME.

Source: National Center for Education Statistics, *Youth Indicators 1996*, Indicator No. 33.

* The NAEP scores range from 0 to 500, but have been evaluated at certain performance levels. A score of 300 implies an ability to find, understand, summarize, and explain relatively complicated literary and informational material. A score of 250 implies an ability to search for specific information, interrelate ideas, and to make generalizations about rather lengthy literature, science, and social studies materials. A score of 200 implies an ability to understand, combine ideas, and to make inferences based on short uncomplicated passages about specific or sequentially related information. A score of 150 implies an ability to follow written directions and select phrases to describe pictures.

TABLE A3.5

MATHEMATICS PROFICIENCY IN THE UNITED STATES AS GAUGED BY THE NATIONAL ASSESSMENT OF EDUCATIONAL PROGRESS*, BY AGE AND BY SELECTED CHARACTERISTICS OF STUDENTS: 1978, 1990 AND 1992

SELECTED CHARACTERISTICS OF STUDENTS	9-YEAR-OLDS			13-YEAR-OLDS			17-YEAR-OLDS		
	1978	1990	1992	1978	1990	1992	1978	1990	1992
ALL STUDENTS	219	230	230	264	270	273	300	305	307
SEX									
MALE	217	229	231	264	271	274	304	306	309
FEMALE	220	230	228	265	270	272	297	303	304
RACE/ETHNICITY									
WHITE	224	235	235	272	276	279	306	310	312
BLACK	192	208	208	230	249	250	268	288	286
HISPANIC	203	214	212	238	255	259	276	284	292
TELEVISION WATCHED PER DAY									
0-2 HOURS	—	231	231	—	277	280	305	312	314
3-5 HOURS	—	234	233	—	271	273	296	300	300
6 OR MORE HOURS	—	221	219	—	258	255	278	287	285
READING MATERIALS IN THE HOME [1]									
0-2 ITEMS	202	217	216	240	255	257	277	289	291
3 ITEMS	221	232	231	268	268	272	296	300	304
4 ITEMS	231	241	240	276	278	281	308	311	313
LANGUAGE OTHER THAN ENGLISH									
OFTEN	—	209	212	—	259	261	288	295	296
SOMETIMES	—	231	232	—	277	278	300	305	306
NEVER	—	232	231	—	270	273	303	306	308
TYPES OF SCHOOL									
PUBLIC	217	229	228	243	269	272	300	304	305
NON-PUBLIC	231	238	242	279	280	283	314	318	320

[1] THE 4 ITEMS IN THE SCALE WERE: NEWSPAPER SUBSCRIPTION; MAGAZINE SUBSCRIPTION; MORE THAN 25 BOOKS IN THE HOME; AND ENCYCLOPEDIA IN THE HOME.

Source: National Center for Education Statistics, *Youth Indicators 1996*, Indicator No. 35.

*The NAEP scores range from 0 to 500, but have been evaluated at certain performance levels. Performers at the 150 level know some basic addition and subtraction facts, and most can add two-digit numbers without regrouping. They recognize simple situations in which addition and subtraction apply. Performers at the 200 level have considerable understanding of two-digit numbers and know some basic multiplication and division facts. Performers at the 250 level have an initial understanding of the four basic operations. They can also compare information from graphs and charts, and are developing an ability to analyze simple logical relations. Performers at the 300 level can compute decimals, simple fractions, and percents. They can identify geometric figures, measure lengths and angles, and calculate areas of rectangles. They are developing the skills to operate with signed numbers, exponents, and square roots. Performers at the 350 level can apply a range of reasoning skills to solve multi-step problems. They can solve routine problems involving fractions and percents, recognize properties of basic geometric figures, and work with exponents and square roots.

TABLE A3.6

SCIENCE PROFICIENCY IN THE UNITED STATES AS GAUGED BY THE NATIONAL ASSESSMENT OF EDUCATIONAL PROGRESS*, BY AGE AND BY SELECTED CHARACTERISTICS OF STUDENTS: 1977, 1990, AND 1992

SELECTED CHARACTERISTICS OF STUDENTS	9-YEAR-OLDS			13-YEAR-OLDS			17-YEAR-OLDS		
	1978	1990	1992	1978	1990	1992	1978	1990	1992
ALL STUDENTS	220	229	230	247	255	258	290	290	294
SEX									
MALE	222	230	235	251	259	260	297	296	299
FEMALE	218	227	226	244	252	256	282	285	289
RACE/ETHNICITY									
WHITE, NON-HISPANIC	230	238	239	256	264	267	298	301	304
BLACK, NON-HISPANIC	175	196	200	208	226	224	240	253	256
HISPANIC	192	206	205	213	232	238	262	262	270
REGION									
NORTHEAST	224	231	234	255	257	257	296	293	300
SOUTHEAST	205	220	223	235	251	254	276	284	283
CENTRAL	225	234	238	254	260	263	294	300	304
WEST	221	230	227	243	253	258	287	286	290
PARENTAL EDUCATION (AS REPORTED BY STUDENTS) [1]									
NOT HIGH SCHOOL GRADUATE	199	210	217	224	233	234	265	261	262
GRADUATED HIGH SCHOOL	223	226	222	245	247	246	284	276	280
SOME COLLEGE	237	238	237	260	263	266	296	297	296
GRADUATED COLLEGE	232	236	239	266	268	269	309	306	308
TYPE OF SCHOOL									
PUBLIC	218	228	229	245	254	257	288	289	292
PRIVATE	235	237	240	268	269	265	308	308	312

[1] ONE QUARTER TO ONE THIRD OF THE 9-YEAR-OLDS DID NOT KNOW THEIR PARENTS' EDUCATION LEVEL.

Source: National Center for Education Statistics, Youth Indicators 1996, Indicator No. 36.

*The NAEP scores range from 0 to 500, but have been evaluated at certain performance levels. A score of 300 implies the ability to evaluate the appropriateness of the design of an experiment and the skill to apply scientific knowledge in interpreting information from text and graphs. These students also exhibit a growing understanding of principles from the physical sciences. Performers at the 250 level can interpret data from simple tables and make inferences about the outcomes of experimental procedures. They exhibit knowledge and understanding of the life sciences, and also demonstrate some knowledge of basic information from the physical sciences. Performers at the 200 level are developing some understanding of simple scientific principles, particularly in the life sciences. Performers at the 150 level know some general scientific facts of the kind that can be learned from everyday experiences.

TABLE A3.7

SCHOLASTIC APTITUDE TEST-TAKERS (SAT) IN THE UNITED STATES AS A PERCENTAGE OF HIGH SCHOOL GRADUATES, PERCENTAGE OF TEST-TAKERS WHO ARE MINORITIES, SAT MEAN SCORES, STANDARD DEVIATIONS, AND PERCENTAGE SCORING 600 OR HIGHER: 1972–1995

| YEAR | NUMBER OF HIGH SCHOOL GRADUATES[1] | SAT TEST-TAKERS VERBAL | | | | VERBAL | | | MATHEMATICS | | |
		NUMBER[1]	AS A PERCENT OF HIGH SCHOOL GRADUATES[2]	PERCENT MINORITY	TOTAL MEAN	MEAN	STANDARD DEVIATION	PERCENTAGE SCORING 600 OR HIGHER	MEAN	STANDARD DEVIATION	PERCENTAGE SCORING 600 OR HIGHER
1995	[4]2,553	1068	41.8	31.0	910	428	113	8	482	127	21
1994	[3,4]2,479	1050	42.4	31.0	902	423	113	7	479	124	18
1993	[3]2,481	1044	[3]42.1	30.0	902	424	113	7	478	125	19
1992	[3]2,483	1034	[3]41.6	28.5	899	423	112	7	476	123	18
1991	[3]2,493	1033	[3]41.4	28.0	896	422	111	7	474	123	17
1990	2588	1026	39.7	26.6	900	424	111	7	476	123	18
1989	2727	1088	39.9	25.3	903	427	111	8	476	121	18
1988	2773	1134	40.9	23.0	904	428	109	7	476	120	17
1987	2694	1080	40.1	21.8	906	430	111	8	476	122	18
1986	2643	1001	37.9	—	906	431	110	8	475	121	17
1985	2677	977	36.5	20.0	906	431	111	7	475	119	17
1984	2767	965	34.9	19.7	897	426	110	7	471	119	17
1983	2888	963	33.3	18.9	893	425	109	7	468	119	16
1982	2995	989	33.0	18.3	893	426	110	7	467	117	15
1981	3020	994	32.9	18.1	890	424	110	7	466	117	14
1980	3043	992	32.6	17.9	890	424	110	7	466	117	15
1979	3117	992	31.8	17.1	894	427	110	7	467	117	15
1978	3127	989	31.6	17.0	897	429	110	8	468	118	15
1977	3155	979	31.0	16.1	899	429	110	8	470	119	16
1976	3148	1000	32.1	—	903	431	110	8	472	120	17
1975	3133	996	31.8	—	906	434	109	8	472	115	15
1974	3073	985	32.1	—	924	444	110	10	480	116	17
1973	3036	1015	33.4	—	926	445	108	10	481	113	16
1972	3001	1023	34.1	—	937	453	111	11	484	115	17

[1] INCLUDES THOSE IN PUBLIC AND PRIVATE SCHOOLS.

[2] THIS FIGURE REPRESENTS HIGH SCHOOL GRADUATES WHO TOOK THE SAT AT ANY TIME WHILE THEY WERE IN HIGH SCHOOL AS A PERCENTAGE OF ALL HIGH SCHOOL GRADUATES.

[3] DATA HAVE BEEN REVISED FROM PREVIOUSLY PUBLISHED FIGURES.

[4] NUMBER OF PUBLIC HIGH SCHOOL GRADUATES IS BASED ON STATE ESTIMATES.

Source: National Center for Education Statistics, The Condition of Education 1996. Table 22-1, P239.

TABLE A3.8

USE OF COMPUTERS AT HOME AND SCHOOL IN THE UNITED STATES BY PERSONS 3-17 YEARS OLD: OCTOBER 1993

(NUMBERS IN THOUSANDS. CIVILIAN NONINSTITUTIONAL POPULATION.)

ALL CHARACTERISTICS	ALL PERSONS	USES COMPUTERS ANYWHERE	WITH COMPUTERS AT HOME	USES COMPUTER AT HOME		USES COMPUTER AT SCHOOL	
				NUMBER	PERCENT WITH COMPUTERS	NUMBER	PERCENT ENROLLED
3 TO 17 YEARS	55,827	58.5	31.9	12,527	74.7	28,848	60.6
3 YEARS	4,053	9.6	25.1	305	32.7	117	11.2
4 YEARS	4,044	15.8	25.2	426	46.5	291	13.9
5 YEARS	3,857	40.3	25.8	567	61.8	1,263	37.3
6 YEARS	3,794	57.9	29.5	726	69.0	1,974	54.9
7 YEARS	3,842	66.2	29.0	786	75.6	2,368	64.9
8 YEARS	3,727	74.0	30.2	858	79.4	2,619	72.7
9 YEARS	3,705	74.8	31.3	936	84.8	2,625	73.8
10 YEARS	3,772	76.8	33.8	950	79.0	2,757	76.9
11 YEARS	3,806	74.3	33.6	1,022	84.0	2,652	72.9
12 YEARS	3,593	71.3	34.4	1,005	85.2	2,345	67.9
13 YEARS	3,798	71.7	36.8	1,115	84.8	2,412	66.5
14 YEARS	3,590	66.6	36.8	1,023	82.4	2,044	60.7
15 YEARS	3,502	63.8	36.6	979	80.0	1,904	59.4
16 YEARS	3,465	63.0	36.1	939	79.1	1,813	58.9
17 YEARS	3,280	60.8	37.9	892	76.1	1,664	60.6
RACE							
WHITE	44,242	61.4	35.8	11,248	75.3	23,799	62.7
BLACK	8,836	45.6	13.0	721	67.3	3,786	50.9
OTHER	2,749	52.7	31.1	558	72.2	1,263	56.8
HISPANIC ORIGIN							
HISPANIC	6,569	45.5	12.1	459	68.4	2,829	52.7
NOT HISPANIC	49,257	60.2	34.6	12,068	74.9	26,018	61.6
GENDER							
MALE	28,602	58.3	31.5	6,385	75.1	14,766	60.3
FEMALE	27,224	58.7	32.4	6,143	74.2	14,081	60.8
HOUSEHOLD TYPE							
MARRIED COUPLE	40,057	62.3	38.3	10,981	75.8	21,590	62.6
FEMALE HOUSEHOLDER	12,741	48.6	13.9	1,095	65.5	5,904	55.2
MALE HOUSEHOLDER	3,000	50.0	23.2	452	72.2	1,337	55.5
USES COMPUTER							
AT HOME	12,527	100.0	100.0	12,527	100.0	8,716	72.2
REGION							
NORTHEAST	10,377	58.5	35.3	2,593	76.8	5,275	59.9
MIDWEST	13,897	61.1	32.5	3,196	74.2	7,608	63.8
SOUTH	18,958	57.2	26.9	3,593	74.2	9,779	60.3
WEST	12,595	57.7	36.1	3,145	74.0	6,187	57.9
EDUCATION OF HOUSEHOLDER							
LESS THAN 9TH GRADE	3,660	40.3	5.7	93	60.6	1,438	48.3
9TH -11TH GRADE	6,413	46.7	8.7	332	66.9	2,870	55.6
HIGH SCHOOL GRADUATE	19,014	54.5	20.7	2,625	71.1	9,579	59.1
SOME COLLEGE	14,292	61.9	37.4	3,747	74.3	7,670	62.2
BACHELORS +	12,418	72.2	62.7	5,731	77.5	7,274	66.6
EMPLOYMENT STATUS							
OF HOUSEHOLDER							
EMPLOYED	45,484	61.3	35.6	11,540	75.5	24,329	62.0
FULL-TIME (& AF)	42,388	61.6	36.3	10,955	75.4	22,769	62.2
PART-TIME	3,096	56.1	26.2	585	77.0	1,561	59.6
UNEMPLOYED	2,592	52.7	19.1	318	70.3	1,286	58.9
NOT LABOR FORCE	7,723	44.1	14.9	669	64.1	3,216	51.8
FAMILY INCOME							
LESS THAN $10,000	7,813	42.6	5.6	242	61.5	3,272	52.3
$10,000 - 14,999	5,183	48.2	10.7	279	52.2	2,419	56.6
$15,000 - 19,999	3,760	52.9	16.2	370	66.2	1,890	60.3
$20,000 - 24,999	4,531	52.9	19.0	583	69.9	2,210	57.0

TABLE A3.8

USE OF COMPUTERS AT HOME AND SCHOOL IN THE UNITED STATES BY PERSONS 3-17 YEARS OLD: OCTOBER 1993

(NUMBERS IN THOUSANDS. CIVILIAN NONINSTITUTIONAL POPULATION.)

ALL CHARACTERISTICS	ALL PERSONS	USES COMPUTERS ANYWHERE	WITH COMPUTERS AT HOME	USES COMPUTER AT HOME		USES COMPUTER AT SCHOOL	
				NUMBER	PERCENT WITH COMPUTERS	NUMBER	PERCENT ENROLLED
$25,000 - 34,999	8,180	59.0	27.4	1557	73.8	4,331	62.1
$35,000 - 49,999	9,593	63.5	37.5	2,591	76.3	5,289	62.5
$50,000 - 74,999	8,395	71.8	55.8	3,476	77.5	4,892	65.0
$75,000 AND OVER	5,136	76.4	75.2	2,862	79.0	3,142	67.7
INCOME NOT REPORTED	3,236	48.5	30.6	567	67.4	1,402	56.4
HOUSEHOLD SIZE							
1-3 PERSONS	11,791	55.4	24.4	2,061	76.5	5,851	59.1
4-5 PERSONS	33,805	61.0	35.6	8,751	76.5	17,998	61.6
6-7 PERSONS	8104	56.3	28.9	1,429	67.2	4,142	60.8
8+ PERSONS	2127	45.2	26.9	286	54.7	856	50.0
OCCUPATION OF HOUSEHOLDER							
MANAGERIAL AND							
PROFESSIONAL	12,887	71.0	59.3	5,676	78.3	7,468	65.8
TECHNICIAN, SALES,							
ADMINISTRATIVE	10,884	59.8	35.4	2,575	70.8	5,698	60.4
SERVICE	5,313	52.1	16.7	639	74.9	2,582	57.7
PRECISION PRODUCTION, CRAFT	8527	58.3	26.7	1586	74.8	4,445	61.7
OPERATORS, LABOR	8,721	54.8	15.7	921	72.9	4,502	60.5
FARM, FOREST, FISH	1,745	54.4	22.0	274	78.3	886	61.2A
NOT IN LABOR FORCE							
OR ARMED SERVICES	7,722	45.5	18.3	857	65.7	3,250	51.9
INDUSTRY OF HOUSEHOLDER							
AGRICULTURE	1,572	56.1	23.6	261	74.5	817	61.7
MINING	561	64.6	34.5	150	82.0	315	62.8
CONSTRUCTION	4,510	59.1	26.0	797	72.9	2,446	64.7
MANUFACTURING	10,537	60.2	33.0	2,535	76.8	5,508	60.8
TRANSPORTATION,							
COMMUNICATIONS, UTILITIES	4410	62.3	35.4	1,124	76.2	2,397	62.1
WHOLESALE/RETAIL	7,999	57.5	27.4	1,420	69.5	4,179	61.3
FINANCE, INSURANCE	2,358	63.5	48.0	774	73.0	1,263	62.5
SERVICES	13,405	62.0	39.1	3,775	76.5	7,179	61.8
FOREST/FISHERIES	72	37.0	17.6	2	(B)	26	(B)
PUBLIC ADMINISTRATION	2,652	64.2	40.2	832	80.9	1,450	62.1
NOT IN LABORFORCE							
OR ARMED FORCES	7,722	45.5	18.3	857	65.7	3,250	51.9

* "USES COMPUTER ANYWHERE" = USES COMPUTER AT HOME AND/OR AT SCHOOL.

* "WITH COMPUTER AT HOME" = THERE IS A COMPUTER IN THE HOUSEHOLD.

PERSONS OF HISPANIC ORIGIN MAY BE OF ANY RACE.

(B) BASE LESS THAN 75,000.

Source: Education and Social Stratification Branch, Population Division, U.S. Bureau of the Census.

Note: The data were collected in October 1993 in the Current Population Survey which is an ongoing monthly survey of approximately 55,000 households. The tables are consistent with Current Population Reports (CPR), Series P-23, No. 171, Computer Use in the United States: 1989" and No. 155.

TABLE A3.9

YEARS OF SCHOOL COMPLETED IN THE UNITED STATES BY PERSONS 25 YEARS OLD AND OVER, BY AGE AND SEX: 1940–1995

(NUMBERS IN THOUSANDS. NONINSTITUTIONAL POPULATION.)

AGE AND YEARS	TOTAL	YEARS OF SCHOOL COMPLETED						MEDIAN
		ELEMENTARY		HIGH SCHOOL		COLLEGE		
		0–4 YEARS	5–7 YEARS	1–3 YEARS	4 YEARS	1–3 YEARS	4 YEARS	
25 YEARS OLD AND OVER								
BOTH SEXES								
1995	166,438	3,074	10,873	16,566	56,450	41,249	38,226	NA
1994	164,512	3,156	11,359	16,925	56,515	40,014	36,544	NA
1993	162,826	3,380	11,747	17,067	57,589	37,451	35,590	NA
1992	160,827	3,449	11,989	17,672	57,860	35,520	34,337	NA
1991	158,694	3,803	13,046	17,379	61,272	29,170	34,026	12.7
1990	156,538	3,833	13,758	17,461	60,119	28,075	33,291	12.7
1989	154,155	3,861	14,061	17,719	59,336	26,614	32,565	12.7
1988	151,635	3,714	14,550	17,847	58,940	25,799	30,787	12.7
1987	149,144	3,640	15,301	17,417	57,669	25,479	29,637	12.7
1986	146,606	3,894	15,672	17,484	56,338	24,729	28,489	12.6
1985	143,524	3,873	16,020	17,553	54,866	23,405	27,808	12.6
1984	140,794	3,884	16,258	17,433	54,073	22,281	26,862	12.6
1983	138,020	4,119	16,714	17,681	52,060	21,531	25,915	12.6
1982	135,526	4,119	17,232	18,006	51,426	20,692	24,050	12.6
1981	132,899	4,358	17,868	18,041	49,915	20,042	22,674	12.5
1980	130,409	4,390	18,426	18,086	47,934	19,379	22,193	12.5
1979	125,295	4,324	18,504	17,579	45,915	18,393	20,579	12.5
1978	123,019	4,445	19,309	18,175	44,381	17,379	19,332	12.4
1977	120,870	4,509	19,567	18,318	43,602	16,247	18,627	12.4
1976	118,848	4,601	19,912	18,204	43,157	15,477	17,496	12.4
1975	116,897	4,912	20,633	18,237	42,353	14,518	16,244	12.3
1974	115,005	5,106	21,200	18,274	41,460	13,665	15,300	12.3
1973	112,866	5,100	21,838	18,420	40,448	12,831	14,228	12.3
1972	111,133	5,124	22,503	18,855	39,171	12,117	13,364	12.2
1971	110,627	5,574	24,029	18,601	38,029	11,782	12,612	12.2
1970	109,310	5,747	24,519	18,682	37,134	11,164	12,062	12.2
1969	107,750	6,014	24,976	18,527	36,133	10,564	11,535	12.1
1968	106,469	6,248	25,467	18,724	34,603	10,254	11,171	12.1
1967	104,864	6,400	26,178	18,647	33,173	9,914	10,550	12.0
1966	103,876	6,705	26,478	18,859	32,391	9,235	10,212	12.0
1965	103,245	6,982	27,063	18,617	31,703	9,139	9,742	11.8
1964	102,421	7,295	27,551	18,419	30,728	9,085	9,345	11.7
1962	100,664	7,826	28,438	17,751	28,477	9,170	9,002	11.4
1960	99,465	8,303	31,218	19,140	24,440	8,747	7,617	10.6
1959	97,478	7,816	28,490	17,520	26,219	7,888	7,734	11.0
1957	95,630	8,561	29,316	16,951	24,832	6,985	7,172	10.6
1952	88,358	8,004	30,274	15,228	21,074	6,714	6,118	10.1
1950	87,484	9,491	31,617	14,817	17,625	6,246	5,272	9.3
1947	82,578	8,611	32,308	13,487	16,926	5,533	4,424	9.0
1940	74,776	10,105	34,413	11,182	10,552	4,075	3,407	8.6
MALE								
1995	79,463	1,598	5,231	7,691	25,378	18,933	20,631	NA
1994	78,539	1,669	5,427	7,789	25,404	18,544	19,705	NA
1993	77,644	1,709	5,594	7,821	25,766	17,521	19,234	NA
1992	76,579	1,737	5,726	8,085	25,774	16,631	18,627	NA
1991	75,487	2,018	6,299	7,887	27,189	13,720	18,373	12.8
1990	74,421	2,004	6,557	8,000	26,426	13,271	18,164	12.8
1989	73,225	1,956	6,659	8,076	25,897	12,725	17,913	12.8
1988	71,911	1,852	6,849	8,247	25,638	12,057	17,268	12.7
1987	70,677	1,794	7,259	7,909	24,998	12,062	16,654	12.7
1986	69,503	1,978	7,446	7,872	24,260	11,856	16,091	12.7
1985	67,756	1,947	7,629	7,783	23,552	11,164	15,682	12.7
1984	66,350	1,945	7,688	7,837	22,990	10,678	15,211	12.7

TABLE A3.9 (CONTINUED)

YEARS OF SCHOOL COMPLETED IN THE UNITED STATES BY PERSONS 25 YEARS OLD AND OVER, BY AGE AND SEX: 1940–1995

(NUMBERS IN THOUSANDS. NONINSTITUTIONAL POPULATION.)

AGE AND YEARS	TOTAL	YEARS OF SCHOOL COMPLETED						
		ELEMENTARY		HIGH SCHOOL		COLLEGE		
		0–4 YEARS	5–7 YEARS	1–3 YEARS	4 YEARS	1–3 YEARS	4 YEARS	MEDIAN
1983	65,004	2,103	7,750	7,867	22,048	10,310	14,926	12.7
1982	63,764	2,074	7,987	7,960	21,749	10,020	13,974	12.6
1981	62,509	2,141	8,322	8,084	21,019	9,734	13,208	12.6
1980	61,389	2,212	8,627	8,046	20,080	9,593	12,832	12.6
1979	58,986	2,190	8,785	7,636	19,250	9,100	12,025	12.6
1978	57,922	2,230	9,195	7,821	18,620	8,657	11,398	12.5
1977	56,917	2,296	9,330	7,969	18,290	8,104	10,926	12.5
1976	55,902	2,371	9,463	7,923	18,048	7,699	10,397	12.5
1975	55,036	2,568	9,760	7,985	17,769	7,274	9,679	12.4
1974	54,167	2,637	10,186	7,966	17,488	6,756	9,135	12.4
1973	53,067	2,598	10,488	8,120	17,011	6,376	8,473	12.3
1972	52,351	2,634	10,854	8,413	16,424	5,972	8,055	12.3
1971	52,357	2,933	11,703	8,264	16,008	5,798	7,653	12.2
1970	51,784	3,031	11,925	8,355	15,571	5,580	7,321	12.2
1969	51,031	3,095	12,182	8,398	15,177	5,263	6,917	12.1
1968	50,510	3,261	12,407	8,564	14,613	4,945	6,721	12.1
1967	49,756	3,417	12,736	8,463	14,015	4,755	6,372	12.0
1966	49,410	3,614	12,992	8,611	13,672	4,342	6,180	11.8
1965	49,242	3,774	13,308	8,529	13,334	4,370	5,923	11.7
1964	48,975	3,959	13,467	8,537	12,902	4,394	5,714	11.5
1962	48,283	4,213	13,927	8,399	11,932	4,315	5,497	11.1
1960	47,997	4,522	15,562	8,988	10,175	4,127	4,626	10.3
1959	47,041	4,257	14,039	8,326	10,870	3,801	4,765	10.7
1957	46,208	4,610	14,634	8,003	10,230	3,347	4,359	10.3
1952	42,368	4,396	14,876	7,048	8,760	3,164	3,480	9.7
1950	42,627	5,074	15,852	6,974	7,511	2,888	3,008	9.0
1947	40,483	4,615	16,086	6,535	7,353	2,625	2,478	8.9
1940	37,463	5,550	17,639	5,333	4,507	1,824	2,021	8.6
FEMALE								
1995	86,975	1,476	5,642	8,874	31,072	22,317	17,594	NA
1994	85,973	1,487	5,932	9,135	31,111	21,470	16,838	NA
1993	85,181	1,672	6,154	9,246	31,823	19,930	16,357	NA
1992	84,248	1,712	6,263	9,587	32,086	18,889	15,709	NA
1991	83,207	1,784	6,747	9,491	34,083	15,449	15,652	12.7
1990	82,116	1,829	7,200	9,462	33,693	14,806	15,126	12.7
1989	80,930	1,904	7,402	9,643	33,440	13,888	14,652	12.6
1988	79,724	1,862	7,700	9,599	33,303	13,741	13,519	12.6
1987	78,467	1,846	8,042	9,508	32,671	13,417	12,983	12.6
1986	77,102	1,916	8,226	9,612	32,078	12,874	12,399	12.6
1985	75,768	1,926	8,390	9,770	31,314	12,242	12,126	12.6
1984	74,444	1,939	8,571	9,596	31,083	11,603	11,651	12.6
1983	73,016	2,015	8,964	9,814	30,012	11,220	10,990	12.5
1982	71,762	2,045	9,245	10,046	29,677	10,673	10,076	12.5
1981	70,390	2,217	9,545	9,957	28,896	10,309	9,466	12.5
1980	69,020	2,178	9,800	10,040	27,854	9,786	9,362	12.4
1979	66,309	2,133	9,720	9,945	26,665	9,293	8,554	12.4
1978	65,097	2,214	10,114	10,353	25,761	8,721	7,934	12.4
1977	63,953	2,213	10,236	10,349	25,312	8,142	7,701	12.4
1976	62,946	2,230	10,449	10,281	25,109	7,779	7,098	12.3
1975	61,861	2,344	10,871	10,252	24,584	7,243	6,565	12.3
1974	60,838	2,469	11,015	10,308	23,972	6,910	6,165	12.3
1973	59,799	2,502	11,350	10,300	23,437	6,454	5,755	12.2
1972	58,782	2,490	11,649	10,442	22,746	6,145	5,309	12.2
1971	58,270	2,641	12,327	10,339	22,021	5,984	4,959	12.2
1970	57,527	2,716	12,595	10,327	21,563	5,584	4,743	12.1

TABLE A3.9 (CONTINUED)

YEARS OF SCHOOL COMPLETED IN THE UNITED STATES BY PERSONS 25 YEARS OLD AND OVER, BY AGE AND SEX: 1940–1995

(NUMBERS IN THOUSANDS. NONINSTITUTIONAL POPULATION.)

| AGE AND YEARS | TOTAL | YEARS OF SCHOOL COMPLETED | | | | | | MEDIAN |
| | | ELEMENTARY | | HIGH SCHOOL | | COLLEGE | | |
		0–4 YEARS	5–7 YEARS	1–3 YEARS	4 YEARS	1–3 YEARS	4 YEARS	
1969	56,719	2,919	12,796	10,131	20,955	5,301	4,619	12.1
1968	55,959	2,987	13,060	10,160	19,991	5,309	4,450	12.1
1967	55,107	2,985	13,439	10,185	19,157	5,162	4,178	12.0
1966	54,467	3,090	13,488	10,246	18,719	4,892	4,032	12.0
1965	54,004	3,207	13,753	10,085	18,369	4,767	3,820	12.0
1964	53,447	3,333	14,086	9,881	17,825	4,686	3,629	11.8
1962	52,381	3,613	14,511	9,352	16,545	4,855	3,505	11.6
1960	51,468	3,781	15,656	10,151	14,267	4,620	2,991	10.9
1959	50,437	3,559	14,451	9,194	15,349	4,087	2,969	11.2
1957	49,422	3,951	14,682	8,948	14,602	3,638	2,813	10.9
1952	45,990	3,608	15,398	8,180	12,314	3,550	2,638	10.4
1950	44,857	4,417	15,824	7,843	10,114	3,358	2,264	9.6
1947	42,095	3,996	16,222	6,952	9,573	2,908	1,946	8.9
1940	37,313	4,554	16,773	5,849	6,044	2,251	1,386	8.7

NA=NOT AVAILABLE.

Source: 1947, and 1952 to 1995 March Current Population Survey, noninstitutional population, excluding members of the Armed Forces living in Barracks; 1960 Census of Population, 1950 Census Population, and 1940 Census of Population resident population.

Begining with data for 1992, a new question results in different categories than for earlier years. Data shown as 'High School, 4 years', is now collected by the category 'High School Graduate'; Data shown as 'College 1 to 3 years', is now collected by 'Some College'; and two 'Associate degree' categories. Data shown as 'College 4 years or more', is now collected by the categories, 'Bachelor's degree'; 'Master's degree'; 'Doctorate degree'; and Professional degree.' Due to the change in question format, median years of schooling can not be derived. Total includes persons who did not report on years of school completed.

TABLE A3.10

PERCENTAGE OF PERSONS 25 YEARS OLD AND OVER IN THE UNITED STATES WHO HAVE COMPLETED HIGH SCHOOL OR COLLEGE, BY RACE, HISPANIC ORIGIN AND SEX: 1940–95

(NONINSTITUTIONAL POPULATION.)

YEAR & AGE	ALL RACES			WHITE			BLACK[1]			HISPANIC ORIGIN[2]		
	BOTH SEXES	MALE	FEMALE	BOTH SEXES	MALE	FEMALE	BOTH SEXES	MALE	FEMALE	BOTH SEXES	MALE	FEMALE
25 YEARS AND OVER												
COMPLETED 4 YEARS OF HIGH SCHOOL OR MORE												
1995	81.7	81.7	81.6	83.0	83.0	83.0	73.8	73.4	74.1	53.4	52.9	53.8
1994	80.9	81.0	80.7	82.0	82.1	81.9	72.9	71.7	73.8	53.3	53.4	53.2
1993	80.2	80.5	80.0	81.5	81.8	81.3	70.4	69.6	71.1	53.1	52.9	53.2
1992	79.4	79.7	79.2	80.9	81.1	80.7	67.7	67.0	68.2	52.6	53.7	51.5
1991	78.4	78.5	78.3	79.9	79.8	79.9	66.7	66.7	66.7	51.3	51.4	51.2
1990	77.6	77.7	77.5	79.1	79.1	79.0	66.2	65.8	66.5	50.8	50.3	51.3
1989	76.9	77.2	76.6	78.4	78.6	78.2	64.6	64.2	65.0	50.9	51.0	50.7
1988	76.2	76.4	76.0	77.7	77.7	77.6	63.5	63.7	63.4	51.0	52.0	50.0
1987	75.6	76.0	75.3	77.0	77.3	76.7	63.4	63.0	63.7	50.9	51.8	50.0
1986	74.7	75.1	74.4	76.2	76.5	75.9	62.3	61.5	63.0	48.5	49.2	47.8
1985	73.9	74.4	73.5	75.5	76.0	75.1	59.8	58.4	60.8	47.9	48.5	47.4
1984	73.3	73.7	73.0	75.0	75.4	74.6	58.5	57.1	59.7	47.1	48.6	45.7
1983	72.1	72.7	71.5	73.8	74.4	73.3	56.8	56.5	57.1	46.2	48.6	44.2
1982	71.0	71.7	70.3	72.8	73.4	72.3	54.9	55.7	54.3	45.9	48.1	44.1
1981	69.7	70.3	69.1	71.6	72.1	71.2	52.9	53.2	52.6	44.5	45.5	43.6
1980	68.6	69.2	68.1	70.5	71.0	70.1	51.2	51.1	51.3	45.3	46.4	44.1
1979	67.7	68.4	67.1	69.7	70.3	69.2	49.4	49.2	49.5	42.0	42.3	41.7
1978	65.9	66.8	65.2	67.9	68.6	67.2	47.6	47.9	47.3	40.8	42.2	39.6
1977	64.9	65.6	64.4	67.0	67.5	66.5	45.5	45.6	45.4	39.6	42.3	37.2
1976	64.1	64.7	63.5	66.1	66.7	65.5	43.8	42.3	45.0	39.3	41.4	37.3
1975	62.5	63.1	62.1	64.5	65.0	64.1	42.5	41.6	43.3	37.9	39.5	36.7
1974	61.2	61.6	60.9	63.3	63.6	63.0	40.8	39.9	41.5	36.5	38.3	34.9
1973	59.8	60.0	59.6	61.9	62.1	61.7	39.2	38.2	40.1	NA	NA	NA
1972	58.2	58.2	58.2	60.4	60.3	60.5	36.6	35.7	37.2	NA	NA	NA
1971	56.4	56.3	56.6	58.6	58.4	58.8	34.7	33.8	35.4	NA	NA	NA
1970	55.2	55.0	55.4	57.4	57.2	57.6	33.7	32.4	34.8	NA	NA	NA
1969	54.0	53.6	54.4	56.3	55.7	56.7	32.3	31.9	32.6	NA	NA	NA
1968	52.6	52.0	53.2	54.9	54.3	55.5	30.1	28.9	31.0	NA	NA	NA
1967	51.1	50.5	51.7	53.4	52.8	53.8	29.5	27.1	31.5	NA	NA	NA
1966	49.9	49.0	50.8	52.2	51.3	53.0	27.8	25.8	29.5	NA	NA	NA
1965	49.0	48.0	49.9	51.3	50.2	52.2	27.2	25.8	28.4	NA	NA	NA
1964	48.0	47.0	48.9	50.3	49.3	51.2	25.7	23.7	27.4	NA	NA	NA
1962	46.3	45.0	47.5	48.7	47.4	49.9	24.8	23.2	26.2	NA	NA	NA
1959	43.7	42.2	45.2	46.1	44.5	47.7	20.7	19.6	21.6	NA	NA	NA
1957	41.6	39.7	43.3	43.2	41.1	45.1	18.4	16.9	19.7	NA	NA	NA
1952	38.8	36.9	40.5	NA	NA	NA	15.0	14.0	15.7	NA	NA	NA
1950	34.3	32.6	36.0	NA	NA	NA	13.7	12.5	14.7	NA	NA	NA
1947	33.1	31.4	34.7	35.0	33.2	36.7	13.6	12.7	14.5	NA	NA	NA
1940	24.5	22.7	26.3	26.1	24.2	28.1	7.7	6.9	8.4	NA	NA	NA
COMPLETED 4 YEARS OF COLLEGE OR MORE												
1995	23.0	26.0	20.2	24.0	27.2	21.0	13.2	13.6	12.9	9.3	10.1	8.4
1994	22.2	25.1	19.6	22.9	26.1	20.0	12.9	12.8	13.0	9.1	9.6	8.6
1993	21.9	24.8	19.2	22.6	25.7	19.7	12.2	11.9	12.4	9.0	9.5	8.5
1992	21.4	24.3	18.6	22.1	25.2	19.1	11.9	11.9	12.0	9.3	10.2	8.5
1991	21.4	24.3	18.8	22.2	25.4	19.3	11.5	11.4	11.6	9.7	10.0	9.4
1990	21.3	24.4	18.4	22.0	25.3	19.0	11.3	11.9	10.8	9.2	9.8	8.7
1989	21.1	24.5	18.1	21.8	25.4	18.5	11.8	11.7	11.9	9.9	11.0	8.8
1988	20.3	24.0	17.0	20.9	25.0	17.3	11.2	11.1	11.4	10.1	12.3	8.1
1987	19.9	23.6	16.5	20.5	24.5	16.9	10.7	11.0	10.4	8.6	9.7	7.5
1986	19.4	23.2	16.1	20.1	24.1	16.4	10.9	11.2	10.7	8.4	9.5	7.4
1985	19.4	23.1	16.0	20.0	24.0	16.3	11.1	11.2	11.0	8.5	9.7	7.3
1984	19.1	22.9	15.7	19.8	23.9	16.0	10.4	10.4	10.4	8.2	9.5	7.0
1983	18.8	23.0	15.1	19.5	24.0	15.4	9.5	10.0	9.2	7.9	9.2	6.8

TABLE A3.10 (CONTINUED)

PERCENTAGE OF PERSONS 25 YEARS OLD AND OVER IN THE UNITED STATES WHO HAVE COMPLETED HIGH SCHOOL OR COLLEGE, BY RACE, HISPANIC ORIGIN AND SEX: 1940–1995

(NONINSTITUTIONAL POPULATION.)

YEAR & AGE	ALL RACES			WHITE			BLACK[1]			HISPANIC ORIGIN[2]		
	BOTH SEXES	MALE	FEMALE	BOTH SEXES	MALE	FEMALE	BOTH SEXES	MALE	FEMALE	BOTH SEXES	MALE	FEMALE
1982	17.7	21.9	14.0	18.5	23.0	14.4	8.8	9.1	8.5	7.8	9.6	6.2
1981	17.1	21.1	13.4	17.8	22.2	13.8	8.2	8.2	8.2	7.7	9.7	5.9
1980	17.0	20.9	13.6	17.8	22.1	14.0	7.9	7.7	8.1	7.9	9.7	6.2
1979	16.4	20.4	12.9	17.2	21.4	13.3	7.9	8.3	7.5	6.7	8.2	5.3
1978	15.7	19.7	12.2	16.4	20.7	12.6	7.2	7.3	7.1	7.0	8.6	5.7
1977	15.4	19.2	12.0	16.1	20.2	12.4	7.2	7.0	7.4	6.2	8.1	4.4
1976	14.7	18.6	11.3	15.4	19.6	11.6	6.6	6.3	6.8	6.1	8.6	4.0
1975	13.9	17.6	10.6	14.5	18.4	11.0	6.4	6.7	6.2	6.3	8.3	4.6
1974	13.3	16.9	10.1	14.0	17.7	10.6	5.5	5.7	5.3	5.5	7.1	4.0
1973	12.6	16.0	9.6	13.1	16.8	9.9	6.0	5.9	6.0	NA	NA	NA
1972	12.0	15.4	9.0	12.6	16.2	9.4	5.1	5.5	4.8	NA	NA	NA
1971	11.4	14.6	8.5	12.0	15.5	8.9	4.5	4.7	4.3	NA	NA	NA
1970	11.0	14.1	8.2	11.6	15.0	8.6	4.5	4.6	4.4	NA	NA	NA
1969	10.7	13.6	8.1	11.2	14.3	8.5	4.6	4.8	4.5	NA	NA	NA
1968	10.5	13.3	8.0	11.0	14.1	8.3	4.3	3.7	4.8	NA	NA	NA
1967	10.1	12.8	7.6	10.6	13.6	7.9	4.0	3.4	4.4	NA	NA	NA
1966	9.8	12.5	7.4	10.4	13.3	7.7	3.8	3.9	3.7	NA	NA	NA
1965	9.4	12.0	7.1	9.9	12.7	7.3	4.7	4.9	4.5	NA	NA	NA
1964	9.1	11.7	6.8	9.6	12.3	7.1	3.9	4.5	3.4	NA	NA	NA
1962	8.9	11.4	6.7	9.5	12.2	7.0	4.0	3.9	4.0	NA	NA	NA
1959	8.1	10.3	6.0	8.6	11.0	6.2	3.3	3.8	2.9	NA	NA	NA
1957	7.6	9.6	5.8	8.0	10.1	6.0	2.9	2.7	3.0	NA	NA	NA
1952	7.0	8.3	5.8	NA	NA	NA	2.4	2.0	2.7	NA	NA	NA
1950	6.2	7.3	5.2	NA	NA	NA	2.3	2.1	2.4	NA	NA	NA
1947	5.4	6.2	4.7	5.7	6.6	4.9	2.5	2.4	2.6	NA	NA	NA
1940	4.6	5.5	3.8	4.9	5.9	4.0	1.3	1.4	1.2	NA	NA	NA

[1] DATA ARE FOR BLACK AND OTHER RACES. FOR 1940 TO 1962: FOR 1963 TO 1981, DATA ARE FOR BLACK PERSONS ONLY.

[2] PERSONS OF HISPANIC ORIGIN MAY BE OF ANY RACE.

NA=NOT AVAILABLE.

Source: U.S. Bureau of the Census, 1947, and 1952 to 1995 March Current Population Survey, noninstitutional population, excluding members of the Armed Forces living in barracks. 1950 Census of Population and 1940 Census of Population resident population.

TABLE A3.11

MEAN EARNINGS OF WORKERS 18 YEARS OLD AND OVER IN THE UNITED STATES, BY EDUCATIONAL ATTAINMENT AND SEX: 1975–1994

(MEAN ANNUAL EARNINGS IN CURRENT DOLLARS. TOTAL NUMBER WITH EARNINGS IN THOUSANDS. STANDARD ERROR OF THE MEAN.)

EARN-INGS YEAR	TOTAL			NOT A HIGH SCHOOL GRADUATE			HIGH SCHOOL GRADUATE			SOME COLLEGE /ASSOCIATE DEGREE			BACHELOR'S DEGREE			ADVANCED DEGREE		
	MEAN	NUMBER WITH EARNINGS	STAND-ARD ERROR	MEAN	NUMBER WITH EARNINGS	STAND-ARD ERROR	MEAN	NUMBER WITH EARNINGS	STAND-ARD ERROR	MEAN	NUMBER WITH EARNINGS	STAND-ARD ERROR	MEAN	NUMBER WITH EARNINGS	STAND-ARD ERROR	MEAN	NUMBER WITH EARNINGS	STAND-ARD ERROR
TOTAL BOTH SEXES																		
1994	25,852	135,096	153	13,697	16,479	288	20,248	44,614	170	22,226	40,135	193	37,224	22,712	491	56,105	11,155	961
1993	24,674	133,119	148	12,820	16,575	237	19,422	44,779	162	21,539	39,429	173	35,121	21,815	425	55,789	10,521	1,140
1992	23,227	130,860	99	12,809	16,612	152	18,737	45,340	110	20,867	37,339	109	32,629	21,091	288	48,652	10,479	571
1991	22,332	130,371	93	12,613	17,553	153	18,261	46,508	104	20,551	35,732	116	31,323	20,475	275	46,039	10,103	571
1990	21,793	130,080	91	12,582	18,698	115	17,820	51,977	95	20,694	28,993	165	31,112	18,128	300	41,458	12,285	488
1989	21,414	129,094	92	12,242	19,137	112	17,594	51,846	100	20,255	28,078	161	30,736	17,767	304	41,019	12,265	506
1988	20,060	127,564	88	11,889	19,635	118	16,750	51,297	98	19,066	27,217	171	28,344	17,308	286	37,724	12,109	458
1987	19,016	124,874	83	11,824	19,748	133	15,939	50,815	91	18,054	26,404	156	26,919	16,497	289	35,968	11,411	447
1986	18,149	122,757	72	11,203	19,665	149	15,120	50,104	77	17,073	26,113	135	26,511	15,788	251	34,787	11,087	393
1985	17,181	120,651	67	10,726	19,692	133	14,457	49,674	74	16,349	25,402	127	24,877	15,373	238	32,909	10,510	367
1984	16,083	118,183	57	10,384	20,206	130	13,893	48,452	68	14,936	24,463	107	23,072	14,653	191	30,192	10,410	281
1983	15,137	115,095	NA	9,853	20,020	NA	13,044	47,560	NA	14,245	23,208	NA	21,532	13,929	NA	28,333	10,377	NA
1982	14,351	113,451	52	9,387	20,789	101	12,560	46,584	64	13,503	22,602	105	20,272	13,425	181	26,915	10,051	272
1981	13,624	113,301	48	9,357	22,296	110	12,109	47,332	59	13,176	21,759	101	19,006	12,579	173	25,281	9,336	266
1980	12,665	111,919	45	8,845	23,028	95	11,314	46,795	54	12,409	21,384	97	18,075	12,175	171	23,308	8,535	254
1979	11,795	110,826	43	8,420	23,783	75	10,624	45,497	50	11,377	21,174	90	16,514	11,751	163	21,874	8,621	251
1978	10,812	106,436	41	7,759	23,787	71	9,834	43,510	49	10,357	20,121	85	15,291	11,001	159	20,173	8,017	248
1977	9,887	103,119	35	7,066	24,854	60	9,013	41,696	41	9,607	18,905	76	14,207	10,357	136	19,077	7,309	222
1976	9,180	100,510	32	6,720	25,035	57	8,393	40,570	39	8,813	17,786	76	13,033	10,132	120	17,911	6,985	218
1975	8,552	97,881	31	6,198	24,916	53	7,843	39,827	38	8,388	16,917	70	12,332	9,764	121	16,725	6,457	206
MALE																		
1994	32,087	72,246	251	16,633	9,981	457	25,038	23,418	286	27,636	19,859	324	46,278	12,324	796	67,032	6,663	1,422
1993	30,568	71,183	244	14,946	10,151	233	23,973	23,388	259	26,614	19,532	301	43,499	11,810	669	68,221	6,302	1,756
1992	28,448	71,138	158	14,934	10,335	212	22,978	23,610	173	25,660	18,768	169	40,039	11,353	456	58,324	6,344	837
1991	27,494	70,145	148	15,056	10,679	187	22,663	24,110	163	25,345	18,076	183	38,484	11,126	432	54,449	6,154	837
1990	27,164	70,218	151	14,991	11,412	155	22,378	26,753	158	26,120	14,844	288	38,901	9,807	505	49,768	7,402	751
1989	27,025	69,798	155	14,727	11,774	150	22,508	26,469	172	25,555	14,384	278	38,692	9,737	510	50,144	7,434	777
1988	25,344	69,006	146	14,551	11,993	163	21,481	26,080	166	23,827	14,019	285	35,906	9,466	479	45,677	7,449	689
1987	24,015	67,951	138	14,544	12,117	188	20,364	25,981	150	22,781	13,433	268	33,677	9,286	472	43,140	7,134	663
1986	23,057	67,189	120	13,703	12,208	217	19,453	25,562	131	21,784	13,502	229	33,376	8,908	406	41,836	7,009	583
1985	21,823	66,439	111	13,124	12,137	185	18,575	25,496	125	20,698	13,385	208	31,433	8,794	386	39,768	6,627	548
1984	20,452	65,005	92	12,775	12,325	170	18,016	24,827	116	18,863	12,818	178	29,203	8,387	301	35,804	6,648	403
1983	19,175	63,816	89	12,052	12,376	160	16,728	24,449	108	18,052	12,261	187	27,239	8,010	295	33,635	6,719	388
1982	18,244	63,489	85	11,513	12,868	144	16,160	24,059	107	17,108	12,103	172	25,758	7,865	285	32,109	6,594	390
1981	17,542	63,547	79	11,668	13,701	146	15,900	24,435	101	16,870	11,784	168	24,353	7,393	273	30,072	6,235	376
1980	16,382	62,825	73	11,042	14,273	129	15,002	24,023	92	15,871	11,663	158	23,340	7,132	272	27,846	5,733	360
1979	15,430	62,464	70	10,628	14,711	102	14,317	23,318	87	14,716	11,781	145	21,482	6,889	260	26,411	5,765	358
1978	14,154	60,586	67	9,894	14,550	93	13,188	22,650	85	13,382	11,352	137	19,861	6,611	250	24,274	5,422	351
1977	12,888	59,441	56	8,939	15,369	81	12,092	21,846	70	12,393	10,848	122	18,187	6,341	210	22,786	5,038	311
1976	11,923	58,419	52	8,522	15,634	79	11,189	21,499	65	11,376	10,282	122	16,714	6,135	186	21,202	4,868	301
1975	11,091	57,297	49	7,843	15,613	71	10,475	21,347	64	10,805	9,851	112	15,758	5,960	188	19,672	4,526	283
FEMALE																		
1994	18,684	62,850	143	9,189	6,498	165	14,955	21,195	149	16,928	20,276	199	26,483	10,388	463	39,905	4,493	1,040
1993	17,900	61,937	141	9,462	6,425	482	14,446	21,391	174	16,555	19,897	155	25,232	10,005	441	37,212	4,281	986
1992	17,145	60,451	96	9,311	6,277	178	14,128	21,730	117	16,023	18,571	138	23,991	9,738	272	33,814	4,135	594
1991	16,320	60,226	91	8,818	6,875	161	13,523	22,398	109	15,643	17,657	141	22,802	9,348	258	32,929	3,948	594
1990	15,493	59,862	86	8,808	7,286	169	12,986	25,224	103	15,002	14,149	154	21,933	8,321	270	28,862	4,883	459
1989	14,809	59,296	84	8,268	7,363	167	12,468	25,377	98	14,688	13,694	155	21,089	8,030	264	26,977	4,831	469
1988	13,833	58,558	84	7,711	7,642	165	11,857	25,217	100	14,009	13,198	179	19,216	7,842	253	25,010	4,660	451
1987	13,049	56,923	80	7,504	7,631	171	11,309	24,834	100	13,158	12,971	155	18,217	7,211	261	24,004	4,277	447

TABLE A3.11 (CONTINUED)

MEAN EARNINGS OF WORKERS 18 YEARS OLD AND OVER IN THE UNITED STATES, BY EDUCATIONAL ATTAINMENT AND SEX: 1975–1994

(MEAN ANNUAL EARNINGS IN CURRENT DOLLARS. TOTAL NUMBER WITH EARNINGS IN THOUSANDS. STANDARD ERROR OF THE MEAN.)

EARN-INGS YEAR	TOTAL			NOT A HIGH SCHOOL GRADUATE			HIGH SCHOOL GRADUATE			SOME COLLEGE /ASSOCIATE DEGREE			BACHELOR'S DEGREE			ADVANCED DEGREE		
	MEAN	NUMBER WITH EARNINGS	STAND-ARD ERROR	MEAN	NUMBER WITH EARNINGS	STAND-ARD ERROR	MEAN	NUMBER WITH EARNINGS	STAND-ARD ERROR	MEAN	NUMBER WITH EARNINGS	STAND-ARD ERROR	MEAN	NUMBER WITH EARNINGS	STAND-ARD ERROR	MEAN	NUMBER WITH EARNINGS	STAND-ARD ERROR
1986	12,214	55,568	67	7,109	7,457	169	10,606	24,542	78	12,029	12,611	133	17,623	6,880	233	22,672	4,078	367
1985	11,493	54,212	63	6,874	7,555	179	10,115	24,178	76	11,504	12,017	134	16,114	6,579	207	21,202	3,883	334
1984	10,742	53,178	56	6,644	7,881	203	9,561	23,625	69	10,614	11,645	110	14,865	6,266	193	20,275	3,762	313
1983	10,111	51,279	NA	6,292	7,644	NA	9,147	23,111	NA	9,981	10,947	NA	13,808	5,919	NA	18,593	3,658	NA
1982	9,403	49,962	50	5,932	7,921	123	8,715	22,525	66	9,348	10,499	108	12,511	5,560	167	17,009	3,457	272
1981	8,619	49,754	44	5,673	8,595	165	8,063	22,897	57	8,811	9,975	98	11,384	5,186	156	15,647	3,101	264
1980	7,909	49,094	42	5,263	8,755	134	7,423	22,772	53	8,256	9,721	99	10,628	5,043	152	14,022	2,802	241
1979	7,099	48,362	38	4,840	9,072	106	6,741	22,179	48	7,190	9,393	89	9,474	4,862	137	12,717	2,856	231
1978	6,396	45,850	35	4,397	9,237	111	6,192	20,860	46	6,441	8,769	79	8,408	4,390	128	11,603	2,595	222
1977	5,804	43,678	30	4,032	9,485	86	5,624	19,850	39	5,856	8,057	69	7,923	4,016	115	10,848	2,271	191
1976	5,373	42,091	28	3,723	9,401	76	5,240	19,071	37	5,301	7,504	70	7,383	3,997	102	10,345	2,117	199
1975	4,968	40,584	26	3,438	9,303	75	4,802	18,480	34	5,019	7,066	62	6,963	3,804	98	9,818	1,931	187

NA=NOT AVAILABLE

Source: U.S. Bureau of the Census, Current Population Survey.

TABLE A3.12

NATIONAL INDEX OF PUBLIC EFFORT TO FUND EDUCATION IN THE UNITED STATES (PUBLIC REVENUES PER STUDENT IN RELATION TO PER CAPITA PERSONAL INCOME), BY LEVEL: SELECTED SCHOOL YEARS ENDING: 1930–1993

(SELECTED YEARS)

| SCHOOL YEAR ENDING | PUBLIC EDUCATION REVENUES | | | | | | PER CAPITA PERSONAL INCOME [2,3] |
| | NATIONAL INDEX [1] | | PER STUDENT [2] | | AS A PERCENTAGE OF GDP | | |
	ELEMENTARY/ SECONDARY	HIGHER EDUCATION	ELEMENTARY/ SECONDARY	HIGHER EDUCATION	ELEMENTARY/ SECONDARY	HIGHER EDUCATION	
1930 [4]	10.6	22.5	$658	$1,391	2.0	0.2	$6,192
1940 [4]	14.6	26.0	881	1,568	2.5	0.2	6,041
1950	13.9	29.4	1,230	2,613	2.1	0.4	8,873
1960	17.2	33.5	1,876	3,660	3.0	0.5	10,922
1966	19.3	36.1	2,503	4,677	3.6	0.8	12,940
1970	20.7	31.9	3,189	4,903	4.2	1.0	15,377
1972	23.0	31.0	3,619	4,881	4.6	1.1	15,739
1974	22.4	29.5	3,781	4,987	4.3	1.1	16,896
1976	23.2	27.5	4,016	4,749	4.5	1.2	17,289
1978	23.1	27.7	4,076	4,883	4.1	1.1	17,621
1980	21.7	25.1	4,085	4,716	3.9	1.1	18,804
1982	21.5	23.1	3,926	4,211	3.6	1.1	18,254
1984	23.1	23.6	4,206	4,295	3.7	1.0	18,173
1986	23.9	25.3	4,653	4,918	3.7	1.1	19,445
1988	23.9	24.3	4,914	4,997	3.7	1.1	20,601
1990	25.7	23.4	5,464	4,975	4.0	1.1	21,278
1992	25.4	21.7	5,486	4,688	4.1	1.1	21,620
1993	25.9	21.9	5,526	4,665	4.1	1.0	21,335

[1] REVISED FROM PREVIOUSLY PUBLISHED FIGURES.

[2] IN CONSTANT 1995 DOLLARS.

[3] FOR THE CALENDAR YEAR IN WHICH THE SCHOOL YEAR BEGAN.

[4] INCOME AND POPULATION ARE FOR THE CALENDAR YEAR IN WHICH THE SCHOOL YEAR ENDED.

Source: National Center for Education Statistics, The Condition of Education 1996, P160.

Note: Public funds for education may be used at many types of institutions, both publicly and privately controlled. For comparability across levels of education, enrollment in both publicly and privately controlled institutions is included.

DETAILED TABLES

HEALTH

TABLE A4.1

NUMBER OF DEATHS, DEATH RATES, AND AGE-ADJUSTED DEATH RATES IN THE UNITED STATES, BY RACE AND SEX: 1940, 1950, 1960, 1970, AND 1975–95

(CRUDE RATES ON AN ANNUAL BASIS PER 100,000 POPULATION IN SPECIFIED GROUP; AGE-ADJUSTED RATES PER 100,000 U.S. STANDARD MILLION POPULATION.)

YEAR	ALL RACES BOTH SEXES	MALE	FEMALE	WHITE BOTH SEXES	MALE	FEMALE	BLACK BOTH SEXES	MALE	FEMALE	AMERICAN INDIAN BOTH SEXES	MALE	FEMALE	ASIAN OR PACIFIC ISLANDER BOTH SEXES	MALE	FEMALE
NUMBER															
1995	2,312,180	1,172,507	1,139,672	19,907,278	998,666	992,062	283,748	152,657	131,091	9,962	5,557	4,404	27,742	15,628	12,114
1994	2,278,994	1,162,747	1,116,247	1,959,875	988,823	971,052	282,379	153,019	129,360	9,637	5,497	4,140	27,103	15,408	11,695
1993	2,268,553	1,161,797	1,106,756	1,951,437	988,329	963,108	282,151	153,502	128,649	9,579	5,434	4,145	25,386	14,532	10,854
1992	2,175,613	1,122,336	1,053,277	1,873,781	956,957	916,824	269,219	146,630	122,589	8,953	5,181	3,772	23,660	13,568	10,092
1991	2,169,518	1,121,665	1,047,853	1,868,904	956,497	912,407	269,525	147,331	122,194	8,621	4,948	3,673	22,173	12,727	9,446
1990	2,148,463	1,113,417	1,035,046	1,853,254	950,812	902,442	265,498	145,359	120,139	8,316	4,877	3,439	21,127	12,211	8,916
1989	2,150,466	1,114,190	1,036,276	1,853,841	950,852	902,989	267,642	146,393	121,249	8,614	5,066	3,548	20,042	11,688	8,354
1988	2,167,999	1,125,540	1,042,459	1,876,906	965,419	911,487	264,019	144,228	119,791	7,917	4,617	3,300	18,963	11,155	7,808
1987	2,123,323	1,107,958	1,015,365	1,843,067	953,382	889,685	254,814	139,551	115,263	7,602	4,432	3,170	17,689	10,496	7,193
1986	2,105,361	1,104,005	1,001,356	1,831,083	952,554	878,529	250,326	137,214	113,112	7,301	4,365	2,936	16,514	9,795	6,719
1985	2,086,440	1,097,758	988,682	1,819,054	950,455	868,599	244,207	133,610	110,597	7,154	4,181	2,973	15,887	9,441	6,446
1984	2,039,369	1,076,514	962,855	1,781,897	934,529	847,368	235,884	129,147	106,737	6,949	4,117	2,832	14,483	8,627	5,856
1983	2,019,201	1,071,923	947,278	1,765,582	931,779	833,803	233,124	127,911	105,213	6,839	4,064	2,775	13,554	8,126	5,428
1982	1,974,797	1,056,440	918,357	1,729,085	919,239	809,846	226,513	125,610	100,903	6,679	3,974	2,705	12,430	7,564	4,866
1981	1,977,981	1,063,772	914,209	1,731,233	925,490	805,743	228,560	127,296	101,264	6,608	4,016	2,592	11,475	6,908	4,567
1980	1,989,841	1,075,078	914,763	1,738,607	933,878	804,729	233,135	130,138	102,997	6,923	4,193	2,730	11,071	6,809	4,262
1979	1,913,841	1,044,959	868,882	1,676,145	910,137	766,008	220,818	124,433	96,385	6,728	4,171	2,557	NA	NA	NA
1978	1,927,788	1,055,290	872,498	1,689,722	920,123	769,599	221,340	124,663	96,677	6,959	4,343	2,616	NA	NA	NA
1977	1,899,597	1,046,243	853,354	1,664,100	912,670	751,430	220,076	123,894	96,182	6,454	4,019	2,435	NA	NA	NA
1976	1,909,440	1,051,983	857,457	1,674,989	918,589	756,400	219,442	123,977	95,465	6,300	3,883	2,417	NA	NA	NA
1975	1,892,879	1,050,819	842,060	1,660,366	917,804	742,562	217,932	123,770	94,162	6,166	3,838	2,328	NA	NA	NA
1970	1,921,031	1,078,478	842,553	1,682,096	942,437	739,659	225,647	127,540	98,107	5,675	3,391	2,284	NA	NA	NA
1960	1,711,982	975,648	736,334	1,505,335	860,857	644,478	196,010	107,701	88,309	4,528	2,658	1,870	NA	NA	NA
1950	1,452,454	827,749	624,705	1,276,085	731,366	544,719	169,606	92,004	77,602	4,440	2,497	1,943	NA	NA	NA
1940	1,417,269	791,003	626,266	1,231,223	690,901	540,322	178,743	95,517	83,226	4,791	2,527	2,264	NA	NA	NA
DEATH RATE															
1995	880.0	913.8	847.7	912.8	933.4	893.0	856.2	971.0	752.5	444.3	500.7	388.9	298.7	348.1	252.5
1994	875.4	915.0	837.6	905.4	931.6	880.1	864.3	987.8	752.9	436.1	502.6	371.0	301.5	354.0	252.2
1993	880.0	923.5	838.6	908.5	938.8	879.4	876.8	1,006.3	760.1	440.0	503.9	377.3	293.9	346.6	244.2
1992	852.9	901.6	806.5	880.0	917.2	844.3	850.5	977.5	736.2	417.7	487.7	348.9	283.1	332.7	235.8
1991	860.3	912.1	811.0	886.2	926.2	847.7	864.9	998.7	744.5	407.2	471.2	343.9	277.3	325.6	231.1
1990	863.8	918.4	812.0	888.0	930.9	846.9	871.0	1,008.0	747.9	402.8	476.4	330.4	283.3	334.3	234.3
1989	871.3	926.3	818.9	893.2	936.5	851.8	887.9	1,026.7	763.2	430.5	510.7	351.3	280.9	334.5	229.4
1988	886.7	945.1	831.2	910.5	957.9	865.3	888.3	1,026.1	764.6	411.7	485.0	339.9	282.0	339.0	227.4
1987	876.4	939.3	816.7	900.1	952.7	849.8	868.9	1,006.2	745.7	410.7	483.8	339.0	278.9	338.3	222.0
1986	876.7	944.7	812.3	900.1	958.6	844.3	864.9	1,002.6	741.5	409.5	494.9	325.9	276.2	335.1	219.9
1985	876.9	948.6	809.1	900.4	963.6	840.1	854.8	989.3	734.2	416.4	492.5	342.5	283.4	344.6	224.9
1984	864.8	938.8	794.7	887.8	954.1	824.6	836.1	968.5	717.4	419.6	502.7	338.4	275.9	336.5	218.1
1983	863.7	943.2	788.4	885.4	957.7	816.4	836.6	971.2	715.9	428.5	515.1	343.9	276.1	339.1	216.1
1982	852.4	938.4	771.2	873.1	951.8	798.2	823.4	966.2	695.5	434.5	522.9	348.1	271.3	338.3	207.4
1981	862.0	954.0	775.0	880.4	965.2	799.8	842.4	992.6	707.7	445.6	547.9	345.6	272.3	336.2	211.5
1980	878.3	976.9	785.3	892.5	983.3	806.1	875.4	1,034.1	733.3	487.4	597.1	380.1	296.9	375.3	222.5
1979	852.2	957.5	752.7	865.2	963.3	771.8	839.3	999.6	695.3	NA	NA	NA	NA	NA	NA
1978	868.0	977.5	764.5	880.2	982.7	782.7	855.1	1,016.9	709.5	NA	NA	NA	NA	NA	NA
1977	864.4	978.9	756.0	874.6	983.0	771.3	864.0	1,026.0	718.0	NA	NA	NA	NA	NA	NA
1976	877.6	993.8	767.6	887.7	997.3	783.1	875.0	1,041.6	724.5	NA	NA	NA	NA	NA	NA
1975	878.5	1,002.0	761.4	886.9	1,004.1	775.1	882.5	1,055.4	726.1	NA	NA	NA	NA	NA	NA
1970	945.3	1,090.3	807.8	946.3	1,086.7	812.6	999.3	1,186.6	829.2	NA	NA	NA	NA	NA	NA
1960	954.7	1,104.5	809.2	947.8	1,098.5	800.9	1,038.6	1,181.7	905.0	NA	NA	NA	NA	NA	NA
1950	963.8	1,106.1	823.5	945.7	1,089.5	803.3	NA	NA	NA	NA	NA	NA	NA	NA	NA
1940	1,076.4	1,197.4	954.6	1,041.5	1,162.2	919.4	NA	NA	NA	NA	NA	NA	NA	NA	NA
AGE-ADJUSTED DEATH RATE															
1995	503.7	645.8	385.2	477.6	611.2	365.6	758.6	1,006.9	566.2	467.1	578.6	366.8	293.2	377.2	266.9
1994	507.4	654.6	385.2	479.8	617.9	364.9	772.1	1,029.9	572.0	460.7	585.9	350.8	299.2	386.5	229.3

TABLE A4.1 (CONTINUED)

NUMBER OF DEATHS, DEATH RATES, AND AGE-ADJUSTED DEATH RATES IN THE UNITED STATES, BY RACE AND SEX: 1940, 1950, 1960, 1970, AND 1975–95

(CRUDE RATES ON AN ANNUAL BASIS PER 100,000 POPULATION IN SPECIFIED GROUP; AGE-ADJUSTED RATES PER 100,000 U.S. STANDARD MILLION POPULATION.)

	ALL RACES			WHITE			BLACK			AMERICAN INDIAN			ASIAN OR PACIFIC ISLANDER		
YEAR	BOTH SEXES	MALE	FEMALE	BOTH SEXES	MALE	FEMALE	BOTH SEXES	MALE	FEMALE	BOTH SEXES	MALE	FEMALE	BOTH SEXES	MALE	FEMALE
1993	513.3	664.9	388.3	485.1	627.5	367.7	785.2	1,052.2	578.8	468.9	589.6	364.5	295.9	381.4	226.7
1992	504.5	656.0	380.3	477.5	620.9	359.9	767.5	1,026.9	568.4	453.1	579.6	343.1	285.8	364.1	220.5
1991	513.7	669.9	386.5	486.8	634.4	366.3	780.7	1,048.8	575.1	441.8	562.6	335.9	283.2	360.2	218.3
1990	520.2	680.2	390.6	492.8	644.3	369.9	789.2	1,061.3	581.6	445.1	573.1	335.1	297.6	377.8	228.9
1989	528.0	689.3	397.3	499.6	652.2	376.0	805.9	1,082.8	594.3	475.7	622.8	353.4	295.8	378.9	225.2
1988	539.9	706.1	406.1	512.8	671.3	385.3	809.7	1,083.0	601.0	456.3	585.7	343.2	300.2	385.4	226.5
1987	539.2	706.8	404.6	513.7	674.2	384.8	796.4	1,063.6	592.4	456.7	580.8	351.3	297.0	386.2	221.3
1986	544.8	716.2	407.6	520.1	684.9	388.1	796.8	1,061.9	594.1	451.4	591.6	328.4	296.7	385.3	220.3
1985	548.9	723.0	410.3	524.9	693.3	391.0	793.6	1,053.4	594.8	468.2	602.6	353.3	305.7	396.9	228.5
1984	548.1	721.6	410.5	525.2	693.6	391.7	783.3	1,035.9	590.1	476.9	614.2	347.3	299.4	386.0	223.0
1983	552.5	729.4	412.5	529.4	701.6	393.3	787.4	1,037.5	595.3	485.9	634.0	360.1	298.9	388.6	218.0
1982	554.7	734.2	411.9	532.3	706.8	393.6	782.1	1,035.4	585.9	494.3	634.6	371.6	293.6	389.2	212.8
1981	568.6	753.8	420.8	544.8	724.8	401.5	807.0	1,068.8	602.7	514.0	676.7	368.5	293.2	382.3	213.9
1980	585.8	777.2	432.6	559.4	745.3	411.1	842.5	1,112.8	631.1	564.1	732.5	414.1	315.6	416.6	224.6
1979	577.0	768.6	423.1	551.9	738.4	402.5	812.1	1,073.3	605.0	NA	NA	NA	NA	NA	NA
1978	595.0	791.4	437.4	569.5	761.1	416.4	831.8	1,093.9	622.7	NA	NA	NA	NA	NA	NA
1977	602.1	801.3	441.8	575.7	770.6	419.6	849.3	1,112.1	639.6	NA	NA	NA	NA	NA	NA
1976	618.5	820.9	455.0	591.3	789.3	432.5	870.5	1,138.3	654.5	NA	NA	NA	NA	NA	NA
1975	630.4	837.2	462.5	602.2	804.3	439.0	890.8	1,163.0	670.6	NA	NA	NA	NA	NA	NA
1970	714.3	931.6	532.5	679.6	893.4	501.7	1,044.0	1,318.6	814.4	NA	NA	NA	NA	NA	NA
1960	760.9	949.3	590.6	727.0	917.7	555.0	1,073.3	1,246.1	916.9	NA	NA	NA	NA	NA	NA
1950	841.5	1,001.6	688.4	800.4	963.1	645.0	NA	NA	NA	NA	NA	NA	NA	NA	NA
1940	1,076.1	1,213.0	938.9	1,017.2	1,155.1	879.0	NA	NA	NA	NA	NA	NA	NA	NA	NA

NA = DATA NOT AVAILABLE.

Source: G.K. Singh, K.D. Kochanck, and M.D. MacDorman, "Advance Report of Final Mortality Statistics," Monthly Vital Statistics Report, vol. 45 no. 3, supp (1966): 15 (Hyattsville, MD, National Center for Health Statistics).

TABLE A4.2

DEATHS AND DEATH RATES FOR THE 10 LEADING CAUSES OF DEATH IN SPECIFIED AGE GROUPS IN THE UNITED STATES, PRELIMINARY 1995

(RATES PER 100,000 POPULATION IN SPECIFIED GROUP.)

RANK [1]	CAUSE OF DEATH AND AGE (BASED ON NINTH REVISION, INTERNATIONAL CLASSIFICATION OF DISEASES, 1975)	NUMBER	RATE
ALL AGES [2]			
	ALL CAUSES	2,312,203	880.0
1	DISEASES OF HEART	738,781	281.2
2	MALIGNANT NEOPLASMS, INCLUDING NEOPLASMS OF LYMPHATIC AND HEMATOPOIETIC TISSUES	537,969	204.7
3	CEREBROVASCULAR DISEASES	158,061	60.2
4	CHRONIC OBSTRUCTIVE PULMONARY DISEASES AND ALLIED CONDITIONS	104,756	39.9
5	ACCIDENTS AND ADVERSE EFFECTS	89,703	34.1
	MOTOR VEHICLE ACCIDENTS	41,786	15.9
	ALL OTHER ACCIDENTS AND ADVERSE EFFECTS	47,916	18.2
6	PNEUMONIA AND INFLUENZA	83,528	31.8
7	DIABETES MELLITUS	59,085	22.5
8	HUMAN IMMUNODEFICIENCY VIRUS INFECTION	42,506	16.2
9	SUICIDE	30,893	11.8
10	CHRONIC LIVER DISEASE AND CIRRHOSIS	24,848	9.5
	ALL OTHER CAUSES (RESIDUAL)	442,073	168.2
1-4 YEARS			
	ALL CAUSES	6,355	40.4
1	ACCIDENTS AND ADVERSE EFFECTS	2277	14.5
	MOTOR VEHICLE ACCIDENTS	814	5.2
	ALL OTHER ACCIDENTS AND ADVERSE EFFECTS	1,463	9.3
2	CONGENITAL ANOMALIES	692	4.4
3	MALIGNANT NEOPLASMS, INCLUDING NEOPLASMS OF LYMPHATIC AND HEMATOPOIETIC TISSUES	487	3.1
4	HOMICIDE AND LEGAL INTERVENTION	414	2.6
5	DISEASES OF HEART	256	1.6
6	HUMAN IMMUNODEFICIENCY VIRUS INFECTION	205	1.3
7	PNEUMONIA AND INFLUENZA	138	0.9
8	CERTAIN CONDITIONS ORIGINATING IN THE PERINATAL PERIOD	96	0.6
9	SEPTICEMIA	67	0.4
10	BENIGN NEOPLASMS, CARCINOMA IN SITU, AND NEOPLASMS OF UNCERTAIN BEHAVIOR AND OF UNSPECIFIED NATURE	60	0.4
	ALL OTHER CAUSES (RESIDUAL)	1,663	10.6
5-14 YEARS			
	ALL CAUSES	8,412	22.1
1	ACCIDENTS AND ADVERSE EFFECTS	3,481	9.1
	MOTOR VEHICLE ACCIDENTS	1,997	5.2
	ALL OTHER ACCIDENTS AND ADVERSE EFFECTS	1,484	3.9
2	MALIGNANT NEOPLASMS, INCLUDING NEOPLASMS OF LYMPHATIC AND HEMATOPOIETIC TISSUES	999	2.6
3	HOMICIDE AND LEGAL INTERVENTION	494	1.3
4	CONGENITAL ANOMALIES	457	1.2
5	SUICIDE	329	0.9
6	DISEASES OF HEART	269	0.7
7	HUMAN IMMUNODEFICIENCY VIRUS INFECTION	174	0.5
8	CHRONIC OBSTRUCTIVE PULMONARY DISEASES AND ALLIED CONDITIONS	137	0.4
9	BENIGN NEOPLASMS, CARCINOMA IN SITU, AND NEOPLASMS OF UNCERTAIN BEHAVIOR AND OF UNSPECIFIED NATURE	120	0.3
10	PNEUMONIA AND INFLUENZA	115	0.3
	ALL OTHER CAUSES (RESIDUAL)	1,837	4.8
15-24 YEARS			
	ALL CAUSES	33,569	93.4
1	ACCIDENTS AND ADVERSE EFFECTS	1,3532	37.6
	MOTOR VEHICLE ACCIDENTS	1,0354	28.8
	ALL OTHER ACCIDENTS AND ADVERSE EFFECTS	3,179	8.8
2	MALIGNANT NEOPLASMS, INCLUDING NEOPLASMS OF LYMPHATIC AND HEMATOPOIETIC TISSUES	6,827	19.0
3	HOMICIDE AND LEGAL INTERVENTION	4,789	13.3
4	CONGENITAL ANOMALIES	1,599	4.4
5	SUICIDE	964	2.7
6	DISEASES OF HEART	643	1.8
7	HUMAN IMMUNODEFICIENCY VIRUS INFECTION	425	1.2

TABLE A4.2 (CONTINUED)

DEATHS AND DEATH RATES FOR THE 10 LEADING CAUSES OF DEATH IN SPECIFIED AGE GROUPS IN THE UNITED STATES, PRELIMINARY 1995

(RATES PER 100,000 POPULATION IN SPECIFIED GROUP.)

RANK [1]	CAUSE OF DEATH AND AGE (BASED ON NINTH REVISION, INTERNATIONAL CLASSIFICATION OF DISEASES, 1975)	NUMBER	RATE
15-24 YEARS (CONTINUED)			
8	CHRONIC OBSTRUCTIVE PULMONARY DISEASES AND ALLIED CONDITIONS	220	0.6
9	BENIGN NEOPLASMS, CARCINOMA IN SITU, AND NEOPLASMS OF UNCERTAIN BEHAVIOR AND OF UNSPECIFIED NATURE	19 3	0.5
10	PNEUMONIA AND INFLUENZA	166	0.5
	ALL OTHER CAUSES (RESIDUAL)	4,211	11.7
25-44 YEARS			
	ALL CAUSES	15,7971	189.5
1	HUMAN IMMUNODEFICIENCY VIRUS INFECTION	30,465	36.6
2	ACCIDENTS AND ADVERSE EFFECTS	25,995	31.2
	MOTOR VEHICLE ACCIDENTS	14,087	16.9
	ALL OTHER ACCIDENTS AND ADVERSE EFFECTS	11,909	14.3
3	MALIGNANT NEOPLASMS, INCLUDING NEOPLASMS OF LYMPHATIC AND HEMATOPOIETIC TISSUES	21,983	26.4
4	DISEASES OF HEART	16,719	20.1
5	SUICIDE	12,518	15.0
6	HOMICIDE AND LEGAL INTERVENTION	9,693	11.6
7	CHRONIC LIVER DISEASE AND CIRRHOSIS	4,146	5.0
8	CEREBROVASCULAR DISEASES	3,407	4.1
9	DIABETES MELLITUS	2,417	2.9
10	PNEUMONIA AND INFLUENZA	2,076	2.5
	ALL OTHER CAUSES (RESIDUAL)	28,552	34.3
45-64 YEARS			
	ALL CAUSES	376,337	720.8
1	MALIGNANT NEOPLASMS, INCLUDING NEOPLASMS OF LYMPHATIC AND HEMATOPOIETIC TISSUES	131,808	252.5
2	DISEASES OF HEART	101,975	195.3
3	ACCIDENTS AND ADVERSE EFFECTS	15,021	28.8
	MOTOR VEHICLE ACCIDENTS	7,004	13.4
	ALL OTHER ACCIDENTS AND ADVERSE EFFECTS	8,016	15.4
4	CEREBROVASCULAR DISEASES	15,015	28.8
5	CHRONIC OBSTRUCTIVE PULMONARY DISEASES AND ALLIED CONDITIONS	12,889	24.7
6	DIABETES MELLITUS	12,039	23.1
7	CHRONIC LIVER DISEASE AND CIRRHOSIS	10,310	19.7
8	HUMAN IMMUNODEFICIENCY VIRUS INFECTION	10,202	19.5
9	SUICIDE	7,175	13.7
10	PNEUMONIA AND INFLUENZA	5,528	10.6
	ALL OTHER CAUSES (RESIDUAL)	54,375	104.1
65 YEARS AND OVER			
	ALL CAUSES	1,699,752	5069.0
1	DISEASES OF HEART	617,844	1842.5
2	MALIGNANT NEOPLASMS, INCLUDING NEOPLASMS OF LYMPHATIC AND HEMATOPOIETIC TISSUES	381,004	1136.2
3	CEREBROVASCULAR DISEASES	139,134	414.9
4	CHRONIC OBSTRUCTIVE PULMONARY DISEASES AND ALLIED CONDITIONS	90,299	269.3
5	PNEUMONIA AND INFLUENZA	74,995	223.7
6	DIABETES MELLITUS	44,472	132.6
7	ACCIDENTS AND ADVERSE EFFECTS	28,545	85.1
	MOTOR VEHICLE ACCIDENTS	7,327	21.9
	ALL OTHER ACCIDENTS AND ADVERSE EFFECTS	21,218	63.3
8	NEPHRITIS, NEPHROTIC SYNDROME, AND NEPHROSIS	20,325	60.6
9	ALZHEIMER'S DISEASE	20,042	59.8
10	SEPTICEMIA	17,035	50.8
	ALL OTHER CAUSES (RESIDUAL)	266,057	793.4

[1] RANK BASED ON NUMBER OF DEATHS.

[2] INCLUDES DEATHS UNDER 1 YEAR OF AGE.

Source: H.M. Rosenberg, S.J. Ventura, J.D. Maurer, et al. "Births and Deaths: United States, 1995," Monthly Vital Statistics Report, vol. 45 no. 3, supp 2, p 31. Hyattsville, MD: National Center for Health Statistics.

TABLE A4.3

PERCENTAGE OF PERSONS RESIDING IN U.S. COUNTIES THAT MET NATIONAL AMBIENT AIR QUALITY STANDARDS THROUGHOUT THE YEAR, BY RACE AND HISPANIC ORIGIN: 1988–1993

(SELECTED YEARS)

TYPE OF POLLUTANT, RACE, AND HISPANIC ORIGIN	PERCENT OF POPULATION					
	1993	1992	1991	1990	1989	1988
ALL POLLUTANTS						
ALL RACES	76.5	78.4	65.2	71.0	65.3	49.7
WHITE	76.9	79.1	66.0	71.8	NA	NA
BLACK	75.2	76.5	63.4	71.5	NA	NA
AMERICAN INDIAN OR ALASKAN NATIVE	82.4	83.0	75.2	76.8	NA	NA
ASIAN OR PACIFIC ISLANDER	62.8	64.4	46.7	49.6	NA	NA
HISPANIC	57.7	56.8	45.2	49.3	NA	NA
OZONE						
ALL RACES	79.5	81.9	71.9	76.3	72.6	53.6
WHITE	79.9	82.7	72.7	76.9	NA	NA
BLACK	79.3	79.8	69.7	77.0	NA	NA
AMERICAN INDIAN OR ALASKAN NATIVE	85.5	88.4	84.8	83.0	NA	NA
ASIAN OR PACIFIC ISLANDER	64.5	67.0	55.2	58.0	NA	NA
HISPANIC	60.2	61.2	53.4	57.1	NA	NA
CARBON MONOXIDE						
ALL RACES	95.4	94.3	92.0	90.8	86.2	87.8
WHITE	95.6	94.4	92.3	91.0	NA	NA
BLACK	96.0	95.5	93.5	93.4	NA	NA
AMERICAN INDIAN OR ALASKAN NATIVE	95.1	92.9	89.9	88.7	NA	NA
ASIAN OR PACIFIC ISLANDER	85.8	84.7	78.0	73.7	NA	NA
HISPANIC	82.2	79.8	75.6	72.5	NA	NA
PARTICULATES (PM-10) [1]						
ALL RACES	97.5	89.6	91.9	92.6	88.8	89.4
WHITE	97.6	90.2	92.1	92.7	NA	NA
BLACK	96.8	87.9	93.6	94.2	NA	NA
AMERICAN INDIAN OR ALASKAN NATIVE	97.4	89.9	90.6	92.4	NA	NA
ASIAN OR PACIFIC ISLANDER	98.5	79.3	80.8	82.7	NA	NA
HISPANIC	97.4	71.3	76.3	76.1	NA	NA
SULFUR DIOXIDE						
ALL RACES	99.4	100.0	97.9	99.4	99.9	99.3
WHITE	99.4	100.0	98.3	99.4	NA	NA
BLACK	99.5	100.0	95.6	99.5	NA	NA
AMERICAN INDIAN OR ALASKAN NATIVE	100.0	100.0	99.4	99.8	NA	NA
ASIAN OR PACIFIC ISLANDER	99.8	100.0	97.4	99.8	NA	NA
HISPANIC	100.0	100.0	96.9	99.9	NA	NA
NITROGEN DIOXIDE						
ALL RACES	100.0	100.0	96.4	96.4	96.5	96.6
WHITE	100.0	100.0	96.8	96.8	NA	NA
BLACK	100.0	100.0	96.6	96.6	NA	NA
AMERICAN INDIAN OR ALASKAN NATIVE	100.0	100.0	97.2	97.2	NA	NA
ASIAN OR PACIFIC ISLANDER	100.0	100.0	86.7	86.7	NA	NA
HISPANIC	100.0	100.0	85.0	85.0	NA	NA
LEAD						
ALL RACES	97.8	98.1	94.1	94.1	99.4	99.3
WHITE	98.2	98.5	94.8	94.9	NA	NA
BLACK	94.8	95.3	91.1	91.5	NA	NA
AMERICAN INDIAN OR ALASKAN NATIVE	99.3	99.4	96.4	96.4	NA	NA
ASIAN OR PACIFIC ISLANDER	98.9	99.0	85.5	85.5	NA	NA
HISPANIC	99.5	99.4	84.0	83.6	NA	NA

[1] PARTICULATE MATTER SMALLER THAN 10 MICRONS.

Sources: Data are based on air quality measurements in counties with monitoring devices; U.S. Environmental Protection Agency, Aerometric Information Retrieval System; Data computed by the National Center for Health Statistics, Division of Health Promotion Statistics from data compiled by the U.S. Environmental Protection Agency, Office of Air Quality and Standards.

Notes: The race groups, White and Black, include persons of Hispanic and non-Hispanic origin. Conversely, persons of Hispanic origin may be of any race. 1988-89 data based on 1987 county population estimates; 1990-93 data based on 1990 county population estimates. Some data have been revised and differ from that published previously in Healthy People 2000 Review.

TABLE A4.4

DEATHS AND DEATH RATES IN THE UNITED STATES FOR ALCOHOL-INDUCED CAUSES, BY RACE AND SEX: 1980–93

(AGE-ADJUSTED RATES PER 100,000).

YEAR	ALL RACES			WHITE			BLACK AND OTHER					
							TOTAL			BLACK		
	BOTH SEXES	MALE	FEMALE	BOTH SEXES	MALE	FEMALE	BOTH SEXES	MALE	FEMALE	BOTH SEXES	MALE	FEMALE
NUMBER												
1980	19,765	14,447	5,318	14,815	10,936	3,879	4,950	3,511	1,439	4,451	3,170	1,281
1985	17,741	13,216	4,525	13,216	9,922	3,294	4,525	3,294	1,231	4,114	3,030	1,084
1990	19,757	14,842	4,915	14,904	11,334	3,570	4,853	3,508	1,345	4,337	3,172	1,165
1991	19,233	14,467	4,766	14,825	11,286	3,539	4,408	3,181	1,227	3,883	2,816	1,067
1992	19,568	14,926	4,642	15,143	11,701	3,442	4,425	3,225	1,200	3,809	2,800	1,009
1993	19,557	14,873	4,684	15,293	11,716	3,577	4,264	3,157	1,107	3,663	2,759	904
RATE [1]												
1980	8.4	13.0	4.3	6.9	10.8	3.5	18.8	29.5	10.0	20.4	32.4	10.6
1985	7.0	11.0	3.4	5.8	9.2	2.8	14.6	23.5	7.2	16.8	27.7	8.0
1990	7.2	11.4	3.4	6.2	9.9	2.8	13.6	22.0	6.8	16.1	26.6	7.7
1991	6.8	10.9	3.2	6.0	9.7	2.7	11.8	19.2	5.9	13.9	22.9	6.8
1992	6.8	11.0	3.1	6.1	9.9	2.6	11.6	18.9	5.6	13.4	22.3	6.3
1993	6.7	10.8	3.0	6.1	9.7	2.7	10.8	17.8	5.0	12.5	21.3	5.5

[1] AGE-ADJUSTED DEATH RATE. FOR METHOD OF COMPUTATION SEE SOURCE.

Source: U.S. Bureau of the Census, "Statistical Abstract of United States 1996:" Table No. 144.

TABLE A4.5

NUMBER OF SELECTED REPORTED CHRONIC CONDITIONS PER 1,000 PERSONS, BY SEX AND AGE: UNITED STATES, 1994

TYPE OF CHRONIC CONDITION	NUMBER OF CHRONIC CONDITIONS PER 1,000 PERSONS									
	MALE					FEMALE				
	UNDER 45 YEARS	45-64 YEARS	65 YEARS AND OVER			UNDER 45 YEARS	45-64 YEARS	65 YEARS AND OVER		
			TOTAL	65-74 YEARS	75 YEARS AND OVER			TOTAL	65-74 YEARS	75 YEARS AND OVER
SELECTED SKIN AND MUSCULOSKELETAL CONDITIONS										
ARTHRITIS	27.4	176.8	428.6	430.8	424.9	38.2	297.0	553.5	513.6	604.4
GOUT, INCLUDING GOUTY ARTHRITIS	3.2	31.7	54.5	57.1	50.4	*1.0	7.3	24.4	*13.4	38.5
INTERVERTEBRAL DISC DISORDERS	16.2	52.4	35.2	42.3	*23.2	11.3	49.3	29.2	32.4	25.2
BONE SPUR OR TENDINITIS, UNSPECIFIED	4.0	20.8	15.7	*15.7	*15.6	6.8	26.9	18.9	26.8	*8.8
DISORDERS OF BONE OR CARTILAGE	3.2	*3.7	*8.1	*10.0	*4.8	2.6	13.0	26.0	22.2	30.8
TROUBLE WITH BUNIONS	2.2	11.5	13.9	*10.0	*20.5	10.3	30.7	51.3	40.9	64.6
BURSITIS, UNCLASSIFIED	8.7	34.0	38.4	52.6	*14.3	11.0	49.6	50.6	49.3	52.3
SEBACEOUS SKIN CYST	5.3	*5.3	*11.2	*10.0	*13.3	3.0	*4.2	*6.1	*9.9	*1.4
TROUBLE WITH ACNE	23.6	*2.8	*3.2	*3.1	*3.3	31.6	7.1	*2.3	*4.1	*-
PSORIASIS	5.4	20.2	14.5	21.6	*2.5	8.7	14.2	14.5	*10.2	*20.0
DERMATITIS	29.3	21.8	22.4	25.3	*17.6	43.6	44.6	39.4	38.6	40.2
TROUBLE WITH DRY (ITCHING) SKIN, UNCLASSIFIED	17.1	29.6	40.4	36.6	46.7	20.5	36.1	35.0	30.8	40.5
TROUBLE WITH INGROWN NAILS	16.0	32.1	40.1	40.9	38.8	16.4	29.7	56.6	52.9	61.4
TROUBLE WITH CORNS AND CALLUSES	6.9	25.3	19.8	21.0	*17.8	12.2	32.5	51.6	46.5	58.1
IMPAIRMENTS										
VISUAL IMPAIRMENT	29.5	52.7	91.6	78.4	113.7	12.9	38.0	75.5	48.0	110.7
COLOR BLINDNESS	16.6	33.0	28.3	35.6	*16.0	2.0	7.9	*8.0	*9.5	*6.2
CATARACTS	2.5	12.3	129.6	79.0	214.7	2.5	21.9	192.4	140.0	259.2
GLAUCOMA	2.0	13.2	48.0	32.3	74.3	*1.8	10.4	58.2	34.7	88.2
HEARING IMPAIRMENT	43.2	191.9	354.1	298.8	447.1	30.4	87.5	238.0	183.3	307.8
TINNITUS	11.6	60.4	113.8	118.1	106.6	9.8	33.2	73.1	67.7	79.9
SPEECH IMPAIRMENT	19.2	11.0	13.7	*14.2	*13.1	8.3	7.0	*5.6	*8.6	*1.8
ABSENCE OF EXTREMITIES (EXCLUDES TIPS OF FINGERS OR TOES ONLY)	4.2	14.0	34.7	34.1	35.7	*0.9	*2.0	*5.7	*3.3	*8.9
PARALYSIS OF EXTREMITIES, COMPLETE OR PARTIAL	3.1	11.3	19.2	*14.1	*27.8	2.5	6.9	12.0	*9.6	*15.1
DEFORMITY OR ORTHOPEDIC IMPAIRMENT	93.5	166.7	153.7	144.4	169.3	101.3	173.2	174.1	161.8	189.9
BACK	55.2	94.5	83.3	88.6	74.3	71.5	109.6	93.1	90.9	95.8
UPPER EXTREMITIES	12.5	29.5	22.7	*11.0	42.5	8.4	21.8	30.3	25.4	36.6
LOWER EXTREMITIES	40.5	68.4	67.6	66.1	70.1	33.0	71.5	84.9	66.7	108.0
SELECTED DIGESTIVE CONDITIONS										
ULCER	11.3	27.4	28.5	27.1	*30.9	13.3	23.3	33.8	42.8	22.3
HERNIA OF ABDOMINAL CAVITY	7.8	31.2	55.1	54.7	55.6	5.8	31.3	71.0	70.0	72.3
GASTRITIS OR DUODENITIS	7.9	18.8	15.7	*13.4	*19.3	10.5	16.5	37.4	39.3	34.7
FREQUENT INDIGESTION	20.5	42.8	47.2	44.6	51.5	18.9	39.0	42.8	41.0	45.3
ENTERITIS OR COLITIS	3.7	*5.9	*4.9	*4.6	*5.6	6.7	19.8	20.4	18.9	22.3
SPASTIC COLON	2.0	*3.5	*8.0	*7.8	*8.5	8.5	21.0	21.5	22.3	20.5
DIVERTICULA OF INTESTINES	*1.6	15.5	23.4	22.3	*25.3	*1.2	19.3	39.6	38.7	40.7
FREQUENT CONSTIPATION	4.3	6.8	31.1	*13.8	60.2	15.1	17.3	71.5	47.3	102.2
SELECTED CONDITIONS OF THE GENITOURINARY, NERVOUS, ENDOCRINE, METABOLIC, AND BLOOD AND BLOOD-FORMING SYSTEMS										
GOITER OR OTHER DISORDERS OF THE THYROID	2.4	7.8	22.0	*13.1	36.9	14.6	50.5	66.7	74.8	56.2
DIABETES	7.3	63.3	107.3	102.4	115.6	8.9	63.0	96.9	101.0	91.8
ANEMIAS	6.0	*4.5	*11.4	*7.3	*18.5	29.3	29.9	26.8	24.3	30.1
EPILEPSY	5.7	*5.6	*8.0	*5.5	*12.0	5.3	*3.8	*4.0	*6.2	*1.3
MIGRAINE HEADACHE	22.0	24.2	12.7	*17.1	*5.2	67.1	78.9	28.2	29.9	26.2
NEURALGIA OR NEURITIS, UNSPECIFIED	*0.2	*2.0	*7.3	*4.4	*12.2	*1.6	*5.4	*6.6	*7.1	*6.0
KIDNEY TROUBLE	5.3	16.3	23.2	*16.1	35.1	16.6	18.0	21.9	*13.5	32.6
BLADDER DISORDERS	2.8	*5.4	22.3	*15.4	33.8	15.9	27.7	52.1	52.8	51.3
DISEASES OF PROSTATE	3.5	28.3	126.5	105.8	161.2	NA	NA	NA	NA	NA
DISEASE OF FEMALE GENITAL ORGANS	NA	NA	NA	NA	NA	39.1	51.1	13.3	16.4	*9.2

TABLE A4.5 (CONTINUED)

NUMBER OF SELECTED REPORTED CHRONIC CONDITIONS PER 1,000 PERSONS, BY SEX AND AGE: UNITED STATES, 1994

	NUMBER OF CHRONIC CONDITIONS PER 1,000 PERSONS									
	MALE					FEMALE				
			65 YEARS AND OVER					65 YEARS AND OVER		
TYPE OF CHRONIC CONDITION	UNDER 45 YEARS	45-64 YEARS	TOTAL	65-74 YEARS	75 YEARS AND OVER	UNDER 45 YEARS	45-64 YEARS	TOTAL	65-74 YEARS	75 YEARS AND OVER
SELECTED CIRCULATORY CONDITIONS										
RHEUMATIC FEVER WITH OR WITHOUT HEART DISEASE	2.9	8.5	*10.8	*12.5	*7.9	7.7	16.0	19.8	23.6	*15.2
HEART DISEASE	27.0	162.0	360.5	319.3	429.9	33.1	111.0	299.4	250.8	361.4
ISCHEMIC HEART DISEASE	3.8	81.9	191.8	183.4	205.8	*1.3	32.5	123.3	94.5	160.1
HEART RHYTHM DISORDERS	16.5	41.8	78.8	63.7	104.1	25.8	53.1	96.2	83.1	112.8
TACHYCARDIA OR RAPID HEART	3.0	14.4	27.4	27.1	*27.8	4.8	16.3	38.7	29.0	51.2
HEART MURMURS	11.5	15.8	15.2	*15.3	*14.9	18.5	29.0	25.3	21.8	29.8
OTHER AND UNSPECIFIED HEART RHYTHM DISORDERS	2.0	11.6	36.3	21.3	61.4	2.5	7.7	32.1	32.3	31.8
OTHER SELECTED DISEASES OF HEART, EXCLUDING HYPERTENSION	6.8	38.3	89.9	72.1	119.7	6.0	25.4	80.0	73.3	88.7
HIGH BLOOD PRESSURE (HYPERTENSION)	31.9	220.0	319.5	307.7	339.2	32.4	224.5	395.8	378.7	417.5
CEREBROVASCULAR DISEASE	*1.3	20.4	53.1	39.6	75.9	1.9	16.2	60.5	41.6	84.4
HARDENING OF THE ARTERIES	*0.4	14.0	69.1	47.2	105.8	*-	8.4	41.3	30.7	55.1
VARICOSE VEINS OF LOWER EXTREMITIES	3.7	17.8	42.3	32.5	58.5	23.3	81.0	97.9	109.0	83.8
HEMORRHOIDS	19.1	68.7	56.9	51.0	66.6	29.0	55.8	65.1	70.2	58.6
SELECTED RESPIRATORY CONDITIONS										
CHRONIC BRONCHITIS	43.6	43.8	51.5	41.7	68.0	56.5	82.7	67.0	79.0	51.7
ASTHMA	57.1	32.3	50.9	39.3	70.3	60.0	68.0	50.2	62.8	34.1
HAY FEVER OR ALLERGIC RHINITIS WITHOUT ASTHMA	98.0	107.3	71.1	79.6	56.6	99.2	133.4	86.3	92.2	78.8
CHRONIC SINUSITIS	101.9	147.5	116.5	118.2	113.9	135.5	210.2	175.7	175.5	176.1
DEVIATED NASAL SEPTUM	4.3	14.5	16.3	22.3	*6.2	6.8	12.3	*8.2	*11.3	*4.3
CHRONIC DISEASE OF TONSILS OR ADENOIDS	11.7	*1.6	*-	*-	*-	19.3	*4.2	*0.7	*1.2	*-
EMPHYSEMA	*1.2	10.3	67.9	59.9	81.3	*0.1	9.5	29.6	36.7	20.4

NA=NOT APPLICABLE

* FIGURE DOES NOT MEET STANDARD OF RELIABILITY OR PRECISION.

- QUANTITY ZERO.

Source: Data are based on household interviews of the civilian noninstitutionalized population. P.F. Adams, M.A. Marano, "Current Estimates from the National Health Interview Survey, 1994," Vital Health Stat 10, 193 (1995): 83-4. National Center for Health Statistics.

TABLE A4.6

SERUM CHOLESTEROL LEVELS AMONG PERSONS 20 YEARS OF AGE AND OVER, IN THE UNITED STATES BY SEX, AGE, RACE, AND HISPANIC ORIGIN: 1960–62, 1971–74, 1976–80, AND 1988–91

(DATA ARE BASED ON PHYSICAL EXAMINATIONS OF A SAMPLE OF THE CIVILIAN NONINSTITUTIONALIZED POPULATION).

SEX, AGE, RACE, AND HISPANIC ORIGIN[1]	PERCENT OF POPULATION WITH HIGH SERUM CHOLESTEROL				MEAN SERUM CHOLESTEROL LEVEL, MG/DL			
	1988-91	1976-80[2]	1971-74	1960-62	1988-91	1976-80[2]	1971-74	1960-62
20-74 YEARS, AGE ADJUSTED								
BOTH SEXES	19.5	26.3	27.2	31.8	205	213	214	220
MALE	18.8	24.6	25.8	28.7	204	211	213	217
FEMALE	20.0	27.6	28.2	34.5	205	214	215	222
WHITE MALE	19.1	24.6	25.9	29.4	205	211	213	218
WHITE FEMALE	20.2	28.0	28.1	35.1	205	214	215	223
BLACK MALE	16.1	24.1	25.1	24.5	200	208	212	210
BLACK FEMALE	19.7	24.9	29.2	30.7	203	213	217	216
WHITE, NON-HISPANIC MALE	18.8	24.7	NA	NA	205	211	NA	NA
WHITE, NON-HISPANIC FEMALE	20.1	28.3	NA	NA	205	214	NA	NA
BLACK, NON-HISPANIC MALE	16.3	24.0	NA	NA	201	208	NA	NA
BLACK, NON-HISPANIC FEMALE	19.7	24.9	NA	NA	204	214	NA	NA
MEXICAN-AMERICAN MALE	19.9	18.8	NA	NA	206	207	NA	NA
MEXICAN-AMERICAN FEMALE	19.8	20.0	NA	NA	205	207	NA	NA
20-74 YEARS, CRUDE								
BOTH SEXES	19.4	26.8	28.2	33.6	205	213	216	222
MALE	18.8	24.9	26.8	30.7	204	211	214	220
FEMALE	20.0	28.5	29.6	36.3	205	215	217	225
WHITE MALE	19.2	25.0	26.9	31.4	205	211	215	221
WHITE FEMALE	20.7	29.2	29.8	37.5	206	216	217	227
BLACK MALE	14.7	23.9	25.1	26.7	198	208	212	214
BLACK FEMALE	16.8	23.7	28.8	29.9	200	212	216	216
WHITE, NON-HISPANIC MALE	19.3	25.1	NA	NA	206	211	NA	NA
WHITE, NON-HISPANIC FEMALE	21.0	29.8	NA	NA	206	216	NA	NA
BLACK, NON-HISPANIC FEMALE	14.9	23.7	NA	NA	198	208	NA	NA
BLACK, NON-HISPANIC FEMALE	17.0	23.7	NA	NA	200	212	NA	NA
MEXICAN-AMERICAN MALE	16.9	16.6	NA	NA	201	203	NA	NA
MEXICAN-AMERICAN FEMALE	15.7	16.5	NA	NA	199	202	NA	NA
MALE								
20-34 YEARS	9.1	11.9	12.4	15.1	188	192	194	198
35-44 YEARS	19.9	27.9	31.8	33.9	207	217	221	227
45-54 YEARS	25.1	36.9	37.5	39.2	217	227	229	231
55-64 YEARS	31.3	36.8	36.2	41.6	222	229	229	233
65-74 YEARS	27.1	31.7	34.7	38.0	217	221	226	230
75 YEARS AND OVER	19.5	NA	NA	NA	205	NA	NA	NA
FEMALE								
20-34 YEARS	8.0	9.8	10.9	12.4	185	189	191	194
35-44 YEARS	10.9	20.7	19.3	23.1	194	207	207	214
45-54 YEARS	25.0	40.5	38.7	46.9	216	232	232	237
55-64 YEARS	40.3	52.9	53.1	70.1	236	249	245	262
65-74 YEARS	44.8	51.6	57.7	68.5	235	246	250	266
75 YEARS AND OVER	39.0	NA	NA	NA	230	NA	NA	NA

NA=NOT AVAILABLE.

[1] THE RACE GROUPS, WHITE AND BLACK, INCLUDE PERSONS OF HISPANIC AND NON-HISPANIC ORIGIN. CONVERSELY, PERSONS OF HISPANIC ORIGIN MAY BE OF ANY RACE.

[2] DATA FOR MEXICAN AMERICANS ARE FOR 1982-84.

Source: National Center for Health Statistics, Health, United States, 1995, (Hyattsville, MD: Public Health Service, 1996), 182.

Notes: High serum cholesterol is defined as greater than or equal to 240 mg/dL (6.20 mmol/L). Risk levels have been defined by the second report of the National Cholesterol Education Program Expert Panel on Detection, Evaluation, and Treatment of High Blood Cholesterol in Adults. National Heart, Lung, and Blood Institute, National Institutes of Health. September 1993. (Summarized in JAMA 269 (23): 3015-23. June 16, 1993.) Some data have been revised and differ from previous editions of Health, United States.

TABLE A4.7

HYPERTENSION AMONG PERSONS 20 YEARS OF AGE AND OVER, IN THE UNITED STATES BY SEX, AGE, RACE, AND HISPANIC ORIGIN: 1960–62, 1971–74, 1976–80, AND 1988–91

(DATA ARE BASED ON PHYSICAL EXAMINATIONS OF A SAMPLE OF THE CIVILIAN NONINSTITUTIONALIZED POPULATION).

SEX, AGE, RACE, AND HISPANIC ORIGIN [1]	PERCENT OF POPULATION			
	1988-91	1976-80 [2]	1971-74	1960-62
20-74 YEARS, AGE ADJUSTED				
BOTH SEXES [3]	23.1	39.0	38.3	36.9
MALE	26.4	44.0	42.4	40.0
FEMALE [3]	19.7	34.0	34.3	33.7
WHITE MALE	25.1	43.5	41.7	39.3
WHITE FEMALE [3]	18.3	32.3	32.4	31.7
BLACK MALE	37.4	48.7	51.8	48.1
BLACK FEMALE [3]	31.0	47.5	50.3	50.8
WHITE, NON-HISPANIC MALE	25.3	43.9	NA	NA
WHITE, NON-HISPANIC FEMALE [3]	18.3	32.1	NA	NA
BLACK, NON-HISPANIC MALE	37.2	48.7	NA	NA
BLACK, NON-HISPANIC FEMALE [3]	31.1	47.6	NA	NA
MEXICAN-AMERICAN MALE	26.7	25.0	NA	NA
MEXICAN-AMERICAN FEMALE [3]	21.0	21.8	NA	NA
20-74 YEARS, CRUDE				
BOTH SEXES [3]	23.0	39.7	39.7	39.0
MALE	25.6	44.0	43.3	41.7
FEMALE [3]	20.5	35.6	36.5	36.6
WHITE MALE	24.7	43.8	42.8	41.0
WHITE FEMALE [3]	19.7	34.2	34.9	34.9
BLACK MALE	33.5	47.4	52.1	50.5
BLACK FEMALE [3]	27.5	46.1	50.2	52.0
WHITE, NON-HISPANIC MALE	25.6	44.3	NA	NA
WHITE, NON-HISPANIC FEMALE [3]	20.1	34.4	NA	NA
BLACK, NON-HISPANIC MALE	33.3	47.5	NA	NA
BLACK, NON-HISPANIC FEMALE [3]	28.1	46.1	NA	NA
MEXICAN-AMERICAN MALE	18.6	18.8	NA	NA
MEXICAN-AMERICAN FEMALE [3]	14.7	16.7	NA	NA
MALE				
20-34 YEARS	9.6	28.9	24.8	22.8
35-44 YEARS	19.9	40.5	39.1	37.7
45-54 YEARS	35.5	53.6	55.0	47.6
55-64 YEARS	46.2	61.8	62.5	60.3
65-74 YEARS	59.5	67.1	67.2	68.8
75 YEARS AND OVER	64.4	NA	NA	NA
FEMALE [3]				
20-34 YEARS	2.4	11.1	11.2	9.3
35-44 YEARS	11.5	28.8	28.2	24.0
45-54 YEARS	22.6	47.1	43.6	43.4
55-64 YEARS	46.6	61.1	62.5	66.4
65-74 YEARS	56.6	71.8	78.3	81.5
75 YEARS AND OVER	77.2	NA	NA	NA

NA=NOT AVAILABLE.

[1] THE RACE GROUPS, WHITE AND BLACK, INCLUDE PERSONS OF HISPANIC AND NON-HISPANIC ORIGIN. CONVERSELY, PERSONS OF HISPANIC ORIGIN MAY BE OF ANY RACE.

[2] DATA FOR MEXICAN AMERICANS ARE FOR 1982-84

[3] EXCLUDES PREGNANT WOMEN.

Source: National Center for Health Statistics. Health, United States, 1995, (Hyattsville, MD: Public Health Service, 1996), 181.

Notes: A person with hypertension is defined by either having elevated blood pressure (systolic pressure of at least 140 mmHg or diastolic pressure of at least 90 mmHg) or taking antihypertensive medication. Percents are based on a single measurement of blood pressure to provide comparable data across the four time periods. In 1976-80, 31.3 percent of persons 20-74 years of age had hypertension, based on the average of three blood pressure measurements, in contrast to 39.7 percent when a single measurement is used. Some data have been revised and differ from previous editions of Health, United States.

TABLE A4.8

OVERWEIGHT PERSONS 20 TO 74 YEARS OF AGE IN THE UNITED STATES BY SEX, RACE, AND HISPANIC ORIGIN: 1960–62, 1971–74, 1976–80, AND 1988–91

SEX, AGE, RACE, AND HISPANIC ORIGIN [1] 20-74 YEARS, AGE ADJUSTED	PERCENT OF POPULATION			
	1988-91	1976-80 [2]	1971-74	1960-62
BOTH SEXES	33.0	25.4	24.9	24.4
MALE	31.9	24.0	23.6	22.9
FEMALE [3]	34.1	26.5	25.9	25.6
WHITE MALE	32.3	24.2	23.8	23.1
WHITE FEMALE [3]	32.6	24.4	24.0	23.5
BLACK MALE	32.9	25.7	24.3	22.2
BLACK FEMALE [3]	49.6	44.3	42.9	41.7
WHITE, NON-HISPANIC MALE	32.4	24.1	NA	NA
WHITE, NON-HISPANIC FEMALE [3]	31.0	23.9	NA	NA
BLACK, NON-HISPANIC MALE	32.9	25.6	NA	NA
BLACK, NON-HISPANIC FEMALE [3]	49.8	44.1	NA	NA
MEXICAN-AMERICAN MALE	39.9	31.0	NA	NA
MEXICAN-AMERICAN FEMALE [3]	48.2	41.4	NA	NA

NA=NOT AVAILABLE

[1] THE RACE GROUPS, WHITE AND BLACK, INCLUDE PERSONS OF HISPANIC AND NON-HISPANIC ORIGIN. CONVERSELY, PERSONS OF HISPANIC ORIGIN MAY BE OF ANY RACE."

[2] DATA FOR MEXICAN AMERICANS ARE FOR 1982-84.

[3] EXCLUDES PREGNANT WOMEN.

Source: Centers for Disease Control and Prevention, National Center for Health Statistics, Division of Health Examination Statistics. Unpublished data.

Notes: Data are based on physical examinations of a sample of the civilian noninstitutionalized population. Overweight is defined for men as body mass index greater than or equal to 27.8 kilograms/meter2/, and for women as body mass index greater than or equal to 27.3 kilograms/meter2/. These cut points were used because they represent the sex-specific 85th percentiles for persons 20-29 years of age in the 1976-80 National Health and Nutrition Examination Survey. Height was measured without shoes; two pounds are deducted from data for 1960-62 to allow for weight of clothing. Some data have been revised and differ from previous editions of Health, United States.

TABLE A4.9

AGE-ADJUSTED PREVALENCE OF CURRENT CIGARETTE SMOKING BY PERSONS 25 YEARS OF AGE AND OVER, BY SEX, RACE, AND EDUCATION: 1974–93

(SELECTED YEARS)

SEX, RACE, AND EDUCATION	PERCENT OF PERSONS 25 YEARS OF AGE AND OVER, AGE ADJUSTED									
	1993	1992	1991	1990	1988	1987	1985	1983	1979	1974
ALL PERSONS [1]	24.8	26.5	26.0	25.6	28.4	29.1	30.2	31.7	33.3	37.1
LESS THAN 12 YEARS	35.8	36.7	37.4	36.7	39.4	40.6	41.0	40.8	41.1	43.8
12 YEARS	28.3	30.7	29.7	29.3	31.8	31.8	32.1	33.6	33.7	36.4
13-15 YEARS	24.5	24.6	24.7	23.5	26.4	27.2	29.7	30.3	33.2	35.8
16 OR MORE YEARS	13.6	15.3	13.9	14.1	16.3	16.7	18.6	20.7	22.8	27.5
ALL MALES [1]	27.2	28.2	28.4	28.3	31.1	31.5	32.9	35.1	37.6	43.0
LESS THAN 12 YEARS	41.0	41.2	42.4	41.8	44.9	45.7	46.0	47.2	48.1	52.4
12 YEARS	30.5	33.3	32.9	33.2	35.2	35.2	35.6	37.4	39.1	42.6
13-15 YEARS	27.4	26.1	27.2	25.9	29.0	28.4	33.0	33.0	36.5	41.6
16 OR MORE YEARS	14.6	15.8	14.8	14.6	17.2	17.3	19.7	21.8	23.1	28.6
WHITE MALES [1]	26.3	27.6	27.3	27.7	30.1	30.6	31.9	34.5	36.9	41.9
LESS THAN 12 YEARS	39.7	41.4	41.8	41.7	44.8	45.3	45.2	47.9	48.0	51.6
12 YEARS	29.7	32.9	32.4	33.0	34.2	34.6	34.8	37.1	38.6	42.2
13-15 YEARS	26.9	25.9	26.0	25.4	28.2	28.0	32.3	32.6	36.4	41.4
16 OR MORE YEARS	14.1	15.0	14.7	14.5	17.1	17.4	19.2	21.1	22.8	28.1
BLACK MALES [1]	36.0	35.3	38.8	34.5	40.3	41.9	42.5	42.8	44.9	53.8
LESS THAN 12 YEARS	47.2	44.5	47.8	41.4	45.3	49.4	51.1	46.0	50.1	58.3
12 YEARS	36.4	38.7	39.6	37.4	48.3	43.6	41.9	47.2	48.4	*51.2
13-15 YEARS	30.1	27.0	32.7	28.3	34.8	32.4	42.3	44.7	39.3	*45.7
16 OR MORE YEARS	*16.0	*26.9	18.3	20.6	21.5	20.9	*32.0	*31.3	*37.9	*41.8
ALL FEMALES [1]	22.7	24.8	23.9	23.2	25.9	26.9	27.8	28.8	29.6	32.2
LESS THAN 12 YEARS	31.0	32.4	33.0	32.1	34.5	36.1	36.7	35.3	35.0	36.8
12 YEARS	26.7	28.7	27.1	26.3	29.1	29.2	29.6	30.9	29.9	32.5
13-15 YEARS	21.8	23.3	22.5	21.1	24.1	26.0	26.7	27.5	30.0	30.2
16 OR MORE YEARS	12.4	14.6	12.8	13.6	15.3	16.1	17.4	19.2	22.5	26.1
WHITE FEMALES [1]	23.1	25.1	24.0	23.6	25.9	27.0	27.6	28.8	29.8	31.9
LESS THAN 12 YEARS	31.7	33.1	33.7	33.6	35.2	37.0	37.1	35.5	36.1	37.0
12 YEARS	27.6	29.5	27.5	26.8	29.3	29.4	29.4	30.9	29.9	32.1
13-15 YEARS	21.9	23.6	22.3	21.4	23.8	26.2	27.1	28.0	30.6	30.5
16 OR MORE YEARS	12.5	14.2	13.3	13.7	15.1	16.4	16.8	18.9	21.9	25.8
BLACK FEMALES [1]	22.2	26.8	25.5	22.6	28.2	28.6	32.1	31.8	30.6	35.9
LESS THAN 12 YEARS	29.8	33.2	33.3	26.8	33.9	35.0	39.2	36.9	31.9	36.4
12 YEARS	23.9	25.9	26.0	24.0	30.1	28.1	32.3	35.2	33.0	41.9
13-15 YEARS	22.7	27.0	24.8	23.1	26.8	27.2	23.7	26.5	*28.8	33.2
16 OR MORE YEARS	*13.3	*25.8	14.4	16.9	22.2	19.5	27.5	*38.7	*43.4	*35.2

[1] INCLUDES UNKNOWN EDUCATION.

* THESE AGE-ADJUSTED PERCENTS SHOULD BE CONSIDERED UNRELIABLE BECAUSE OF SMALL SAMPLE SIZE. FOR AGE GROUPS WHERE PERCENT SMOKING WAS 0 OR 100, THE AGE-ADJUSTMENT 'PROCEDURE WAS MODIFIED TO SUBSTITUTE THE PERCENT FROM THE NEXT LOWER EDUCATION GROUP.

Sources: Data computed by the Centers for Disease Control and Prevention, National Center for Health Statistics, Division of Health and Utilization Analysis from data compiled by the Division of Health Interview Statistics.

Notes: Data are based on household interviews of a sample of the civilian noninstitutionalized population. Estimates for 1992 and beyond are not strictly comparable with those for earlier Years, and estimates for 1992 and 1993 are not strictly comparable with each other due to a change in the definition of current smoker in 1992 and the use of a split sample in 1992.

TABLE A4.10

USE OF SELECTED SUBSTANCES IN THE PAST MONTH IN THE UNITED STATES BY PERSONS 12 YEARS OF AGE AND OVER, BY AGE, SEX, RACE, AND HISPANIC ORIGIN: 1974–94

(SELECTED YEARS)

SUBSTANCE, AGE, SEX, RACE, AND HISPANIC ORIGIN	PERCENT OF POPULATION											
	1994	1993	1992	1991	1990	1988	1985	1982	1979	1977	1976	1974
CIGARETTES												
12-17 YEARS	10	10	10	11	12	12	15	15	-1	22	23	25
12-13 YEARS	3	3	2	3	2	3	6	*3	-1	10	11	13
14-15 YEARS	10	9	10	9	14	11	14	10	-1	22	20	25
16-17 YEARS	17	18	18	21	18	20	25	30	-1	35	39	38
12-17 YEARS												
MALE	10	9	10	12	12	12	16	16	-1	23	21	27
FEMALE	10	10	10	10	11	11	15	13	-1	22	26	24
WHITE, NON-HISPANIC	11	11	12	13	14	14	17	NA	NA	NA	NA	NA
BLACK, NON-HISPANIC	8	4	3	4	4	5	9	NA	NA	NA	NA	NA
HISPANIC	6	8	7	9	11	8	11	NA	NA	NA	NA	NA
ALCOHOL 2												
12 YEARS AND OVER	53	50	48	51	51	53	58	55	60	54	52	54
12-17 YEARS	16	18	16	20	25	25	31	27	37	31	32	34
12-13 YEARS	4	6	4	7	8	7	11	10	20	13	19	19
14-15 YEARS	22	17	15	19	26	23	34	23	36	28	31	32
16-17 YEARS	24	33	30	35	38	42	46	45	55	52	47	51
18-25 YEARS	64	59	59	64	63	65	71	68	76	70	69	69
26-34 YEARS	64	63	61	62	63	64	69	71	70	70	68	68
35 YEARS AND OVER	53	49	46	49	49	52	56	52	58	50	52	49
12-17 YEARS												
MALE	14	18	17	22	25	27	33	27	39	37	36	39
FEMALE	19	18	15	18	24	23	29	27	36	25	29	29
WHITE, NON-HISPANIC	17	19	17	20	28	27	34	NA	NA	NA	NA	NA
BLACK, NON-HISPANIC	11	13	13	20	15	16	22	NA	NA	NA	NA	NA
HISPANIC	17	18	16	23	19	25	21	NA	NA	NA	NA	NA
18-25 YEARS												
MALE	70	65	66	70	74	75	78	75	84	82	79	NA
FEMALE	58	54	53	58	53	57	64	61	68	59	58	NA
WHITE, NON-HISPANIC	71	65	63	67	66	69	75	NA	NA	NA	NA	NA
BLACK, NON-HISPANIC	40	45	51	56	59	50	57	NA	NA	NA	NA	NA
HISPANIC	53	50	53	53	57	61	60	NA	NA	NA	NA	NA
MARIJUANA												
12 YEARS AND OVER	5	4	4	5	5	6	9	11	13	10	9	8
12-17 YEARS	7	5	4	4	5	6	12	12	17	17	12	12
12-13 YEARS	2	1	1	*	*	1	*3	*2	4	*4	*3	*2
14-15 YEARS	11	4	4	4	5	5	11	8	17	16	13	12
16-17 YEARS	9	11	8	9	10	12	21	23	28	30	21	20
18-25 YEARS	12	11	11	13	13	15	22	27	35	27	25	25
26-34 YEARS	6	7	8	7	9	11	17	17	17	12	11	8
35 YEARS AND OVER	2	2	2	2	2	1	2	3	2	1	1	*
12-17 YEARS												
MALE	8	6	5	5	6	6	13	13	19	20	14	12
FEMALE	7	4	3	4	4	7	11	10	14	13	11	11
WHITE, NON-HISPANIC	7	5	4	4	6	7	13	NA	NA	NA	NA	NA
BLACK, NON-HISPANIC	8	6	3	4	3	4	9	NA	NA	NA	NA	NA
HISPANIC	8	7	5	5	4	5	9	NA	NA	NA	NA	NA

TABLE A4.10 (CONTINUED)

USE OF SELECTED SUBSTANCES IN THE PAST MONTH IN THE UNITED STATES BY PERSONS 12 YEARS OF AGE AND OVER, BY AGE, SEX, RACE, AND HISPANIC ORIGIN: 1974–94 (SELECTED YEARS)

SUBSTANCE, AGE, SEX, RACE, AND HISPANIC ORIGIN	PERCENT OF POPULATION											
	1994	1993	1992	1991	1990	1988	1985	1982	1979	1977	1976	1974
MARIJUANA (CONTINUED)												
18-25 YEARS												
MALE	15	17	15	16	17	20	27	36	45	35	31	NA
FEMALE	10	6	8	10	9	11	17	19	26	20	19	NA
WHITE, NON-HISPANIC	14	13	12	14	14	16	22	NA	NA	NA	NA	NA
BLACK, NON-HISPANIC	13	9	11	15	13	15	24	NA	NA	NA	NA	NA
HISPANIC	7	8	8	9	8	14	16	NA	NA	NA	NA	NA
COCAINE												
12 YEARS AND OVER	0.6	0.6	0.6	0.9	0.8	1.5	2.7	2.3	2.4	1.0	0.7	0.2
12-17 YEARS	0.4	0.4	0.3	0.4	0.6	1.1	1.4	1.6	1.4	*0.8	*1.0	*1.0
18-25 YEARS	1.0	1.5	1.8	2.0	2.2	4.5	7.5	6.8	9.3	3.7	2.0	3.1
26-34 YEARS	1.5	1.0	1.4	1.8	1.7	2.6	5.9	3.3	NA	NA	NA	NA
35 YEARS AND OVER	0.3	0.4	0.2	0.5	0.2	0.4	0.4	0.5	NA	NA	NA	NA
12-17 YEARS												
MALE	*	0.4	0.2	0.5	0.7	0.9	1.8	1.8	NA	NA	NA	NA
FEMALE	0.3	0.4	0.3	0.3	0.4	1.4	1.0	*1.5	NA	NA	NA	NA
WHITE, NON-HISPANIC	0.5	0.3	0.1	*0.3	0.4	1.3	1.4	NA	NA	NA	NA	NA
BLACK, NON-HISPANIC	0.0	0.3	0.2	*0.5	0.7	0.5	1.2	NA	NA	NA	NA	NA
HISPANIC	0.6	1.0	1.2	1.3	1.9	1.3	2.4	NA	NA	NA	NA	NA
18-25 YEARS												
MALE	1.5	1.7	2.9	2.8	2.8	6.0	8.8	9.1	NA	NA	NA	NA
FEMALE	0.5	1.4	0.8	1.3	1.6	3.0	6.3	4.7	NA	NA	NA	NA
WHITE, NON-HISPANIC	0.9	1.6	2.0	1.7	1.9	4.1	8.0	NA	NA	NA	NA	NA
BLACK, NON-HISPANIC	1.8	1.3	1.4	3.1	3.6	4.3	6.2	NA	NA	NA	NA	NA
HISPANIC	1.3	2.1	1.8	2.7	3.1	6.7	6.3	NA	NA	NA	NA	NA

NA=NOT AVAILABLE

1 DATA NOT COMPARABLE BECAUSE DEFINITIONS DIFFER.

2 IN SURVEYS CONDUCTED IN 1979 AND LATER YEARS, PRIVATE ANSWER SHEETS WERE USED FOR ALCOHOL QUESTIONS; PRIOR TO 1979 RESPONDENTS ANSWERED QUESTIONS ALOUD.

* RELATIVE STANDARD ERROR GREATER THAN 30 PERCENT. ESTIMATES WITH RELATIVE STANDARD ERROR GREATER THAN 50 PERCENT ARE NOT SHOWN.

Sources: P. M. Fishburne, H.I. Abelson, and I. Cisn, "National Household Survey on Drug Abuse: Main Findings," National Institute on Drug Abuse DHHS Pub No. (ADM) 80-976 (1979). Alcohol, Drug Abuse, and Mental Health Administration, Washington, D.C., 1980; J.D. Miller, et. Al.

Notes: Data are based on household interviews of a sample of the population 12 years of age and over in the coterminous United States. Estimates of the use of substances from the National Household Survey on Drug Abuse and the Monitoring the Future Study differ because of different methodologies, sampling frames, and tabulation categories.

TABLE A4.11

METHODS OF CONTRACEPTION RELIED ON BY WOMEN 15-44 YEARS OF AGE IN THE UNITED STATES,
BY RACE AND AGE: 1982, 1988, AND 1990

METHOD OF CONTRACEPTION AND AGE	ALL RACES			WHITE			BLACK		
	1990	1988	1982	1990	1988	1982	1990	1988	1982
NUMBER OF WOMEN IN THOUSANDS									
15-44 YEARS	58,381	57,900	54,099	47,342	47,076	45,367	7,846	7,679	6,985
15-19 YEARS	8,483	9,179	9,521	6,533	7,313	7,815	1,344	1,409	1,416
20-24 YEARS	9,154	9,413	10,629	7,344	7,401	8,855	1,327	1,364	1,472
25-34 YEARS	21,728	21,726	19,644	17,501	17,682	16,485	2,923	2,865	2,479
35-44 YEARS	19,016	17,582	14,305	15,964	14,681	12,212	2,251	2,041	1,618
PRECENT OF WOMEN USING CONTRACEPTIVES									
ALL METHODS									
15-44 YEARS	59.3	60.3	55.7	59.9	61.8	56.7	58.0	56.7	52.0
15-19 YEARS	31.5	32.1	24.2	29.7	32.2	23.4	42.9	35.1	30.0
20-24 YEARS	55.3	59.0	55.8	55.6	60.2	56.6	58.4	61.1	52.5
25-34 YEARS	63.2	66.3	66.7	63.2	67.7	67.7	65.7	63.8	64.0
35-44 YEARS	68.9	68.3	61.6	70.2	70.2	63.1	57.0	58.9	52.3
FEMALE STERILIZATION									
15-44 YEARS	29.5	27.5	23.2	27.7	26.1	22.1	41.8	38.1	30.0
15-19 YEARS	NA	*1.5	NA	NA	*1.6	NA	NA	*1.6	NA
20-24 YEARS	8.0	4.6	4.5	8.1	3.9	*3.8	*9.3	9.1	9.8
25-34 YEARS	25.6	25.0	22.1	22.7	23.2	20.2	43.3	39.9	33.5
35-44 YEARS	47.8	47.6	43.5	44.5	44.7	41.9	78.1	70.5	56.8
MALE STERILIZATION									
15-44 YEARS	12.6	11.7	10.9	14.8	13.6	12.2	*1.5	*0.9	*1.4
15-19 YEARS	NA	*0.2	*0.4	NA	*0.3	*0.5	NA	NA	NA
20-24 YEARS	*1.8	*1.8	*3.6	*2.2	*2.3	*4.2	NA	NA	*0.5
25-34 YEARS	9.3	10.2	10.1	10.8	11.7	11.3	*2.7	*1.1	*1.4
35-44 YEARS	22.9	20.8	19.9	25.7	23.7	21.6	*1.5	*1.5	*3.1
BIRTH CONTROL PILL									
15-44 YEARS	28.5	30.7	28.0	28.8	29.8	26.7	27.9	38.0	38.0
15-19 YEARS	52.0	58.8	63.9	53.2	55.9	62.1	42.6	74.2	70.8
20-24 YEARS	55.4	68.2	55.1	57.1	67.9	53.5	51.7	70.3	65.0
25-34 YEARS	34.7	32.6	25.7	36.3	32.4	24.8	30.0	35.7	33.7
35-44 YEARS	6.8	4.3	3.7	7.0	4.5	3.7	*3.7	*4.2	*5.1
INTRAUTERINE DEVICE									
15-44 YEARS	1.4	2.0	7.1	1.4	1.8	6.9	*1.4	3.1	9.1
15-19 YEARS	NA	NA	*1.3	NA	NA	*0.5	NA	NA	*4.9
20-24 YEARS	*0.8	*0.3	4.2	*0.9	*0.3	*3.5	NA	*0.9	*6.2
25-34 YEARS	*0.7	2.1	9.7	*0.6	1.7	9.4	*1.6	*4.1	13.0
35-44 YEARS	2.6	3.1	6.9	2.5	3.0	7.0	*2.4	*4.3	*6.5
DIAPHRAGM									
15-44 YEARS	2.8	5.7	8.1	2.8	6.2	8.8	*1.6	1.9	3.5
15-19 YEARS	NA	*1.0	*6.0	NA	*1.3	*7.1	NA	NA	*1.8
20-24 YEARS	*0.6	3.7	10.2	*0.7	4.1	11.3	*0.5	*1.6	*2.8
25-34 YEARS	3.6	7.3	10.3	3.9	8.0	11.3	*2.1	*1.7	*3.0
35-44 YEARS	3.5	6.0	4.0	2.9	6.2	3.8	*2.1	*3.3	*6.0
CONDOM									
15-44 YEARS	17.7	14.6	12.0	17.0	14.9	12.7	19.2	10.3	6.2
15-19 YEARS	44.0	32.8	20.8	43.3	34.2	22.6	52.4	22.7	*12.6
20-24 YEARS	25.3	14.5	10.7	23.1	15.8	11.4	29.9	9.6	*6.4
25-34 YEARS	17.3	13.7	11.4	17.1	14.0	12.0	13.2	9.4	5.3
35-44 YEARS	9.8	11.2	11.3	10.3	11.3	12.0	6.7	7.0	*4.5

NA=NOT AVAILABLE
* RELATIVE STANDARD ERROR GREATER THAN 30 PERCENT.

Sources: Data are based on household interviews of samples of women in the childbearing ages. Centers for Disease Control and Prevention, National Center for Health Statistics, Division of Vital Statistics. Data from the National Survey of Family Growth.

TABLE A4.12

ABORTIONS IN THE UNITED STATES - NUMBER, RATE, AND RATIO, BY RACE: 1975–92

	ALL RACES				WHITE				BLACK AND OTHER			
		ABORTIONS				ABORTIONS				ABORTIONS		
YEAR	WOMEN 15-44 YEARS OLD (1,000)	NUMBER (1,000)	RATE PER 1,000 WOMEN	RATIO PER 1,000 LIVE BIRTHS [1]	WOMEN 15-44 YEARS OLD (1,000)	NUMBER (1,000)	RATE PER 1,000 WOMEN	RATIO PER 1,000 LIVE BIRTHS [1]	WOMEN 15-44 YEARS OLD (1,000)	NUMBER (1,000)	RATE PER 1,000 WOMEN	RATIO PER 1,000 LIVE BIRTHS [1]
1992	59,020	1,529	25.9	379	NA	NA	NA	NA	NA	NA	NA	NA
1991	59,080	1,557	26.3	379	48,406	982	20.3	303	10,674	574	53.8	661
1990 [2]	58,700	1,609	27.4	389	48,224	1,039	21.5	318	10,476	570	54.4	655
1989 [2]	58,365	1,567	26.8	380	48,104	1,006	20.9	309	10,261	561	54.7	650
1988	58,192	1,591	27.3	401	48,325	1,026	21.2	333	9,867	565	57.3	638
1987	57,964	1,559	27.1	405	48,288	1,017	21.1	338	9,676	542	56.0	648
1986 [2]	57,483	1,574	27.4	416	48,010	1,045	21.8	350	9,473	529	55.9	661
1985	56,754	1,589	28.0	422	47,512	1,076	22.6	360	9,242	513	55.5	659
1984	56,061	1,577	28.1	423	47,023	1,087	23.1	366	9,038	491	54.3	646
1983 [2]	55,340	1,575	28.5	436	46,506	1,084	23.3	376	8,834	491	55.5	670
1982	54,679	1,574	28.8	428	46,049	1,095	23.8	373	8,630	479	55.5	646
1981	53,901	1,577	29.3	430	45,494	1,108	24.3	377	8,407	470	55.9	645
1980	53,048	1,554	29.3	428	44,942	1,094	24.3	376	8,106	460	56.5	642
1979	52,016	1,498	28.8	420	44,266	1,062	24.0	373	7,750	435	56.2	625
1975	47,606	1,034	21.7	331	40,857	701	17.2	276	6,749	333	49.3	565

NA=NOT AVAILABLE.

[1] LIVE BIRTHS ARE THOSE WHICH OCCURRED FROM JULY 1 OF YEAR SHOWN THROUGH JUNE 30 OF THE FOLLOWING YEAR (TO MATCH TIME OF CONCEPTION WITH ABORTIONS). BIRTHS ARE CLASSIFIED BY RACE OF CHILD 1972-88, AND BY RACE OF MOTHER AFTER 1988.

[2] TOTAL NUMBERS OF ABORTIONS IN 1983 AND 1986 HAVE BEEN ESTIMATED BY INTERPOLATION; 1989 AND 1990 HAVE BEEN ESTIMATED USING TRENDS IN CENTERS FOR DISEASE CONTROL DATA.

Source: U.S. Bureau of the Census, Statistical Abstract of the United States 1996. Table No. 115.

TABLE 4.13

SELECTED NOTIFIABLE SEXUALLY TRANSMITTED DISEASE RATES IN THE UNITED STATES, BY DISEASE: 1950–94
(SELECTED YEARS)

DISEASE	1994	1993	1992	1991	1990	1989	1988	1985	1980	1970	1960	1950
CASES PER 100,000 POPULATION												
SYPHILIS [1]	32.00	39.70	44.20	51.00	54.30	46.60	42.53	28.50	30.51	45.26	68.78	146.02
PRIMARY AND SECONDARY	8.10	10.40	13.30	17.00	20.30	18.60	16.47	11.45	12.06	10.89	9.06	16.73
EARLY LATENT	12.50	16.40	19.60	21.40	22.30	18.40	14.63	9.15	9.00	8.08	10.11	39.71
LATE AND LATE LATENT	10.50	11.60	9.80	10.90	10.40	8.90	11.13	7.77	9.30	24.94	45.91	70.22
CONGENITAL [2]	0.90	1.30	1.50	1.80	1.60	0.73	0.30	0.14	0.12	0.97	2.48	8.97
GONORRHEA [3]	168.40	173.80	196.70	247.10	278.00	297.10	300.30	384.28	444.99	297.22	145.33	192.45
CHANCROID	0.30	0.50	0.70	1.40	1.70	1.90	2.04	0.87	0.35	0.70	0.94	3.34
GRANULOMA INGUINALE	0.00	0.00	0.00	0.00	0.00	0.00	0.00	0.02	0.02	0.06	0.17	1.19
LYMPHOGRANULOMA VENEREUM	0.10	0.10	0.10	0.20	0.10	0.10	0.08	0.10	0.09	0.30	0.47	0.95
NUMBER OF CASES												
SYPHILIS [1]	81,696	101,333	112,816	128,637	135,043	115,067	104,546	67,563	68,832	91,382	122,538	217,558
PRIMARY AND SECONDARY	20,627	26,496	33,962	42,950	50,578	45,826	40,474	27,131	27,204	21,982	16,145	23,939
EARLY LATENT	32,012	41,902	49,903	53,855	55,397	45,394	35,968	21,689	20,297	16,311	18,017	59,256
LATE AND LATE LATENT	26,840	29,675	25,084	27,490	25,750	22,032	27,363	18,414	20,979	50,348	81,798	113,569
CONGENITAL [2]	2,217	3,260	3,889	4,424	3,865	1,837	741	329	277	1,953	4,416	13,377
GONORRHEA [3]	418,068	443,278	501,777	623,009	691,368	733,294	738,160	911,419	1,004,029	600,072	258,933	286,746
CHANCROID	773	1,229	1,885	3,476	4,212	4,697	4,891	2,067	788	1,416	1,680	4,977
GRANULOMA INGUINALE	3	19	6	29	97	7	11	44	51	124	296	1,783
LYMPHOGRANULOMA VENEREUM	235	286	289	471	277	182	194	226	199	612	835	1,427

[1] INCLUDES STAGE OF SYPHILIS NOT STATED.

[2] DATA REPORTED FOR 1989 AND LATER YEARS REFLECT CHANGE IN CASE DEFINITION INTRODUCED IN 1988.

[3] DATA FOR 1994 DO NOT INCLUDE CASES FROM GEORGIA.

Sources: Data are based on reporting by State health departments. Centers for Disease Control and Prevention. Summary of Notifiable Diseases, United States, 1994. Morbidity and Mortality Weekly Report 43(53), Atlanta, Georgia: Public Health Service. 1995; National Center for HIV, STD, and TB Prevention, Division of STD Prevention. Sexually Transmitted Disease Surveillance, 1994. 'Atlanta, Georgia: Public Health Service. Centers for Disease Control and Prevention, 1995.

Note: Rates greater than 0 but less than 0.005 are shown as 0.00. The total resident population was used to calculate all rates except sexually transmitted diseases, for which the civilian resident population was used prior to 1991. Population data from those States where diseases were not notifiable or not available were excluded from rate calculation. Some numbers in this table have been revised and differ from previous editions of Health, United States, by the National Center of Health Statistics

TABLE A4.14

NUMBER AND PERCENT OF PERSONS WITH DISABILITIES IN THE UNITED STATES, BY SEX AND TYPE OF DISABILITY: 1991–92

(NUMBERS IN THOUSANDS)

CHARACTERISTICS	BOTH SEXES		MALES		FEMALES	
	NUMBER	PERCENT DISTRIBUTION	NUMBER	PERCENT DISTRIBUTION	NUMBER	PERCENT DISTRIBUTION
ALL AGES						
TOTAL	251,796	100.0	122,692	100.0	129,104	100.0
WITH A DISABILITY	48,936	19.4	22,916	18.7	26,020	20.2
SEVERE	24,117	9.6	9,929	8.1	14,187	11.0
NOT SEVERE	24,819	9.9	12,987	10.6	11,833	9.2
PERSONS 0–15 YEARS OLD AND OLDER						
TOTAL	56,067	100.0	28,707	100.0	27,360	100.0
WITH A DISABILITY	2,913	5.2	1,876	6.5	1,038	3.8
SEVERE	529	0.9	336	1.2	192	0.7
NOT SEVERE	2,384	4.3	1,540	5.4	846	3.1
PERSONS 15 YEARS AND OVER						
TOTAL	195,729	100.0	93,985	100.0	101,744	100.0
WITH A DISABILITY	46,023	23.5	21,040	22.4	24,982	24.6
SEVERE	23,588	12.1	9,593	10.2	13,995	13.8
NOT SEVERE	22,435	11.5	11,447	12.2	10,987	10.8
WITH A FUNCTIONAL LIMITATION	34,163	17.5	14,774	15.7	19,389	19.1
SEVERE	15,173	7.8	5,558	5.9	9,614	9.5
SEEING WORDS AND LETTERS	9,685	5.0	4,006	4.3	5,679	5.6
UNABLE	1,590	0.8	661	0.7	929	0.9
HEARING NORMAL CONVERSATION	10,928	5.6	6,421	6.8	4,506	4.4
UNABLE	924	0.5	529	0.6	396	0.4
HAVING SPEECH UNDERSTOOD	2,284	1.2	1,316	1.4	968	1.0
UNABLE	237	0.1	141	0.2	95	0.1
LIFTING AND CARRYING 10 LBS	16,205	8.3	5,218	5.6	10,987	10.8
UNABLE	7,734	4.0	2,375	2.5	5,359	5.3
CLIMBING STAIRS WITHOUT RESTING	17,469	8.9	6,465	6.9	11,003	10.8
UNABLE	9,116	4.7	3,277	3.5	5,839	5.7
WALKING 3 CITY BLOCKS	17,319	8.9	6,653	7.1	10,665	10.5
UNABLE	8,972	4.6	3,236	3.4	5,736	5.6
NUMBER OF FUNCTIONAL LIMITATIONS						
1	14,463	7.4	7,099	7.6	7,364	7.2
2	7,093	3.6	3,057	3.3	4,036	4.0
3 OR MORE	12,608	6.4	4,619	4.9	7,989	7.9
NUMBER OF SEVERE FUNCTIONAL LIMITATIONS						
1	6,979	3.6	2,710	2.9	4270	4.2
2	3,956	2.0	1,460	1.6	2496	2.5
3 OR MORE	4,286	2.2	1,422	1.5	2864	2.8
WITH AN ADL LIMITATION	7,919	4.1	3,013	3.2	4907	4.8
NEEDS PERSONAL ASSISTANCE	3,886	2.0	1,481	1.6	2405	2.4
GETTING AROUND INSIDE THE HOME	3,664	1.9	1,376	1.5	2,288	2.3
NEEDS PERSONAL ASSISTANCE	1,706	0.9	698	0.7	1,008	1.0
GETTING IN OR OUT OF BED OR A CHAIR	5,280	2.7	2,006	2.1	3,274	3.2
NEEDS PERSONAL ASSISTANCE	2,022	1.0	796	0.9	1,227	1.2
TAKING BATH OR SHOWER	4,501	2.3	1,550	1.7	2,951	2.9
NEEDS PERSONAL ASSISTANCE	2,718	1.4	1,028	1.1	1,691	1.7
DRESSING	3,234	1.7	1,262	1.3	1,971	1.9
NEEDS PERSONAL ASSISTANCE	2,060	1.1	866	0.9	1,193	1.2
EATING	1,077	0.6	437	0.5	640	0.6
NEEDS PERSONAL ASSISTANCE	487	0.3	226	0.2	261	0.3

TABLE A4.14 (CONTINUED)

NUMBER AND PERCENT OF PERSONS WITH DISABILITIES IN THE UNITED STATES, BY SEX AND TYPE OF DISABILITY: 1991–92

(NUMBERS IN THOUSANDS)

CHARACTERISTICS	BOTH SEXES		MALES		FEMALES	
	NUMBER	PERCENT DISTRIBUTION	NUMBER	PERCENT DISTRIBUTION	NUMBER	PERCENT DISTRIBUTION
NUMBER OF SEVERE FUNCTIONAL LIMITATIONS (CONTINUED)						
USING THE TOILET, INCLUDING GETTING						
TO THE TOILET	2,084	1.1	767	0.8	1,317	1.3
NEEDS PERSONAL ASSISTANCE	1,157	0.6	477	0.5	680	0.7
NUMBER OF ADL LIMITATIONS						
1	3,337	1.7	1,364	1.5	1,973	1.9
2	1,394	0.7	478	0.5	915	0.9
3 OR MORE	3,189	1.6	1,171	1.2	2,018	2.0
NUMBER OF ADL'S FOR WHICH PERSONAL ASSISTANCE NEEDED:						
1	1,490	0.8	505	0.5	985	1.0
2	778	0.4	304	0.3	474	0.5
3 OR MORE	1,618	0.8	672	0.7	944	0.9
WITH AN IADL LIMITATION	11,694	6.0	4,601	4.9	7,093	7.0
NEEDS PERSONAL ASSISTANCE	8,705	4.5	3,145	3.4	5,560	5.5
GOING OUTSIDE OF THE HOME, FOR EXAMPLE						
TO SHOP OR VISIT A DOCTOR'S OFFICE	7,809	4.0	2,759	2.9	5,050	5.0
NEEDS PERSONAL ASSISTANCE	6,011	3.1	2,017	2.2	3,994	3.9
KEEPING TRACK OF MONEY AND BILLS	3,901	2.0	1,621	1.7	2,280	2.2
NEEDS PERSONAL ASSISTANCE	3,425	1.8	1,460	1.6	1,965	1.9
PREPARING MEALS	4,530	2.3	1,699	1.8	2,831	2.8
NEEDS PERSONAL ASSISTANCE	3,685	1.9	1,447	1.5	2,238	2.2
DOING LIGHT HOUSEWORK, SUCH AS						
WASHING DISHES OR SWEEPING A FLOOR	6,313	3.2	2,191	2.3	4,122	4.1
NEEDS PERSONAL ASSISTANCE	4,745	2.4	1,626	1.7	3,119	3.1
USING THE TELEPHONE	3,130	1.6	1,749	1.9	1,381	1.4
UNABLE TO USE	933	0.5	509	0.5	424	0.4
NUMBER OF IADL LIMITATIONS:						
1	5,021	2.6	2,117	2.3	2,904	2.9
2	2,482	1.3	918	1.0	1,564	1.5
3 OR MORE	4,190	2.1	1,567	1.7	2,624	2.6
NUMBER OF IADL'S FOR WHICH PERSONAL ASSISTANCE NEEDED:						
1	3,668	1.9	1,292	1.4	2,375	2.3
2	1,980	1.0	674	0.7	1,306	1.3
3 OR MORE	3,057	1.6	1,178	1.3	1,879	1.8
USES A WHEELCHAIR	1,494	0.8	575	0.6	919	0.9
DOES NOT USE A WHEELCHAIR BUT HAS USED A CANE, CRUTCHES, OR A WALKER						
FOR SIX MONTHS OR LONGER	3,962	2.0	1547	1.7	2,415	2.4
NEEDS PERSONAL ASSISTANCE						
WITH AN ADL OR IADL	9,211	4.7	3,383	3.6	5,828	5.7
WITH A MENTAL OR EMOTIONAL DISABILITY	6,879	3.5	3,534	3.8	3,345	3.3
MENTAL RETARDATION	1,224	0.6	716	0.8	508	0.5

TABLE A4.14 (CONTINUED)

NUMBER AND PERCENT OF PERSONS WITH DISABILITIES IN THE UNITED STATES BY SEX AND TYPE OF DISABILITY: 1991–92

(NUMBERS IN THOUSANDS)

CHARACTERISTICS	BOTH SEXES		MALES		FEMALES	
	NUMBER	PERCENT DISTRIBUTION	NUMBER	PERCENT DISTRIBUTION	NUMBER	PERCENT DISTRIBUTION
PERSONS 16–67 YEARS OLD						
TOTAL	167,899	100.0	82,261	100.0	85,638	100.0
WITH A WORK DISABILITY	19,544	11.6	9,620	11.7	9,924	11.6
PREVENTED FROM WORKING	8,632	5.1	3,922	4.8	4,710	5.5
PERSONS 18 YEARS OLD AND OVER						
TOTAL	192,348	100.0	92,220	100.0	100,128	100.0
WITH A HOUSEWORK DISABILITY	18,088	9.4	7,477	8.1	10,611	10.6
UNABLE TO DO HOUSEWORK	3,591	1.9	1,691	1.8	1,900	1.9

ADL = ACTIVITIES OF DAILY LIVING SUCH AS WASHING, EATING OR DRESSING.

IADL = INSTRUMENTAL ACTIVITIES OF DAILY LIVING SUCH AS DIFFICULTY GOING OUTSIDE OF THE HOME, OR PAYING BILLS.

Source: U.S. Census Bureau, Survey of Income and Program Participation.

TABLE A4.15

HEALTH INSURANCE COVERAGE STATUS AND TYPE OF COVERAGE IN THE UNITED STATES, BY SEX: 1987–1995

(NUMBERS IN THOUSANDS. PERSONS AS OF MARCH OF THE FOLLOWING YEAR.)

YEAR	TOTAL PERSONS	COVERED BY PRIVATE OR GOVERNMENT HEALTH INSURANCE		
		TOTAL	PRIVATE HEALTH INSURANCE	
			TOTAL	GROUP HEALTH
ALL RACES **BOTH SEXES** **NUMBERS**				
1995	264,314	223,733	185,881	161,453
1994 2	262,105	222,387	184,318	159,634
1993 3	259,753	220,040	182,351	148,318
1992 4	256,830	218,189	181,466	148,796
1991	251,447	216,003	181,375	150,077
1990	248,886	214,167	182,135	150,215
1989	246,191	212,807	183,610	151,644
1988	243,685	211,005	182,019	150,940
1987 5	241,187	210,161	182,160	149,739
PERCENTS				
1995	100.0	84.6	70.3	61.1
1994 2	100.0	84.8	70.3	60.9
1993 3	100.0	84.7	70.2	57.1
1992 4	100.0	85	70.7	57.9
1991	100.0	85.9	72.1	59.7
1990	100.0	86.1	73.2	60.4
1989	100.0	86.4	74.6	61.6
1988	100.0	86.6	74.7	61.9
1987 5	100.0	87.1	75.5	62.1

YEAR	COVERED BY PRIVATE OR GOVERNMENT HEALTH INSURANCE-CONTINUED				NOT COVERED
	GOVERNMENT HEALTH INSURANCE				
	TOTAL	MEDICAID	MEDICARE	MILITARY HEALTH CARE[1]	
ALL RACES **BOTH SEXES** **NUMBERS**					
1995	69,776	31,877	34,655	9,375	40,582
1994 2	70,163	31,645	33,901	11,165	39,718
1993 3	68,554	31,749	33,097	9,560	39,713
1992 4	66,244	29,416	33,230	9,510	38,641
1991	63,882	26,880	32,907	9,820	35,445
1990	60,965	24,261	32,260	9,922	34,719
1989	57,382	21,185	31,495	9,870	33,385
1988	56,850	20,728	30,925	10,105	32,680
1987 5	56,282	20,211	30,458	10,542	31,026
PERCENTS					
1995	26.4	12.1	13.1	3.5	15.4
1994 2	26.8	12.1	12.9	4.3	15.2
1993 3	26.4	12.2	12.7	3.7	15.3
1992 4	25.8	11.5	12.9	3.7	15.0
1991	25.4	10.7	13.1	3.9	14.1
1990	24.5	9.7	13.0	4.0	13.9
1989	23.3	8.6	12.8	4.0	13.6
1988	23.3	8.5	12.7	4.1	13.4
1987 5	23.3	8.4	12.6	4.4	12.9

Table A4.15 (Continued)

Health Insurance Coverage Status and Type of Coverage in the United States, by Sex: 1987–1995

(Numbers in thousands. Persons as of March of the following year.)

		Covered by Private or Government Health Insurance		
			Private Health Insurance	
Year	Total Persons	Total	Total	Group Health
ALL RACES **MALE** **NUMBERS**				
1995	129,143	107,496	91,275	80,744
1994 [2]	128,072	106,762	90,438	79,743
1993 [3]	126,914	105,261	89,385	74,192
1992 [4]	125,437	104,300	88,613	74,069
1991	122,528	103,130	88,410	74,666
1990	121,191	102,478	88,828	74,724
1989	119,811	102,134	89,691	75,702
1988	118,474	101,035	88,786	75,316
1987 [5]	117,217	100,707	88,616	74,716
PERCENTS				
1995	100.0	83.2	70.7	62.5
1994 [2]	100.0	83.4	70.6	62.3
1993 [3]	100.0	82.9	70.4	58.5
1992 [4]	100.0	83.1	70.6	59.0
1991	100.0	84.2	72.2	60.9
1990	100.0	84.6	73.3	61.7
1989	100.0	85.2	74.9	63.2
1988	100.0	85.3	74.9	63.6
1987 [5]	100.0	85.9	75.6	63.7

	Covered by Private or Government Health Insurance-Continued				
Year	Government Health Insurance				
	Total	Medicaid	Medicare	Military Health Care[1]	Not Covered
ALL RACES **MALE** **NUMBERS**					
1995	30,666	13,425	14,886	5,038	21,647
1994 [2]	30,894	13,218	14,513	6,032	21,310
1993 [3]	29,705	13,043	14,053	5,052	21,653
1992 [4]	28,645	12,048	14,045	5,035	21,337
1991	27,584	10,808	13,938	5,232	19,398
1990	26,483	9,962	13,680	5,246	18,712
1989	24,895	8,528	13,424	5,216	17,678
1988	24,725	8,192	13,113	5,470	17,439
1987 [5]	24,576	8,251	12,886	5,629	16,510
PERCENTS					
1995	23.7	10.4	11.5	3.9	16.8
1994 [2]	24.1	10.3	11.3	4.7	16.6
1993 [3]	23.4	10.3	11.1	4.0	17.1
1992 [4]	22.8	9.6	11.2	4.0	16.9
1991	22.5	8.8	11.4	4.3	15.8
1990	21.9	8.2	11.3	4.3	15.4
1989	20.8	7.1	11.2	4.4	14.8
1988	20.9	6.9	11.1	4.6	14.7
1987 [5]	21.0	7.0	11.0	4.8	14.1

TABLE A4.15 (CONTINUED)

HEALTH INSURANCE COVERAGE STATUS AND TYPE OF COVERAGE IN THE UNITED STATES, BY SEX: 1987–1995

(NUMBERS IN THOUSANDS. PERSONS AS OF MARCH OF THE FOLLOWING YEAR.)

YEAR	TOTAL PERSONS	COVERED BY PRIVATE OR GOVERNMENT HEALTH INSURANCE		
		TOTAL	PRIVATE HEALTH INSURANCE	
			TOTAL	GROUP HEALTH
ALL RACES **FEMALE** **NUMBERS**				
1995	135,171	116,237	94,606	80,709
1994 [2]	134,033	115,625	93,880	79,891
1993 [3]	132,838	114,779	92,965	74,126
1992 [4]	131,393	113,890	92,853	74,726
1991	128,919	112,873	92,964	75,411
1990	127,695	111,688	93,307	75,491
1989	126,380	110,673	93,919	75,941
1988	125,211	109,970	93,233	75,624
1987 [5]	123,970	109,454	93,544	75,023
PERCENTS				
1995	100.0	86.0	70.0	59.7
1994 [2]	100.0	86.3	70.0	59.6
1993 [3]	100.0	86.4	70.0	55.8
1992 [4]	100.0	86.7	70.7	56.9
1991	100.0	87.6	72.1	58.5
1990	100.0	87.5	73.1	59.1
1989	100.0	87.6	74.3	60.1
1988	100.0	87.8	74.5	60.4
1987 [5]	100.0	88.3	75.5	60.5

YEAR	COVERED BY PRIVATE OR GOVERNMENT HEALTH INSURANCE-CONTINUED				NOT COVERED
	GOVERNMENT HEALTH INSURANCE				
	TOTAL	MEDICAID	MEDICARE	MILITARY HEALTH CARE[1]	
ALL RACES **FEMALE** **NUMBERS**					
1995	39,110	18,452	19,769	4,338	18,934
1994 [2]	39,269	18,428	19,388	5,134	18,408
1993 [3]	38,849	18,705	19,044	4,508	18,060
1992 [4]	37,599	17,368	19,185	4,475	17,503
1991	36,298	16,072	18,969	4,588	16,046
1990	34,481	14,299	18,580	4,676	16,007
1989	32,487	12,657	18,072	4,654	15,707
1988	32,125	12,535	17,812	4,635	15,241
1987 [5]	31,706	11,959	17,571	4,913	14,516
PERCENTS					
1995 [2]	28.9	13.7	14.6	3.2	14.0
1994	29.3	13.7	14.5	3.8	13.7
1993 [3]	29.2	14.1	14.3	3.4	13.6
1992 [4]	28.6	13.2	14.6	3.4	13.3
1991	28.2	12.5	14.7	3.6	12.4
1990	27.0	11.2	14.6	3.7	12.5
1989	25.7	10.0	14.3	3.7	12.4
1988	25.7	10.0	14.2	3.7	12.2
1987 [5]	25.6	9.6	14.2	4.0	11.7

[1] INCLUDES CHAMPUS (COMPREHENSIVE HEALTH AND MEDICAL PLAN FOR UNIFORMED SERVICES), VETERANS, AND MILITARY HEALTH CARE.

[2] HEALTH INSURANCE QUESTIONS WERE REDESIGNED, DECREASES IN ESTIMATES OF GROUP HEALTH AND MILITARY HEALTH CARE COVERAGE MAY BE PARTIALLY DUE TO QUESTIONNAIRE CHANGES. OVERALL COVERAGE ESTIMATES WERE NOT AFFECTED.

[3] DATA COLLECTION METHOD CHANGED FROM PAPER AND PENCIL TO COMPUTER ASSISTED INTERVIEWING.

[4] IMPLEMENTATION OF 1990 CENSUS POPULATION CONTROLS.

[5] IMPLEMENTATION OF A NEW MARCH CPS PROCESSING SYSTEM.

Source: U.S. Bureau of the Census, unpublished March Current Population Survey Data prior to 1989 and Current Population Reports, Series P60 for 1989 forward.

LABOR FORCE AND JOB CHARACTERISTICS

TABLE A5.1

EMPLOYMENT STATUS OF THE CIVILIAN NON-INSTITUTIONAL POPULATION, 1947–1996

(NUMBERS IN THOUSANDS)

YEAR	CIVILIAN NON-INSTITUTIONAL POPULATION	CIVILIAN LABOR FORCE								NOT IN LABOR FORCE
		TOTAL	PERCENT OF POPULATION	EMPLOYED			UNEMPLOYED			
				TOTAL	AGRICULTURE	NON AGRICULTURAL	NUMBER	PERCENT OF LABOR FORCE		
1947	101,827	59,350	58.3	57,038	7,890	49,148	2,311	3.9		42,477
1948	103,068	60,621	58.8	58,343	7,629	50,714	2,276	3.8		42,447
1949	103,994	61,286	58.9	57,651	7,658	49,993	3,637	5.9		42,708
1950	104,995	62,208	59.2	58,918	7,160	51,758	3,288	5.3		42,787
1951	104,621	62,017	59.2	59,961	6,726	53,235	2,055	3.3		42,604
1952	105,231	62,138	59.0	60,250	6,500	53,749	1,883	3.0		43,093
1954	108,321	63,643	58.8	60,109	6,205	53,904	3,532	5.5		44,678
1955	109,683	65,023	59.3	62,170	6,450	55,722	2,852	4.4		44,660
1956	110,954	66,552	60.0	63,799	6,283	57,514	2,750	4.1		44,402
1957	112,265	66,929	59.6	64,071	5,947	58,123	2,859	4.3		45,336
1958	113,727	67,639	59.5	63,036	5,586	57,450	4,602	6.8		46,088
1959	115,329	68,369	59.3	64,630	5,565	59,065	3,740	5.5		46,960
1961	118,771	70,459	59.3	65,746	5,200	60,546	4,714	6.7		48,312
1963	122,416	71,833	58.7	67,762	4,687	63,076	4,070	5.7		50,583
1964	124,485	73,091	58.7	69,305	4,523	64,782	3,786	5.2		51,394
1965	126,513	74,455	58.9	71,088	4,361	66,726	3,366	4.5		52,058
1966	128,058	75,770	59.2	72,895	3,979	68,915	2,875	3.8		52,288
1967	129,874	77,347	59.6	74,372	3,844	70,527	2,975	3.8		52,527
1968	132,028	78,737	59.6	75,920	3,817	72,103	2,817	3.6		53,291
1969	134,335	80,734	60.1	77,902	3,606	74,296	2,832	3.5		53,602
1970	137,085	82,771	60.4	78,678	3,463	75,215	4,093	4.9		54,315
1971	140,216	84,382	60.2	79,367	3,394	75,972	5,016	5.9		55,834
1974	150,120	91,949	61.3	86,794	3,515	83,279	5,156	5.6		58,171
1975	153,153	93,775	61.2	85,846	3,408	82,438	7,929	8.5		59,377
1976	156,150	96,158	61.6	88,752	3,331	85,421	7,406	7.7		59,991
1977	159,033	990,09	62.3	92,017	3,283	88,734	6,991	7.1		60,025
1979	164,863	104,962	63.7	98,824	3,347	95,477	6,137	5.8		59,900
1980	167,745	106,940	63.8	99,303	3,364	95,938	7,637	7.1		60,806
1981	170,130	108,670	63.9	100,397	3,368	97,030	8,273	7.6		61,460
1982	172,271	110,204	64.0	99,526	3,401	96,125	10,678	9.7		62,067
1983	174,215	111,550	64.0	100,834	3,383	97,450	10,717	9.6		62,665
1984	176,383	113,544	64.4	105,005	3,321	101,685	8,539	7.5		62,839
1985	178,206	115,461	64.8	107,150	3,179	103,971	8,312	7.2		62,744
1987	182,753	119,865	65.6	112,440	3,208	109,232	7,425	6.2		62,888
1988	184,613	121,669	65.9	114,968	3,169	111,800	6,701	5.5		62,944
1989	186,393	123,869	66.5	117,342	3,199	114,142	6,528	5.3		62,523
1991	190,925	126,346	66.2	117,718	3,269	114,449	8,628	6.8		64,578
1992	192,805	128,105	66.4	118,492	3,247	115,245	9,613	7.5		64,700
1993	194,838	129,200	66.3	120,259	3,115	117,144	8,940	6.9		65,638
1995	198,584	132,304	66.6	124,900	3,440	121,460	7,404	5.6		66,280
1996	200,591	133,943	66.8	126,708	3,443	123,264	7,236	5.4		66,647
1953 [1]	107,056	63,015	58.9	61,179	6,260	54,919	1,834	2.9		44,041
1960 [1]	117,245	69,628	59.4	65,778	5,458	60,318	3,852	5.5		47,617
1962 [1]	120,153	70,614	58.8	66,702	4,944	61,759	3,911	5.5		49,539
1972 [1]	144,126	87,034	60.4	82,153	3,484	78,669	4,882	5.6		57,091
1973 [1]	147,096	89,429	60.8	85,064	3,470	81,594	4,365	4.9		57,667
1978 [1]	161,910	102,251	63.2	96,048	3,387	92,661	6,202	6.1		59,659
1986 [1]	180,587	117,834	65.3	109,597	3,163	106,434	8,237	7.0		62,752
1990 [2]	189,164	125,840	66.5	118,793	3,223	115,570	7,047	5.6		63,324
1994 [2]	196,814	131,056	66.6	123,060	3,409	119,651	7,996	6.1		65,758

[1] NOT STRICTLY COMPARABLE WITH DATA FOR PRIOR YEARS.

[2] DATA, BEGINNING IN 1994, ARE NOT STRICTLY COMPARABLE WITH DATA FOR 1993 AND PRIOR YEARS BECAUSE OF THE INTRODUCTION OF A MAJOR REDESIGN OF THE CURRENT POPULATION SURVEY (HOUSEHOLD SURVEY) QUESTIONNAIRE AND COLLECTION METHODOLOGY. FOR ADDITIONAL "BEGINNING IN 1990," DATA INCORPORATE 1990 CENSUS-BASED POPULATION CONTROLS, ADJUSTED FOR THE ESTIMATED UNDERCOUNT.

Source: U.S. Bureau of Labor Statistics.

TABLE A5.2

CIVILIAN LABOR FORCE PARTICIPATION RATES IN THE UNITED STATES, BY SEX AND AGE: 1948–1995

YEAR, SEX, RACE, AND HISPANIC ORIGIN	18 YEARS AND OVER	16–19 YEARS	20 YEARS AND OVER						
			TOTAL	20–24 YEARS	25–34 YEARS	35–44 YEARS	45–54 YEARS	55–64 YEARS	65 YEARS AND OVER
TOTAL									
1995	66.6	53.5	67.7	76.6	83.8	84.6	81.4	57.2	12.1
1994	66.6	52.7	67.7	77.0	83.2	84.8	81.7	56.8	12.4
1993	66.3	51.5	67.5	77.0	83.3	84.9	81.6	56.4	11.2
1992	66.4	51.3	67.6	77.0	83.7	85.1	81.5	56.2	11.5
1991	66.2	51.6	67.3	76.7	83.2	85.2	81.0	55.5	11.5
1990	66.5	53.7	67.6	77.8	83.6	85.2	80.7	55.9	11.8
1989	66.5	55.9	67.3	78.7	83.8	85.1	80.5	55.5	11.8
1988	65.9	55.3	66.8	78.7	83.3	84.6	79.6	54.6	11.5
1987	65.6	54.7	66.5	78.9	83.3	84.3	78.6	54.4	11.1
1986	65.3	54.7	66.2	78.9	82.9	83.7	78.0	54.0	10.9
1985	64.8	54.5	65.7	78.2	82.5	83.1	77.3	54.2	10.8
1984	64.4	53.9	65.3	77.6	81.8	82.4	76.5	54.2	11.1
1983	64.0	53.5	65.0	77.2	81.3	81.6	76.0	54.5	11.7
1982	64.0	54.1	65.0	77.1	81.0	81.2	75.9	55.1	11.9
1981	63.9	55.4	64.8	77.3	80.5	80.7	75.7	55.0	12.2
1980	63.8	56.7	64.5	77.2	79.9	80.0	74.9	55.7	12.5
1979	63.7	57.9	64.3	77.5	79.2	79.2	74.3	56.2	13.1
1978	63.2	57.8	63.8	76.8	78.3	78.1	73.5	56.3	13.3
1977	62.3	56.0	63.0	75.7	77.0	77.0	72.8	56.3	13.0
1976	61.6	54.5	62.4	74.7	75.7	76.0	72.5	56.6	13.1
1975	61.2	54.0	62.1	73.9	74.4	75.0	72.6	57.2	13.7
1974	61.3	54.8	62.0	74.0	73.6	74.6	72.7	57.8	14.0
1973	60.8	53.7	61.7	72.6	72.3	74.0	72.5	58.4	14.6
1972	60.4	51.9	61.4	70.8	70.9	73.3	72.7	60.0	15.6
1971	60.2	49.7	61.4	69.3	69.9	73.2	73.2	61.3	16.2
1970	60.4	49.9	61.6	69.2	69.7	73.1	73.5	61.8	17.0
1969	60.1	49.4	61.3	68.2	69.1	72.5	73.4	62.1	17.3
1968	59.6	48.3	60.9	67.0	68.6	72.0	72.8	62.2	17.2
1967	59.6	48.4	60.9	67.1	68.2	71.6	72.7	62.3	17.2
1966	59.2	48.2	60.5	66.5	67.1	71.0	72.7	62.2	17.2
1965	58.9	45.7	60.3	66.4	66.4	70.7	72.5	61.9	17.8
1964	58.7	44.5	60.2	66.3	65.8	70.0	72.9	61.9	18.0
1963	58.7	45.2	60.1	65.1	65.6	70.1	72.5	62.0	17.9
1962	58.8	46.1	60.0	65.3	65.2	69.7	72.2	61.5	19.1
1961	59.3	46.9	60.5	65.7	65.6	69.5	72.1	61.5	20.1
1960	59.4	47.5	60.5	65.2	65.4	69.4	72.2	60.9	20.8
1959	59.3	46.7	60.4	64.3	65.0	69.5	71.9	61.0	21.1
1958	59.5	47.4	60.5	64.4	65.0	69.6	71.5	60.5	21.8
1957	59.6	49.6	60.4	64.0	64.9	69.5	70.9	60.1	22.9
1956	60.0	50.9	60.7	64.1	64.8	69.5	70.5	60.8	24.3
1955	59.3	48.9	60.1	62.7	64.8	68.9	69.7	59.5	24.1
1954	58.8	48.3	59.6	61.6	64.3	68.8	68.4	58.7	23.9
1953	58.9	50.2	59.6	61.2	64.0	68.9	68.1	58.0	24.8
1952	59.0	51.3	59.7	62.2	64.7	68.0	67.5	57.5	24.8
1951	59.2	52.2	59.8	64.8	64.2	67.6	67.2	56.9	25.8
1950	59.2	51.8	59.9	65.9	63.5	67.5	66.4	56.7	26.7
1949	58.9	52.2	59.5	64.9	63.2	67.2	65.3	56.2	27.3
1948	58.8	52.5	59.4	64.1	63.1	66.7	65.1	56.9	27.0
MEN									
1995	75.0	54.8	76.7	83.1	93.0	92.3	88.8	66.0	16.8
1994	75.1	54.1	76.8	83.1	92.6	92.8	89.1	65.5	16.8
1993	75.4	53.2	77.3	83.2	93.4	93.4	90.1	66.5	15.6
1992	75.8	53.4	77.7	83.3	93.8	93.7	90.7	67.0	16.1
1991	75.8	53.2	77.7	83.5	93.6	94.1	90.5	67.0	15.7
1990	76.4	55.7	78.2	84.4	94.1	94.3	90.7	67.8	16.3

TABLE A5.2 (CONTINUED)

CIVILIAN LABOR FORCE PARTICIPATION RATES IN THE UNITED STATES, BY SEX AND AGE: 1948–1995

YEAR, SEX, RACE, AND HISPANIC ORIGIN	18 YEARS AND OVER	16–19 YEARS	20 YEARS AND OVER						
			TOTAL	20–24 YEARS	25–34 YEARS	35–44 YEARS	45–54 YEARS	55–64 YEARS	65 YEARS AND OVER
MEN (CONTINUED)									
1989	76.4	57.9	78.1	85.3	94.4	94.5	91.1	67.2	16.6
1988	76.2	56.9	77.9	85.0	94.3	94.5	90.9	67.0	16.5
1987	76.2	56.1	78.0	85.2	94.6	94.6	90.7	67.6	16.3
1986	76.3	56.4	78.1	85.8	94.6	94.8	91.0	67.3	16.0
1985	76.3	56.8	78.1	85.0	94.7	95.0	91.0	67.9	15.8
1984	76.4	56.0	78.3	85.0	94.4	95.4	91.2	68.5	16.3
1983	76.4	56.2	78.5	84.8	94.2	95.2	91.2	69.4	17.4
1982	76.6	56.7	78.7	84.9	94.7	95.3	91.2	70.2	17.8
1981	77.0	59.0	79.0	85.5	94.9	95.4	91.4	70.6	18.4
1980	77.4	60.5	79.4	85.9	95.2	95.5	91.2	72.1	19.0
1979	77.8	61.5	79.8	86.4	95.3	95.7	91.4	72.8	19.9
1978	77.9	62.0	79.8	85.9	95.3	95.7	91.3	73.3	20.4
1977	77.7	60.9	79.7	85.6	95.3	95.7	91.1	73.8	20.0
1976	77.5	59.3	79.8	85.2	95.2	95.4	91.6	74.3	20.2
1975	77.9	59.1	80.3	84.5	95.2	95.6	92.1	75.6	21.6
1974	78.7	60.7	81.0	85.9	95.8	96.0	92.2	77.3	22.4
1973	78.8	59.7	81.3	85.2	95.7	96.2	93.0	78.2	22.7
1972	78.9	58.1	81.6	83.9	95.7	96.4	93.2	80.4	24.3
1971	79.1	56.1	82.1	83.0	95.9	96.5	93.9	82.1	25.5
1970	79.7	56.1	82.6	83.3	96.4	96.9	94.3	83.0	26.8
1969	79.8	55.9	82.8	82.8	96.7	96.9	94.6	83.4	27.2
1968	80.1	55.1	83.1	82.8	96.9	97.1	94.9	84.3	27.3
1967	80.4	55.6	83.4	84.4	97.2	97.3	95.2	84.4	27.1
1966	80.4	55.3	83.6	85.1	97.3	97.2	95.3	84.5	27.1
1965	80.7	53.8	83.9	85.8	97.2	97.3	95.6	84.6	27.9
1964	81.0	52.4	84.2	86.1	97.3	97.3	95.7	85.6	28.0
1963	81.4	52.9	84.4	86.1	97.1	97.5	95.7	86.2	28.4
1962	82.0	53.8	84.8	86.9	97.2	97.6	95.6	86.2	30.3
1961	82.9	54.6	85.7	87.8	97.5	97.6	95.6	87.3	31.7
1960	83.3	56.1	86.0	88.1	97.5	97.7	95.7	86.8	33.1
1959	83.7	55.8	86.3	87.8	97.4	97.8	96.0	87.4	34.2
1958	84.2	56.6	86.6	86.9	97.1	97.9	96.3	87.8	35.6
1957	84.8	59.1	86.9	87.1	97.1	97.9	96.3	87.5	37.5
1956	85.5	60.5	87.6	87.8	97.3	97.9	96.6	88.5	40.0
1955	85.4	58.9	87.6	86.9	97.6	98.1	96.4	87.9	39.6
1954	85.5	58.0	87.8	86.9	97.3	98.1	96.5	88.7	40.5
1953	86.0	60.7	88.0	87.7	97.4	98.2	96.5	87.9	41.6
1952	86.3	61.3	88.3	88.1	97.5	97.8	96.2	87.5	42.6
1951	86.3	63.0	88.2	88.4	96.9	97.5	95.9	87.2	44.9
1950	86.4	63.2	88.4	87.9	96.0	97.6	95.8	86.9	45.8
1949	86.4	62.8	88.5	86.6	95.8	97.9	95.6	87.5	47.0
1948	86.6	63.7	88.6	84.6	95.9	97.9	95.8	89.5	46.8
WOMEN									
1995	58.9	52.2	59.4	70.3	74.9	77.2	74.4	49.2	8.8
1994	58.8	51.3	59.3	71.0	74.0	77.1	74.6	48.9	9.2
1993	57.9	49.7	58.5	70.9	73.4	76.6	73.5	47.2	8.1
1992	57.8	49.1	58.5	70.9	73.9	76.7	72.6	46.5	8.3
1991	57.4	50.0	57.9	70.1	73.1	76.5	72.0	45.2	8.5
1990	57.5	51.6	58.0	71.3	73.5	76.4	71.2	45.2	8.6
1989	57.4	53.9	57.7	72.4	73.5	76.0	70.5	45.0	8.4
1988	56.6	53.6	56.8	72.7	72.7	75.2	69.0	43.5	7.9
1987	56.0	53.3	56.2	73.0	72.4	74.5	67.1	42.7	7.4
1986	55.3	53.0	55.5	72.4	71.6	73.1	65.9	42.3	7.4
1985	54.5	52.1	54.7	71.8	70.9	71.8	64.4	42.0	7.3
1984	53.6	51.8	53.7	70.4	69.8	70.1	62.9	41.7	7.5

TABLE A5.2 (CONTINUED)

CIVILIAN LABOR FORCE PARTICIPATION RATES IN THE UNITED STATES, BY SEX AND AGE: 1948–1995

YEAR, SEX, RACE, AND HISPANIC ORIGIN	18 YEARS AND OVER	16–19 YEARS	20 YEARS AND OVER						
			TOTAL	20–24 YEARS	25–34 YEARS	35–44 YEARS	45–54 YEARS	55–64 YEARS	65 YEARS AND OVER
WOMEN (CONTINUED)									
1983	52.9	50.8	53.1	69.9	69.0	68.7	61.9	41.5	7.8
1982	52.6	51.4	52.7	69.8	68.0	68.0	61.6	41.8	7.9
1981	52.1	51.8	52.1	69.6	66.7	66.8	61.1	41.4	8.0
1980	51.5	52.9	51.3	68.9	65.5	65.5	59.9	41.3	8.1
1979	50.9	54.2	50.6	69.0	63.9	63.6	58.3	41.7	8.3
1978	50.0	53.7	49.6	68.3	62.2	61.6	57.1	41.3	8.3
1977	48.4	51.2	48.1	66.5	59.7	59.6	55.8	40.9	8.1
1976	47.3	49.8	47.0	65.0	57.3	57.8	55.0	41.0	8.2
1975	46.3	49.1	46.0	64.1	54.9	55.8	54.6	40.9	8.2
1974	45.7	49.1	45.3	63.1	52.6	54.7	54.6	40.7	8.1
1973	44.7	47.8	44.4	61.1	50.4	53.3	53.7	41.1	8.9
1972	43.9	45.8	43.7	59.1	47.8	52.0	53.9	42.1	9.3
1971	43.4	43.4	43.3	57.7	45.6	51.6	54.3	42.9	9.5
1970	43.3	44.0	43.3	57.7	45.0	51.1	54.4	43.0	9.7
1969	42.7	43.2	42.7	56.7	43.7	49.9	53.8	43.1	9.9
1968	41.6	41.9	41.6	54.5	42.6	48.9	52.3	42.4	9.6
1967	41.1	41.6	41.1	53.3	41.9	48.1	51.8	42.4	9.6
1966	40.3	41.4	40.1	51.5	39.8	46.8	51.7	41.8	9.6
1965	39.3	38.0	39.4	49.9	38.5	46.1	50.9	41.1	10.0
1964	38.7	37.0	38.9	49.4	37.2	45.0	51.4	40.2	10.1
1963	38.3	38.0	38.3	47.5	37.2	44.9	50.6	39.7	9.6
1962	37.9	39.0	37.8	47.3	36.3	44.1	50.0	38.7	10.0
1961	38.1	39.7	38.0	47.0	36.4	43.8	50.1	37.9	10.7
1960	37.7	39.3	37.6	46.1	36.0	43.4	49.9	37.2	10.8
1959	37.1	38.2	37.1	45.1	35.3	43.4	49.0	36.6	10.2
1958	37.1	39.0	36.9	46.3	35.6	43.4	47.8	35.2	10.3
1957	36.9	41.1	36.5	45.9	35.6	43.3	46.5	34.5	10.5
1956	36.9	42.2	36.4	46.3	35.4	43.1	45.5	34.9	10.8
1955	35.7	39.7	35.4	45.9	34.9	41.6	43.8	32.5	10.6
1954	34.6	39.4	34.2	45.1	34.4	41.2	41.2	30.0	9.3
1953	34.4	40.7	33.9	44.3	34.0	41.3	40.4	29.1	10.0
1952	34.7	42.2	34.1	44.7	35.4	40.4	40.1	28.7	9.1
1951	34.6	42.4	34.0	46.5	35.4	39.8	39.7	27.6	8.9
1950	33.9	41.0	33.3	46.0	34.0	39.1	37.9	27.0	9.7
1949	33.1	42.4	32.3	45.0	33.4	38.1	35.9	25.3	9.6
1948	32.7	42.0	31.8	45.3	33.2	36.9	35.0	24.3	9.1

Note: Data not available for Blacks, ages 20 years and over.

Source: U.S. Bureau of Labor Statistics

TABLE A5.3

EMPLOYMENT STATUS OF WOMEN IN THE UNITED STATES, BY MARITAL STATUS AND PRESENCE AND AGE OF CHILDREN: 1960-1995

(AS OF MARCH. FOR 1960, CIVILIAN NONINSTITUTIONAL PERSONS 14 YEARS AND OVER, THEREAFTER 16 YEARS OLD AND OVER. BASED ON CURRENT POPULATION SURVEY.)

| | TOTAL | | | WITH ANY CHILDREN | | | | | | | | |
| | | | | TOTAL | | | CHILDREN 6-17 ONLY | | | CHILDREN UNDER 6 | | |
ITEM	SINGLE	MARRIED [1]	OTHER [2]	SINGLE	MARRIED [1]	OTHER [2]	SINGLE	MARRIED [1]	OTHER [2]	SINGLE	MARRIED [1]	OTHER [2]
IN LABOR FORCE (MIL.)												
1995	15.0	33.6	12.0	2.1	18.0	4.6	0.8	10.2	3.3	1.3	7.8	1.3
1994 [3]	14.9	32.9	11.9	2.2	17.6	4.4	0.8	9.9	3.2	1.4	7.7	1.2
1993	14.1	32.2	11.3	1.9	16.9	4.2	0.7	9.7	3.0	1.1	7.3	1.2
1992	14.1	31.7	11.5	1.7	16.8	4.2	0.7	9.5	3.0	1.0	7.3	1.2
1990	14.0	31.0	11.2	1.5	16.5	4.2	0.6	9.3	3.0	0.9	7.2	1.2
1985	12.9	27.7	10.3	1.1	14.9	4.0	0.4	8.5	2.9	0.7	6.4	1.1
1980	11.2	24.9	8.8	0.6	13.7	3.6	0.2	8.4	2.6	0.3	5.2	1.0
1970	7.0	18.4	5.9	NA	10.2	1.9	NA	6.3	1.3	NA	3.9	0.6
1960	5.4	12.3	4.9	NA	6.6	1.5	NA	4.1	1.0	NA	2.5	0.4
PARTICIPATION RATE [4]												
1995	65.5	61.1	47.3	57.5	70.2	75.3	67.0	76.2	79.5	53.0	63.5	66.3
1994 [3]	65.1	60.6	47.3	56.9	69.0	73.1	67.5	76.0	78.4	52.2	61.7	62.2
1993	64.5	59.4	45.9	54.4	67.5	72.1	70.2	74.9	78.3	47.4	59.6	60.0
1992	64.7	59.3	46.7	52.5	67.8	73.2	67.2	75.4	80.0	45.8	59.9	60.5
1990	66.4	58.2	46.8	55.2	66.3	74.2	69.7	73.6	79.7	48.7	58.9	63.6
1985	65.2	54.2	45.6	51.6	60.8	71.9	64.1	67.8	77.8	46.5	53.4	59.7
1980	61.5	50.1	44.0	52.0	54.1	69.4	67.6	61.7	74.6	44.1	45.1	60.3
1970	53.0	40.8	39.1	NA	39.7	60.7	NA	49.2	66.9	NA	30.3	52.2
1960	44.1	30.5	40.0	NA	27.6	56.0	NA	39.0	65.9	NA	18.6	40.5
EMPLOYMENT (MIL.)												
1995	13.7	32.3	11.3	1.8	17.2	4.2	0.7	9.8	3.1	1.1	7.3	1.2
1994 [3]	13.4	31.4	11.0	1.7	16.8	4.0	0.7	9.5	2.9	1.1	7.3	1.0
1993	12.7	30.8	10.5	1.5	16.1	3.9	0.6	9.3	2.8	0.9	6.8	1.1
1992	12.8	30.1	10.6	1.4	15.9	3.7	0.6	9.1	2.7	0.8	6.8	1.0
1990	12.9	29.9	10.5	1.2	15.8	3.8	0.5	8.9	2.7	0.7	6.9	1.1
1985	11.6	26.1	9.4	0.9	13.9	3.5	0.3	8.1	2.6	0.5	5.9	0.9
1980	10.1	23.6	8.2	0.4	12.8	3.3	0.2	8.1	2.4	0.2	4.8	0.9
1970	6.5	17.5	5.6	NA	9.6	1.8	NA	6.0	1.2	NA	3.6	0.6
1960	5.1	11.6	4.6	NA	6.2	1.3	NA	3.9	0.9	NA	2.3	0.4
UNEMPLOYMENT RATE [5]												
1995	8.7	3.9	5.8	16.6	4.3	8.1	11.8	3.6	7.1	19.5	5.3	10.8
1994 [3]	10.0	4.5	7.4	19.5	5.0	9.8	13.2	4.5	7.7	23.0	5.6	15.1
1993	9.8	4.4	6.9	19.2	4.8	8.5	13.7	3.8	7.0	22.8	6.2	12.5
1992	9.1	4.9	7.6	17.3	5.7	10.8	14.1	4.6	8.6	19.4	7.0	16.3
1990	8.2	3.5	5.7	18.4	4.2	8.5	14.5	3.8	7.7	20.8	4.8	10.2
1985	10.2	5.7	8.5	23.8	6.6	12.1	15.4	5.5	10.6	28.5	8.0	16.1
1980	10.3	5.3	6.4	23.2	5.9	9.2	15.6	4.4	7.9	29.2	8.3	12.8
1970	7.1	4.8	4.8	NA	6.0	7.2	NA	4.8	5.9	NA	7.9	9.8
1960	6.0	5.4	6.2	NA	6.0	8.4	NA	4.9	6.8	NA	7.8	12.5

NA = NOT AVAILABLE.

[1] HUSBAND PRESENT.

[2] WIDOWED, DIVORCED, OR SEPARATED.

[3] DATA BEGINNING 1994 NOT STRICTLY COMPARABLE WITH DATA FOR EARLIER YEARS.

[4] PERCENT OF WOMEN IN EACH SPECIFIC CATEGORY IN THE LABOR FORCE.

[5] UNEMPLOYED AS A PERCENT OF CIVILIAN LABOR FORCE IN SPECIFIED GROUP.

Source: U.S. Bureau of Labor Statistics, *Bulletin 2307*; and unpublished data.

TABLE A5.4

UNEMPLOYMENT RATES IN NINE COUNTRIES, CIVILIAN LABOR FORCE BASIS APPROXIMATING U.S. CONCEPTS, SEASONALLY ADJUSTED: 1975-1996

PERIOD	UNITED STATES	CANADA	AUSTRALIA	JAPAN	FRANCE	GERMANY[1]	ITALY[2]	SWEDEN	UNITED KINGDOM
1996	5.4	9.7	8.6	3.4	12.6	7.2P	12.1P	9.9	8.2P
1995	5.6	9.5	8.5	3.2	11.8	6.5P	12.0P	9.1	8.7
1994	6.1[3]	10.4	9.7	2.9	12.3	6.5P	11.3P	9.6	9.7
1993	6.9	11.2	10.9	2.5	11.8	5.7P	10.2P [3]	9.3	10.5
1992	7.5	11.3	10.8	2.2	10.4[3]	4.6P	7.3P	5.6	10.1
1991	6.8	10.4	9.6	2.1	9.6	4.3P	6.93	3.1	8.8
1990	5.6[3]	8.1	6.9	2.1	9.1	5.0	7.0	1.8	6.9
1989	5.3	7.5	6.2	2.3	9.6	5.7	7.8	1.6	7.2
1988	5.5	7.8	7.2	2.5	10.3	6.3	7.9	1.9	8.6
1987	6.2	8.9	8.1	2.9	10.8	6.3	7.9	2.2 [3]	10.3
1986	7.0	9.6	8.1	2.8	10.6	6.6	7.5 [3]	2.6	11.2
1985	7.2	10.5	8.3	2.6	10.5	7.2	6.0	2.8	11.2
1984	7.5	11.3	9.0	2.8	10.0	7.1	5.9	3.1	11.7
1983	9.6	11.9	10.0	2.7	8.6	6.9 [3]	5.9	3.5	11.8
1982	9.7	11.0	7.2	2.4	8.3	5.6	5.4	3.1	11.3
1981	7.6	7.6	5.8	2.2	7.6	4.0	4.9	2.5	10.5
1980	7.1	7.5	6.1	2.0	6.5	2.8	4.4	2.0	7.0
1979	5.8	7.5	6.3	2.1	6.1	2.9	4.4	2.1	5.4
1978	6.1	8.4	6.3	2.3	5.4	3.3	4.1	2.2	6.3
1977	7.1	8.1	5.6	2.0	5.2	3.4	4.1	1.8	6.4
1976	7.7	7.2	4.8	2.0	4.6	3.4	3.9	1.6	5.9
1975	8.5	6.9	4.9	1.9	4.2	3.4	3.4	1.6	4.6

P = PRELIMINARY.

[1] FORMER WEST GERMANY.

[2] QUARTERLY RATES ARE FOR THE FIRST MONTH OF THE QUARTER.

[3] BREAK IN SERIES.

Note: Quarterly and monthly figures for France and Germany are calculated by applying annual adjustment factors to current published data and therefore should be viewed as less precise indicators of unemployment under U.S. concepts than the annual figures.

Source: Data from U.S. Bureau of Labor Statistics, published in *Handbook of U.S. Labor Statistics*, second edition (Bernan Press 1998).

TABLE A5.5

NUMBER OF PERSONS WITH WORK EXPERIENCE DURING THE YEAR IN THE UNITED STATES BY SEX AND EXTENT OF EMPLOYMENT: 1987–1994

(NUMBERS IN THOUSANDS)

YEAR AND SEX	TOTAL	FULL-TIME				PART-TIME			
		TOTAL	50–52 WEEKS	27–49 WEEKS	1–26 WEEKS	TOTAL	50-52 WEEKS	27-49 WEEKS	1-26 WEEKS
TOTAL									
1987	128,315	100,288	77,015	13,361	9,912	28,027	10,973	6,594	10,460
1988	130,451	102,131	79,627	12,875	9,629	28,320	11,384	6,624	10,312
1989	132,817	104,876	81,117	14,271	9,488	27,941	11,275	6,987	9,679
1990	133,535	105,323	80,932	14,758	9,633	28,212	11,507	7,012	9,693
1991	133,410	104,472	80,385	14,491	9,596	28,938	11,946	7,003	9,989
1992	133,912	104,813	81,523	13,587	9,703	29,099	12,326	6,841	9,932
1993	136,354	106,299	83,384	13,054	9,861	30,055	12,818	6,777	10,460
1994	138,468	108,141	85,764	13,051	9,326	30,327	12,936	6,956	10,435
MEN									
1987	69,144	59,736	47,040	7,503	5,193	9,408	3,260	2,191	3,957
1988	70,021	60,504	48,299	7,329	4,876	9,517	3,468	2,199	3,850
1989	71,640	62,108	49,693	7,642	4,773	9,532	3,619	2,254	3,659
1990	71,953	62,319	49,175	8,188	4,956	9,634	3,650	2,322	3,662
1991	71,700	61,636	47,895	8,324	5,417	10,064	3,820	2,342	3,902
1992	72,007	61,722	48,300	7,965	5,457	10,285	3,864	2,354	4,067
1993	72,872	62,513	49,832	7,317	5,364	10,359	4,005	2,144	4,210
1994	73,958	63,634	51,582	7,094	4,958	10,324	3,948	2,358	4,018
WOMEN									
1987	59,171	40,552	29,975	5,858	4,719	18,619	7,713	4,403	6,503
1988	60,430	41,627	31,328	5,546	4,753	18,803	7,916	4,425	6,462
1989	61,178	42,768	31,424	6,629	4,715	18,410	7,656	4,733	6,021
1990	61,582	43,004	31,757	6,570	4,677	18,578	7,857	4,690	6,031
1991	61,712	42,837	32,491	6,167	4,179	18,875	8,126	4,662	6,087
1992	61,904	43,090	33,223	5,621	4,246	18,814	8,462	4,487	5,865
1993	63,481	43,785	33,552	5,736	4,497	19,696	8,813	4,633	6,250
1994	64,511	44,508	34,182	5,957	4,369	20,003	8,988	4,598	6,417

Source: U.S. Bureau of Labor Statistics.

TABLE A5.6

WORK EXPERIENCE OF THE U.S. POPULATION DURING THE YEAR, BY RACE, HISPANIC ORIGIN, AND SEX: 1995–1996

(NUMBERS IN THOUSANDS)

EXTENT OF EMPLOYMENT, RACE, AND HISPANC ORIGIN	TOTAL		MEN		WOMEN	
	1995	1996	1995	1996	1995	1996
WHITE						
CIVILIAN NONINSTITUTIONAL POPULATION	167,865	169,555	81,253	82,324	86,612	87,230
TOTAL WHO WORKED OR LOOKED FOR WORK	119,833	121,113	64,289	65,152	55,545	55,962
PERCENT OF THE POPULATION	71.4	71.4	79.1	79.1	64.1	64.2
TOTAL WHO WORKED DURING THE YEAR [1]	118,107	119,579	63,478	64,484	54,630	55,094
PERCENT OF THE POPULATION	70.4	70.5	78.1	78.3	63.1	63.2
PERCENT WHO WORKED DURING THE YEAR [1]	100.0	100.0	100.0	100.0	100.0	100.0
FULL TIME [2]	78.2	78.3	86.2	86.3	68.9	69.0
50–52 WEEKS	62.8	63.3	71.0	71.5	53.3	53.7
27–49 WEEKS	9.3	9.1	9.4	9.1	9.1	9.2
1–26 WEEKS	6.1	5.9	5.8	5.7	6.5	6.2
PART-TIME [3]	21.8	21.7	13.8	13.7	31.1	31.0
50–52 WEEKS	9.5	9.8	5.5	5.8	14.1	14.6
27–49 WEEKS	5.1	4.9	3.1	2.9	7.4	7.3
1–26 WEEKS	7.2	6.9	5.1	5.0	9.7	9.1
BLACK						
CIVILIAN NONINSTITUTIONAL POPULATION	23,482	23,893	10,515	10,709	12,967	13,184
TOTAL WHO WORKED OR LOOKED FOR WORK	15,855	16140	7,567	7484	8,288	8,656
PERCENT OF THE POPULATION	67.5	67.6	72	69.9	63.9	65.7
TOTAL WHO WORKED DURING THE YEAR [1]	15,059	15,485	7,153	7,206	7,905	8,279
PERCENT OF THE POPULATION	64.1	64.8	68	67.3	61	62.8
PERCENT WHO WORKED DURING THE YEAR [1]	100.0	100.0	100.0	100.0	100.0	100.0
FULL TIME [2]	81.8	82.3	85.3	85.1	78.6	79.8
50–52 WEEKS	63.4	63.2	66.3	65.3	60.7	61.3
27–49 WEEKS	10.1	9.8	10.3	10.4	9.9	9.2
1–26 WEEKS	8.3	9.3	8.7	9.3	8.0	9.3
PART-TIME [3]	18.2	17.7	14.7	14.9	21.4	20.2
50–52 WEEKS	7.1	7.0	5.1	5.5	8.9	8.3
27–49 WEEKS	3.6	3.1	2.7	2.2	4.4	3.9
1–26 WEEKS	7.5	7.6	6.8	7.2	8.1	8.0
HISPANIC ORIGIN						
CIVILIAN NONINSTITUTIONAL POPULATION	19,028	20,114	9,518	10,257	9,510	9,857
TOTAL WHO WORKED OR LOOKED FOR WORK	13,081	13,973	7,640	8,256	5,442	5,717
PERCENT OF THE POPULATION	68.7	69.5	80.3	80.5	57.2	58.0
TOTAL WHO WORKED DURING THE YEAR [1]	12,627	13,600	7,422	8,084	5,205	5516
PERCENT OF THE POPULATION	66.4	67.6	78.0	78.8	54.7	56.0
PERCENT WHO WORKED DURING THE YEAR [1]	100.0	100.0	100.0	100.0	100.0	100.0
FULL TIME [2]	81.2	81.4	87.0	87.0	73.0	73.2
50–52 WEEKS	60.9	62.1	66.2	67.9	53.2	53.5
27–49 WEEKS	10.7	10.7	11.7	11.2	9.3	10.0
1–26 WEEKS	9.6	8.7	9.0	7.9	10.5	9.8
PART-TIME [3]	18.8	18.6	13.0	13.0	27.0	26.8
50–52 WEEKS	8.1	8.5	5.2	5.7	12.4	12.5
27–49 WEEKS	3.3	3.5	2.3	2.5	4.6	5.1
1–26 WEEKS	7.4	6.6	5.5	4.7	10.0	9.2

[1] TIME WORKED INCLUDES PAID VACATION AND SICK LEAVE.

[2] USUALLY WORKED 35 HOURS OR MORE PER WEEK.

[3] USUALLY WORKED 1 TO 34 HOURS PER WEEK.

Source: U.S. Bureau of Labor Statistics.

Note: Detail for the above race and Hispanic origin groups will not sum to totals because data for the other races group are not presented and Hispanics are included in both the White and Black Population groups. Data refer to persons 16 years and over.

TABLE A5.7

CIVILIAN EMPLOYMENT IN U.S. OCCUPATIONS WITH THE LARGEST JOB GROWTH: 1994-2005

(OCCUPATIONS ARE IN DESCENDING ORDER OF ABSOLUTE EMPLOYMENT CHANGE 1994–2005 (MODERATE GROWTH). INCLUDES WAGE AND SALARY JOBS, SELF-EMPLOYED, AND UNPAID FAMILY MEMBERS. ESTIMATES BASED ON THE CURRENT EMPLOYMENT STATISTICS ESTIMATES AND THE OCCUPATIONAL EMPLOYMENT STATISTICS ESTIMATES. SEE SOURCE FOR METHODOLOGICAL ASSUMPTIONS.)

| | | EMPLOYMENT (1,000) | | | PERCENT CHANGE, 1994-2005 | | |
| | | 2005 [1] | | | | | |
	1994	LOW	MODERATE	HIGH	LOW	MODERATE	HIGH
TOTAL, ALL OCCUPATIONS [2]	127,015	140, 261	144,706	150,212	10.4	13.9	18.3
CASHIERS	3,005	3,493	3,567	3,645	16.2	18.7	21.3
JANITORS AND CLEANERS [3]	3,043	3,483	3,602	3,745	14.5	18.4	23.1
SALESPERSONS, RETAIL	3,842	4,244	4,374	4,508	10.5	13.8	17.3
WAITERS AND WAITRESSES	1,847	2,361	2,326	2,291	27.8	25.9	24.0
REGISTERED NURSES	1,906	2,318	2,379	2,481	21.6	24.8	30.2
GENERAL MANAGERS AND TOP EXECUTIVES	3,046	3,403	3,512	3,641	11.7	15.3	19.5
SYSTEMS ANALYSTS	483	893	928	972	84.9	92.1	101.3
HOME HEALTH AIDES	420	832	848	863	98.3	102.0	105.7
GUARDS	867	1,248	1,282	1,322	44.0	47.9	52.5
NURSING AIDES, ORDERLIES, AND ATTENDANTS	1,265	1,624	1,652	1,709	28.4	30.6	35.1
TEACHERS, SECONDARY SCHOOL	1,340	1,585	1,726	1,885	18.3	28.8	40.7
MARKETING AND SALES WORKER SUPERVISORS	2,293	2,628	2,673	2,728	14.6	16.6	18.9
TEACHER AIDES AND EDUCATIONAL ASSISTANTS	932	1,211	1,296	1,393	29.9	39.0	49.5
RECEPTIONISTS AND INFORMATION CLERKS	1,019	1,311	1,337	1,367	28.7	31.2	34.2
TRUCK DRIVERS LIGHT AND HEAVY	2,565	2,744	2,837	2,944	7.0	10.6	14.7
SECRETARIES, EXCEPT LEGAL AND MEDICAL	2,842	2,983	3,109	3,258	5.0	9.4	14.6
CLERICAL SUPERVISORS AND MANAGERS	1,340	1,550	1,600	1,658	15.7	19.5	23.8
CHILD CARE WORKERS	757	1,009	1,005	1,006	33.2	32.8	33.0
MAINTENANCE REPAIRERS, GENERAL UTILITY	1,273	1,431	1,505	1,597	12.4	18.2	25.4
TEACHERS, ELEMENTARY	1,419	1,509	1,639	1,787	6.3	15.5	25.9
PERSONAL AND HOME CARE AIDES	179	382	391	397	114.0	118.7	122.3
TEACHERS, SPECIAL EDUCATION	388	545	593	648	40.6	53.0	67.2
LICENSED PRACTICAL NURSES	702	882	899	927	25.7	28.0	32.1
FOOD SERVICE AND LODGING MANAGERS	579	776	771	769	34.0	33.2	32.9
FOOD PREPARATION WORKERS	1,190	1,368	1,378	1,393	14.9	15.7	17.0
SOCIAL WORKERS	557	712	744	778	27.9	33.5	39.8
LAWYERS	656	824	839	856	25.6	27.9	30.6
FINANCIAL MANAGERS	768	919	950	988	19.7	23.6	28.5
COMPUTER ENGINEERS	195	355	372	394	81.8	90.4	101.9
HAND PACKERS AND PACKAGERS	942	1,070	1,102	1,137	13.6	17.0	20.7
CORRECTION OFFICERS	310	430	468	513	38.5	50.9	65.2
COLLEGE AND UNIVERSITY FACULTY	823	893	972	1,062	8.6	18.2	29.1
ADJUSTMENT CLERKS	373	505	521	540	35.1	39.6	44.6
TEACHERS, PRESCHOOL AND KINDERGARTEN	462	588	602	620	27.2	30.3	34.2
AMUSEMENT AND RECREATION ATTENDANTS	267	398	406	414	49.2	52.0	55.2
AUTOMOTIVE MECHANICS	736	840	862	882	14.2	17.1	19.9
RESIDENTIAL COUNSELORS	165	284	290	295	72.7	76.5	79.5
GENERAL OFFICE CLERKS	2,946	2,959	3,071	3,204	0.5	4.3	8.8
HUMAN SERVICES WORKERS	168	284	293	303	68.8	74.5	80.0
COOKS, RESTAURANT	704	839	827	815	19.3	17.5	15.8
MEDICAL ASSISTANTS	206	329	327	324	59.9	59.0	57.9
ACCOUNTANTS AND AUDITORS	962	1,056	1,083	1,119	9.7	12.6	16.3
PHYSICIANS	539	659	659	661	22.3	22.3	22.7
MARKETING, ADVERTISING, AND PUBLIC RELATIONS MANAGERS	461	558	575	595	21.1	24.8	29.2
POLICE PATROL OFFICERS	400	469	511	560	17.3	27.9	40.2
COUNTER AND RENTAL CLERKS	341	438	451	464	28.3	32.0	36.0
COOKS, SHORT ORDER AND FAST FOOD	760	884	869	855	16.2	14.3	12.4
INSTRUCTORS AND COACHES, SPORTS AND PHYSICAL TRAINING	282	365	381	399	29.2	34.8	41.1
ENGINEERING, MATHEMATICAL, AND NATURAL SCIENCE MANAGERS	337	415	432	453	23.3	28.1	34.5
BILL AND ACCOUNT COLLECTORS	250	334	342	351	33.3	36.5	40.1
SECURITIES AND FINANCIAL SERVICES SALES WORKERS	246	328	335	343	33.6	36.6	39.5
INSTRUCTORS, ADULT (NONVOCATIONAL) EDUCATION	290	366	376	387	26.1	29.4	33.4
HAIRDRESSERS, HAIRSTYLISTS, AND COSMETOLOGISTS	595	675	677	680	13.4	13.8	14.3
CARPENTERS	992	1,044	1,074	1,122	5.2	8.3	13.2

Table A5.7 (Continued)

Civilian Employment in U.S. Occupations With the Largest Job Growth: 1994-2005

(Occupations are in descending order of absolute employment change 1994–2005 (moderate growth). Includes wage and salary jobs, self-employed, and unpaid family members. Estimates based on the Current Employment Statistics estimates and the Occupational Employment Statistics estimates. See source for methodological assumptions.)

| | | Employment (1,000) | | | Percent Change, 1994-2005 | | |
| | | 2005[1] | | | | | |
	1994	Low	Moderate	High	Low	Moderate	High
Management Analysts	231	308	312	319	33.4	35.4	38.2
Teachers and Instructors, Vocational Ed and Training	299	356	381	409	19.0	27.2	36.6
Physical Therapists	102	182	183	185	78.9	80.0	81.9
Dental Assistants	190	271	269	266	43.1	41.9	40.0
Designers, Except Interior Designers	238	308	314	322	29.3	31.9	35.1
Painters and Paperhangers, Construction and Maintenance	439	497	509	529	13.3	16.0	20.6
Electrical and Electronics Engineers	349	402	417	439	15.3	19.7	25.9
Legal Secretaries	281	341	350	358	21.3	24.3	27.3
Helpers, Construction Trades	513	549	581	630	6.9	13.2	22.8
Personnel, Training, and Labor Relations Specialists	307	360	374	391	17.2	21.9	27.4
Heat, Air Conditioning, and Refrigeration Mechanics [4]	233	286	299	319	22.9	28.5	36.8
Education Administrators	393	431	459	491	9.8	16.9	25.0
Bus Drivers, School	404	439	470	503	8.7	16.4	24.6
Computer Programmers	537	577	601	631	7.4	12.0	17.6

[1] Based on low, moderate, or high trend assumptions.

[2] Includes other occupations, not shown separately.

[3] Includes maids and housekeepers.

[4] Includes installers.

Source: U. S. Bureau of Labor Statistics, Monthly Labor Review, November 1995.

TABLE A5.8

LABOR UNION MEMBERSHIP IN THE UNITED STATES, BY SECTOR: 1983–1995

(SELECTED YEARS)

SECTOR	1983	1985	1989	1990	1991	1992	1993	1994	1995
TOTAL (1,000)									
WAGE AND SALARY WORKERS:									
UNION	17,717.40	16,996.10	16,960.50	16,739.80	16,568.40	16,390.30	16,598.10	16,740.30	16,359.60
COVERED	20,532.10	19,358.10	19,197.60	19,057.80	18,733.80	18,540.10	18,646.40	18,842.50	18,346.30
PUBLIC SECTOR WORKERS:									
UNION	5,737.20	5,743.10	6,424.20	6,485.00	6,632.00	6,653.10	7,017.80	7,091.00	6,927.40
COVERED	7,112.20	6,920.60	7,614.40	7,691.40	7,796.00	7,840.60	8,162.40	8,191.80	7,986.60
PRIVATE SECTOR WORKERS:									
UNION	11,980.20	11,253.00	10,536.20	10,254.80	9,936.50	9,737.20	9,580.30	9,649.40	9,432.10
COVERED	13,419.90	12,437.50	11,583.10	11,366.40	10,937.80	10,699.50	10,484.00	10,650.60	10,359.80
PERCENT:									
WAGE AND SALARY WORKERS:									
UNION	20.1	18.0	16.4	16.1	16.1	15.8	15.8	15.5	14.9
COVERED	23.3	20.5	18.6	18.3	18.2	17.9	17.7	17.4	16.7
PUBLIC SECTOR WORKERS:									
UNION	36.7	35.7	36.7	36.5	36.9	36.6	37.7	38.7	37.7
COVERED	45.5	43.1	43.5	43.3	43.3	43.2	43.8	44.7	43.5
PRIVATE SECTOR WORKERS:									
UNION	16.5	14.3	12.3	11.9	11.7	11.4	11.1	10.8	10.3
COVERED	18.5	15.9	13.5	13.2	12.9	12.5	12.1	11.9	11.3

Source: Barry Hirsch, *Union Membership and Earnings Data Book: Compilations from the Current Population Survey* (Washington, D.C.: Bureau of National Affairs, 1996); Internet site http://www.bna.com/bnaplus.

TABLE A5.9

EMPLOYEE BENEFITS IN PRIVATE ESTABLISHMENTS IN THE UNITED STATES: 1993 AND 1994

(COVERS FULL-TIME EMPLOYEES IN PRIVATE INDUSTRY. MEDIUM AND LARGE ESTABLISHMENTS EXCLUDES ESTABLISHMENTS WITH FEWER THAN 100 WORKERS, EXECUTIVE AND TRAVELING OPERATING EMPLOYEES, AND ALASKA AND HAWAII. SMALL ESTABLISHMENTS INCLUDE THOSE WITH FEWER THAN 100 EMPLOYEES. COVERS ONLY BENEFITS FOR WHICH THE EMPLOYER PAYS PART OR ALL OF THE PREMIUM OR EXPENSES INVOLVED, EXCEPT UNPAID PARENTAL LEAVE AND LONG-TERM CARE INSURANCE.)

PERCENT OF EMPLOYEES PARTICIPATING IN—	ALL EMPLOYEES	PROFESSIONAL, TECHNICAL AND RELATED	CLERICAL AND SALES	PRODUCTION AND SERVICE
PAID				
VACATIONS	97	97	98	96
HOLIDAYS	91	89	93	92
JURY DUTY LEAVE	90	95	92	85
FUNERAL LEAVE	83	86	85	80
REST TIME	68	54	66	76
MILITARY LEAVE	53	66	54	44
SICK LEAVE	65	85	80	45
PERSONAL LEAVE	21	27	31	13
LUNCH TIME	9	5	5	13
MATERNITY LEAVE	3	4	3	1
PATERNITY LEAVE	1	2	1	(Z)
UNPAID				
MATERNITY LEAVE	60	63	60	59
PATERNITY LEAVE	53	55	51	52
INSURANCE PLANS				
MEDICAL CARE	82	84	79	82
NONCONTRIBUTORY	37	31	32	44
HOSPITAL/ ROOM AND BOARD	82	84	79	82
INPATIENT SURGERY	82	84	79	82
MENTAL HEALTH CARE				
INPATIENT CARE	80	83	77	80
OUTPATIENT CARE	80	82	77	79
DENTAL	62	68	63	58
EXTENDED CARE FACILITY	67	71	68	66
HOME HEALTH CARE	71	74	70	68
HOSPICE CARE	53	56	54	52
VISION	26	27	26	27
IN HMO'S	19	24	21	15
ALCOHOL ABUSE TREATMENT				
INPATIENT DETOXIFICATION	80	82	77	80
INPATIENT REHABILITATION	66	66	63	58
OUTPATIENT	67	69	65	68
DRUG ABUSE TREATMENT				
INPATIENT DETOXIFICATION	80	82	77	80
INPATIENT REHABILITATION	64	65	60	66
OUTPATIENT	66	68	64	65
LIFE INSURANCE	91	95	92	89
NONCONTRIBUTORY	87	84	87	89
ACCIDENT/ SICKNESS	44	28	37	57
NONCONTRIBUTORY	75	65	67	81
LONG-TERM DISABILITY	41	64	50	23
NONCONTRIBUTORY	73	69	71	80
RETIREMENT AND SAVINGS PLANS [1]	78	83	78	76
DEFINED BENEFIT PENSION	56	57	54	56
EARNINGS-BASED [2]	40	50	45	32
DEFINED CONTRIBUTION	49	60	54	40
SAVINGS AND THRIFT	29	38	34	21
EMPLOYEE STOCK OWNERSHIP	3	3	4	2
DEFERRED PROFIT SHARING	13	12	16	12
MONEY PURCHASE PENSION	8	13	7	6
ADDITIONAL BENEFITS				
PARKING [3]	88	86	85	92
EDUCATIONAL ASSISTANCE	72	85	72	65
TRAVEL ACCIDENT INSURANCE	44	59	52	32

TABLE A5.9 (CONTINUED)

EMPLOYEE BENEFITS IN PRIVATE ESTABLISHMENTS IN THE UNITED STATES: 1993 AND 1994

(COVERS FULL-TIME EMPLOYEES IN PRIVATE INDUSTRY. MEDIUM AND LARGE ESTABLISHMENTS EXCLUDES ESTABLISHMENTS WITH FEWER THAN 100 WORKERS, EXECUTIVE AND TRAVELING OPERATING EMPLOYEES, AND ALASKA AND HAWAII. SMALL ESTABLISHMENTS INCLUDE THOSE WITH FEWER THAN 100 EMPLOYEES. COVERS ONLY BENEFITS FOR WHICH THE EMPLOYER PAYS PART OR ALL OF THE PREMIUM OR EXPENSES INVOLVED, EXCEPT UNPAID PARENTAL LEAVE AND LONG-TERM CARE INSURANCE.)

PERCENT OF EMPLOYEES PARTICIPATING IN—	ALL EMPLOYEES	PROFESSIONAL, TECHNICAL AND RELATED	CLERICAL AND SALES	PRODUCTION AND SERVICE
ADDITIONAL BENEFITS (CONTINUED)				
SEVERANCE PAY	42	56	48	31
RELOCATION ALLOWANCE [3]	31	50	30	21
RECREATION FACILITIES [3]	26	34	25	23
NONPRODUCTION BONUSES, CASH	38	37	38	38
CHILD CARE	7	12	6	4
FLEXIBLE BENEFITS PLANS	12	21	13	6
REIMBURSEMENT ACCOUNTS [4]	52	68	62	37
ELDERCARE	31	33	32	29
LONG-TERM CARE INSURANCE	6	8	8	3
WELLNESS PROGRAMS	37	51	38	29
EMPLOYEE ASSISTANCE PROGRAMS	62	74	64	53
PAID TIME OFF				
HOLIDAYS	82	91	89	75
VACATIONS	88	92	93	83
PERSONAL LEAVE	13	21	17	7
FUNERAL LEAVE	50	58	55	45
JURY DUTY LEAVE	58	74	66	48
MILITARY LEAVE	17	23	19	13
FAMILY LEAVE	2	5	2	1
UNPAID FAMILY LEAVE	47	53	50	43
DISABILITY BENEFITS				
SHORT- TERM DISABILITY	61	75	69	50
PAID SICK LEAVE	50	69	61	36
SICKNESS AND ACCIDENT INSURANCE	26	27	27	25
LONG- TERM DISABILITY	20	36	27	10
SURVIVOR BENEFITS				
LIFE INSURANCE	61	73	68	52
ACCIDENTAL DEATH AND DISMEMBERMENT	48	60	52	40
HEALTH CARE BENEFITS				
MEDICAL CARE	66	80	70	57
DENTAL CARE	28	40	31	22
VISION CARE	10	11	11	10
OUTPATIENT PRESCRIPTION DRUG COVERAGE	60	75	64	51
RETIREMENT INCOME BENEFITS				
ALL RETIREMENT [1]	42	53	47	35
DEFINED BENEFIT	15	16	16	15
DEFINED CONTRIBUTION	34	45	39	26
SAVINGS AND THRIFT	17	23	20	13
DEFERRED PROFIT SHARING	13	16	17	10
EMPLOYEE STOCK OWNERSHIP	1	2	1	1
MONEY PURCHASE PENSION	5	9	5	4
CASH OR DEFERRED ARRANGEMENTS				
WITH EMPLOYER CONTRIBUTIONS	20	28	23	15
NO EMPLOYER CONTRIBUTIONS	3	5	3	2
INCOME CONTINUATION PLANS				
SEVERANCE PAY	15	24	22	8
SUPPLEMENTAL UNEMPLOYMENT BENEFITS	(Z)	(Z)	(Z)	(Z)
FAMILY BENEFITS				
EMPLOYER ASSISTANCE FOR CHILDCARE	1	2	1	1
EMPLOYER PROVIDED FUNDS	1	1	1	(Z)
ON-SITE CHILD CARE	1	1	(Z)	1
OFF-SITE CHILD CARE	(Z)	-	(Z)	(Z)
ELDERCARE	33	38	35	29
LONG-TERM CARE INSURANCE	1	1	1	(Z)

TABLE A5.9 (CONTINUED)

EMPLOYEE BENEFITS IN PRIVATE ESTABLISHMENTS IN THE UNITED STATES: 1993 AND 1994

(COVERS FULL-TIME EMPLOYEES IN PRIVATE INDUSTRY. MEDIUM AND LARGE ESTABLISHMENTS EXCLUDES ESTABLISHMENTS WITH FEWER THAN 100 WORKERS, EXECUTIVE AND TRAVELING OPERATING EMPLOYEES, AND ALASKA AND HAWAII. SMALL ESTABLISHMENTS INCLUDE THOSE WITH FEWER THAN 100 EMPLOYEES. COVERS ONLY BENEFITS FOR WHICH THE EMPLOYER PAYS PART OR ALL OF THE PREMIUM OR EXPENSES INVOLVED, EXCEPT UNPAID PARENTAL LEAVE AND LONG-TERM CARE INSURANCE.)

PERCENT OF EMPLOYEES PARTICIPATING IN—	ALL EMPLOYEES	PROFESSIONAL, TECHNICAL AND RELATED	CLERICAL AND SALES	PRODUCTION AND SERVICE
HEALTH PROMOTION PROGRAMS				
WELLNESS PROGRAMS	6	8	8	3
EMPLOYEE ASSISTANCE	15	19	18	11
MISCELLANEOUS BENEFITS:				
EMPLOYER-SUBSIDIZED RECREATION FACILITIES	5	7	5	4
JOB-RELATED TRAVEL ACCIDENT INSURANCE	13	18	14	10
NONPRODUCTION BONUSES	47	48	49	46
FINANCIAL COUNSELING	2	3	2	2
SUBSIDIZED COMMUTING	1	2	(Z)	(Z)
SABBATICAL LEAVE	1	3	1	1
EDUCATION ASSISTANCE:				
JOB-RELATED	37	49	46	27
NOT JOB-RELATED	6	7	8	4
FLEXIBLE BENEFIT PLANS	3	2	5	2
REIMBURSEMENT ACCOUNTS [4]	19	28	23	13

- REPRESENTS ZERO.

Z = LESS THAN .5 PERCENT.

[1] EMPLOYEES MAY PARTICIPATE IN BOTH DEFINED BENEFIT AND CONTRIBUTION PLANS.

[2] EARNINGS- BASED FORMULAS PAY A PERCENT OF EMPLOYEE'S ANNUAL EARNINGS (USUALLY EARNINGS IN THE FINAL YEARS OF EMPLOYMENT) PER YEAR OF SERVICE.

[3] 1991 DATA.

[4] ACCOUNT WHICH IS USED THROUGHOUT THE YEAR TO PAY FOR PLAN PREMIUMS OR TO REIMBURSE THE EMPLOYEE FOR BENEFIT-RELATED EXPENSES. ACCOUNT MAY BE FINANCED BY EMPLOYER, EMPLOYEE, OR BOTH.

Source: U. S. Bureau of Labor Statistics.

INCOME, WEALTH, AND POVERTY

TABLE A6.1

INCOME LIMITS FOR EACH FIFTH AND TOP 5 PERCENT OF HOUSEHOLDS IN THE UNITED STATES (ALL RACES): 1967–96

(HOUSEHOLDS AS OF MARCH OF THE FOLLOWING YEAR. INCOME IN CURRENT AND 1996 CPI-U-X1 ADJUSTED DOLLARS. DATA FOR THE YEARS 1974 THROUGH 1986 WERE REVISED IN MARCH 1996. FOR FURTHER DETAILS, SEE NOTE AT END OF TABLE.)

| YEAR | NUMBER (THOUS.) | UPPER LIMIT OF EACH FIFTH | | | | LOWER LIMIT OF TOP 5 PERCENT |
		LOWEST	SECOND	THIRD	FOURTH	
IN CURRENT DOLLARS						
1996	101,018	$14,768	$27,760	$44,006	$68,015	$119,540
1995 [14]	99,627	14,400	26,914	42,002	65,124	113,000
1994 [13]	98,990	13,426	25,200	40,100	62,841	109,821
1993 [12]	97,107	12,967	24,679	38,793	60,300	104,639
1992 [11]	96,426	12,600	24,140	37,900	58,007	99,020
1991	95,699	12,588	24,000	37,070	56,760	96,400
1990	94,312	12,500	23,662	36,200	55,205	94,748
1989	93,347	12,096	23,000	35,350	53,710	91,750
1988	92,830	11,382	21,500	33,506	50,593	85,640
1987 [10]	91,124	10,800	20,500	32,000	48,363	80,928
1986	89,479	10,358	19,783	30,555	46,120	78,226
1985 [9]	88,458	10,000	18,852	29,022	43,809	73,263
1984	86,789	9,600	17,904	27,506	41,600	69,590
1983 [8]	85,290	9,000	16,773	25,718	38,898	64,600
1982	83,918	8,520	16,010	24,560	36,670	61,107
1981	83,527	8,160	15,034	23,396	34,600	56,300
1980	82,368	7,556	14,100	21,610	31,700	51,500
1979 [7]	80,776	7,009	13,035	20,025	29,097	47,465
1978	77,330	6,384	12,000	18,146	26,425	42,572
1977	76,030	5,813	10,900	16,531	24,100	38,961
1976 [6]	74,142	5,479	10,133	15,423	22,192	35,382
1975 [5]	72,867	5,025	9,450	14,246	20,496	32,681
1974 [5, 4]	71,163	4,923	9,094	13,400	19,453	31,085
1973	69,859	4,418	8,393	12,450	17,985	28,509
1972 [3]	68,251	4,050	7,800	11,530	16,500	26,560
1971 [2]	66,676	3,800	7,244	10,660	15,200	24,138
1970	64,374	3,687	7,064	10,276	14,661	23,178
1969	63,401	3,574	6,860	9,920	13,900	21,800
1968	61,805	3,323	6,300	9,030	12,688	19,850
1967 [1]	60,446	3,000	5,850	8,306	11,841	19,000
IN 1996 DOLLARS						
1996	101,018	$14,768	$27,760	$44,006	$68,015	$119,540
1995 [14]	99,627	14,825	27,709	43,242	67,047	116,337
1994 [13]	98,990	14,214	26,679	42,454	66,530	116,268
1993 [12]	97,107	14,080	26,797	42,122	65,475	113,618
1992 [11]	96,426	14,091	26,996	42,384	64,870	110,736
1991	95,699	14,501	27,648	42,704	65,386	111,051
1990	94,312	15,006	28,405	43,457	66,271	113,741
1989	93,347	15,305	29,102	44,729	67,960	116,093
1988	92,830	15,096	28,515	44,439	67,101	113,583
1987 [10]	91,124	14,917	28,314	44,197	66,797	111,775
1986	89,479	14,828	28,321	43,742	66,024	111,986
1985 [9]	88,458	14,582	27,490	42,319	63,881	106,830
1984	86,789	14,497	27,037	41,537	62,820	105,088
1983 [8]	85,290	14,178	26,423	40,514	61,276	101,764
1982	83,918	13,983	26,276	40,308	60,183	100,290
1981	83,527	14,210	26,180	40,742	60,252	98,041
1980	82,368	14,405	26,881	41,198	60,434	98,182
1979 [7]	80,776	14,861	27,638	42,458	61,693	100,639
1978	77,330	14,839	27,893	42,179	61,423	98,956
1977	76,030	14,431	27,060	41,040	59,831	96,724
1976 [6]	74,142	14,472	26,765	40,739	58,618	93,459
1975 [5]	72,867	14,029	26,383	39,772	57,221	91,239
1974 [5, 4]	71,163	14,883	27,492	40,510	58,809	93,974
1973	69,859	14,686	27,900	41,386	59,785	94,768

TABLE A6.1 (CONTINUED)

INCOME LIMITS FOR EACH FIFTH AND TOP 5 PERCENT OF HOUSEHOLDS IN THE UNITED STATES (ALL RACES): 1967-96

(HOUSEHOLDS AS OF MARCH OF THE FOLLOWING YEAR. INCOME IN CURRENT AND 1996 CPI-U-X1 ADJUSTED DOLLARS. DATA FOR THE YEARS 1974 THROUGH 1986 WERE REVISED IN MARCH 1996. FOR FURTHER DETAILS, SEE NOTE AT END OF TABLE).

YEAR	NUMBER (THOUS.)	UPPER LIMIT OF EACH FIFTH				LOWER LIMIT OF TOP 5 PERCENT
		LOWEST	SECOND	THIRD	FOURTH	
1972 [3]	68,251	14,312	27,564	40,745	58,307	93,857
1971 [2]	66,676	13,833	26,371	38,806	55,334	87,871
1970	64,374	14,007	26,836	39,039	55,698	88,054
1969	63,401	14,233	27,318	39,504	55,353	86,813
1968	61,805	13,830	26,219	37,581	52,805	82,612
1967 [1]	60,446	12,967	25,286	35,901	51,181	82,124

NA = NOT AVAILABLE.

[1] IMPLEMENTATION OF A NEW MARCH CPS PROCESSING SYSTEM.

[2] INTRODUCTION OF 1970 CENSUS SAMPLE DESIGN AND POPULATION CONTROLS.

[3] FULL IMPLEMENTATION OF 1970 CENSUS-BASED SAMPLE DESIGN.

[4] IMPLEMENTATION OF A NEW MARCH CPS PROCESSING SYSTEM. QUESTIONNAIRE EXPANDED TO ASK ELEVEN INCOME QUESTIONS.

[5] THESE ESTIMATES WERE DERIVED USING PARETO INTERPOLATION AND MAY DIFFER FROM PUBLISHED DATA WHICH WERE DERIVED USING LINEAR INTERPOLATION.

[6] FIRST YEAR MEDIANS ARE DERIVED USING BOTH PARETO AND LINEAR INTERPOLATION. PRIOR TO THIS YEAR ALL MEDIANS WERE DERIVED USING LINEAR INTERPOLATION.

[7] IMPLEMENTATION OF 1980 CENSUS POPULATION CONTROLS. QUESTIONNAIRE EXPANDED TO SHOW 27 POSSIBLE VALUES FROM 51 POSSIBLE SOURCES OF INCOME.

[8] IMPLEMENTATION OF HISPANIC POPULATION WEIGHTING CONTROLS AND INTRODUCTION OF 1980 CENSUS SAMPLE DESIGN.

[9] RECORDING OF AMOUNTS FOR EARNINGS FROM LONGEST JOB INCREASED TO $299,999. FULL IMPLEMENTATION OF 1980 CENSUS-BASED SAMPLE DESIGN.

[10] IMPLEMENTATION OF A NEW MARCH CPS PROCESSING SYSTEM.

[11] IMPLEMENTATION OF 1990 CENSUS POPULATION CONTROLS.

[12] DATA COLLECTION METHOD CHANGED FROM PAPER AND PENCIL TO COMPUTER-ASSISTED INTERVIEWING. IN ADDITION, THE MARCH 1994 INCOME SUPPLEMENT WAS REVISED TO ALLOW FOR THE CODING OF DIFFERENT INCOME AMOUNTS ON SELECTED QUESTIONNAIRE ITEMS. LIMITS EITHER INCREASED OR DECREASED IN THE FOLLOWING CATEGORIES: EARNINGS INCREASED TO $999,999; SOCIAL SECURITY INCREASED TO $49,999; SUPPLEMENTAL SECURITY INCOME AND PUBLIC ASSISTANCE INCREASED TO $24,999; VETERANS' BENEFITS INCREASED TO $99,999; CHILD SUPPORT AND ALIMONY DECREASED TO $49,999.

[13] INTRODUCTION OF 1990 CENSUS SAMPLE DESIGN.

[14] FULL IMPLEMENTATION OF THE 1990 CENSUS-BASED SAMPLE DESIGN AND METROPOLITAN DEFINITIONS, 7,000 HOUSEHOLD SAMPLE REDUCTION, AND REVISED RACE EDITS.

Notes: It appears that between the years 1974 and 1986 negative amounts were included in the aggregate. These data were revised to maintain comparability with the majority of years where negative amounts were treated as zeros.

Source: U.S. Bureau of the Census, March Current Population Survey.

TABLE A6.2

SHARE OF AGGREGATE INCOME RECEIVED BY EACH FIFTH AND TOP 5 PERCENT OF HOUSEHOLDS IN THE UNITED STATES (ALL RACES): 1967–96

(HOUSEHOLDS AS OF MARCH OF THE FOLLOWING YEAR)

YEAR	NUMBER (THOUS.)	SHARES OF AGGREGATE INCOME					
		LOWEST FIFTH	SECOND FIFTH	THIRD FIFTH	FOURTH FIFTH	HIGHEST FIFTH	TOP 5 PERCENT
1996	101,018	3.7	9.0	15.1	23.3	49.0	21.4
1995 [14]	99,627	3.7	9.1	15.2	23.3	48.7	21.0
1994 [13]	98,990	3.6	8.9	15.0	23.4	49.1	21.2
1993 [12]	97,107	3.6	9.0	15.1	23.5	48.9	21.0
1992 [11]	96,426	3.8	9.4	15.8	24.2	46.9	18.6
1991	95,699	3.8	9.6	15.9	24.2	46.5	18.1
1990	94,312	3.9	9.6	15.9	24.0	46.6	18.6
1989	93,347	3.8	9.5	15.8	24.0	46.8	18.9
1988	92,830	3.8	9.6	16.0	24.3	46.3	18.3
1987 [10]	91,124	3.8	9.6	16.1	24.3	46.2	18.2
1986	89,479	3.9	9.7	16.2	24.5	45.7	17.5
1985 [9]	88,458	4.0	9.7	16.3	24.6	45.3	17.0
1984	86,789	4.1	9.9	16.4	24.7	44.9	16.5
1983 [8]	85,290	4.1	10.0	16.5	24.7	44.7	16.4
1982	83,918	4.1	10.1	16.6	24.7	44.5	16.2
1981	83,527	4.2	10.2	16.8	25.0	43.8	15.6
1980	82,368	4.3	10.3	16.9	24.9	43.7	15.8
1979 [7]	80,776	4.2	10.3	16.9	24.7	44.0	16.4
1978	77,330	4.3	10.3	16.9	24.8	43.7	16.2
1977	76,030	4.4	10.3	17.0	24.8	43.6	16.1
1976 [6]	74,142	4.4	10.4	17.1	24.8	43.3	16.0
1975 [5]	72,867	4.4	10.5	17.1	24.8	43.2	15.9
1974 [5, 4]	71,163	4.4	10.6	17.1	24.7	43.1	15.9
1973	69,859	4.2	10.5	17.1	24.6	43.6	16.6
1972 [3]	68,251	4.1	10.5	17.1	24.5	43.9	17.0
1971 [2]	66,676	4.1	10.6	17.3	24.5	43.5	16.7
1970	64,778	4.1	10.8	17.4	24.5	43.3	16.6
1969	63,401	4.1	10.9	17.5	24.5	43.0	16.6
1968	62,214	4.2	11.1	17.5	24.4	42.8	16.6
1967 [1]	60,813	4.0	10.8	17.3	24.2	43.8	17.5

NOTE: IT APPEARS THAT BETWEEN THE YEARS 1974 AND 1986 NEGATIVE AMOUNTS WERE INCLUDED IN THE AGGREGATE. THESE DATA WERE REVISED TO MAINTAIN COMPARABILITY WITH THE MAJORITY OF YEARS WHERE NEGATIVE AMOUNTS WERE TREATED AS ZEROS.

NA = NOT AVAILABLE.

1   IMPLEMENTATION OF A NEW MARCH CPS PROCESSING SYSTEM.

2   INTRODUCTION OF 1970 CENSUS SAMPLE DESIGN AND POPULATION CONTROLS.

3   FULL IMPLEMENTATION OF 1970 CENSUS-BASED SAMPLE DESIGN.

4   IMPLEMENTATION OF A NEW MARCH CPS PROCESSING SYSTEM. QUESTIONNAIRE EXPANDED TO ASK ELEVEN INCOME QUESTIONS.

5   THESE ESTIMATES WERE DERIVED USING PARETO INTERPOLATION AND MAY DIFFER FROM PUBLISHED DATA WHICH WERE DERIVED USING LINEAR INTERPOLATION.

6   FIRST YEAR MEDIANS ARE DERIVED USING BOTH PARETO AND LINEAR INTERPOLATION. PRIOR TO THIS YEAR ALL MEDIANS WERE DERIVED USING LINEAR INTERPOLATION.

7   IMPLEMENTATION OF 1980 CENSUS POPULATION CONTROLS. QUESTIONNAIRE EXPANDED TO SHOW 27 POSSIBLE VALUES FROM 51 POSSIBLE SOURCES OF INCOME.

8   IMPLEMENTATION OF HISPANIC POPULATION WEIGHTING CONTROLS AND INTRODUCTION OF 1980 CENSUS SAMPLE DESIGN.

9   RECORDING OF AMOUNTS FOR EARNINGS FROM LONGEST JOB INCREASED TO $299,999. FULL IMPLEMENTATION OF 1980 CENSUS-BASED SAMPLE DESIGN.

10 IMPLEMENTATION OF A NEW MARCH CPS PROCESSING SYSTEM.

11 IMPLEMENTATION OF 1990 CENSUS POPULATION CONTROLS.

12 DATA COLLECTION METHOD CHANGED FROM PAPER AND PENCIL TO COMPUTER-ASSISTED INTERVIEWING. IN ADDITION, THE MARCH 1994 INCOME SUPPLEMENT WAS REVISED TO ALLOW FOR THE CODING OF DIFFERENT INCOME AMOUNTS ON SELECTED QUESTIONNAIRE ITEMS. LIMITS EITHER INCREASED OR DECREASED IN THE FOLLOWING CATEGORIES: EARNINGS INCREASED TO $999,999; SOCIAL SECURITY INCREASED TO $49,999; SUPPLEMENTAL SECURITY INCOME AND PUBLIC ASSISTANCE INCREASED TO $24,999; VETERANS' BENEFITS INCREASED TO $99,999; CHILD SUPPORT AND ALIMONY DECREASED TO $49,999.

13 INTRODUCTION OF 1990 CENSUS SAMPLE DESIGN.

14 FULL IMPLEMENTATION OF THE 1990 CENSUS-BASED SAMPLE DESIGN AND METROPOLITAN DEFINITIONS, 7,000 HOUSEHOLD SAMPLE REDUCTION, AND REVISED RACE EDITS.

Source: U.S. Bureau of the Census.

TABLE A6.3

RACE AND HISPANIC ORIGIN OF HOUSEHOLDER-FAMILIES IN THE UNITED STATES BY MEDIAN AND MEAN INCOME: 1947–96

(FAMILIES AS OF MARCH OF THE FOLLOWING YEAR. INCOME IN CURRENT AND 1996 CPI-U-X1 ADJUSTED DOLLARS[1])

RACE AND YEAR	NUMBER (THOUSANDS)	MEDIAN INCOME		MEAN INCOME	
		CURRENT DOLLARS	1996 DOLLARS	CURRENT DOLLARS	1996 DOLLARS
ALL RACES					
1996	70,241	$42,300	$42,300	$53,676	$53,676
1995 [24]	69,597	40,611	41,810	51,353	52,869
1994 [23]	69,313	38,782	41,059	49,340	52,236
1993 [22]	68,506	36,959	40,131	47,221	51,273
1992 [21]	68,216	36,573	40,900	44,221	49,453
1991	67,173	35,939	41,401	43,237	49,808
1990	66,322	35,353	42,440	42,652	51,202
1989	66,090	34,213	43,290	41,506	52,518
1988	65,837	32,191	42,695	38,608	51,205
1987 [20]	65,204	30,970	42,775	36,884	50,943
1986	64,491	29,458	42,171	34,924	49,996
1985 [19]	63,558	27,735	40,443	32,944	48,038
1984 [18]	62,706	26,433	39,917	31,052	46,892
1983	61,997	24,580	38,721	28,638	45,113
1982	61,393	23,433	38,459	27,391	44,954
1981	61,019	22,388	38,986	25,838	44,994
1980	60,309	21,023	40,079	23,974	45,705
1979 [17]	59,550	19,587	41,530	22,316	47,316
1978	57,804	17,640	41,003	20,091	46,700
1977	57,215	16,009	39,744	18,264	45,342
1976 [16]	56,710	14,958	39,510	16,870	44,561
1975 [15]	56,245	13,719	38,301	15,546	43,402
1974 [15, 14]	55,698	12,902	39,004	14,711	44,473
1973	55,053	12,051	40,059	13,622	45,282
1972 [15]	54,373	11,116	39,282	12,625	44,614
1971 [14]	53,296	10,285	37,441	11,583	42,166
1970	52,227	9,867	37,485	11,106	42,192
1969	51,586	9,433	37,564	10,577	42,120
1968	50,823	8,632	35,925	9,670	40,245
1967 [15]	50,111	7,933	34,289	8,801	38,041
1966 [14]	49,214	7,532	33,573	8,395	37,420
1965 [7]	48,509	6,957	31,917	7,704	35,344
1964	47,956	6,569	30,584	7,336	34,155
1963	47,540	6,249	29,443	6,998	32,973
1962 [6]	47,059	5,956	28,491	6,670	31,906
1961 [5]	46,418	5,735	27,687	6,471	31,240
1960	45,539	5,620	27,384	6,227	30,342
1959	45,111	5,417	26,896	5,976	29,672
1958	44,232	5,087	25,419	5,565	27,807
1957	43,696	4,966	25,546	5,443	28,000
1956	43,497	4,780	25,337	5,341	28,311
1955	42,889	4,418	23,821	4,962	26,754
1954	41,951	4,167	22,390	4,684	25,168
1953	41,202	4,242	22,951	4,706	25,461
1952 [4]	40,832	3,890	21,192	4,457	24,281
1951	40,578	3,709	20,563	4,194	23,252
1950	39,929	3,319	19,876	3,815	22,846
1949 [3]	39,303	3,107	18,822	3,569	21,621
1948	38,624	3,187	19,086	3,671	21,984
1947 [2]	37,237	3,031	19,651	3,546	22,990

TABLE A6.3 (CONTINUED)

RACE AND HISPANIC ORIGIN OF HOUSEHOLDER-FAMILIES IN THE UNITED STATES BY MEDIAN AND MEAN INCOME: 1947–96

(FAMILIES AS OF MARCH OF THE FOLLOWING YEAR. INCOME IN CURRENT AND 1996 CPI-U-X1 ADJUSTED DOLLARS[1])

NA = NOT AVAILABLE.

[1] PRIOR TO 1967, CPI FACTORS ARE EXTRAPOLATED.

[2] PRIOR TO 1967, DATA ARE FOR BLACK AND OTHER RACES.

[3] PERSONS OF HISPANIC ORIGIN MAY BE OF ANY RACE.

[4] BASED ON 1940 CENSUS POPULATION CONTROLS.

[5] IMPLEMENTATION OF EXPANDED INCOME QUESTIONS TO SHOW WAGE AND SALARY, FARM SELF-EMPLOYMENT, NONFARM SELF-EMPLOYMENT AND ALL OTHER NONEARNED INCOME SEPARATELY.

[6] IMPLEMENTATION OF 1950 CENSUS POPULATION CONTROLS.

[7] IMPLEMENTATION OF FIRST HOTDECK PROCEDURE TO IMPUTE MISSING INCOME ENTRIES (ALL INCOME DATA IMPUTED IF ANY MISSING). INTRODUCTION OF 1960 CENSUS SAMPLE DESIGN.

[8] FULL IMPLEMENTATION OF 1960 CENSUS-BASED SAMPLE DESIGN AND POPULATION CONTROLS.

[9] IMPLEMENTATION OF NEW PROCEDURES TO IMPUTE MISSING DATA ONLY.

[10] QUESTIONNAIRE EXPANDED TO ASK EIGHT INCOME QUESTIONS.

[11] IMPLEMENTATION OF A NEW MARCH CPS PROCESSING SYSTEM.

[12] INTRODUCTION OF 1970 CENSUS SAMPLE DESIGN AND POPULATION CONTROLS.

[13] FULL IMPLEMENTATION OF 1970 CENSUS-BASED SAMPLE DESIGN.

[14] IMPLEMENTATION OF A NEW MARCH CPS PROCESSING SYSTEM. QUESTIONNAIRE EXPANDED TO ASK ELEVEN INCOME QUESTIONS.

[15] THESE ESTIMATES WERE DERIVED USING PARETO INTERPOLATION AND MAY DIFFER FROM PUBLISHED DATA WHICH WERE DERIVED USING LINEAR INTERPOLATION.

[16] FIRST YEAR MEDIANS ARE DERIVED USING BOTH PARETO AND LINEAR INTERPOLATION. PRIOR TO THIS YEAR ALL MEDIANS WERE DERIVED USING LINEAR INTERPOLATION.

[17] IMPLEMENTATION OF 1980 CENSUS POPULATION CONTROLS. QUESTIONNAIRE EXPANDED TO SHOW 27 POSSIBLE VALUES FROM 51 POSSIBLE SOURCES OF INCOME.

[18] IMPLEMENTATION OF HISPANIC POPULATION WEIGHTING CONTROLS AND INTRODUCTION OF 1980 CENSUS SAMPLE DESIGN.

[19] RECORDING OF AMOUNTS FOR EARNINGS FROM LONGEST JOB INCREASED TO $299,999. FULL IMPLEMENTATION OF 1980 CENSUS-BASED SAMPLE DESIGN.

[20] IMPLEMENTATION OF A NEW MARCH CPS PROCESSING SYSTEM.

[21] IMPLEMENTATION OF 1990 CENSUS POPULATION CONTROLS.

[22] DATA COLLECTION METHOD CHANGED FROM PAPER AND PENCIL TO COMPUTER-ASSISTED INTERVIEWING. IN ADDITION, THE MARCH 1994 INCOME SUPPLEMENT WAS REVISED TO ALLOW FOR THE CODING OF DIFFERENT INCOME AMOUNTS ON SELECTED QUESTIONNAIRE ITEMS. LIMITS EITHER INCREASED OR DECREASED IN THE FOLLOWING CATEGORIES: EARNINGS INCREASED TO $999,999; SOCIAL SECURITY INCREASED TO $49,999; SUPPLEMENTAL SECURITY INCOME AND PUBLIC ASSISTANCE INCREASED TO $24,999; VETERANS' BENEFITS INCREASED TO $99,999; CHILD SUPPORT

AND ALIMONY DECREASED TO $49,999.

[23] INTRODUCTION OF 1990 CENSUS SAMPLE DESIGN.

[24] FULL IMPLEMENTATION OF THE 1990 CENSUS-BASED SAMPLE DESIGN AND METROPOLITAN DEFINITIONS, 7,000 HOUSEHOLD SAMPLE REDUCTION, AND REVISED RACE EDITS.

Source: U.S. Bureau of the Census, Income Statistics Branch/HHES Division.

TABLE A6.4

TYPE OF FAMILY (ALL RACES) IN THE UNITED STATES BY MEDIAN AND MEAN INCOME: 1947–1996

(FAMILIES AS OF MARCH OF THE FOLLOWING YEAR. INCOME IN CURRENT AND 1996 CPI-U-X1 ADJUSTED DOLLARS[1])

TYPE OF FAMILY AND YEAR	NUMBER (THOUS.)	MEDIAN INCOME		MEAN INCOME	
		CURRENT DOLLARS	1996 DOLLARS	CURRENT DOLLARS	1996 DOLLARS
ALL FAMILIES					
1996	70,241	$42,300	$42,300	$53,676	$53,676
1995 [24]	69,597	40,611	41,810	51,353	52,869
1994 [23]	69,313	38,782	41,059	49,340	52,236
1993 [22]	68,506	36,959	40,131	47,221	51,273
1992 [21]	68,216	36,573	40,900	44,221	49,453
1991	67,173	35,939	41,401	43,237	49,808
1990	66,322	35,353	42,440	42,652	51,202
1989	66,090	34,213	43,290	41,506	52,518
1988	65,837	32,191	42,695	38,608	51,205
1987 [20]	65,204	30,970	42,775	36,884	50,943
1986	64,491	29,458	42,171	34,924	49,996
1985 [19]	63,558	27,735	40,443	32,944	48,038
1984 [18]	62,706	26,433	39,917	31,052	46,892
1983	61,997	24,580	38,721	28,638	45,113
1982	61,393	23,433	38,459	27,391	44,954
1981	61,019	22,388	38,986	25,838	44,994
1980	60,309	21,023	40,079	23,974	45,705
1979 [17]	59,550	19,587	41,530	22,316	47,316
1978	57,804	17,640	41,003	20,091	46,700
1977	57,215	16,009	39,744	18,264	45,342
1976 [16]	56,710	14,958	39,510	16,870	44,561
1975 [15]	56,245	13,719	38,301	15,546	43,402
1974 [15, 14]	55,698	12,902	39,004	14,711	44,473
1973	55,053	12,051	40,059	13,622	45,282
1972 [13]	54,373	11,116	39,282	12,625	44,614
1971 [12]	53,296	10,285	37,441	11,583	42,166
1970	52,227	9,867	37,485	11,106	42,192
1969	51,586	9,433	37,564	10,577	42,120
1968	50,823	8,632	35,925	9,670	40,245
1967 [11]	50,111	7,933	34,289	8,801	38,041
1966 [10]	49,214	7,532	33,573	NA	NA
1965 [9]	48,509	6,957	31,917	NA	NA
1964	47,956	6,569	30,584	NA	NA
1963	47,540	6,249	29,443	NA	NA
1962 [8]	47,059	5,956	28,491	NA	NA
1961 [7]	46,418	5,735	27,687	NA	NA
1960	45,539	5,620	27,384	NA	NA
1959	45,111	5,417	26,896	NA	NA
1958	44,232	5,087	25,419	NA	NA
1957	43,696	4,966	25,546	NA	NA
1956	43,497	4,780	25,337	NA	NA
1955	42,889	4,418	23,821	NA	NA
1954	41,951	4,167	22,390	NA	NA
1953	41,202	4,242	22,951	NA	NA
1952 [6]	40,832	3,890	21,192	NA	NA
1951	40,578	3,709	20,563	NA	NA
1950	39,929	3,319	19,876	NA	NA
1949 [5]	39,303	3,107	18,822	NA	NA
1948	38,624	3,187	19,086	NA	NA
1947 [4]	37,237	3,031	19,651	NA	NA

TABLE A6.4 (CONTINUED)

TYPE OF FAMILY (ALL RACES) IN THE UNITED STATES BY MEDIAN AND MEAN INCOME: 1947–1996

(FAMILIES AS OF MARCH OF THE FOLLOWING YEAR. INCOME IN CURRENT AND 1996 CPI-U-X1 ADJUSTED DOLLARS[1])

TYPE OF FAMILY AND YEAR	NUMBER (THOUS.)	MEDIAN INCOME		MEAN INCOME	
		CURRENT DOLLARS	1996 DOLLARS	CURRENT DOLLARS	1996 DOLLARS
MARRIED COUPLE FAMILIES					
1996	53,604	$49,707	$49,707	$61,214	$61,214
1995 [24]	53,570	47,062	48,452	58,377	60,101
1994 [23]	53,865	44,959	47,598	55,944	59,228
1993 [22]	53,181	43,005	46,695	53,472	58,061
1992 [21]	53,090	41,890	46,846	49,755	55,642
1991	52,457	40,995	47,226	48,480	55,848
1990	52,147	39,895	47,892	47,528	57,055
1989	52,317	38,547	48,774	45,995	58,199
1988	52,100	36,389	48,262	42,801	56,766
1987 [20]	51,675	34,879	48,174	40,818	56,376
1986	51,537	32,805	46,963	38,672	55,362
1985 [19]	50,933	31,100	45,349	36,267	52,884
1984 [18]	50,350	29,612	44,717	34,156	51,579
1983	50,090	27,286	42,984	31,467	49,570
1982	49,908	26,019	42,703	29,992	49,223
1981	49,630	25,065	43,648	28,253	49,200
1980	49,294	23,141	44,117	26,128	49,811
1979 [17]	49,112	21,429	45,435	24,222	51,357
1978	47,692	19,340	44,955	21,804	50,682
1977	47,385	17,616	43,733	19,798	49,150
1976 [16]	47,497	16,203	42,799	18,206	48,090
1975 [15]	47,318	14,867	41,506	16,693	46,604
1974 [15, 14]	47,069	13,923	42,091	15,767	47,666
1973	46,812	13,028	43,307	14,594	48,513
1972 [13]	46,314	11,903	42,063	13,477	47,625
1971 [12]	45,752	10,990	40,008	12,336	44,908
1970	44,739	10,516	39,951	11,774	44,730
1969	44,436	10,001	39,826	11,187	44,549
1968	43,841	9,144	38,056	10,222	42,542
1967 [11]	43,292	8,441	36,485	9,508	41,097
1966 [10]	42,553	7,838	34,937	NA	NA
1965 [9]	42,108	7,265	33,330	NA	NA
1964	41,647	6,932	32,274	NA	NA
1963	41,311	6,593	31,064	NA	NA
1962 [8]	40,923	6,263	29,959	NA	NA
1961 [7]	40,405	6,037	29,145	NA	NA
1960	39,624	5,873	28,617	NA	NA
1959	39,335	5,662	28,113	NA	NA
1958	38,585	5,315	26,558	NA	NA
1957	38,112	5,157	26,529	NA	NA
1956	37,849	4,973	26,360	NA	NA
1955	37,200	4,599	24,797	NA	NA
1954	36,395	4,333	23,282	NA	NA
1953	NA	4,371	23,649	NA	NA
1952 [6]	35,782	4,061	22,124	NA	NA
1951	35,196	3,837	21,273	NA	NA
1950	34,556	3,446	20,637	NA	NA
1949 [5]	34,291	3,195	19,355	NA	NA
1948	33,538	3,272	19,595	NA	NA
1947 [4]	32,288	3,109	20,157	NA	NA

TABLE A6.4 (CONTINUED)

TYPE OF FAMILY (ALL RACES) IN THE UNITED STATES BY MEDIAN AND MEAN INCOME: 1947–1996

(FAMILIES AS OF MARCH OF THE FOLLOWING YEAR. INCOME IN CURRENT AND 1996 CPI-U-X1 ADJUSTED DOLLARS[1])

TYPE OF FAMILY AND YEAR	NUMBER (THOUS.)	MEDIAN INCOME		MEAN INCOME	
		CURRENT DOLLARS	1996 DOLLARS	CURRENT DOLLARS	1996 DOLLARS
WIFE IN PAID LABOR FORCE					
1996	33,242	$58,381	$58,381	NA	NA
1995 [24]	32,677	55,823	57,471	NA	NA
1994 [23]	32,902	53,309	56,438	NA	NA
1993 [22]	32,194	51,204	55,598	NA	NA
1992 [21]	31,389	49,775	55,664	NA	NA
1991	30,923	48,169	55,490	NA	NA
1990	30,298	46,777	56,154	NA	NA
1989	30,188	45,266	57,276	NA	NA
1988	29,713	42,709	56,644	NA	NA
1987 [20]	29,010	40,751	56,284	NA	NA
1986	28,498	38,346	54,895	$43,635	$62,467
1985 [19]	27,489	36,431	53,123	41,058	59,870
1984 [18]	26,938	34,668	52,352	38,570	58,245
1983	26,177	32,107	50,578	35,751	56,319
1982	25,480	30,342	49,798	33,729	55,356
1981	25,002	29,247	50,931	31,757	55,302
1980	24,752	26,879	51,243	29,291	55,842
1979 [17]	24,187	24,861	52,712	27,236	57,748
1978	23,005	22,109	51,391	24,445	56,821
1977	21,936	20,268	50,317	22,153	54,997
1976 [16]	21,554	18,731	49,476	20,396	53,874
1975 [15]	20,833	17,237	48,123	18,633	52,020
1974 [15, 14]	20,404	16,221	49,038	17,538	53,019
1973	19,464	15,237	50,650	16,439	54,646
1972 [13]	18,888	13,897	49,109	15,094	53,339
1971 [12]	18,274	12,853	46,790	13,882	50,536
1970	17,568	12,276	46,637	13,315	50,584
1969	17,464	11,629	46,309	12,576	50,081
1968	16,638	10,686	44,473	11,490	47,819
1967 [11]	15,845	9,956	43,033	10,803	46,694
1966 [10]	15,005	9,246	41,213	NA	NA
1965 [9]	14,183	8,597	39,441	NA	NA
1964	13,647	8,170	38,038	NA	NA
1963	13,398	7,789	36,700	NA	NA
1962 [8]	13,028	7,461	35,690	NA	NA
1961 [7]	12,366	7,188	34,701	NA	NA
1960	12,007	6,900	33,621	NA	NA
1959	11,265	6,705	33,292	NA	NA
1958	11,014	6,214	31,050	NA	NA
1957	10,696	6,141	31,591	NA	NA
1956	10,266	5,957	31,576	NA	NA
1955	9,786	5,622	30,312	NA	NA
1954	9,005	5,336	28,672	NA	NA
1953	NA	5,405	29,243	NA	NA
1952 [6]	9,154	4,900	26,695	NA	NA
1951	8,044	4,631	25,675	NA	NA
1950	NA	4,003	23,972	NA	NA
1949 [5]	NA	3,857	23,365	NA	NA

TABLE A6.4 (CONTINUED)

TYPE OF FAMILY (ALL RACES) IN THE UNITED STATES BY MEDIAN AND MEAN INCOME: 1947–1996

(FAMILIES AS OF MARCH OF THE FOLLOWING YEAR. INCOME IN CURRENT AND 1996 CPI-U-X1 ADJUSTED DOLLARS[1])

TYPE OF FAMILY AND YEAR	NUMBER (THOUS.)	MEDIAN INCOME		MEAN INCOME	
		CURRENT DOLLARS	1996 DOLLARS	CURRENT DOLLARS	1996 DOLLARS
WIFE NOT IN PAID LABOR FORCE					
1996	20,362	$33,748	$33,748	NA	NA
1995 [24]	20,893	32,375	33,331	NA	NA
1994 [23]	20,962	31,176	33,006	NA	NA
1993 [22]	20,988	30,218	32,811	NA	NA
1992 [21]	21,701	30,174	33,744	NA	NA
1991	21,534	30,075	34,646	NA	NA
1990	21,849	30,265	36,332	NA	NA
1989	22,129	28,747	36,374	NA	NA
1988	22,387	27,220	36,102	NA	NA
1987 [20]	22,664	26,640	36,794	NA	NA
1986	23,038	25,803	36,939	$32,533	$46,573
1985 [19]	23,445	24,556	35,807	30,650	44,693
1984 [18]	23,412	23,582	35,611	29,078	43,911
1983	23,913	21,890	34,483	26,777	42,182
1982	24,428	21,299	34,956	26,094	42,826
1981	24,628	20,325	35,394	24,696	43,006
1980	24,542	18,972	36,169	22,938	43,730
1979 [17]	24,925	17,706	37,542	21,297	45,155
1978	24,686	16,156	37,554	19,343	44,962
1977	25,449	15,063	37,395	17,768	44,111
1976 [16]	25,944	13,931	36,798	16,386	43,282
1975 [15]	26,486	12,752	35,601	15,166	42,341
1974 [15, 14]	26,665	12,231	36,976	14,411	43,566
1973	27,348	11,418	37,955	13,281	44,148
1972 [13]	27,426	10,556	37,303	12,363	43,688
1971 [12]	27,478	9,744	35,472	11,307	41,162
1970	27,172	9,304	35,346	10,778	40,946
1969	26,972	8,879	35,358	10,288	40,969
1968	27,203	8,215	34,189	9,447	39,317
1967 [11]	27,447	7,611	32,897	8,760	37,863
1966 [10]	27,548	7,128	31,772	NA	NA
1965 [9]	27,925	6,592	30,242	NA	NA
1964	28,000	6,338	29,508	NA	NA
1963	27,913	6,039	28,454	NA	NA
1962 [8]	27,895	5,764	27,572	NA	NA
1961 [7]	28,039	5,592	26,996	NA	NA
1960	27,617	5,520	26,897	NA	NA
1959	28,070	5,317	26,400	NA	NA
1958	27,571	4,983	24,899	NA	NA
1957	27,416	4,833	24,862	NA	NA
1956	27,583	4,645	24,622	NA	NA
1955	27,414	4,326	23,325	NA	NA
1954	27,390	4,051	21,767	NA	NA
1953	NA	4,117	22,274	NA	NA
1952 [6]	26,628	3,812	20,767	NA	NA
1951	27,152	3,634	20,148	NA	NA
1950	NA	3,315	19,852	NA	NA
1949 [5]	NA	3,058	18,525	NA	NA

TABLE A6.4 (CONTINUED)

TYPE OF FAMILY (ALL RACES) IN THE UNITED STATES BY MEDIAN AND MEAN INCOME: 1947–1996

(FAMILIES AS OF MARCH OF THE FOLLOWING YEAR. INCOME IN CURRENT AND 1996 CPI-U-X1 ADJUSTED DOLLARS[1])

TYPE OF FAMILY AND YEAR	NUMBER (THOUS.)	MEDIAN INCOME		MEAN INCOME	
		CURRENT DOLLARS	1996 DOLLARS	CURRENT DOLLARS	1996 DOLLARS
MALE HOUSEHOLDER, NO WIFE PRESENT					
1996	3,847	$31,600	$31,600	$40,013	$40,013
1995 [24]	3,513	30,358	31,254	37,238	38,338
1994 [23]	3,228	27,751	29,380	34,663	36,698
1993 [22]	2,914	26,467	28,738	33,585	36,467
1992 [21]	3,065	27,576	30,839	34,070	38,101
1991	3,025	28,351	32,660	34,611	39,871
1990	2,907	29,046	34,869	34,685	41,638
1989	2,884	27,847	35,235	34,756	43,978
1988	2,847	26,827	35,580	32,501	43,106
1987 [20]	2,834	25,208	34,816	30,786	42,520
1986	2,510	24,962	35,735	29,472	42,191
1985 [19]	2,414	22,622	32,987	27,525	40,136
1984 [18]	2,228	23,325	35,223	27,037	40,829
1983	2,030	21,845	34,412	24,949	39,302
1982	2,016	20,140	33,054	22,907	37,595
1981	1,986	19,889	34,635	22,607	39,368
1980	1,933	17,519	33,399	20,820	39,692
1979 [17]	1,733	16,808	35,637	20,047	42,505
1978	1,655	15,966	37,112	18,784	43,662
1977	1,594	14,518	36,042	16,355	40,603
1976 [16]	1,500	12,860	33,969	14,733	38,916
1975 [15]	1,444	12,995	36,280	14,686	41,001
1974 [15, 14]	1,399	11,658	35,244	13,343	40,338
1973	1,438	10,742	35,708	12,219	40,618
1972 [13]	1,453	10,305	36,416	11,657	41,193
1971 [12]	1,353	8,722	31,751	9,911	36,080
1970	1,258	9,012	34,237	10,476	39,799
1969	1,221	8,340	33,212	9,662	38,476
1968	1,229	7,321	30,469	8,185	34,064
1967 [11]	1,210	6,814	29,452	7,899	34,142
1966 [10]	1,197	6,432	28,670	NA	NA
1965 [9]	1,179	6,148	28,205	NA	NA
1964	1,182	5,792	26,966	NA	NA
1963	1,243	5,710	26,904	NA	NA
1962 [8]	1,334	5,711	27,319	NA	NA
1961 [7]	1,293	5,069	24,472	NA	NA
1960	1,202	4,860	23,681	NA	NA
1959	1,233	4,613	22,904	NA	NA
1958	1,285	4,260	21,286	NA	NA
1957	1,292	4,581	23,566	NA	NA
1956	1,230	4,167	22,088	NA	NA
1955	1,404	4,190	22,591	NA	NA
1954	1,314	4,014	21,568	NA	NA
1953	NA	4,113	22,253	NA	NA
1952 [6]	1,396	3,615	19,694	NA	NA
1951	1,216	3,452	19,138	NA	NA
1950	1,226	3,115	18,654	NA	NA
1949 [5]	1,265	2,821	17,089	NA	NA
1948	1,287	3,295	19,732	NA	NA
1947 [4]	1,234	2,936	19,035	NA	NA

TABLE A6.4 (CONTINUED)

TYPE OF FAMILY (ALL RACES) IN THE UNITED STATES BY MEDIAN AND MEAN INCOME: 1947–1996

(FAMILIES AS OF MARCH OF THE FOLLOWING YEAR. INCOME IN CURRENT AND 1996 CPI-U-X1 ADJUSTED DOLLARS[1])

TYPE OF FAMILY AND YEAR	NUMBER (THOUS.)	MEDIAN INCOME		MEAN INCOME	
		CURRENT DOLLARS	1996 DOLLARS	CURRENT DOLLARS	1996 DOLLARS
FEMALE HOUSEHOLDER, NO HUSBAND PRESENT					
1996	12,790	$19,911	$19,911	$26,196	$26,196
1995 [24]	12,514	19,691	20,272	25,249	25,995
1994 [23]	12,220	18,236	19,307	24,105	25,520
1993 [22]	12,411	17,443	18,940	23,635	25,663
1992 [21]	12,061	17,025	19,039	22,441	25,096
1991	11,692	16,692	19,229	21,946	25,281
1990	11,268	16,932	20,326	22,140	26,578
1989	10,890	16,442	20,804	21,730	27,495
1988	10,890	15,346	20,353	20,144	26,717
1987 [20]	10,696	14,683	20,280	19,489	26,917
1986	10,445	13,647	19,537	17,743	25,400
1985 [19]	10,211	13,660	19,919	17,647	25,732
1984 [18]	10,129	12,803	19,334	16,501	24,918
1983	9,878	11,789	18,571	15,052	23,711
1982	9,469	11,484	18,848	14,635	24,019
1981	9,403	10,960	19,086	13,773	23,984
1980	9,082	10,408	19,842	12,953	24,694
1979 [17]	8,705	9,880	20,948	12,014	25,473
1978	8,458	8,537	19,844	10,689	24,846
1977	8,236	7,765	19,277	9,811	24,357
1976 [16]	7,713	7,211	19,047	9,058	23,926
1975 [15]	7,482	6,844	19,107	8,463	23,627
1974 [15, 14]	7,230	6,488	19,614	8,106	24,505
1973	6,804	5,797	19,270	7,228	24,027
1972 [13]	6,607	5,342	18,877	6,862	24,249
1971 [12]	6,191	5,114	18,617	6,388	23,255
1970	5,950	5,093	19,348	6,213	23,603
1969	5,580	4,822	19,202	5,915	23,555
1968	5,439	4,477	18,632	5,549	23,094
1967 [11]	5,333	4,294	18,560	5,305	22,930
1966 [10]	5,172	4,010	17,874	NA	NA
1965 [9]	4,992	3,532	16,204	NA	NA
1964	5,006	3,458	16,100	NA	NA
1963	4,882	3,211	15,129	NA	NA
1962 [8]	4,741	3,131	14,977	NA	NA
1961 [7]	4,643	2,993	14,449	NA	NA
1960	4,609	2,968	14,462	NA	NA
1959	4,494	2,764	13,724	NA	NA
1958	4,332	2,741	13,696	NA	NA
1957	4,310	2,763	14,214	NA	NA
1956	4,366	2,754	14,598	NA	NA
1955	4,239	2,471	13,323	NA	NA
1954	4,225	2,294	12,326	NA	NA
1953	NA	2,455	13,282	NA	NA
1952 [6]	3,842	2,235	12,176	NA	NA
1951	4,030	2,220	12,308	NA	NA
1950	4,040	1,922	11,510	NA	NA
1949 [5]	3,637	2,103	12,740	NA	NA
1948	3,713	2,064	12,360	NA	NA
1947 [4]	3,757	2,172	14,082	NA	NA

TABLE A6.4 (CONTINUED)

TYPE OF FAMILY (ALL RACES) IN THE UNITED STATES BY MEDIAN AND MEAN INCOME: 1947–1996

(FAMILIES AS OF MARCH OF THE FOLLOWING YEAR. INCOME IN CURRENT AND 1996 CPI-U-X1 ADJUSTED DOLLARS[1])

NA = NOT AVAILABLE.

1 PRIOR TO 1967, CPI FACTORS ARE EXTRAPOLATED.

2 PRIOR TO 1967, DATA ARE FOR BLACK AND OTHER RACES.

3 PERSONS OF HISPANIC ORIGIN MAY BE OF ANY RACE.

4 BASED ON 1940 CENSUS POPULATION CONTROLS.

5 IMPLEMENTATION OF EXPANDED INCOME QUESTIONS TO SHOW WAGE AND SALARY, FARM SELF-EMPLOYMENT, NONFARM SELF-EMPLOYMENT AND ALL OTHER NONEARNED INCOME SEPARATELY.

6 IMPLEMENTATION OF 1950 CENSUS POPULATION CONTROLS.

7 IMPLEMENTATION OF FIRST HOTDECK PROCEDURE TO IMPUTE MISSING INCOME ENTRIES (ALL INCOME DATA IMPUTED IF ANY MISSING). INTRODUCTION OF 1960 CENSUS SAMPLE DESIGN.

8 FULL IMPLEMENTATION OF 1960 CENSUS-BASED SAMPLE DESIGN AND POPULATION CONTROLS.

9 IMPLEMENTATION OF NEW PROCEDURES TO IMPUTE MISSING DATA ONLY.

10 QUESTIONNAIRE EXPANDED TO ASK EIGHT INCOME QUESTIONS.

11 IMPLEMENTATION OF A NEW MARCH CPS PROCESSING SYSTEM.

12 INTRODUCTION OF 1970 CENSUS SAMPLE DESIGN AND POPULATION CONTROLS.

13 FULL IMPLEMENTATION OF 1970 CENSUS-BASED SAMPLE DESIGN.

14 IMPLEMENTATION OF A NEW MARCH CPS PROCESSING SYSTEM. QUESTIONNAIRE EXPANDED TO ASK ELEVEN INCOME QUESTIONS.

15 THESE ESTIMATES WERE DERIVED USING PARETO INTERPOLATION AND MAY DIFFER FROM PUBLISHED DATA WHICH WERE DERIVED USING LINEAR INTERPOLATION.

16 FIRST YEAR MEDIANS ARE DERIVED USING BOTH PARETO AND LINEAR INTERPOLATION. PRIOR TO THIS YEAR ALL MEDIANS WERE DERIVED USING LINEAR INTERPOLATION.

17 IMPLEMENTATION OF 1980 CENSUS POPULATION CONTROLS. QUESTIONNAIRE EXPANDED TO SHOW 27 POSSIBLE VALUES FROM 51 POSSIBLE SOURCES OF INCOME.

18 IMPLEMENTATION OF HISPANIC POPULATION WEIGHTING CONTROLS AND INTRODUCTION OF 1980 CENSUS SAMPLE DESIGN.

19 RECORDING OF AMOUNTS FOR EARNINGS FROM LONGEST JOB INCREASED TO $299,999. FULL IMPLEMENTATION OF 1980 CENSUS-BASED SAMPLE DESIGN.

20 IMPLEMENTATION OF A NEW MARCH CPS PROCESSING SYSTEM.

21 IMPLEMENTATION OF 1990 CENSUS POPULATION CONTROLS.

22 DATA COLLECTION METHOD CHANGED FROM PAPER AND PENCIL TO COMPUTER-ASSISTED INTERVIEWING. IN ADDITION, THE MARCH 1994 INCOME SUPPLEMENT WAS REVISED TO ALLOW FOR THE CODING OF DIFFERENT INCOME AMOUNTS ON SELECTED QUESTIONNAIRE ITEMS. LIMITS EITHER INCREASED OR DECREASED IN THE FOLLOWING CATEGORIES: EARNINGS INCREASED TO $999,999; SOCIAL SECURITY INCREASED TO $49,999; SUPPLEMENTAL SECURITY INCOME AND PUBLIC ASSISTANCE INCREASED TO $24,999; VETERANS' BENEFITS INCREASED TO $99,999; CHILD SUPPORT

AND ALIMONY DECREASED TO $49,999.

23 INTRODUCTION OF 1990 CENSUS SAMPLE DESIGN.

24 FULL IMPLEMENTATION OF THE 1990 CENSUS-BASED SAMPLE DESIGN AND METROPOLITAN DEFINITIONS, 7,000 HOUSEHOLD SAMPLE REDUCTION, AND REVISED RACE EDITS.

Source: U.S. Bureau of the Census, Income Statistics Branch/HHES Division.

TABLE A6.5

TOTAL CPS POPULATION AND PER CAPITA MONEY INCOME IN THE UNITED STATES: 1967-96

(NUMBERS IN THOUSANDS. POPULATION AS OF MARCH OF THE FOLLOWING YEAR. INCOME IN CURRENT AND 1996 CPI-U-X1 ADJUSTED DOLLARS.)

YEAR	POPULATION	PER CAPITA INCOME	
		CURRENT DOLLARS	1996 DOLLARS
1996	266,792	$18,136	$18,136
1995 [14]	264,314	17,227	17,736
1994 [13]	262,105	16,555	17,527
1993 [12]	259,753	15,777	17,131
1992 [11]	256,830	14,847	16,604
1991	251,434	14,617	16,839
1990	248,886	14,387	17,271
1989	246,191	14,056	17,785
1988	243,685	13,123	17,405
1987 [10]	241,187	12,391	17,114
1986	238,789	11,670	16,706
1985 [9]	236,749	11,013	16,059
1984 [8]	234,066	10,328	15,596
1983	231,852	9,494	14,956
1982	229,587	8,980	14,738
1981	227,375	8,476	14,760
1980	225,242	7,787	14,845
1979 [7]	223,160	7,168	15,198
1978	215,935	6,455	15,004
1977	214,159	5,785	14,362
1976 [6]	212,566	5,271	13,923
1975 [5]	211,140	4,818	13,451
1974 [5,4]	209,572	4,445	13,438
1973	207,949	4,141	13,765
1972 [3]	206,302	3,769	13,319
1971 [2]	204,840	3,417	12,439
1970	205,214	3,177	12,070
1969	202,189	3,007	11,975
1968	200,139	2,731	11,366
1967 [1]	198,120	2,464	10,650

NA = NOT AVAILABLE.

[1] IMPLEMENTATION OF A NEW MARCH CPS PROCESSING SYSTEM.

[2] INTRODUCTION OF 1970 CENSUS SAMPLE DESIGN AND POPULATION CONTROLS.

[3] FULL IMPLEMENTATION OF 1970 CENSUS-BASED SAMPLE DESIGN.

[4] IMPLEMENTATION OF A NEW MARCH CPS PROCESSING SYSTEM. QUESTIONNAIRE EXPANDED TO ASK ELEVEN INCOME QUESTIONS.

[5] THESE ESTIMATES WERE DERIVED USING PARETO INTERPOLATION AND MAY DIFFER FROM PUBLISHED DATA WHICH WERE DERIVED USING LINEAR INTERPOLATION.

[6] FIRST YEAR MEDIANS ARE DERIVED USING BOTH PARETO AND LINEAR INTERPOLATION. PRIOR TO THIS YEAR ALL MEDIANS WERE DERIVED USING LINEAR INTERPOLATION.

[7] IMPLEMENTATION OF 1980 CENSUS POPULATION CONTROLS.

[8] IMPLEMENTATION OF HISPANIC POPULATION WEIGHTING CONTROLS AND INTRODUCTION OF 1980 CENSUS SAMPLE DESIGN.

[9] RECORDING OF AMOUNTS FOR EARNINGS FROM LONGEST JOB INCREASED TO $299,999. FULL IMPLEMENTATION OF 1980 CENSUS-BASED SAMPLE DESIGN.

[10] IMPLEMENTATION OF A NEW MARCH CPS PROCESSING SYSTEM.

[11] IMPLEMENTATION OF 1990 CENSUS POPULATION CONTROLS.

[12] DATA COLLECTION METHOD CHANGED FROM PAPER AND PENCIL TO COMPUTER-ASSISTED INTERVIEWING. IN ADDITION, THE MARCH 1994 INCOME SUPPLEMENT WAS REVISED TO ALLOW FOR THE CODING OF DIFFERENT INCOME AMOUNTS ON SELECTED QUESTIONNAIRE ITEMS. LIMITS EITHER INCREASED OR DECREASED IN THE FOLLOWING CATEGORIES: EARNINGS INCREASED TO $999,999; SOCIAL SECURITY INCREASED TO $49,999; SUPPLEMENTAL SECURITY INCOME AND PUBLIC ASSISTANCE INCREASED TO $24,999; VETERANS' BENEFITS INCREASED TO $99,999; CHILD SUPPORT AND ALIMONY DECREASED TO $49,999.

[13] INTRODUCTION OF 1990 CENSUS SAMPLE DESIGN.

[14] FULL IMPLEMENTATION OF THE 1990 CENSUS-BASED SAMPLE DESIGN AND METROPOLITAN DEFINITIONS, 7,000 HOUSEHOLD SAMPLE REDUCTION, AND REVISED RACE EDITS.

Source: U.S. Department of the Census.

TABLE A6.6

PERSONS 15 YEARS OLD AND OVER IN THE UNITED STATES BY MEDIAN INCOME AND SEX: 1947-96

(NUMBERS IN THOUSANDS. PERSONS 15 YEARS OLD AND OVER BEGINNING WITH MARCH 1980, AND PERSONS 14 YEARS OLD AND OVER AS OF MARCH OF THE FOLLOWING YEAR FOR PREVIOUS YEARS. INCOME IN CURRENT AND 1996 CPI-U-X1 ADJUSTED DOLLARS.[1])

| | MALE | | | FEMALE | | |
| | | MEDIAN INCOME | | | MEDIAN INCOME | |
AGE AND YEAR	NUMBER WITH INCOME	CURRENT DOLLARS	1996 DOLLARS	NUMBER WITH INCOME	CURRENT DOLLARS	1996 DOLLARS
15 YEARS AND OVER						
1996	93,439	$23,834	$23,834	96,558	$12,815	$12,815
1995 [24]	92,066	22,562	23,228	96,007	12,130	12,488
1994 [23]	91,254	21,720	22,995	95,147	11,466	12,139
1993 [22]	90,194	21,102	22,913	94,417	11,046	11,994
1992 [21]	90,175	20,455	22,875	93,517	10,714	11,982
1991	88,653	20,469	23,580	92,569	10,476	12,068
1990	88,220	20,293	24,361	92,245	10,070	12,089
1989	87,454	19,893	25,171	91,399	9,624	12,177
1988	86,584	18,908	25,077	90,593	8,884	11,783
1987 [20]	85,713	17,786	24,565	89,661	8,295	11,457
1986	84,471	17,114	24,500	87,822	7,610	10,894
1985 [19]	83,631	16,311	23,784	86,531	7,217	10,524
1984 [18]	82,183	15,600	23,558	85,555	6,868	10,371
1983	80,909	14,631	23,048	83,830	6,319	9,954
1982	79,722	13,950	22,895	82,505	5,887	9,662
1981	79,688	13,473	23,462	82,139	5,458	9,505
1980	78,661	12,530	23,888	80,826	4,920	9,380
1979 [17]	78,129	11,779	24,975	79,921	4,352	9,227
1978	75,609	10,935	25,418	71,864	4,068	9,456
1977	74,015	10,123	25,131	65,407	3,941	9,784
1976 [16]	72,775	9,426	24,898	63,170	3,576	9,446
1975 [15]	71,234	8,853	24,716	60,807	3,385	9,450
1974 [15, 14]	70,863	8,452	25,551	59,642	3,082	9,317
1973	69,387	8,056	26,779	57,029	2,796	9,294
1972 [13]	67,474	7,450	26,327	54,487	2,599	9,184
1971 [12]	66,486	6,903	25,129	52,603	2,408	8,766
1970	65,008	6,670	25,340	51,647	2,237	8,498
1969	63,882	6,429	25,602	50,224	2,132	8,490
1968	62,501	5,980	24,888	48,544	2,019	8,403
1967 [11]	61,454	5,571	24,080	46,927	1,819	7,862
1966 [10]	60,088	5,306	23,651	44,067	1,638	7,301
1965 [9]	59,172	4,824	22,131	42,223	1,564	7,175
1964	58,533	4,647	21,635	41,704	1,449	6,746
1963	57,686	4,511	21,255	40,364	1,372	6,464
1962 [8]	56,624	4,372	20,914	38,988	1,342	6,420
1961 [7]	55,839	4,189	20,223	38,076	1,279	6,175
1960	55,172	4,081	19,885	36,526	1,262	6,149
1959	54,285	3,996	19,841	34,380	1,222	6,067
1958	53,543	3,742	18,698	33,340	1,176	5,876
1957	52,877	3,684	18,951	32,702	1,199	6,168
1956	52,016	3,608	19,125	31,823	1,146	6,075
1955	51,446	3,354	18,084	29,791	1,116	6,017
1954	49,712	3,199	17,189	27,715	1,161	6,238
1953	49,667	3,223	17,438	27,379	1,168	6,319
1952 [6]	49,242	3,105	16,916	27,150	1,147	6,249
1951	47,497	2,952	16,366	25,179	1,045	5,794
1950	47,585	2,570	15,391	24,651	953	5,707
1949 [5]	48,258	2,346	14,212	23,510	960	5,816
1948	47,370	2,396	14,349	22,725	1,009	6,042
1947 [4]	46,813	2,230	14,458	21,479	1,017	6,594

TABLE A6.6 (CONTINUED)

PERSONS 15 YEARS OLD AND OVER IN THE UNITED STATES BY MEDIAN INCOME AND SEX: 1947–96

(NUMBERS IN THOUSANDS. PERSONS 15 YEARS OLD AND OVER BEGINNING WITH MARCH 1980, AND PERSONS 14 YEARS OLD AND OVER AS OF MARCH OF THE FOLLOWING YEAR FOR PREVIOUS YEARS. INCOME IN CURRENT AND 1996 CPI-U-X1 ADJUSTED DOLLARS.[1])

NA = NOT AVAILABLE.

[1] PRIOR TO 1967, CPI FACTORS ARE EXTRAPOLATED.

[2] PRIOR TO 1967, DATA ARE FOR BLACK AND OTHER RACES.

[3] PERSONS OF HISPANIC ORIGIN MAY BE OF ANY RACE.

[4] BASED ON 1940 CENSUS POPULATION CONTROLS.

[5] IMPLEMENTATION OF EXPANDED INCOME QUESTIONS TO SHOW WAGE AND SALARY, FARM SELF-EMPLOYMENT, NONFARM SELF-EMPLOYMENT AND ALL OTHER NONEARNED INCOME SEPARATELY.

[6] IMPLEMENTATION OF 1950 CENSUS POPULATION CONTROLS.

[7] IMPLEMENTATION OF FIRST HOTDECK PROCEDURE TO IMPUTE MISSING INCOME ENTRIES (ALL INCOME DATA IMPUTED IF ANY MISSING). INTRODUCTION OF 1960 CENSUS SAMPLE DESIGN.

[8] FULL IMPLEMENTATION OF 1960 CENSUS-BASED SAMPLE DESIGN AND POPULATION CONTROLS.

[9] IMPLEMENTATION OF NEW PROCEDURES TO IMPUTE MISSING DATA ONLY.

[10] QUESTIONNAIRE EXPANDED TO ASK EIGHT INCOME QUESTIONS.

[11] IMPLEMENTATION OF A NEW MARCH CPS PROCESSING SYSTEM.

[12] INTRODUCTION OF 1970 CENSUS SAMPLE DESIGN AND POPULATION CONTROLS.

[13] FULL IMPLEMENTATION OF 1970 CENSUS-BASED SAMPLE DESIGN.

[14] IMPLEMENTATION OF A NEW MARCH CPS PROCESSING SYSTEM. QUESTIONNAIRE EXPANDED TO ASK ELEVEN INCOME QUESTIONS.

[15] THESE ESTIMATES WERE DERIVED USING PARETO INTERPOLATION AND MAY DIFFER FROM PUBLISHED DATA WHICH WERE DERIVED USING LINEAR INTERPOLATION.

[16] FIRST YEAR MEDIANS ARE DERIVED USING BOTH PARETO AND LINEAR INTERPOLATION. PRIOR TO THIS YEAR ALL MEDIANS WERE DERIVED USING LINEAR INTERPOLATION.

[17] IMPLEMENTATION OF 1980 CENSUS POPULATION CONTROLS. QUESTIONNAIRE EXPANDED TO SHOW 27 POSSIBLE VALUES FROM 51 POSSIBLE SOURCES OF INCOME.

[18] IMPLEMENTATION OF HISPANIC POPULATION WEIGHTING CONTROLS AND INTRODUCTION OF 1980 CENSUS SAMPLE DESIGN.

[19] RECORDING OF AMOUNTS FOR EARNINGS FROM LONGEST JOB INCREASED TO $299,999. FULL IMPLEMENTATION OF 1980 CENSUS-BASED SAMPLE DESIGN.

[20] IMPLEMENTATION OF A NEW MARCH CPS PROCESSING SYSTEM.

[21] IMPLEMENTATION OF 1990 CENSUS POPULATION CONTROLS.

[22] DATA COLLECTION METHOD CHANGED FROM PAPER AND PENCIL TO COMPUTER-ASSISTED INTERVIEWING. IN ADDITION, THE MARCH 1994 INCOME SUPPLEMENT WAS REVISED TO ALLOW FOR THE CODING OF DIFFERENT INCOME AMOUNTS ON SELECTED QUESTIONNAIRE ITEMS. LIMITS EITHER INCREASED OR DECREASED IN THE FOLLOWING CATEGORIES: EARNINGS INCREASED TO $999,999; SOCIAL SECURITY INCREASED TO $49,999; SUPPLEMENTAL SECURITY INCOME AND PUBLIC ASSISTANCE INCREASED TO $24,999; VETERANS' BENEFITS INCREASED TO $99,999; CHILD SUPPORT AND ALIMONY DECREASED TO $49,999.

[23] INTRODUCTION OF 1990 CENSUS SAMPLE DESIGN.

[24] FULL IMPLEMENTATION OF THE 1990 CENSUS-BASED SAMPLE DESIGN AND METROPOLITAN DEFINITIONS, 7,000 HOUSEHOLD SAMPLE REDUCTION, AND REVISED RACE EDITS.

Source: U.S. Bureau of the Census, U.S. Department of Commerce.

* Data on persons 15 to 24 years are not available prior to 1974 and data on persons 15 to 19 and 20 to 24 years old are not available after 1986. Data on persons 65 to 74 and 75 years and over are not available prior to 1987.

TABLE A6.7

YEAR-ROUND, FULL-TIME WORKERS IN THE UNITED STATES—PERSONS (ALL RACES) 15 YEARS OLD AND OVER, BY MEDIAN EARNINGS AND SEX: 1960–96

(NUMBERS IN THOUSANDS. PERSONS 15 YEARS OLD AND OVER WITH EARNINGS BEGINNING IN MARCH 1980, AND PERSONS 14 YEARS OLD AND OVER AS OF MARCH OF THE FOLLOWING YEAR FOR PREVIOUS YEARS. PRIOR TO 1989 EARNINGS ARE FOR CIVILIAN WORKERS ONLY. EARNINGS IN CURRENT AND 1996 CPI-U-X1 ADJUSTED DOLLARS.[1])

| | MALE | | | FEMALE | | |
| | | MEDIAN INCOME | | | MEDIAN INCOME | |
AGE AND YEAR	NUMBER WITH EARNINGS	CURRENT DOLLARS	1996 DOLLARS	NUMBER WITH INCOME	CURRENT DOLLARS	1996 DOLLARS
1995 [19]	52,667	31,496	32,426	35,482	22,497	23,161
1994 [18]	51,580	30,854	32,665	34,155	22,205	23,509
1993 [17]	49,818	30,407	33,016	33,524	21,747	23,613
1992 [16]	48,551	30,197	33,770	33,241	21,375	23,904
1991	47,888	29,421	33,892	32,436	20,553	23,677
1990	49,171	27,678	33,226	31,682	19,822	23,795
1989	49,678	27,331	34,583	31,340	18,769	23,749
1988	48,285	26,656	35,354	31,237	17,606	23,351
1987 [15]	47,013	25,946	35,836	29,912	16,911	23,357
1986	45,912	25,256	36,156	28,420	16,232	23,237
1985 [14]	44,943	24,195	35,281	27,383	15,624	22,783
1984 [13]	43,808	23,218	35,062	26,466	14,780	22,319
1983	41,528	21,881	34,469	25,166	13,915	21,920
1982	40,105	21,077	34,592	23,702	13,014	21,359
1981	41,773	20,260	35,281	23,329	12,001	20,899
1980	41,881	18,612	35,483	22,859	11,197	21,346
1979 [12]	42,437	17,014	36,074	22,082	10,151	21,523
1978	41,036	15,730	36,564	20,914	9,350	21,734
1977	39,263	14,626	36,310	19,238	8,618	21,395
1976 [11]	38,184	13,455	35,540	18,073	8,099	21,393
1975 [10]	37,267	12,758	35,618	17,452	7,504	20,950
1974 [9] [8]	37,916	11,863	35,863	16,945	6,970	21,071
1973	39,581	11,186	37,184	17,195	6,335	21,059
1972 [7]	38,184	10,202	36,052	16,675	5,903	20,860
1971 [6]	36,819	9,399	34,216	16,002	5,593	20,361
1970	36,132	8,966	34,062	15,476	5,323	20,222
1969	37,008	8,455	33,670	15,374	4,977	19,820
1968	37,068	7,664	31,896	15,013	4,457	18,549
1967 [5]	36,645	7,182	31,043	14,846	4,150	17,938
1966 [4]	(NA)	6,856	30,560	NA	3,946	17,589
1965 [3]	(NA)	6,388	29,306	NA	3,828	17,562
1964	(NA)	6,203	28,880	NA	3,669	17,082
1963	(NA)	5,980	28,176	NA	3,525	16,609
1962 [2]	(NA)	5,754	27,524	NA	3,412	16,321
1961 [1]	(NA)	5,595	27,011	NA	3,315	16,004
1960	(NA)	5,368	26,156	NA	3,257	15,870

TABLE A6.7 (CONTINUED)

YEAR-ROUND, FULL-TIME WORKERS IN THE UNITED STATES—PERSONS (ALL RACES) 15 YEARS OLD AND OVER, BY MEDIAN EARNINGS AND SEX: 1960—96

(NUMBERS IN THOUSANDS. PERSONS 15 YEARS OLD AND OVER WITH EARNINGS BEGINNING IN MARCH 1980, AND PERSONS 14 YEARS OLD AND OVER AS OF MARCH OF THE FOLLOWING YEAR FOR PREVIOUS YEARS. PRIOR TO 1989 EARNINGS ARE FOR CIVILIAN WORKERS ONLY. EARNINGS IN CURRENT AND 1996 CPI-U-X1 ADJUSTED DOLLARS.[1])

NA = NOT AVAILABLE.

[1] PRIOR TO 1967, CPI FACTORS ARE EXTRAPOLATED.

[2] PRIOR TO 1967, DATA ARE FOR BLACK AND OTHER RACES.

[3] PERSONS OF HISPANIC ORIGIN MAY BE OF ANY RACE.

[4] BASED ON 1940 CENSUS POPULATION CONTROLS.

[5] IMPLEMENTATION OF EXPANDED INCOME QUESTIONS TO SHOW WAGE AND SALARY, FARM SELF-EMPLOYMENT, NONFARM SELF-EMPLOYMENT AND ALL OTHER NONEARNED INCOME SEPARATELY.

[6] IMPLEMENTATION OF 1950 CENSUS POPULATION CONTROLS.

[7] IMPLEMENTATION OF FIRST HOTDECK PROCEDURE TO IMPUTE MISSING INCOME ENTRIES (ALL INCOME DATA IMPUTED IF ANY MISSING). INTRODUCTION OF 1960 CENSUS SAMPLE DESIGN.

[8] FULL IMPLEMENTATION OF 1960 CENSUS-BASED SAMPLE DESIGN AND POPULATION CONTROLS.

[9] IMPLEMENTATION OF NEW PROCEDURES TO IMPUTE MISSING DATA ONLY.

[10] QUESTIONNAIRE EXPANDED TO ASK EIGHT INCOME QUESTIONS.

[11] IMPLEMENTATION OF A NEW MARCH CPS PROCESSING SYSTEM.

[12] INTRODUCTION OF 1970 CENSUS SAMPLE DESIGN AND POPULATION CONTROLS.

[13] FULL IMPLEMENTATION OF 1970 CENSUS-BASED SAMPLE DESIGN.

[14] IMPLEMENTATION OF A NEW MARCH CPS PROCESSING SYSTEM. QUESTIONNAIRE EXPANDED TO ASK ELEVEN INCOME QUESTIONS.

[15] THESE ESTIMATES WERE DERIVED USING PARETO INTERPOLATION AND MAY DIFFER FROM PUBLISHED DATA WHICH WERE DERIVED USING LINEAR INTERPOLATION.

[16] FIRST YEAR MEDIANS ARE DERIVED USING BOTH PARETO AND LINEAR INTERPOLATION. PRIOR TO THIS YEAR ALL MEDIANS WERE DERIVED USING LINEAR INTERPOLATION.

[17] IMPLEMENTATION OF 1980 CENSUS POPULATION CONTROLS. QUESTIONNAIRE EXPANDED TO SHOW 27 POSSIBLE VALUES FROM 51 POSSIBLE SOURCES OF INCOME.

[18] IMPLEMENTATION OF HISPANIC POPULATION WEIGHTING CONTROLS AND INTRODUCTION OF 1980 CENSUS SAMPLE DESIGN.

[19] RECORDING OF AMOUNTS FOR EARNINGS FROM LONGEST JOB INCREASED TO $299,999. FULL IMPLEMENTATION OF 1980 CENSUS-BASED SAMPLE DESIGN.

[20] IMPLEMENTATION OF A NEW MARCH CPS PROCESSING SYSTEM.

[21] IMPLEMENTATION OF 1990 CENSUS POPULATION CONTROLS.

[22] DATA COLLECTION METHOD CHANGED FROM PAPER AND PENCIL TO COMPUTER-ASSISTED INTERVIEWING. IN ADDITION, THE MARCH 1994 INCOME SUPPLEMENT WAS REVISED TO ALLOW FOR THE CODING OF DIFFERENT INCOME AMOUNTS ON SELECTED QUESTIONNAIRE ITEMS. LIMITS EITHER INCREASED OR DECREASED IN THE FOLLOWING CATEGORIES: EARNINGS INCREASED TO $999,999; SOCIAL SECURITY INCREASED TO $49,999; SUPPLEMENTAL SECURITY INCOME AND PUBLIC ASSISTANCE INCREASED TO $24,999; VETERANS' BENEFITS INCREASED TO $99,999; CHILD SUPPORT AND ALIMONY DECREASED TO $49,999.

[23] INTRODUCTION OF 1990 CENSUS SAMPLE DESIGN.

[24] FULL IMPLEMENTATION OF THE 1990 CENSUS-BASED SAMPLE DESIGN AND METROPOLITAN DEFINITIONS, 7,000 HOUSEHOLD SAMPLE REDUCTION, AND REVISED RACE EDITS.

Source: U.S. Bureau of the Census, Income Statistics Branch/HHES Division.

TABLE A6.8

WOMEN'S EARNINGS AS A PERCENTAGE OF MEN'S EARNINGS IN THE UNITED STATES BY RACE AND HISPANIC ORIGIN: 1960–96

(YEAR-ROUND, FULL-TIME WORKERS 15 YEARS OLD AND OVER AS OF MARCH OF THE FOLLOWING YEAR. PRIOR TO 1989 EARNINGS ARE FOR CIVILIAN WORKERS ONLY)

YEAR	ALL RACES	WHITE	BLACK	ASIAN PACIFIC ISLANDER	HISPANIC ORIGIN [3]	WHITE NOT HISPANIC
1996	73.8	73.3	81.3	74.2	88.6	70.2
1995 [19]	71.4	71.2	84.6	78.8	84.3	68.8
1994 [18]	72.0	71.6	83.9	76.3	86.5	71.1
1993 [17]	71.5	70.8	86.1	78.8	83.2	70.0
1992 [16]	70.8	70.0	88.2	74.7	87.4	69.0
1991	69.9	68.7	84.8	70.2	82.2	67.9
1990	71.6	69.4	85.4	79.7	81.9	67.6
1989	68.7	66.3	85.1	75.9	85.3	64.2
1988	66.0	65.4	81.2	71.3	83.2	64.1
1987 [15]	65.2	64.4	82.4	NA	83.3	63.5
1986	64.3	63.3	80.3	NA	82.3	NA
1985 [14]	64.6	63.0	81.9	NA	76.6	NA
1984 [13]	63.7	62.2	82.5	NA	74.1	NA
1983	63.6	62.7	78.6	NA	72.1	NA
1982	61.7	60.9	78.3	NA	72.2	NA
1981	59.2	58.5	76.0	NA	72.9	NA
1980	60.2	58.9	78.8	NA	71.4	NA
1979 [12]	59.7	58.8	74.6	NA	68.2	NA
1978	59.4	58.9	71.5	NA	68.8	NA
1977	58.9	57.6	77.5	NA	69.7	NA
1976 [11]	60.2	59.0	75.7	NA	68.0	NA
1975 [10]	58.8	57.6	74.6	NA	68.3	NA
1974 [9][8]	58.8	57.9	75.3	NA	66.7	NA
1973	56.6	55.9	69.6	NA	NA	NA
1972 [7]	57.9	56.6	70.5	NA	NA	NA
1971 [6]	59.5	58.5	75.2	NA	NA	NA
1970	59.4	58.7	69.8	NA	NA	NA
1969	58.9	58.1	68.2	NA	NA	NA
1968	58.2	58.2	65.6	NA	NA	NA
1967 [5]	57.8	57.9	66.9	NA	NA	NA
1966 [4]	57.6	NA	NA	NA	NA	NA
1965 [3]	59.9	NA	NA	NA	NA	NA
1964	59.1	NA	NA	NA	NA	NA
1963	58.9	NA	NA	NA	NA	NA
1962 [2]	59.3	NA	NA	NA	NA	NA
1961 [1]	59.2	NA	NA	NA	NA	NA
1960	60.7	NA	NA	NA	NA	NA

NA = NOT AVAILABLE.

[1] PRIOR TO 1967, CPI FACTORS ARE EXTRAPOLATED.

[2] PRIOR TO 1967, DATA ARE FOR BLACK AND OTHER RACES.

[3] PERSONS OF HISPANIC ORIGIN MAY BE OF ANY RACE.

[4] BASED ON 1940 CENSUS POPULATION CONTROLS.

[5] IMPLEMENTATION OF EXPANDED INCOME QUESTIONS TO SHOW WAGE AND SALARY, FARM SELF-EMPLOYMENT, NONFARM SELF-EMPLOYMENT AND ALL OTHER NONEARNED INCOME SEPARATELY.

[6] IMPLEMENTATION OF 1950 CENSUS POPULATION CONTROLS.

[7] IMPLEMENTATION OF FIRST HOTDECK PROCEDURE TO IMPUTE MISSING INCOME ENTRIES (ALL INCOME DATA IMPUTED IF ANY MISSING). INTRODUCTION OF 1960 CENSUS SAMPLE DESIGN.

[8] FULL IMPLEMENTATION OF 1960 CENSUS-BASED SAMPLE DESIGN AND POPULATION CONTROLS.

[9] IMPLEMENTATION OF NEW PROCEDURES TO IMPUTE MISSING DATA ONLY.

[10] QUESTIONNAIRE EXPANDED TO ASK EIGHT INCOME QUESTIONS.

[11] IMPLEMENTATION OF A NEW MARCH CPS PROCESSING SYSTEM.

[12] INTRODUCTION OF 1970 CENSUS SAMPLE DESIGN AND POPULATION CONTROLS.

[13] FULL IMPLEMENTATION OF 1970 CENSUS-BASED SAMPLE DESIGN.

[14] IMPLEMENTATION OF A NEW MARCH CPS PROCESSING SYSTEM. QUESTIONNAIRE EXPANDED TO ASK ELEVEN INCOME QUESTIONS.

TABLE A6.8

WOMEN'S EARNINGS AS A PERCENTAGE OF MEN'S EARNINGS IN THE UNITED STATES BY RACE AND HISPANIC ORIGIN: 1960–96

[15] THESE ESTIMATES WERE DERIVED USING PARETO INTERPOLATION AND MAY DIFFER FROM PUBLISHED DATA WHICH WERE DERIVED USING LINEAR INTERPOLATION.

[16] FIRST YEAR MEDIANS ARE DERIVED USING BOTH PARETO AND LINEAR INTERPOLATION. PRIOR TO THIS YEAR ALL MEDIANS WERE DERIVED USING LINEAR INTERPOLATION.

[17] IMPLEMENTATION OF 1980 CENSUS POPULATION CONTROLS. QUESTIONNAIRE EXPANDED TO SHOW 27 POSSIBLE VALUES FROM 51 POSSIBLE SOURCES OF INCOME.

[18] IMPLEMENTATION OF HISPANIC POPULATION WEIGHTING CONTROLS AND INTRODUCTION OF 1980 CENSUS SAMPLE DESIGN.

[19] RECORDING OF AMOUNTS FOR EARNINGS FROM LONGEST JOB INCREASED TO $299,999. FULL IMPLEMENTATION OF 1980 CENSUS-BASED SAMPLE DESIGN.

[20] IMPLEMENTATION OF A NEW MARCH CPS PROCESSING SYSTEM.

[21] IMPLEMENTATION OF 1990 CENSUS POPULATION CONTROLS.

[22] DATA COLLECTION METHOD CHANGED FROM PAPER AND PENCIL TO COMPUTER-ASSISTED INTERVIEWING. IN ADDITION, THE MARCH 1994 INCOME SUPPLEMENT WAS REVISED TO ALLOW FOR THE CODING OF DIFFERENT INCOME AMOUNTS ON SELECTED QUESTIONNAIRE ITEMS. LIMITS EITHER INCREASED OR DECREASED IN THE FOLLOWING CATEGORIES: EARNINGS INCREASED TO $999,999; SOCIAL SECURITY INCREASED TO $49,999; SUPPLEMENTAL SECURITY INCOME AND PUBLIC ASSISTANCE INCREASED TO $24,999; VETERANS' BENEFITS INCREASED TO $99,999; CHILD SUPPORT AND ALIMONY DECREASED TO $49,999.

[23] INTRODUCTION OF 1990 CENSUS SAMPLE DESIGN.

[24] FULL IMPLEMENTATION OF THE 1990 CENSUS-BASED SAMPLE DESIGN AND METROPOLITAN DEFINITIONS, 7,000 HOUSEHOLD SAMPLE REDUCTION, AND REVISED RACE EDITS.

Source: U.S. Bureau of the Census, Income Statistics Branch/HHES Division.

TABLE A6.9

POVERTY STATUS OF FAMILIES, BY TYPE OF FAMILY AND PRESENCE OF RELATED CHILDREN: 1959–1996

(NUMBERS IN THOUSANDS. FAMILIES AS OF MARCH OF THE FOLLOWING YEAR).

YEAR AND CHARACTERISTIC	ALL FAMILIES			MARRIED-COUPLE FAMILIES			MALE HOUSEHOLDER, NO HUSBAND PRESENT			FEMALE HOUSEHOLDER, NO WIFE PRESENT		
		BELOW POVERTY LEVEL			BELOW POVERTY LEVEL			BELOW POVERTY LEVEL			BELOW POVERTY LEVEL	
	TOTAL	NUMBER	PERCENT	TOTAL	NUMBER	PERCENT	TOTAL	NUMBER	PERCENT	TOTAL	NUMBER	PERCENT
ALL RACES												
WITH & WITHOUT CHILDREN UNDER 18 YEARS												
1996	70,241	7,708	11.0	53,604	3,010	5.6	3,847	531	13.8	12,790	4,167	32.6
1995	69,597	7,532	10.8	53,570	2,982	5.6	3,513	493	14.0	12,514	4,057	32.4
1994	69,313	8,053	11.6	53,865	3,272	6.1	3,228	549	17.0	12,220	4,232	34.6
1993 [1]	68,506	8,393	12.3	53,181	3,481	6.5	2,914	488	16.8	12,411	4,424	35.6
1992 [2]	68,216	8,144	11.9	53,090	3,385	6.4	3,065	484	15.8	12,061	4,275	35.4
1991	67,173	7,712	11.5	52,457	3,158	6.0	3,024	393	13.0	11,692	4,161	35.6
1990	66,322	7,098	10.7	52,147	2,981	5.7	2,907	349	12.0	11,268	3,768	33.4
1989	66,090	6,784	10.3	52,137	2,931	5.6	2,884	348	12.1	10,890	3,504	32.2
1988	65,837	6,874	10.4	52,100	2,897	5.6	2,847	336	11.8	10,890	3,642	33.4
1987 [3]	65,204	7,005	10.7	51,675	3,011	5.8	2,833	340	12.0	10,696	3,654	34.2
1986	64,491	7,023	10.9	51,537	3,123	6.1	2,510	287	11.4	10,445	3,613	34.6
1985	63,558	7,223	11.4	50,933	3,438	6.7	2,414	311	12.9	10,211	3,474	34
1984	62,706	7,277	11.6	50,350	3,488	6.9	2,228	292	13.1	10,129	3,498	34.5
1983 [4]	62,015	7,647	12.3	50,081	3,815	7.6	2,038	268	13.2	9,896	3,564	36
1982	61,393	7,512	12.2	49,908	3,789	7.6	2,016	290	14.4	9,469	3,434	36.3
1981	61,019	6,851	11.2	49,630	3,394	6.8	1,986	205	10.3	9,403	3,252	34.6
1980	60,309	6,217	10.3	49,294	3,032	6.2	1,933	213	11.0	9,082	2,972	32.7
1979 [5]	59,550	5,461	9.2	49,112	2,640	5.4	1,733	176	10.2	8,705	2,645	30.4
1978	57,804	5,280	9.1	47,692	2,474	5.2	1,654	152	9.2	8,458	2,654	31.4
1977	57,215	5,311	9.3	47,385	2,524	5.3	1,594	177	11.1	8,236	2,610	31.7
1976	56,710	5,311	9.4	47,497	2,606	5.5	1,500	162	10.8	7,713	2,543	33
1975	56,245	5,450	9.7	47,318	2,904	6.1	1,445	116	8.0	7,482	2,430	32.5
1974 [6]	55,698	4,922	8.8	47,069	2,474	5.3	1,399	125	8.9	7,230	2,324	32.1
1973	55,053	4,828	8.8	46,812	2,482	5.3	1,438	154	10.7	6,804	2,193	32.2
1972	54,373	5,075	9.3	46,314	NA	NA	1,452	NA	NA	6,607	2,158	32.7
1971 [7]	53,296	5,303	10.0	45,752	NA	NA	1,353	NA	NA	6,191	2,100	33.9
1970	52,227	5,260	10.1	44,739	NA	NA	1,487	NA	NA	6,001	1,952	32.5
1969	51,586	5,008	9.7	44,436	NA	NA	1,559	NA	NA	5,591	1,827	32.7
1968	50,511	5,047	10.0	43,842	NA	NA	1,228	NA	NA	5,441	1,755	32.3
1967 [8]	49,835	5,667	11.4	43,292	NA	NA	1,210	NA	NA	5,333	1,774	33.3
1966	48,921	5,784	11.8	42,553	NA	NA	1,197	NA	NA	5,171	1,721	33.1
1965	48,278	6,721	13.9	42,107	NA	NA	1,179	NA	NA	4,992	1,916	38.4
1964	47,836	7,160	15.0	41,648	NA	NA	1,182	NA	NA	5,006	1,822	36.4
1963	47,436	7,554	15.9	41,311	NA	NA	1,243	NA	NA	4,882	1,972	40.4
1962	46,998	8,077	17.2	40,923	NA	NA	1,334	NA	NA	4,741	2,034	42.9
1961	46,341	8,391	18.1	40,405	NA	NA	1,293	NA	NA	4,643	1,954	42.1
1960	45,435	8,243	18.1	39,624	NA	NA	1,202	NA	NA	4,609	1,955	42.4
1959	45,054	8,320	18.5	39,335	NA	NA	1,226	NA	NA	4,493	1,916	42.6

TABLE A6.9 (CONTINUED)

POVERTY STATUS OF FAMILIES, BY TYPE OF FAMILY AND PRESENCE OF RELATED CHILDREN: 1959–1996

(NUMBERS IN THOUSANDS. FAMILIES AS OF MARCH OF THE FOLLOWING YEAR).

YEAR AND CHARACTERISTIC	ALL FAMILIES			MARRIED-COUPLE FAMILIES			MALE HOUSEHOLDER, NO HUSBAND PRESENT			FEMALE HOUSEHOLDER, NO WIFE PRESENT		
	TOTAL	BELOW POVERTY LEVEL		TOTAL	BELOW POVERTY LEVEL		TOTAL	BELOW POVERTY LEVEL		TOTAL	BELOW POVERTY LEVEL	
		NUMBER	PERCENT		NUMBER	PERCENT		NUMBER	PERCENT		NUMBER	PERCENT
ALL RACES **WITH CHILDREN UNDER 18 YEARS**												
1996	37,204	6,131	16.5	26,184	1,964	7.5	2,063	412	20.0	8,957	3,755	41.9
1995	36,719	5,976	16.3	26,034	1,961	7.5	1,934	381	19.7	8,751	3,634	41.5
1994	36,782	6,408	17.4	26,367	2,197	8.3	1,750	395	22.6	8,665	3,816	44
1993[1]	36,456	6,751	18.5	26,121	2,363	9.0	1,577	354	22.5	8,758	4,034	46.1
1992[2]	35,851	6,457	18.0	25,907	2,237	8.6	1,569	353	22.5	8,375	3,867	46.2
1991	34,861	6,170	17.7	25,357	2,106	8.3	1,513	297	19.6	7,991	3,767	47.1
1990	34,503	5,676	16.4	25,410	1,990	7.8	1,386	260	18.8	7,707	3,426	44.5
1989	34,279	5,308	15.5	25,476	1,872	7.3	1,358	246	18.1	7,445	3,190	42.8
1988	34,251	5,373	15.7	25,598	1,847	7.2	1,292	232	18.0	7,361	3,294	44.7
1987[3]	33,996	5,465	16.1	25,464	1,963	7.7	1,316	221	16.8	7,216	3,281	45.5
1986	33,801	5,516	16.3	25,571	2,050	8.0	1,136	202	17.8	7,094	3,264	46
1985	33,536	5,586	16.7	25,496	2,258	8.9	1,147	197	17.1	6,892	3,131	45.4
1984	32,942	5,662	17.2	25,038	2,344	9.4	1,072	194	18.1	6,832	3,124	45.7
1983[4]	32,787	5,871	17.9	25,216	2,557	10.1	949	192	20.2	6,622	3,122	47.1
1982	32,565	5,712	17.5	25,276	2,470	9.8	892	184	20.6	6,397	3,059	47.8
1981	32,587	5,191	15.9	25,278	2,199	8.7	822	115	14.0	6,488	2,877	44.3
1980	32,773	4,822	14.7	25,671	1,974	7.7	802	144	18.0	6,299	2,703	42.9
1979[5]	32,397	4,081	12.6	25,615	1,573	6.1	747	116	15.5	6,035	2,392	39.6
1978	31,735	4,060	12.8	25,199	1,495	5.9	699	103	14.7	5,837	2,462	42.2
1977	31,637	4,081	12.9	25,284	1,602	6.3	644	95	14.8	5,709	2,384	41.8
1976	31,434	4,060	12.9	25,515	1,623	6.4	609	94	15.4	5,310	2,343	44.1
1975	31,377	4,172	13.3	25,704	1,855	7.2	554	65	11.7	5,119	2,252	44
1974[6]	31,319	3,789	12.1	25,857	1,558	6.0	545	84	15.4	4,917	2,147	43.7
1973	30,977	3,520	11.4	25,983	NA	NA	397	NA	NA	4,597	1,987	43.2
1972	30,807	3,621	11.8	26,085	NA	NA	401	NA	NA	4,321	1,925	44.5
1971[7]	30,725	3,683	12.0	26,201	NA	NA	447	NA	NA	4,077	1,830	44.9
1970	30,070	3,491	11.6	25,789	NA	NA	444	NA	NA	3,837	1,680	43.8
1969	29,827	3,226	10.8	26,083	NA	NA	360	NA	NA	3,384	1,519	44.9
1968	29,325	3,347	11.4	25,684	NA	NA	372	NA	NA	3,269	1,459	44.6
1967[8]	29,032	3,586	12.4	25,482	NA	NA	360	NA	NA	3,190	1,418	44.5
1966	28,592	3,734	13.4	25,197	NA	NA	436	NA	NA	2,959	1,410	47.1
1965	28,100	4,379	15.6	24,829	NA	NA	398	NA	NA	2,873	1,499	52.2
1964	28,277	4,771	16.9	25,017	NA	NA	367	NA	NA	2,893	1,439	49.7
1963	28,317	4,991	17.6	25,084	NA	NA	400	NA	NA	2,833	1,578	55.7
1962	28,174	5,460	19.4	24,990	NA	NA	483	NA	NA	2,701	1,613	59.7
1961	27,600	5,500	19.9	24,509	NA	NA	404	NA	NA	2,687	1,505	56
1960	27,102	5,328	19.7	24,164	NA	NA	319	NA	NA	2,619	1,476	56.3
1959	26,992	5,443	20.3	24,099	NA	NA	349	NA	NA	2,544	1,525	59.9

TABLE A6.9

POVERTY STATUS OF FAMILIES, BY TYPE OF FAMILY AND PRESENCE OF RELATED CHILDREN: 1959–1996

(NUMBERS IN THOUSANDS. FAMILIES AS OF MARCH OF THE FOLLOWING YEAR).

NA=NOT AVAILABLE.

1 DATA COLLECTION METHOD CHANGED FROM PAPER AND PENCIL TO COMPUTER-ASSISTED INTERVIEWING. IN ADDITION, THE MARCH 1994 INCOME SUPPLEMENT WAS REVISED TO ALLOW FOR THE CODING OF DIFFERENT INCOME AMOUNTS ON SELECTED QUESTIONNAIRE ITEMS. LIMITS EITHER INCREASED OR DECREASED IN THE FOLLOWING CATEGORIES: EARNINGS INCREASED TO $999,999; SOCIAL SECURITY INCREASED TO $49,999; SUPPLEMENTAL SECURITY INCOME AND PUBLIC ASSISTANCE INCREASED TO $24,999; VETERANS' BENEFITS INCREASED TO $99,999; CHILD SUPPORT AND ALIMONY DECREASED TO $49,999.

2 IMPLEMENTATION OF 1990 CENSUS POPULATION CONTROLS.

3 IMPLEMENTATION OF A NEW MARCH CPS PROCESSING SYSTEM.

4 IMPLEMENTATION OF HISPANIC POPULATION WEIGHTING CONTROLS.

5 IMPLEMENTATION OF 1980 CENSUS POPULATION CONTROLS. QUESTIONNAIRE EXPANDED TO SHOW 27 POSSIBLE VALUES FROM 51 POSSIBLE SOURCES OF INCOME.

6 IMPLEMENTATION OF A NEW MARCH CPS PROCESSING SYSTEM. QUESTIONNAIRE EXPANDED TO ASK ELEVEN INCOME QUESTIONS.

7 IMPLEMENTATION OF 1970 CENSUS POPULATION CONTROLS.

8 IMPLEMENTATION OF A NEW MARCH CPS PROCESSING SYSTEM.

9 PERSONS OF HISPANIC ORIGIN MAY BE OF ANY RACE. DATA FOR HISPANIC ORIGIN NOT AVAILABLE PRIOR TO 1972. PRIOR TO 1979 UNRELATED SUBFAMILES WERE INCLUDED IN ALL FAMILIES. BEGINNING IN 1979 UNRELATED SUBFAMILES ARE EXCLUDED FROM ALL FAMILIES.

Source: U.S. Bureau of the Census, Poverty and Health Statistics Branch/HHES Division, *March Current Population Survey.*

TABLE A6.10

NUMBER OF FAMILIES BELOW THE POVERTY LEVEL AND POVERTY RATE IN THE UNITED STATES: 1959–96

(NUMBERS IN THOUSANDS. FAMILIES AS OF MARCH OF THE FOLLOWING YEAR.)

YEAR	NUMBER OF POOR FAMILIES	POVERTY RATES FOR FAMILIES	NUMBER OF POOR FAMILIES WITH FEMALE (NSP) HOUSEHOLDER	POVERTY RATE FOR FAMILIES WITH FEMALE HOUSEHOLDER	FAMILIES WITH FEMALE HOUSEHOLDER AS A PERCENT OF ALL FAMILIES	POOR FAMILIES WITH FEMALE HOUSEHOLDER AS A PERCENT OF ALL POOR FAMILIES	NONPOOR FAMILIES WITH FEMALE HOUSEHOLDER AS A PERCENT OF ALL NON-POOR FAMILIES
1996	7,708	11.0	4,167	32.6	18.2	54.1	13.8
1995	7,532	10.8	4,057	32.4	18.0	53.9	13.6
1994	8,053	11.6	4,232	34.6	17.6	52.6	13.0
1993 [1]	8,393	12.3	4,424	35.6	18.1	52.7	13.3
1992 [2]	8,144	11.9	4,275	35.4	17.7	52.5	13.0
1991	7,712	11.5	4,161	35.6	17.4	54.0	12.7
1990	7,098	10.7	3,768	33.4	17.0	53.1	12.7
1989	6,784	10.3	3,504	32.2	16.5	51.7	12.5
1988	6,874	10.4	3,642	33.4	16.5	53.0	12.3
1987 [3]	7,005	10.7	3,654	34.2	16.4	52.2	12.1
1986	7,023	10.9	3,613	34.6	16.2	51.4	11.9
1985	7,223	11.4	3,474	34.0	16.1	48.1	12.0
1984	7,277	11.6	3,498	34.5	16.2	48.1	12.0
1983 [4]	7,647	12.3	3,564	36.0	16.0	46.6	11.6
1982	7,512	12.2	3,434	36.3	15.4	45.7	11.2
1981	6,851	11.2	3,252	34.6	15.4	47.5	11.4
1980	6,217	10.3	2,972	32.7	15.1	47.8	11.3
1979 [5]	5,461	9.2	2,645	30.4	14.6	48.4	11.2
1978	5,280	9.1	2,654	31.4	14.6	50.3	11.1
1977	5,311	9.3	2,610	31.7	14.4	49.1	10.8
1976	5,311	9.4	2,543	33.0	13.6	47.9	10.1
1975	5,450	9.7	2,430	32.5	13.3	44.6	9.9
1974 [6]	4,922	8.8	2,324	32.1	13.0	47.2	9.7
1973	4,828	8.8	2,193	32.2	12.4	45.4	9.2
1972	5,075	9.3	2,158	32.7	12.2	42.5	9.0
1971 [7]	5,303	10.0	2,100	33.9	11.6	39.6	8.5
1970	5,260	10.1	1,951	32.5	11.5	37.1	8.6
1969	5,008	9.7	1,827	32.7	10.8	36.5	8.2
1968	5,047	10.0	1,755	32.3	10.7	34.8	8.0
1967 [8]	5,667	11.4	1,774	33.3	10.6	31.3	8.0
1966	5,784	11.8	1,721	33.1	10.5	29.8	7.9
1965	6,721	13.9	1,916	38.4	10.3	28.5	7.3
1964	7,160	15.0	1,822	36.4	10.4	25.4	7.8
1963	7,554	15.9	1,972	40.4	10.2	26.1	7.2
1962	8,077	17.2	2,034	42.9	10.0	25.2	6.8
1961	8,391	18.1	1,954	42.1	9.9	23.3	7.0
1960	8,243	18.1	1,955	42.4	10.1	23.7	7.0
1959	8,320	18.5	1,916	42.6	9.8	23.0	6.8

NSP - NO SPOUSE PRESENT.

[1] DATA COLLECTION METHOD CHANGED FROM PAPER AND PENCIL TO COMPUTER-ASSISTED INTERVIEWING. IN ADDITION, THE MARCH 1994 INCOME SUPPLEMENT WAS REVISED TO ALLOW FOR THE CODING OF DIFFERENT INCOME AMOUNTS ON SELECTED QUESTIONNAIRE ITEMS. LIMITS EITHER INCREASED OR DECREASED IN THE FOLLOWING CATEGORIES: EARNINGS INCREASED TO $999,999; SOCIAL SECURITY INCREASED TO $49,999; SUPPLEMENTAL SECURITY INCOME AND PUBLIC ASSISTANCE INCREASED TO $24,999; VETERANS' BENEFITS INCREASED TO $99,999; CHILD SUPPORT AND ALIMONY DECREASED TO $49,999.

[2] IMPLEMENTATION OF 1990 CENSUS POPULATION CONTROLS.

[3] IMPLEMENTATION OF A NEW MARCH CPS PROCESSING SYSTEM.

[4] IMPLEMENTATION OF HISPANIC POPULATION WEIGHTING CONTROLS.

[5] IMPLEMENTATION OF 1980 CENSUS POPULATION CONTROLS. QUESTIONNAIRE EXPANDED TO SHOW 27 POSSIBLE VALUES FROM 51 POSSIBLE SOURCES OF INCOME.

[6] IMPLEMENTATION OF A NEW MARCH CPS PROCESSING SYSTEM. QUESTIONNAIRE EXPANDED TO ASK ELEVEN INCOME QUESTIONS.

[7] IMPLEMENTATION OF 1970 CENSUS POPULATION CONTROLS.

[8] IMPLEMENTATION OF A NEW MARCH CPS PROCESSING SYSTEM. PRIOR TO 1979 UNRELATED SUBFAMILES WERE INCLUDED IN ALL FAMILIES. BEGINNING IN 1979 UNRELATED SUBFAMILIES ARE EXCLUDED FROM ALL FAMILIES.

Source: U.S. Bureau of the Census, Poverty and Health Statistics Branch/HHES Division, March Current Population Survey.

TABLE A6.11

PERCENT OF PERSONS BY RATIO OF INCOME TO POVERTY LEVEL: 1970–1996

YEAR	RATIO OF INCOME TO POVERTY LEVEL LESS THAN						
	0.50	0.75	1.00	1.25	1.50	1.75	2.00
ALL PERSONS							
1996	5.4	9.3	13.7	18.5	23.4	28.5	33.5
1995	5.3	9.3	13.8	18.5	23.5	28.6	33.6
1994	5.9	10.1	14.5	19.3	24.3	29.3	34.3
1993 [1]	6.2	10.5	15.1	20.0	25.0	30.3	35.2
1992 [2]	6.1	10.2	14.8	19.7	24.5	29.4	34.4
1991	5.6	9.7	14.2	18.9	23.8	28.7	33.5
1990	5.2	9.1	13.5	18.0	22.7	27.6	32.3
1989	4.9	8.4	12.8	17.3	22.0	26.6	31.4
1988	5.2	8.8	13.0	17.5	22.2	26.8	31.7
1987 [3]	5.2	9.0	13.4	17.9	22.3	26.9	31.7
1986	5.3	9.4	14.0	18.7	23.9	28.9	33.9
1985	5.2	9.4	13.6	18.7	23.9	28.9	33.9
1984	5.5	9.7	14.4	19.4	24.3	29.3	34.6
1983 [4]	5.9	10.2	15.2	20.3	25.6	30.8	36.1
1982	5.6	10.1	15.0	20.3	25.5	30.9	36.6
1981	4.9	9.1	14.0	19.3	24.7	30.1	35.7
1980	4.4	8.3	13.0	18.1	23.1	28.4	33.9
1979 [5]	3.8	7.3	11.7	16.4	21.1	26.1	31.3
1978	3.6	6.9	11.4	15.8	20.5	25.9	31.0
1977	3.5	7.0	11.6	16.7	21.8	27.2	32.7
1976	3.3	7.0	11.8	16.7	22.2	27.8	33.5
1975	3.7	7.3	12.3	17.6	23.3	28.8	34.6
1974 [6]	NA	NA	11.2	16.5	21.6	NA	NA
1973	NA	NA	11.1	15.8	20.7	NA	NA
1972	NA	NA	NA	16.8	NA	NA	NA
1971 [7]	NA	NA	NA	17.8	NA	NA	NA
1970	NA	NA	NA	17.6	NA	NA	NA
PERSONS AGE 65 YEARS AND OVER							
1996	2.1	4.9	10.8	18.4	25.2	33.0	40.2
1995	1.9	4.7	10.5	17.7	25.3	32.5	39.6
1994	2.5	5.6	11.7	18.7	26.3	33.8	41.2
1993 [1]	2.4	5.6	12.2	19.7	27.4	35.2	42.0
1992 [2]	2.3	5.6	12.9	20.5	27.7	34.6	41.5
1991	2.2	5.2	12.4	19.7	26.8	33.9	40.4
1990	2.1	5.2	12.2	19.0	26.3	33.2	39.2
1989	2.0	4.6	11.4	19.1	27.2	34.3	40.5
1988	1.9	4.7	12.0	20.0	27.5	33.9	40.4
1987 [3]	1.9	5.3	12.5	20.2	27.4	33.6	40.3
1986	2.1	4.7	12.4	20.5	28.0	34.5	40.8
1985	2.0	5.0	12.6	20.9	28.6	35.7	42.0
1984	1.7	4.6	12.4	21.2	29.1	36.1	42.6
1983 [4]	2.2	5.3	13.8	22.0	29.5	36.9	43.5
1982	2.5	6.0	14.6	23.7	31.8	39.2	46.0
1981	2.0	6.3	15.3	25.2	33.7	40.8	48.0
1980	2.1	6.3	15.7	25.7	34.4	42.1	49.2
1979 [5]	2.4	6.6	15.2	24.7	32.9	41.0	48.2
1978	1.7	5.3	14.0	23.4	32.4	40.6	47.3
1977	1.7	5.4	14.1	24.5	34.2	42.7	50.0
1976	1.9	5.8	15.0	25.0	34.0	42.5	49.7
1975	2.0	5.7	15.3	25.4	35.0	42.8	50.3
1974 [6]	NA	NA	14.6	25.9	35.1	NA	NA
1973	NA	NA	16.3	26.8	35.7	NA	NA
1972	NA	NA	NA	NA	NA	NA	NA
1971 [7]	NA	NA	NA	NA	NA	NA	NA
1970	NA	NA	NA	NA	NA	NA	NA

TABLE A6.11 (CONTINUED)

PERCENT OF PERSONS BY RATIO OF INCOME TO POVERTY LEVEL: 1970-96

NA = NOT AVAILABLE.

[1] DATA COLLECTION METHOD CHANGED FROM PAPER AND PENCIL TO COMPUTER-ASSISTED INTERVIEWING. IN ADDITION, THE MARCH 1994 INCOME SUPPLEMENT WAS REVISED TO ALLOW FOR THE CODING OF DIFFERENT INCOME AMOUNTS ON SELECTED QUESTIONNAIRE ITEMS. LIMITS EITHER INCREASED OR DECREASED IN THE FOLLOWING CATEGORIES: EARNINGS INCREASED TO $999,999; SOCIAL SECURITY INCREASED TO $49,999; SUPPLEMENTAL SECURITY INCOME AND PUBLIC ASSISTANCE INCREASED TO $24,999; VETERANS' BENEFITS INCREASED TO $99,999; CHILD SUPPORT AND ALIMONY DECREASED TO $49,999.

[2] IMPLEMENTATION OF 1990 CENSUS POPULATION CONTROLS.

[3] IMPLEMENTATION OF A NEW MARCH CPS PROCESSING SYSTEM.

[4] INCOME.

[6] IMPLEMENTATION OF A NEW MARCH CPS PROCESSING SYSTEM. QUESTIONNAIRE EXPANDED TO ASK ELEVEN INCOME QUESTIONS.

[7] IMPLEMENTATION OF 1970 CENSUS POPULATION CONTROLS.

[8] IMPLEMENTATION OF A NEW MARCH CPS PROCESSING SYSTEM.

[9] PERSONS OF HISPANIC ORIGIN MAY BE OF ANY RACE. DATA FOR HISPANIC ORIGIN NOT AVAILABLE PRIOR TO 1972.

Source: U.S. Bureau of the Census, Poverty and Health Statistics Branch/HHES Division, *March Current Population Survey.*

TABLE A6.12

DISTRIBUTION OF THE POOR BY RACE AND HISPANIC ORIGIN: 1966-96

(NUMBERS IN THOUSANDS)

YEAR	TOTAL		WHITE		BLACK		HISPANIC ORIGIN		WHITE, NOT HISPANIC		ASIAN & PACIFIC ISLANDER	
	NUMBER	PERCENT	NUMBER	PERCENT	NUMBER	PERCENT	NUMBER	PERCENT	NUMBER	PERCENT	NUMBER	PERCENT
1996	36,529	100	24,650	67.5	9,694	26.5	8,697	23.8	16,462	45.1	1,454	4.0
1995	36,425	100	24,423	67.1	9,872	27.1	8,574	23.5	16,267	44.7	1,411	3.9
1994	38,059	100	25,379	66.7	10,196	26.8	8,416	22.1	18,110	47.6	974	2.6
1993 [1]	39,265	100	26,226	66.8	10,877	27.7	8,126	20.7	18,882	48.1	1,134	2.9
1992 [2]	38,014	100	25,259	66.4	10,827	28.5	7,592	20.0	18,202	47.9	985	2.6
1992	36,880	100	24,523	66.5	10,613	28.8	6,655	18.0	18,613	50.5	912	2.5
1991	35,708	100	23,747	66.5	10,242	28.7	6,339	17.8	17,741	49.7	996	2.8
1990	33,585	100	22,326	66.5	9,837	29.3	6,006	17.9	16,622	49.5	858	2.6
1989	31,528	100	20,785	65.9	9,302	29.5	5,430	17.2	15,599	49.5	939	3.0
1988	31,745	100	20,715	65.3	9,356	29.5	5,357	16.9	15,565	49.0	1,117	3.5
1987 [3]	32,221	100	21,195	65.8	9,520	29.5	5,422	16.8	16,029	49.7	1,021	3.2
1986	32,370	100	22,183	68.5	8,983	27.8	5,117	15.8	17,244	53.3	NA	NA
1985	33,064	100	22,860	69.1	8,926	27	5,236	15.8	17,839	54.0	NA	NA
1984	33,700	100	22,955	68.1	9,490	28.2	4,806	14.3	18,300	54.3	NA	NA
1983 [4]	35,303	100	23,984	67.9	9,882	28	4,633	13.1	19,538	55.3	NA	NA
1982	34,398	100	23,517	68.4	9,697	28.2	4,301	12.5	19,362	56.3	NA	NA
1981	31,822	100	21,553	67.7	9,173	28.8	3,713	11.7	17,987	56.5	NA	NA
1980	29,272	100	19,699	67.3	8,579	29.3	3,491	11.9	16,365	55.9	NA	NA
1979 [5]	26,072	100	17,214	66	8,050	30.9	2,921	11.2	14,419	55.3	NA	NA
1978	24,497	100	16,259	66.4	7,625	31.1	2,607	10.6	NA	NA	NA	NA
1977	24,720	100	16,416	66.4	7,726	31.3	2,700	10.9	NA	NA	NA	NA
1976	24,975	100	16,713	66.9	7,595	30.4	2,783	11.1	NA	NA	NA	NA
1975	25,877	100	17,770	68.7	7,545	29.2	2,991	11.6	NA	NA	NA	NA
1974 [6]	23,370	100	15,736	67.3	7,182	30.7	2,575	11.0	NA	NA	NA	NA
1973	22,973	100	15,142	65.9	7,388	32.2	2,366	10.3	NA	NA	NA	NA
1972	24,460	100	16,203	66.2	7,710	31.5	NA	NA	NA	NA	NA	NA
1971 [7]	25,559	100	17,780	69.6	7,396	28.9	NA	NA	NA	NA	NA	NA
1970	25,420	100	17,484	68.8	7,548	29.7	NA	NA	NA	NA	NA	NA
1969	24,147	100	16,659	69	7,095	29.4	NA	NA	NA	NA	NA	NA
1968	25,389	100	17,395	68.5	7,616	30.0	NA	NA	NA	NA	NA	NA
1967 [8]	27,769	100	18,983	68.4	8,486	30.6	NA	NA	NA	NA	NA	NA
1966	28,510	100	19,290	67.7	8,867	31.1	NA	NA	NA	NA	NA	NA

NA = NOT AVAILABLE.

[1] DATA COLLECTION METHOD CHANGED FROM PAPER AND PENCIL TO COMPUTER-ASSISTED INTERVIEWING. IN ADDITION, THE MARCH 1994 INCOME SUPPLEMENT WAS REVISED TO ALLOW FOR THE CODING OF DIFFERENT INCOME AMOUNTS ON SELECTED QUESTIONNAIRE ITEMS. LIMITS EITHER INCREASED OR DECREASED IN THE FOLLOWING CATEGORIES: EARNINGS INCREASED TO $999,999; SOCIAL SECURITY INCREASED TO $49,999; SUPPLEMENTAL SECURITY INCOME AND PUBLIC ASSISTANCE INCREASED TO $24,999; VETERANS' BENEFITS INCREASED TO $99,999; CHILD SUPPORT AND ALIMONY DECREASED TO $49,999.

[2] IMPLEMENTATION OF 1990 CENSUS POPULATION CONTROLS.

[3] IMPLEMENTATION OF A NEW MARCH CPS PROCESSING SYSTEM.

[4] IMPLEMENTATION OF HISPANIC POPULATION WEIGHTING CONTROLS.

[5] IMPLEMENTATION OF 1980 CENSUS POPULATION CONTROLS. QUESTIONNAIRE EXPANDED TO SHOW 27 POSSIBLE VALUES FROM 51 POSSIBLE SOURCES OF INCOME.

[6] IMPLEMENTATION OF A NEW MARCH CPS PROCESSING SYSTEM. QUESTIONNAIRE EXPANDED TO ASK ELEVEN INCOME QUESTIONS.

[7] IMPLEMENTATION OF 1970 CENSUS POPULATION CONTROLS.

[8] IMPLEMENTATION OF A NEW MARCH CPS PROCESSING SYSTEM.

[9] PERSONS OF HISPANIC ORIGIN MAY BE OF ANY RACE. DATA FOR HISPANIC ORIGIN NOT AVAILABLE PRIOR TO 1972.

Source: U.S. Bureau of the Census, Poverty and Health Statistics Branch/HHES Division, *March Current Population Survey.*

TABLE A6.13

PERCENTAGE OF PERSONS IN POVERTY IN THE UNITED STATES, BY STATE: 1994, 1995, AND 1996

STATE	1996 PERCENT	1996 STANDARD ERROR	1995 PERCENT	1995 STANDARD ERROR	1994 PERCENT	1994 STANDARD ERROR
ALABAMA	14.0	1.7	20.1	2.0	16.4	1.9
ALASKA	8.2	1.3	7.1	1.3	10.2	1.4
ARIZONA	20.5	1.8	16.1	1.8	15.9	1.8
ARKANSAS	17.2	1.8	14.9	1.8	15.3	1.8
CALIFORNIA	16.9	0.8	16.7	0.8	17.9	0.7
COLORADO	10.6	1.5	8.8	1.4	9.0	1.5
CONNECTICUT	11.7	1.8	9.7	1.7	10.8	1.8
DELAWARE	8.6	1.6	10.3	1.7	8.3	1.6
D.C.	24.1	2.4	22.2	2.3	21.2	2.4
FLORIDA	14.2	0.9	16.2	1.0	14.9	0.9
GEORGIA	14.8	1.6	12.1	1.5	14.0	1.7
HAWAII	12.1	1.8	10.3	1.7	8.7	1.6
IDAHO	11.9	1.6	14.5	1.7	12.0	1.5
ILLINOIS	12.1	1.0	12.4	1.0	12.4	0.9
INDIANA	7.5	1.3	9.6	1.5	13.7	1.8
IOWA	9.6	1.5	12.2	1.6	10.7	1.6
KANSAS	11.2	1.6	10.8	1.6	14.9	1.8
KENTUCKY	17.0	1.9	14.7	1.8	18.5	2.0
LOUISIANA	20.5	1.9	19.7	1.9	25.7	2.3
MAINE	11.2	1.8	11.2	1.8	9.4	1.6
MARYLAND	10.3	1.6	10.1	1.6	10.7	1.6
MASSACHUSETTS	10.1	1.1	11.0	1.2	9.7	0.8
MICHIGAN	11.2	1.0	12.2	1.0	14.1	0.9
MINNESOTA	9.8	1.5	9.2	1.4	11.7	1.7
MISSISSIPPI	20.6	2.0	23.5	2.1	19.9	2.0
MISSOURI	9.5	1.5	9.4	1.5	15.6	2.0
MONTANA	17.0	1.8	15.3	1.8	11.5	1.6
NEBRASKA	10.2	1.6	9.6	1.5	8.8	1.4
NEVADA	8.1	1.4	11.1	1.7	11.1	1.5
NEW HAMPSHIRE	6.4	1.4	5.3	1.3	7.7	1.6
NEW JERSEY	9.2	1.0	7.8	0.9	9.2	0.8
NEW MEXICO	25.5	2.1	25.3	2.1	21.1	2.0
NEW YORK	16.7	0.8	16.5	0.8	17.0	0.8
NORTH CAROLINA	12.2	1.2	12.6	1.2	14.2	0.9
NORTH DAKOTA	11.0	1.6	12.0	1.7	10.4	1.5
OHIO	12.7	1.0	11.5	1.0	14.1	0.9
OKLAHOMA	16.6	1.8	17.1	1.8	16.7	1.9
OREGON	11.8	1.7	11.2	1.7	11.8	1.7
PENNSYLVANIA	11.6	0.9	12.2	0.9	12.5	0.9
RHODE ISLAND	11.0	1.8	10.6	1.8	10.3	1.8
SOUTH CAROLINA	13.0	1.8	19.9	2.1	13.8	1.6
SOUTH DAKOTA	11.8	1.6	14.5	1.8	14.5	1.6
TENNESSEE	15.9	1.8	15.5	1.8	14.6	1.7
TEXAS	16.6	1.0	17.4	1.0	19.1	1.0
UTAH	7.7	1.3	8.4	1.3	8.0	1.3
VERMONT	12.6	1.9	10.3	1.7	7.6	1.5
VIRGINIA	12.3	1.6	10.2	1.5	10.7	1.4
WASHINGTON	11.9	1.7	12.5	1.8	11.7	1.6
WEST VIRGINIA	18.5	1.9	16.7	1.8	18.6	2.0
WISCONSIN	8.8	1.4	8.5	1.4	9.0	1.4
WYOMING	11.9	1.6	12.2	1.7	9.3	1.7
LOS ANGELES CMSA	18.8	0.9	18.6	0.9	19.8	0.9
NEW YORK CMSA	15.2	0.7	15.0	0.7	14.9	0.7

Source: U.S. Bureau of the Census, Poverty and Health Statistics Branch/HHES Division, *March Current Population Survey.*

TABLE A6.14

AGE DISTRIBUTION OF THE POOR IN THE UNITED STATES: 1966–96

(NUMBERS IN THOUSANDS)

YEAR	TOTAL POOR		CHILDREN UNDER 18		RELATED CHILDREN UNDER 18		PERSONS 18 TO 64 YEARS		PERSONS 65 AND OVER	
	NUMBER	PERCENT	NUMBER	PERCENT	NUMBER	PERCENT	NUMBER	PERCENT	NUMBER	PERCENT
1996	36,529	100	14,463	39.6	13,764	37.7	18,638	51.0	3,428	9.4
1995	36,425	100	14,665	40.3	13,999	38.4	18,442	50.6	3,318	9.1
1994	38,059	100	15,289	40.2	14,610	38.4	19,107	50.2	3,663	9.6
1993 [1]	39,265	100	15,727	40.1	14,961	38.1	19,783	50.4	3,755	9.6
1992 [2]	38,014	100	15,294	40.2	14,521	38.2	18,793	49.4	3,928	10.3
1991	35,708	100	14,341	40.2	13,658	38.2	17,585	49.2	3,781	10.6
1990	33,585	100	13,431	40.0	12,715	37.9	16,496	49.1	3,658	10.9
1989	31,528	100	12,590	39.9	12,001	38.1	15,575	49.4	3,363	10.7
1988	31,745	100	12,455	39.2	11,935	37.6	15,809	49.8	3,481	11.0
1987 [3]	32,221	100	12,843	39.9	12,275	38.1	15,815	49.1	3,563	11.1
1986	32,370	100	12,876	39.8	12,257	37.9	16,017	49.5	3,477	10.7
1985	33,064	100	13,010	39.3	12,483	37.8	16,598	50.2	3,456	10.5
1984	33,700	100	13,420	39.8	12,929	38.4	16,952	50.3	3,330	9.9
1983 [4]	35,303	100	13,911	39.4	13,427	38.0	17,767	50.3	3,625	10.3
1982	34,398	100	13,647	39.7	13,139	38.2	17,000	49.4	3,751	10.9
1981	31,822	100	12,505	39.3	12,068	37.9	15,464	48.6	3,853	12.1
1980	29,272	100	11,543	39.4	11,114	38.0	13,858	47.3	3,871	13.2
1979 [5]	26,072	100	10,377	39.8	9,993	38.3	12,014	46.1	3,682	14.1
1978	24,497	100	9,931	40.5	9,722	39.7	11,332	46.3	3,233	13.2
1977	24,720	100	10,288	41.6	10,028	40.6	11,316	45.8	3,177	12.9
1976	24,975	100	10,273	41.1	10,081	40.4	11,389	45.6	3,313	13.3
1975	25,877	100	11,104	42.9	10,882	42.1	11,456	44.3	3,317	12.8
1974 [6]	23,370	100	10,156	43.5	9,967	42.6	10,132	43.4	3,085	13.2
1973	22,973	100	9,642	42.0	9,453	41.1	9,977	43.4	3,354	14.6
1972	24,460	100	10,284	42.0	10,082	41.2	10,438	42.7	3,738	15.3
1971 [7]	25,559	100	10,551	41.3	10,344	40.5	10,735	42.0	4,273	16.7
1970	25,420	100	10,440	41.1	10,235	40.3	10,187	40.1	4,793	18.9
1969	24,147	100	9,691	40.1	9,501	39.3	9,669	40.0	4,787	19.8
1968	25,389	100	10,954	43.1	10,739	42.3	9,803	38.6	4,632	18.2
1967 [8]	27,769	100	11,656	42.0	11,427	41.2	10,725	38.6	5,388	19.4
1966	28,510	100	12,389	43.5	12,146	42.6	11,007	38.6	5,114	17.9

[1] DATA COLLECTION METHOD CHANGED FROM PAPER AND PENCIL TO COMPUTER-ASSISTED INTERVIEWING. IN ADDITION, THE MARCH 1994 INCOME SUPPLEMENT WAS REVISED TO ALLOW FOR THE CODING OF DIFFERENT INCOME AMOUNTS ON SELECTED QUESTIONNAIRE ITEMS. LIMITS EITHER INCREASED OR DECREASED IN THE FOLLOWING CATEGORIES: EARNINGS INCREASED TO $999,999; SOCIAL SECURITY INCREASED TO $49,999; SUPPLEMENTAL SECURITY INCOME AND PUBLIC ASSISTANCE INCREASED TO $24,999; VETERANS' BENEFITS INCREASED TO $99,999; CHILD SUPPORT AND ALIMONY DECREASED TO $49,999.

[2] IMPLEMENTATION OF 1990 CENSUS POPULATION CONTROLS.

[3] IMPLEMENTATION OF A NEW MARCH CPS PROCESSING SYSTEM.

[4] IMPLEMENTATION OF HISPANIC POPULATION WEIGHTING CONTROLS.

[5] IMPLEMENTATION OF A NEW MARCH CPS PROCESSING SYSTEM.

[6] IMPLEMENTATION OF A NEW MARCH CPS PROCESSING SYSTEM. QUESTIONNAIRE EXPANDED TO ASK ELEVEN INCOME QUESTIONS.

[7] IMPLEMENTATION OF 1970 CENSUS POPULATION CONTROLS.

[8] IMPLEMENTATION OF A NEW MARCH CPS PROCESSING SYSTEM. PRIOR TO 1979 UNRELATED SUBFAMILES WERE INCLUDED IN ALL FAMILIES. BEGINNING IN 1979 UNRELATED SUBFAMILIES ARE EXCLUDED FROM ALL FAMILIES.

Source: U.S. Bureau of the Census, Poverty and Health Statistics Branch/HHES Division, *March Current Population Survey.*

TABLE A6.15

PERCENT OF PERSONS IN POVERTY IN THE UNITED STATES, BY DEFINITION OF INCOME: 1979–1996

(POVERTY THRESHOLDS BASED ON CPI-U. PERSONS AS OF MARCH OF THE FOLLOWING YEAR.)

YEAR	TOTAL (THOUSANDS)	EXCLUDING CAPITAL GAINS (CURRENT OFFICIAL MEASURE)	MONEY INCOME- DEFINITION 1 LESS TAXES PLUS CAPITAL GAINS (LOSSES)	
------	-------------------	---	WITHOUT EIC	WITH EIC
			WITHOUT EIC	WITH EIC
1996	266,218	13.7	14.9	13.3
1995	263,733	13.8	14.8	13.4
1994	261,616	14.5	15.8	14.6
1993	259,278	15.1	16.3	15.5
1992R	256,549	14.8	16.2	15.2
1992	253,969	14.5	15.8	14.9
1991	251,179	14.2	NA	NA
1990	248,644	13.5	NA	NA
1989	245,992	12.8	NA	NA
1988	243,530	13.0	NA	NA
1987	240,982	13.4	NA	NA
1986	238,554	13.6	NA	NA
1985	236,594	14.0	NA	NA
1984	233,816	14.4	NA	NA
1983	231,700	15.2	NA	NA
1982	229,412	15.0	NA	NA
1981	227,157	14.0	NA	NA
1980	225,027	13.0	NA	NA
1979	222,903	11.7	NA	NA

	BEFORE TAXES			
	MONEY INCOME			
	DEFINITION 1	DEFINITION 2	DEFINITION 3	DEFINITION 4
YEAR	LESS GOVERNMENT TRANSFERS	PLUS CAPITAL GAINS (LOSSES)	PLUS HEALTH INSURANCE SUPPLEMENTS TO WAGE OR SALARY INCOME	LESS SOCIAL SECURITY PAYROLL TAXES
1996	21.6	21.5	20.8	21.8
1995	21.9	21.8	21.1	22.0
1994	22.8	22.7	22.0	23.0
1993	23.4	23.3	22.6	23.6
1992R	22.8	22.7	22.1	23.2
1992	22.6	22.5	21.9	22.9
1991	21.8	21.8	21.1	22.0
1990	20.5	20.4	19.9	20.9
1989	20.0	19.9	19.4	20.3
1988	20.2	20.2	19.7	20.6
1987	20.4	20.2	19.7	20.5
1986	20.8	20.4	19.9	20.7
1985	21.3	20.9	20.4	21.3
1984	21.8	21.4	20.8	21.6
1983	23.0	22.5	21.8	22.6
1982	23.0	22.7	22.0	22.9
1981	22.0	21.8	21.1	22.0
1980	20.8	20.7	20.1	20.8
1979	19.5	19.3	18.8	19.4

TABLE A6.15 (CONTINUED)

PERCENT OF PERSONS IN POVERTY IN THE UNITED STATES, BY DEFINITION OF INCOME: 1979–1996

(POVERTY THRESHOLDS BASED ON CPI-U. PERSONS AS OF MARCH OF THE FOLLOWING YEAR.)

	AFTER TAXES			
	DEFINITION 5	DEFINITION 6	DEFINITION 7	DEFINITION 8
YEAR	LESS FEDERAL INCOME TAXES	PLUS EARNED INCOME CREDIT	LESS STATE INCOME TAXES	PLUS NONMEANS-TESTED GOVERNMENT CASH TRANSFERS
1996	22.0	20.5	20.7	13.9
1995	22.1	20.9	21.0	14.1
1994	23.2	22.0	22.2	15.1
1993	23.8	23.1	23.2	16.1
1992R	23.4	22.6	22.8	15.8
1992	23.2	22.4	22.6	15.5
1991	22.3	21.6	21.8	15.1
1990	21.1	20.6	20.8	14.7
1989	20.5	20.1	20.3	14.0
1988	20.7	20.3	20.5	14.1
1987	20.7	20.4	20.6	14.3
1986	21.1	20.9	21.0	14.7
1985	21.6	21.5	21.7	15.2
1984	22.0	21.9	22.0	15.5
1983	23.0	22.8	22.9	16.1
1982	23.3	23.1	23.3	16.0
1981	22.5	22.3	22.4	15.3
1980	21.1	20.8	20.9	14.1
1979	19.6	19.2	19.3	12.7

	AFTER TAXES - CONTINUED			
	DEFINITION 9	DEFINITION 10	DEFINITION 11	DEFINITION 12
YEAR	PLUS MEDICARE	PLUS REGULAR-PRICE SCHOOL LUNCHES	PLUS NONMEANS-TESTED GOVERNMENT CASH TRANSFERS	PLUS MEDICAID
1996	13.5	13.5	12.4	11.5
1995	13.7	13.7	12.5	11.7
1994	14.8	14.7	13.5	12.6
1993	15.6	15.6	14.5	13.5
1992R	15.4	15.4	14.3	13.3
1992	15.1	15.1	14.0	13.0
1991	14.7	14.6	13.6	12.9
1990	14.2	14.2	13.2	12.4
1989	13.5	13.5	12.5	11.7
1988	13.6	13.6	12.7	12.1
1987	13.8	13.8	13.0	12.4
1986	14.2	14.2	13.3	12.8
1985	14.8	14.8	13.8	13.2
1984	15.1	15.1	14.2	13.5
1983	15.7	15.7	14.8	14.2
1982	15.5	15.5	14.6	14.0
1981	14.8	14.8	13.7	13.0
1980	13.7	13.6	12.5	11.7
1979	12.4	12.4	11.2	10.4

TABLE A6.15 (CONTINUED)

PERCENT OF PERSONS IN POVERTY IN THE UNITED STATES, BY
DEFINITION OF INCOME: 1979–1996
POVERTY THRESHOLDS BASED ON CPI-U. PERSONS AS OF MARCH OF THE FOLLOWING YEAR.)

| | AFTER TAXES - CONTINUED | | |
| | DEFINITION 13 | | DEFINITION 14 |
YEAR	NONCASH TRANSFERS	NONCASH TRANSFERS LESS MEDICAL PROGRAMS	PLUS NET IMPUTED RETURN ON EQUITY IN OWN HOME
1996	10.2	11.1	9.3
1995	10.3	11.1	9.4
1994	11.1	12.0	10.0
1993	12.1	13.1	11.2
1992R	11.9	12.8	10.7
1992	11.7	12.6	10.4
1991	11.4	NA	10.3
1990	10.9	NA	9.8
1989	10.4	NA	9.1
1988	10.8	NA	9.4
1987	11.0	NA	9.7
1986	11.3	NA	10.1
1985	11.7	NA	9.9
1984	12.0	NA	9.9
1983	12.7	NA	10.4
1982	12.3	NA	9.9
1981	11.5	NA	8.7
1980	10.1	NA	8.2
1979	8.9	NA	7.5

R = REVISED.
NA = NOT AVAILABLE.

Source: U.S. Bureau of the Census, H.H.E.S. Division.

TABLE A6.16

FAMILY NET WORTH, BY SELECTED CHARACTERISTICS OF FAMILIES: 1989, 1992, AND 1995

(THOUSANDS OF 1995 DOLLARS, EXCEPT AS NOTED.)

FAMILY CHARACTERISTIC	1989			1992			1995		
	MEDIAN	MEAN	PERCENTAGE OF FAMILIES	MEDIAN	MEAN	PERCENTAGE OF FAMILIES	MEDIAN	MEAN	PERCENTAGE OF FAMILIES
ALL FAMILIES	56.5	216.7	100.0	52.8	200.5	100.0	56.4	205.9	100.0
INCOME (1995 DOLLARS) [1]									
LESS THAN 10,000	1.6	26.1	15.4	3.3	30.9	15.5	4.8	45.6	16.0
10,000– 24,999	25.6	77.9	24.3	28.2	71.2	27.8	30.0	74.6	26.5
25,000– 49,999	56.0	121.8	30.3	54.8	124.4	29.5	54.9	119.3	31.1
50,000– 99,999	128.1	229.5	22.3	121.2	240.8	20.0	121.1	256.0	20.2
100,000 AND MORE	474.7	1372.9	7.7	506.1	1283.6	7.1	485.9	1465.2	6.1
AGE OF FAMILY HEAD (YEARS)									
LESS THAN 35	9.2	66.3	27.2	10.1	50.3	25.8	11.4	47.2	24.8
35– 44	69.2	171.3	23.4	46.0	144.3	22.8	48.5	144.5	23.2
45– 54	114.0	338.9	14.4	83.4	287.8	16.2	90.5	277.8	17.8
55– 64	110.5	334.4	13.9	122.5	358.6	13.2	110.8	356.2	12.5
65– 74	88.4	336.8	12.0	105.8	308.3	12.6	104.1	331.6	11.9
75 AND MORE	83.2	250.8	9.0	92.8	231.0	9.4	95.0	276.0	9.8
EDUCATION OF FAMILY HEAD									
NO HIGH SCHOOL DIPLOMA	28.5	92.1	24.3	21.6	75.8	20.4	26.3	87.2	19.0
HIGH SCHOOL DIPLOMA	43.4	134.4	32.1	41.4	120.6	29.9	50.0	138.2	31.6
SOME COLLEGE	56.4	213.8	15.1	62.6	185.4	17.7	43.2	186.6	19.0
COLLEGE DEGREE	132.1	416.9	28.5	103.1	363.3	31.9	104.1	361.8	30.5
RACE OR ETHNICITY OF HEAD									
WHITE NON- HISPANIC	84.7	261.4	75.1	71.7	237.8	75.1	73.9	244.0	77.5
NONWHITE OR HISPANIC	6.8	82.1	24.9	16.9	87.9	24.9	16.5	74.4	22.5
CURRENT WORK STATUS OF FAMILY HEAD									
PROFESSIONAL, MANAGERIAL	106.6	262.7	16.9	78.8	248.5	16.8	89.3	252.8	15.9
TECHNICAL, SALES, CLERICAL	40.9	98.9	13.4	48.0	105.4	14.8	43.3	109.3	14.9
PRECISION PRODUCTION	58.4	94.2	9.6	38.4	85.5	7.0	43.5	79.3	8.2
MACHINE OPERATORS AND LABORERS	23.1	67.2	10.6	23.5	56.8	10.0	37.3	70.0	13.1
SERVICE OCCUPATIONS	9.3	53.2	6.6	15.7	52.9	6.2	15.8	60.0	6.6
SELF- EMPLOYED	200.7	765.4	11.2	155.6	644.3	10.9	152.9	731.5	9.7
RETIRED	77.5	199.2	25.0	76.3	201.2	26.0	81.6	218.3	25.0
OTHER NOT WORKING	0.7	62.9	6.7	5.5	68.5	8.2	4.5	60.4	6.5
HOUSING STATUS									
OWNER	119.9	311.7	63.8	106.1	289.6	63.9	102.3	295.4	64.7
RENTER OR OTHER	2.4	49.4	36.2	3.6	42.7	36.1	4.5	42.2	35.3

NA = NOT AVAILABLE.

[1] FOR THE CALENDAR YEAR PRECEDING THE SURVEY.

Source: Aurthur B. Kennickell et al. *Family Finances in the U.S.: Recent Evidence from the Survey of Consumer Finances,* Federal Reserve Bulletin, January 1997.

TABLE A6.17

FAMILY HOLDINGS OF FINANCIAL ASSETS IN THE UNITED STATES, BY SELECTED CHARACTERISTICS OF FAMILIES AND TYPE OF ASSET: 1995

FAMILY CHARACTERISTIC	TRANS-ACTION ACCOUNTS	CDs	SAVINGS BONDS	BONDS	STOCKS	MUTUAL FUNDS	RETIREMENT ACCOUNTS	LIFE INSURANCE	OTHER MANAGED	OTHER FINANCIAL	ANY FINANCIAL ASSET
	MEDIAN VALUE OF HOLDINGS FOR FAMILIES HOLDING ASSET (THOUSANDS OF 1995 DOLLARS)										
ALL FAMILIES	2.5	11.2	0.7	32.6	8.7	17.4	15.2	3.3	21.7	2.7	12.0
INCOME (1995 DOLLARS)											
LESS THAN 10,000	0.5	6.5	0.2	*	4.0	15.2	7.9	1.1	*	1.1	1.1
10,000– 24,999	1.2	14.6	0.5	14.1	4.3	7.6	5.8	1.7	17.4	2.3	4.1
25,000– 49,999	2.3	11.2	0.5	41.2	5.2	16.3	9.0	3.0	19.5	2.2	11.7
50,000– 99,999	4.9	9.8	1.1	21.7	5.7	21.7	23.3	5.4	21.7	3.3	37.7
100,000 AND MORE	20.3	21.7	1.1	97.6	38.0	32.6	55.6	11.4	71.2	27.1	197.5
AGE OF HOUSEHOLD HOUSEHOLD HEAD (YEARS)											
LESS THAN 35	1.4	4.9	0.4	10.9	2.2	2.7	5.4	2.0	21.7	1.1	4.0
35– 44	2.2	5.4	0.7	21.7	4.3	19.5	9.8	3.8	8.7	3.3	10.5
45– 54	3.2	8.7	0.9	43.4	11.3	16.3	28.2	4.9	21.7	5.4	20.0
55– 64	3.3	16.3	1.1	54.2	14.1	23.9	30.4	7.3	43.4	5.4	29.9
65– 74	3.9	21.7	0.7	34.7	16.3	32.6	21.7	2.5	34.7	7.6	26.0
75 AND MORE	4.3	23.9	1.2	38.0	27.1	22.8	30.4	2.1	21.7	5.4	22.3
RACE OR ETHNICITY OF HOUSEHOLD HOUSEHOLD HEAD											
WHITE NON- HISPANIC	3.0	11.9	0.7	32.6	8.7	17.4	16.3	3.3	24.1	3.1	16.3
NONWHITE OR HISPANIC	1.1	8.7	0.6	32.0	6.5	18.4	10.9	3.5	9.8	1.4	3.4
CURRENT WORK STATUS OF HOUSEHOLD HEAD											
PROFESSIONAL, MANAGERIAL	3.7	7.1	1.1	38.0	8.1	16.3	21.9	4.3	21.7	3.3	25.8
TECHNICAL, SALES, CLERICAL	2.2	10.3	0.5	16.3	6.8	10.9	10.9	3.3	43.4	2.2	10.9
PRECISION PRODUCTION	2.2	2.8	0.3	*	4.0	5.1	11.1	4.1	11.4	2.2	9.9
MACHINE OPERATORS											
AND LABORERS	1.3	7.6	0.5	*	2.2	15.6	5.4	3.0	*	1.8	4.2
SERVICE OCCUPATIONS	0.9	16.3	0.5	*	4.3	6.5	6.3	3.0	3.3	0.6	2.6
SELF- EMPLOYED	5.4	10.9	0.5	43.4	10.9	27.1	27.1	6.9	99.8	7.6	21.5
RETIRED	3.3	21.7	1.1	34.7	17.8	27.1	18.4	2.5	21.7	6.5	16.8
OTHER NOT WORKING	1.1	7.1	0.5	48.3	11.3	11.5	9.5	4.9	6.5	2.0	3.5
HOUSING STATUS											
OWNER	3.6	12.0	0.8	32.6	10.9	19.5	19.0	3.8	21.7	5.4	22.8
RENTER OR OTHER	1.1	8.1	0.5	27.1	4.0	10.9	5.4	2.2	21.7	1.6	3.2

* FEWER THAN FIVE OBSERVATIONS

Source: Aurthur B. Kennickell et al. *Family Finances in the U.S.: Recent Evidence from the Survey of Consumer Finances*, Federal Reserve Bulletin, January 1997.

TABLE A6.18

FAMILY HOLDINGS OF NONFINANCIAL ASSETS IN THE UNITED STATES, BY SELECTED CHARACTERISTICS OF FAMILIES AND TYPE OF ASSET: 1995

FAMILY CHARACTERISTIC	VEHICLES	PRIMARY RESIDENCE	INVESTMENT REAL ESTATE	BUSINESS	OTHER NON-FINANCIAL	ANY NON-FINANCIAL ASSET
MEDIAN VALUE OF HOLDINGS FOR FAMILIES HOLDING ASSET (THOUSANDS OF 1995 DOLLARS)						
ALL FAMILIES	7.4	86.8	48.8	65.1	7.6	74.2
INCOME (1995 DOLLARS)						
LESS THAN 10,000	2.6	38.8	26.0	29.0	1.6	19.3
10,000– 24,999	4.5	54.2	21.7	32.6	4.9	39.4
25,000– 49,999	7.8	81.4	43.4	54.2	5.4	71.1
50,000– 99,999	11.8	108.5	51.5	65.1	13.0	134.6
100,000 AND MORE	17.8	217.0	130.2	260.4	27.1	391.0
AGE OF HOUSEHOLD HEAD (YEARS)						
LESS THAN 35	6.4	72.7	34.7	32.6	4.3	18.1
35– 44	8.1	97.6	38.0	48.8	8.7	88.4
45– 54	9.1	97.6	57.5	108.5	12.5	102.4
55– 64	9.0	90.1	54.2	119.3	10.9	115.5
65– 74	5.4	70.5	51.5	162.7	9.8	82.6
75 AND MORE	4.8	75.9	54.2	86.8	7.1	75.5
RACE OR ETHNICITY OF HOUSEHOLD HEAD						
WHITE NON- HISPANIC	7.8	92.2	48.8	70.5	7.6	85.5
NONWHITE OR HISPANIC	5.3	54.2	48.8	48.8	9.2	40.4
CURRENT WORK STATUS OF HOUSEHOLD HEAD						
PROFESSIONAL, MANAGERIAL	9.4	121.5	70.5	54.2	8.7	108.1
TECHNICAL, SALES, CLERICAL	8.0	84.4	41.2	48.8	7.6	74.1
PRECISION PRODUCTION	8.2	81.4	32.6	13.6	5.4	69.2
MACHINE OPERATORS AND LABORERS	6.4	60.8	27.1	19.0	3.3	40.0
SERVICE OCCUPATIONS	5.5	52.1	54.2	32.6	5.4	26.0
SELF- EMPLOYED	11.8	135.6	83.5	97.6	16.3	195.4
RETIRED	4.9	70.5	46.7	65.1	6.0	70.9
OTHER NOT WORKING	4.5	60.8	32.6	30.5	9.8	22.8
HOUSING STATUS						
OWNER	9.0	86.8	48.8	86.8	8.7	111.9
RENTER OR OTHER	4.6	*	54.2	27.1	5.4	5.7

* FEWER THAN FIVE OBSERVATIONS.

Source: Aurthur B. Kennickell et al. *Family Finances in the U.S.: Recent Evidence from the Survey of Consumer Finances,* Federal Reserve Bulletin, January 1997.

TABLE A6.19

FAMILY HOLDINGS OF DEBT IN THE UNITED STATES, BY SELECTED CHARACTERISTICS OF FAMILIES AND TYPE OF DEBT: 1995

FAMILY CHARACTERISTIC	MORTGAGE AND HOME EQUITY	INSTAL- LMENT	OTHER LINES OF CREDIT	CREDIT CARD	INVESTMENT REAL ESTATE	OTHER DEBT	ANY DEBT
MEDIAN VALUE OF HOLDINGS FOR FAMILIES HOLDING DEBT (THOUSANDS OF 1995 DOLLARS)							
ALL FAMILIES	47.4	5.0	2.2	1.1	26.0	2.7	19.5
INCOME (1995 DOLLARS)							
LESS THAN 10,000	15.2	2.1	*	0.5	38.0	1.6	2.5
10,000– 24,999	20.6	3.1	2.9	0.9	6.5	1.1	6.3
25,000– 49,999	42.3	5.7	1.5	1.2	16.3	2.2	19.3
50,000– 99,999	60.8	8.1	2.0	1.6	27.1	3.3	59.3
100,000 AND MORE	99.7	11.2	4.3	2.7	74.9	6.5	120.1
AGE OF FAMILY HEAD (YEARS)							
LESS THAN 35	55.3	5.0	1.3	1.0	14.2	1.5	11.5
35– 44	59.7	5.4	2.0	1.3	27.1	3.3	39.1
45– 54	43.4	5.1	5.4	1.6	36.9	3.3	31.3
55– 64	32.6	4.8	4.3	1.1	29.5	3.3	22.6
65– 74	18.4	4.3	4.3	0.9	16.3	1.6	5.4
75 AND MORE	30.4	3.4	*	0.6	82.7	2.9	2.6
RACE OR ETHNICITY OF FAMILY HEAD							
WHITE NON- HISPANIC	48.8	5.5	2.2	1.1	26.6	3.3	23.9
NONWHITE OR HISPANIC	33.8	3.5	2.4	0.9	19.5	2.2	9.7
CURRENT WORK STATUS OF FAMILY HEAD							
PROFESSIONAL, MANAGERIAL	65.1	6.2	3.3	1.5	35.8	3.3	42.4
TECHNICAL, SALES, CLERICAL	51.5	5.6	1.3	1.1	13.6	2.2	24.8
PRECISION PRODUCTION	47.7	5.0	1.4	1.1	15.2	3.3	25.3
MACHINE OPERATORS AND LABORERS	28.1	5.2	1.1	1.1	9.8	2.2	16.3
SERVICE OCCUPATIONS	32.9	3.8	2.2	0.9	*	1.6	7.4
SELF- EMPLOYED	73.0	6.9	4.3	1.9	58.6	5.4	57.3
RETIRED	19.6	3.7	4.3	0.8	19.5	2.2	6.2
OTHER NOT WORKING	28.5	2.8	*	0.8	29.3	2.7	5.1
HOUSING STATUS							
OWNER	47.4	6.1	3.0	1.2	29.5	3.3	41.2
RENTER OR OTHER	*	4.0	1.3	1.0	17.5	1.5	4.2

* FEWER THAN FIVE OBSERVATIONS.

Source: Aurthur B. Kennickell et al. *Family Finances in the U.S.: Recent Evidence from the Survey of Consumer Finances,* Federal Reserve Bulletin, January 1997.

HOUSING

TABLE A7.1

INTRODUCTORY CHARACTERISTICS - ALL HOUSING UNITS IN THE UNITED STATES: 1995

(NUMBERS IN THOUSANDS. CONSISTENT WITH THE 1990 CENSUS).

CHARACTERISTICS	TOTAL HOUSING UNITS	SEASONAL	YEAR ROUND TOTAL	OCCUPIED TOTAL	OCCUPIED OWNER	OCCUPIED RENTER	VACANT TOTAL
TOTAL	109,457	3,054	104,401	97,693	63,544	34,150	8,710
UNITS IN STRUCTURE							
1, DETACHED	66,169	1,804	64,365	60,826	52,257	8,569	3,539
1, ATTACHED	6,213	41	6,172	5,545	2,936	2,609	627
2 TO 4	10,700	124	10,576	9,299	1,734	7,565	1,277
5 TO 9	5,594	102	5,492	4,803	520	4,283	690
10 TO 19	5,092	93	4,999	4,342	368	3,974	657
20 TO 49	3,901	74	3,827	3,244	342	2,903	583
50 OR MORE	4,140	55	4,085	3,470	550	2,920	615
MOBILE HOME OR TRAILER	7,647	761	6,888	6,164	4,837	1,328	722
COOPERATIVES AND CONDOMINIUMS							
COOPERATIVES	772	24	748	639	371	268	109
CONDOMINIUMS	4,962	286	4,677	3,783	2,736	1,047	894
YEAR STRUCTURE BUILT*							
1995 -99	986	28	957	810	598	212	148
1990 -94	7,573	122	7,452	6,978	5,712	1,266	473
1985 -89	9,033	247	8,786	8,118	5,350	2,768	668
1980 -84	8,257	257	8,000	7,295	4,651	2,644	705
1975 -79	12,314	322	11,992	11,108	7,301	3,806	884
1970 -74	11,403	462	10,940	9,925	6,046	3,879	1,015
1960 -69	15,806	472	15,334	14,267	9,349	4,918	1,068
1950 -59	13,569	371	13,198	12,398	8,798	3,600	800
1940 -49	8,400	228	8,172	7,487	4,671	2,817	685
1930 -39	6,552	231	6,320	5,744	3,201	2,542	577
1920 -29	5,545	86	5,459	4,893	2,828	2,065	568
1919 OR EARLIER	10,019	227	9,792	8,671	5,039	2,632	1,120
MEDIAN	1967	1968	1967	1967	1968	1965	1966
METROPOLITAN/NONMETROPOLITAN AREAS							
INSIDE METROPOLITAN STATISTICAL AREAS	83,349	1,021	82,327	76,107	47,689	28,418	6,220
IN CENTER CITIES	33,513	128	33,385	30,243	14,808	15,434	3,142
SUBURBS	49,836	894	48,942	45,864	328,890	12,984	3,078
OUTSIDE METROPOLITAN STATISTICAL AREAS	26,108	2,032	24,076	21,586	15,885	5,731	2,489
REGIONS							
NORTHEAST	21,461	714	20,747	19,200	11,861	7,338	1,548
MIDWEST	26,056	648	25,410	23,200	16,567	7,096	1,748
SOUTH	39,148	1,235	37,912	34,236	22,959	11,277	3,677
WEST	22,791	458	22,333	20,596	12,157	8,439	1,738

*FOR MOBILE HOME, OLDEST CATEGORY IS 1939 OR EARLIER.

Source: U.S. Bureau of the Census, Series H-150A, *American Housing Survey For The United States*, 1995.

TABLE A7.2

INTRODUCTORY CHARACTERISTICS - OCCUPIED UNITS IN THE UNITED STATES: 1995

(NUMBERS IN THOUSANDS. CONSISTENT WITH THE 1990 CENSUS).

CHARACTERISTICS	TOTAL OCCUPIED UNITS	TENURE		HOUSING UNIT CHARACTERISTICS		HOUSEHOLD CHARACTERISTICS			
				PHYSICAL PROBLEMS					BELOW POVERTY LEVEL
		OWNER	RENTER	SEVERE	MODERATE	BLACK	HISPANIC	ELDERLY	
TOTAL	97,693	63,544	34,150	2,022	4,348	11,773	7,757	20,541	14,695
TENURE									
OWNER OCCUPIED	63544	63,544	NA	1,173	2,071	5,137	3,245	16,299	6,034
PERCENT OF ALL OCCUPIED	65.0%	100.0%	NA	58.0%	47.6%	43.6%	41.8%	78.2%	41.1%
RENTER OCCUPIED	34,150	NA	34,150	849	2,277	6,637	4,512	4,542	8,661
RACE AND ORIGIN									
WHITE	81,611	56,507	25,104	1,437	2,989	NA	6,454	18,598	10,127
NON-HISPANIC	7,515	53,627	21,530	1,285	2,454	NA		17,869	8,402
HISPANIC	6,454	2,880	3,574	153	535	NA	6,454	729	1,726
BLACK	11,773	5,137	6,637	448	1,148	11,773	238	1,882	3,627
AMERICAN INDIAN, ESKIMO, AND ALEUT	601	287	314	24	39	NA	57	89	198
ASIAN AND PACIFIC ISLANDER	2,430	1,295	1,135	44	83	NA	45	210	387
OTHER	1,278	318	960	69	89	NA	963	62	358
TOTAL HISPANIC	7,757	3,245	4,512	227	622	238	7,757	838	2,089
UNITS IN STRUCTURE									
1, DETACHED	60,826	52,257	8,569	1,198	2,545	5,601	3,699	13,992	6,810
1, ATTACHED	5,545	2,936	2,609	103	211	1,971	393	1,064	916
2 TO 4	9,299	1,734	7,565	211	563	1,754	1,170	1,451	2,201
5 TO 9	4,803	520	4,283	120	223	988	687	545	1,214
10 TO 19	4,342	368	3,974	98	183	742	561	500	884
20 TO 49	3,244	342	2,903	80	154	495	568	645	713
50 OR MORE	3,470	550	2,920	110	131	724	387	1,322	833
MOBILE HOME OR TRAILER	6,164	4,837	1,328	102	340	398	292	1,320	1,123
COOPERATIVES AND CONDOMINIUMS									
COOPERATIVES	639	371	268	8	24	118	32	221	90
CONDOMINIUMS	3,783	2,736	1,047	45	50	235	226	1,030	271
YEAR STRUCTURE BUILT*									
1995 -99	810	598	212		114	33	34	40	42
1990 -94	6,978	5,712	1,266	65	79	465	376	815	538
1985 -89	8,118	5,350	2,768	127	179	626	475	1,033	756
1980 -84	7,295	4,651	2,644	102	132	776	571	1,140	936
1975 -79	11,108	7,301	3,806	190	329	1,050	866	1,903	1,525
1970 -74	9,925	6,046	3,879	126	402	1,324	712	1,989	1,728
1960 -69	14,267	9,349	4,918	309	551	1,852	1,170	3,437	2,141
1950 -59	12,398	8,798	3,600	226	626	1,616	1,112	3,808	1,882
1940 -49	7,487	4,671	2,817	198	585	1,259	850	2,088	1,472
1930 -39	5,744	3,201	2,542	171	465	1,001	638	1,301	1,150
1920 -29	4,893	2,828	2,065	161	396	769	389	1,207	924
1919 OR EARLIER	8,671	5,039	2,632	347	591	1,003	503	2,080	1,600
MEDIAN	1967	1968	1965	1956	1952	1961	1963	1960	1951

TABLE A7.2

INTRODUCTORY CHARACTERISTICS - OCCUPIED UNITS IN THE UNITED STATES: 1995

(NUMBERS IN THOUSANDS. CONSISTENT WITH THE 1990 CENSUS).

CHARACTERISTICS	TOTAL OCCUPIED UNITS	TENURE		HOUSING UNIT CHARACTERISTICS		HOUSEHOLD CHARACTERISTICS			
				PHYSICAL PROBLEMS					BELOW POVERTY LEVEL
		OWNER	RENTER	SEVERE	MODERATE	BLACK	HISPANIC	ELDERLY	
METROPOLITAN/NONMETROPOLITAN AREAS									
INSIDE METROPOLITAN STATISTICAL									
AREAS	76,107	47,689	28,418	1,549	3,048	10,155	7,037	15,084	10,928
IN CENTER CITIES	30,243	14,808	15,434	746	1,662	6,699	3,803	5,916	5,925
SUBURBS	45,864	32,880	12,984	803	1,386	3,457	3,234	9,169	5,004
OUTSIDE METROPOLITAN									
STATISTICAL AREAS	21,586	15,885	5,731	474	1,300	1,618	720	5,756	3,767
REGIONS									
NORTHEAST	19,200	11,861	7,338	545	668	2,147	1,294	4,563	2,675
MIDWEST	23,662	16,567	7,096	512	690	2,227	510	5,112	3,282
SOUTH	34,236	22,959	11,277	11,277	2,296	6,295	2,686	7,230	5,725
WEST	20,596	12,157	8,439	8,439	693	1,104	3,267	3,935	3,014

NA = NOT APPLICABLE OR SAMPLE TOO SMALL - MEANS ZERO OR ROUNDS TO ZERO.

Source: U.S. Bureau of the Census, Series H-150A, *American Housing Survey For The United States,* 1995.

TABLE A7.3

SIZE OF UNIT AND LOT - OCCUPIED UNITS IN THE UNITED STATES: 1995

(NUMBERS IN THOUSANDS. CONSISTENT WITH THE 1990 CENSUS.)

CHARACTERISTICS	TOTAL OCCUPIED UNITS	TENURE OWNER	TENURE RENTER	HOUSING UNIT CHARACTERISTICS — PHYSICAL PROBLEMS SEVERE	HOUSING UNIT CHARACTERISTICS — PHYSICAL PROBLEMS MODERATE	HOUSEHOLD CHARACTERISTICS BLACK	HOUSEHOLD CHARACTERISTICS HISPANIC	HOUSEHOLD CHARACTERISTICS ELDERLY	BELOW POVERTY LEVEL
ROOMS									
1 ROOM	550	22	528	97	94	93	73	95	164
2 ROOMS	958	60	898	54	93	162	135	181	313
3 ROOMS	8,311	859	7,452	293	444	1,411	1,109	2,020	2,164
4 ROOMS	17,062	6,069	10,993	346	1,014	2,591	2,087	3,614	3,837
5 ROOMS	21,600	13,895	7,705	417	1,108	3,004	1,808	5,269	3,648
6 ROOMS	20,700	16,686	4,014	378	809	2,378	1,381	4,829	2,462
7 ROOMS	13,560	12,007	1,554	243	420	1,160	670	2,665	1,177
8 ROOMS	8,041	7,447	594	127	206	541	263	1,268	488
9 ROOMS	3,984	3,734	250	87	86	254	134	525	274
10 ROOMS OR MORE	2,927	2,765	162	71	74	180	96	375	168
MEDIAN	5.5	6.2	4.2	5.2	5.0	5.0	4.8	5.4	4.7
BEDROOMS									
NONE	1,047	52	995	118	119	153	129	174	300
1	11,777	1,734	10,043	282	644	1,925	1,441	2,804	2,823
2	29,146	14,532	14,613	559	1,591	3,864	2,862	7,141	5,526
3	40,302	33,332	6,970	767	1,508	4,517	2,566	8,376	4,681
4 OR MORE	15,421	13,784	1,528	295	487	1,315	759	2,345	1,364
MEDIAN	2.7	3.0	1.9	2.6	2.4	2.5	2.3	2.5	2.3
COMPLETE BATHROOMS									
NONE	465	195	270	319	18	95	52	109	183
1	43,777	19,069	24,709	884	2,991	7,102	4,646	9,973	9,791
1 AND ONE-HALF	14,780	11,319	3,461	274	483	1,842	787	3,692	1,775
2 OR MORE	38,671	32,961	5,710	545	857	2,734	2,272	7,066	2,946
SQUARE FOOTAGE OF UNIT									
SINGLE DETACHED AND MOBILE HOMES	66,990	57,094	9,897	1,300	2,885	5,999	3,991	15,312	7,933
LESS THAN 500	667	379	288	53	59	90	95	164	186
500 - 749	2,356	1,386	969	76	274	345	258	618	663
750 - 999	5,697	4,126	1,571	115	481	657	540	1,433	1,158
1,000 - 1,499	15,450	12,697	2,753	278	771	1,655	1,131	3,973	2,150
1,500 - 1,999	13,785	12,218	1,567	242	448	1,068	746	3,109	1,284
2,000 - 2,499	9,943	9,211	732	175	195	542	380	2,070	756
2,500 - 2,999	5,486	5,147	339	94	153	322	136	1,130	360
3,000 - 3,999	4,956	4,737	219	92	138	221	122	991	291
4,000 OR MORE	2,785	2,597	189	59	60	151	82	576	183
NOT REPORTED	5,867	4,596	1,271	116	306	949	501	1,247	903
MEDIAN	1,732	1,814	1,270	1,644	1,309	1,433	1,377	1,636	1,351
LOT SIZE									
LESS THAN ONE-EIGHTH ACRE	6,292	5,367	924	114	299	634	540	1,750	766
ONE-EIGHTH UP TO ONE-QUARTER ACRE	12,184	11,077	1107	155	383	821	789	3,309	1,085
ONE-QUARTER UP TO ONE-HALF ACRE	10,077	9,303	774	192	277	581	410	2,336	737
ONE-HALF UP TO ONE ACRE	7,394	6,656	738	127	202	486	225	1,466	610
1 - 4 ACRES	10,450	9,398	1,051	211	503	711	250	2,154	1,113
5 - 9 ACRES	1,713	1,574	139	22	61	60	22	307	176
10 ACRES OR MORE	3,670	3,185	485	116	199	118	77	1,081	503
DON'T KNOW	14,239	8,539	5,700	257	953	2,524	1,602	2,349	2,636
NOT REPORTED	6,503	4,921	1,582	211	220	1,135	467	1,625	1,219
MEDIAN	.43	.43	.44	.53	.51	.36	.22	.37	.47

TABLE A7.3

SIZE OF UNIT AND LOT - OCCUPIED UNITS IN THE UNITED STATES: 1995
(NUMBERS IN THOUSANDS. CONSISTENT WITH THE 1990 CENSUS.)

CHARACTERISTICS	TOTAL OCCUPIED UNITS	TENURE		HOUSING UNIT CHARACTERISTICS		HOUSEHOLD CHARACTERISTICS			
				PHYSICAL PROBLEMS					BELOW POVERTY LEVEL
		OWNER	RENTER	SEVERE	MODERATE	BLACK	HISPANIC	ELDERLY	
PERSON PER ROOM									
0.50 OR LESS	67,043	46,210	20,832	1,224	2,505	7,073	3,172	19,249	8,796
0.51 - 1.00	28,097	16,453	11,644	680	1,520	4,248	3,469	1,524	4,774
1.01 - 1.50	2,059	782	1,276	78	236	363	834	59	849
1.51 OR MORE	495	98	397	11	40	87	89	281	275
SQUARE FOOT PER PERSON									
SINGLE DETACHED AND MOBILE									
HOMES	66,990	57,094	9,897	1,300	2,885	5,999	3,991	15,312	7,933
LESS THAN 200	1,779	1,070	709	66	226	268	469	102	609
200 - 299	4,223	2,889	1,334	97	335	540	578	299	790
300 - 399	6,403	5,019	1,384	150	344	779	571	538	818
400 - 499	6,741	5,627	1,114	126	282	616	430	883	654
500 - 599	5,906	5,222	684	117	241	489	295	993	571
600 - 699	5,882	5,161	721	106	187	422	276	1214	517
700 - 799	4,966	4,450	516	94	155	337	165	1,275	443
800 - 899	3,696	3,321	375	57	114	264	146	904	383
900 - 999	3,490	3,187	302	53	112	246	101	1,065	352
1,000 - 1,499	10,005	9,150	854	184	331	617	278	3,437	1,040
1,500 OR MORE	8,034	7,401	632	134	253	473	180	3,355	854
NOT REPORTED	5,867	4,596	1,271	116	306	949	501	1,247	903
MEDIAN	694	728	480	634	543	566	429	977	614

Source: U.S. Bureau of the Census, Series H-150A, *American Housing Survey For The United States, 1995.*

TABLE A7.4

SELECTED EQUIPMENT AND PLUMBING - OCCUPIED UNITS IN THE UNITED STATES: 1995

(NUMBERS IN THOUSANDS. CONSISTENT WITH THE 1990 CENSUS).

CHARACTERISTICS	TOTAL OCCUPIED UNITS	TENURE		HOUSING UNIT CHARACTERISTICS		HOUSEHOLD CHARACTERISTICS			
		OWNER	RENTER	PHYSICAL PROBLEMS		BLACK	HISPANIC	ELDERLY	BELOW POVERTY LEVEL
				SEVERE	MODERATE				
EQUIPMENT									
LACKING COMPLETE KITCHEN FACILITIES	1,075	481	614	197	808	197	151	180	293
WITH COMPLETE KITCHEN (SINK, REFRIGERATOR, OVEN, AND BURNERS)	96,618	63,083	33,536	1,825	3,540	11,576	7,606	20,661	14,402
KITCHEN SINK	97,034	63,231	33,803	1,858	3,854	11,685	7,679	20,722	14,523
REFRIGERATOR	97,433	63,469	33,964	1,938	4,172	11,711	7,720	20,806	14,593
LESS THAN 5 YEARS OLD	35,847	23,572	12,274	650	1,350	4,678	3,047	6,409	5,331
AGE NOT REPORTED	2,479	620	1,859	39	126	439	246	292	517
BURNERS AND OVEN	97,207	6,343	33,764	1,920	4,033	11,691	7,658	20,779	14,537
LESS THAN 5 YEARS OLD	28,768	19,770	8,998	508	949	3,748	2,427	4,770	4,176
AGE NOT REPORTED	2,680	729	1,951	41	97	453	238	285	499
BURNERS ONLY	105	31	74	15	21	9	33	8	29
LESS THAN 5 YEARS OLD	28	13	15	3	4	NA	14	3	5
AGE NOT REPORTED	17	2	15	2	9	2	NA	2	7
OVEN ONLY	99	32	68	8	91	10	7	21	22
LESS THAN 5 YEARS OLD	34	11	23	3	31	4	3	8	12
AGE NOT REPORTED	12	2	10	1	11	NA	NA	3	1
NEITHER BURNERS NOR OVEN	282	38	244	79	203	63	59	33	108
DISHWASHER	52,508	40,236	12,272	772	1,060	3,466	2,717	9,373	4,130
LESS THAN 5 YEARS OLD	19,273	15,275	3,998	251	301	1,132	916	2,666	1,373
AGE NOT REPORTED	1,724	563	1,161	26	28	219	140	174	191
WASHING MACHINE	75,745	60,034	15,711	1,373	2,812	7,148	4,581	16,710	8,925
LESS THAN 5 YEARS OLD	27,863	21,287	6,576	466	1,020	2,958	2,007	4,358	3,260
AGE NOT REPORTED	959	468	491	19	37	160	62	149	128
CLOTHES DRYER	70,756	57,184	13,571	181	2,270	5,700	3,497	14,918	7,149
LESS THAN 5 YEARS OLD	23,974	18,545	5,429	406	754	2,228	1,442	3,560	2,365
AGE NOT REPORTED	899	444	455	16	23	121	56	145	99
DISPOSAL IN KITCHEN SINK	42,451	28,793	13,659	636	875	3,487	3,213	7,840	4,195
LESS THAN 5 YEARS OLD	16,127	11,867	4,260	253	280	1,177	1,200	2,681	1,445
AGE NOT REPORTED	2,186	550	1,636	33	64	295	234	192	304
AIR CONDITIONING									
CENTRAL	46,577	34,161	12,415	666	932	4,609	2,878	9,481	4,718
1 ROOM UNIT	17,137	9,053	8,083	370	1,255	2,568	1,523	3,990	3,613
2 ROOM UNIT	7,339	4,906	2,433	180	508	1,093	600	1,737	1,127
3 ROOM UNITS OR MORE	2,705	2,167	538	34	169	392	177	612	297
MAIN HEATING EQUIPMENT									
WARM-AIR FURNACE	53,165	38,301	14,863	918	1,223	5,762	2,921	11,181	6,768
STEAM OR HOT WATER SYSTEM	13,689	7,323	6,345	432	554	1,963	1,124	3,188	2,171
ELECTRIC HEAT PUMP	9,406	7,027	2,379	118	158	888	578	1,680	795
BUILT-IN ELECTRIC UNITS	7,035	2,870	4,166	113	180	856	608	1,518	1,221
FLOOR, WALL, OR OTHER BUILT-IN HOT AIR UNITS WITHOUT DUCTS	4,963	2,148	2,815	77	239	733	1,205	1,076	1,212
ROOM HEATERS WITH FLUE	1,620	889	752	63	101	384	137	499	481
ROOM HEATERS WITHOUT FLUE	1,642	984	878	63	1,579	544	263	499	598
PORTABLE ELECTRIC HEATERS	809	413	395	44	50	159	248	175	303
STOVES	2,320	1,735	585	120	109	192	178	457	544
FIREPLACES WITH INSERTS	511	429	81	12	3	33	22	111	87
FIREPLACES WITHOUT INSERTS	339	232	106	13	14	28	47	42	53
OTHER	1,171	788	403	26	43	139	94	291	266
NONE	1,044	483	581	23	96	115	334	148	213

TABLE A7.4

SELECTED EQUIPMENT AND PLUMBING - OCCUPIED UNITS IN THE UNITED STATES: 1995

(NUMBERS IN THOUSANDS. CONSISTENT WITH THE 1990 CENSUS).

CHARACTERISTICS	TOTAL OCCUPIED UNITS	TENURE		HOUSING UNIT CHARACTERISTICS		HOUSEHOLD CHARACTERISTICS			
				PHYSICAL PROBLEMS					BELOW POVERTY LEVEL
		OWNER	RENTER	SEVERE	MODERATE	BLACK	HISPANIC	ELDERLY	
OTHER HEATING EQUIPMENT									
WITH OTHER HEATING EQUIPMENT	26,636	21,529	5,107	493	1,078	2,120	1,245	5,317	2,669
WARM AIR FURNACE	1,161	916	245	19	79	73	48	196	145
STEAM OR HOT WATER SYSTEM	201	161	40	2	7	14	NA	36	13
ELECTRIC HEAT PUMP	311	284	26	5	9	18	9	50	29
BUILT-IN ELECTRIC UNITS	2,229	1,758	470	19	84	128	94	405	182
FLOOR, WALL OR OTHER BUILT-IN HOT-AIR UNITS WITHOUT DUCTS	473	381	112	4	23	38	31	102	78
ROOM HEATERS WITH FLUE	946	748	200	21	44	115	33	234	153
ROOM HEATERS WITHOUT FLUE	1,488	1,158	333	39	53	210	47	295	233
PORTABLE ELECTRIC HEATERS	5,443	3,731	1,712	153	501	880	354	1,390	807
STOVES	3,305	2,871	433	63	135	168	149	626	324
FIREPLACES WITH INSERTS	4,307	3,954	354	62	76	252	149	809	266
FIREPLACES WITHOUT INSERTS	8,669	7,316	1,354	137	147	516	390	1,528	510
OTHER	1,002	819	183	19	25	79	25	197	118
PLUMBING									
WITH ALL PLUMBING FACILITIES	96,234	62,572	33,663	563	4,348	11,522	7,637	20,466	14,329
LACKING SOME PLUMBING FACILITIES	188	80	107	188	NA	33	16	52	70
NO HOT PIPED WATER	42	26	16	42	NA	6	6	25	23
NO BATHTUB OR SHOWER	141	49	93	141	NA	24	8	38	50
NO FLUSH TOILET	85	24	62	85	NA	15	8	6	33
NO PLUMBING FACILITIES FOR EXCLUSIVE USE	1,271	892	380	1,271	NA	218	104	322	294

NA = MEANS NOT APPLICABLE OR SAMPLE TOO SMALL – MEANS ZERO OR ROUNDS TO ZERO.

Source: U.S. Bureau of the Census, Series H-150A, *American Housing Survey For The United States*, 1995.

TABLE A7.5

FUELS - OCCUPIED UNITS IN THE UNITED STATES: 1995

(NUMBERS IN THOUSANDS. CONSISTENT WITH THE 1990 CENSUS.)

CHARACTERISTICS	TOTAL OCCUPIED UNITS	TENURE		HOUSING UNIT CHARACTERISTICS — PHYSICAL PROBLEMS		HOUSEHOLD CHARACTERISTICS			
		OWNER	RENTER	SEVERE	MODERATE	BLACK	HISPANIC	ELDERLY	BELOW POVERTY LEVEL
TOTAL	97,693	63,544	34,150	2,022	4,348	11,773	7,757	20,841	14,695
MAIN HOUSE HEATING FUEL									
HOUSING UNITS WITH HEATING FUEL	96,650	63,081	33,589	1,999	4,252	11,658	7,423	20,693	14,482
ELECTRICITY	26,711	15,485	11,286	415	827	3,438	2,198	4,858	3,732
PIPED GAS	49,203	33,438	15,785	960	2,324	6,105	4,009	10,734	7,277
BOTTLED GAS	4251	3318	933	88	461	375	122	1096	724
FUEL OIL	10,974	6,871	4,104	346	448	1,209	752	2,869	1,643
KEROSENE OR OTHER LIQUID FUEL	1,055	756	298	22	227	163	32	257	225
COAL OR COKE	210	177	33	13	11	8	7	72	39
WOOD	3,533	2,708	825	147	133	272	250	664	699
SOLAR ENERGY	16	13	3	-	-	-	-	6	-
OTHER	637	315	321	10	21	88	52	137	143
OTHER HOUSE HEATING FUELS									
WITH OTHER HEATING FUELS*	16,141	13,013	3,128	345	727	1,313	720	3,002	1,746
ELECTRICITY	5,299	3,924	1,375	133	420	578	290	1,096	671
PIPED GAS	848	618	229	15	30	108	62	145	156
BOTTLED GAS	558	490	68	11	16	47	26	119	83
FUEL OIL	451	357	94	3	17	24	4	93	40
KEROSENE OR OTHER LIQUID FUEL	1,159	887	272	52	70	188	19	148	250
COAL OR COKE	157	140	17	9	8	8	-	39	18
WOOD	7,949	6,899	1,050	127	205	390	336	1,391	547
SOLAR ENERGY	111	107	3	1	5	12	4	12	2
OTHER	484	353	131	15	3	51	19	91	65
NOT REPORTED	665	499	166	11	44	80	51	149	108
COOKING FUEL									
WITH COOKING FUEL	97,406	63,502	33,904	1,943	4,145	11,710	7,697	20,806	14,587
ELECTRICITY	57,621	38,628	18,994	903	1,753	5,269	3,040	12,320	7,237
PIPED GAS	35,001	21,048	13,953	876	1,974	5,941	4,430	7,251	6,417
BOTTLED GAS	4,217	3,385	832	127	366	474	200	1,096	824
KEROSENE OR OTHER LIQUID FUEL	301	252	49	13	34	16	90	69	65
COAL OR COKE	7	7	-	-	-	3	-	2	-
OTHER	33	28	5	21	2	3	3	10	17
	225	154	71	3	15	4	15	58	27
WATER HEATING FUEL									
WITH HOT PIPED WATER	97,522	63,456	34,067	1,851	4,348	11,725	7,737	20,782	14,598
ELECTRICITY	36,630	23,419	13,211	543	1,474	4,126	2,161	7,701	5,403
PIPED GAS	50,558	33,354	17,205	1,015	2,309	6,258	4,743	10,545	7,574
BOTTLED GAS	3,239	2,540	699	57	259	233	161	780	545
FUEL OIL	5,808	3,395	2,413	210	246	722	552	1,489	835
KEROSENE OR OTHER LIQUID FUEL	331	259	72	8	21	16	13	73	45
COAL OR COKE	28	26	2	-	2	-	2	16	4
WOOD	44	32	12	5	2	2	2	7	11
SOLAR ENERGY	251	211	40	9	-	5	11	55	13
OTHER	633	220	414	5	34	91	91	115	167

TABLE A7.5 (CONTINUED)

FUELS - OCCUPIED UNITS IN THE UNITED STATES: 1995

(NUMBERS IN THOUSANDS. CONSISTENT WITH THE 1990 CENSUS.)

CHARACTERISTICS	TOTAL OCCUPIED UNITS	TENURE		HOUSING UNIT CHARACTERISTICS		HOUSEHOLD CHARACTERISTICS			
				PHYSICAL PROBLEMS					BELOW POVERTY LEVEL
		OWNER	RENTER	SEVERE	MODERATE	BLACK	HISPANIC	ELDERLY	
CENTRAL AIR CONDITIONING FUEL									
WITH CENTRAL AIR CONDITIONING	46,577	34,161	12,415	666	932	4,609	2,878	9,481	4,718
ELECTRICITY	43,120	31,398	11,721	601	866	4,235	2,707	8,533	4,335
PIPED GAS	2,971	2,375	597	58	48	317	154	804	331
OTHER	485	388	97	7	17	57	17	145	52
CLOTHES DRYER FUEL									
WITH CLOTHES DRYER	70,756	57,184	13,571	1,181	2,270	5,700	3,497	14,918	7,149
ELECTRICITY	53,666	42,438	11,228	844	1,804	4,287	2,378	11,238	5,540
PIPED GAS	15,998	13,781	2,216	305	425	1,369	1,083	3,448	1,487
OTHER	1,093	965	127	31	41	43	37	231	122
UNITS USING EACH FUEL*									
ELECTRICITY	97,680	63,515	34,145	1,989	4,348	11,771	7,757	20,833	14,680
ALL-ELECTRIC UNITS	20,891	12,292	8,599	282	409	2,493	1,380	3,938	2,722
PIPED GAS	60,243	38,625	21,618	1,310	2,875	8,105	5,731	12,767	9,511
BOTTLED GAS	7,830	6,213	1,617	185	630	661	296	1,973	1,306
FUEL OIL	13,485	8,324	5,160	429	558	1,544	949	3,444	2,122
KEROSENE OR OTHER LIQUID FUEL	2,421	1,811	610	84	318	366	64	449	520
COAL OR COKE	373	323	50	22	19	18	7	111	57
WOOD	11,488	9,609	1,879	274	340	663	586	2,057	1,246
SOLAR ENERGY	382	319	43	10	5	17	16	70	15
OTHER	1,555	813	742	30	64	192	129	324	310

- MEANS ZERO OR ROUNDS TO ZERO.

*MAY NOT ADD TO TOTAL BECAUSE MORE THAN ONE CATEGORY MAY APPLY TO A UNIT.

Source: U.S. Bureau of the Census, Series H-150A, *American Housing Survey For The United States, 1995.*

TABLE A7.6

INDICATORS OF HOUSING QUALITY - OCCUPIED UNITS IN THE UNITED STATES: 1995

(NUMBERS IN THOUSANDS. CONSISTENT WITH THE 1990 CENSUS.)

CHARACTERISTICS	TOTAL OCCUPIED UNITS	TENURE		HOUSING UNIT CHARACTERISTICS		HOUSEHOLD CHARACTERISTICS			
				PHYSICAL PROBLEMS					BELOW POVERTY LEVEL
		OWNER	RENTER	SEVERE	MODERATE	BLACK	HISPANIC	ELDERLY	
SELECTED AMENITIES*									
PORCH, DECK, BALCONY, OR PATIO	75,657	54,319	21,338	1,367	3,117	7,925	5,005	16,063	9,645
NOT REPORTED	270	167	103	7	17	37	18	83	41
TELEPHONE AVAILABLE	91,544	61,676	29,868	1,767	3,753	10,404	6,725	20,081	12,761
USABLE FIREPLACE	31,734	27,280	4,454	517	599	1,992	1,422	5,965	2,257
SEPARATE DINING ROOM	46,657	36,374	10,283	847	1,604	5,008	2,807	9,320	4,940
WITH 2 OR MORE LIVING ROOMS									
OR RECREATION ROOMS, ETC.	28,941	26,179	2,762	494	752	2,014	1,123	5,956	2,006
GARAGE OR CARPORT INCLUDED									
WITH HOME	57,352	46,906	10,446	918	1,624	3,975	3,689	13,458	5,47
NOT INCLUDED	40,036	16,514	23,522	1,100	2,707	7,728	4,038	7,322	9,144
OFFSTREET PARKING INCLUDED	30,330	13,342	16,988	682	1,838	5,200	2,752	5,318	6,494
OFFSTREET PARKING NOT REPORTED	422	450	377	33	7	27	39	91	116
GARAGE OR CARPORT NOT REPORTED	305	123	182	9	4	18	70	61	73
SELECTED DEFICIENCIES*									
SIGNS OF RATS IN LAST 3 MONTHS	2,708	1,219	1,489	247	760	786	656	395	872
HOLES IN FLOORS	1,074	503	571	198	543	283	195	119	348
OPEN CRACKS OR HOLES (INTERIOR)	4,527	1,943	2,584	393	1,656	1106	594	523	1,267
BROKEN PLASTER OR PEELING PAINT									
(INTERIOR)	3,873	1,672	2,002	339	1,377	857	NA	5	15
NO ELECTRICAL WIRING	26	22	4	26	NA	NA	225	366	410
EXPOSED WIRING	1,760	873	887	152	278	358	191	373	540
ROOMS WITHOUT ELECTRIC OUTLETS	1,818	891	925	135	290	399	478	542	1,033
WATER LEAKAGE DURING LAST 12 MONTHS									
NO LEAKAGE FROM INSIDE STRUCTURE	88,008	57,058	28,950	1,591	2,957	9,903	6,724	19,277	12,605
WITH LEAKAGE FROM INSIDE STRUCTURE*	11,411	6,325	5,088	423	1,378	1,838	1,018	1,509	2,051
FIXTURES BACKED UP OR OVERFLOWED	3,728	2,123	1,605	139	488	623	370	425	718
PIPES LEAKED	5,456	2,824	2,632	238	723	958	517	748	1,057
OTHER OR UNKNOWN									
(INCLUDES NOT REPORTED)	2,604	1,545	1,059	71	272	330	167	371	370
INTERIOR LEAKAGE NOT REPORTED	274	161	114	8	13	32	18	54	39
NO LEAKAGE FROM OUTSIDE STRUCTURE	81,330	51,787	29,543	1,458	2,675	9780	6,701	17,944	12,381
WITH LEAKAGE FROM OUTSIDE STRUCTURE*	15,999	11,542	4,457	557	1,661	1972	1,032	2,836	2,274
ROOF	7,566	4,950	2,316	345	1,025	1115	640	1,659	1,285
BASEMENT	4,944	4,195	479	112	265	422	88	917	443
WALLS, CLOSED WINDOWS, OR DOORS	3,075	1,837	1,238	111	354	410	258	417	478
OTHER OR UNKNOWN									
(INCLUDES NOT REPORTED)	1,778	1,345	461	61	161	171	119	289	246
EXTERIOR LEAKAGE NOT REPORTED	385	215	149	7	12	41	24	61	40
OVERALL OPINION OF STRUCTURE									
1 (WORST)	540	159	381	75	167	175	96	94	228
2	399	122	276	48	103	110	49	70	146
3	751	213	537	64	138	158	97	95	261
4	1,088	379	709	72	190	201	126	115	282
5	5,844	2,374	3,470	217	678	985	721	1,098	1,407
6	4,738	2,091	2,647	125	379	813	433	689	877
7	10,998	5,632	5,388	215	883	1,491	932	1,375	1,699
8	24,256	15,274	8,982	385	818	2,841	1,884	4,257	3,151
9	15,173	10,994	4,179	207	335	1,486	1,091	2,979	1,695
10 (BEST)	32,826	25,753	7,073	552	791	3,359	2,224	9,707	4,681
NOT REPORTED	1,080	551	530	62	67	155	104	361	268

TABLE A7.6

INDICATORS OF HOUSING QUALITY - OCCUPIED UNITS IN THE UNITED STATES: 1995

(NUMBERS IN THOUSANDS. CONSISTENT WITH THE 1990 CENSUS.)

CHARACTERISTICS	TOTAL OCCUPIED UNITS	TENURE		HOUSING UNIT CHARACTERISTICS PHYSICAL PROBLEMS		HOUSEHOLD CHARACTERISTICS			
		OWNER	RENTER	SEVERE	MODERATE	BLACK	HISPANIC	ELDERLY	BELOW POVERTY LEVEL
SELECTED PHYSICAL PROBLEMS									
SEVERE PHYSICAL PROBLEMS*	2,022	1,173	849	2,022	NA	448	227	431	584
PLUMBING	1,459	972	487	1,459	NA	251	120	374	366
HEATING	361	116	245	367	NA	124	66	33	119
ELECTRIC	61	38	25	61	NA	7	7	9	31
UPKEEP	182	67	115	182	NA	76	38	18	87
HALLWAYS	6	-	6	6	NA	4	1	-	4
MODERATE PHYSICAL PROBLEMS*	4,348	2,071	2,277	NA	4,348	1,148	622	820	1,303
PLUMBING	276	107	169	NA	276	79	46	34	95
HEATING	1,579	930	650	NA	1,579	509	252	468	553
UPKEEP	1887	767	1121	NA	1887	495	260	217	572
HALLWAYS	36	2	34	NA	36	15	10	3	11
KITCHEN	794	355	438	NA	794	133	97	141	182

NA = NOT APPLICABLE OR SAMPLE TOO SMALL - MEANS ZERO OR ROUNDS TO ZERO.)

*FIGURES MAY NOT ADD TO TOTAL BECAUSE MORE THAN ONE CATEGORY MAY APPLY TO A UNIT.

Source: U.S. Bureau of the Census, Series H-150A, *American Housing Survey For The United States, 1995*.

TABLE A7.7

NEIGHBORHOOD - OCCUPIED UNITS IN THE UNITED STATES: 1995

(NUMBERS IN THOUSANDS. CONSISTENT WITH THE 1990 CENSUS.)

CHARACTERISTICS	TOTAL OCCUPIED UNITS	TENURE		HOUSING UNIT CHARACTERISTICS		HOUSEHOLD CHARACTERISTICS			
				PHYSICAL PROBLEMS					BELOW POVERTY LEVEL
		OWNER	RENTER	SEVERE	MODERATE	BLACK	HISPANIC	ELDERLY	
TOTAL	97,693	63,544	34,150	2,022	4,348	11,773	7,757	20,841	14,695
OVERALL OPINION OF NEIGHBORHOOD									
1 (WORST)	1,349	447	902	84	185	443	216	254	576
2	795	324	471	47	97	189	81	132	243
3	1,208	482	726	45	102	255	159	185	330
4	1813	764	1049	66	138	280	211	220	366
5	7,011	3,387	3,623	177	474	1,249	793	1,288	1,558
6	4,919	2,521	2,398	147	289	800	504	737	846
7	10,173	5,943	4,230	192	447	1,410	764	1,442	1,301
8	22,242	14,692	7,551	404	838	2,522	1,606	4,256	2,779
9	14,361	10,311	4,050	202	433	1,277	972	2,780	1540
10 (BEST)	31,623	23,354	8,269	581	1,228	3,125	2,264	8,842	4,695
NO NEIGHBORHOOD	872	628	244	11	55	20	42	226	122
NOT REPORTED	1,326	691	636	66	62	205	144	480	340
NEIGHBORHOOD CONDITIONS									
OCCUPIED UNITS WITH NEIGHBORHOOD	95,495	62,225	33,270	1,945	4,231	11,549	7,571	20,135	14,233
NO PROBLEMS	60,176	40,612	19,563	1,073	2,347	6,711	4,657	14,577	8,831
WITH PROBLEMS	34,852	21,308	13,543	858	1,860	4,756	2,892	5,458	5,325
CRIME	6,926	2,920	4,007	228	553	1649	871	812	1,554
NOISE	7,396	3,505	3,891	217	464	1,148	751	1,166	1,333
TRAFFIC	7,319	4,478	2,842	173	410	712	484	1,000	957
LITTER OR HOUSING DETERIORATION	4,058	2,680	1,378	138	284	750	398	832	696
POOR CITY OR COUNTY SERVICES	1,179	777	402	51	94	206	128	152	199
UNDESIRABLE COMMERCIAL, INSTITUTIONAL, INDUSTRIAL	1,335	870	465	33	74	167	89	229	194
PEOPLE	11,161	6,147	5,013	319	691	1,680	1,146	1,694	2,157
OTHER	9,441	6,683	2,758	227	460	1,113	623	1,571	1,176
TYPE OF PROBLEM NOT REPORTED	604	395	208	7	26	70	47	75	77
PRESENCE OF PROBLEMS NOT REPORTED	468	304	164	14	24	82	22	101	78
OTHER BUILDINGS VANDALIZED OR WITH INTERIOR EXPOSED**									
NONE	22,065	3,070	18,995	499	1,022	3,878	2,940	3,855	4,956
1 BUILDING	443	44	399	20	41	160	102	52	146
MORE THAN 1 BUILDING	664	64	601	56	102	345	143	73	308
NO BUILDINGS WITHIN 300 FEET	390	59	332	7	12	80	26	125	110
NOT REPORTED	1,606	283	1,322	37	76	240	165	359	328
BARS ON WINDOWS OF BUILDINGS**									
WITH OTHER BUILDINGS WITHIN 300 FEET	23,172	3,177	19,995	575	1,164	4,383	3,185	3,981	5,411
NO BARS ON WINDOWS	19,514	2,729	16,785	408	810	3,116	2,208	3,411	4,163
1 BUILDING WITH BARS	544	79	465	17	66	133	136	74	187
2 OR MORE BUILDINGS WITH BARS	2,948	358	2,590	144	282	1,083	816	446	1,003
NOT REPORTED	166	11	155	6	6	51	25	50	...
CONDITION OF STREETS**									
NO REPAIRS NEEDED	17,909	2,676	15,233	364	774	2,925	2,277	3,244	3,788
MINOR REPAIRS NEEDED	5,039	509	4,530	213	349	1,328	845	759	1,554
MAJOR REPAIRS NEEDED	520	59	460	21	58	182	101	89	181
NO STREETS WITHIN 300 FEET	295	18	277	2	9	58	27	38	43
NOT REPORTED	1405	257	1149	19	63	211	126	333	283

TABLE A7.7 (CONTINUED)

NEIGHBORHOOD - OCCUPIED UNITS IN THE UNITED STATES: 1995
(NUMBERS IN THOUSANDS. CONSISTENT WITH THE 1990 CENSUS.)

CHARACTERISTICS	TOTAL OCCUPIED UNITS	TENURE		HOUSING UNIT CHARACTERISTICS		HOUSEHOLD CHARACTERISTICS			
				PHYSICAL PROBLEMS					BELOW POVERTY LEVEL
		OWNER	RENTER	SEVERE	MODERATE	BLACK	HISPANIC	ELDERLY	
TRASH, LITTER, OR JUNK ON STREETS OR ANY PROPERTIES**									
NONE	17,367	2,754	14,614	321	623	2,453	1,976	3,337	3,323
MINOR ACCUMULATION	5,808	462	5,346	227	472	1,769	1,101	727	1,960
MAJOR ACCUMULATION	609	62	547	50	94	273	174	54	284
NOT REPORTED	1,384	242	1,142	21	62	208	126	346	283

NA = NOT APPLICABLE OR SAMPLE TOO SMALL - MEANS ZERO OR ROUNDS TO ZERO.

* FIGURES MAY NOT ADD TO TOTAL BECAUSE MORE THAN ONE CATEGORY MAY APPLY TO A UNIT.

**LIMITED TO MULTI-UNIT STRUCTURES.

Source: U.S. Bureau of the Census, Series H-150A, *American Housing Survey For The United States, 1995.*

TABLE A7.8

SELECTED HOUSING COSTS - OCCUPIED UNITS IN THE UNITED STATES: 1995

(NUMBERS IN THOUSANDS. CONSISTENT WITH THE 1990 CENSUS)

CHARACTERISTICS	TOTAL OCCUPIED UNITS	TENURE		HOUSING UNIT CHARACTERISTICS		HOUSEHOLD CHARACTERISTICS			
		OWNER	RENTER	PHYSICAL PROBLEMS					BELOW POVERTY LEVEL
				SEVERE	MODERATE	BLACK	HISPANIC	ELDERLY	
TOTAL	97,693	63,644	34,260	2,022	4,348	11,773	7,767	20,841	14,696
MONTHLY HOUSING COSTS									
LESS THAN $100	1,365	1,049	317	59	178	295	107	614	596
$100 - $199	8,493	7,269	1,224	231	652	1,210	593	4,447	2,274
$200 - $249	5,619	4,675	944	143	353	667	326	2,654	1,115
$250 - $299	5,211	4,034	1,177	128	270	602	237	2,176	887
$300 - $349	5,101	3,375	1,730	125	308	691	347	1,695	970
$350 - $399	5,228	2,985	2,243	101	259	754	417	1,351	889
$400 - $449	5,411	2,702	2,709	137	322	761	469	1,158	914
$450 - $499	5,337	2,566	2,771	92	273	800	513	879	853
$500 - $599	9,877	4921	4,955	170	423	1,306	1,008	1,418	1,247
$600 - $699	8,495	4,356	4,139	130	258	1,060	862	967	851
$700 - $799	7,017	4,142	2,874	132	202	719	585	686	628
$800 - $999	9,504	6,684	2,819	132	271	909	653	817	574
$1,000 - $1,249	6,695	5,477	1,218	93	148	474	478	437	327
$1,250 - $1,499	3,937	3,518	419	90	72	230	260	245	174
$1,500 OR MORE	6,156	5,791	365	93	117	236	333	368	305
NO CASH RENT	4,244	NA	4,244	165	241	1,060	569	929	2,092
MORTGAGE PAYMENT NOT REPORTED	NA	NA	NA	NA	NA	NA	NA	NA	NA
MEDIAN (EXCLUDES NO CASH RENT)	550	563	537	452	405	474	558	302	376
MEDIAN MONTHLY HOUSING COSTS FOR OWNERS									
MONTHLY COSTS INCLUDING ALL MORTGAGES PLUS MAINTENANCE COSTS	593	593	NA	485	313	497	614	299	320
MONTHLY COSTS EXCLUDING 2ND AND SUBSEQUENT MORTGAGES AND MAINTENANCE COSTS	549	549	NA	446	293	451	577	282	299
MONTHLY HOUSING COSTS AS PERCENT OF CURRENT INCOME*									
LESS THAN 5 PERCENT	3,014	2,845	170	44	135	188	117	680	29
5 - 9 PERCENT	10,458	9,570	888	185	346	783	530	2,814	132
10 - 14 PERCENT	13,885	11,260	2,624	246	568	1,236	643	3,344	301
15 - 19 PERCENT	14,556	10,637	3,919	256	559	1,440	878	2,551	424
20 - 24 PERCENT	12,115	8,174	3,941	191	456	1,395	842	2,060	543
25 - 29 PERCENT	9,165	5,523	3,641	149	395	1,057	764	1,648	698
30 - 34 PERCENT	6,327	3,586	2,741	134	253	771	587	1,297	700
35 - 39 PERCENT	4,588	2,402	2,186	118	199	606	512	952	606
40 - 49 PERCENT	5,299	2,688	2,611	125	303	864	632	1,168	1,123
50 - 59 PERCENT	3,074	1,525	1,549	77	182	474	398	756	872
60 - 69 PERCENT	2,039	950	1,088	59	142	367	250	504	748
70 - 99 PERCENT	2,662	1,185	1,677	53	237	515	434	716	1,517
MONTHLY HOUSING COSTS AS PERCENT OF CURRENT INCOME* (CONT.)									
100 PERCENT OR MORE	4,268	2,029	2,239	145	241	718	461	1,011	3,207
ZERO OR NEGATIVE INCOME	1,800	1,169	631	76	90	301	141	392	1,703
NO CASH RENT	4,244	NA	4,244	165	241	1,060	569	929	2,092
MORTGATE PAYMENT NOT REPORTED	NA	NA	NA	NA	NA	NA	NA	NA	NA
MEDIAN (EXCLUDES 3 PREVIOUS LINES)	22	19	29	24	24	26	28	21	60
MEDIAN (EXCLUDES 4 LINES BEFORE MEDIANS)	21	18	28	22	23	24	27	20	44

TABLE A7.8 (CONTINUED)

SELECTED HOUSING COSTS - OCCUPIED UNITS IN THE UNITED STATES: 1995

(NUMBERS IN THOUSANDS. CONSISTENT WITH THE 1990 CENSUS)

CHARACTERISTICS	TOTAL OCCUPIED UNITS	TENURE		HOUSING UNIT CHARACTERISTICS		HOUSEHOLD CHARACTERISTICS			
		OWNER	RENTER	PHYSICAL PROBLEMS		BLACK	HISPANIC	ELDERLY	BELOW POVERTY LEVEL
				SEVERE	MODERATE				
RENT PAID BY LODGERS									
LODGERS IN HOUSING UNITS	980	503	477	22	71	76	143	64	94
LESS THAN $100 PER MONTH	42	25	17	3	3	3	10	3	4
$100 - $199	146	63	83	5	10	21	25	19	15
$200 - $299	246	122	124	6	18	24	32	13	46
$300 - $399	164	81	83	4	19	7	22	6	13
$400 OR MORE PER MONTH	186	96	90	2	8	7	28	5	9
NOT REPORTED	197	117	80	3	13	13	25	19	6
MEDIAN	283	286	279	NA	289	230	273	205	253
MONTHLY COST PAID FOR ELECTRICITY									
ELECTRICITY USED	97,660	63,515	34,145	1,989	4,348	11,771	7,757	20,833	14,680
LESS THAN $25	7,368	2,825	4,544	178	369	929	905	2,091	1,699
$25 - $49	24,913	14,714	10,199	478	1,341	2,913	2,222	6,380	4,109
$50 - $74	22,396	15,885	6,510	367	1,000	2,585	1,552	4,774	3,031
$75 - $99	14,253	11,054	3,199	245	486	1,498	738	2,555	1,588
$100 - $149	23,254	9,923	2,331	230	417	1,316	672	1,897	1,261
$150 - $199	4,100	3,555	545	98	131	488	209	613	374
$200 OR MORE	1,982	1,655	328	20	58	224	159	354	194
MEDIAN	63	69	48	60	55	61	52	55	53
INCLUDED IN RENT, OTHER FEE, OR OBTAINED FREE	10,393	3,904	6,490	372	547	1,818	1,300	2,170	2,426
MONTHLY COST PAID FOR PIPED GAS									
PIPED GAS USED	60,243	38,625	21,618	1,310	2,875	8,105	5,731	12,767	9,511
LESS THAN $25	14,450	7,840	6,610	282	857	1,765	2,317	2,999	2,699
$25 - $49	19,757	14,492	5,265	297	932	2,164	1,425	4,341	2,605
$50 - $74	9,686	7,808	1,878	218	304	1,243	381	2,163	1,116
$75 - $99	3,468	2,746	723	71	168	522	152	749	450
$100 - $149	1,887	1,606	280	64	82	322	75	495	213
$150 - $199	579	469	110	24	18	123	26	158	81
$200 OR MORE	366	268	98	5	21	95	26	70	63
MEDIAN	38	42	29	42	34	41	25-	39	34
INCLUDED IN RENT, OTHER FEE, OR OBTAINED FREE	10,050	3,395	6,655	349	493	1,871	1,330	1,792	2,284
AVERAGE MONTHLY COST FOR FUEL OIL									
FUEL OIL USED	13,485	8,324	5,160	429	558	1,544	949	3,444	2,122
LESS THAN $25	1,257	820	437	29	82	166	68	291	195
$25 - $49	2,691	2,047	644	58	112	174	133	739	389
$50 - $74	2,993	2,396	598	77	81	158	65	889	345
$75 - $99	1,355	1,113	242	20	41	49	48	390	140
$100 - $149	1,231	1,038	192	37	32	69	38	308	91
$150 - $199	356	227	128	1	10	122	20	79	61
$200 OR MORE	196	176	20	3	5	20	7	61	15
MEDIAN	59	61	52	58	47	56	48	60	52
INCLUDED IN RENT, OTHER FEE, OR OBTAINED FREE	3,406	507	2,899	203	195	786	570	688	886
PROPERTY INSURANCE									
PROPERTY INSURANCE PAID	68,453	59,753	8,699	1,129	1,886	5,585	3,080	16,859	6,154
MEDIAN PER MONTH	33	35	17	33	31	30	36	32	27

NA = NOT APPLICABLE OR SAMPLE TOO SMALL - MEANS ZERO OR ROUNDS TO ZERO.

Source: U.S. Bureau of the Census, Series H-150A, *American Housing Survey For The United States*, 1995.

TABLE A7.9

CONSUMPTION AND EXPENDITURES IN U.S. HOUSEHOLDS: 1993

| CHARACTERISTICS | TOTAL HOUSEHOLDS (MILLIONS) | CONSUMPTION | | EXPENDITURES | |
		PER HOUSEHOLD (MILLION BTU)	PER HOUSEHOLD MEMBER (MILLION BTU)	PER HOUSEHOLD (DOLLARS)	PER HOUSEHOLD MEMBER (DOLLARS)
TOTAL U.S. HOUSEHOLDS	96.6	103.6	40	1,282	491
TYPE OF HOUSING UNIT					
SINGLE-FAMILY	66.8	118.5	43	1,441	517
DETACHED	59.5	121.2	43	1,462	520
ATTACHED	7.3	96.3	37	1,266	487
MOBILE HOME	5.6	81.9	31	1,203	454
MULTIFAMILY	24.2	67.3	32	863	406
2-4 UNITS	8.0	99.5	41	1,112	461
5 OR MORE UNITS	16.2	51.5	26	740	373
EDUCATION OF HOUSEHOLDER					
12 YEARS OR FEWER	51.5	100.6	38	1,226	463
13-16 YEARS	33.6	105.0	40	1,330	512
17 YEARS OR MORE	11.5	112.4	45	1,394	556
RACE OF HOUSEHOLDER					
WHITE	80.2	105.3	41	1,307	513
BLACK	10.9	106.7	39	1,250	461
OTHER*	5.5	72.7	22	988	295
HOUSEHOLDER OF HISPANIC DESCENT					
YES	7.9	81.2	25	1,065	332
NO	88.7	105.5	41	1,302	508
HOUSEHOLD SIZE					
1 PERSON	23.5	76.7	77	904	904
2 PERSONS	31.7	101.3	51	1,253	626
3 PERSONS	16.6	112.9	38	1,416	472
4 PERSONS	14.6	125.2	31	1561	390
5 PERSONS	6.8	122.3	24	1588	318
6 OR MORE PERSONS	3.5	133.9	20	1708	251
OWNERSHIP OF UNIT					
OWNED	63.2	118.5	44	1,457	537
RENTED	33.4	75.2	31	953	393
AGE OF HOUSEHOLDER					
UNDER 25 YEARS	5.7	75.4	30	956	377
25-34 YEARS	19.9	95.4	32	1187	394
35-44 YEARS	21.4	105.9	32	1380	417
45-59 YEARS	21.9	113.5	43	1429	546
60 YEARS AND OVER	27.8	105.6	59	1227	681

*INCLUDES 1.7 MILLION HOUSEHOLDERS WHO DESCRIBED THEMSELVES AS HISPANIC RATHER THAN WHITE, BLACK, OR OTHER.

Source: U.S. Department of Energy, Energy Information Administration, DOE/EIA-0464(94), *Household Energy Consumption and Expenditures*, August 1997.

TABLE A7.10

U.S. AVERAGE HOUSEHOLD AND VEHICLE ENERGY EXPENDITURES: 1994

(DOLLARS PER HOUSEHOLD)

1993 HOUSEHOLD CHARACTERISTICS	ALL HOUSEHOLDS		HOUSEHOLDS WITHOUT VEHICLES		HOUSEHOLDS WITH VEHICLES			
	NUMBER OF HOUSEHOLDS (MILLIONS)	HOUSEHOLD & VEHICLE ENERGY EXPENDITURES (DOLLARS)	NUMBER OF HOUSEHOLDS (MILLIONS)	HOUSEHOLD ENERGY EXPENDITURES (DOLLARS)	NUMBER OF HOUSEHOLDS (MILLIONS)	HOUSEHOLD & VEHICLE ENERGY EXPENDITURES (DOLLARS)	HOUSEHOLD ENERGY EXPENDITURES (DOLLARS)	MOTOR FUEL ENERGY EXPENDITURES (DOLLARS)
TOTAL	97.3	2,365	12.5	962	84.9	2,571	1,337	1,234
ENERGY USED IN HOME— JAN. THROUGH DEC. 1993 (MILLION BTU/ HOUSEHOLD)								
50 OR LESS	20.0	1,415	4.7	569	15.3	1,677	715	962
51 - 75	17.4	2,083	2.1	858	15.3	2,251	1,069	1,182
76 - 100	16.0	2,362	1.8	1,019	14.2	2,536	1,275	1,260
101 - 125	13.8	2,566	1.4	1,260	12.4	2,713	1,429	1,284
126 - 150	10.0	2,629	0.7	1,259	9.2	2,807	1,530	1,277
151 OR OVER	20.1	3,256	1.7	1,770	18.5	3,389	1,964	1,425
ENERGY USED IN HOME— JAN. THROUGH DEC. 1993 (DOLLARS PER HOUSEHOLD)								
600 OR LESS	10.5	998	3.4	430	7.1	1,273	453	820
601 - 800	10.8	1,450	2.3	702	8.5	1,648	701	947
800 - 1,000	13.4	1,830	2.0	910	11.4	1,989	905	1,084
1,001 - 1,200	14.2	2,115	1.5	1,094	12.7	2,232	1,101	1,131
1,201 - 1,600	23.2	2,554	1.8	1,354	21.4	2,655	1,392	1,263
1,601 OR OVER	25.3	3,576	1.5	2,017	23.7	3,676	2,116	1,561
MEASURE HEATED AREA OF RESIDENCE (SQUARE FEET)								
FEWER THAN 600	8.0	1,099	3.5	636	4.5	1,459	711	748
600 - 999	22.0	1,730	4.8	892	17.1	1,965	972	993
1,000 - 1,599	26.9	2,338	2.5	1,239	24.3	2,453	1,247	1,205
1,600 - 1,999	12.8	2,604	0.7	1,361	12.1	2,681	1,417	1,264
2,000 - 2,399	9.9	2,848	NA	NA	9.6	2,899	1,576	1,323
2,400 - 2,999	8.1	3,224	NA	NA	7.9	3,256	1,707	1,549
3,000 OR MORE	9.8	3,385	0.4	1,652	9.4	3,461	1,878	1,583
MAIN HEATING FUEL								
NATURAL GAS	52.1	2,331	7.0	1,013	45.1	2,536	1,343	1,193
ELECTRICITY	25.0	2,264	2.7	763	22.3	2,445	1,219	1,226
FUEL OIL OR KEROSENE	11.6	2,528	2.0	1,075	9.6	2,828	1,594	1,233
WOOD	3.1	2,757	NA	NA	2.9	2,903	1,184	1,719
LIQUIFIED PETROLEUM GAS	4.4	2,840	0.4	1,197	4.0	3,002	1,571	1,431
OTHE/NONE	1.2	1,589	NA	NA	1.0	1,791	731	1,060

NA = NOT APPLICABLE OR SAMPLE TOO SMALL.

Source: U.S. Department of Energy, Energy Information Administration, DOE/EIA-0464(94), Household Vehicles Energy Consumption, 1994, August 1997.

CRIME AND CRIMINAL JUSTICE

TABLE A8.1

ESTIMATED NUMBER AND RATE (PER 100,000 INHABITANTS) OF OFFENSES IN THE U.S. KNOWN TO POLICE, BY OFFENSE: 1960–1995

YEAR	TOTAL CRIME INDEX	VIOLENT CRIME	PROPERTY CRIME	MURDER AND NON-NEGLIGENT MANSLAUGHTER	FORCIBLE RAPE	ROBBERY	AGGRAVATED ASSAULT	BURGLARY	LARCENY- THEFT	MOTOR VEHICLE THEFT
NUMBER OF OFFENSES										
1960	3,384,200	288,460	3,095,700	9,110	17,190	107,840	154,320	912,100	1,855,400	328,200
1961	3,488,000	289,390	3,198,600	8,740	17,220	106,670	156,760	949,600	1,913,000	336,000
1962	3,752,200	301,510	3,450,700	8,530	17,550	110,860	164,570	994,300	2,089,600	366,800
1963	3,109,500	316,970	3,792,500	8,640	17,650	116,470	174,210	1,086,400	2,297,800	408,300
1964	4,564,600	364,220	4,200,400	9,360	21,420	130,390	203,050	1,213,200	2,514,400	472,800
1965	4,739,400	387,390	4,352,000	9,960	23,410	138,690	215,330	1,282,500	2,572,600	496,900
1966	5,223,500	430,180	4,793,300	11,040	25,820	157,990	235,330	1,410,100	2,822,000	561,200
1967	5,903,400	499,930	5,403,500	12,240	27,620	202,910	257,160	1,632,100	3,111,600	659,800
1968	6,720,200	595,010	6,125,200	13,800	31,670	262,840	286,700	1,858,900	3,482,700	783,600
1969	7,410,900	661,870	6,749,000	14,760	37,170	298,850	311,090	1,981,900	3,888,600	878,500
1970	8,098,000	738,820	7,359,200	16,000	37,990	349,860	334,970	2,205,000	4,225,800	928,400
1971	8,588,200	816,500	7,771,700	17,780	42,260	387,700	368,760	2,399,300	4,424,200	948,200
1972	8,248,800	834,900	7,413,900	18,670	46,850	376,290	393,090	2,375,500	4,151,200	887,200
1973	8,718,100	875,910	7,842,200	19,640	51,400	384,220	420,650	2,565,500	4,347,900	928,800
1974	10,253,400	974,720	9,278,700	20,710	55,400	442,400	456,210	3,039,200	5,262,500	977,100
1975	11,292,400	1,039,710	10,252,700	20,510	56,090	470,500	492,620	3,265,300	5,977,700	1,009,600
1976	11,349,700	1,004,210	10,345,500	18,780	57,080	427,810	500,530	3,108,700	6,270,800	966,000
1977	10,984,500	1,029,580	9,955,000	19,120	63,500	412,610	534,350	3,071,500	5,905,700	977,700
1978	11,209,000	1,085,550	10,123,400	19,560	67,610	426,930	571,460	3,128,300	5,991,000	1,004,100
1979	12,249,500	1,208,030	11,041,500	21,460	76,390	480,700	629,480	3,327,700	6,601,000	1,112,800
1980	13,408,300	1,344,520	12,063,700	23,040	82,990	565,840	672,650	3,795,200	7,136,900	1,131,700
1981	13,423,800	1,361,820	12,061,900	22,520	82,500	592,910	663,900	3,779,700	7,194,400	1,087,800
1982	12,974,400	1,322,390	11,652,000	21,010	78,770	553,130	669,480	3,447,100	7,142,500	1,062,400
1983	12,108,600	1,258,090	10,850,500	19,310	78,920	506,570	653,290	3,129,900	6,712,800	1,007,900
1984	11,881,800	1,273,280	10,608,500	18,960	84,230	485,010	685,350	2,984,400	6,591,900	1,032,200
1985	12,431,400	1,328,800	11,102,600	18,980	88,670	497,870	723,250	3,073,300	6,926,400	1,102,900
1986	13,211,900	1,489,170	11,722,700	20,610	91,460	542,780	834,320	3,241,400	7,257,200	1,224,100
1987	13,508,700	1,484,000	12,024,700	20,100	91,110	517,700	855,090	3,236,200	7,499,900	1,288,700
1988	13,923,100	1,566,220	12,356,900	20,680	92,490	542,970	910,090	3,218,100	7,705,900	1,432,900
1989	14,251,400	1,646,040	12,605,400	21,500	94,500	578,330	951,710	3,168,200	7,872,400	1,564,800
1990	14,475,600	1,820,130	12,655,500	23,440	102,560	639,270	1,054,860	3,073,900	7,945,700	1,635,900
1991	14,872,900	1,911,770	12,961,100	24,700	106,590	687,730	1,092,740	3,157,200	8,142,200	1,661,700
1992	14,438,200	1,932,270	12,505,900	23,760	109,060	672,480	1,126,970	2,979,900	7,915,200	1,610,800
1993	14,141,800	1,926,020	12,218,800	24,530	106,010	659,870	1,135,610	2,834,800	7,820,900	1,563,100
1994	13,989,500	1,857,670	12,131,900	23,330	102,220	618,950	1,113,180	2,712,800	7,879,800	1,539,300
1995	13,867,100	1,798,790	12,068,400	21,600	97,460	580,550	1,099,180	2,595,000	8,000,600	1,472,700
NUMBER OF OFFENSES										
1960	1,887.20	160.9	1,726.30	5.1	9.6	60.1	86.1	508.6	1,034.70	183
1961	1,906.10	158.1	1,747.90	4.8	9.4	58.3	85.7	518.9	1,045.40	183.6
1962	2,019.80	162.3	1,857.50	4.6	9.4	59.7	88.6	535.2	1,124.80	197.4
1963	2,180.30	168.2	2,012.10	4.6	9.4	61.8	92.4	576.4	1,219.10	216.6
1964	2,388.10	190.6	2,197.50	4.9	11.2	68.2	106.2	634.7	1,315.50	247.4
1965	2,449.00	200.2	2,248.80	5.1	12.1	71.7	111.3	662.7	1,329.30	256.8
1966	2,670.80	220	2,450.90	5.6	13.2	80.8	120.3	721	1,442.90	286.9
1967	2,989.70	253.2	2,736.50	6.2	14	102.8	130.2	826.6	1,575.80	334.1
1968	3,370.20	298.4	3,071.80	6.9	15.9	131.8	143.8	932.3	1,746.60	393
1969	3,680.00	328.7	3,351.30	7.3	18.5	148.4	154.5	984.1	1,930.90	436.2
1970	3,984.50	363.5	3,621.00	7.9	18.7	172.1	164.8	1,084.90	2,079.30	456.8
1971	4,164.70	396	3,768.80	8.6	20.5	188	178.8	1,163.50	2,145.50	459.8
1972	3,961.40	401	3,560.40	9	22.5	180.7	188.8	1,140.80	1,993.60	426.1
1973	4,154.40	417.4	3,737.00	9.4	24.5	183.1	200.5	1,222.50	2,071.90	442.6
1974	4,850.40	461.1	4,389.30	9.8	26.2	209.3	215.8	1,437.70	2,489.50	462.2
1975	5,298.50	487.8	4,810.70	9.6	26.3	220.8	231.1	1,532.10	2,804.80	473.7

TABLE A8.1 (CONTINUED)

ESTIMATED NUMBER AND RATE (PER 100,000 INHABITANTS) OF OFFENSES IN THE U.S. KNOWN TO POLICE, BY OFFENSE: 1960–1995

YEAR	TOTAL CRIME INDEX	VIOLENT CRIME	PROPERTY CRIME	MURDER AND NON-NEGLIGENT MANSLAUGHTER	FORCIBLE RAPE	ROBBERY	AGGRAVATED ASSAULT	BURGLARY	LARCENY-THEFT	MOTOR VEHICLE THEFT
NUMBER OF OFFENSES (CONTINUED)										
1976	5,287.30	467.8	4,819.50	8.8	26.6	199.3	233.2	1,448.20	2,921.30	450
1977	5,077.60	475.9	4,601.70	8.8	29.4	190.7	240	1,419.80	2,729.90	451.9
1978	5,140.30	497.8	4,642.50	9	31	195.8	262.1	1,434.60	2,747.40	460.5
1979	5,565.50	548.9	5,016.60	9.7	34.7	218.4	286	1,511.90	2,999.10	505.6
1980	5,950.00	596.6	5,353.30	10.2	36.8	251.1	298.5	1,684.10	3,167.00	502.2
1981	5,858.20	594.3	5,263.90	9.8	36	258.7	289.7	1,649.50	3,139.70	474.7
1982	5,603.60	571.1	5,032.50	9.1	34	238.9	289.2	1,488.80	3,084.80	458.8
1983	5,175.00	537.7	4,637.40	8.3	33.7	216.5	279.2	1,337.70	2,868.90	430.8
1984	5,031.30	539.2	4,492.10	7.9	35.7	205.4	290.2	1,263.70	2,791.30	437.1
1985	5,207.10	556.6	4,650.50	7.9	37.1	208.5	302.9	1,287.30	2,901.20	462
1986	5,480.40	617.7	4,862.60	8.6	37.9	225.1	346.1	1,344.60	3,010.30	507.8
1987	5,550.00	609.7	4,940.30	8.3	37.4	212.7	351.3	1,329.60	3,081.30	529.4
1988	5,664.20	637.2	5,027.10	8.4	37.6	220.9	370.2	1,309.20	3,134.90	582.9
1989	5,741.00	663.7	5,077.90	8.7	38.1	233	383.4	1,276.30	3,171.30	630.4
1990	5,820.30	731.8	5,088.50	9.4	41.2	257	424.1	1,235.90	3,194.80	657.8
1991	5,897.80	758.1	5,139.70	9.8	42.3	272.7	433.3	1,252.00	3,228.80	659
1992	5,660.20	757.5	4,902.70	9.3	42.8	263.6	441.8	1,168.20	3,103.00	631.5
1993	5,484.40	746.8	4,737.60	9.5	41.1	255.9	440.3	1,099.20	3,032.40	606.1
1994	5,373.50	713.6	4,660.00	9	39.3	237.7	427.6	1,042.00	3,026.70	591.3
1995	5,277.60	684.6	4,593.00	8.2	37.1	220.9	418.3	987.6	3,044.90	560.5

Source: U.S. Department of Justice, Federal Bureau of Investigation, Crime in the United States, 1975, p. 49, Table 2; 1995, p. 58 (Washington, DC: USGPO).

TABLE A8.2

ESTIMATED NUMBER, PERCENT DISTRIBUTION, AND RATE OF PERSONAL AND PROPERTY VICTIMIZATION IN THE UNITED STATES, BY TYPE OF CRIME: 1994 [1]

TYPE OF CRIME	NUMBER OF VICTIMIZATIONS	PERCENT OF ALL VICTIM- IZATIONS [2]	RATE PER 1,000 PERSONS OR HOUSEHOLDS
ALL CRIMES	42,359,370	100	NA
PERSONAL CRIMES	11,348,630	26.8	53.1
CRIMES OF VIOLENCE	10,859,700	25.6	50.8
COMPLETED VIOLENCE	3,205,230	7. 6	15
ATTEMPTED/ THREATENED VIOLENCE	7,654,470	18.1	35.8
RAPE/ SEXUAL ASSAULT	432,700	1. 0	2. 0
RAPE/ ATTEMPTED RAPE	316,140	0. 7	1. 5
RAPE	167,530	0. 4	0. 8
ATTEMPTED RAPE [3]	148,610	0. 4	0. 7
SEXUAL ASSAULT [4]	116,570	0. 3	0. 5
ROBBERY	1,298,590	3. 1	6. 1
COMPLETED/ PROPERTY TAKEN	795,030	1. 9	3. 7
WITH INJURY	287,600	0. 7	1. 3
WITHOUT INJURY	507,430	1. 2	2. 4
ATTEMPTED TO TAKE PROPERTY	503,560	1. 2	2. 4
WITH INJURY	121,790	0. 3	0. 6
WITHOUT INJURY	381,770	0. 9	1. 8
ASSAULT	9,128,400	21.5	42.7
AGGRAVATED	2,477,940	5. 8	11.6
WITH INJURY	678,540	1. 6	3. 2
THREATENED WITH WEAPON	1,799,400	4. 2	8. 4
SIMPLE	6,650,470	15.7	31.1
WITH MINOR INJURY	1,466,070	3. 5	6. 9
WITHOUT INJURY	5,184,400	12.2	24.3
PURSE SNATCHING/ POCKET PICKING	488,930	1. 2	2. 3
COMPLETED PURSE SNATCHING	90,150	0. 2	0. 4
ATTEMPTED PURSE SNATCHING	23,150	0. 1	0. 1
POCKET PICKING	375,630	0. 9	1. 8
TOTAL POPULATION AGE 12 AND OLDER	213,747,400	X	X
PROPERTY CRIMES	31,010,740	73.2	307.6
HOUSEHOLD BURGLARY	5,482,300	12.9	54.4
COMPLETED	4,572,560	10.8	45.4
FORCIBLE ENTRY	1,725,400	4. 1	17.1
UNLAWFUL ENTRY WITHOUT FORCE	2,847,160	6. 7	28.2
ATTEMPTED FORCIBLE ENTRY	909,750	2. 1	9. 0
MOTOR VEHICLE THEFT	1,763,540	4. 2	17.5
COMPLETED	1,172,200	2. 8	11.6
ATTEMPTED	591,340	1. 4	5. 9
THEFT [5]	23,764,900	56.1	235.7
COMPLETED	22,743,000	53.7	225.6
LESS THAN $50	9,376,580	22.1	93
$50 TO $249	7,874,460	18.6	78.1
$250 OR MORE	4,250,850	10	42.2
AMOUNT NOT AVAILABLE	1,241,110	2. 9	12.3
ATTEMPTED	1,021,900	2. 4	10.1
TOTAL NUMBER OF HOUSEHOLDS	100,808,030	X	X

X = NOT APPLICABLE

NA = NOT AVAILABLE.

[1] DETAIL MAY NOT ADD TO TOTAL BECAUSE OF ROUNDING.

[2] PERCENT DISTRIBUTION IS BASED ON UNROUNDED FIGURES.

[3] INCLUDES VERBAL THREATS OF RAPE.

[4] INCLUDES THREATS.

[5] INCLUDES CRIMES PREVIOUSLY CLASSIFIED AS PERSONAL LARCENY WITHOUT CONTACT AND HOUSEHOLD LARCENY.

TABLE A8.2 (CONTINUED)

ESTIMATED NUMBER, PERCENT DISTRIBUTION, AND RATE OF PERSONAL AND PROPERTY VICTIMIZATION IN THE UNITED STATES, BY TYPE OF CRIME: 1994 [1]

Source: U. S. Department of Justice, Bureau of Justice Statistics, Criminal Victimization in the United States, 1994, NCJ- 162126 (Washington, DC: U.S. Department of Justice, forthcoming), Soucebook of Criminal Justice Statistics 1995, page 230.

Note: The National Crime Victimization Survey (NCVS) is conducted annually for the Department of Justice, Bureau of Justice Statistics by the U.S. Bureau of the Census. These estimates are based on data derived from a continuous survey of a representative sample of housing units in The United States. For the 1994 survey, approximately 120,000 residents in 56,000 housing units were interviewed about the crimes they had experienced in the previous 6 months. Response rates were 96 percent of eligible housing units and 92 percent of individuals in interviewed households. Readers should note that murder is not measured by the NCVS because of the inability to question the victim. The NCVS has undergone a redesign and all data presented are based on the redesigned survey. The redesign was implemented during 1993 and data based on the redesign are not comparable to data prior to 1993.

TABLE A8.3

ESTIMATED NUMBER OF ARRESTS[1] IN THE U.S. BY OFFENSE CHARGED: 1995

OFFENSE CHARGED	
TOTAL [2]	15,119,800
MURDER AND NONNEGLIGENT MANSLAUGHTER	21,230
FORCIBLE RAPE	34,650
ROBBERY	171,870
AGGRAVATED ASSAULT	568,480
BURGLARY	386,500
LARCENY- THEFT	1,530,200
MOTOR VEHICLE THEFT	191,900
ARSON	20,000
VIOLENT CRIME [3]	796,250
PROPERTY CRIME [4]	2,128,600
TOTAL CRIME INDEX [5]	2,924,800
OTHER ASSAULTS	1,290,400
FORGERY AND COUNTERFEITING	122,300
FRAUD	436,400
EMBEZZLEMENT	15,200
STOLEN PROPERTY; BUYING, RECEIVING, POSSESSING	166,500
VANDALISM	311,100
WEAPONS; CARRYING, POSSESSING, ETC.	243,900
PROSTITUTION AND COMMERCIALIZED VICE	97,700
SEX OFFENSES (EXCEPT FORCIBLE RAPE AND PROSTITUTION)	94,500
DRUG ABUSE VIOLATIONS	1,476,100
GAMBLING	19,500
OFFENSES AGAINST FAMILY AND CHILDREN	142,900
DRIVING UNDER THE INFLUENCE	1,436,000
LIQUOR LAWS	594,900
DRUNKENNESS	708,100
DISORDERLY CONDUCT	748,600
VAGRANCY	25,900
ALL OTHER OFFENSES (EXCEPT TRAFFIC)	3,865,400
SUSPICION (NOT INCLUDED IN TOTAL)	12,100
CURFEW AND LOITERING LAW VIOLATIONS	149,800
RUNAWAYS	249,500

[1] ARREST TOTALS BASED ON ALL REPORTING AGENCIES AND ESTIMATES FOR UNREPORTED AREAS.

[2] BECAUSE OF ROUNDING, FIGURES MAY NOT ADD TO TOTAL.

[3] VIOLENT CRIMES ARE OFFENSES OF MURDER AND NONNEGLIGENT MANSLAUGHTER, FORCIBLE RAPE, ROBBERY, AND AGGRAVATED ASSAULT.

[4] PROPERTY CRIMES ARE OFFENSES OF BURGLARY, LARCENY- THEFT, MOTOR VEHICLE THEFT, AND ARSON.

[5] INCLUDES ARSON.

Source: U. S. Department of Justice, Federal Bureau of Investigation, Crime in the United States, 1995 (Washington, DC: USGPO, 1996), p. 208.

TABLE A8.4

ARREST RATES (PER 100,000 INHABITANTS) BY OFFENSE, 1971–95

(RATE PER 100,000 INHABITANTS)

	TOTAL CRIME INDEX A	VIOLENT CRIME B	PROPERTY- CRIME C
1971	897.1	175.8	721.4
1972	881.5	186.5	695.0
1973	883.4	187.3	696.1
1974	1,098.00	219.7	878.3
1975	1,059.60	206.7	852.9
1976	1,016.80	193.1	823.7
1977	1,039.40	202.7	836.7
1978	1,047.60	215.5	832.2
1979	1,057.20	212.5	844.7
1980	1,055.80	214.4	841.4
1981	1,070.00	216.8	853.2
1982	1,148.90	236.9	912.0
1983	1,071.90	221.1	850.8
1984	1,019.80	212.5	807.3
1985	1,046.50	212.4	834.0
1986	1,091.80	234.5	857.3
1987	1,120.10	233.8	886.4
1988	1,123.50	243.8	879.7
1989	1,173.10	268.6	904.4
1990	1,203.20	290.7	912.5
1991	1,198.80	293.0	905.8
1992	1,162.40	300.5	861.9
1993	1,131.60	302.9	828.8
1994	1,148.40	310.7	837.7
1995	1,140.30	315.2	825.0

Source: United States Department of Justice, Federal Bureau of Investigation, Crime in the United States, annual (USGPO Washington, DC).

TABLE A8.5

OFFENDERS SENTENCED TO PRISON IN U.S. DISTRICT COURTS[1], BY OFFENSE: 1982, 1988–1992

MOST SERIOUS CONVICTION OFFENSE	1982		1988		1989		1990		1991		1992 R	
	NUMBER	PERCENT	NUMBER	PERCENT	NUMBER	PERCENT	NUMBER	PERCENT	NUMBER	PERCENT	NUMBER	PERCENT
ALL OFFENSES [2]	17,481	51.1	23,450	53.8	27,377	58.5	28,659	60.3	30,555	62.4	34,352	65.6
VIOLENT OFFENSES	2,027	86.1	1,733	81	1,892	86.8	2,032	87.2	2,260	89.9	2,675	90.9
MURDER	100	90.9	88	94.6	92	90.2	124	93.2	111	90.2	117	94
NEGLIGENT MANSLAUGHTER	8	R	25	92. 6	43	89. 6	20	87. 0	29	93. 5	20	72. 4
ASSAULT	275	63.2	286	63.8	257	64.6	282	62	283	67.4	288	65.9
ROBBERY	1,453	92.9	1,059	94	1,237	97.7	1,313	98.2	1,504	98.5	1,900	99.1
RAPE	44	91.7	97	83.6	101	77.7	120	80.5	161	83.9	179	88.7
OTHER SEX OFFENSES	37	62.7	112	44.4	75	51.7	106	66.7	93	67.9	98	65.3
KIDNAPPING	64	97	44	91.7	56	96.6	48	90.6	66	98.5	56	88.5
THREATS AGAINST THE PRESIDENT	46	74.2	22	78.6	31	93.9	19	86.4	13	B	15	84.5
PROPERTY OFFENSES	5,834	45.6	5,723	42.6	5,974	44.1	5,885	43.3	6,033	45.8	6,699	46.8
FRAUDULENT OFFENSES	3,873	44.1	4,182	43.6	4,400	44.4	4,464	44.1	4,542	47.9	5,148	49.8
EMBEZZLEMENT	592	30	490	27.6	510	28.4	520	28.4	614	34.9	734	41.8
FRAUD [3]	1,976	43.8	2,915	47.1	3,028	46.3	3,230	46.9	3,251	50.7	3,749	51.5
FORGERY	806	54.8	459	45.6	518	50.8	397	43.8	361	48.2	343	46.9
COUNTERFEITING	499	59.7	318	52.3	344	60.4	317	62.6	316	57.1	323	56.3
OTHER OFFENSES	1,961	49.2	1,541	40	1,574	43.3	1,421	41	1,491	40.2	1,551	38.8
BURGLARY	96	64.4	84	84	93	82.3	83	83.8	119	83.8	108	86
LARCENY	1,223	43.7	978	33	1,036	36.9	940	34.7	951	32.6	921	29.6
MOTOR VEHICLE THEFT	338	70.3	293	71.6	239	71.3	200	72.7	170	68	256	76.2
ARSON	0	X	2	R	11	R	1	R	2	R	6	87. 6
TRANSPORTATION OF STOLEN PROPERTY	268	67.5	132	62	161	69.4	171	73.1	191	79.3	215	78.8
OTHER	36	22.8	52	32.5	34	26.2	26	17.6	58	38.4	45	31.4
DRUG OFFENSES	5,138	73.6	10,599	79.2	13,306	84.2	14,092	86.4	15,012	86.5	16,757	88.9
TRAFFICKING	4,417	82.1	10,197	88.2	12,832	91.5	13,640	90.9	14,558	89.9	16,334	92.2
POSSESSION AND OTHER	721	44.9	402	22.1	474	26.7	452	34.7	454	39	423	37.5
PUBLIC- ORDER OFFENSES	1,516	37.1	5,395	37	6,194	40.6	6,650	43.6	7,250	45.6	8,220	50.6
REGULATORY OFFENSES	516	28.5	640	32.6	746	36.9	799	38.9	884	37.8	875	39.8
AGRICULTURE	31	15.3	52	19.9	37	15.2	49	18.9	40	13.8	47	17.4
ANTITRUST	54	33.1	43	24.2	22	19.6	22	26.5	25	27.2	14	20.6
FAIR LABOR STANDARDS	4	15.4	6	17.6	2	6.9	3	8.8	8	19.5	14	35.8
FOOD AND DRUG	4	4. 0	8	16. 0	24	20. 0	16	16. 5	7	11. 5	13	16.1
MOTOR CARRIER	7	10.9	27	40.9	21	35.6	19	37.3	24	40	12	40.9
OTHER REGULATORY OFFENSES	416	33	504	36.6	640	43.8	690	45.1	780	43.5	773	45.4
OTHER OFFENSES	3,966	38.6	4,755	37.7	5,448	41.2	5,851	44.3	6,366	46.9	7,345	52.3
WEAPONS OFFENSES	1,000	62.3	1,262	70	1,647	76.6	1,894	77.6	2,632	83.9	3,500	87.1
IMMIGRATION OFFENSES	1,117	53.2	1,287	69.5	1,658	67.8	1,876	73	1,742	75.5	1,779	74.7
TAX LAW VIOLATIONS INCLUDING TAX FRAUD	508	45.8	629	44	543	46.8	507	43.5	434	41.4	445	41.6
BRIBERY	74	47.4	81	44	103	43.3	111	50.5	122	50.4	135	44.3
PERJURY, CONTEMPT, AND INTIMIDATION	67	69.8	73	70.2	65	60.2	62	71.3	75	70.1	55	62.9
NATIONAL DEFENSE	31	23.5	49	24.1	88	43.1	61	43.3	53	39.3	60	39.6
ESCAPE	577	87.2	566	86.9	580	89.5	545	89.1	470	89.5	485	92.1
RACKETEERING AND EXTORTION	316	72.3	418	74.5	459	78.1	404	78	437	84.4	535	85.4
GAMBLING OFFENSES	50	40.7	67	40.9	69	40.4	113	53.6	83	31.7	85	38.4
LIQUOR OFFENSES	9	33.3	3	R	3	R	11	50	0	X	1	4.8
MAIL OR TRANSPORT OF OBSCENE MATERIAL	10	50	14	25	9	16.7	19	26.4	17	37.8	10	25
TRAFFIC OFFENSES	185	5. 1	279	5. 1	207	4. 0	233	4. 7	275	5. 5	237	5. 3
MIGRATORY BIRDS	0	X	8	24. 2	9	12. 9	2	3. 5	3	10. 0	0	X
OTHER	22	28.9	19	19	8	5.8	13	12.3	23	12.3	16	13.2

R = DATA HAVE BEEN REVISED BY THE SOURCE.

[1] INCLUDES SENTENCES TO PRISON WITH OR WITHOUT PROBATION.

[2] TOTALS MAY INCLUDE DEFENDANTS FOR WHICH OFFENSE CATEGORY COULD NOT BE DETERMINED, BUT EXCLUDE CASES FOR WHICH SENTENCES CATEGORY COULD NOOT BE DETERMINED.

[3] EXCLUDES TAX FRAUD.

Source: U. S. Department of Justice, Bureau of Justice Statistics, Federal Criminal Case Processing, 1982- 93, With Preliminary Data for 1994, NCJ- 160088 Washington, DC: USGPO, 1996), pp.15, 16. Sourcebook of criminal justice statistics 1995, pages 472, 473.

TABLE A8.6

AVERAGE LENGTH OF PRISON SENTENCES IMPOSED FOR OFFENDERS CONVICTED IN U.S. DISTRICT COURTS BY OFFENSE: 1982, 1988–1994

(IN MONTHS. AVERAGE SENTENCE LENGTH IMPOSED FOR CONVICTED OFFENDERS SENTENCED TO PRISON.)

MOST SERIOUS CONVICTION OFFENSE	1982	1988	1989	1990	1991 [1]	1992 R	1993	1994
ALL OFFENSES [2]	47.8	55.1	54.5	57.2	61.9	62.6	60.6	60.9
VIOLENT OFFENSES	133.3	110.7	90.6	89.2	90.7	94.8	88.8	88.2
MURDER	161.9	162.7	180.1	134.7	172.3	143.8	118.9	117
NEGLIGENT MANSLAUGHTER	R	29. 2	23.3	19.9	21.8	22.6	15	14.4
ASSAULT	43. 1	39. 7	34.4	34.8	37.8	43.9	34.5	41
ROBBERY	153.1	131.4	101	100.7	98.6	101.5	96.4	94.6
RAPE	113.2	95.8	90.1	78.9	72.3	82.4	73.8	68.4
OTHER SEX OFFENSES	73. 5	75. 1	44.7	33.1	31.7	48.9	40.2	56.9
KIDNAPPING	147.1	190.5	147.9	178.5	189.9	146.8	142	152.7
THREATS AGAINST THE PRESIDENT	42. 4	44. 1	35.9	R	R	R	18.6	24.1
PROPERTY OFFENSES	31. 1	31. 5	26	22	21.2	21.8	23.7	25.1
FRAUDULENT OFFENSES	28. 3	31. 0	26.1	21.9	20.1	20.3	19.2	20.7
EMBEZZLEMENT	20. 2	19. 6	16.5	17.5	15.5	16.3	12.3	14.3
FRAUD [3]	27.9	32.9	29.8	23.4	21.6	21.1	20.6	22.1
FORGERY	33. 0	32.1	18.3	16.9	16.6	18.7	14.9	16.8
COUNTERFEITING	31. 6	29.1	20.1	19.4	18.5	20	18.7	17
OTHER OFFENSES	36. 5	32.7	25.7	22.4	24.6	27.6	38.8	39.9
BURGLARY	74. 5	55.6	41.7	34.4	59.5	52.9	79.1	59.7
LARCENY	32. 0	27.5	22.7	18.8	17.5	18.6	22.2	25
MOTOR VEHICLE THEFT	42. 3	38	28.6	27.6	29.8	21.8	68.8	86.1
ARSON	(4)	19	45.3	R	R	R	R	R
TRANSPORTATION OF STOLEN PROPERTY	40. 0	51.1	33.3	31.8	38.6	21.9	32.8	24.2
OTHER	10. 7	17.7	12.2	11.5	8.8	12.1	66.9	11.9
DRUG OFFENSES	54.6	71.3	74.9	80.9	85.7	82.9	79.7	80.1
TRAFFICKING	59. 3	73.6	77.3	83.1	87.4	84.3	82.2	82.5
POSSESSION AND OTHER	26. 2	13.6	8.1	14.9	21.7	22.1	18	22
PUBLIC- ORDER OFFENSES	25. 6	30.7	27.6	28.3	37.8	40.5	42.1	46
REGULATORY OFFENSES	25. 7	30.4	24	26.7	26.5	28.8	26.8	31.7
AGRICULTURE	12. 0	7.4	7. 9	9. 1	6. 9	8. 6	8. 0	10. 3
ANTITRUST	6. 9	8. 3	13.5	12.9	17.2	R	R	R
FAIR LABOR STANDARDS	R	8. 7	5. 0	R	R	R	16. 3	R
FOOD AND DRUG	R	12.6	11.3	R	R	R	12.3	25.4
MOTOR CARRIER	R	23.6	13	R	11.8	28	19.6	R
OTHER REGULATORY OFFENSES	29. 5	35.6	26.2	29.1	28.6	33.3	29.1	33.1
OTHER OFFENSES	25. 6	30.7	28.1	28.5	39.3	40.9	44.1	47.8
WEAPONS OFFENSES	34. 3	52.3	47.1	47.3	63	64.6	66.6	81.2
IMMIGRATION OFFENSES	16. 4	11.7	9.3	10.5	12.5	15	18.8	19.9
TAX LAW VIOLATIONS INCLUDING TAX FRAUD	15. 1	22.8	25.2	24.3	24.9	22.2	21.1	15.7
BRIBERY	26. 7	27	21	24.8	23.9	28.5	24.5	24.3
PERJURY, CONTEMPT, AND INTIMIDATION	22. 5	18.9	17.2	22.5	32.2	32.2	25.2	24.8
NATIONAL DEFENSE	19. 0	14.3	13.8	15.9	16.1	29.7	13.9	39.4
ESCAPE	21. 6	23.9	23.6	22.2	21.8	21.3	19.7	21.2
RACKETEERING AND EXTORTION	70. 7	72.3	57.4	61.4	63	81.7	78.3	62
GAMBLING OFFENSES	25. 1	12.6	12	13.6	20.1	24.7	35.3	19.7
LIQUOR OFFENSES	R	4. 7	3. 7	R	(4)	R	R	(4)
MAIL OR TRANSPORT OF OBSCENE MATERIAL	R	44.3	22.2	R	R	R	R	R
TRAFFIC OFFENSES	2. 5	3. 9	3. 2	4. 5	5. 3	5. 2	8. 5	7. 5
MIGRATORY BIRDS	(4)	5. 1	11.3	R	R	(4)	R	R
OTHER	14. 8	9. 0	3. 4	R	R	9. 2	19. 0	21. 3

R = DATA HAVE BEEN REVISED BY THE SOURCE.

[1] 1,688 OFFENDERS WERE EXCLUDED FROM THE 1991 DATA BECAUSE OF UNCLEAR SENTENCING INFORMATION.

[2] TOTALS MAY INCLUDE OFFENDERS FOR WHICH OFFENSE CATEGORY COULD NOT BE DETERMINED.

[3] EXCLUDES TAX FRAUD.

[4] NO CASES OF THIS TYPE OCCURRED IN THE DATA.

Source: U. S. Department of Justice, Bureau of Justice Statistics, Federal Criminal Case Processing, 1982- 93, With Preliminary Data for 1994, NCJ- 160088 (Washington, DC: USGPO, 1996), p. 17.

Note: Data for 1990 through 1994 reflect a change in the Administrative Office of the United States Courts' file closeout procedures and are not exactly comparable to data for earlier years.

TABLE A8.7

AVERAGE MAXIMUM LENGTH OF FELONY SENTENCES IMPOSED BY U.S. STATE COURTS BY OFFENSE U.S.: 1994

(IN MONTHS)

MOST SERIOUS CONVICTION OFFENSE	TOTAL	MAXIMUM SENTENCE LENGTH FOR FELONS SENTENCED TO:		
		INCARCERATION		STRAIGHT PROBATION
		PRISON	JAIL	
AVERAGE SENTENCE				
ALL OFFENSES	49	71	6	40
VIOLENT OFFENSES	93	118	6	45
MURDER [1]	262	269	7	59
RAPE	133	158	7	60
ROBBERY	104	116	9	51
AGGRAVATED ASSAULT	54	79	6	42
OTHER VIOLENT [2]	47	70	6	43
PROPERTY OFFENSES	39	57	6	42
BURGLARY	52	69	7	47
LARCENY [3]	29	45	6	40
FRAUD [4]	32	51	5	41
DRUG OFFENSES	40	61	6	38
POSSESSION	28	50	4	37
TRAFFICKING	48	66	7	40
WEAPONS OFFENSES	31	47	5	32
OTHER OFFENSES [5]	26	41	5	36
MEDIAN SENTENCE				
ALL OFFENSES	24	48	4	36
VIOLENT OFFENSES	60	72	6	36
MURDER [1]	300	300	6	60
RAPE	84	120	6	48
ROBBERY	72	84	9	48
AGGRAVATED ASSAULT	36	54	4	36
OTHER VIOLENT [2]	24	48	5	36
PROPERTY OFFENSES	24	42	4	36
BURGLARY	36	49	6	36
LARCENY [3]	16	36	4	36
FRAUD [4]	23	36	3	36
DRUG OFFENSES	24	48	4	30
POSSESSION	12	36	3	24
TRAFFICKING	36	48	6	36
WEAPONS OFFENSES	18	36	4	24
OTHER OFFENSES [5]	12	30	3	30

[1] INCLUDES NONNEGLIGENT MANSLAUGHTER.
[2] INCLUDES OFFENSES SUCH AS NEGLIGENT MANSLAUGHTER, SEXUAL ASSAULT, AND KIDNAPPING.
[3] INCLUDES MOTOR VEHICLE THEFT.
[4] INCLUDES FORGERY AND EMBEZZLEMENT.
[5] COMPOSED OF NONVIOLENT OFFENSES SUCH AS RECEIVING STOLEN PROPERTY AND VANDALISM.

Note: The median sentence is the sentence length that marks the point below which 50% of all sentence lengths fall. Average exclude sentences to death or to life in prison. Sentence length data were available for 834,124 cases sentenced to incarceration or probation.

Source: U. S. Department of Justice, Bureau of Justice Statistics, Felony Sentences in State Courts. Sourcebook of Criminal Justice Statistics Online Table 5.53.

TABLE A8.8

AVERAGE MAXIMUM LENGTH OF FELONY SENTENCES IMPOSED BY STATE COURTS BY RACE OF OFFENDER AND OFFENSE, UNITED STATES, 1992

(IN MONTHS)

OFFENSE	WHITE	BLACK
ALL OFFENSES	45	63
VIOLENT OFFENSES	84	101
MURDER [1]	208	241
RAPE	120	148
ROBBERY	90	100
AGGRAVATED ASSAULT	47	62
OTHER VIOLENT [2]	62	49
PROPERTY OFFENSES	45	51
BURGLARY	58	58
LARCENY [3]	31	40
FRAUD [4]	45	62
DRUG OFFENSES	30	52
POSSESSION	22	39
TRAFFICKING	35	59
WEAPONS OFFENSES	29	43
OTHER OFFENSES [5]	23	56

[1] INCLUDES NONNEGLIGENT MANSLAUGHTER.
[2] INCLUDES OFFENSES SUCH AS NEGLIGENT MANSLAUGHTER, SEXUAL ASSAULT, AND KIDNAPPING.
[3] INCLUDES MOTOR VEHICLE THEFT.
[4] INCLUDES FORGERY AND EMBEZZLEMENT.
[5] COMPOSED OF NONVIOLENT OFFENSES SUCH AS RECEIVING STOLEN PROPERTY AND DRIVING WHILE INTOXICATED.

Source: U. S. Department of Justice, Bureau of Justice Statistics, State Court Sentencing of NCJ-152696 (Washington, DC: U.S. Department of Justice, Convicted Felons, 1992).

TABLE A8.9

AVERAGE PRISON SENTENCE FOR DEFENDANTS SENTENCED FOR VIOLATION OF DRUG LAWS IN U.S. DISTRICT COURTS

YEAR ENDING	AVERAGE PRISON SENTENCE (IN MONTHS)
1945	22.2
1946	18.7
1947	19.7
1948	18.6
1949	18.9
1950	21.9
1951	27.1
1952	35.2
1953	38.4
1954	41.3
1955	43.5
1956	45.8
1957	66.0
1958	69.4
1959	74.2
1960	72.8
1961	74.0
1962	70.5
1963	70.1
1964	63.7
1965	60.3
1966	61.3
1967	62.0
1968	64.4
1969	63.7
1970	64.8
1971	58.5
1972	46.4
1973	45.5
1974	43.7
1975	45.3
1976	47.6
1977	47.3
1978	51.3
1979	50.8
1980	54.5
1981	55.5
1982	61.4
1983	63.8
1984	65.7
1985	64.8
1986	70.0
1987	73.0
1988	78.0
1989	73.8
1990	79.3
1991	95.7
1992	87.5
1993	84.0
1994	84.3
1995	88.7
1996	82.5

Source: U. S. Department of Justice, Bureau of Justice Statistics, State Court Sentencing of NCJ-152696 (Washington, DC: U.S. Department of Justice, Convicted Felons, 1992).

TABLE A8.10

U.S. PRISONERS UNDER JURISDICTION OF STATE AND FEDERAL CORRECTIONAL AUTHORITIES

(BY RACE, REGION, AND JURISDICTION, 1993)

REGION AND JURISDICTION	PRISONER POPULATION DEC. 31, 1993	WHITE	BLACK	AMERICAN INDIAN/ ALASKA NATIVE	ASIAN/PACIFIC ISLANDER	NOT KNOWN
UNITED STATES, TOTAL	946,946	431,780	456,570	8,300	5,408	44,888
FEDERAL	89,587	56,536	30,169	1,310	1,114	458
STATE	857,359	375,244	426,401	6,990	4,294	44,430
NORTHEAST	145,425	57,175	75,971	257	445	11,577
CONNECTICUT [2,3]	13,691	3,672	6,310	8	30	3,671
MAINE	1,469	1,414	37	11	3	4
MASSACHUSETTS [2]	10,034	4,808	3,022	11	60	2,133
NEW HAMPSHIRE	1,775	1,691	76	1	7	0
NEW JERSEY [2]	23,831	6,639	15,671	3	41	1,477
NEW YORK	64,569	26,954	35,275	177	220	1,943
PENNSYLVANIA [2]	26,050	8,892	14,706	40	63	2,349
RHODE ISLAND [1]	2,783	1,882	874	6	21	0
VERMONT [1,2]	1,223	1,223	NA	NA	NA	NA
MIDWEST	173,277	76,745	90,386	1,444	209	4,493
ILLINOIS [2]	34,495	8,569	22,535	45	57	3,289
INDIANA	14,470	8,506	5,906	44	14	0
IOWA [2]	4,898	3,458	1,221	65	17	137
KANSAS [4]	5,727	3,392	2,223	76	36	0
MICHIGAN [2]	39,318	16,243	22,099	168	33	775
MINNESOTA [2]	4,200	2,209	1,404	318	NA	269
MISSOURI	16,178	8,403	7,728	35	10	2
NEBRASKA [4]	2,518	1,568	874	74	2	0
NORTH DAKOTA	498	392	12	92	2	0
OHIO [4]	40,641	18,415	22,226	NA	NA	NA
SOUTH DAKOTA	1,553	1,148	47	358	0	0
WISCONSIN	8,781	4,442	4,111	169	38	21
SOUTH	350,825	116,948	209,288	1,545	312	22,732
ALABAMA	18,624	6,411	12,179	4	3	27
ARKANSAS [2]	8,625	3,653	4,925	9	6	32
DELAWARE [1,2]	4,210	1,326	2,800	0	2	82
DISTRICT OF COLOMBIA [1,4]	10,845	162	10,683	0	0	0
FLORIDA	53,048	21,029	30,997	21	158	843
GEORGIA	27,783	8,761	18,855	24	48	95
KENTUCKY	10,440	6,923	3,503	0	0	14
LOUISIANA	22,468	5,221	17,201	3	2	41
MARYLAND	20,264	4,662	15,539	3	0	60
MISSISSIPPI [2]	9,907	2,496	7,341	7	11	52
NORTH CAROLINA	21,892	7,223	13,977	446	13	233
OKLAHOMA [2]	16,409	9,042	5,784	1,011	3	569
SOUTH CAROLINA	18,704	5,736	12,890	13	6	59
TENNESSEE [5]	12,824	6,595	6,182	NA	NA	47
TEXAS [2]	70,127	18,359	31,277	NA	NA	20,491
VIRGINIA [2]	22,850	7,815	14,886	3	59	87
WEST VIRGINIA	1,805	1,534	269	1	1	0
WEST	187,832	124,376	50,756	3,744	3,328	5,628
ALASKA [1,2,3]	2,703	1,385	336	887	33	62
ARIZONA	17,811	13,936	3,087	584	23	181
CALIFORNIA [2]	119,951	75,761	39,104	828	1,089	3,169
COLORADO [4]	9,462	6,802	2,327	168	39	126
HAWAII [1,2,4]	3,129	637	163	46	1,747	536
IDAHO [4]	2,606	2,371	49	127	22	37
MONTANA [6]	1,541	1,256	27	253	5	0

TABLE A8.10

U.S. PRISONERS UNDER JURISDICTION OF STATE AND FEDERAL CORRECTIONAL AUTHORITIES

(BY RACE, REGION, AND JURISDICTION, 1993)

REGION AND JURISDICTION	PRISONER POPULATION DEC. 31, 1993	WHITE	BLACK	AMERICAN INDIAN/ ALASKA NATIVE	ASIAN/PACIFIC ISLANDER	NOT KNOWN
WEST (CONTINUED)						
NEVADA 2	6,138	3,544	1,823	92	62	617
NEW MEXICO	3,498	2,943	395	117	5	38
OREGON	6,557	4,814	872	125	60	686
UTAH	2,888	2,450	243	129	42	24
WASHINGTON	10,419	7,471	2,271	333	198	146
WYOMING 2	1,129	1,006	59	55	3	6

1 FIGURES INCLUDE BOTH JAIL AND PRISON INMATES; JAILS AND PRISONS ARE COMBINED IN ONE SYSTEM.

2 SOME OR ALL HISPANIC PRISONERS REPORTED UNDER UNKNOWN RACE.

3 VERMONT INCLUDES ALL INMATES UNDER WHITE.

4 FIGURES FOR RACE WERE ESTIMATED.

5 TENNESSEE REPORTED PERSONS WHOSE RACE WAS NEITHER BLACK NOR WHITE UNDER UNKNOWN RACE.

6 MONTANA INCLUDES ALL HISPANIC INMATES UNDER WHITE.

Source: U.S. Department of Justice, Bureau of Justice Statistics, Correction; Populations in the United States, 1993, NCJ-156241 (Washington, DC: U.S. Department of Justice, 1995), Table 5.6.

Note: All data for Alaska, Arizona, California, Florida, Georgia, Illinois, Iowa, Massachusetts, Michigan, Missouri, and Texas are custody rather than jurisdiction counts.

TABLE A8.11

ADULTS ON PROBATION, IN JAIL OR PRISON, AND ON PAROLE, UNITED STATES, 1990–94

	TOTAL ESTIMATED CORRECTIONAL POPULATION 1	PROBATION	JAIL	PRISON 2	PAROLE
1980	1,840,400	1,118,097	182,288 3	319,598	220,438
1981	2,006,600	1,225,934	195,085 3	360,029	225,539
1982	2,192,600	1,357,264	207,853	402,914	224,604
1983	2,475,100	1,582,947	221,815	423,898	246,440
1984	2,689,200	1,740,948	233,018	448,264	266,992
1985	3,011,500	1,968,712	254,986	487,593	300,203
1986	3,239,400	2,114,621	272,735	526,436	325,638
1987	3,459,600	2,247,158	294,092	562,814	355,505
1988	3,714,100	2,356,483	341,893	607,766	407,977
1989	4,055,600	2,522,125	393,303	683,367	456,803
1990	4,348,000	2,670,234	403,019	743,382	531,407
1991	4,535,600	2,728,472	424,129	792,535	590,442
1992	4,762,600	2,811,611	441,781	850,566	658,601
1993	4,944,000	2,903,061	455,500 3	909,381	676,100
1994	5,129,700	2,964,171	483,717	991,612	690,159
PERCENT CHANGE					
1993 TO 1994	3.8	2.1	6.2	9	2.1
1980 TO 1994	178.7	165.1	165.4	210.3	213.1

1 A SMALL NUMBER OF INDIVIDUALS MAY HAVE MULTIPLE CORRECTIONAL STATUSES; CONSEQUENTLY, THE TOTAL NUMBER OF PERSONS UNDER CORRECTIONAL SUPERVISION MAY BE AN OVERESTIMATE.

2 INCLUDES ONLY PRISONERS UNDER CUSTODY.

3 ESTIMATED.

Source: U. S. Department of Justice, Bureau of Justice Statistics, Correctional Populations in the United States, 1994, NCJ- 160091 (Washington, DC: U.S. Department of Justice, 1996), Table 1.1.

TABLE A8.12

ESTIMATED NUMBER AND PERCENT OF ADULTS UNDER CORRECTIONAL SUPERVISION IN THE U.S., BY SEX AND RACE: 1985–1994

| | ESTIMATED NUMBER OF ADULTS UNDER CORRECTIONAL SUPERVISION [1] | | | | | | ESTIMATED PERCENT OF ADULTS UNDER CORRECTIONAL SUPERVISION [2] | | | | | |
| | | SEX | | RACE | | | | SEX | | RACE | | |
	TOTAL	MALE	FEMALE	WHITE	BLACK	OTHER	TOTAL	MALE	FEMALE	WHITE	BLACK	OTHER
1985	3,011,500	2,606,000	405,500	1,941,600	1,029,600	40,300	1.7	3	0.4	1.2	5.2	0.8
1986	3,239,400	2,829,100	410,300	2,090,100	1,117,200	32,100	1.8	3.3	0.4	1.4	5.7	0.6
1987	3,459,600	3,021,000	438,600	2,192,200	1,231,100	36,300	1.9	3.5	0.5	1.4	6.2	0.6
1988	3,714,100	3,223,000	491,100	2,348,600	1,325,700	39,800	2	3.7	0.5	1.5	6.6	0.7
1989	4,055,600	3,501,600	554,000	2,521,200	1,489,000	45,400	2.2	4	0.6	1.6	7.3	0.7
1990	4,348,000	3,746,300	601,700	2,665,500	1,632,700	49,800	2.3	4.2	0.6	1.7	7.9	0.7
1991	4,535,600	3,913,000	622,600	2,742,400	1,743,300	49,900	2.4	4.4	0.6	1.7	8.3	0.7
1992	4,762,600	4,050,300	712,300	2,835,900	1,873,200	53,500	2.5	4.5	0.7	1.8	8.7	0.7
1993	4,944,000	4,215,800	728,200	2,872,200	2,011,600	60,200	2.6	4.6	0.7	1.7	8.8	0.8
1994	5,129,700	4,367,500	762,200	3,051,100	2,013,400	65,200	2.7	4.7	0.8	1.9	9.1	0.8

[1] POPULATIONS ARE ESTIMATED AND ROUNDED TO THE NEAREST 100.

[2] PERCENTAGES ARE BASED ON THE RESIDENT POPULATION AGE 18 OR OLDER ON JULY 1 OF EACH REFERENCE YEAR.

Source: U. S. Department of Justice, Bureau of Justice Statistics, Correctional Populations in the United States, 1994, NCJ-160091 (Washington, DC: U.S. Department of Justice, 1996), Table 1.3 and 1.4.

TABLE A8.13

NUMBER AND RATE (PER 100,000 RESIDENTS) OF ADULTS IN CUSTODY OF U.S. STATE OR FEDERAL PRISONS OR LOCAL JAILS: 1980, 1985, 1990–94

	TOTAL CUSTODY [1]	FEDERAL PRISONS	STATE PRISONS	LOCAL JAILS [2]	TOTAL RATE [3]
1980 [4]	501,886	23,779	295,819	182,288	221
1985	742,579	35,781	451,812	254,986	312
1990	1,146,401	58,838	684,544	403,019	460
1991	1,216,664	63,930	728,605	424,129	482
1992	1,292,347	72,071	778,495	441,781	507
1993 [4]	1,364,881	80,815	828,566	455,500	526
1994	1,475,329	85,500	906,112	483,717	565
PERCENT CHANGE					
1993 TO 1994	8.7	5.8	10.3	6.2	X
1980 TO 1994	195.6	259.6	209	165.4	X

[1] STATE AND FEDERAL INMATE COUNTS EXCLUDE THOSE UNDER STATE OR FEDERAL JURISDICTION WHO WERE HOUSED ELSEWHERE, AS IN COUNTY OR LOCAL JAILS.

[2] NUMBER OF ADULTS HELD IN LOCAL JAILS.

[3] TOTAL NUMBER OF ADULTS HELD IN THE CUSTODY OF STATE, FEDERAL, OR LOCAL JURISDICTIONS PER 100,000 U.S. RESIDENTS.

[4] JAIL POPULATION COUNTS ARE ESTIMATED.

Source: U. S. Department of Justice, Bureau of Justice Statistics, Correctional Populations in the United States, 1994, NCJ- 160091 (Washington, DC: U.S. Department of Justice, 1996), Table 1.5. Sourcebook of Criminal Justice Statistics 1995, page 548.

TABLE A8.14

NUMBER AND RATE (PER 100,000 RESIDENT POPULATION IN EACH GROUP) OF SENTENCED PRISONERS IN U.S. STATE AND FEDERAL INSTITUTIONS ON DECEMBER 31, BY SEX: 1925–1994

(RATE PER 100,000 RESIDENT POPULATION IN EACH GROUP)

YEAR	TOTAL	RATE	MALE NUMBER	MALE RATE	FEMALE NUMBER	FEMALE RATE	YEAR	TOTAL	RATE	MALE NUMBER	MALE RATE	FEMALE NUMBER	FEMALE RATE
1925	91,669	79	88,231	149	3,438	6	1960	212,953	117	205,265	230	7,688	8
1926	97,991	83	94,287	157	3,704	6	1961	220,149	119	212,268	234	7,881	8
1927	109,983	91	104,983	173	4,363	7	1962	218,830	117	210,823	229	8,007	8
1928	116,390	96	111,836	182	4,554	8	1963	217,283	114	209,538	225	7,745	8
1929	120,496	98	115,876	187	4,620	8	1964	214,336	111	206,632	219	7,704	8
							1965	210,895	108	203,327	213	7,568	8
1930	129,453	104	124,785	200	4,668	8	1966	199,654	102	192,703	201	6,951	7
1931	137,082	110	132,638	211	4,444	7	1967	194,896	98	188,661	195	6,235	6
1932	137,997	110	133,573	211	4,424	7	1968	187,914	94	182,102	187	5,812	6
1933	136,810	109	132,520	209	4,290	7	1969	196,007	97	189,413	192	6,594	6
1934	138,316	109	133,769	209	4,547	7							
1935	144,180	113	139,278	217	4,902	8	1970	196,429	96	190,794	191	5,635	5
1936	145,038	113	139,990	217	5,048	8	1971	198,061	95	191,732	189	6,329	6
1937	152,741	118	147,375	227	5,366	8	1972	196,092	93	189,823	185	6,269	6
1938	160,285	123	154,826	236	5,459	8	1973	204,211	96	197,523	191	6,004	6
1939	179,818	137	173,143	263	6,675	10	1974	218,466	102	211,077	202	7,389	7
							1975	240,593	111	231,918	220	8,675	8
1940	173,706	131	167,345	252	6,361	10	1976	262,833	120	252,794	238	10,039	9
1941	165,439	124	159,228	239	6,211	9	1977 [1]	278,141	126	267,097	249	11,044	10
1942	150,384	112	144,167	217	6,217	9	1977 [2]	285,456	129	274,244	255	11,212	10
1943	137,220	103	131,054	202	6,166	9	1978	294,396	132	282,813	261	11,583	10
1944	132,456	100	126,350	200	6,106	9	1979	301,470	133	289,465	264	12,005	10
1945	133,649	98	127,609	193	6,040	9							
1946	140,079	99	134,075	191	6,004	8	1980	315,974	139	303,643	275	12,331	11
1947	151,304	105	144,961	202	6,343	9	1981	353,167	154	338,940	304	14,227	12
1948	155,977	106	149,739	205	6,238	8	1982	394,374	171	378,045	337	16,329	14
1949	163,749	109	157,663	211	6,086	8	1983	419,820	179	402,391	354	17,429	15
							1984	443,398	188	424,193	370	19,205	16
1950	166,123	109	160,309	211	5,814	8	1985	480,568	202	458,972	397	21,296	17
1951	165,680	107	159,610	208	6,070	8	1986	522,084	217	497,540	426	24,544	20
1952	168,233	107	161,994	208	6,239	8	1987	560,812	231	533,990	453	26,822	22
1953	173,579	108	166,909	211	6,670	8	1988	603,732	247	573,587	482	30,145	24
1954	182,901	112	175,907	218	6,994	8	1989	680,907	276	643,643	535	37,264	29
1955	185,780	112	178,655	217	7,125	8							
1956	189,565	112	182,190	218	7,375	9	1990	739,980	297	699,416	575	40,564	32
1957	195,414	113	188,113	221	7,301	8	1991	789,610	313	745,808	606	43,802	34
1958	205,643	117	198,208	229	7,435	8	1992	846,277	332	799,776	642	46,501	36
1959	208,105	117	200,469	228	7,636	8	1993	932,074	359	878,037	698	54,037	41
							1994	1,016,760	389	956,691	753	60,069	45

[1] CUSTODY COUNTS.

[2] JURISDICTION COUNTS.

Source: U. S. Department of Justice, Bureau of Justice Statistics, Sourcebook of Criminal Justice Statistics, 1995 table 621 (Washington DC, 1996).

Note: These data represent prisoners sentenced to more than 1 year. Both custody and jurisdiction figures are shown for 1977 to facilitate year to year comparison.

TABLE A8.15

FELONY SENTENCES IMPOSED BY U.S. STATE COURTS, BY OFFENSE: 1994

MOST SERIOUS CONVICTION OFFENSE	TOTAL	TOTAL	PERCENT OF FELONS SENTENCED TO:		
			INCARCERATION		STRAIGHT PROBATION
			PRISON	JAIL	
ALL OFFENSES	100	71	45	26	29
VIOLENT OFFENSES	100	82	62	20	18
MURDER [1]	100	97	95	2	3
RAPE	100	88	71	17	12
ROBBERY	100	88	77	11	12
AGGRAVATED ASSAULT	100	75	48	27	25
OTHER VIOLENT [2]	100	75	45	30	25
PROPERTY OFFENSES	100	68	42	26	32
BURGLARY	100	75	53	22	25
LARCENY [3]	100	66	38	28	34
FRAUD [4]	100	60	32	28	40
DRUG OFFENSES	100	69	42	27	31
POSSESSION	100	66	34	32	34
TRAFFICKING	100	71	48	23	29
WEAPONS OFFENSES	100	69	42	27	31
OTHER OFFENSES [5]	100	66	36	30	34

[1] INCLUDES NONNEGLIGENT MANSLAUGHTER.

[2] INCLUDES OFFENSES SUCH AS NEGLIGENT MANSLAUGHTER, SEXUAL ASSAULT, AND KIDNAPPING.

[3] INCLUDES MOTOR VEHICLE THEFT.

[4] INCLUDES FORGERY AND EMBEZZLEMENT.

[5] COMPOSED OF NONVIOLENT OFFENSES SUCH AS RECEIVING STOLEN PROPERTY AND VANDALISM.

Note: Data on sentence type were available for 867,709 of the estimated total of 872,217 convicted felons. For persons receiving a combination of sentences, the sentence designation came from the most serious penalty imposed — prison being the most serious, followed by jail, then probation. Prison included sentences to death. Straight probation includes probation sentences not combined with a term of incarceration in prison or jail.

Source: U. S. Department of Justice, Bureau of Justice Statistics, Felony Sentences in State Courts, 1994, Bulletin NCJ- 163391 (Washington, DC: U.S. Department of Justice, January 1997), p. 2, Table 2. Sourcebook of Criminal Justice Statistics Online.

TABLE A8.16

AVERAGE TIME SERVED UNTIL FIRST RELEASE FOR OFFENDERS SENTENCED TO PRISON IN U.S. DISTRICT COURTS, BY OFFENSE: 1986, 1988–94

(IN MONTHS. AVERAGE TIME SERVED UNTIL FIRST RELEASE.)

MOST SERIOUS CONVICTION OFFENSE [1]	1986	1988	1989	1990	1991	1992	1993	1994
				PRELIMINARY				
ALL OFFENSES [2]	14.6	17.9	17.7	18.2	20.1	21.7	23.9	25.1
VIOLENT OFFENSES	46.4	49.8	48.0	52.9	54.5	54.4	55.9	53.5
MURDER/ MANSLAUGHTER	41.8	52.8	43.5	62.5	55.8	49.9	64.0	51.3
ASSAULT	40.4	40.5	38.9	45.5	49.8	48.2	57.4	52.1
ROBBERY	50.1	54.2	54.2	56.3	57.8	59.6	56.8	56.2
RAPE	(2)	48.3	71.4	59.4	72.2	69.4	(2)	(2)
OTHER SEX OFFENSES	24.8	29.8	30.6	32.4	26.6	23.8	31.0	28.7
KIDNAPPING	66.1	93.6	67.9	104.6	95.3	93.5	93.4	97.2
THREATS AGAINST THE PRESIDENT	26.3	26.6	23.7	21.0	23.9	30.8	21.6	29.3
PROPERTY OFFENSES	15.6	16.3	15.8	15.7	15.9	15.8	15.4	15.3
FRAUDULENT OFFENSES	13.3	14.4	14.7	14.4	14.6	14.8	14.5	14.6
EMBEZZLEMENT	9.8	10.5	10.0	11.4	10.8	10.0	9.1	9.4
FRAUD [3]	12.7	14.1	14.7	14.3	14.5	15.1	15.2	15.1
FORGERY	14.8	16.7	16.1	14.5	16.7	14.9	13.6	13.0
COUNTERFEITING	18.8	19.0	18.6	18.1	18.5	20.1	17.6	17.9
OTHER OFFENSES	19.7	20.5	18.0	18.8	19.0	18.4	18.1	17.5
BURGLARY	17.3	24.5	24.9	25.3	24.2	23	23.8	23.9
LARCENY	18.3	17.4	15.8	16.2	14.1	14.6	13.4	11.3
MOTOR VEHICLE THEFT	24.1	27.4	21.6	21.7	29.8	24.8	20.5	21.3
ARSON	26.5	28.0	33.2	36.8	39.7	35.5	37.7	39.7
TRANSPORTATION OF STOLEN PROPERTY	22.8	27.1	24.3	28.7	23.2	24.6	25.4	22.2
OTHER	9.9	9.0	5.8	14.3	17.1	17.6	19.8	22.7
DRUG OFFENSES	20.6	23.2	24.3	27.1	28.4	29.7	33	35.0
TRAFFICKING	21.1	23.9	25.2	28.1	30.0	31.5	35.1	36.6
POSSESSION AND OTHER	8.0	9.2	8.7	9.1	8.2	7.1	7.2	7.7
PUBLIC- ORDER OFFENSES	6.3	8.9	8.3	7.8	9.1	11.0	12.4	13.7
REGULATORY OFFENSES	14.8	17.2	16.6	16.6	17.2	16.2	18.0	19.2
OTHER OFFENSES	5.9	8.3	7.8	7.4	8.6	10.7	12.1	13.3
WEAPONS OFFENSES	18.2	19.5	18.7	19.1	18.9	20.4	23.5	27.8
IMMIGRATION OFFENSES	3.3	4.4	3.9	3.6	4.2	5.3	5.5	6.2
TAX LAW VIOLATIONS INCLUDING TAX FRAUD	9.3	10.7	10.9	11.8	12.1	13.5	13.8	14
BRIBERY	11.4	12.8	13.3	10.8	11.0	12.1	13.0	14.2
PERJURY	10.3	11.0	16.1	12.9	13.8	16.1	15.8	15.6
NATIONAL DEFENSE	17.5	15.1	20.9	22.8	23.0	24.2	16.6	26.1
ESCAPE	21.4	17.0	19.1	19.0	19.5	19.0	22.9	18.4
RACKETEERING AND EXTORTION	22.1	26.1	29.7	29.8	31.4	36.2	36.7	36.0
GAMBLING OFFENSES	(2)	(2)	(2)	(2)	(2)	(2)	(2)	(2)
LIQUOR OFFENSES	(2)	(2)	(2)	(2)	(2)	(2)	(2)	(2)
MAIL OR TRANSPORT OF OBSCENE MATERIAL	21.0	34.1	20.1	23.1	17.7	16.3	25.8	29.4
TRAFFIC OFFENSES	2.0	2.2	2.6	1.9	2.4	2.4	3.0	2.9
MIGRATORY BIRDS	5.1	4.8	5.7	6.1	7.7	6.9	7.0	7.1
OTHER	13.8	15.5	10.8	12.6	15.4	14.7	16.4	13.2

1 PRISONERS ARE CLASSIFIED ACCORDING TO THE OFFENSE ASSOCIATED WITH THE LONGEST SENTENCE ACTUALLY IMPOSED. OFFENSE CATEGORIES ARE BASED ON COMBINATIONS OF OFFENSE DESIGNATIONS USED BY THE BUREAU OF PRISONS. THEY ARE SIMILAR TO THE CATEGORIES IN OTHER TABLES, BUT MAY NOT BE DIRECTLY COMPARABLE.

2 TOTAL INCLUDES OFFENDERS WHOSE OFFENSE CATEGORY COULD NOT BE DETERMINED.

3 EXCLUDES TAX FRAUD.

Note: Time- served data in this table are based on a new method and supersede time- served in prior Federal Justice Statistics reports. These data include only prisoners serving U.S. District Court sentences first released in the indicated calendar year, regardless of sentences length. The data exclude subsequent releases (e.g., parole violators).

Source: U. S. Department of Justice, Bureau of Justice Statistics, Federal Criminal Case Processing, 1982- 93, With Preliminary Data for 1994, NCJ-160088 (Washington, DC: USGPO, 1996), p.18.

Table A8.17

U.S. Justice System Direct and Intergovernmental Expenditures, by Type of Activity and Level of Government: Fiscal Years 1980–1993[1]

(In thousands)

Level of Government and Fiscal Year	Total Justice Expenditure			
	Total Justice System	Police Protection	Judicial and Legal	Corrections
All Governments				
1980	NA	$15,163,029	NA	$6,900,751
1981	NA	16,822,094	NA	7,868,822
1982	$35,841,916	19,022,184	$7,770,785	9,048,947
1983	39,680,167	20,648,200	8,620,604	10,411,363
1984	43,942,690	22,685,766	9,463,180	11,793,744
1985	48,563,068	24,399,355	10,628,816	13,534,897
1986	53,499,805	26,254,993	11,485,446	15,759,366
1987	58,871,348	28,767,553	12,555,026	17,548,769
1988	65,230,542	30,960,824	13,970,563	20,299,155
1989	70,949,468	32,794,182	15,588,664	22,566,622
1990	79,433,959	35,923,479	17,356,826	26,153,654
1991	87,566,819	38,971,240	19,298,379	29,297,200
1992	93,776,852	41,326,531	20,988,888	31,461,433
1993	97,541,826	44,036,756	21,558,403	31,946,667
Percent Change				
1980 to 1982	NA	25.5	NA	31.1
1980 to 1993	NA	190.2	NA	363.3
1982 to 1987	64.3	51.2	61.6	93.9
1988 to 1993	49.6	42.1	54.4	57.5
1982 to 1993	172.2	131.3	177.6	253.3
Federal				
1980	NA	$1,941,000	NA	$408,000
1981	NA	2,118,000	NA	436,000
1982	$4,458,000	2,527,000	$1,390,000	541,000
1983	4,844,000	2,815,000	1,523,000	606,000
1984	5,868,000	3,396,000	1,785,000	687,000
1985	6,416,000	3,495,000	2,129,000	792,000
1986	6,595,000	3,643,000	2,090,000	862,000
1987	7,496,000	4,231,000	2,271,000	994,000
1988	8,851,000	4,954,000	2,639,000	1,258,000
1989	9,674,000	5,307,000	2,949,000	1,418,000
1990	12,798,000	5,666,000	5,398,000	1,734,000
1991	15,231,000	6,725,000	6,384,000	2,122,000
1992	17,423,000	7,400,000	7,377,000	2,646,000
1993	18,591,000	8,069,000	7,832,000	2,690,000
Percent Change				
1980 to 1982	NA	30.2	NA	32.6
1980 to 1993	NA	315.7	NA	559.3
1982 to 1987	68.1	67.4	63.4	83.7
1988 to 1993	110	62.9	196.8	113.8
1982 to 1993	317	219.3	463.5	397.2
Total State and Local B				
1980	NA	$13,424,029	NA	$6,515,689
1981	NA	14,918,094	NA	7,458,133
1982	$31,572,916	16,656,184	$6,380,785	8,535,947
1983	34,836,167	17,903,200	7,097,604	9,835,363
1984	38,155,690	19,330,766	7,678,180	11,146,744
1985	42,284,068	20,969,355	8,499,816	12,814,897
1986	47,069,805	22,712,993	9,395,446	14,961,366
1987	51,640,348	24,731,553	10,284,026	16,624,769
1988	56,766,542	26,303,824	11,331,563	19,131,155
1989	61,745,468	27,842,182	12,639,664	21,263,622
1990	69,214,959	30,579,479	14,075,826	24,559,654
1991	75,460,819	32,801,240	15,303,379	27,356,200
1992	80,247,852	34,623,531	16,573,888	29,050,433
1993	83,112,826	36,691,756	16,896,403	29,524,667

TABLE A8.17

U.S. JUSTICE SYSTEM DIRECT AND INTERGOVERNMENTAL EXPENDITURES, BY TYPE OF ACTIVITY AND LEVEL OF GOVERNMENT: FISCAL YEARS 1980–1993[1]

(IN THOUSANDS)

LEVEL OF GOVERNMENT AND FISCAL YEAR	TOTAL JUSTICE EXPENDITURE			
	TOTAL JUSTICE SYSTEM	POLICE PROTECTION	JUDICIAL AND LEGAL	CORRECTIONS
PERCENT CHANGE				
1980 TO 1982	NA	24.1	NA	31
1980 TO 1993	NA	173.3	NA	353.1
1982 TO 1987	63.6	48.5	61.2	94.8
1988 TO 1993	46.4	39.5	49.1	54.3
1982 TO 1993	163.2	120.3	164.8	245.9
STATE				
1980	$9,256,443	$2,194,349	$2,051,108	$4,547,667
1981	10,372,682	2,479,905	2,332,434	5,179,448
1982	11,601,780	2,833,370	2,748,364	6,020,046
1983	12,785,244	2,963,067	2,949,598	6,872,579
1984	14,212,842	3,173,297	3,271,076	7,768,469
1985	16,252,377	3,468,821	3,635,984	9,147,572
1986	18,555,723	3,749,413	4,004,720	10,801,590
1987	20,157,123	4,066,692	4,339,306	11,691,125
1988	22,836,919	4,531,184	4,885,843	13,419,892
1989	25,268,915	4,780,353	5,441,743	15,046,819
1990	28,345,066	5,163,475	5,970,895	17,210,696
1991	31,484,371	5,507,249	6,754,491	19,222,631
1992	33,755,092	5,592,791	7,722,882	20,439,419
1993	34,227,194	5,603,484	7,820,251	20,803,459
PERCENT CHANGE				
1980 TO 1982	25.3	29.1	34	32.4
1980 TO 1993	269.8	155.4	281.3	357.5
1982 TO 1987	73.7	43.5	57.9	94.2
1988 TO 1993	49.9	23.7	60.1	55
1982 TO 1993	195	97.8	184.5	245.6
LOCAL, TOTAL B				
1980	NA	$11,398,808	NA	$2,277,257
1981	NA	12,678,955	NA	2,636,064
1982	$20,967,562	14,172,313	$3,784,285	3,010,964
1983	23,186,040	15,276,352	4,361,362	3,548,326
1984	25,154,172	16,515,727	4,627,473	4,010,972
1985	27,461,643	17,847,016	5,090,344	4,524,283
1986	30,178,432	19,355,599	5,690,544	5,132,289
1987	33,265,315	21,089,053	6,229,510	5,946,752
1988	36,097,549	22,370,517	6,826,419	6,900,613
1989	38,825,015	23,671,582	7,682,188	7,471,245
1990	43,558,671	26,097,219	8,675,732	8,785,720
1991	47,075,424	28,017,151	9,418,374	9,639,899
1992	50,115,498	29,658,955	10,052,330	10,404,213
1993	52,561,979	31,733,159	10,282,702	10,546,118
PERCENT CHANGE				
1980 TO 1982	NA	24.3	NA	32.2
1980 TO 1993	NA	178.4	NA	363.1
1982 TO 1987	58.7	48.8	64.6	97.5
1988 TO 1993	45.6	41.9	50.6	52.8
1982 TO 1993	150.7	123.9	171.7	250.3

[1] DETAIL MAY NOT ADD TO TOTAL BECAUSE OF ROUNDING.

[2] DATA FOR LOCAL GOVERNMENTS ARE ESTIMATES SUBJECT TO SAMPLING VARIATION.

Note: Duplicative transactions between levels of government are excluded from the total for all governments, the State and local total, and the local total. Such intergovernmental expenditure consists of payments from one government to another and eventually will show up as a direct expenditure of a recipient government. The State government total for 1980 and 1981 includes a residual other category not displayed separately.

Source: U. S. Department of Justice, Bureau of Justice Statistics, Justice Expenditure and Employment Extracts: 1993, NcJ- 163068 (Washington, DC: forthcoming). Table E. Table adapted by SOURCEBOOK staff. Sourcebook of criminal justice statistics Online.

TABLE A8.18

U.S. JUSTICE SYSTEM PER CAPITA EXPENDITURES, BY TYPE OF ACTIVITY: FISCAL YEARS 1980–93[1]

FISCAL YEAR	JULY 1 POPULATION IN TOUSANDS [2]	TOTAL JUSTICE SYSTEM	POLICE PROTECTION	JUDICIAL AND LEGAL	CORRECTIONS
1980	227,225	NA	$66.73	NA	$30.37
1981	229,466	NA	73.31	NA	34.29
1982	231,664	$154.72	82.11	$33.54	39.06
1983	233,792	169.72	88.32	36.87	44.53
1984	235,825	186.34	96.20	40.13	50.01
1985	237,924	204.11	102.55	44.67	56.89
1986	240,133	222.79	109.34	47.83	65.63
1987	242,289	242.98	118.73	51.82	72.43
1988	244,499	266.79	126.63	57.14	83.02
1989	246,819	287.46	132.87	63.16	91.43
1990	249,402	318.5	144.04	69.59	104.87
1991	252,131	347.31	154.57	76.54	116.2
1992	255,028	367.71	162.05	82.3	123.36
1993	257,783	378.39	162.05	83.63	123.93
PERCENT CHANGE [3]					
1980 TO 1993	13.4	NA	142.8	NA	308.1
1982 TO 1987	4.6	57	44.6	54.5	85.4
1988 TO 1993	5.4	41.8	28.0	46.4	49.3
1982 TO 1993	11.3	144.6	97.4	149.3	217.3

[1] DETAIL MAY NOT ADD TO TOTAL BECAUSE OF ROUNDING.

[2] POPULATION FIGURES ARE FOR JULY 1 OF EACH YEAR FROM THE U. S. BUREAU OF THE CENSUS, CURRENT POPUALTION REPORTS. THEY ARE CONSISTENT WITH THE 1980 AND 1990 DECENNIAL ENUMERATIONS.

[3] PERCENT CHANGE COMPUTATIONS WERE PERFORMED ON UNROUNDED DATA.

Source: U. S. Department of Justice, Bureau of Justice Statistics, Justice Expenditure and Employment Extracts: 1992, NCJ- 148821 (Washington, DC: forthcoming). Table K.

TABLE A8.19

U.S. ATTITUDES TOWARD WHETHER VIOLENT CRIMINALS CAN BE REHABILITATED, BY DEMOGRAPHIC CHARACTERISTICS: 1995

QUESTION: THINKING OF CRIMINALS WHO COMMIT VIOLENT CRIMES DO YOU THINK MOST, SOME, ONLY A FEW, OR NONE OF THEM CAN BE REHABILITATED GIVEN EARLY INTERVENTION WITH THE RIGHT PROGRAM?

	MOST	SOME	ONLY A FEW	NONE
NATIONAL	14.4	44.8	28.7	9.1
SEX				
MALE	12.2	42.7	30.9	10.7
FEMALE	16.5	46.7	26.6	7.7
RACE				
WHITE	13	44.3	30.2	9.9
BLACK	25	46.2	22.1	3.8
HISPANIC	14.9	41.9	28.4	6.8
AGE				
18 TO 29 YEARS	20.3	45	25.2	8.1
30 TO 39 YEARS	13.3	49.5	26.9	9
40 TO 59 YEARS	12.9	47	29.3	7.3
60 YEARS AND OLDER	11.6	35.3	34.7	12.7
EDUCATION				
COLLEGE GRADUATE	13.3	49.6	28.1	6.8
SOME COLLEGE	17.1	45.8	26.6	7.3
HIGH SCHOOL GRADUATE	12.6	42.9	29.1	12
LESS THAN HIGH SCHOOL GRADUATE	16.7	41.2	30.4	8.8
INCOME				
OVER $60,000	11.3	51.6	26.9	8.1
BETWEEN $30,000 AND $60,000	15.5	46.3	28.5	7.8
BETWEEN $15,000 AND $29,999	12.9	43.6	30.7	9.5
LESS THAN $15,000	15	44.2	25	9.2
COMMUNITY				
URBAN	22.9	33.8	33.1	5.7
SUBURBAN	10.6	50.8	27.3	9.5
SMALL CITY	11.1	54	25.9	6.3
RURAL/ SMALL TOWN	15.5	41.5	28.6	11.5
REGION				
NORTHEAST	11.9	42.6	32.4	8
MIDWEST	13.9	45.8	27.7	8
SOUTH	13.2	45.3	29.2	11.7
WEST	18.2	44.6	26.4	7.9
POLITICS				
REPUBLICAN	11.9	46.9	31.3	7.8
DEMOCRAT	16.4	47.5	26.1	7.9
INDEPENDENT/ OTHER	16.4	43.1	26.2	10.3

Source: Data provided by Survey Research Program, College of Criminal Justice, Sam Houston State University. Sourcebook of Criminal Justice Statistics 1995, page 177.

Note: See Note, table 2.21. The don't know and refused categories have been omitted; therefore percents may not sum to 100.

TABLE A8.20

POLICE CHIEFS' ATTITUDES TOWARD FEDERAL PROGRAMS DEALING WITH DRUG ABUSEIN THE U.S., BY SIZE OF COMMUNITY: 1996

QUESTION: AS YOU MAY KNOW, CONGRESS HAS CONSIDERED CHANGES IN LEGISLATION THAT AFFECT FEDERAL PROGRAMS DEALING WITH CRIME AND DRUG ABUSE. LET ME READ YOU SOME OF THE MEASURES THAT WILL BE CONSIDERED, AND FOR EACH ONE, PLEASE TELL ME WHETHER YOU FEEL IT WOULD BE A STEP IN THE RIGHT DIRECTION OR A STEP IN THE WRONG DIRECTION.

	A STEP IN THE RIGHT DIRECTION	A STEP IN THE WRONG DIRECTION	NOT SURE
SHIFTING FEDERAL FUNDING FOR DRUG PREVENTION AND TREATMENT PROGRAMS TO LAW ENFORCEMENT AND PRISON CONSTRUCTION			
ALL POLICE CHIEFS	57	40	3
LARGE CITIES	29	68	3
MEDIUM COMMUNITIES	61	37	2
SMALL TOWNS	69	27	4
SHIFTING FEDERAL FUNDING FROM DRUG PREVENTION AND TREATMENT PROGRAMS TO BORDER PATROLS AND INTERCEPTING DRUGS BEFORE THEY REACH THE U.S.			
ALL POLICE CHIEFS	55	39	6
LARGE CITIES	32	58	10
MEDIUM COMMUNITIES	43	52	5
SMALL TOWNS	70	25	5
CUTTING BACK ON FEDERAL FUNDING FOR COMMUNITY DRUG COURTS IN WHICH NONVIOLENT DRUG OFFENDERS ARE GIVEN A CHOICE BETWEEN PRISON AND SUPERVISED TREATMENT			
ALL POLICE CHIEFS	25	69	6
LARGE CITIES	23	74	3
MEDIUM COMMUNITIES	20	73	7
SMALL TOWNS	28	65	7

Source: Police Foundation and Drug Strategies, Drugs and Crime Across America: Police Chiefs Speak Out (Washington, DC: Police Foundation and Drug Stategies, 1996), p. 16. Reprinted by permission. Sourcebook of Criminal Justice Statistics, 1995 Table 255.

TABLE A8.21

U.S. ATTITUDES TOWARD WHETHER GOVERNMENT SHOULD REHABILITATE OR PUNISH CRIMINALS, BY DEMOGRAPHIC CHARACTERISTICS: 1995

QUESTION: IN YOUR OPINION WHERE DOES GOVERNMENT NEED TO MAKE A GREATER EFFORT THESE DAYS: REHABILITATE CRIMINALS WHO COMMIT VIOLENT CRIMES OR PUNISH AND PUT AWAY CRIMINALS WHO COMMIT VIOLENT CRIMES?

	REHABILITATE	PUNISH	BOTH	NEITHER
NATIONAL	26.1	58.2	12.3	1.1
SEX				
MALE	26.7	60.3	9.7	1.4
FEMALE	25.5	56.2	14.8	0.8
RACE				
WHITE	22.6	62.2	11.5	1.4
BLACK	44.2	37.5	15.4	0
HISPANIC	38.4	50.7	11	0
AGE				
18 TO 29 YEARS	36	54.1	7.2	1.4
30 TO 39 YEARS	24.5	58.6	15.5	0.7
40 TO 59 YEARS	26.2	56.8	12.9	0.3
60 YEARS AND OLDER	17.3	64.2	12.7	2.3
EDUCATION				
COLLEGE GRADUATE	31.2	53	13.6	2.2
SOME COLLEGE	28.4	55.8	14.4	0.7
HIGH SCHOOL GRADUATE	21.2	63.4	11.1	0.6
LESS THAN HIGH SCHOOL GRADUATE	24.5	61.8	6.9	1
INCOME				
OVER $60,000	36	51.6	9.1	2.2
BETWEEN $30,000 AND $60,000	24.7	59	14.1	0.8
BETWEEN $15,000 AND $29,999	20.9	62.8	14.2	0.4
LESS THAN $15,000	30.5	54.2	8.5	1.7
COMMUNITY				
URBAN	32.1	55.8	8.3	0.6
SUBURBAN	28.9	53.6	14.4	2.3
SMALL CITY	20.1	56.6	16.4	2.1
RURAL/ SMALL TOWN	24.6	63.1	10.5	0.3
REGION				
NORTHEAST	31.1	54.2	13.6	0
MIDWEST	26.1	61.3	10.1	0.4
SOUTH	22.6	60.2	11.7	2.3
WEST	27.3	55	14.9	0.8
POLITICS				
REPUBLICAN	21.1	63.6	11.9	1.7
DEMOCRAT	25.4	56.1	16.8	0.4
INDEPENDENT/ OTHER	30.9	55.1	9.8	1.1

Note: The don't know category has been omitted; therefore percents may not sum to 100

Source: Data provided by Survey Research Program, College of Criminal Justice, Sam Houston State University. Sourcebook of Criminal Justice Statistics 1995, page 177.

VOTING

TABLE A9.1

PERCENTAGE WHO REPORTED VOTING AND REGISTERING IN THE UNITED STATES, BY RACE, HISPANIC ORIGIN AND SEX: NOVEMBER 1964–NOVEMBER 1996

YEAR	TOTAL	WHITE	BLACK	HISPANIC [1]	MALE	FEMALE
PERCENT VOTED						
1996	54.2	56.0	50.6	26.7	52.8	55.5
1994	45.0	47.3	37.1	20.2	44.7	45.3
1992	61.3	63.6	54.0	28.9	60.2	62.3
1990	45.0	46.7	39.2	21.0	44.6	45.4
1988	57.4	59.1	51.5	28.8	56.4	58.3
1986	46.0	47.0	43.2	24.2	45.8	46.1
1984	59.9	61.4	55.8	32.6	59.0	60.8
1982	48.5	49.9	43.0	25.3	48.7	48.4
1980	59.2	60.9	50.5	29.9	59.1	59.4
1978	45.9	47.3	37.2	23.5	46.6	45.3
1976	59.2	60.9	48.7	31.8	59.6	58.8
1974	44.7	46.3	33.8	22.9	46.2	43.4
1972	63.0	64.5	52.1	37.5	64.1	62.0
1970	54.6	56.0	43.5	NA	56.8	52.7
1968	67.8	69.1	57.6	NA	69.8	66.0
1966	55.4	57.0	41.7	NA	58.2	53.0
1964	69.3	70.7	58.5	NA	71.9	67.0
PERCENT REGISTERED						
1996	65.9	67.7	63.5	35.7	64.4	67.3
1994	62.5	64.6	58.5	31.3	61.2	63.7
1992	68.2	70.1	63.9	35.0	66.9	69.3
1990	62.2	63.8	58.8	32.3	61.2	63.1
1988	66.6	67.9	64.5	35.5	65.2	67.8
1986	64.3	65.3	64.0	35.9	63.4	65.0
1984	68.3	69.6	66.3	40.1	67.3	69.3
1982	64.1	65.6	59.1	35.3	63.7	64.4
1980	66.9	68.4	60.0	36.3	66.6	67.1
1978	62.6	63.8	57.1	32.9	62.6	62.5
1976	66.7	68.3	58.5	37.8	67.1	66.4
1974	62.2	63.5	54.9	34.9	62.8	61.7
1972	72.3	73.4	65.5	44.4	73.1	71.6
1970	68.1	69.1	60.8	NA	69.6	66.8
1968	74.3	75.4	66.2	NA	76.0	72.8
1966	70.3	71.6	60.2	NA	72.2	68.6
1964	NA	NA	NA	NA	NA	NA

[1] PERSONS OF HISPANIC ORIGIN MAY BE OF ANY RACE. PRIOR TO 1972, DATA ARE FOR PERSONS OF VOTING AGE, 21 YEARS OLD AND OVER, IN MOST STATES. REGISTRATION DATA WERE NOT COLLECTED IN THE 1964 CURRENT POPULATION SURVEY.

NA = NOT AVAILABLE.

Source: U.S. Department of the Census, *Current Population Reports*, Series P20, No.466, Voting and Registration in the Election of November 1992, and earlier reports.

TABLE A9.2

PERCENTAGE WHO REPORTED VOTING AND REGISTERING IN THE U.S., BY AGE AND REGION OF RESIDENCE: NOVEMBER 1964–NOVEMBER 1996

YEAR	AGE (IN YEARS)				REGION [1]			
	18-24	25-44	45-64	65 AND OVER	NORTHEAST	MIDWEST	SOUTH	WEST
PERCENT VOTED								
1996	32.4	49.2	64.4	67.0	54.5	59.3	52.2	51.8
1994	20.1	39.4	56.7	61.3	45.6	48.9	40.9	47.1
1992	42.8	58.3	70.0	70.1	61.2	67.2	59.0	58.5
1990	20.4	40.7	55.8	60.3	45.2	48.6	42.4	45.0
1988	36.2	54.0	67.9	68.8	57.4	62.9	54.5	55.6
1986	21.9	41.4	58.7	60.9	44.4	49.5	43.0	48.4
1984	40.8	58.4	69.8	67.7	59.7	65.7	56.8	58.5
1982	24.8	45.4	62.2	59.9	49.8	54.7	41.8	50.7
1980	39.9	58.7	69.3	65.1	58.5	65.8	55.6	57.2
1978	23.5	43.1	58.5	55.9	48.1	50.5	39.6	47.5
1976	42.2	58.7	68.7	62.2	59.5	65.1	54.9	57.5
1974	23.8	42.2	56.9	51.4	48.7	49.3	36.0	48.1
1972	49.6	62.7	70.8	63.5	66.4	NA	55.4	NA
1970	30.4	51.9	64.2	57.0	59.0	NA	44.7	NA
1968	50.4	66.6	74.9	65.8	71.0	NA	60.1	NA
1966	31.2	53.1	64.5	56.1	60.9	NA	43.0	NA
1964	50.9	69.0	75.9	66.3	74.4	76.2	56.7	71.9
PERCENT REGISTERED								
1996	48.8	61.9	73.5	77.0	64.7	71.6	65.9	60.8
1994	42.3	57.9	71.7	76.3	61.5	68.9	61.1	58.9
1992	52.5	64.8	75.3	78.0	67.0	74.6	67.2	63.6
1990	39.9	58.4	71.4	76.5	61.0	68.2	61.3	57.7
1988	48.2	63.0	75.5	78.4	64.8	72.5	65.6	63.0
1986	42.0	61.1	74.8	76.9	62.0	70.7	63.0	60.8
1984	51.3	66.6	76.6	76.9	66.6	74.6	66.9	64.7
1982	42.4	61.5	75.6	75.2	62.5	71.1	61.7	60.6
1980	49.2	65.6	75.8	74.6	64.8	73.8	64.8	63.3
1978	40.5	60.2	74.3	72.8	62.3	68.2	60.1	59.1
1976	51.3	65.5	75.5	71.4	65.9	72.3	64.6	63.2
1974	41.3	59.9	73.6	70.2	62.2	66.6	59.8	59.8
1972	58.9	71.3	79.7	75.6	73.9	NA	68.7	NA
1970	40.9	65.0	77.5	73.7	70.0	NA	63.8	NA
1968	56.0	72.4	81.1	75.6	76.5	NA	69.2	NA
1966	44.1	67.6	78.9	73.5	73.8	NA	62.2	NA
1964	NA	NA	NA	NA	NA	NA	NA	NA

[1] FOR YEARS 1966 TO 1972 DATA WERE AVAILABLE FOR THE WEST AND SOUTH REGIONS ONLY. PRIOR TO 1972, DATA ARE FOR PERSONS OF VOTING AGE, 21 YEARS OLD AND OVER, IN MOST STATES. REGISTRATION DATA WERE NOT COLLECTED IN THE 1964 CURRENT POPULATION SURVEY.

NA = NOT AVAILABLE.

Source: U.S. Department of the Census, Current Population Reports, Series P20-466. *Voting and Registration in the Election of November 1992*, and earlier reports.

TABLE A9.3

PERCENTAGE OF PERSONS IN THE UNITED STATES AGE 18-24 YEARS WHO REPORTED VOTING, BY RACE AND HISPANIC ORIGIN: NOVEMBER 1964–NOVEMBER 1996

(NUMBERS IN THOUSANDS)

YEAR	WHITE		BLACK		HISPANIC [1]	
	NUMBER	PERCENT VOTED	NUMBER	PERCENT VOTED	NUMBER	PERCENT VOTED
1996	19,669	33.3	3,613	32.4	3,452	15.1
1994	20,151	21.1	3,638	17.4	3,512	10.1
1992	19,682	45.4	3,543	36.6	2,795	17.6
1990	20,357	20.8	3,525	20.2	2,711	8.70
1988	21,092	37.0	3,567	35.0	2,661	16.8
1986	21,957	21.6	3,651	25.1	2,543	11.6
1984	23,227	41.6	3,875	40.6	2,064	21.9
1982	24,133	25.0	3,850	25.5	2,019	14.2
1980	23,976	41.8	3,559	30.1	2,047	15.9
1978	23,669	24.2	3,462	20.1	1,606	11.5
1976	23,141	44.7	3,323	27.9	1,559	21.8
1974	22,187	25.2	3,113	16.1	1,481	13.3
1972	21,339	51.9	2,994	34.7	1,338	30.9
1970	11,345	31.5	1,542	22.4	NA	NA
1968	9,820	52.8	1,255	38.9	NA	NA
1966	9,405	32.6	1,208	21.9	NA	NA
1964	8,715	52.1	1,115	44.2	NA	NA

[1] PERSONS OF HISPANIC ORIGIN MAY BE OF ANY RACE.

NA = NOT AVAILABLE.

Source: U.S. Bureau of the Census, Current Population Reports, Series P20-466, Voting and Registration in the Election of November 1992, and earlier reports.

Note: Data are for persons of voting age, 21 years old and over, in most states prior to 1972.

TABLE A9.4

PERCENTAGE OF PERSONS IN THE UNITED STATES AGE 65 YEARS AND OVER WHO REPORTED VOTING, BY RACE AND HISPANIC ORIGIN: NOVEMBER 1964–NOVEMBER 1996

(NUMBERS IN THOUSANDS)

	WHITE		BLACK		HISPANIC [1]	
YEAR	NUMBER	PERCENT VOTED	NUMBER	PERCENT VOTED	NUMBER	PERCENT VOTED
1996	28,456	68.1	2,623	63.7	1,488	47.6
1994	27,890	62.8	2,538	51.6	1,356	37.6
1992	27,592	71.5	2,644	64.1	1,184	39.7
1990	26,807	61.7	2,528	51.3	1,072	40.5
1988	25,908	69.8	2,422	63.5	862	45.6
1986	24,982	61.9	2,318	53.3	881	36.5
1984	24,081	68.7	2,203	61.5	674	40.5
1982	23,139	61.1	2,132	50.8	599	29.5
1980	21,748	66.0	2,039	59.4	538	36.8
1978	20,798	57.2	1,943	45.6	511	24.9
1976	19,943	63.2	1,848	54.3	509	29.9
1974	19,058	52.8	1,710	38.5	413	28.1
1972	18,307	64.8	1,613	50.6	412	26.7
1970	17,583	58.6	1,413	39.3	NA	NA
1968	16,989	67.4	1,363	49.9	NA	NA
1966	16,413	57.9	1,316	35.3	NA	NA
1964	15,924	68.1	1,266	45.3	NA	NA

[1] PERSONS OF HISPANIC ORIGIN MAY BE OF ANY RACE.

NA=Not available.

Source: U.S. Bureau of the Census, *Current Population Reports*, Series P20-466, *Voting and Registration in the Election of November 1992*, and earlier reports.

Note: Data are for persons of voting age, 21 years old and over, in most states prior to 1972.

TABLE A9.5

PERCENTAGE WHO REPORTED VOTING IN THE U.S., BY AGE AND SEX: NOVEMBER 1964–NOVEMBER 1996

(NUMBERS IN THOUSANDS)

	TOTAL		18–44 YEARS		45 YEARS AND OVER	
	MEN	WOMEN	MEN	WOMEN	MEN	WOMEN
1996						
NUMBER	92,632	101,020	53,277	54,765	39,353	46,256
PERCENT VOTED	52.8	55.5	42.9	47.8	66.2	64.7
1994						
NUMBER	91,006	99,260	53,406	54,783	37,601	44,478
PERCENT VOTED	44.7	45.3	33.9	35.9	60.2	57.0
1992						
NUMBER	88,557	97,126	52,008	53,682	36,549	43,445
PERCENT VOTED	60.2	62.3	52.3	57.1	71.5	68.9
1990						
NUMBER	86,621	95,496	51,695	53,677	34,927	41,819
PERCENT VOTED	44.6	45.4	34.6	37.2	59.5	55.9
1988						
NUMBER	84,531	93,568	50,652	52,781	33,878	40,788
PERCENT VOTED	56.4	58.3	47.4	51.6	69.9	66.8
1986						
NUMBER	82,364	91,526	49,558	51,795	32,806	39,732
PERCENT VOTED	45.8	46.1	35.3	37.2	61.6	57.8
1984						
NUMBER	80,327	89,636	48,428	50,571	31,899	39,065
PERCENT VOTED	59.0	60.8	51.3	55.5	70.6	67.8
1982						
NUMBER	78,046	87,437	46,656	49,049	31,389	38,388
PERCENT VOTED	48.7	48.4	38.7	39.7	63.7	59.5
1980						
NUMBER	74,082	83,003	43,326	46,096	30,756	36,906
PERCENT VOTED	59.1	59.4	51.3	54.2	70.0	66.0
1978						
NUMBER	71,465	80,181	41,228	43,986	30,238	36,196
PERCENT VOTED	46.6	45.3	36.2	37.2	60.7	55.1
1976						
NUMBER	68,957	77,591	39,259	41,995	29,699	35,596
PERCENT VOTED	59.6	58.8	52.3	54.1	69.2	64.3
1974						
NUMBER	66,393	74,906	37,260	40,123	29,133	34,782
PERCENT VOTED	46.2	43.4	36.2	36.0	59.0	51.9
1972						
NUMBER	63,833	72,370	35,395	38,390	28,439	33,979
PERCENT VOTED	64.1	62.0	57.9	58.7	71.7	65.7
1970						
NUMBER	56,431	64,270	28,583	31,503	27,848	32,767
PERCENT VOTED	56.8	52.7	47.8	46.7	66.1	58.4
1968						
NUMBER	54,464	62,071	27,077	30,195	27,180	31,651
PERCENT VOTED	69.8	66.0	64.2	63.1	75.6	69.0
1966						
NUMBER	52,799	60,001	26,290	29,522	26,509	30,479
PERCENT VOTED	58.2	50.3	50.1	47.8	66.1	58.1
1964						
NUMBER	52,123	58,482	26,144	29,070	25,977	29,413
PERCENT VOTED	71.9	67.0	66.8	64.8	77.1	69.2

Source: U.S. Department of the Census, *Current Population Reports*, Series P20-466, *Voting and Registration in the Election of November 1992*, and earlier reports.

Note: Prior to 1972, data are for persons of voting age, 21 years old and over, in most states.

TABLE A9.6

SELECTED CHARACTERISTICS OF PERSONS OF VOTING AGE IN THE UNITED STATES, BY WHETHER REPORTED VOTING AND REGISTERING: NOVEMBER 1996

CHARACTERISTICS	VOTING-AGE POPULATION	REGISTERED		VOTED	
		NUMBER	PERCENT	NUMBER	PERCENT
GENDER AND AGE					
BOTH SEXES	193,651	127,661	65.9	105,017	54.2
18 - 20 YRS	10,785	4,919	45.6	3,366	31.2
21 - 24 YRS	13,865	7,099	51.2	4,630	33.4
25 - 44 YRS	83,393	51,606	61.9	41,050	49.2
45 - 64 YRS	53,721	39,489	73.5	34,615	64.4
65 YRS AND OVER	31,888	24,547	77	21,356	67
MALE	92,632	59,672	64.4	48,909	52.8
18 - 20 YRS	5,372	2,294	42.7	1,521	28.3
21 - 24 YRS	6,901	3,417	49.5	2,140	31
25 - 44 YRS	41,005	24,453	59.6	19,211	46.8
45 - 64 YRS	25,945	18,829	72.6	16,530	63.7
65 YRS AND OVER	13,408	10,680	79.7	9,507	70.9
FEMALE	101,020	67,989	67.3	56,108	55.5
18 - 20 YRS	5,413	2,625	48.5	1,845	34.1
21 - 24 YRS	6,964	3,681	52.9	2,490	35.8
25 - 44 YRS	42,388	27,153	64.1	21,840	51.5
45 - 64 YRS	27,776	20,662	74.4	18,085	65.1
65 YRS AND OVER	18,480	13,867	75	11,849	64.1
RACE AND HISPANIC ORIGIN					
WHITE	162,779	110,259	67.7	91,208	56
BLACK	22,483	14,267	63.5	11,386	50.6
HISPANIC [1]	18,426	6,573	35.7	4,928	26.7
REGION					
NORTHEAST	38,263	24,772	64.7	20,852	54.5
MIDWEST	45,177	32,364	71.6	26,798	59.3
SOUTH	68,080	44,891	65.9	35,550	52.2
WEST	42,131	25,634	60.8	21,816	51.8
EDUCATION					
LESS THAN HIGH SCHOOL	13,986	5,697	40.7	4,188	29.9
SOME HIGH SCHOOL	21,002	10,059	47.9	7,099	33.8
HIGH SCHOOL GRADUATE	65,208	40,542	62.2	32,019	49.1
SOME COLLEGE, INCLUDING ASSOCIATE DEGREE	50,939	37,160	72.9	30,835	60.5
BACHELOR'S DEGREE OR HIGHER	42,517	34,203	80.4	30,877	72.6
LABOR FORCE					
IN LABOR FORCE	132,043	87,532	66.3	71,682	54.3
EMPLOYED	125,634	84,166	67	69,300	55.2
UNEMPLOYED	6,409	3,365	52.5	2,383	37.2
NOT IN LABOR FORCE	61,608	40,129	65.1	33,335	54.1

[1] PERSONS OF HISPANIC ORIGIN MAY BE OF ANY RACE.

Source: U.S. Bureau of the Census, *Current Population Reports*, Series P20-504, Voting and Registration in the Election of November 1996.

LEISURE, VOLUNTEERISM, AND RELIGIOSITY

TABLE A10.1

PARTICIPATION IN SELECTED SPORTS ACTIVITIES IN THE UNITED STATES: 1994

(IN THOUSANDS, EXCEPT RANK. FOR PERSONS 7 YEARS OF AGE OR OLDER. EXCEPT AS INDICATED, A PARTICIPANT PLAYS A SPORT MORE THAN ONCE IN THE YEAR. BASED ON A SAMPLING OF 10,000 HOUSEHOLDS).

ACTIVITY	ALL PERSONS		SEX		AGE								HOUSEHOLD INCOME (DOL.)					
	NUMBER	RANK	MALE	FEMALE	7-11 YEARS	12-17 YEARS	18-24 YEARS	25-34 YEARS	35-44 YEARS	45-54 YEARS	55-64 YEARS	65 YEARS AND OVER	UNDER 15,000	15,000-24,999	25,000-34,999	35,000-49,999	50,000-74,999	75,000+
TOTAL NUMBER PARTICIPATED IN:	232,986	X	113,093	119,892	18,773	21,579	25,846	42,225	41,264	29,001	21,132	33,166	42,890	35,670	35,957	45,148	48,155	25,166
AEROBIC EXERCISING 1	23,200	11	4,435	18,765	464	1,083	4,566	6,945	4,994	2,236	1,280	1,633	3,161	2,898	3,281	4,799	5,404	3,657
BACKPACKING 2	9,809	23	5,880	3,928	859	1,427	1,501	2,769	2,073	519	367	293	1,500	1,304	1,783	2,335	1,740	1,145
BADMINTON	5,424	26	2,413	3,011	1,073	1,099	733	1,104	778	447	165	24	1,010	928	992	854	1,167	473
BASEBALL	15,096	17	12,254	2,842	5,107	4,148	1,548	1,820	1,623	418	203	229	1,979	2,061	1,999	3,584	3,523	1,950
BASKETBALL	28,191	8	20,492	7,699	5,554	7,951	5,165	4,768	3,462	797	287	208	3,537	4,394	4,428	5,580	6,603	3,649
BICYCLE RIDING 1	49,818	3	26,945	22,872	11,403	9,363	4,707	8,460	7,580	3,750	2,202	2,353	6,614	6,414	7,634	10,298	12,226	6,632
BOWLING	37,356	7	19,544	17,812	4,501	4,833	6,476	9,215	6,185	2,846	1,346	1,954	5,217	5,708	5,892	8,154	7,995	4,389
CALISTHENICS 1	8,536	24	3,634	4,902	1,178	1,259	1,414	1,654	1,239	682	371	738	924	1,159	1,189	1,851	2,170	1,243
CAMPING 3	42,932	5	23,066	19,866	6,100	5,566	4,280	9,580	8,832	4,258	2,420	1,896	5,584	6,141	6,616	10,127	10,090	4,374
EXERCISE WALKING 1	70,794	1	25,451	45,344	2,218	2,850	5,870	13,032	14,336	11,198	8,596	12,695	12,471	11,257	10,788	12,369	16,037	7,873
EXERCISING WITH EQUIPMENT 1	43,784	4	21,173	22,611	770	3,063	6,984	10,975	9,145	5,795	3,379	3,672	5,276	5,366	6,290	8,932	10,749	7,171
FISHING—FRESH WATER	40,477	6	27,477	13,000	4,883	4,632	3,548	9,408	7,599	4,791	2,581	3,035	6,580	6,558	7,172	8,929	7,997	3,241
FISHING—SALT WATER	11,515	21	7,941	3,574	855	1,037	1,026	2,532	2,668	1,353	784	1,260	1,374	1,399	1,941	2,572	2,786	1,444
FOOTBALL	15,574	16	13,203	2,371	3,021	4,958	3,255	2,484	1,105	271	228	253	2,692	2,466	2,274	2,626	3,586	1,929
GOLF	24,551	10	18,662	5,889	670	1,885	2,868	5,988	4,901	3,283	2,207	2,748	2,025	2,414	3,087	4,935	7,113	4,978
HIKING	25,301	9	13,976	11,326	2,710	2,811	3,125	5,690	5,440	2,808	1,432	1,285	3,350	3,826	3,248	5,058	6,339	3,480
HUNTING WITH FIREARMS	16,369	15	14,099	2,270	297	2,130	1,693	4,292	3,674	2,206	1,245	831	2,360	2,712	2,852	4,014	3,103	1,328
RACQUETBALL	5,340	27	3,971	1,369	255	438	1,637	1,634	821	351	191	12	897	831	398	1,073	1,547	595
RUNNING/JOGGING 1	20,640	12	11,981	8,659	1,661	3,399	4,614	4,782	3,112	1,844	759	470	2,396	2,668	3,447	3,498	5,195	3,435
SKIING—ALPINE/DOWNHILL	10,620	22	6,356	4,264	646	1,966	2,493	2,683	1,620	931	173	107	741	883	1,167	2,011	2,881	2,936
SKIING—CROSS COUNTRY	3,627	28	1,744	1,883	216	467	395	599	861	518	396	176	327	150	398	1,170	845	737
SOCCER	12,508	18	8,223	4,284	5,494	3,536	1,394	1,023	778	157	59	67	1,262	1,614	1,507	2,640	3,414	2,070
SOFTBALL	18,143	13	10,162	7,982	3,292	3,567	3,070	4,340	2,667	893	246	68	1,941	2,783	3,019	3,666	4,551	2,183
SWIMMING 1	60,277	2	28,960	31,317	10,669	9,335	6,565	10,645	10,470	5,261	2,742	4,591	7,206	7,696	9,399	12,741	14,608	8,627
TABLE TENNIS	7,817	25	4,965	2,852	1,056	1,283	1,517	1,600	1,124	702	276	258	833	945	1,026	1,338	2,199	1,478
TARGET SHOOTING	12,231	19	9,617	2,614	878	1,401	1,484	3,427	2,394	1,420	603	624	1,657	2,008	2,354	2,801	2,071	1,342
TENNIS	11,590	20	6,535	5,055	941	2,083	2,155	2,655	1,725	1,172	480	378	1,254	1,491	1,058	1,972	3,450	2,364
VOLLEYBALL	17,383	14	8,492	8,891	1,739	4,222	3,374	4,538	2,551	591	314	55	2,455	2,744	2,627	3,689	3,984	1,882

X = NOT APPLICABLE.
1 PARTICIPANT ENGAGED IN ACTIVITY AT LEAST SIX TIMES IN THE YEAR.   2 INCLUDES WILDERNESS CAMPING.   3 VACATION/OVERNIGHT

Source: National Sporting Goods Association, Mt. Prospect, IL, Sports Participation in 1994: Series I.

TABLE A10.2

HOUSEHOLD PARTICIPATION IN LAWN AND GARDEN ACTIVITIES IN THE UNITED STATES: 1990–1994

(BASED ON NATIONAL HOUSEHOLD SAMPLE SURVEY CONDUCTED BY THE GALLUP ORGANIZATION. SUBJECT TO SAMPLING VARIABLITY.)

ACTIVITY	PERCENTAGE OF HOUSEHOLDS ENGAGED IN—					RETAIL SALES (MILLIONS OF DOLLARS)				
	1990	1991	1992	1993	1994	1990	1991	1992	1993	1994
TOTAL	80	78	75	71	74	20,802	22,134	22,824	22,410	25,897
LAWN CARE	66	62	54	54	56	6,412	6,890	7,460	6,446	8,417
INDOOR HOUSEPLANTS	43	42	34	31	37	928	852	926	689	999
FLOWER GARDENING	48	41	39	39	44	2,275	2,302	2,167	2,396	3,147
INSECT CONTROL	39	35	27	24	28	1,370	1,260	1,593	1,080	1,127
SHRUB CARE	38	32	27	28	30	1,099	1,030	1,437	1,274	1,133
VEGETABLE GARDENING	37	31	31	26	31	1,384	1,652	1,440	1,063	1,476
TREE CARE	31	27	20	21	22	1,445	1,443	1,664	2,011	1,408
LANDSCAPING	31	26	22	24	26	3,837	4,828	4,444	5,006	5,797
FLOWER BULBS	31	26	23	22	28	579	520	503	453	635
FRUIT TREES	19	15	13	13	14	502	371	350	759	389
CONTAINER GARDENING	15	13	9	11	12	359	330	239	441	359
RAISING TRANSPLANTS1	15	12	8	10	11	181	141	169	201	182
HERB GARDENING	9	9	7	8	10	84	161	135	175	112
GROWING BERRIES	9	7	6	6	6	79	90	62	126	85
ORNAMENTAL GARDENING	7	7	5	6	5	268	264	235	290	264
WATER GARDENING	NA	NA	NA	NA	5	NA	NA	NA	NA	367

NA=NOT AVAILABLE.

1 STARTING PLANTS IN ADVANCE OF PLANTING IN GROUND.

Source: The National Gardening Association, Burlington, VT, *National Gardening Survey*, annual.

TABLE A10.3

PARTICIPATION IN VARIOUS LEISURE ACTIVITIES IN THE UNITED STATES: 1992

(IN PERCENT, EXCEPT AS INDICATED. COVERS ACTIVITIES ENGAGED IN AT LEAST ONCE IN THE PRIOR 12 MONTHS.)

| ITEM | ADULT POPULATION (MIL.) | ATTENDANCE AT— | | | PARTICIPATION IN— | | | | |
		MOVIES	SPORTS EVENTS	AMUSEMENT PARK	EXERCISE PROGRAM	PLAYING SPORTS	OUTDOOR ACTIVITIES [1]	HOME IMPROVEMENT/ REPAIR	GARDENING
TOTAL	185.8	59	37	50	60	39	34	48	55
SEX									
MALE	89	60	44	51	61	50	39	53	46
FEMALE	96.8	59	30	50	59	29	29	42	62
RACE									
WHITE	158.8	60	38	51	61	40	37	50	57
BLACK	21.1	54	32	45	51	32	10	32	39
OTHER	5.9	62	20	46	51	38	28	31	42
AGE									
18 - 24	24.1	82	51	68	67	59	43	33	31
25 - 34	42.4	70	47	68	67	52	41	47	51
35 - 44	39.8	68	43	58	62	44	42	58	57
45 - 54	27.7	58	35	44	62	34	36	57	64
55 - 64	21.2	40	23	30	56	21	21	53	63
65 - 74	18.3	34	20	29	50	18	21	42	63
75 - 96	12.3	19	7	14	34	7	5	20	55
EDUCATION									
GRADE SCHOOL	14.3	16	9	24	24	10	11	24	44
SOME HIGH SCHOOL	18.6	35	19	35	39	18	21	34	50
HIGH SCHOOL GRADUATE	69.4	54	33	51	55	34	31	47	53
SOME COLLEGE	39.2	21	45	59	71	49	42	53	55
COLLEGE GRADUATE	26.2	77	51	58	75	55	42	52	61
GRADUATE SCHOOL	18.1	81	51	54	79	57	51	65	65

[1] CAMPING, HIKING, AND CANOEING.

Source: U.S. National Endowment for the Arts, *Arts Participation in America: 1982-92.*

ENVIRONMENT

TABLE A11.1

U.S. THREATENED AND ENDANGERED PLANT AND ANIMAL GROUPS, 1980–1995

YEAR	THREATENED ANIMAL GROUPS (NUMBER OF SPECIES)										THREATENED PLANTS	TOTAL
	MAMMALS	BIRDS	REPTILES	AMPHIBIANS	FISH	CRUSTACEANS	SNAILS	INSECTS	ARACHNIDS	CLAMS		
1995	9	16	19	5	40	3	7	9	0	6	92	206
1994	6	8	15	4	30	3	7	9	0	6	76	164
1993	6	8	14	4	31	2	7	9	0	5	69	155
1992	6	7	14	4	30	2	6	9	0	2	62	142
1991	8	12	18	5	34	2	6	9	0	2	61	157
1990	5	7	13	4	25	1	6	7	0	0	46	114
1989	6	7	14	4	25	1	6	7	0	0	42	112
1988	3	7	14	4	25	1	5	7	0	0	31	97
1987	7	10	18	4	30	1	5	7	0	0	44	126
1986	4	4	11	3	21	1	5	5	0	0	23	77
1985	4	3	8	3	14	1	5	4	0	0	10	52
1984	3	3	8	3	12	1	5	4	0	0	9	48
1983	3	3	12	3	12	1	5	6	0	0	10	55
1982	3	3	8	3	12	1	5	4	0	0	8	47
1981	3	3	8	3	12	0	5	4	0	0	7	45
1980	3	3	10	3	12	0	5	6	0	0	7	49

YEAR	ENDANGERED ANIMAL GROUPS (NUMBER OF SPECIES)										ENDANGERED PLANTS	TOTAL
	MAMMALS	BIRDS	REPTILES	AMPHIBIANS	FISH	CRUSTACEANS	SNAILS	INSECTS	ARACHNIDS	CLAMS		
1995	55	74	14	7	65	14	15	20	5	51	434	754
1994	36	58	8	6	62	14	14	16	4	50	404	672
1993	37	57	8	6	55	11	12	13	5	51	317	572
1992	37	57	8	6	52	8	7	13	3	40	274	505
1991	55	73	16	6	54	8	7	13	3	40	229	504
1990	33	60	8	6	49	8	3	10	3	35	163	378
1989	32	61	9	6	49	8	3	10	3	34	163	378
1988	28	61	8	5	41	5	3	8	0	29	139	327
1987	50	76	15	5	47	7	3	10	3	30	158	404
1986	45	72	12	5	46	3	3	8	0	24	87	305
1985	20	59	8	5	30	3	3	8	0	22	67	225
1984	15	52	8	5	30	3	3	7	0	22	60	205
1983	33	66	14	5	33	2	3	7	0	23	55	241
1982	15	52	8	5	28	2	3	7	0	23	55	198
1981	15	52	7	5	29	1	2	7	0	23	48	189
1980	32	66	3	5	34	1	2	7	0	23	51	234

Source: U.S. Department of the Interior (DOI), Fish and Wildlife Service (FWS), Endangered Species Bulletin(Washington, D.C.:, annual December issue).

Notes: Separate populations of a species listed both as Threatened and Endangered are tallied twice. Those species are the grizzly bear, gray wolf, bald eagle, piping plover, roseate tern, green sea turtle, and olive ridley sea turtle.

TABLE A11.2

INVENTORY OF U.S. GREENHOUSE GAS EMISSIONS AND SINKS: 1990–1994

(IN MILLION METRIC TONS)

GAS / SOURCE	1990	1991	1992	1993	1994
CARBON DIOXIDE					
FOSSIL FUEL COMBUSTION	1336	1320	1340	1369	1390
OTHER	17	17	17	18	17
TOTAL	1353	1336	1357	1387	1408
FORESTS (SINKS)	-125	-125	-125	NA	NA
NET TOTAL	1228	1211	1232	NA	NA
METHANE					
LANDFILLS	66	67	66	67	68
AGRICULTURE	56	57	59	59	61
COAL MINING	29	28	27	24	29
OIL AND GAS SYSTEMS	22	22	22	22	22
OTHER	6	7	7	6	6
TOTAL	181	182	182	179	188
NITROUS OXIDE					
AGRICULTURE	16	17	17	17	19
FOSSIL FUEL COMBUSTION	12	12	12	12	12
INDUSTRIAL PROCESSES	8	9	8	9	9
TOTAL	37	37	37	38	41
HFCS AND PFCS	18.8	19.3	21.1	19.8	23.5
SF6	6.4	6.5	6.7	6.8	7
TOTAL U.S. EMISSIONS	1595	1582	1604	1630	1666
NET, INCLUDING SINKS	1470	1457	1479	NA	NA

NA = NOT AVAILABLE.

Source: U.S. Environmental Protection Agency (EPA), Office of Policy, Planning and Evaluation (OPPE), Inventory of U.S. Greenhouse Gas Emissions and Sinks: 1990-1994, EPA-230-R-96-006 (Washington, D.C.: 1995).

Notes: HFCs=hydrofluorocarbons. PFCs=perfluorocarbons. SF6=sulfur hexafluoride. Emissions include direct and indirect effects. Other carbon emissions come from fuel production and processing, cement and lime production, limestone consumption, soda ash production and consumption, and carbon dioxide manufacture. Total carbon dioxide does not include emissions from bunker fuels used in international transport activities. U.S. emissions from bunker fuels were approximately 23 million metric tons (carbon-equivalent) in 1994. Other methane emissions come from fuel combustion by stationary and mobile sources and from wastewater facilities.

TABLE A11.3

AIR QUALITY TRENDS IN SELECTED U.S. URBAN AREAS, 1985–1994

(NUMBER OF PSI DAYS GREATER THEN 100)

PMSA	TREND SITES NUMBER	1985	1986	1987	1988	1989	1990	1991	1992	1993	1994
ATLANTA	7	9	18	27	21	3	17	6	5	17	4
BALTIMORE	15	25	23	28	43	9	12	20	5	14	17
BOSTON	24	3	2	5	15	4	1	3	1	3	1
CHICAGO	40	9	9	17	22	4	3	8	7	1	8
CLEVELAND	25	1	2	7	21	6	2	7	1	2	4
DALLAS	9	27	9	13	14	7	8	1	3	5	1
DENVER	20	38	49	37	19	11	9	7	7	3	2
DETROIT	25	2	5	9	17	10	3	8	0	2	8
EL PASO	16	32	43	32	16	33	27	10	13	6	10
HOUSTON	28	64	55	67	61	42	61	42	31	26	29
KANSAS CITY	19	3	4	6	4	2	2	1	1	2	0
LOS ANGELES	37	208	226	201	239	226	178	182	185	146	136
MIAMI	7	5	4	4	5	4	1	2	0	0	0
MINN/ST. PAUL	22	14	13	7	1	5	1	0	1	0	3
NEW YORK	24	65	58	44	46	18	18	22	4	6	8
PHILADELPHIA	36	31	23	36	35	20	14	25	3	22	6
PHOENIX	22	88	88	42	26	30	9	4	9	7	7
PITTSBURGH	31	9	8	13	25	9	11	4	2	5	2
SAN DIEGO	21	88	70	61	84	90	60	39	37	17	16
SAN FRANCISCO	11	5	4	1	2	1	1	0	0	0	0
SEATTLE	13	25	13	14	20	8	5	2	1	0	0
ST. LOUIS	46	10	13	17	18	13	8	6	3	5	11
WASH, DC	32	17	12	26	37	8	5	17	2	13	7
SUBTOTAL	522	778	751	714	791	563	456	416	321	302	280
OTHER SITES	682	878	816	824	1,163	687	552	578	357	374	333
ALL SITES	1,204	1,656	1,567	1,538	1,954	1,250	1,008	994	678	676	613

Source: U.S. Environmental Protection Agency (EPA), Office of Air Quality Planning and Standards (OAQPS), *National Air Quality and Emissions Trends Report, 1994*, Data Appendix, Table A-13 (Research Triangle Park, N.C.: 1995).

Notes: PMSA=Primary Metropolitan Statistical Area. PSI=Pollutant Standards Index. Minn=Minneapolis. The PSI index integrates information from many pollutants across an entire monitoring network into a single number which represents the worst daily air quality experienced in an urban area. Only carbon monoxide and ozone monitoring sites with adequate historical data are included in the PSI trend analysis above, except for Pittsburgh, where sulfur dioxide contributes a significant number of days in the PSI high range. PSI index ranges and health effect descriptor words are as follows: 0-50 (good); 51-100 (moderate); 101-199 (unhealthful); 200-299 (very unhealthful); and 300 and above (hazardous). The table above shows the number of days when the PSI was greater than 100 (=unhealthy or worse days).

Table A11.4

Water Use in the United States by Source and End-use Sector, 1900–1990
(Selected Years)

	Source		End-use Sector					
(Billions of Gallons per Day)								
Year	Ground Water	Surface Water	Public Supply	Rural Domestic & Livestock	Irrigation	Thermo-Electric Utility	Other Industrial	Total
1990	80.6	327.2	38.5	7.9	137	195	29.9	408.8
1985	73.7	320	37.0	7.8	140	190	31	405.8
1980	83.9	361	34.0	5.6	150	210	45	444.6
1975	83.0	329	29.0	4.9	140	200	45	418.9
1970	69.0	303	27.0	4.5	130	170	47	378.5
1965	60.5	253	24.0	4.0	120	130	46	324.0
1960	50.4	221	21.0	3.6	110	100	38	272.6
1955	47.6	198	17.0	3.6	110	72	39	241.6
1950	34.0	150	14.0	3.6	89	40	37	183.6
1945	NA	NA	12.0	3.4	80	31.5	35	161.9
1940	NA	NA	10.0	3.1	71	23	29	136.1
1930	NA	NA	8.0	2.9	60	18	21	109.9
1920	NA	NA	6.0	2.4	56	9	18	91.4
1910	NA	NA	5.0	2.2	39	7	14	67.2
1900	NA	NA	3.0	2.0	20	5	10	40.0

NA = Not Available.

Sources: U.S. Department of Commerce, Bureau of the Census, Historical Statistics of the United States: *Colonial Times to 1970*, Series J 92-103 (Washington, D.C.: 1975), W.B. Solley, R.R. Pierce and H.A. Perlman, *Estimated Water Use in the United States in 1990*, Circular 1081 (Reston, VA: U.S. Department of the Interior, Geological Survey, 1993) and earlier reports in this series.

TABLE A11.5

AMBIENT WATER QUALITY IN U.S. RIVERS AND STREAMS, VIOLATION RATES: 1975–1994

(PERCENT OF ALL MEASUREMENTS EXCEEDING NATIONAL WATER QUALITY CRITERIA)

YEAR	FECAL COLIFORM BACTERIA	DISSOLVED OXYGEN	TOTAL PHOSPHORUS	TOTAL CADMIUM, DISSOLVED	TOTAL LEAD, DISSOLVED
1994	29	<1	4	NA	NA
1993	31	1	2	NA	NA
1992	28	2	2	<1	<1
1991	15	2	2	<1	<1
1990	26	2	3	<1	<1
1989	30	3	2	<1	<1
1988	22	2	4	<1	<1
1987	23	2	3	<1	<1
1986	24	3	3	<1	<1
1985	28	3	3	<1	<1
1984	30	3	4	<1	<1
1983	34	4	3	1	5
1982	33	5	3	1	2
1981	30	4	4	1	3
1980	31	5	4	1	5
1979	34	4	3	4	13
1978	35	5	5	*	*
1977	34	11	5	*	*
1976	32	6	5	*	*
1975	36	5	5	*	*

*BASE FIGURE TOO SMALL TO MEET STATISTICAL STANDARDS FOR RELIABILITY OF DERIVED FIGURES.
NA = NOT AVAILABLE.

Source: U.S. Geological Survey, unpublished, Reston, VA, 1995.

Notes: Violation levels are based on the following U.S. Environmental Protection Agency water quality criteria: fecal coliform bacteria—above 200 cells per 100 ml; dissolved oxygen—below 5 mg per liter; total phosphorus—above 1.0 mg per liter; cadmium, dissolved—above 10 ug per liter; lead, dissolved—above 50 ug per liter.

TABLE A11.6

OIL POLLUTING INCIDENTS REPORTED IN AND AROUND U.S. WATERS: 1970–1994

YEAR	THOUSANDS NUMBER	MILLION GALLONS VOLUME
1994	9.44	19.51
1993	8.97	2.08
1992	4.49	1.88
1991	10.41	2.16
1990	8.18	7.97
1989	6.61	13.48
1988	5.00	6.59
1987	4.84	3.61
1986	4.99	4.28
1985	6.17	8.47
1984	8.26	19.01
1983	7.92	8.38
1982	7.48	10.34
1981	7.81	8.92
1980	8.38	12.6
1979	9.83	20.89
1978	10.64	10.86
1977	9.46	8.19
1976	9.42	18.52
1975	9.3	21.52
1974	9.99	15.72
1973	9.01	15.25
1972	9.93	18.81
1971	8.74	8.84
1970	3.71	15.25

Source: U.S. Department of Transportation, United States Coast Guard, Response Division, G-MRO, Oil Spill Database, unpublished, Washington, D.C., 1996.

TABLE A11.7

WATERBORNE DISEASE OUTBREAKS AND CASES IN THE UNITED STATES: 1971-94

| YEAR | WATER SUPPLY SYSTEM (NUMBER OF OUTBREAKS) | | | TOTAL | (NUMBER) TOTAL CASES |
	COMMUNITY	NON-COMMUNITY	INDIVIDUAL		
1994	5	5	2	12	649
1993	9	4	5	18	404,190
1992	6	10	3	19	4,504
1991	2	13	0	15	12,960
1990	6	7	2	15	1,748
1989	6	6	1	13	2,670
1988	6	10	1	16	2,169
1987	8	6	1	15	22,149
1986	10	10	2	22	1,569
1985	7	14	1	22	1,946
1984	12	5	10	27	1,800
1983	30	9	4	43	21,036
1982	26	15	3	44	3,588
1981	14	18	4	36	4,537
1980	26	20	7	53	20,045
1979	24	13	8	45	9,841
1978	10	19	3	32	11,435
1977	14	18	2	34	3,860
1976	9	23	3	35	5,068
1975	6	16	2	24	10,879
1974	11	9	5	25	8,356
1973	6	16	3	25	1,762
1972	9	19	2	30	1,650
1971	8	8	4	20	5,184

Source: M.H. Kramer, B.L. Herwaldt, G.F. Craun, R.L. Calderon and D.D. Juranek, "Surveillance for Waterborne-Disease Outbreaks - United States, 1993-1994," CDC Surveillance Summaries, April 12, 1996, *Morbidity and Mortality Weekly Report* 42(SS-5) (U.S. Department of Health and Human Services, Public Health Service, Centers for Disease Control and Prevention, Atlanta, GA), 7-8, and earlier reports.

Notes: The number of waterborne disease outbreaks and the number of affected people (=cases) reported to the Centers for Disease Control and Prevention and to the U.S. Environmental Protection Agency represents a fraction of the total number that occur. Therefore, these data should not be used to draw firm conclusions about the true incidence of waterborne disease outbreaks.

TABLE A11.8

LAND USE AND OWNERSHIP IN THE UNITED STATES: 1900–1992
(SELECTED YEARS)

YEAR	LAND USE (MILLION ACRES)					OWNERSHIP (PERCENT)	
	PRIVATE & CROP-LAND	GRAZING LAND	FORESTLAND	OTHER LAND	TOTAL	OTHER PUBLIC	FEDERAL
1900	319	1044	366	175	1904	52.7	47.3
1910	347	814	562	181	1904	68.5	31.5
1920	402	750	567	185	1904	73.8	26.2
1930	413	708	607	176	1904	74.0	26.0
1945	451	660	602	193	1905	73.7	26.3
1949	478	631	606	189	1904	73.5	26.5
1954	465	632	615	191	1904	73.5	26.5
1959	458	633	728	452	2271	61.0	39.0
1964	444	640	732	450	2266	60.4	39.6
1969	472	604	723	465	2264	66.5	33.5
1974	465	598	718	483	2264	66.5	33.5
1978	471	587	703	503	2264	67.2	32.9
1982	469	597	655	544	2265	67.9	32.2
1987	464	591	648	562	2265	68.1	31.9
1992	460	591	648	564	2263	71.3	28.7

Sources: A.B. Daugherty, *Major Uses of Land in the United States: 1992*, Table 1, p. 4, *Agricultural Economic Report* No. 723 (Washington, D.C., 1995) and earlier reports in this series. U.S. Department of Commerce, Bureau of the Census, Statistical Abstract of the United States(GPO, Washington, DC, annual).

Notes: Prior to 1959, excludes Alaska and Hawaii. Other changes in total land area result from refinements in measuring techniques. Federal includes original public-domain lands vested in the U.S. government by virtue of its sovereignty as well as lands acquired by the U.S. government by purchase, condemnation, and gift. Historical estimates are based on imperfect data. Other land includes rural transportation areas, areas used primarily for recreation and wildlife purposes, various public installations and facilities, farmsteads and farm roads, urban areas, areas in miscellaneous uses not inventoried, marshes, open swamps, bare rock areas, desert, tundra, and other land generally having low value for agricultural purposes. Land-use and land-ownership estimates are not strictly comparable. Totals may not agree with sum of components due to independent rounding.

TABLE A11.9

U.S. COMMERCIAL FERTILIZER USE
IN THE UNITED STATES: 1960-95

YEAR	TOTAL QUANTITY	ACTIVE INGREDIENTS (MILLION TONS)			
		NITROGEN	PHOSPHATE	POTASH	TOTAL
1995	50.7	11.7	4.4	5.1	21.3
1994	52.3	12.6	4.5	5.3	22.4
1993	49.1	11.4	4.4	5.1	20.9
1992	48.8	11.5	4.2	5.0	20.7
1991	47.3	11.3	4.2	5.0	20.5
1990	47.7	11.1	4.3	5.2	20.6
1989	44.9	10.6	4.1	4.8	19.6
1988	44.5	10.5	4.1	5.0	19.6
1987	43.0	10.2	4.0	4.8	19.1
1986	44.1	10.4	4.2	5.1	19.7
1985	49.1	11.5	4.7	5.6	21.7
1984	50.1	11.1	4.9	5.8	21.8
1983	41.8	9.1	4.1	4.8	18.1
1982	48.7	11.0	4.8	5.6	21.4
1981	54.0	11.9	5.4	6.3	23.7
1980	52.8	11.4	5.4	6.2	23.1
1979	51.5	10.7	5.6	6.2	22.6
1978	47.5	10.0	5.1	5.5	20.6
1977	51.6	10.6	5.6	5.8	22.1
1976	49.2	10.4	5.2	5.2	20.8
1975	42.5	8.6	4.5	4.4	17.6
1974	47.1	9.2	5.1	5.1	19.3
1973	43.3	8.3	5.1	4.6	18.0
1972	41.2	8.0	4.9	4.3	17.2
1971	41.1	8.1	4.8	4.2	17.2
1970	39.6	7.5	4.6	4.0	16.1
1969	38.9	6.9	4.7	3.9	15.5
1968	38.7	6.8	4.4	3.8	15.0
1967	37.1	6.0	4.3	3.6	14.0
1966	34.5	5.3	3.9	3.2	12.4
1965	31.8	4.6	3.5	2.8	10.9
1964	30.7	4.4	3.4	2.7	10.5
1963	28.8	3.9	3.1	2.5	9.5
1962	26.6	3.4	2.8	2.3	8.4
1961	25.6	3.0	2.6	2.2	7.8
1960	24.9	2.7	2.6	2.2	7.5

Sources: Tennessee Valley Authority, Environmental Research Center, Commercial Fertilizers, 1994 (Oak Ridge, TN: 1995) and earlier issues, The Association of American Plant Food Control Officials (AAPFCO), *Commercial Fertilizers*, 1995 (Lexington, KY: 1996), U.S. Department of Agriculture, Economic Research Service, AREI UPDATES: *Nutrient Use and Management*, Table 1, p. 2 (Washington, D.C.: 1995).

Notes: Quantity refers to total fertilizer materials. Fertilizer use estimates for 1960-84 are based on USDA data; those for 1985-94 are TVA estimates. The 1995 data are from AAPFCO. Includes fertilizer use on farms, lawns, golf courses, home gardens, and other nonfarm lands. Includes Puerto Rico.

TABLE A11.10

U.S. COMMERCIAL PESTICIDE USE, BY SECTOR AND TYPE: 1979-93
(MILLION POUNDS OF ACTIVE INGREDIENTS)

YEAR	AGRICULTURE				INDUSTRY, COMMERCIAL, AND GOVERNMENT			
	HERBICIDES	INSECTICIDES	FUNGICIDES	TOTAL	HERBICIDES	INSECTICIDES	FUNGICIDES	TOTAL
1979	488	302	90	840	84	38	18	140
1980	445	306	95	846	82	47	18	147
1981	456	309	95	860	86	48	19	153
1982	430	295	90	815	86	48	19	153
1983	445	185	103	733	105	40	20	165
1984	545	200	105	850	105	40	20	165
1985	525	225	111	861	115	40	21	176
1986	500	210	110	820	125	45	25	195
1987	505	179	130	814	115	45	40	200
1988	510	185	150	845	120	45	40	205
1989	520	151	135	806	110	45	40	195
1990	516	173	145	834	103	42	38	183
1991	496	175	147	817	108	44	39	191
1992	511	181	147	839	110	43	40	193
1993	481	171	159	811	112	44	41	197

YEAR	HOME AND GARDEN				TOTAL			
	HERBICIDES	INSECTICIDES	FUNGICIDES	TOTAL	HERBICIDES	INSECTICIDES	FUNGICIDES	TOTAL
1979	28	38	12	77	560	378	120	1058
1980	28	42	12	82	555	395	125	1075
1981	28	48	12	85	570	405	126	1101
1982	28	48	12	88	544	391	121	1056
1983	25	30	10	65	575	255	133	963
1984	25	30	10	65	675	270	135	1080
1985	30	35	10	75	670	300	142	1112
1986	30	40	11	81	655	395	146	1096
1987	25	36	12	73	645	260	182	1087
1988	30	38	12	80	660	268	202	1130
1989	25	30	14	78	655	226	189	1070
1990	25	30	14	69	644	245	197	1086
1991	25	30	14	69	628	249	200	1077
1992	26	31	14	71	647	255	201	1103
1993	27	32	14	73	620	247	214	1081

Notes: Estimates for total fungicide use also include other pesticides. Totals may not agree with sum of components due to independent rounding.

Source: U.S. Environmental Protection Agency (EPA), Office of Pesticide Programs (OPP), Biological and Economic Analysis Division (BEAD), *Pesticide Industry Sales and Usage: 1992 and 1993 Market Estimates*, Tables 13, p. 26, and Table 14, pp. 27-29 (Washington, D.C.: 1994).

TABLE A11.11

U.S. MUNICIPAL SOLID WASTE TRENDS, BY WASTE TYPE: 1960-94

(MILLION TONS)

YEAR	PAPER		GLASS		METALS [1]		ALUMINUM		PLASTICS	
	GENERATION	RECOVERY	GENERATION	RECOVERY	GENERATION	RECOVERY	GENERATION	RECOVERY	GENERATION	RECOVERY
1994	81.3	28.73	13.27	3.11	12.73	4.52	3.06	1.15	19.84	0.93
1990	72.72	20.23	13.11	2.63	13.54	2.44	2.85	1.01	16.89	0.37
1980	55.16	11.74	14.99	0.75	12.89	0.91	1.77	0.31	7.74	0.2
1970	44.31	6.77	12.75	0.16	13.56	0.47	0.85	0.01	3.07	(Z)
1960	29.98	5.08	6.68	0.1	10.11	0.5	0.36	(Z)	0.36	(Z)

YEAR	RUBBER AND LEATHER		TEXTILES		WOOD		FOOD		YARD	
	GENERATION	RECOVERY	GENERATION	RECOVERY	GENERATION	RECOVERY	GENERATION	RECOVERY	GENERATION	RECOVERY
1994	6.37	0.45	6.56	0.77	14.59	1.43	14.07	0.48	30.6	7.0
1990	6.25	0.37	5.15	0.57	12.31	0.39	13.2	(Z)	35.0	4.2
1980	4.49	0.13	2.61	0.03	7.44	(Z)	13	(Z)	27.5	(Z)
1970	3.27	0.25	2.00	0.01	4.22	(Z)	12.8	(Z)	23.2	(Z)
1960	2.03	0.32	1.73	0.01	3.01	(Z)	12.2	(Z)	20.0	(Z)

[1] FERROUS AND NONFERROUS METALS.

(Z) = NEGLIGIBLE (LESS THAN 50, 000 TONS OR 0.05 PERCENT).

Source: U.S. Environmental Protection Agency, Office of Solid Waste and Emergency Response. *Characterization of Municipal Solid Waste in the United States: 1995 Update*, Table 1, p. 26 and Table 2, p. 27 (EPA, Washington, DC, 1996).

TABLE A11.12

U.S. INVENTORY OF LOW-LEVEL NUCLEAR WASTE, HIGH-LEVEL NUCLEAR WASTE, AND SPENT NUCLEAR FUEL: 1962–1995

(SELECTED YEARS)

	LOW-LEVEL WASTES AT COMMERCIAL DISPOSAL SITES				
YEAR	CUMULATIVE VOLUME MILLION M3	CUMULATIVE RADIOACTIVITY	YEAR	CUMULATIVE VOLUME (MILLION M3)	CUMULATIVE RADIOACTIVITY (MILLION CURIES)
1978	0.593	4.383	1995	1.543	5.944
1977	0.514	3.765	1994	1.519	5.841
1976	0.442	3.268	1993	1.495	5.709
1975	0.367	3.04	1992	1.472	5.708
1974	0.309	2.754	1991	1.423	5.272
1973	0.255	2.732	1990	1.384	4.979
1972	0.208	2.287	1989	1.352	5.284
1971	0.169	2.000	1988	1.306	4.793
1970	0.138	0.855	1987	1.265	4.924
1969	0.112	0.687	1986	1.213	5.059
1968	0.091	0.529	1985	1.16	5.282
1967	0.071	0.428	1984	1.083	4.954
1966	0.049	0.355	1983	1.007	4.732
1965	0.034	0.273	1982	0.929	4.568
1964	0.02	0.204	1981	0.852	4.483
1963	0.008	0.042	1980	0.768	4.547
1962	0.002	NA	1979	0.676	4.539

	HIGH-LEVEL NUCLEAR WASTE AT DOE/DEFENSE AND COMMERCIAL SITES			SPENT NUCLEAR FUEL AT COMMERCIAL SITES	
YEAR	CUMULATIVE VOLUME MILLION M3	CUMULATIVE RADIOACTIVITY	YEAR	CUMULATIVE VOLUME (MILLION M3)	CUMULATIVE RADIOACTIVITY (MILLION CURIES)
1995	371.7	916.7	1995	32,200	30,200
1994	378.4	958.8	1994	29,811	26,661
1993	403.5	1,045.30	1993	27,929	27,516
1992	398.3	1,081.20	1992	25,697	26,136
1991	396.5	1,007.40	1991	23,406	22,825
1990	398.5	1,050.80	1990	21,547	22,910
1989	381.1	1,113.90	1989	19,410	20,209
1988	384.9	1,206.70	1988	17,497	18,207
1987	381.4	1,303.10	1987	15,844	17,292
1986	365.9	1,419.00	1986	14,139	15,308
1985	357.1	1,459.50	1985	12,684	14,228
1984	363.5	1,355.20	1984	11,291	13,222
1983	352.7	1,299.70	1983	9,952	12,088
1982	342	1,369.40	1982	8,690	10,400
1981	339.3	1,628.50	1981	7,692	10,552
1980	329.7	1,362.60	1980	6,558	10,137

NA = NOT AVAILABLE.

Source: U.S. Department of Energy, Integrated Data Base Report - 1994: U.S. Spent Fuel and Radioactive Waste Inventories, Projections, and Characteristics(Washington, D.C.: 1995).

TABLE A11.13

PESTICIDE RESIDUES IN U.S. DOMESTIC SURVEILLANCE FOOD SAMPLES, BY COMMODITY GROUP: 1978–1994

				(PERCENT OF SAMPLES WITH RESIDUES FOUND)			
YEAR	GRAINS AND GRAIN PRODUCTS	MILK, DAIRY PRODUCTS AND EGGS	FISH, SHELLFISH AND MEATS	FRUITS	VEGETABLES	OTHER	TOTAL
1994	39	7	41	56	34	12	37
1993	34	6	47	30	61	17	36
1992	39	6	52	49	31	19	35
1991	42	22	42	51	32	19	36
1990	46	9	68	49	38	21	40
1989	44	13	65	44	32	20	35
1988	49	19	72	51	35	28	40
1987	57	24	73	50	37	37	42
1986	60	21	68	57	39	48	44
1985	52	22	65	36	34	22	35
1984	54	31	75	38	33	31	37
1983	42	32	61	52	41	31	43
1982	42	34	72	49	36	32	41
1981	43	32	77	56	37	34	44
1980	52	36	71	53	40	36	46
1979	54	47	81	58	35	47	49
1978	54	43	80	48	34	42	47

Source: Food and Drug Administration, *Pesticide Program Residues Monitoring 1994*, J. Assoc. Off. Anal. Chem. Vol. 78 (Washington, DC: FDA, 1995), and earlier issues.

Notes: Domestic food samples are collected as close as possible to the point of production. Fresh produce is analyzed as the unwashed whole, raw commodity. Although a percentage of samples contain pesticide residues, the percent of samples with over-tolerance residues (as set by EPA) is low. Between 1973 and 1986. 3 percent of samples were classed as violative; since 1987, less than 1 percent were violative.

TABLE A11.14

U.S. ENERGY PRODUCTION BY SOURCE: 1960–1995

(QUADRILLION BTU)

YEAR	COAL	CRUDE OIL AND NPGL	NATURAL GAS	HYDROELECTRIC POWER	NUCLEAR	GEOTHERMAL AND OTHER RENEWABLES	TOTAL
1960	10.82	16.39	12.66	1.61	0.01	<0.01	41.49
1961	10.45	16.76	13.1	1.66	0.02	<0.01	41.99
1962	10.9	17.11	13.72	1.82	0.03	<0.01	43.58
1963	11.85	17.68	14.51	1.77	0.04	<0.01	45.85
1964	12.52	17.96	15.3	1.89	0.04	<0.01	47.72
1965	13.06	18.4	15.78	2.06	0.04	<0.01	49.34
1966	13.47	19.56	17.01	2.06	0.06	<0.01	52.17
1967	13.83	20.83	17.94	2.35	0.09	0.01	55.04
1968	13.61	21.63	19.07	2.35	0.14	0.01	56.81
1969	13.86	21.98	20.45	2.65	0.15	0.01	59.1
1970	14.61	22.91	21.67	2.63	0.24	0.01	62.07
1971	13.19	22.57	22.28	2.82	0.41	0.01	61.29
1972	14.09	22.64	22.21	2.86	0.58	0.03	62.42
1973	13.99	22.06	22.19	2.86	0.91	0.04	62.06
1974	14.07	21.04	21.21	3.18	1.27	0.05	60.84
1975	14.99	20.1	19.64	3.15	1.9	0.07	59.86
1976	15.65	19.59	19.48	2.98	2.11	0.08	59.89
1977	15.76	19.78	19.57	2.33	2.7	0.09	60.22
1978	14.91	20.68	19.49	2.94	3.02	0.06	61.1
1979	17.54	20.39	20.08	2.93	2.78	0.09	63.8
1980	18.6	20.5	19.91	2.9	2.74	0.11	64.76
1981	18.38	20.46	19.7	2.76	3.01	0.12	64.42
1982	18.64	20.5	18.32	3.27	3.13	0.1	63.96
1983	17.25	20.57	16.59	3.53	3.2	0.13	61.28
1984	19.72	21.12	18.01	3.39	3.55	0.17	65.96
1985	19.33	21.23	16.98	2.97	4.15	0.21	64.87
1986	19.51	20.53	16.54	3.07	4.47	0.23	64.35
1987	20.14	19.89	17.14	2.63	4.91	0.25	64.95
1988	20.74	19.54	17.6	2.33	5.66	0.24	66.1
1989	21.35	18.28	17.85	2.77	5.68	0.22	66.13
1990	22.46	17.74	18.36	2.99	6.16	3.05	70.75
1991	21.59	18.01	18.23	2.94	6.58	3.07	70.41
1992	21.59	17.58	18.38	2.57	6.61	3.23	69.96
1993	20.22	16.9	18.58	2.84	6.52	3.25	68.32
1994	22.07	16.49	19.26	2.64	6.84	3.31	70.62
1995	21.91	16.27	19.23	3.17	7.19	3.4	71.16

Source: U.S. Department of Energy, Energy Information Administration, Annual Energy Review 1995, DOE/EIA-0384(95) (Washington, D.C.: 1996), Table 1.2, 7.

Notes: NGPL=Natural gas plant liquids. Hydroelectric power includes hydroelectric pumped storage. Other renewables include electricity produced from wood, waste, wind, photovoltaic, and solar thermal sources. There is a discontinuity in this time series between 1989 and 1990 due to expanded coverage of nonelectric utility use of renewable energy beginning in 1990. Previous-year data may have been revised. Current-year data are preliminary and may be revised in future publications.

GOVERNMENT

TABLE A12.1

TOTAL TAX REVENUE IN SELECTED COUNTRIES AS A PERCENTAGE OF GDP AT MARKET PRICES: 1980–1994

(RANKED BY THE 1994 FIGURES)

COUNTRY	1980	1985	1990	1991	1992	1993	1994
DENMARK	45.5	49.0	48.7	48.8	49.2	50.3	51.6
SWEDEN	48.8	50.0	55.6	53.7	51.0	50.1	51.0
CZECH REP.	(X)	(X)	(X)	(X)	(X)	47.8	47.3
FINLAND	36.9	40.8	45.4	46.9	46.8	45.4	47.3
BELGIUM	44.4	47.7	44.8	44.9	44.9	45.6	46.6
NETHERLANDS	45.0	44.1	44.6	47.2	46.8	47.7	45.9
LUXEMBOURG	46.3	46.7	43.6	42.9	42.5	44.3	45.0
FRANCE	41.7	44.5	43.7	43.9	43.7	43.9	44.1
POLAND	NA	NA	NA	37.2	38.2	42.4	43.2
AUSTRIA	41.2	43.1	41.3	41.9	43.2	43.5	42.8
GREECE	29.4	35.1	37.5	39.0	40.8	41.2	42.5
ITALY	30.2	34.5	39.1	39.7	42.1	43.8	41.7
NORWAY	47.1	47.6	41.8	41.8	41.0	40.2	41.2
HUNGARY	NA	NA	NA	42.4	42.4	42.0	41.0
GERMANY [1]	38.2	38.1	36.7	38.2	39.0	39.1	39.3
IRELAND	33.8	36.4	35.2	35.8	36.2	36.4	37.5
NEW ZEALAND	32.9	33.3	37.6	36.3	36.2	35.6	37.0
CANADA	31.6	33.1	36.5	36.7	36.4	35.8	36.1
SPAIN	24.1	28.8	34.4	34.7	36.0	35.0	35.8
UNITED KINGDOM	35.3	37.9	36.4	35.7	35.1	33.4	34.1
SWITZERLAND	30.8	32.0	31.5	31.2	31.9	33.2	33.9
PORTUGAL	25.2	27.8	31.0	31.7	33.4	31.4	33.0
ICELAND	29.2	28.4	31.4	31.4	32.2	31.3	30.9
AUSTRALIA	28.4	30.0	30.8	29.1	28.7	28.8	29.9
JAPAN	25.4	27.6	31.3	30.8	29.2	29.1	27.8
UNITED STATES	26.9	29.0	26.7	26.8	26.7	27.0	27.6
TURKEY	17.9	15.4	20.0	21.0	22.4	22.7	22.2
MEXICO	17.4	18.3	18.6	18.9	19.4	19.7	18.8

[1] UNIFIED GERMANY BEGINNING IN 1991.

(X) NOT APPLICABLE

NA = NOT AVAILABLE

Source: OECD Internet table (Address: http://www.oecd.org/news_and _events/publish/stat.pdf)

TABLE A12.2

REAL GROSS STATE PRODUCT (TOTAL AND FOR GOVERNMENT) IN THE UNITED STATES: 1987 AND 1994

(MILLIONS OF CHAINED [1992] DOLLARS. RANKED ACCORDING TO GOVERNMENT AS A PERCENT OF TOTAL REAL GROSS STATE PRODUCT FOR 1994).

STATE	TOTAL STATE GSP		GOVERNMENT PORTION OF GSP		GOVERNMENT PORTION AS % OF GSP		RANK	DIFFERENCE 1987 TO 1994
	1987	1994	1987	1994	1987	1994		
DISTRICT OF COLUMBIA	40,492	44,715	16,105	17,598	39.8	39.4	1	-0.4
HAWAII	28,156	34,748	6,766	7,438	24.0	21.4	2	-2.6
ALASKA	23,881	22,308	4,408	4,490	18.5	20.1	3	1.7
VIRGINIA	147,245	170,594	30,599	33,523	20.8	19.7	4	-1.1
NEW MEXICO	26,647	36,473	5,895	6,485	22.1	17.8	5	-4.3
MARYLAND	110,588	125,585	20,461	21,893	18.5	17.4	6	-1.1
OKLAHOMA	56,578	63,541	10,172	10,257	18.0	16.1	7	-1.8
MONTANA	13,406	16,046	2,438	2,574	18.2	16.0	8	-2.1
NORTH DAKOTA	11,805	12,966	2,248	2,079	19.0	16.0	9	-3.0
ALABAMA	71,618	84,630	12,987	13,562	18.1	16.0	10	-2.1
UTAH	29,718	39,666	5,665	6,231	19.1	15.7	11	-3.4
SOUTH CAROLINA	62,733	76,721	11,653	12,023	18.6	15.7	12	-2.9
WASHINGTON	104,079	136,328	17,690	20,473	17.0	15.0	13	-2.0
MISSISSIPPI	39,070	48,176	6,561	7,190	16.8	14.9	14	-1.9
NEBRASKA	31,268	39,613	5,612	5,834	17.9	14.7	15	-3.2
KANSAS	52,243	58,981	7,656	8,652	14.7	14.7	16	0.0
MAINE	23,141	24,629	3,426	3,478	14.8	14.1	17	-0.7
COLORADO	74,413	95,327	12,326	13,224	16.6	13.9	18	-2.7
ARIZONA	69,802	89,450	10,860	12,312	15.6	13.8	19	-1.8
IDAHO	16,094	23,000	2,581	3,130	16.0	13.6	20	-2.4
SOUTH DAKOTA	12,832	16,254	2,043	2,201	15.9	13.5	21	-2.4
KENTUCKY	67,105	83,249	9,869	11,203	14.7	13.5	22	-1.2
WEST VIRGINIA	27,871	33,485	4,127	4,379	14.8	13.1	23	-1.7
GEORGIA	138,624	175,034	20,063	22,870	14.5	13.1	24	-1.4
NORTH CAROLINA	143,379	177,167	19,491	22,998	13.6	13.0	25	-0.6
FLORIDA	246,059	301,800	32,674	38,399	13.3	12.7	26	-0.6
OREGON	53,487	70,122	7,516	8,915	14.1	12.7	27	-1.3
UNITED STATES	5,543,830	6,518,459	744,156	815,597	13.4	12.5	X	0.9
WYOMING	11,979	15,582	1,958	1,919	16.3	12.3	28	-4.0
VERMONT	10,941	12,641	1,289	1,537	11.8	12.2	29	0.4
CALIFORNIA	742,606	833,935	94,439	100,712	12.7	12.1	30	-0.6
LOUISIANA	91,146	97,022	10,950	11,710	12.0	12.1	31	0.1
TENNESSEE	96,687	120,661	13,637	14,560	14.1	12.1	32	-2.0
TEXAS	357,257	461,547	48,732	55,344	13.6	12.0	33	-1.6
RHODE ISLAND	21,391	22,686	2,665	2,699	12.5	11.9	34	-0.6
ARKANSAS	37,931	48,344	5,180	5,684	13.7	11.8	35	-1.9
IOWA	52,631	65,314	7,092	7,666	13.5	11.7	36	-1.7
NEW YORK	505,203	544,749	57,899	61,242	11.5	11.2	37	-0.2
MISSOURI	107,337	121,801	12,859	13,529	12.0	11.1	38	-0.9
MINNESOTA	98,419	118,672	11,633	13,144	11.8	11.1	39	-0.7
WISCONSIN	96,448	119,713	11,238	13,147	11.7	11.0	40	-0.7
NEW JERSEY	209,961	242,171	22,653	26,205	10.8	10.8	41	0.0
MICHIGAN	197,688	227,368	22,524	24,402	11.4	10.7	42	-0.7
PENNSYLVANIA	244,940	279,897	27,825	29,769	11.4	10.6	43	-0.7
OHIO	228,154	261,625	25,090	27,822	11.0	10.6	44	-0.4
NEVADA	25,879	41,547	3,242	4,365	12.5	10.5	45	-2.0
INDIANA	108,053	131,629	11,945	13,549	11.1	10.3	46	-0.8
ILLINOIS	272,412	317,166	29,409	31,926	10.8	10.1	47	-0.7
NEW HAMPSHIRE	25,262	28,066	2,411	2,668	9.5	9.5	48	-0.0
CONNECTICUT	96,819	104,319	9,276	9,798	9.6	9.4	49	-0.2
MASSACHUSETTS	166,090	177,313	16,321	16,551	9.8	9.3	50	-0.5
DELAWARE	19,687	25,194	1,985	2,232	10.1	8.9	51	-1.2

(X) = NOT APPLICABLE

Source: U. S. Bureau of Economic Analysis, *Survey of Current Business*, (June 1997), Table 10.

TABLE A12.3

POLL OPINIONS ABOUT GOVERNMENTS AND TAXES IN THE UNITED STATES: 1972–1993
(PERCENT)

| YEAR | FROM WHICH LEVEL OF GOVERNMENT DO YOU FEEL YOU GET THE MOST FOR YOUR MONEY? | | | | WHICH DO YOU THINK IS THE WORST TAX, THAT IS, THE LEAST FAIR? | | | | |
	FEDERAL	STATE	LOCAL	DON'T KNOW / NO ANSWER	FEDERAL INCOME TAX	STATE INCOME TAX	STATE SALES TAX	LOCAL PROPERTY TAX	DON'T KNOW/ NO ANSWER
1993	23	20	38	20	36	10	16	26	14
1992	QUESTION NOT ASKED				QUESTION NOT ASKED				
1991	26	22	31	22	26	12	19	30	14
1990	QUESTION NOT ASKED				QUESTION NOT ASKED				
1989	33	23	29	15	27	10	18	32	13
1988	28	27	29	16	33	10	18	28	11
1987	28	22	29	21	30	12	21	24	13
1986	32	22	33	13	37	8	17	28	10
1985	32	22	31	15	38	10	16	24	12
1984	24	27	35	14	36	10	15	29	10
1983	31	20	31	19	35	11	13	26	15
1982	35	20	28	17	36	11	14	30	9
1981	30	25	33	14	36	9	14	33	9
1980	33	22	26	19	36	10	19	25	10
1979	29	22	33	16	37	8	15	27	13
1978	35	20	26	19	30	11	18	32	10
1977	36	20	25	18	28	11	17	33	11
1976	36	20	25	19	NA	NA	NA	NA	NA
1975	38	20	25	17	28	11	23	29	10
1974	29	24	28	19	30	10	20	28	14
1973	35	18	25	22	30	10	20	31	11
1972	39	18	26	17	19	13	13	45	11

NA = NOT AVAILABLE.

Source: Gallup Poll results as reported in the U. S. Advisory Commission on Intergovernmental Relations, *Changing Public Attitudes on Government and Taxes*, 1993 (S-22).

TABLE A12.4

NUMBER OF LOCAL GOVERNMENTS IN THE UNITED STATES, BY TYPE AND STATE: 1992

| | GENERAL PURPOSE | | | | | SPECIAL PURPOSE | |
| | | SUBCOUNTY | | | | | |
STATE	TOTAL	COUNTY	TOTAL	MUNICIPAL	TOWNSHIP	SPECIAL DISTRICT	SCHOOL DISTRICT
UNITED STATES	84,955	3,043	35,935	19,279	16,656	31,555	14,422
ALABAMA	1,121	67	438	438	0	487	129
ALASKA	174	12	148	148	0	14	0
ARIZONA	590	15	86	86	0	261	228
ARKANSAS	1,446	75	489	489	0	561	321
CALIFORNIA	4,392	57	460	460	0	2,797	1,078
COLORADO	1,760	62	266	266	0	1,252	180
CONNECTICUT	563	0	178	29	149	368	17
DELAWARE	275	3	57	57	0	196	19
DISTRICT OF COLUMBIA	2	0	1	1	0	1	0
FLORIDA	1,013	66	390	390	0	462	95
GEORGIA	1,297	157	536	536	0	421	183
HAWAII	20	3	1	1	0	16	0
IDAHO	1,086	44	199	199	0	728	115
ILLINOIS	6,722	102	2,715	1,282	1,433	2,920	985
INDIANA	2,898	91	1,574	566	1,008	939	294
IOWA	1,880	99	952	952	0	388	441
KANSAS	3,891	105	1,980	627	1,353	1,482	324
KENTUCKY	1,320	119	435	435	0	590	176
LOUISIANA	458	61	301	301	0	30	66
MAINE	796	16	490	22	468	199	91
MARYLAND	401	23	155	155	0	223	0
MASSACHUSETTS	843	12	351	39	312	396	84
MICHIGAN	2,721	83	1,776	534	1,242	277	585
MINNESOTA	3,579	87	2,657	854	1,803	377	458
MISSISSIPPI	869	82	294	294	0	320	173
MISSOURI	3,309	114	1,257	933	324	1,386	552
MONTANA	1,275	54	128	128	0	556	537
NEBRASKA	2,923	93	986	534	452	1,047	797
NEVADA	207	16	18	18	0	156	17
NEW HAMPSHIRE	527	10	234	13	221	116	167
NEW JERSEY	1,512	21	567	320	247	374	550
NEW MEXICO	341	33	98	98	0	116	94
NEW YORK	3,298	57	1,548	619	929	980	713
NORTH CAROLINA	937	100	516	516	0	321	0
NORTH DAKOTA	2,764	53	1,714	364	1,350	722	275
OHIO	3,523	88	2,256	942	1,314	513	666
OKLAHOMA	1,794	77	588	588	0	524	605
OREGON	1,450	36	239	239	0	835	340
PENNSYLVANIA	5,158	66	2,570	1,022	1,548	2,006	516
RHODE ISLAND	125	0	39	8	31	83	3
SOUTH CAROLINA	697	46	269	269	0	291	91
SOUTH DAKOTA	1,785	64	1,279	310	969	262	180
TENNESSEE	923	93	339	339	0	477	14
TEXAS	4,791	254	1,171	1,171	0	2,266	1,100
UTAH	626	29	228	228	0	329	40
VERMONT	681	14	287	50	237	104	276
VIRGINIA	454	95	230	230	0	129	0
WASHINGTON	1,760	39	268	268	0	1,157	296
WEST VIRGINIA	691	55	231	231	0	350	55
.WISCONSIN	2,738	72	1,849	583	1,266	377	440
WYOMING	549	23	97	97	0	373	56

Source: U. S. Bureau of the Census, *Government Organization*, vol. 1, no. 1, (1992) Census of Governments, Table 3.

TABLE A12.5

RANK OF 50 U.S. STATE GOVERNMENTS IN COMBINED RANKING WITH THE FORTUNE 500 INDUSTRIAL CORPORATIONS

(CORPORATIONS BASED ON SALES, STATE GOVERNMENTS BASED ON GENERAL REVENUE)

STATE	COMBINED RANK OF STATES WITH FORTUNE 500 CORPORATIONS
CALIFORNIA	4
NEW YORK	8
TEXAS	15
PENNSYLVANIA	19
FLORIDA	20
ILLINOIS	21
OHIO	22
MICHIGAN	24
NEW JERSEY	25
MASSACHUSETTS	33
NORTH CAROLINA	40
WASHINGTON	42
VIRGINIA	47
GEORGIA	50
WISCONSIN	51
MINNESOTA	52
INDIANA	57
MARYLAND	60
LOUISIANA	69
CONNECTICUT	76
KENTUCKY	77
MISSOURI	80
TENNESSEE	83
ALABAMA	85
ARIZONA	88
SOUTH CAROLINA	90
OKLAHOMA	106
OREGON	108
COLORADO	111
IOWA	113
ALASKA	128
MISSISSIPPI	135
KANSAS	139
HAWAII	148
NEW MEXICO	149
ARKANSAS	151
WEST VIRGINIA	152
UTAH	165
NEBRASKA	185
MAINE	200
RHODE ISLAND	212
NEVADA	221
DELAWARE	236
IDAHO	241
MONTANA	266
NORTH DAKOTA	271
WYOMING	273
NEW HAMPSHIRE	281
VERMONT	306
SOUTH DAKOTA	320

Source: Robert D. Behn and John S. Clendinen,
The Fortune 500 and the Fifty States: A Combined Ranking,
Governors Center at Duke University, 1993.

TABLE A12.6

ANNUAL SALARIES OF U.S. GOVERNORS BY STATE

STATE	ANNUAL SALARY
ALABAMA	$ 81,151
ALASKA	81,648
ARIZONA	75,000
ARKANSAS	60,000
CALIFORNIA	120,000
COLORADO	70,000
CONNECTICUT	78,000
DELAWARE	95,000
FLORIDA	101,764
GEORGIA	103,074
HAWAII	94,780
IDAHO	85,000
ILLINOIS	119,439
INDIANA	77,199
IOWA	98,200
KANSAS	80,340
KENTUCKY	88,645
LOUISIANA	73,440
MAINE	69,992
MARYLAND	120,000
MASSACHUSETTS	75,000
MICHIGAN	121,166
MINNESOTA	114,506
MISSISSIPPI	83,160
MISSOURI	98,345
MONTANA	59,310
NEBRASKA	65,000
NEVADA	90,000
NEW HAMPSHIRE	86,235
NEW JERSEY	85,000
NEW MEXICO	90,000
NEW YORK	130,000
NORTH CAROLINA	98,576
NORTH DAKOTA	69,648
OHIO	115,762
OKLAHOMA	70,000
OREGON	80,000
PENNSYLVANIA	105,000
RHODE ISLAND	69,900
SOUTH CAROLINA	106,078
SOUTH DAKOTA	82,700
TENNESSEE	85,000
TEXAS	99,122
UTAH	82,000
VERMONT	80,724
VIRGINIA	110,000
WASHINGTON	121,000
WEST VIRGINIA	72,000
WISCONSIN	101,861
WYOMING	95,000

Source: The Book of the States, 1996-97 Edition, vol.
31, Table 2.3 (Lexington, KY: Council of State
Governments, 1996).

TABLE A12.7

PERCENTAGE OF ELEMENTARY-SECONDARY EDUCATION REVENUE IN THE U.S. FUNDED BY FEDERAL, STATE AND LOCAL GOVERNMENT SOURCES, BY STATE: 1993-94

(RANKED BY PERCENT FROM STATE SOURCES)

		ELEMENTARY-SECONDARY REVENUE			
		FROM FEDERAL	FROM LOCAL	FROM STATE SOURCES	
AREA	TOTAL	SOURCES	SOURCES	PERCENT	RANK
HAWAII	100.0	6.9	2.7	90.5	1
NEW MEXICO	100.0	11.1	14.8	74.2	2
WASHINGTON	100.0	5.8	24.5	69.8	3
DELAWARE	100.0	7.4	27.6	65.0	4
NEVADA	100.0	4.5	30.8	64.7	5
KENTUCKY	100.0	10.4	25.1	64.5	6
WEST VIRGINIA	100.0	7.9	28.1	63.9	7
ALASKA	100.0	12.8	23.7	63.5	8
NORTH CAROLINA	100.0	8.1	29.0	62.9	9
ALABAMA	100.0	11.2	26.4	62.4	10
ARKANSAS	100.0	9.3	29.9	60.8	11
IDAHO	100.0	8.2	31.1	60.7	12
OKLAHOMA	100.0	8.0	32.0	60.0	13
KANSAS	100.0	5.0	37.5	57.5	14
CALIFORNIA	100.0	7.1	36.7	56.2	15
MISSISSIPPI	100.0	15.5	29.5	54.9	16
MINNESOTA	100.0	4.4	40.7	54.9	17
UTAH	100.0	7.0	38.1	54.9	18
LOUISIANA	100.0	12.2	34.1	53.6	19
WYOMING	100.0	5.8	42.0	52.2	20
GEORGIA	100.0	6.6	42.2	51.1	21
MONTANA	100.0	9.5	39.6	51.0	22
FLORIDA	100.0	7.2	42.8	50.0	23
IOWA	100.0	5.1	46.4	48.6	24
TENNESSEE	100.0	9.7	42.1	48.2	25
MISSOURI	100.0	6.6	46.5	46.9	26
MAINE	100.0	5.9	47.4	46.7	27
SOUTH CAROLINA	100.0	9.0	44.6	46.3	28
INDIANA	100.0	4.8	48.9	46.3	29
UNITED STATES AVERAGE	100.0	6.5	47.6	45.9	X
TEXAS	100.0	7.4	49.1	43.5	30
NORTH DAKOTA	100.0	11.5	45.2	43.3	31
WISCONSIN	100.0	4.2	53.8	42.0	32
ARIZONA	100.0	9.8	48.5	41.7	33
COLORADO	100.0	4.9	54.6	40.5	34
OREGON	100.0	7.0	52.9	40.1	35
PENNSYLVANIA	100.0	5.4	54.5	40.1	36
OHIO	100.0	5.0	54.9	40.0	37
VIRGINIA	100.0	6.2	54.1	39.7	38
NEW JERSEY	100.0	3.6	56.8	39.6	39
MARYLAND	100.0	5.0	56.0	39.0	40
RHODE ISLAND	100.0	4.8	56.9	38.3	41
NEW YORK	100.0	6.1	55.6	38.3	42
CONNECTICUT	100.0	3.4	60.4	36.2	43
MASSACHUSETTS	100.0	4.9	61.9	33.2	44
ILLINOIS	100.0	5.6	61.4	33.0	45
NEBRASKA	100.0	6.1	62.0	31.8	46
VERMONT	100.0	5.0	63.7	31.3	47
MICHIGAN	100.0	5.7	64.1	30.2	48
SOUTH DAKOTA	100.0	10.3	64.2	25.5	49
NEW HAMPSHIRE	100.0	3.4	88.4	8.2	50
DISTRICT OF COLUMBIA	100.0	10.8	89.2	0.0	51

X = NOT APPLICABLE

Source: U. S. Bureau of the Census, Annual Survey of Government Finance.

TABLE A12.8

RANK OF STATE AND LOCAL GOVERNMENT TAXES IN THE UNITED STATES PER $100 PERSONAL INCOME: FY 1994

(WHOLE DOLLARS)

STATE RANK	AREA	TAXES PER $100 PERSONAL INCOME	PERCENT DIFFERENCE FROM U.S. AVERAGE
	U.S. AVERAGE	11.67	X
1	NEW YORK	15.54	33.1
2	DISTRICT OF COLUMBIA	14.62	25.3
3	ALASKA	14.18	21.5
4	WISCONSIN	13.73	17.7
5	HAWAII	13.71	17.5
6	NEW MEXICO	13.17	12.8
7	MINNESOTA	13.15	12.6
8	WYOMING	12.90	10.5
9	VERMONT	12.86	10.2
10	IOWA	12.60	8.0
11	MAINE	12.53	7.3
12	MICHIGAN	12.45	6.7
13	ARIZONA	12.44	6.6
14	CONNECTICUT	12.30	5.4
15	UTAH	12.21	4.6
16	WASHINGTON	12.12	3.9
17	NEW JERSEY	12.07	3.4
18	NORTH DAKOTA	11.91	2.1
19	OREGON	11.86	1.6
20	RHODE ISLAND	11.75	0.6
21	KANSAS	11.73	0.5
22	NEBRASKA	11.71	0.3
23	MASSACHUSETTS	11.64	-0.3
24	DELAWARE	11.57	-0.9
25	IDAHO	11.51	-1.4
26	KENTUCKY	11.50	-1.5
27	NORTH CAROLINA	11.49	-1.5
28	MONTANA	11.43	-2.1
29	WEST VIRGINIA	11.40	-2.3
30	MISSISSIPPI	11.35	-2.7
31	OHIO	11.24	-3.7
32	GEORGIA	11.23	-3.7
33	MARYLAND	11.20	-4.0
34	INDIANA	11.14	-4.6
35	CALIFORNIA	11.06	-5.2
36	ILLINOIS	11.03	-5.5
37	PENNSYLVANIA	11.03	-5.5
38	OKLAHOMA	10.93	-6.4
39	NEVADA	10.86	-7.0
40	TEXAS	10.80	-7.5
41	SOUTH CAROLINA	10.77	-7.7
42	FLORIDA	10.77	-7.8
43	COLORADO	10.72	-8.2
44	ARKANSAS	10.62	-9.0
45	LOUISIANA	10.42	-10.7
46	SOUTH DAKOTA	10.20	-12.6
47	VIRGINIA	10.13	-13.2
48	NEW HAMPSHIRE	9.98	-14.5
49	TENNESSEE	9.70	-16.9
50	MISSOURI	9.62	-17.6
51	ALABAMA	9.43	-19.2

X = NOT APPLICABLE

Source: U. S. Bureau of the Census, Annual Survey of Government Finance.

TABLE A12.9

STATE RANKINGS IN THE UNITED STATES FOR PER CAPITA DISTRIBUTION OF FEDERAL FUNDS: FISCAL YEAR 1996

STATE	TOTAL	GRANTS TO STATE AND LOCAL GOVERNMENTS	SALARIES AND WAGES	DIRECT PAYMENTS FOR INDIVIDUALS	PROCUREMENT	OTHER
VIRGINIA	1	50	3	22	1	14
MARYLAND	2	43	4	19	4	3
ALASKA	3	1	1	50	5	13
NEW MEXICO	4	8	6	35	2	15
HAWAII	5	15	2	27	11	19
MISSOURI	6	30	22	14	3	10
MASSACHUSETTS	7	9	34	7	7	6
RHODE ISLAND	8	4	18	4	31	21
MONTANA	9	11	14	24	42	1
MISSISSIPPI	10	14	25	8	12	37
NORTH DAKOTA	11	7	5	37	39	4
WEST VIRGINIA	12	6	38	2	43	35
ALABAMA	13	28	15	5	19	25
FLORIDA	13	48	29	1	23	41
MAINE	15	10	24	13	17	42
CONNECTICUT	16	16	41	12	8	18
PENNSYLVANIA	17	21	35	3	29	22
SOUTH DAKOTA	18	5	13	30	37	5
WASHINGTON	19	32	8	31	13	16
COLORADO	20	46	7	47	6	12
WYOMING	21	2	10	42	40	34
NEW YORK	22	3	44	11	36	27
TENNESSEE	23	20	32	15	14	44
LOUISIANA	24	12	33	18	27	26
OKLAHOMA	25	36	9	9	33	33
KENTUCKY	26	18	19	16	25	32
SOUTH CAROLINA	27	24	21	20	20	48
CALIFORNIA	28	22	28	39	10	24
ARIZONA	29	42	26	23	16	45
ARKANSAS	30	19	42	6	50	17
NEW JERSEY	31	25	39	10	28	49
KANSAS	32	45	17	26	30	9
GEORGIA	33	37	11	44	21	43
VERMONT	34	13	37	40	26	28
IOWA	35	41	48	29	44	2
DELAWARE	36	23	27	17	48	29
NEVADA	37	49	30	34	9	50
IDAHO	38	34	31	45	15	38
NEBRASKA	39	35	20	38	35	7
TEXAS	40	44	23	46	18	39
OHIO	41	26	43	21	32	47
NORTH CAROLINA	42	39	16	33	41	40
OREGON	43	17	40	25	49	20
ILLINOIS	44	27	36	32	45	30
NEW HAMPSHIRE	45	29	45	43	22	36
INDIANA	46	47	47	36	34	11
UTAH	47	38	12	49	24	31
MICHIGAN	48	33	49	28	46	46
MINNESOTA	49	31	46	48	38	8
WISCONSIN	50	40	50	41	47	23

Source: U. S. Bureau of the Census, *Federal Expenditures by State for Fiscal Year 1996.*

Note: Excludes Federal funds for loans and insurance.

TABLE A12.10

ADJUSTED FEDERAL EXPENDITURES IN THE UNITED STATES PER DOLLAR OF TAXES: FISCAL YEARS 1986 AND 1996

STATE	FISCAL YEAR 1996 EXPENDITURE PER $1 TAX	RANK	FISCAL YEAR 1986 EXPENDITURE PER $1 TAX	RANK	DIFFERENCE IN RANK, 1986-96
NEW MEXICO	1.83	1	1.89	1	0
MISSISSIPPI	1.64	2	1.61	2	0
WEST VIRGINIA	1.52	3	1.21	16	13
VIRGINIA	1.42	4	1.43	5	1
MONTANA	1.41	5	1.31	10	5
MISSOURI	1.38	6	1.31	11	5
NORTH DAKOTA	1.35	7	1.46	3	-4
HAWAII	1.33	8	1.40	6	-2
ALABAMA	1.33	9	1.30	12	3
OKLAHOMA	1.31	10	0.99	32	22
LOUISIANA	1.30	11	1.01	30	19
MAINE	1.29	12	1.22	15	3
ARKANSAS	1.28	13	1.32	9	-4
KENTUCKY	1.27	14	1.38	8	-6
SOUTH DAKOTA	1.27	15	1.44	4	-11
ALASKA	1.26	16	1.05	26	10
MARYLAND	1.24	17	1.20	17	0
SOUTH CAROLINA	1.23	18	1.23	14	-4
IDAHO	1.15	19	1.20	18	-1
ARIZONA	1.15	20	1.18	19	-1
TENNESSEE	1.14	21	1.23	13	-8
RHODE ISLAND	1.08	22	0.98	33	11
IOWA	1.06	23	1.02	28	5
UTAH	1.06	24	1.39	7	-17
WYOMING	1.05	25	0.92	38	13
FLORIDA	1.05	26	1.03	27	1
VERMONT	1.03	27	0.96	34	7
PENNSYLVANIA	1.02	28	0.96	35	7
GEORGIA	1.01	29	1.06	25	-4
NORTH CAROLINA	1.00	30	0.92	39	9
KANSAS	1.00	31	1.08	22	-9
NEBRASKA	1.00	32	1.08	23	-9
TEXAS	0.98	33	0.84	45	12
COLORADO	0.97	34	1.01	31	-3
WASHINGTON	0.97	35	1.14	20	-15
CALIFORNIA	0.94	36	1.02	29	-7
MASSACHUSETTS	0.94	37	1.06	24	-13
OREGON	0.92	38	0.94	36	-2
OHIO	0.92	39	0.92	37	-2
INDIANA	0.87	40	0.88	42	2
NEW YORK	0.86	41	0.86	43	2
NEVADA	0.82	42	1.11	21	-21
DELAWARE	0.82	43	0.74	48	5
WISCONSIN	0.79	44	0.84	44	0
MINNESOTA	0.76	45	0.9	40	-5
MICHIGAN	0.76	46	0.76	47	1
NEW HAMPSHIRE	0.74	47	0.8	46	-1
ILINOIS	0.73	48	0.71	49	1
CONNECTICUT	0.71	49	0.88	41	-8
NEW JERSEY	0.69	50	0.65	50	0
DISTRICT OF COLUMBIA	5.59	X	5.03	X	X

(X) = NOT APPLICABLE

Source: *1997 Federal Tax Burden by State, Tax Foundation,* (Washington, D.C., July 1997), no. 70.

TABLE 12.11

CATEGORICAL GOVERNMENT EXPENDITURES IN THE UNITED STATES AS A PERCENT OF TOTAL EXPENDITURES, BY LEVEL OF GOVERNMENT: 1993–1994

	ALL GOVERNMENTS [1]	FEDERAL GOVERNMENT	STATE AND LOCAL GOVERNMENTS [1]	STATE GOVERNMENTS	LOCAL GOVERNMENTS
EXPENDITURE, TOTAL	100.00	100.00	100.00	100.00	100.00
INTERGOVERNMENTAL EXPENDITURE	0.00	13.37	0.29	29.00	1.22
CURRENT OPERATION	53.20	30.32	73.39	47.48	77.86
CAPITAL OUTLAY	8.13	4.90	10.88	6.82	11.76
CONSTRUCTION	4.18	0.59	8.07	5.37	8.39
EQUIPMENT, LAND, AND EXISTING STRUCTURES	3.95	4.30	2.81	1.45	3.37
ASSISTANCE AND SUBSIDIES	5.54	6.92	2.79	2.86	1.82
INTEREST ON DEBT	9.99	12.43	5.10	3.16	5.56
INSURANCE BENEFITS AND REPAYMENTS	23.13	32.07	7.55	10.67	1.78
SALARIES & WAGES	21.45	9.98	32.48	15.53	40.36
GENERAL EXPENDITURE	73.46	67.93	85.24	88.08	86.90
CURRENT EXPENDITURE	66.01	63.04	75.80	81.53	77.37
CAPITAL OUTLAY	7.45	4.90	9.44	6.55	9.53
NATIONAL DEFENSE	12.47	20.45	0.00	0.00	0.00
POSTAL SERVICE	1.73	2.83	0.00	0.00	0.00
SPACE RESEARCH	0.51	0.83	0.00	0.00	0.00
EDUCATION	14.09	3.07	27.94	29.72	35.98
LIBRARIES	0.20	0.04	0.39	0.09	0.65
PUBLIC WELFARE	8.83	10.50	14.51	23.54	5.12
HOSPITALS	2.86	0.72	5.15	3.64	5.24
HEALTH	1.69	1.14	2.79	3.66	2.30
SOCIAL INSURANCE ADMINISTRATION	0.37	0.56	0.32	0.52	0.00
VETERANS SERVICES	0.83	1.34	0.01	0.02	0.00
HIGHWAYS	2.72	1.22	5.70	6.89	3.95
AIR TRANSPORTATION	0.59	0.50	0.74	0.15	1.20
WATER TRANSPORT AND TERMINALS	0.20	0.17	0.21	0.09	0.28
OTHER TRANSPORTATION	0.04	0.00	0.09	0.02	0.14
POLICE PROTECTION	1.72	0.49	3.06	0.77	4.63
FIRE PROTECTION	0.60	0.00	1.28	0.00	2.25
CORRECTION	1.30	0.17	2.55	2.98	1.55
PROTECTIVE INSPECTION	0.25	0.00	0.53	0.57	0.32
NATURAL RESOURCES	2.42	3.27	1.11	1.53	0.40
PARKS AND RECREATION	0.70	0.14	1.32	0.41	1.93
HOUSING AND COMMUNITY DEVELOPMENT	1.34	2.26	1.57	0.41	2.49
SEWERAGE	0.81	0.00	1.71	0.26	2.84
SOLID WASTE MANAGEMENT	0.63	0.32	1.11	0.21	1.76
FINANCIAL ADMINISTRATION	1.21	0.73	1.63	1.47	1.29
JUDICIAL	0.85	0.50	1.41	1.04	1.53
PUBLIC BUILDING	0.24	0.00	0.51	0.17	0.72
OTHER GOVERNMENT ADMINISTRATION	0.47	0.10	0.85	0.35	1.13
INTEREST ON GENERAL DEBT	9.64	12.43	4.35	3.06	4.34
GENERAL EXPENDITURE, NEC	4.15	4.13	4.40	6.51	4.87
UTILITY AND LIQUOR STORES	3.41	0.00	7.21	1.25	11.33
INSURANCE TRUST EXPENDITURE	23.13	32.07	7.55	10.67	1.78
SOCIAL SECURITY AND MEDICARE	17.68	28.98	0.00	0.00	0.00
UNEMPLOYMENT COMPENSATION	1.07	0.01	2.26	3.67	0.02
EMPLOYEE RETIREMENT	3.46	2.25	4.40	5.55	1.75
OTHER INSURANCE TRUST EXPEND	0.92	0.83	0.88	1.44	0.00

[1] EXCLUDES INTERGOVERNMENTAL FINANCIAL FLOWS TO AVOID DUPLICATION.

Source: U. S. Bureau of the Census, Annual Survey of Government Finance.

TABLE A12.12

TOTAL EMPLOYEES OF STATE AND LOCAL GOVERNMENTS IN THE UNITED STATES: 1977-92

LEVEL OF GOVERNMENT	TOTAL	EDUCATION	NONEDUCATION
NUMBER OF EMPLOYEES (IN THOUSANDS)			
1992			
STATE AND LOCAL	15,117	7,642	7,475
STATE	4,587	2,027	2,560
LOCAL	10,531	5,616	4,915
1987			
STATE AND LOCAL	14,121	7,397	6,724
STATE	4,116	1,802	2,314
LOCAL	10,005	5,595	4,410
1982			
STATE AND LOCAL	12,993	6,728	6,265
STATE	3,744	1,618	2,126
LOCAL	9,249	5,110	4,139
1977			
STATE AND LOCAL	12,765	6,703	6,062
STATE	3,491	1,484	2,007
LOCAL	9,274	5,219	4,055

Source: U. S. Bureau of the Census, *1992 Census of Governments*, vol. 3 and 2, Compendium of Government Employment.

Bernan Associates Order Form

4611-F Assembly Drive ■ Lanham, MD 20706 USA

If using a purchase order, please attach this form

Quantity	ISBN	Title	Begin Standing Order?		Price
	0-89059-083-4	Business Statistics of the U.S., 1997 Ed.	Yes ☐	No ☐	$65.00
	0-89059-094-X	Handbook of U.S. Labor Statistics, Second Ed.	Yes ☐	No ☐	$65.00
	0-89059-065-6	Housing Statistics of the U.S., First Ed.	Yes ☐	No ☐	$59.00

Subtotal	
Tax*	
Postage & Handling**	
Total	

*MD, DC, and NY add applicable sales tax; Canada add GST

**Add Postage and Handling as follows:
U.S.: 6%, minimum $5.00
Canada and Mexico: 10%, minimum $6.00
Outside North America: 30%, minimum $15.00

Rush Service
Rush Service is available for an additional $15.

Prices are subject to change

Terms: Net 30 days

Return Policy
You may review any Bernan Press publication for 30 days. If you are not completely satisfied, you may return it (in saleable condition) for a full refund or credit to your account.

Methods of Payment

Deposit Account
Requires a minimum initial deposit of $100.00 and an ongoing balance of $50.00. Upon receipt of the check or money order, an account will be established and a special account number will be assigned. The cost of ordered publications will be deducted from the funds on deposit.

Invoice Statement Account
Send in the order on an authorized purchase order, and an invoice will be included with the shipment of publications. An account number will be assigned after the first purchase. All future orders can be charged against this account number with an authorized purchase order.

Prepayment
Prepay all orders with a check or money order in U.S. dollars, drawn from a U.S. bank, payable to Bernan Associates.

MAKE RE-ORDERING EASY WITH STANDING ORDERS!

Place your publications on *Standing Order* and you are guaranteed automatic delivery of each new edition as it is published!

☐ Check or Money Order enclosed

☐ Bill Me P.O.# _____ Date _____

☐ MC ☐ Visa ☐ Am Ex Exp. Date ____

Card # _____

Signature _____

YES!
I'd like to open a Deposit Account.
Enclosed is a check for _____
(minimum $100)
Account # _____
Tax Exempt # _____

Bill To

Name _____

Organization _____

Street Address _____

City/State/Zip _____

Phone _____ Fax _____

Ship To

Name _____

Organization _____

Street Address _____

City/State/Zip _____

Phone _____ Fax _____

Call Toll Free 1•800•865•3457   Fax Toll Free 1•800•865•3450   e-mail: order@bernan.com

Bernan Associates
Specialists in Government Information

A unique, one-stop source for U.S. government and international agency publications

For over 40 years, Bernan Associates has been providing centralized access to a wide variety of government and intergovernmental titles from some of the largest, most prolific publishers in the world. Our vision is to be recognized as the premier source for worldwide and intergovernmental publications by supplying you with valuable product expertise and effective distribution services. We offer:

- Complimentary subscription to *The Bernan Bulletin*
- Knowledgeable customer service representatives
- Experienced publications/acquisitions specialists
- Comprehensive Standing Order services
- Trouble-free payment plans
- Toll-free phone and fax lines
- Timely delivery
- Subscription services

Visit our Web site at www.bernan.com

We distribute titles from the following publishers:

U.S. Government Publishers
- Executive Branch
- Judicial Branch
- Legislative Branch
- District of Columbia
- Smithsonian Institution Press
- Independent U.S. Government Agencies
- Boards, Committees, Commissions, Councils

U.K. Government Publisher
- The Stationery Office (formerly HMSO)

Private Publishers
- **Bernan Press** (U.S.A.)
- Editions Delta (Belgium)
- EUROPA Publications (U.K.)
- Library Association Publishing, Ltd. (U.K.)

Intergovernmental Publishers
- Asian Productivity Organization (APO)
- The Nordic Council of Ministers
- Office for Official Publications of the European Communities (EC)
- Organization for Economic Cooperation and Development (OECD)

United Nations & U.N. Specialized Agencies
- United Nations (UN)
- Food and Agriculture Organization (FAO)
- International Atomic Energy Agency (IAEA)
- International Labour Organisation (ILO)
- International Monetary Fund (IMF)
- United Nations Educational, Scientific, and Cultural Organization (UNESCO)
- UNESCO Bangkok
- World Bank
- World Tourism Organization (WTO)
- World Trade Organization (WTO), formerly the General Agreement on Tariffs and Trade (GATT)

BERNAN
Associates

The Bernan Press
U.S. DataBook Series™

The Bernan Press U.S. DataBook Series™ is designed to provide essential, yet hard-to-find government statistics in a convenient printed format. Our well-known editors have held high-ranking positions in the Department of Commerce, the Bureau of the Census, the Bureau of Labor Statistics, and other federal and national organizations. Their experience is your assurance of statistical information that is timely and authoritative.

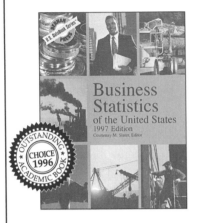

Business Statistics of the United States: 1997 Edition
Courtenay M. Slater, Editor

Based on the popular *Business Statistics* (formerly published by the Bureau of Economic Analysis), this essential reference work contains 29 years of annual time series data, with monthly data for 1993 through 1996, and an update of key data through the first half of 1997. You'll find current information on: construction and housing; mining, oil, and gas; manufacturing; transportation, communications, and utilities; retail and wholesale trade; services; and government.

It also features a full statistical picture of the overall U.S. economy, including data on: gross domestic product; consumer income and spending; industrial production; money and financial markets; and more. It contains numerous charts and tables illustrating economic trends.

December 1997. Paperback. 432 pages. ISBN 0-89059-083-4. $65.00.

Handbook of U.S. Labor Statistics: Employment, Earnings, Prices, Productivity, and Other Labor Data: Second Edition
Eva E. Jacobs, Editor

Based on the *Handbook of Labor Statistics* (formerly published by the Bureau of Labor Statistics), the new Second Edition of this comprehensive research tool incorporates annual data for 1996-1997 and newly available employment projections for the year 2006. Topics include: population, labor force, and employment status; consumer prices; producer prices; export and import prices; consumer expenditures; and productivity.

June 1998. Paperback. 354 pages. ISBN 0-89059-094-X. $65.00.

Housing Statistics of the United States: First Edition
Patrick A. Simmons, Editor

Here is the first ever comprehensive source for current and historical information on households, housing, and housing finance. Data include: household characteristics; prices, rents, and affordability; housing production and investment; home mortgage lending; housing stock characteristics; and federal housing programs. This is an ideal source for data that can be used for producing or benchmarking market reports, trend analysis, and research.

October 1997. Paperback. 442 pages. ISBN 0-89059-065-6. $59.00.